International Schools for Computer Scientists

Series Editors

ALFREDO FERRO

Department of Mathematics
University of Catania
Viale A. Doria 6
I-95125 Catania
Italy

DANIELE MUNDICI

Department of Computer Science
University of Milan
Via Comelico 39-41
I-20135 Milan
Italy

Advisory Editor

DOV M. GABBAY

Department of Computing
Imperial College
180 Queen's Gate
London SW7 2BZ
UK

International Schools for Computer Scientists

Giorgio Levi (ed.): *Advances in logic programming theory*
Egon Börger (ed.): *Specification and validation methods*

Specification and Validation Methods

Edited by

EGON BÖRGER

*Dipartimento di Informatica, Università di Pisa,
Corso Italia 40, I-56125, Pisa, Italy*

CLARENDON PRESS • OXFORD

1995

Oxford University Press, Walton Street, Oxford OX2 6DP
Oxford New York
Athens Auckland Bangkok Bombay
Calcutta Cape Town Dar es Salaam Delhi
Florence Hong Kong Istanbul Karachi
Kuala Lumpur Madras Madrid Melbourne
Mexico City Nairobi Paris Singapore
Taipei Tokyo Toronto
and associated companies in
Berlin Ibadan

Oxford is a trade mark of Oxford University Press

Published in the United States
by Oxford University Press Inc., New York

© The contributors listed on p. ix, 1995

All rights reserved. No part of this publication may be
reproduced, stored in a retrieval system, or transmitted, in any
form or by any means, without the prior permission in writing of Oxford
University Press. Within the UK, exceptions are allowed in respect of any
fair dealing for the purpose of research or private study, or criticism or
review, as permitted under the Copyright, Designs and Patents Act, 1988, or
in the case of reprographic reproduction in accordance with the terms of
licences issued by the Copyright Licensing Agency. Enquiries concerning
reproduction outside those terms and in other countries should be sent to
the Rights Department, Oxford University Press, at the address above.

This book is sold subject to the condition that it shall not,
by way of trade or otherwise, be lent, re-sold, hired out, or otherwise
circulated without the publisher's prior consent in any form of binding
or cover other than that in which it is published and without a similar
condition including this condition being imposed
on the subsequent purchaser.

A catalogue record for this book is available from the British Library

Library of Congress Cataloging in Publication Data
Specification and validation methods/
edited by Egon Börger.—1st ed.
Includes bibliographical references.
1. Programming languages (Electronic computers) I. Börger, E. (Egon), 1946–
QA76.7.S64   1995   004'.015113—dc20   95–10608

ISBN 0 19 853854 5

Typeset by the editor and
contributors using LaTeX

Printed in Great Britain by
Biddles Ltd,
Guildford & King's Lynn

Contents

List of contributors   ix

Introduction   1

Survey of the book   3
Bibliography   5

Part I: Evolving Algebras   7

Evolving algebras 1993: Lipari guide   9
Yuri Gurevich

1. Introduction   9
2. Static algebras and updates   11
3. Sequential evolving algebras   15
4. Nondeterministic sequential algebras and some other simple extensions of the basic model   22
5. Parallelism: evolving algebras with variables   27
6. Distributed evolving algebras   30

Bibliography   36

Annotated bibliography on evolving algebras   37
Egon Börger

Bibliography   37

Part II: Programming Languages   53

Program verification and Prolog   55
Krzysztof R. Apt

1. Introduction   55
2. Setting the stage   56
3. Pure Prolog   61
4. Pure Prolog with arithmetic   77
5. Pure Prolog with negation   83
6. Conclusions   90

Bibliography   92

CLAM specification for provably correct compilation of CLP($\mathcal{R}$) programs   97
Egon Börger and Rosario F. Salamone

1	Introduction	97
2	Prerequisites on evolving algebras	98
3	CLP($\mathcal{R}$) with predicate and clause compilation	99
4	Representation of constraints	105
5	Unification	109
6	Compilation of constraints	112
7	CLAM	124
	Bibliography	130

The semantics of the C++ programming language   131
Charles Wallace

1	Introduction	131
2	Class structure and encapsulation	132
3	Programmer-defined class operations	139
4	Object creation and destruction	145
5	Overloading and parameterized types	152
6	Other extensions	157
7	Conclusion	164
	Appendix A Macro definitions	164
	Bibliography	164

Part III: Parallel and Distributed Programs   165

Verification of parameterized programs   167
Zohar Manna and Amir Pnueli

1	Introduction	167
2	Preliminaries	168
3	Parameterized programs	179
4	Verifying invariance properties	185
5	Verifying response properties	190
6	Representation by verification diagrams	197
7	Coordination by add-and-store	209
	Bibliography	230

The Bakery Algorithm: yet another specification and verification   231
Egon Börger, Yuri Gurevich and Dean Rosenzweig

	Introduction	231
1	The algorithms	232
2	Atomic actions interpretation	236
3	Durative actions interpretation	239
	Bibliography	242

Part IV: Protocols 245

Kermit: specification and verification 247
James K. Huggins

1 The alternating bit protocol (ABP) 247
2 Symmetric ABP 256
3 Sliding windows 260
4 Bounded sliding windows 265
5 Alternating bit Kermit: the session layer 268
6 Alternating bit Kermit: the transport layer 279
7 Alternating bit Kermit: the datalink layer 283
8 Sliding windows Kermit 285
Appendix A   Kermit initialization 290
Appendix B   Partially ordered runs of Kermit 292
Bibliography 293

Group membership protocol: specification and verification 295
Yuri Gurevich and Raghu Mani

1 Introduction 295
2 Overview of the protocol 296
3 The program 299
4 Semantics: definitions and discussion 305
5 Proof of protocol 309
Bibliography 328

Part V: Architecture Design 329

Specification and verification of VHDL-based system-level hardware designs 331
Werner Damm, Bernhard Josko and Rainer Schlör

1 Introduction 331
2 Ingredients of VHDL-based system-level design: a short introduction 339
3 A formal semantics for VHDL 351
4 A correctness logic for VHDL 372
5 Symbolic timing diagrams 388
Bibliography 404

Specification and verification of gate-level VHDL models of synchronous and asynchronous circuits 411
David M. Russinoff

1 Introduction 411
2 Definition of the language 414
3 Specification of synchronous circuits 424
4 Asynchronous communication 437
5 Biphase mark 445
Bibliography 460

Contributors

Krzysztof R. Apt, CWI, P.O. Box 94079, 1090 GB, Amsterdam, The Netherlands; and Faculty of Mathematics and Computer Science, University of Amsterdam, Plantage Muidergracht 24, 1018 TV Amsterdam, The Netherlands; E-mail apt@cwi.nl.

Egon Börger, Dipartimento di Informatica, Università di Pisa, Corso Italia 40, I-56125, Pisa, Italy; E-mail boerger@di.unipi.it.

Werner Damm, Universität Oldenburg, FB Informatik, 26111 Oldenburg, Germany; E-mail damm@informatik.uni-oldenburg.de.

Yuri Gurevich, EECS Department, 1301 Beal Avenue, University of Michigan, Ann Arbor, Michigan 48109-2122, USA; E-mail gurevich@umich.edu.

James K. Huggins, EECS Department, 1301 Beal Avenue, University of Michigan, Ann Arbor, Michigan 48109-2122, USA; E-mail huggins@umich.edu.

Bernhard Josko, Kuratorium OFFIS e.V., Escherweg 2, 26121 Oldenburg, Germany; E-mail josko@offis.uni-oldenburg.de.

Raghu Mani, EECS Department, 1301 Beal Avenue, University of Michigan, Ann Arbor, Michigan 48109-2122, USA; E-mail raghu@eecs.umich.edu.

Zohar Manna, Department of Computer Science, Stanford University, Stanford, California 94305, USA; E-mail manna@cs.stanford.edu.

Amir Pnueli, Department of Computer Science, Weizmann Institute of Science, Rehovot, Israel; E-mail amir@wisdom.weizmann.ac.il.

Dean Rosenzweig, University of Zagreb, FSB, Salajeva 5, Zagreb, Croatia; E-mail dean@math.hr.

David M. Russinoff, Computational Logic, Inc., 1717 West 6th Street, Suite 290, Austin, TX 78703, USA; E-mail russ@cli.com.

Rosario F. Salamone, RISC-Linz, Johannes Kepler University, A-4040 Linz, Austria; E-mail rsalamon@risc.uni-linz.ac.at.

Rainer Schlör, Kuratorium OFFIS e.V., Escherweg 2, 26121 Oldenburg, Germany; E-mail schloer@offis.uni-oldenburg.de.

Charles Wallace, EECS Department, 1301 Beal Avenue, University of Michigan, Ann Arbor, Michigan 48109-2122, USA; E-mail wallace@eecs.umich.edu.

Introduction

At first glance, this book may seem to be a volume of conference proceedings, and in a sense it is. But, to a greater extent, it is a graduate course on *Specification and Validation Methods* which does not presuppose any familiarity with the subject and leads the reader to the forefront of the current research in the field.

In 1993, Alfredo Ferro (Catania, Sicily) and myself organized an International Summer School on *Specification and Validation Methods for Programming Languages and Systems*. The School was held during 21 June–3 July 1993 in Lipari (Sicily). The goal of the school was to provide graduate students and young reserachers with a comprehensive presentation of the state of the art. Alfredo Ferro took upon himself the hard and thankless task of administration and organization. He did an excellent job: the school on the beautiful Island of Lipari remains an unforgettable event. My part was to provide good lecturers. I was lucky to attract some leading experts in the field, able to transmit their own enthusiasm to their listeners.

The positive reaction of the participants, who came from all over the world, their critical attention, open discussions and fruitful interaction among the lecturers made the school into a great success. This prompted me to ask the lecturers to considerably expand the course material for this book.[1] I also succeeded in soliciting additional new chapters from other eminent researchers which complement nicely the material presented at the school. The result of this one year endeavour is a book which provides easy access to promising new methods for specification and validation of computing systems.

The methods presented in this book are exemplified on challenging and typical applications. The issues range from semantics of programming languages and their implementation (Part II) to architectural design (Part V), also including parallel and distributed programs (Part III) as well as protocols (Part IV).

The chapters are self-contained and can be read independently of each other. The only exception is this: to understand chapters 4, 5 and 7–9 the reader should know the definition of evolving algebras which can be found

---

[1] See chapters 1, 3, 4, 6 and 10 which are derived from the lectures of Y. Gurevich, K. Apt, E. Börger, A. Pnueli and W. Damm. Due to an unfortunate sequence of technical obstacles, M. Fourman has not been able to turn the material taught in his lectures on *System Specification and Development using Higher–order Logic* into a contribution to this volume.

in chapter 1. Only elementary knowledge in mathematical manipulation and reasoning techniques is assumed.

We are confident that not only the graduate student and young researcher but also and especially the reader who applies formal methods for designing and verifying complex real-life computing systems will find this book useful.

EGON BÖRGER, Pisa, Summer 1994

Survey of the Book

Part I is an introduction to the new specification methodology known as *evolving algebras*. Chapter 1 (written by Y. Gurevich, Ann Arbor, Michigan) contains the basic definition of the notion of *evolving algebra* which is used in chapters 4, 5 and 7–9. Gurevich formulated this notion in order to improve on Turing's thesis by bringing in concern about resources and thereby about data structures (see [Gurevich91]). The notion constitutes a fundamental discovery for the theory of computation models. It quickly turned out to be also the basis for a specification methodology with an apparently unlimited range of applicability for the design and the verification of real-life complex systems. Among other features, Gurevich's contribution to this book provides a remarkable extension of the notion of evolving algebra from sequential to distributed computations.

Part I concludes with an annotated bibliography, compiled by myself, of the work done using evolving algebras and covering the period from the first appearance of the notion in the literature in 1988 (see [Gurevich88]) until the summer of 1994.

Part II is devoted to the semantics of programming languages and their implementations. The case studies come from logic and object-oriented programming languages. Chapter 3 (written by K. Apt, Amsterdam) shows how verification of Prolog programs can be systematically carried out within a simple framework comprising syntactic analysis, declarative semantics, modes and types. The method is applied in particular to the study of termination, partial correctness, occur-check freedom, and the absence of errors or floundering in Prolog programs.

In chapter 4 (written by E. Börger, Pisa and R. Salamone, Linz) the authors prove the correctness of the compilation of a popular constraint logic programming language (CLP($\mathcal{R}$)) into the appropriate implementation (the CLAM machine, developed by Jaffar and his colleagues at IBM Yorktown Heights). This complex case study illustrates the remarkable power of modularization offered by the evolving algebra approach. The modularization deals simultaneously with the specifications and with the related correctness proofs. Indeed, the formal specification of Prolog and the WAM given in [BoeRos94] enters the CLP($\mathcal{R}$) and the CLAM specification as a module; but, also, the correctness proof of a general compilation scheme of Prolog programs to the WAM can be taken as a part of the proof that a natural extension of this scheme to CLP($\mathcal{R}$) programs and the CLAM is also correct.

Chapter 5 (written by C. Wallace, Ann Arbor, Michigan) extends the evolving algebra formalization of the C programming language given by [GurHug93] to C++. This provides another interesting example which shows how fruitfully the well known stepwise refinement techniques can be applied to evolving algebra specifications. Wallace builds his C++ model by incorporating into the evolving algebra model for C the features which support object-oriented programming, namely combination of the definition of types and operations of objects, the creation and destruction of objects, overloading, parameterized type definitions, inheritance and encapsulation.

Part III is devoted to specification and verification of parallel and distributed programs. Chapter 6 (written by Z. Manna, Stanford, California and A. Pnueli, Weizmann Institute, Israel) pioneers the use of temporal logic for the verification of parameterized reactive programs. Parameterization is an important feature which permits one to use compound statements of variable size; in this chapter the challenging case of variable size cooperation statements is considered. The method is explained predominantly by analysis of safety and response statements. This chapter extends considerably the well known method of the authors, published in [ManPnu91].

Chapter 7 (written by E. Börger, Y. Gurevich and by D. Rosenzweig, Zagreb) gives a very simple evolving algebra specification and verification of Lamport's Bakery Algorithm. This is a famous mutual exclusion protocol for distributed environments. In this little example one finds an illustration of how smoothly the evolving algebra approach allows one to combine the stepwise refinement technique with the built-in abstraction principles. The specification and the correctness proof work for both the *atomic* as well as the *durative* interpretation of basic actions. Only the corresponding notion of state has to be refined.

Part IV deals with specification and verification of real-life protocols. The two case studies presented here give faithful and easily readable formal specifications and mathematical verifications without extraneous formal overhead. Chapter 8 (written by J. Huggins, Ann Arbor, Michigan) provides an evolving algebra specification and verification of the widely used communication protocol *Kermit*. The specification and the verification are first given separately for the *alternating bit* and the *sliding window* protocols; next this is extended to the full Kermit protocol. Chapter 9 (written by Y. Gurevich and R. Mani, Ann Arbor, Michigan) contains an evolving algebra specification and verification of an interesting group membership protocol used to enhance fault tolerance of distributed computing services. The particular interest of such protocols stems from the fact that they represent time constrained algorithms. This case study illustrates well the advantage one can take by separating different concerns. Functional and timing properties are specified and verified separately, thus providing simple proofs and avoiding formal overhead.

Part V is devoted to specification and verification methods for architecture design, centered around the IEEE standard hardware description language VHDL. VHDL plays a central role because it is supported by the major CAD (Computer Aided Design) tool suppliers. Both contributions in Part V start from the observation that up to now there has been no comprehensive formal semantics for VHDL. As a validation method they propose to use not a simulation (simulations tend to be unfeasible) but a formal verification—proving that the given model of a hardware device satisfies the given behavioral description. Both contributions make an effort to navigate between Scylla and Charybdis, presenting a specification that (a) is sufficiently abstract (to provide a comprehensive description of desired functionalities), and (b) constitutes a model that is sufficiently concrete (to permit a simple implementation).

Chapter 10 (written by W. Damm, B. Josko and R. Schlör, all Oldenburg) provides a semantic foundation of a formal verification environment for VHDL based system-level design. The environment is currently under development within the ESPRIT project FORMAT. In particular, a tool is developed to support temporal logic specifications and verifications of system-level hardware designs which come expressed in VHDL, using an extension of symbolic timing diagrams.

Chapter 11 (written by D. Russinoff, Austin, Texas) gives a functional definition of a hardware description language based on event driven simulation that admits a semantics-preserving translation to an important subset of VHDL. This language includes basic propagation delay mechanisms and gate-level circuit descriptions. The definition, together with related procedures (for deriving and verifying behavioral specifications of combinatorial and sequential devices), have been formally encoded in Boyer–Moore Computational Logic. This provides a facility for mechanical proof checking by a LISP implementation. The method is used to design, specify and verify an interesting example, namely a circuit that achieves asynchronous communication by means of the biphase mark protocol.

EGON BÖRGER, Pisa, Summer 1994

Bibliography

[BoeRos94] E. Börger and D. Rosenzweig, *The WAM - definition and compiler correctness.* In L. C. Beierle and L. Plümer (Eds.): *Logic Programming: Formal Methods and Practical Applications*, Series in Computer Science and Artificial Intelligence. North–Holland, 1994.

[Gurevich88] Y. Gurevich. *Logic and the challenge of computer science.* In E. Börger, editor, *Current Trends in Theoretical Computer Science*, pages 1–57. Computer Science Press, 1988.

[Gurevich91] Y. Gurevich., *Evolving Algebras. A Tutorial Introduction,*

EATCS Bulletin 43, February 1991, pp. 264–284. A slightly revised version appeared in "Current Trends in Theoretical Computer Science", Eds. G. Rozenberg and A. Salomaa, World Scientific, 1993, 266–292.

[GurHug93] Y. Gurevich and J. Huggins, *The evolving algebra semantics of C.* In E. Börger, H. Kleine Büning, G. Jäger, S. Martini, and M. M. Richter, editors, *Computer Science Logic*, Lecture Notes in Computer Science vol 702. Springer, 1993, pp. 274–309.

[ManPnu91] Z. Manna and A. Pnueli, *Completing the temporal picture.* In *Theor. Comp. Sci.*, 83(1): 97–130, 1991.

Part I: Evolving Algebras

Evolving Algebras 1993: Lipari Guide

Yuri Gurevich*

1 Introduction

Computation models and specification methods seem to be worlds apart. The evolving algebra project started as an attempt to bridge the gap by improving on Turing's thesis [G1, G2]. We sought more versatile machines which would be able to simulate arbitrary algorithms in a direct and essentially coding-free way. Here the term algorithm is taken in a broad sense including programming languages, architectures, distributed and real-time protocols, *etc..* The simulator is not supposed to implement the algorithm on a lower abstraction level; the simulation should be performed on the natural abstraction level of the algorithm.

The evolving algebra thesis asserts that evolving algebras are such versatile machines. The thesis suggests an approach to the notorious correctness problem that arises in mathematical modeling of non-mathematical reality: How can one establish that a model is faithful to reality? The approach is to construct an evolving algebra $\mathcal{A}$ that reflects the given computer system so closely that the correctness can be established by observation and experimentation. (There are tools for running evolving algebras.) $\mathcal{A}$ can then be refined or coarsened and used for numerous purposes. An instructive example is described in [B] by Egon Börger who championed this approach and termed $\mathcal{A}$ the *ground model* of the system. The use of the successive refinement method is facilitated by the ability of evolving algebras to reflect arbitrary abstraction levels. This has been convincingly demonstrated by Börger and Rosenzweig in [BR]; a simpler example is found in [GH].

Evolving algebras have been used to specify languages (*e.g.* C, Prolog and VHDL), to specify real and virtual architectures (*e.g.* APE, PVM and Transputer), to validate standard language implementations (*e.g.* of Prolog, Occam), to validate distributed protocols (see examples in Parts III and IV of this book), to prove complexity results [BG], *etc..* See Börger's annotated bibliography on evolving algebras in this book and the proceedings of the first evolving algebra workshop in [PS].

Here we extend the definition of evolving algebras given in the tutorial [G2] (henceforth "the tutorial"). For the sake of brevity, the term "evolving algebra" is often shortened to "ealgebra" (pronounced e-algebra) or "EA"; the latter term is used mostly as an adjective. Static algebras are discussed in §2. Sequential ealgebras are discussed in §3; first we define basic eal-

---

*Partially supported by ONR grant N00014-91-J-1861 and NSF grant CCR-92-04742.

gebras and then we equip them with the ability to import new elements. Nondeterministic sequential ealgebras and some other simple extensions of basic ealgebras are discussed in §4, parallel ealgebras are discussed in §5, and distributed ealgebras are discussed in §6 which can be read immediately after §3. Admittedly this guide is harder to read than the tutorial, and we intend to write a more popular version of the guide.

Now let us return to the EA thesis. In the tutorial, we defined sequential ealgebras and sketched a speculative philosophical "proof" of the sequential version of the thesis. The definition of sequential ealgebras and the sequential EA thesis have survived several years of intensive application and experimentation. As a matter of fact, we (the EA community) seem to have run out of challenges.

The situation with non-sequential computations is more complicated. It seems that, for every reasonably understood class of algorithms, there is a natural extension of the basic EA model that "captures" that class. That form of the EA thesis also has survived several years of intensive application and experimentation. The philosophy and guiding principles of the EA approach seem quite stable. However, at the current stage of computer science, there is yet no clear understanding of what parallel, distributed or real-time algorithms are in general. Thus, the definitions of parallel and distributed ealgebras given below are necessarily tentative. They provide a foundation for existing EA applications and reflect my anticipation of things to come. (Many existing applications, including those in this volume, were done before this guide have been completed; the terminology there may reflect earlier versions of the guide.)

We try to derive our definitions from first principles. Unfortunately some arbitrariness is inescapable and one has to balance the clarity and simplicity versus programming convenience and efficient execution. When one thinks mostly about applications, as we do, there is a tendency to prefer programming convenience and efficient execution. This is a dangerous trend which leads to an idiosyncratic programming language. For future reference we formulate the following principle:

The Pragmatic Occam's Razor Logic simplicity comes first; it may be sacrificed only in those cases where a slight logic complication is demonstrated to ease programming or improve execution efficiency in a substantial way.

The EA field is quickly expanding in depth and breadth. I hope that this guide lives up to its name and guides the developments in the near future.

Acknowledgment Egon Börger and Dean Rosenzweig generously shared with me their ideas and rich application experience. Discussions with Andreas Blass were indispensable in clarifying things. Numerous working walks with Jim Huggins through the woods of Ann Arbor were very helpful. Raghu Mani raised important implementation issues. Numerous ealgebraists commented on earlier drafts of the guide. I am very thankful to all of them. To an extent, this chapter is a result of a collective effort, though I am responsible for possible blunders.

A preliminary version of the guide has been tried out during the 1993 summer school on Specification and Validation Methods for Programming Languages and Systems on the beautiful island of Lipari in Italy. I use this opportunity to thank the organizers, Egon Börger and Alfredo Ferro, and all participants.

2 Static Algebras and Updates

2.1 Static Algebras: Motivation

In first-order logic, a structure is a nonempty set with operations and relations (called the basic operations and relations of the structure). That is how Tarski defined structures. He could have defined structures differently; there were a number of reasonable options. For our purposes here, a variant of Tarski's notion is more appropriate. Respecting tradition, we do not redefine structures. Rather, we modify the notion of structure and give the new notion a new name.

Structures without relations are called *algebras* in the branch of mathematics called universal algebra. Restrict attention to algebras with distinct nullary operations *true* and *false* and define basic relations as basic operations taking only the Boolean values *true* and *false*. Further restrict attention to algebras with the equality relation and the usual Boolean operations. (We will specify later the values of the Boolean operations outside their natural domains later.) The resulting notion of algebra is our variant of the notion of structure with equality. It allows us to write quantifier-free formulas as terms.

Actually, we are interested in multi-sorted structures with partial operations. The sorts can be given by unary relations (they will be called universes and the whole underlying set of a structure will be called the superuniverse). To deal with partial functions, further restrict attention to algebras with a nullary operation *undef*, different from *true* and *false*, and interpret an operation f as undefined at a tuple $\bar{a}$ if $f(\bar{a}) = undef$. These algebras will be called *static algebras* or *states*. Their operations will be called functions.

In the following subsections, we start anew and define static algebras from scratch, establishing terminology on the way.

2.2 Vocabularies

A *vocabulary* (or *signature*) is a finite collection of function names, each of a fixed arity. Some function names may be marked as *relation names* or *static names*, or both. Every vocabulary contains the following static names: the equality sign, nullary function names *true, false, undef* and the names of the usual Boolean operations. The equality sign and *true, false* are marked as relation names. The Greek letter Υ is reserved to denote vocabularies.

Logic Names The particular function names listed above are *basic logic names*. There are precedents of logic names in mathematical logic, though usually they are called logical constants. For example, the equality sign is a logic name in first-order logic with equality. Usually, logic names are present in every vocabulary and their interpretations satisfy some *a priori* restrictions. Accordingly, we suppose that the basic logic names appear in every vocabulary, and thus there is no need to mention them when a particular vocabulary is described.

An additional logic name is introduced in §3. It does not necessarily appear in every vocabulary and it is not marked static. The latter is one reason why we do not use the term "logical constants".

2.3 Definition of Static Algebras

A *static algebra* or (for the sake of brevity) *state* S of vocabulary Υ is a nonempty set X, the *superuniverse* of S, together with interpretations of the function names in Υ on X. An r-ary function name is interpreted as a function from X^r to X, a *basic function* of S. The interpretation of an r-ary relation name is a function from X^r to $\{true, false\}$, a *basic relation* of S. The vocabulary Υ is called the *vocabulary* of S and denoted $\mathrm{Fun}(S)$.

The interpretations of the nullary logic names *true, false* and *undef* are distinct elements of X. The Boolean operations behave in the usual way on the Boolean values *true* and *false* and produce *undef* if at least one of the arguments is not Boolean. The equality sign is interpreted as the characteristic function of the identity relation on X. If $f(\bar{x})$ evaluates to *true* in S, we say that $f(\bar{x})$ holds in S; and if $f(\bar{x})$ evaluates to *false* in S, we say that $f(\bar{x})$ fails in S.

Formally speaking, basic functions are total. However, we view them as being partial and define the domain $\mathrm{Dom}(f)$ of an r-ary basic function f as the set of r-tuples $\bar{x}$ such that $f(\bar{x}) \neq undef$. Let us stress though that *undef* is an ordinary element of the superuniverse. Often, a basic function produces *undef* if at least one argument equals *undef*, but this is not required and there are exceptions (*e.g.* basic relations).

Universes A basic relation f may be viewed as the set of tuples where it evaluates to *true*. We may write $\bar{x} \in f$ instead of $f(\bar{x})$. If f is unary it can be viewed as a special *universe*. For example, we may have a universe Nodes and declare a binary relation Edge over the universe of Nodes; $\mathrm{Edge}(x,y)$ will hold only if both x and y belong to Nodes. Such universes allow us to view states as many-sorted structures. Sometimes we speak about universe names. These are unary relation names intended to be used as universes.

As a rule, *undef* is not included in universes. Coming back to our example, is it natural that Edge(*undef,undef*) equals *false* rather than *undef*? In a sense, yes. Think about Edge as a set of pairs of nodes. It is natural that the pair (*undef,undef*) does not belong there.

2.4 Terms

Terms are defined recursively, as in first-order logic:

- A variable is a term.
- If f is an r-ary function name and $t_1, \ldots, t_r$ are terms, then $f(t_1, \ldots, t_r)$ is a term.

As usual, *ground terms* are terms without variables. By analogy, other syntactical objects without variables will be called ground.

Atomic Boolean terms are terms of the form $f(\bar{t})$, where f is a relation name. *Boolean terms* are built from atomic Boolean terms by means of the Boolean operations.

Appropriate States and the Fun Notation In addition to terms, we will define various other syntactic objects, *e.g.*, update instructions and transition rules. We call a state S *appropriate* for a syntactic object s if Fun(S) includes the collection of function names that occur in s. By default (that is, unless explicitly defined differently), that collection will be denoted Fun(s).

In an appropriate state S, a ground term $t = f(t_1, \ldots, t_r)$ evaluates to an element $Val_S(t) = f(Val_S(t_1), \ldots, Val_S(t_r))$. If $\bar{t}$ is a tuple $(t_1, \ldots, t_r)$ of terms, define $Val_S(\bar{t}) = (Val_S(t_1), \ldots, Val_S(t_r))$.

An expression $t_1 = t_2$ may be a Boolean term or a metalanguage statement. Often it does not matter which it is. One can use two different equality signs or just try to be careful; we choose the second alternative.

2.5 Locations and Updates

As in first-order logic, the *reduct* of an Υ-state S to a smaller vocabulary Υ' is the Υ'-state S' obtained from S by "disinterpreting" function names in $\Upsilon - \Upsilon'$; S is an *expansion* of S' to Υ.

A *carrier* is a state whose vocabulary contains only static function names. The *carrier* $|S|$ *of a state* S is the reduct of S to the static part of Fun(S).

A *location over a carrier* C is a pair $\ell = (f, \bar{x})$, where f is a function name outside of Fun(C) and $\bar{x}$ is a tuple of elements of C whose length equals the arity of f; location ℓ is *relational* if f is a relation symbol. Loc$_\Upsilon(C)$ is the collection of all locations over C with function names in Υ. An Υ-state S with carrier C will sometimes be viewed as a function from Loc$_\Upsilon(C)$ to (the superuniverse of) C; *locations of* S are locations in Loc$_\Upsilon(C)$.

If a state S is appropriate for a ground term $t_0 = f(\bar{t})$, then the *location* of t_0 in S is the location $(f, Val_S(\bar{t}))$.

An *update* of a state S is a pair $\alpha = (\ell, y)$, where ℓ is a location of S and $y \in |S|$; if ℓ is relational then y is Boolean. (More precisely, y belongs to the superuniverse of static algebra $|S|$; the looser language is common in logic.) The location ℓ is the *location* $\mathrm{Loc}(\alpha)$ of α, and y is the *value* $\mathrm{Val}(\alpha)$ of α. To *fire* α at S, put y into the location ℓ; that is, redefine S to map ℓ to y. The result is a new state S' such that $\mathrm{Fun}(S') = \mathrm{Fun}(S)$, $|S'| = |S|$, $S'(\ell) = y$ and $S'(\ell') = S(\ell')$ for every location ℓ' of S different from ℓ.

2.6 Update Sets and Families of Update Sets

An *update set* β over a state S is a set of updates of S. $\mathrm{Loc}(\beta) = \{\mathrm{Loc}(\alpha) : \alpha \in \beta\}$. For each $\ell \in \mathrm{Loc}(\beta)$, $\mathrm{Val}_\beta(\ell) = \{\mathrm{Val}(\alpha) : \alpha \in \beta \wedge \mathrm{Loc}(\alpha) = \ell\}$.

An update set β is *consistent* at the given state S if every $\mathrm{Val}_\beta(\ell)$ is a singleton set; otherwise β is inconsistent.

To fire a consistent β at the given state S, fire all its members simultaneously. The result is a new state S' with the same vocabulary and carrier as S. If $\ell \in \mathrm{Loc}(\beta)$ then $S'(\ell)$ is the only element of $\mathrm{Val}_\beta(\ell)$; otherwise $S'(\ell) = S(\ell)$. To fire an inconsistent update set β at the given state S, do nothing; the new state S' equals S.

Remark It is reasonable to require that the detection of inconsistency manifest itself in some way; for example, a nullary function *crash* automatically gets value *true*. To keep the EA logic clean and simple, we try to minimize the number of things done automatically, and thus we leave necessary manifestations of inconsistency to the programmer. This is one application of the pragmatic Occam's razor of §1; substantial programming convenience has not been demonstrated yet.

To fire a family γ of update sets over S, nondeterministically choose some update set $\beta \in \gamma$ and fire it at S. If $\gamma = \emptyset$, do nothing. Intentionally, the empty family of update sets means inconsistency.

2.7 Conservative Determinism vs. Local Nondeterminism

The mode of dealing with inconsistent update sets described above can be called conservative determinism. The mode of dealing with inconsistent update sets in the tutorial was different: Fire all updates simultaneously; in case of conflict at any location ℓ, choose the new value for ℓ nondeterministically among all candidate values. It could be called local nondeterminism.

With the exception of this change in the treatment of inconsistent update sets, this guide is compatible with the tutorial. The change is not as big as it may seem because people are usually interested in deterministic programs. As far as we know, no existing EA application is affected. The local nondeterminism has not been exploited. The conservative determinism is simpler, and a more manageable form of nondeterminism will be introduced in §4.

3 Sequential Evolving Algebras

Basic transition rules are defined in subsection 3.1. Subsection 3.2 deals with the problem of extending universes. The reader may skip 3.2 and go directly to subsection 3.3 on programs and runs.

3.1 Basic Transition Rules

In this subsection, terms are ground.

3.1.1 Update Instructions

An *update instruction* R is an expression

$$f(\bar{t}) := t_0$$

where f is a non-static function name (the *subject* of the instruction), $\bar{t}$ is a tuple of terms whose length equals the arity of f, and t_0 is another term; if f is a relation name then t_0 must be a Boolean term. (Update instructions are called local function updates in the tutorial.)

Semantics To execute R at an appropriate state S, fire the update $\alpha = (\ell, y)$ at S, where $\ell = (f, Val_S(\bar{t}))$ and $y = Val_S(t_0)$. For future reference define Updates$(R, S) = \{\alpha\}$.

3.1.2 Two Rule Constructors

Basic rules are constructed recursively from update instructions by means of two rule constructors: the sequence constructor and the conditional constructor. Semantics is defined by means of update sets. For each rule R and every state S appropriate for R, we define an update set Updates(R, S) over S. To fire R at S, fire Updates(R, S).

The Sequence Constructor A sequence of rules is a rule.

  Semantics If R is a sequence of rules $R_1, \ldots, R_k$ then

$$\text{Updates}(R, S) = \text{Updates}(R_1, S) \cup \cdots \cup \text{Updates}(R_k, S).$$

In other words, to fire a sequence of rules, fire all of them simultaneously. Notice that Updates(R, S) is inconsistent if any R_i is so.

  Remark The term "sequence" may be misleading here. We are not executing first R_1, then R_2, then R_3, *etc.*. A better term is "block". (This remark is written at the proofreading stage.)

The Conditional Constructor If k is a natural number, $g_0, \ldots, g_k$ are Boolean terms and $R_0, \ldots, R_k$ are rules, then the following expression is a rule:

```
if g0 then R0
elseif g1 then R1
    ⋮
elseif gk then Rk
endif
```

If the guard g_k is the nullary function *true*, then the last elseif clause may be replaced by "else R_k". For brevity we will say that the conditional rule R above is the conditional rule with clauses $(g_0, R_0), \ldots, (g_k, R_k)$.

Semantics Updates(R, S) = Updates(R_i, S) if g_i holds in S but every g_j with $j < i$ fails in S. Updates$(R, S) = \emptyset$ if every g_i fails in S.

3.1.3 Guarded Multi-updates

A *multi-update instruction* is a sequence of update instructions. A *guarded update instruction* (respectively, *guarded multi-update instruction*) is a rule of the form

```
if g then R endif
```

where R is an update (respectively, a multi-update) instruction.

Lemma 3.1 *For every rule R, there is a sequence R' of guarded updates such that $Fun(R') = Fun(R)$ and $Updates(R', S) = Updates(R, S)$ for all appropriate states S.*

For example, the rule

```
if FirstChild(c)≠ undef then c:=FirstChild(c)
elseif NextSib(c)≠ undef then c:=NextSib(c)
elseif Parent(c)≠ undef then c:=Parent(c)
endif
```

converts to the following sequence of guarded updates:

```
if FirstChild(c)≠ undef then c:=FirstChild(c) endif
if FirstChild(c)=undef and NextSib(c)≠ undef then
    c:=NextSib(c) endif
if FirstChild(c)=undef and NextSib(c)=undef
    and Parent(c)≠ undef then c:=Parent(c) endif
```

The Lemma suggests a simpler definition of rules. The reason for choosing the recursive definition is pragmatic. It is too tedious to write rules as sequences of guarded updates. It is feasible to write them as sequences of guarded multi-updates but it is more convenient and practical to use elseif clauses and nest conditionals. The pragmatic Occam's razor does not cut as much as the original Occam's razor would.

Remark This is another proofreading time remark. The new version of the EA interpreter permits the use of two additional rule constructors.

One is the case constructor, like that in Pascal, which may make the execution substantially more efficient. Of course, the same set of updates is generated by a case command and its case-free equivalent; the difference is in how fast this set is generated. For example, consider a sequence of rules of the form "if $t = i$ then R_i endif" where i ranges from 1 to a relatively large n. This example is extreme, because the the set $\{1, \ldots, n\}$ of alternatives is so easy to deal with; but it is not unusual to have similar long sequences of rules. In addition, the case construct makes it easier to program a sequential execution of a sequence of rules, which is sometimes desirable. The other rule constructor is "let x=t in R", which prevents re-evaluations of term t in R and which has been used informally. The let constructor was advocated by Raghu Mani who is working on the new EA interpreter.

3.2 Importing New Elements

The basic rules suffice for many purposes (*e.g.*, for describing the C programming language [GH]), but they do not suffice to model all sequential algorithms. A sequential algorithm may add a new node to a graph or create a new message. We need rules that allow us to create new nodes, new messages, *etc.*, and such rules are introduced in this subsection. However, we do not create new elements; instead, we use a special universe Reserve from which the new elements come.

In this section we use individual variables, but only in a limited way. (Variables are used more extensively in §5.) Roughly speaking, only bound variables are used; free variables appear only in contexts where some values have been assigned to them.

3.2.1 *Reserve*

In addition to basic logic names, we introduce a new logic name: a universe name Reserve. It is not static, and we do not require that it belong to the vocabulary of every static algebra. If the vocabulary of state S contains Reserve, then the set $\{x : S \models x \in \text{Reserve}\}$ is the *reserve* of S. Intuitively the reserve is a naked set.

Reserve Proviso Every state satisfies the following conditions:

- Every basic relation, with the exception of equality and Reserve, evaluates to *false* if at least one of its arguments belongs to the reserve.
- Every other basic function evaluates to *undef* if at least one of its arguments belongs to the reserve.
- No basic function outputs an element of the reserve.

It follows that every permutation of the reserve is an automorphism of the state.

3.2.2 Transition Rules: Syntax

Generalize the definitions of terms and update instructions in 3.1 as follows:

- allow terms to have variables, and
- forbid mentioning Reserve.

Variables are often treated as auxiliary nullary function names below but *a variable cannot be the subject of an update instruction*. The reason for forbidding to mention Reserve in terms and update instructions is discussed below.

Rules are constructed from update instructions by means of three rule constructors: the sequence constructor, the conditional constructor and the import constructor.

The Import Constructor If v is a variable and R_0 is a rule, then the following expression is a rule with *main existential variable v* and *body R_0*:

import v
   R_0
endimport

In the usual and obvious way define which occurrences of variables are free and which are bound. Call a rule *perspicuous* if no variable has both bound and free occurrences, and no bound variable is declared more than once. (The latter means here that different occurrences of the import command have different main existential variables.)

Let Free(R) be the set of free variables of a rule R. In other words, Free(R) is the set of variables v such that v occurs freely in rule R. Define Bound(R) similarly. If R is an import rule with main existential variable v and body R_0, we have:

$$\text{Free}(R) = \text{Free}(R_0) - \{v\}, \quad \text{and} \quad \text{Bound}(R) = \text{Bound}(R_0) \cup \{v\}.$$

3.2.3 Auxiliary Vocabularies

The names of variables are different from function names of course, but it is convenient to treat free variables of rules as auxiliary nullary functions (which cannot be subjects of update instructions). An *auxiliary vocabulary* has the form $\Upsilon \cup V$, where Υ is a genuine vocabulary and V is a finite set of variables.

If S is a state of an auxiliary vocabulary $\Upsilon' = \Upsilon \cup V$, then Fun($S$) = Υ'. S is *appropriate* for a rule R if Υ contains all function names of R and V contains all free variables of R. R is S-*perspicuous* if it is perspicuous and its bound variables do not occur in V.

3.2.4 Transition Rules: Semantics

An import commands chooses an element of the reserve and removes it from the reserve. To clarify our intentions, we note that the non-perspicuous rule

```
import v
   Parent(v):=CurrentNode
endimport
import v
   Parent(v):=CurrentNode
endimport
```

creates *two* children of CurrentNode. In general, different choices from the reserve produce different elements.

For each rule R and every state S appropriate for R, we define an update set Updates(R, S) over S; to fire R at S, fire Updates(R, S).

First, we consider the case of when R is S-perspicuous. Fix an injective map ξ from Bound(R) to the reserve of the given S. (The injectivity means that ξ assigns different elements to different bound variables.) By induction on subrule R' of R we define sets Updates(R', S', ξ) where S' is an expansion of S appropriate for R' and such that R' is S'-perspicuous. (Recall that S' is an expansion of S if and only if the reduct of S' to Fun(S) equals S.) Let $\Upsilon' = \text{Fun}(S')$.

The cases of update instructions, sequence rules and conditional rules are treated as above. (Variables in Υ' are treated as nullary functions.) Suppose that R' is an import rule with main existential variable v and body R_0. Let $a = \xi(v)$ and S'_a be the expansion of S' to the auxiliary vocabulary $\Upsilon' \cup \{v\}$ where v is interpreted as a. Recall that variables are not subjects of update instructions. Thus Updates(R_0, S'_a, ξ) is an update set over S'. Set

$$\text{Updates}(R', S', \xi) = \{((\text{Reserve}, a), \textit{false})\} \cup \text{Updates}(R_0, S'_a, \xi).$$

Finally Updates(R, S) = Updates(R, S, ξ). Of course, Updates(R, S) is not defined uniquely, because it depends on ξ. It is easy to see, however, the resulting state is unique up to isomorphism.

Second, we stipulate that an arbitrary rule R is equivalent, over the given appropriate state S, to an S-perspicuous rule R' obtained from R by renaming the bound variables. (The desired R' can be obtained by iterating the following transformation: Select an innermost import subrule R_1 whose main existential variable v occurs in the rest of the rule or in Fun(S), and replace v with a fresh variable in R_1.) The stipulation means the following: To fire R at S, fire R' at S.

Discarding Elements from Universes Finally, we explain the reason for forbidding to mention Reserve explicitly in our rules. Terms Reserve(t) always evaluate to *false*, so evaluating Reserve(t) or setting it to *false* is useless. But why not to allow putting the value *true* into Reserve locations? Elements can be discarded from universes, of course; to discard an element (represented by a term) t from a universe U, use the instruction

$U(t) := \textit{false}$. Isn't the reserve a natural place for unwanted elements? Yes, it is. Notice, however, that moving an element into the reserve may necessitate numerous changes of basic functions in order to ensure that the Reserve proviso remains valid. Would such a move contradict the sequential character of our rules? Not necessarily. We could just mark discarded elements as reserve elements, but then it might be necessary to augment rules with numerous guards Reserve$(t) = \textit{false}$, which would be too tedious. It is preferable to leave the discarded elements alone. This pragmatic argument was put forward originally by Egon Börger.

But shouldn't the computational resources of the ealgebra simulating an algorithm A closely reflect the computational resources of A? Yes, but it is important to separate the following concerns: the logic of A and the relevant resources of A. Concentrating on the logic of A may allow one to come up with simpler rules for the simulating ealgebra. And if one needs to track the resources of A, a separate bookkeeping may be set up. This separation of concerns allows us, for example, to use infinite universes. And caring about only particular elements and universes, rather than the whole superuniverse, makes combining ealgebras easier.

3.2.5 Importing Several Elements at a Time

Let v_1, v_2 be distinct variables. Abbreviate

```
import v₁
   import v₂
      R₀
   endimport
endimport
```

to

```
import v₁, v₂
   R₀
endimport
```

In a similar way, define abbreviations

```
import v₁,...,vₖ
   R₀
endimport
```

Abbreviate

```
import v₁,...,vₖ
   U(v₁) := true
     ⋮
   U(vₖ) := true
   R₀
endimport
```

to

```
extend U with v₁,...,vₖ
   R₀
endextend
```

Later (in 5.4) we'll see how to import a number of elements that is not bounded *a priori* by any constant. Here is an example of the extend rule:

```
extend Nodes with v₁, v₂
   FistChild(CurrentNode) := v₁
   SecondChild(CurrentNode) := v₂
   NextSib(v₁) := v₂
endextend
```

3.3 Programs and Runs

3.3.1 *Programs and Pure Runs*

A *program* P is a rule without free variables. A *basic program* is a basic rule without free variables. In applications, a program is usually a sequence of rules referred to as rules of the program. To fire P at an appropriate state S, fire Updates(P, S) at S.

A *pure run* of P is a sequence $\langle S_n : n < \kappa \rangle$ of states of vocabulary Fun(P) such that each S_{n+1} is obtained from S_n by firing P at S_n. Here and henceforth κ is a positive integer or the first infinite ordinal. In the latter case, $\{n : n < \kappa\}$ is the set of all natural numbers.

The adjective "pure" reflects the fact that the run is not affected by the environment.

3.3.2 *External Functions*

In general runs may be affected by the environment. Suppose that the environment manifests itself via some basic functions $e_1, \ldots, e_k$, called *external functions*. A typical external function is the input provided by the user.

Think about an external function as a (dynamic) oracle. The ealgebra provides the arguments and the oracle gives the result. The oracle need not be consistent and may give different results for the same argument at different times. The seeming inconsistency may be quite natural. For example, the argument may specify an input channel. The next time around, another input can come via the same channel.

However, the oracle should be consistent during the execution of any one step of the program. In an implementation, this may be achieved by not reiterating the same question during a one-step execution. Ask the question once and, if necessary, save the result and reuse it.

The computation steps of a program are supposed to be atomic at an appropriate level of abstraction. A computation step is hardly atomic if during that step the ealgebra queries an oracle and then, depending on the result, submits another query to the same or a different oracle. Thus it seems reasonable to forbid nesting of external functions. Indeed, the need to nest external functions has not arisen in applications so far. But we withhold final judgement and wait for more experimentation.

Call non-external basic functions *internal*. If S is an appropriate state for a program P, let S^- be the reduct of S to the internal vocabulary.

Runs A *run* of a program P is a sequence $\langle S_n : n < \kappa \rangle$ of states where:
- every nonfinal S_n is an appropriate state for P and the final state (if any) is a state of the internal vocabulary of P, and
- every S_{n+1}^- is obtained from S_n by firing P at S_n.

Internal and External Locations It may happen that the environment controls only a part of a function e_i and the remaining part of e_i is governed internally. In such a case it is natural to speak about internal and external locations rather than internal and external functions. See an example in [BGR, 3.1]. The generalization to that case is relatively straightforward.

Irrelevant Values of External Functions In order to fire a given program at a given state, we may not need to know all about the state. Only some values of external functions may be needed for firing. We may not care about or even know the values of external functions which are not needed for the execution. Some of those values may even be ill-defined. There is also an issue of influencing the environment by requiring an extra value, *e.g.*, by requiring a user-provided datum.

It is natural to set all irrelevant values of external functions to *undef*. However, caution should be exercised in the distributed situation (see §6) where other agents may have different views of those values.

Sometimes it may be simpler to use partial states. A partial Υ-state S with carrier C can be defined as a partial function from $\text{Loc}_\Upsilon(C)$ to C. See examples in [BGR, GM]. For simplicity, we will not use partial states here.

4 Nondeterministic Sequential Ealgebras and Some Other Simple Extensions of the Basic Model

Describing algorithms on higher abstraction levels, one often comes across the phenomenon of nondeterminism. Nevertheless, the built-in nondeterminism of ealgebras has been rarely used. It is often more appropriate to use external functions to reflect nondeterministic behavior. (In the distributed case, nondeterminism may be often eliminated by introducing additional agents.) Consider for instance the assignment statement of the C programming language. Should one evaluate the left side or the right side first? According to the ANSI standard (ANSI is the American National Standards Institute), the choice of the evaluation order is implementation-dependent. Moreover, an implementation does not have to be consistent; the evaluation order may change when the same assignment statement is executed next time around (say, in a loop). This is an obvious case of nondeterminism and first we, the authors of [GH], were tempted to use a nondeterministic rule to reflect the nondeterminism. But then we realized that C is perfectly deterministic. It is just that execution may depend on information provided by implementation. Thus it is more faithful to the standard (and more convenient) to use an external function that decides the evaluation order.

Still, nondeterministic commands may be desired and we provide such commands in this section. For example, it may be convenient to formalize the environment in a distributed situation, so that an external function of one agent is nondeterministically computed by another agent.

For simplicity, we ignore the import constructor in this section. It is easy to extend the language of this section with the import constructor. Moreover, the choice constructor defined below and the import constructor can be combined into one constructor.

4.1 Basic Evolving Algebras with Choice

4.1.1 *Syntax*

Transition rules are constructed as in 3.2, except that instead of the import constructor, we use the Choose (or Choice) Constructor:

Choose Constructor If U is a universe name different from Reserve, v is a variable and R_0 is a rule then the following expression is a rule with *main existential variable v* that ranges over U and *body R_0*:

choose v in U
   R_0
endchoose

This is the basic version of the choice constructor; a stronger version is defined in 4.2.2. Perspicuity is defined as 3.2.

4.1.2 *Semantics*

For each rule R and each state S appropriate for R, we define a family $\gamma = \text{NUpdates}(R, S)$ of update sets over S. To fire R at S, choose any $\beta \in \gamma$ and fire β at S.

We stipulate that an arbitrary rule R is equivalent, over the given S, to an S-perspicuous rule R' obtained from R by renaming the bound variables. The equivalence means here that $\text{NUpdates}(R, S) = \text{NUpdates}(R', S)$. It remains to define $\gamma = \text{NUpdates}(R, S)$ when S is S-perspicuous.

Global Choice Semantics Semantics is defined as in 3.2.4. On one hand, things are simpler this time around because there is no correlation among individual choices. On the other hand, there is a complication related to attempts to choose an element of the empty set. Such attempt cannot succeed and the execution should be aborted. To deal with this complication, we extend the collection of updates of any state by an ideal element $\bot$ that symbolizes inconsistency. If an update set β contains $\bot$ then firing β does not change the state; we call such β contradictory.

Suppose that a state S is appropriate for a rule R and R is S-perspicuous. Let V be the collection of bound variables of R such that the range of v is not empty in state S. Fix a function ξ on V such that, for each $v \in V$, $\xi(v)$ belongs to the range of v in S. By induction on subrule R' of R define Updates(R', S', ξ) where S' is an expansion of S appropriate for R' and R' is S'-perspicuous.

The cases of update instructions, sequence rules and conditional rule are treated as above. Notice that if R' is a sequence of rules R_i and some Updates(R_i, S', ξ) is contradictory then Updates(R', S', ξ) is so.

Suppose that R' is a choose rule with main existential variable v and body R_0. If the range of v is empty then Updates$(R', S', \xi) = \bot$. Otherwise let $a = \xi(v)$ and S'_a be the expansion of S' to the auxiliary vocabulary $\Upsilon' \cup \{v\}$ where v is interpreted as a. Set Updates$(R', S', \xi) = $ Updates(R_0, S'_a, ξ).

Finally, NUpdates(R, S) is the set of Updates(R, S, ξ) where ξ takes all possible values.

Semantics without Global Choice The global choice semantics is straightforward. However, contrary to the situation 3.2.4, there is no correlation among individual choices this time around, and thus there is no real need for a global choice function ξ. It may be more elegant to define $\gamma = $ NUpdates(R, S) directly by induction on R. We suppose again that S is appropriate to R and R is S-conspicuous.

If R is an update instruction then $\gamma = \{$Updates$(R, S)\}$. If R is a sequence of rules $R_1, \ldots, R_k$, then

$$\gamma = \{\beta_1 \cup \cdots \cup \beta_k : \text{ each } \beta_i \in \text{NUpdates}(R_i, S)\}.$$

Notice that γ is empty if so is some NUpdates(R_i, S).

If R is a conditional rule with clauses $(g_0, R_0), \ldots, (g_k, R_k)$, we have two cases as usual; if all $k+1$ guards fail in S then $\gamma = \{\emptyset\}$, and if g_i is the first guard that holds in S then $\gamma = $ NUpdates(R_i, S). (It would be a mistake to replace $\{\emptyset\}$ with $\emptyset$ above. If NUpdates$(R_1, S) = \emptyset$ then NUpdates$((R_1, R_2), S) = \emptyset$ for every rule R_2, which is not desired.)

Finally, suppose that R is a choose rule with universe name U, main existential variable v and body R_0. For each $a \in U$, let S_a be the expansion of S of the auxiliary vocabulary Fun$(S) \cup \{v\}$ where v is interpreted as a. Then

$$\gamma = \bigcup \{\text{NUpdates}(R_0, S_a) : a \in U\}.$$

Notice that γ is empty if U is empty.

It is easy to check that if R contains no choice subrules then NUpdates$(R, S) = \{$Updates$(R, S)\}$.

Remark In the second approach, $\bot$ is not used. Its role is played by the empty family of update sets. This gives us an idea to eliminate the use of $\bot$ in the first approach: replace Updates(R', S', ξ) with the singleton family $\{$Updates$(R', S', \xi)\}$ and replace $\bot$ with the empty family.

Runs The definition of runs in §3 remains in force.

4.1.3 Abbreviations

Let v_1, v_2 be distinct variables. Abbreviate

choose v_1 in U
  choose v_2 in U choose v_1, v_2 in U
    R_0 to R_0
  endchoose   endchoose
endchoose

In a similar way define abbreviation

choose $v_1, \ldots, v_k$ in U
  R_0
endchoose

4.2 Some Other Simple Extensions of the Basic Model

We consider three extensions, which are simple in the sense that it is easy to define them. The third extension has not been used; it is just a trial balloon.

4.2.1 First-order Guards

In §3, guards were Boolean terms. Now we introduce a separate syntactic category of guards. Intuitively, guards are first-order formulas with bound variables. It is intended that bound variables range over finite domains, though exceptions are possible. Here is a recursive definition:

- If f is an r-ary relation name and $t_1, \ldots, t_r$ are terms, then $f(t_1, \ldots, t_r)$ is a guard.
- Any Boolean combination of guards is a guard.
- If g is a guard and U a universe name, then $(\exists v \in U)g$ and $(\forall v \in U)g$ are guards.

Call a guard closed if it has no free variables. Extend the definition of basic ealgebras by replacing the condition "$g_1, \ldots, g_k$ are Boolean terms" with the condition "$g_1, \ldots, g_k$ are closed guards" in the definition of the conditional rule constructor.

Semantics The definition of the value of a closed guard at an appropriate state mirrors the truth definition of formulas in first-order logic. The semantics of rules is given exactly as in 3.1.

Remark One can go further in this direction and use quantification inside other terms. To formalize this idea, the notion of terms can be redefined as follows:

- A variable v is a term.

- If f is an r-ary function name and $t_1, \ldots, t_r$ are terms, then $f(t_1, \ldots, t_r)$ is a term. The new term is Boolean if f is a relation name.
- Boolean terms are closed under the Boolean operations and quantification, and every Boolean term is a term.

4.2.2 Qualified Choose Construct

Restricting the choice by a Boolean term gives a much more powerful version of the choose constructor.

Qualified Choose Constructor If U is a universe name different from Reserve, v is a variable, $g(v)$ is a Boolean term and R_0 is a rule, then the following expression is a rule with *main existential variable* v that ranges over U and body R_0:

choose v in U satisfying $g(v)$
  R_0
endchoose

Replacing the choose constructor with the qualified choose constructor requires only a small and obvious change in the semantical definition of 4.1.2. We restrict attention to the global choice approach. Consider the case in the inductive definition of Updates(R', S', ξ) where R' is a choose rule and the range U of the main existential variable v of R in S' is not empty. If $g(\xi(v))$ fails in S, set Updates$(R', S', \xi) = \bot$.

It is easy to construct a rule to choose several elements $v_1, \ldots, v_k$ subject to a condition $g(v_1, \ldots, v_k)$.

The qualified choose constructor may be too powerful. The decision problem whether there is any tuple $(v_1, \ldots, v_k)$ in the universe U satisfying the condition g may be hard. If U is the set of natural numbers and g a polynomial, the decision problem may even be undecidable [Mt]. But the logical clarity of the constructor is attractive. It may be used in particular to reflect environmental forces that are not necessarily algorithmic.

4.2.3 Duplication

The powerful extension of basic ealgebras considered in this subsection is logically clear, but untried and computationally expensive. It does not hurt to explore it though.

Call elements a and a' of a state S indistinguishable as arguments for a basic r-ary function f if $f(b_1, \ldots, b_r) = f(c_1, \ldots, c_r)$ for all r-tuples $b_1, \ldots, b_r$ and $c_1, \ldots, c_r$ such that either $b_i = c_i$ or $\{b_i, c_i\} = \{a, a'\}$. Call a, a' indistinguishable as arguments if they are indistinguishable as arguments for any basic function with the exception of equality. Now we are ready to introduce the duplicate constructor:

```
duplicate t as v
  R_0
endduplicate
```

Semantics To execute, calculate $a = Val_S(t)$, get some a' from the reserve and redefine basic functions on tuples involving a' in such a way that a and a' become indistinguishable as arguments. Then execute R_0 with v equal a'.

Duplication can be seen as a powerful inheritance mechanism. It is easy to see that the extend construct is not powerful enough to replace duplication.

5 Parallelism: Evolving Algebras with Variables

What does it mean that an algorithm is sequential? This usually means that the algorithm has the following two features. First, time is sequential. The algorithm proceeds from some initial state S_0 to a state S_1, then to a state S_2, *etc.*, and the steps are atomic. Second, only a bounded amount of work is done at each step. In principle, a single agent is able to move the algorithm from S_0 to S_1, then to S_2, *etc.*.

In this section, we are interested in one-agent algorithms where the agent may perform a substantial amount of work at one step. We use variables to formalize such algorithms. It is intended that non-Reserve variables range over finite (better yet, feasible) domains, though exceptions are possible.

We do not assume any particular sequential order of executing one step of the algorithm. It is possible that this work involves plenty of parallelism and is implemented by a number of auxiliary agents. But on the natural level of abstraction of the given algorithm, those auxiliary agents are invisible, and in principle a single agent may execute the algorithm.

5.1 Variables

In preceding sections, we dealt with implicit variables declarations by means import commands, bounded quantifiers, etc. In this section, we introduce explicit variable declarations.

An *explicit atomic variable declaration* is an expression "Var v ranges over U", where v is a variable and U a universe name. The universe U is the range (or type) of the variable v. An *explicit variable declaration* D is a sequence of explicit atomic variable declarations, and $\text{Var}(D)$ is the collection of variables in D. For brevity, the adjective explicit is often omitted.

Intuitively, D is a set of explicit atomic declarations, but we do not forbid re-declarations of the same variable. The range of a variable $v \in \text{Var}(D)$ is the range in the last declaration of v in D. In other words, later declarations of a variable override the earlier ones. One may use more concise explicit variable declarations, like "Var $v_1, \ldots, v_k$ range over U".

A variable declaration D *covers* a syntactic object s if $\text{Var}(D)$ contains all free (that is undeclared) variables of s.

As in 3.2.3, we use auxiliary vocabularies of the form $\Upsilon \cup V$, where Υ is a genuine vocabulary, V a finite set of variables and each $v \in V$ is treated as a nullary function, except it cannot be the subject of an update instruction. We say that a state S of an auxiliary vocabulary is *appropriate* for a syntactical object s if all function names and all free variables of s occur in $\text{Fun}(S)$.

5.2 Terms and Guards

Terms and Boolean terms are defined in §3. Guards are defined in 4.2.1. The free variables of terms and guards are defined inductively, as in first-order logic. Notice that a bounded quantifier implicitly contains an atomic declaration.

As usual, every guard g is equivalent to a guard g' where no variable is both bound and free and where different quantifier occurrences bind different variables. To reduce g to g', iterate the following transformation: Select an innermost quantifier q whose variable v occurs outside the scope of q and then replace v with a fresh variable in the scope of q.

5.3 A Parallel Version of the Basic EA Model

5.3.1 *Syntax*

Update instructions and basic rules are defined as in 3.1, except that terms may have free variables, and guards are defined as above. In addition, we have the following third rule constructor.

The Declaration Constructor An atomic variable declaration followed by a rule is a rule.

By an obvious induction on rules, define which occurrences of variables are free (or undeclared) and which are bound. Suppose that D is a variable declaration, R is a rule, and S is a state of an auxiliary vocabulary. R is (D, S)-*perspicuous* if it satisfies the following conditions:

- no variable is declared (explicitly or implicitly) more than once in R, and
- $\text{Bound}(R)$ is disjoint from $\text{Free}(R) \cup \text{Var}(D) \cup \text{Fun}(S)$.

Programs A *program* is a rule without any undeclared variables.

5.3.2 *Semantics of Rules*

By induction on R, we define the update set $\beta = \text{Updates}(D, R, S)$ generated by a rule R at an appropriate state S under a declaration D that covers R. To fire R at S under D, fire β.

We stipulate that an arbitrary rule R is equivalent, for given D and S, to a (D, S)-perspicuous rule R' obtained from R by renaming the bound variables. The equivalence means that $\text{Updates}(D, R, S) = \text{Updates}(D, R', S)$.

It remains to define $\beta = \text{Updates}(D, R, S)$ in the case when R is (D, S)-perspicuous.

If D is not empty, then β is the union of $\text{Updates}(\emptyset, R, S')$, where S' ranges over expansions of S such that $\text{Fun}(S') = \text{Fun}(S) \cup \text{Var}(D)$ and S' is consistent with D (so that the values of D variables are within their ranges in S'). Notice that $\beta = \emptyset$ if the range of any D variable is empty.

Suppose $D = \emptyset$. If R is an update instruction then $\beta = \text{Updates}(R, S)$. If R is a sequence of rules $R_1, \ldots, R_k$, then β is the union of the update sets $\text{Updates}(\emptyset, R_i, S)$. Suppose that R is the conditional rule with clauses $(g_0, R_0), \ldots, (g_k, R_k)$. Since R is covered by the empty declaration, the guards g_i have no free variables. We have two cases as usual. If all guards g_i fail in S, then β is empty, and if g_i is the first guard that holds in S then $\beta = \text{NUpdates}(\emptyset, R_i, S)$. Finally, if R is a declaration rule with declaration d and body R' then $\beta = \text{Updates}(d, R', S)$.

Remark Suppose that $D = \emptyset$ and R is a sequence of a declaration-free rule R_1 and a declaration rule R_2 with atomic declaration "Var v ranges over U" followed by a declaration-free body R_2'. Further suppose that U is empty in a state S appropriate for R and thus $\text{Updates}(D, R_2, S) = \emptyset$. Then $\text{Updates}(D, R, S)$ equals $\text{Updates}(D, R_1, S)$ which may be not empty. Contrary to the situation in 4.1.2, the empty range does not give inconsistency here. One cannot choose an element from the empty set, but one can execute a rule $R_2'(v)$ for every v in the empty set: just do not execute anything.

5.4 Importing Elements

The recursive definition of rules in 5.3 can be extended by import commands and/or (qualified) choice commands. The adjustment of the semantic definition is straightforward. For the sake of definiteness, consider the extension by means of the import constructor. The most important novelty, in comparison to 3.2.4, is that reserve elements have to be chosen for all combinations of the values of explicitly declared variables u such that the scope of the declaration of u properly includes the given import or choose subrule. For example, the rule

```
Var u ranges over U
import v
    Parent(v):=u
endimport
```

creates a new child for every element of U, and of course all these new children are different.

To reflect the novelty we redefine the domain of the global choice function. Suppose that D is a variable declaration, R is a rule covered by D, S is a state of an auxiliary vocabulary appropriate for R, and R is (D,S)-perspicuous. For every bound variable v of R, list all explicitly declared variables u such that either u occurs in D or u occurs in R and the scope of the declaration of u properly includes the scope of the declaration of v: $u_1, \ldots, u_l$. (The adverb properly is there to exclude v from the list.) Let $U_1, \ldots, U_l$ be the ranges of $u_1, \ldots, u_l$ in S respectively, and $\bar{U}_v$ be the Cartesian product $U_1 \times \cdots \times U_l$. The desired global function ξ assigns different reserve elements to every pair $(v, \bar{a})$ where $v \in \text{Bound}(R)$ and $\bar{a} \in \bar{U}_v$.

Here is a variant of the example from 3.2.5:

```
Var u ranges over U
extend Nodes with v₁, v₂
    if Leaf(u) then
        FirstChild(u) := v₁
        SecondChild(u) := v₂
        NextSib(v₁) := v₂
    endif endextend
```

Remark Should one provide means to say explicitly that the main existential variable of a given choose rule depends only on such and such of the free variables of the rule? Maybe. But the need for such means has not been demonstrated yet.

5.5 Runs

Runs are defined as above.

6 Distributed Evolving Algebras

In this section we consider multi-agent computations. We do not suppose that agents are deterministic or do only a bounded amount of work at each step. The program of an agent may be any program described above.

Agents may share functions, and it is convenient [GR] to assume that all states of all agents share the same carrier; see the end of 3.2.4 in this connection.

6.1 The Self Function

There is an interesting problem of self identification. It can be illustrated on the example of the following simple version of Dijkstra's dining philosophers protocol (which may deadlock). There are n philosophers, marked with numbers modulo n, each equipped with a fork. A philosopher i may think (which requires no forks) or eat using his/her fork and the fork of philosopher $i+1$. A fork cannot be used by two philosophers at the same time.

Using functions

$$\text{Fork}_i = \begin{cases} \text{up} & \text{if the fork of philosopher } i \text{ is used,} \\ \text{down} & \text{otherwise,} \end{cases}$$

we can write a separate program for each philosopher i. Intuitively, however, all philosophers use the same program in the protocol.

To solve such problems, we suppose that each agent a is represented by an element of the common carrier. For simplicity, we will not distinguish between an agent and the element that represents the agent. Further, we use a special nullary function Self, interpreted differently by different agents. An agent a interprets Self as a. Thus function Self allows an agent to identify itself among other agents. Self is a logic name and cannot be the subject of an update instruction. To make rules sound a little better for humans, we use some capitalized pronouns, e.g. Me, as aliases for Self. Viewing agents as elements of the carrier is useful for other purposes as well. For example, it allows us to model the creation of new agents.

We return to the dining philosophers protocol. Here is a possible program (courtesy of Jim Huggins):

```
if Mode(Me)=think and Fork(Me)=Fork(Me+1)=down then
    Fork(Me):=up, Fork(Me+1):=up, Mode(Me):=eat
elseif Mode(Me)=eat then
    Fork(Me):=down, Fork(Me+1):=down, Mode(Me):=think
endif
```

It may be convenient to suppress the argument Self. For example, terms Mode(Me), Fork(Me) and Fork(Me+1) may be treated as nullary functions and abbreviated, e.g., as mode, lfork and rfork, so that the rfork function of philosopher i is the lfork function of philosopher $i + 1$ and mode is a private function.

6.2 Basic Definition of Distributed Ealgebras

A *distributed ealgebra* $\mathcal{A}$ consists of the following:

- A finite indexed set of single-agent programs π_ν, called *modules*. The *module names* ν are static nullary function names.
- A vocabulary $\Upsilon = \text{Fun}(\mathcal{A})$ which includes each $\text{Fun}(\pi_\nu) - \{\text{Self}\}$ but does not contain Self. In addition, Υ contains a unary function name Mod.
- A collection of Υ-states, called *initial states* of $\mathcal{A}$, satisfying the following conditions:
    * Different module names are interpreted as different elements.
    * There are only finitely many elements a such that, for some module name ν, $\text{Mod}(a) = \nu$.

A state S of vocabulary $\text{Fun}(\mathcal{A})$ is a state of $\mathcal{A}$ if it satisfies the two conditions imposed on initial states. In applications it may make sense to restrict further the notion of state of the ealgebra in question.

An element a is an *agent* at S if there is a module name ν such that $S \models \text{Mod}(a) = \nu$; the corresponding π_ν is the program $\text{Prog}(a)$ of a, and $\text{Fun}(\pi_\nu)$ is the vocabulary $\text{Fun}(a)$ of a. Agent a is deterministic if $\text{Prog}(a)$ is so.

$\text{View}_a(S)$ is the reduct of S to vocabulary $\text{Fun}(a) - \{\text{Self}\}$ expanded with Self, which is interpreted as a. Think about $\text{View}_a(S)$ as the local state of agent a corresponding to the global state S. (It is not necessary to define local states via global states; see [GM] for example.)

An agent a can *make a move* at S by firing $\text{Prog}(a)$ at $\text{View}_a(S)$ and changing S accordingly. As a part of the move, a may create new agents, *e.g.*, by importing reserve elements.

To perform a move of a deterministic agent a, fire

$$\text{Updates}(a, S) = \text{Updates}\Big(\text{Prog}(a), \text{View}_a(S)\Big).$$

Runs of a distributed ealgebra are defined below.

Cooperative Actions Consider a simple scenario with agents Sender and Receiver. If both are in mode Ready then Sender passes a value t_1 to Receiver who stores it at location $f(t_2)$. The transaction is atomic (that is, indivisible), but the Sender does not have access to $f(t_2)$ and the Receiver does not have access to t_1, and thus neither agent is able to perform the transaction. A special auxiliary agent is needed to do the job, and it may be convenient to view the auxiliary agent as a team with members Sender and Receiver. Using functions Member_1 and Member_2 to specify the members of the team, we may write the following rule for the team, where Us is an alias for Self:

```
if Mode(Member₁(Us))=Mode(Member₂(Us))=Ready then
    f(t₂) := t₁
endif
```

In a similar way, one may have larger teams. Depending on need, teams may or may not be ordered.

6.3 Generalizations

6.3.1 *Active Agents*

Alter definition 6.2 as follows: Require that $\text{Fun}(\mathcal{A})$ contains an additional unary relation name Active and that only agents satisfying the relation Active (*active agents*) can make moves. This is essentially a generalization; the original definition can be seen as a special case where all agents are active.

The new definition may be convenient, for example, when the initial state specifies all agents and their programs, and these agents are activated and deactivated during the evolution.

The same convenience can be achieved without altering the original definition. (This may be useful, for example, if you want to prove something about all distributed ealgebras and wish to restrict attention to the basic definition without losing generality.) Here is one way to do that. In order to indicate the program of a potential agent without making it an actual agent, use an auxiliary unary function name Mod'. Active(t) can be viewed as an abbreviation for Mod(t) = Mod'(t) except if Active is the subject of an update instruction.

```
Active(t):=t₀
```

can be viewed as an abbreviation for

```
if t₀ then Mod(t):=Mod'(t)
else Mod(t):=undef
endif
```

6.3.2 *Active Teams*

The generalized definition of distributed ealgebras described in 6.3.1 is used in this sub-subsection. The following problem was raised by Dean Rosenzweig [R].

Consider a scenario with (agents called) players and (additional agents viewed as) teams. Players form a static universe, teams form another static universe, and each agent is assigned a program once and for all. Players are activated and deactivated during the evolution. A team is supposed to be active if and only if its members are active. It follows that activating one player may necessitate the tedious work of activating many teams. Is there a simple and elegant way to ensure that every team is active when and only when all its members are active?

One obvious solution is to make teams active all the time and augment the program of each team with a guard stating that all the members are active. A more radical solution is to make the notion of team a part of the logic of distributed ealgebras. It will be ensured automatically that a team is active if and only if all its members are active. (It may be also required that the moves made by a player or any team involving the player are linearly ordered; see the second property of runs in 6.5.1 in this connection.) If substantial programming convenience is demonstrated, use that solution.

The possibilities to pay a lesser price in logic complication for the advantages of the radical solution will be discussed elsewhere. In this connection, Rosenzweig suggested generalizing further the definition of 6.3.1 by letting a possibly compound Boolean term play the role of Active. For example, Active(v) may say that either v is a player satisfying an auxiliary relation Ac or v is a team with all members satisfying Ac.

6.4 Sequential Runs

We return to the basic definition of distributed ealgebras in 6.2.

A *pure sequential run* ρ of an ealgebra $\mathcal{A}$ is a sequence $\langle S_n : n < \kappa \rangle$ of states of $\mathcal{A}$, where S_0 is an initial state and every S_{n+1} is obtained from S_n by executing a move of an agent. The generalization to the case of external functions or external locations is relatively straightforward.

Stages Since S_i may be equal to S_j for some $i \neq j$, it may be convenient to speak about stages. Starting from stage 0, the run goes through stages 1, 2, *etc.*. Formally, stage i can be defined as the pair (i, S_i).

Quasi-sequential Runs An obvious generalization of a sequential run is a quasi-sequential run $\langle S_n : n < \kappa \rangle$, where each S_{n+1} is obtained from S_n by firing a collection A_n of agents. We do not mean that A_n is a team; since teams are agents, the definition of sequential runs does not exclude team moves. We mean that each $a \in A_n$ makes a move at S_n. If all agents are deterministic, then S_{n+1} is the result of firing $\bigcup \{\text{Updates}(S, a) : a \in A_n\}$.

Quasi-sequential runs may arise, for example, if you order moves in real (physical) time.

6.5 Partially Ordered Runs

Partially ordered computations are well known in the literature [L, Mz, KP, *etc.*] but we need to define our own version of that notion for our purposes here. We restrict attention to the case where moves are atomic and we use global states. Non-atomic moves have been explored in [BGR]. A simple notion of runs in [GM] does not use global states.

Let us recall some well known notions. A *poset* is a partially ordered set. An *initial segment* of a poset P is a substructure X of P such that if $x \in X$ and $y < x$ in P then $y \in X$. Since X is a substructure, $y < x$ in X if and only if $y < x$ in P whenever $x, y \in X$. A *linearization* of a poset P is a linearly ordered set P' with the same elements such that if $x < y$ in P then $x < y$ in P'.

6.5.1 Runs

For simplicity, we restrict attention to pure runs and deterministic agents. A *run* ρ of a distributed ealgebra $\mathcal{A}$ can be defined as a triple (M, A, σ) satisfying the following conditions 1–4.

1 M is a partially ordered set, where all sets $\{y : y \leq x\}$ are finite.

Elements of M represent *moves* made by various agents during the run. If $y < x$ then x starts when y is already finished; that explains why the set $\{y : y \leq x\}$ is finite.

2 A is a function on M such that every nonempty set $\{x : A(x) = a\}$ is linearly ordered.

$A(x)$ is the agent performing move x. The moves of any single agent are supposed to be linearly ordered.

3 σ assigns a state of $\mathcal{A}$ to the empty set and each finite initial segment of M; $\sigma(\emptyset)$ is an initial state.

$\sigma(X)$ is the result of performing all moves in X.

4 The coherence condition: If x is a maximal element in a finite initial segment X of M and $Y = X - \{x\}$, then $A(x)$ is an agent in $\sigma(Y)$ and $\sigma(X)$ is obtained from $\sigma(Y)$ by firing $A(x)$ at $\sigma(Y)$.

Intuitively, a run can be seen as the common part of histories of the same computation recorded by various observers. We hope to address this issue elsewhere.

If agents are not necessarily deterministic, we have to define moves as state transformers and make the coherence condition more precise:

4* If x is a maximal element in a finite initial segment X of M and $Y = X - \{x\}$, then $A(x)$ is an agent in $\sigma(Y)$, x is a move of $A(x)$ and $\sigma(X)$ is obtained from $\sigma(Y)$ by performing x at $\sigma(Y)$.

A run ρ' is an *initial segment* of a run ρ if (i) the move poset of ρ' is an initial segment of the move poset of ρ and (ii) the agent and state functions of ρ' are restrictions of those in ρ. A run ρ' is a *linearization* of ρ if the move poset of ρ' is a linearization of that of ρ, the agent function of ρ' is that of ρ, and the state function of ρ' is a restriction of that of ρ. Linearizations are sequential runs. A state S of is *reachable* in a run ρ if it belongs to the range of the state function of ρ.

Corollary 6.1 *All linearizations of the same finite initial segment of ρ have the same final state.*

Corollary 6.2 *A property holds in every reachable state of a run ρ if and only if it holds in every reachable state of every linearization of ρ.*

6.6 Real-time Computations

Real-time semantics appears in [BGR]. Ealgebras with clocks made their debut in [GM]. We will have to address the issue of real time elsewhere.

Bibliography

B Egon Börger, "Logic Programming: The Evolving Algebra Approach", in [PS].

BG Andreas Blass and Yuri Gurevich, "Evolving Algebras and Linear Time Hierarchy", in [PS].

BGR Egon Börger, Yuri Gurevich and Dean Rosenzweig, "The Bakery Algorithm: Yet Another Specification and Verification", this volume.

BR Egon Börger and Dean Rosenzweig, "The WAM — Definition and Compiler Correctness", to appear in "Logic Programming: Formal Methods and Practical Applications", Eds. C. Beierle and L. Pluemer, North-Holland, 1994.

G1 Yuri Gurevich, "Logic and the challenge of computer science", In "Current Trends in Theoretical Computer Science", Ed. E. Börger, Computer Science Press, 1988, 1–57.

G2 Yuri Gurevich, "Evolving Algebras: An Attempt to Discover Semantics ", Bull. EATCS 43 (1991), 264–284; a slightly revised version in "Current Trends in Theoretical Computer Science", Eds. G. Rozenberg and A. Salomaa, World Scientific, 1993, 266–292.

GH Yuri Gurevich and James K. Huggins, "The Semantics of the C Programming Language", Springer Lecture Notes in Computer Science 702, 1993, 274–308.

GM Yuri Gurevich and Raghu Mani, "Group Membership Protocol: Formal Specification and Verification", this volume.

GR Paola Glavan and Dean Rosenzweig, "Communicating Evolving Algebras", in "Computer Science Logic", eds. E. Börger et al., Lecture Notes in Computer Science 702, Springer, 1993, 182–215.

H James K. Huggins, "Kermit: Specification and Verification", this volume.

KP Shmuel Katz and Doron Peled, "Defining Conditional Independence Using Collapses", Theoretical Computer Science 101 (1992), 337–359.

L Leslie Lamport, "On Interprocess Communication", Distributed Computing 1 (1986), 77–101.

Mt Yuri Matijasevich, "Enumerable sets are Diophantine", Soviet Math. Doklady 11:2 (1970), 354–358.

Mz Antoni Mazurkiewicz, "Trace Theory", Springer Lecture Notes in Computer Science 255 (1987), 279–324.

PS B. Pehrson and I. Simon, Editors, "IFIP 13th World Computer Congress 1994, Volume I: Technology/Foundations", Elsevier, Amsterdam, to appear.

R Dean Rosenzweig, Private Communication.

Annotated Bibliography on Evolving Algebras

Egon Börger

Abstract

This is the current version of an annotated bibliography of papers which deal with or use evolving algebras. It is compiled to a great extent from references and annotations provided by the authors of the listed papers. Thanks to all of them. Comments, additions and corrections are welcome and should be sent to: boerger@di.unipi.it

To submit a new item, please use the format explained below, provide your proposal for the annotation and send a hard copy of the paper to the following address: Egon Börger, Dipartimento di Informatica, Università di Pisa, Corso Italia 40, I-56125 Pisa, Italy.

It is intended to make current updates of this bibliography available for anonymous ftp as dvi-file, as compressed ps-file and as tex-file in the directory pub/Papers/boerger of the machine ftp.di.unipi.it. At the beginning of the tex-file it is indicated how the file can also be edited without the annotations. If you want to use the tex-file to compile your own references, note the following principle which has been used for defining the keys.

The key for a paper published in 1945 by (a single author) Bach is Bach45, i.e. the author's name, where the first letter is a capital, followed by the last two digits of the year of publication of the paper. The key for a paper with two authors, Bach and Beethoven, is BacBee45; if there is a third author, Brahms, it is BaBeBr45; with a fourth author, Bartok, it becomes BaBeBB45, etc.

The order of the references is alphabetical; it is chronological within a group of authors. If for a group of authors there is more than one paper in the one year 1945, these papers receive keys with suffix 45a, 45b, 45c etc.

Some of the papers mentioned in this bibliography can be obtained by anonymous ftp from the following machines in the indicated directory:

(1) ftp.di.unipi.it, directory pub/Papers/boerger

(2) ftp.eecs.umich.edu, directory /groups/Ealgebras

Bibliography

1. C. Beierle. Formal Design of an Abstract Machine for Constraint Logic Programming. In B. Pehrson and I. Simon (Eds.) *IFIP 13th World Computer Congress 1994*, Volume I: *Technology/Foundations*, Elsevier, Amsterdam, 377–382.

Proposes a general implementation scheme for CLP(X) over an unspecified constraint domain X by designing a generic extension WAM(X) of the Warren Abstract Machine and a corresponding generic compilation scheme of CLP(X) programs to WAM(X) code. The scheme is based on the specification and correctness proof for compilation of Prolog programs on the WAM in [32].

2. C. Beierle and E. Börger. A WAM extension for type-constraint logic programming: Specification and correctness proof. Research report IWBS 200, IBM Germany Science Center, Heidelberg, December 1991.

Contains the extension of [3] to the full Protos Abstract Machine by refining the abstract type constraints to the polymorphic order-sorted types of PROTOS-L.

3. C. Beierle and E. Börger. Correctness proof for the WAM with types. In E. Börger, G. Jäger, H. Kleine Büning, and M. M. Richter, editors, *Computer Science Logic*, volume 626 of *Lecture Notes in Computer Science*, pages 15–34. Springer, 1992. = Research Report IWBS 205, pp. ii+23, IBM Germany Science Center, Heidelberg, January 1992.

The Börger–Rosenzweig's specification and correctness proof for compiling Prolog to WAM [32] is extended to the Protos-L language which extends Prolog with polymorphic (dynamic) types. In this paper the type notion is kept abstract (as constraint) in order to allow application to different constraint formalisms. [2] extends the specification and the correctness proof to the full Protos Abstract Machine by refining the abstract type constraints to the polymorphic order-sorted types of PROTOS-L.

4. B. Blakley. *A Smalltalk Evolving Algebra And Its Uses*. PhD thesis, University of Michigan, Ann Arbor MI, 1992.

An early student work on evolving algebras (the late date of 1992 is accidental). A reduced version of Smalltalk is formalized and studied.

5. A. Blass and Y. Gurevich. Evolving Algebras and Linear Time Hierarchy. Extended Abstract. In B. Pehrson and I. Simon (Eds.) *IFIP 13th World Computer Congress 1994*, Volume I: *Technology/Foundations*, Elsevier, Amsterdam, 383-390.

There exists a sequential evolving algebra U (an allusion to "universal") and a constant c such that, under honest time counting, U simulates every other sequential evolving algebra in lock-step with lag factor c. In STOC'92, Neil Jones exhibited simple computation models where the time-speed-up theorem fails and linear time computable functions form a hierarchy. Jones' notion of linear time is too restrictive. To overcome that obstacle, we generalize the linear hierarchy theorem to sequential evolving algebras.

6. E. Börger. A logical operational semantics for full Prolog. Part I: Selection core and control. In E. Börger, H. Kleine Büning, M. M. Richter, and W. Schönfeld, editors, *CSL'89. 3rd Workshop on Computer Science Logic, Lecture Notes in Computer Science*, volume 440, pp. 36–64. Springer, 1990. = IBM Germany Science Center Heidelberg, IWBS Report 111, March 1990. Reprinted in: Proceedings *The 3rd Logic Programming Winter School and Seminar. LOP'91*, Ruprechtov, Czechoslovakia, pp. 65–94.

See comments to [8]

7. E. Börger. A logical operational semantics for full Prolog. Part II: Built-in predicates for database manipulations. In B. Rovan, editor, *Mathematical Foundations of Computer Science*, volume 452 of *Lecture Notes in Computer Science*, pages 1–14. Springer, 1990. = IBM Germany Science Center Heidelberg, IWBS Report 115, April 1990.

See comments to [8]

8. E. Börger. A logical operational semantics for full Prolog. Part III: Built-in predicates for files, terms, arithmetic and input–output. In Y. Moschovakis, editor, *Logic from Computer Science*, Berkeley Mathematical Sciences Research Institute Publications, volume 21, pp. 17–50. Springer, 1992. Preliminary version: IBM Germany Science Center Heidelberg, IWBS Report 117, April 1990.

These are the original 3 papers of Börger where he gives a complete evolving-algebra formalization of Prolog with all features discussed in the international Prolog standardization working group (WG17 of ISO/IEC JTC1 SC22), see [10]. The specification is developed by stepwise refinement, describing orthogonal language features by modular rule sets. An improved (tree instead of stack based) version is found in [27, 30]; the revised final version is in [33].

9. E. Börger. Logic Programming: The Evolving Algebra Approach. In B. Pehrson and I. Simon (Eds.) *IFIP 13th World Computer Congress 1994*, Volume I: *Technology/Foundations*, Elsevier, Amsterdam, 391–395.

The paper surveys the work which has been done from 1986–1994 on specifications of logic programming systems by evolving algebras.

10. E. Börger and K. Dässler. Prolog: DIN papers for discussion. ISO/IEC JTCI SC22 WG17 Prolog standardization document no. 58, National Physical Laboratory, Middlesex, April 1990.

A version of [6, 7, 8] proposed to the international Prolog standardization committee as a complete formal semantics of Prolog. An improved version is in [33].

11. E. Börger, G. Del Castillo, P. Glavan, and D. Rosenzweig. Towards a mathematical specification of the APE100 architecture: the APESE model. In B. Pehrson and I. Simon (Eds.) *IFIP 13th World Computer Congress 1994*, Volume I: *Technology/Foundations*, Elsevier, Amsterdam, 396–401.

Defines a lock–step parallel evolving algebra which models the high level programming view of the APE100 parallel architecture.

12. E. Börger and B. Demoen. A framework to specify database update views for Prolog. In M. J. Maluszynski, editor, *PLILP'91. Third International Symposium on Programming Languages Implementation and Logic Programming*, volume 528 of *Lecture Notes in Computer Science*, pages 147–158. Springer, 1991. Preliminary version: *The view on database updates in Standard Prolog: a proposal and a rationale* in: ISO/IEC JTC1 SC22 WG17 Prolog Standardization Report no. 74, February 1991, pp. 3–10.

Provides a precise definition of the major Prolog database update views (immediate, logical, minimal, maximal), within a framework closely related to [6, 7, 8].

13. E. Börger, I. Durdanović, and D. Rosenzweig. Occam: Specification and compiler correctness. Part I: Simple mathematical interpreters. In U. Montanari, E.-R. Olderog (Eds.), *Proc. PROCOMET'94 (IFIP Working Conference on Programming Concepts, Methods and Calculi)*, pages 489-508, North-Holland, 1994

A truly concurrent evolving algebra model of Occam is defined as basis for a provably correct, smooth transition to the Transputer Instruction Set architecture. This model is stepwise refined, in a provably correct way, providing: (a) an asynchronous implementation of synchronous channel communication, (b) its optimization for internal channels, (c) the sequential implementation of processors using priority and time–slicing.

14. E. Börger and U.Glässer. A formal specification of the PVM architecture. In B. Pehrson and I. Simon (Eds.) *IFIP 13th World Computer Congress 1994*, Volume I: *Technology/Foundations*, Elsevier, Amsterdam, 402–409.

Provides an evolving algebra model for the Parallel Virtual machine (PVM, the Oak Ridge National Laboratory software system that serves as general purpose environment for heterogeneous distributed computing). The model defines PVM at the C–interface, at the level of abstraction which is tailored to the programmer's understanding. Cf. the survey *An abstract model of the parallel virtual machine (PVM)* presented at *7th International Conference on Parallel and Distributed Computing Systems* (PDCS'94), Las Vegas/Nevada, 5.–9.10.1994.

15. E. Börger, U. Glässer, and W. Müller. The semantics of Behavioral VHDL'92 Descriptions. In: EURO–DAC'94. European Design Automation Conference with EURO–VHDL'94. Proceedings IEEE CS Press, Los Alamitos, CA, 1994, pp. 500–505.

Provides a transparent but precise definition of the signal behavior and time model of full *elaborated* VHDL'92. This includes guarded signals, delta and time delays, the two main propagation delay modes *transport,inertial*, and the three process suspensions (wait on/until/for). Shared variables, postponed processes and rejection pulse are covered.

16. E. Börger, U. Glässer, and W. Müller. Formal definition of an abstract VHDL'93 simulator by EA–machines. In C. Delgado Kloos and P. T. Breuer (Eds.), *Formal Semantics for VHDL*, Kluwer Academic Publishers, 1995.

Extends the work in [15] by including the treatment of variable assignments and of value propagation by ports.

17. E. Börger, Y. Gurevich, and D. Rosenzweig. The bakery algorithm: Yet another specification and verification. In E. Börger, editor, *Specification and Validation Methods*. Oxford University Press, 1994.

One evolving algebra A1 is constructed to reflect faithfully the algorithm. Then a more abstract evolving algebra A2 is constructed. It is checked that A2 is safe and fair, and that A1 correctly implements A2. The proofs work for atomic as well as, mutatis mutandis, for durative actions.

18. E. Börger, F. J. López-Fraguas, and M. Rodríguez-Artalejo. Towards a mathematical specification of a narrowing machine. Research report DIA 94/5, pp. I+30, Dep. Informática y Automática, Universidad Complutense, Madrid, March 1994.

Full version of [19], containing optimizations and proofs.

19. E. Börger, F. J. López-Fraguas, and M. Rodríguez-Artalejo. A model for mathematical analysis of functional logic programs and their implementations. In B. Pehrson and I. Simon (Eds.) *IFIP 13th World Computer Congress 1994*, Volume I: *Technology/Foundations*, Elsevier, Amsterdam, 410–415.

Defines an evolving algebra model for the innermost version of the functional logic programming language BABEL, extending the Prolog model of [30, 33] by rules which describe the reduction of expressions to normal form. The model is stepwise refined towards a mathematical specification of the implementation of Babel by a graph–narrowing machine. The refinements are proved to be correct.

20. E. Börger and E. Riccobene. Logical operational semantics of Parlog. Part I: And-parallelism. In H. Boley and M. M. Richter, editors, *Processing Declarative Knowledge*, volume 567 of *Lecture Notes in Artificial Intelligence*, pages 191–198. Springer, 1991.

See comment to [23].

21. E. Börger and E. Riccobene. Logical operational semantics of Parlog. Part II: Or-parallelism. In A.Voronkov, editor, *Logic Programming*, volume 592 of *Lecture Notes in Artificial Intelligence*, pages 27–34. Springer, 1992.

See comment to [23].

22. E. Börger and E. Riccobene. A mathematical model of Concurrent Prolog. Research report CSTR-92-15, Dept. of Computer Science, University of Bristol, Bristol, 1992.

An evolving algebra formalization of Ehud Shapiro's Concurrent Prolog. Adaptation of the model defined for PARLOG in [23].

23. E. Börger and E. Riccobene. A formal specification of Parlog. In M. Droste and Y. Gurevich, editors, *Semantics of Programming Languages and Model Theory*, pages 1–42. Gordon and Breach, 1993. = TR 1/93, Dipartimento di Informatica, Università di Pisa, 1993.

An evolving algebra formalization of Parlog, a well known parallel version of Prolog. This formalization separates explicitly the two kinds of parallelism occurring in Parlog: AND–parallelism and OR–parallelism. It uses an implementation independent, abstract notion of terms and substitutions. Improved and extended version of [20, 21], obtained combining the concurrent features of the Occam model of [52] with the logic programming model of [30, 33].

24. E. Börger and E. Riccobene. Logic + control revisited: an abstract interpreter for Gödel programs. In G. Levi, editor, *Advances in Logic Programming Theory*. Oxford University Press, 1994.

Develops a simple evolving algebra interpreter for Gödel programs. This interpreter abstracts from the deterministic and sequential execution strategies of Prolog [32] and thus provides a precise interface between logic and control components for execution of Gödel programs. The construction is given in abstract terms which cover the general logic programming paradigm and allow for concurrency.

25. E. Börger and D. Rosenzweig. An analysis of Prolog database views and their uniform implementation. Research report CSE-TR-89-91, EECS, University of Michigan, Ann Arbor MI, 1991. Also issued by the international Prolog standardization committee as ISO/IEC JTCI SC22 WG17 document No. 80, National Physical Laboratory, Teddington 1991, pages 87–130.

A mathematical analysis of the Prolog database views defined in [12]. The analysis is derived by stepwise refinement of the stack model for Prolog from [29]. It leads to the proposal of a uniform implementation of the different views which discloses the tradeoffs between semantic clarity and efficiency of database update view implementations.

26. E. Börger and D. Rosenzweig. From Prolog algebras towards WAM— a mathematical study of implementation. In E. Börger, H. Kleine Büning, M. M. Richter, and W. Schönfeld, editors, *CSL'90, 4th Workshop on Computer Science Logic*, volume 533 of *Lecture Notes in Computer Science*, pages 31–66. Springer, 1991.

Refines Börger's Prolog model [7] by elaborating the conjunctive component—as reflected by compilation of clause structure into WAM code—and the disjunctive component—as reflected by compilation of predicate structure into WAM code. The correctness proofs for these refinements include last call optimization, determinacy detection and virtual copying of dynamic code. Improved in [29].

27. E. Börger and D. Rosenzweig. A formal specification of Prolog by tree algebras. In V. Čerić, V. Dobrić, V. Lužar, and R. Paul, editors, *Information Technology Interfaces*, pages 513–518, Zagreb, 1991. University Computing Centre. Cf. abstract *A natural formalization of full Prolog*. In: Newsletter of the Association for Logic Programming, Short Communications, vol. 5/1, February 1992, pp. 8–9.

Prompted by discussion in the international Prolog standardization committee (ISO/IEC JTC1 SC22 WG17), this paper suggests to replace the stack based model of [6] and the stack implementation of the tree based model of [7] by a pure tree model for Prolog. An improved version of the latter is the basis for [30, 33] where also an error in the treatment of the *catch* built-in predicate is corrected.

28. E. Börger and D. Rosenzweig. WAM algebras—a mathematical study of implementation, part 2. In A. Voronkov, editor, *Logic Program-*

ming, volume 592 of *Lecture Notes in Artificial Intelligence*, pages 35–54. Springer, 1992. Preliminary version: Technical Report CSE-TR-88-91, Computer Science and Engineering Division, Department of Electrical Engineering and Computer Science, University of Michigan/Ann Arbor, April 1991, pp. 21.

Refines the Prolog model of [26] by elaborating the WAM code for representation and unification of terms. The correctness proof for this refinement includes environment trimming, Warren's variable classification and switching instructions. Improved in [29].

29. E. Börger and D. Rosenzweig. The WAM – definition and compiler correctness. Research report TR-14/92, Dipartimento di Informatica, Università di Pisa, Pisa, 1992.

Substantial example of the successive refinement method in the area, improving the predecessors [26, 28]. A hierarchy of evolving algebras provides a solid foundation for constructing provably correct compilers from Prolog to WAM. Various refinement steps take care of different distinctive features ("orthogonal components" in the authors' metaphor) of WAM making the specification as well as the correctness proof modular and extendible; examples of such extensions are found in [2, 3, 34, 67]. The revised final version is in [32].

30. E. Börger and D. Rosenzweig. A simple mathematical model for full Prolog. Research report TR-33/92, Dipartimento di Informatica, Università di Pisa, Pisa, October 1992.

An improved version of [6, 7, 27], taking into account the ISO Prolog standardization effort. For the revised final version see [33].

31. E. Börger and D. Rosenzweig. The mathematics of set predicates in Prolog. In G. Gottlob, A. Leitsch, and D. Mundici, editors, *Computational Logic and Proof Theory*, volume 713 of *Lecture Notes in Computer Science*, pages 1–13. Springer, 1993. Also issued as *Prolog. Copenhagen papers 2*, ISO/IEC JTC1 SC22 WG17 Standardization report no. 105, National Physical Laboratory, Middlesex, 1993, pp. 33–42.

Provides a logical (proof–theoretical) specification of the solution collecting predicates *findall, bagof* of Prolog. This abstract definition allows a logico–mathematical analysis, rationale and criticism of various proposals made for implementations of these predicates (in particular of *setof*) in current Prolog systems. Foundational companion to section 5, on solution collecting predicates, in [33].

32. E. Börger and D. Rosenzweig. The WAM – definition and compiler

correctness. In L. C. Beierle and L. Plümer, editors, *Logic Programming: Formal Methods and Practical Applications*, Series in Computer Science and Artificial Intelligence. North–Holland, 1994.

Revised and final version of [29].

33. E. Börger and D. Rosenzweig. A mathematical definition of full Prolog. In *Science of Computer Programming*, 1994. See the abstract *Full Prolog in a Nutshell*. In: *Logic Programming* (Proceedings of the 10th International Conference on Logic Programming) (D. S. Warren, Ed.), MIT Press 1993, p. 832.

An abstract evolving algebra specification of the semantics of Prolog, rigorously defining the international ISO Prolog standard (draft proposal) by stepwise refinement. Revised and final version of [6, 7, 27, 30].

34. E. Börger and R. Salamone. CLAM specification for provably correct compilation of CLP($\mathcal{R}$) programs. In E. Börger, editor, *Specification and Validation Methods*. Oxford University Press, 1994.

Extends the Börger–Rosenzweig's specification and correctness proof, for compiling Prolog programs to the WAM [32], to CLP($\mathcal{R}$) and the constraint logical arithmetical machine (CLAM) developed at IBM Yorktown Heights. Full proofs appear in [67].

35. E. Börger and P. Schmitt. A formal operational semantics for languages of type Prolog III. In E. Börger, H. Kleine Büning, M. M. Richter, and W. Schönfeld, editors, *CSL '90, 4th Workshop on Computer Science Logic*, volume 533 of *Lecture Notes in Computer Science*, pages 67–79. Springer, 1991. Preliminary version: IBM Germany, IWBS Report 144, November 1990, pp. 1–27.

An evolving algebra formalization of Alain Colmerauer's constraint logic programming language Prolog III, obtained from the Prolog model in [6, 7, 8] through extending unifications by constraint systems. This extension was the starting point for the extension of [32] in [3].

36. P. Glavan. Semantička analiza istodobnih logičkih programskih jezika (Semantical analysis of concurrent logic languages). Master's thesis (in Croation), University of Zagreb, Zagreb, 1993.

See comments for [37].

37. P. Glavan and D. Rosenzweig. Communicating evolving algebras. In E. Börger, H. Kleine Büning, G. Jäger, S. Martini, and M. M. Richter, editors, *Computer Science Logic*, Lecture Notes in Computer Science 702, pages 182–215. Springer, 1993.

A theory of concurrent computation within the framework of evolving algebras is developed, generalizing [52, 20, 21, 22]. The power of the framework is demonstrated by modelling the Chemical Abstract Machine of Berry and Boudol and the π-calculus of Milner.

38. P. Glavan and D. Rosenzweig. Evolving Algebra Model of Programming Language Semantics. In B. Pehrson and I. Simon (Eds.) *IFIP 13th World Computer Congress 1994*, Volume I: *Technology/Foundations*, Elsevier, Amsterdam, pp.416–422.

Evolving algebra interpretation of many–step SOS, denotational semantics and Hoare logic for the language of while–programs, based on a simple flowchart model of the language.

39. G. Gottlob, G. Kappel, and M. Schrefl. Semantics of object-oriented data models – the evolving algebra approach. In J. W. Schmidt and A. A. Stogny, editors, *Next Generation Information Technology*, volume 504 of *Lecture Notes in Computer Science*, pages 144–160. Springer, 1991.

Uses evolving algebras to define the operational semantics of object creation, of overriding and dynamic binding, and of inheritance at the type level (type specialization) and at the instance level (object specialization).

40. Y. Gurevich. Logic and the challenge of computer science. In E. Börger, editor, *Current Trends in Theoretical Computer Science*, pages 1–57. Computer Science Press, 1988.

The introduction and the first use of evolving algebras (at the end of the paper).

41. Y. Gurevich. Algorithms in the world of bounded resources. In R. Herken, editor, *The universal Turing machine – a half-century story*, pages 407–416. Oxford University Press, 1988.

Early complexity theoretical motivation for introduction of evolving algebras is discussed.

42. Y. Gurevich. Evolving algebras. A tutorial introduction. *Bulletin of EATCS*, 43: 264–284, 1991. Slightly revised reprinted in *Current Trends in Theoretical Computer Science*, Eds. G. Rozenberg and A. Salomaa, World Scientific, 1993, 266–292.

The first tutorial on evolving algebras. The EA thesis is stated: Every algorithm can be simulated by an appropriate evolving algebra in lock-step on the natural abstraction level of the algorithm.

43. Y. Gurevich. Logic Activities in Europe. ACM SIGACT NEWS, 1994, to appear.

A critical analysis of European logic activities in computer science. The part relevant to evolving algebras is subsection 4.6 called Mathematics and Pedantics.

44. Y. Gurevich. Evolving Algebras 1993: Lipari Guide. *Specification and Validation Methods*, Ed. E. Börger, Oxford University Press, 1994.

The tutorial [42] covered basic evolving algebras. In the meantime, evolving algebras have been extensively used, in particular, for specifying parallel, distributed computations and computations involving real time. It became obvious that a more advanced definition of evolving algebras is needed. The guide addresses this need.

45. Y. Gurevich. Evolving Algebras. In B. Pehrson and I. Simon (Eds.) *IFIP 13th World Computer Congress 1994*, Volume I: *Technology/Foundations*, Elsevier, Amsterdam, 423–427.

The opening talk at the first EA workshop. Sections: Introduction, The EA Thesis, Remarks, Future Work.

46. Y. Gurevich and E. Grädel. Towards a Model Theory of Metafinite Structures. Logic Colloquium 1994.

Seemingly finite objects, like databases or states of algorithms, often have an infinite structure (e.g. arithmetic) somewhere in the background. (The phenomenon is known to evolving algebra practitioners.) A more careful formalizations of such finite objects should reflect the relevant infinite structure in one way or another. The problem is explained and some frameworks of carefully controlled infinity are proposed. The full paper is in preparation.

47. Y. Gurevich and J. Huggins. The semantics of the C programming language. In E. Börger, H. Kleine Büning, G. Jäger, S. Martini, and M. M. Richter, editors, *Computer Science Logic*, Lecture Notes in Computer Science 702, pages 274–309. Springer, 1993.

The method of successive refinements is used to give a succint semantics of the C programming language. See [48].

48. Y. Gurevich and J. Huggins. ERRATA to "The Semantics of the C Programming Language". In E. Börger, Y. Gurevich, K. Meinke, editors, *Computer Science Logic*, Lecture Notes in Computer Science 832, pages 334–336, Springer, 1994.

A correction of minor errors and omissions in [47].

49. Y. Gurevich and J. Huggins. Evolving Algebras and Partial Evaluation. In B. Pehrson and I. Simon (Eds.) *IFIP 13th World Computer Congress 1994*, Volume I: *Technology/Foundations*, Elsevier, Amsterdam, 587–592.

    The paper describes an automated partial evaluator for sequential evolving algebras implemented at the University of Michigan.

50. Y. Gurevich and R. Mani. Group Membership Protocol: Specification and Verification. In *Specification and Validation Methods*, Ed. E. Börger, Oxford University Press, 1994.

    An interesting and useful protocol of Flavio Christian involves timing constraints and its correctness is not obvious. The protocol is formally specified and verified. (The verification proof allowed the authors to simplify the assumptions slightly.)

51. Y. Gurevich and J. Morris. Algebraic operational semantics and Modula-2. In E. Börger, H. Kleine Büning, and M. M. Richter, editors, *CSL'87, 1st Workshop on Computer Science Logic*, volume 329 of *Lecture Notes in Computer Science*, pages 81–101. Springer, 1988.

    An extended abstract of [58].

52. Y. Gurevich and L. Moss. Algebraic operational semantics and Occam. In E. Börger, H. Kleine Büning, and M. M. Richter, editors, *CSL'89, 3rd Workshop on Computer Science Logic*, volume 440 of *Lecture Notes in Computer Science*, pages 176–192. Springer, 1990.

    The first application of evolving algebras to distributed parallel computing with the challenge of true concurrency.

53. J. Huggins. Kermit: Specification and Verification. In *Specification and Validation Methods*, Ed. E. Börger, Oxford University Press, 1994.

    The Kermit file-transfer protocol (including a sliding windows extension to the basic protocol) is specified and verified using evolving algebras at several different layers of abstraction.

54. D. E. Johnson and L. S. Moss. Grammar Formalisms Viewed as Evolving Algebras. submitted to the Proceedings of the *Third Meeting on Mathematics of Language*, 1994.

    Distributed Evolving Algebras are used to model formalisms for natural language syntax. A model of context free derivations is defined which abstracts from the parse tree descriptions used in [52, 23] and from the dynamic tree generation appearing in [27, 30, 33]. It is extended to characterise in a uniform and natural way different context sensitive languages in terms of evolving algebras.

55. A. M. Kappel. Algebraische operationale Semantik und ihre Anwendungen auf Prolog. Master's thesis (in German), Universität Dortmund, Dortmund, 1990.

   See [56].

56. A. M. Kappel. Executable Specifications based on Dynamic Algebras. In A. Voronkov, editor, *Logic Programming and Automated Reasoning*, volume 698 of *LNAI*, pages 229–240. Springer, 1993.

   Defines a language for specification of evolving algebras and designs an abstract target machine (namely a Prolog program) which is specially tailored for executing evolving algebra computations. A prototype of the compiler has been implemented in Prolog. An extended abstract of [55].

57. R. Mani. The evolving algebra static semantics of SML. Preliminary version, 1992.

   An evolving algebra description for the static semantics of Core ML. Preliminary version: a revised version is in preparation.

58. J. Morris. *Algebraic operational semantics for Modula 2*. PhD thesis, University of Michigan, Ann Arbor MI, 1988.

   The earliest formalization of a real-life language. The semantical description is parse tree directed. In the meantime, the methodology has developed enabling more elegant descriptions, but one has to start somewhere. Abstract in [51].

59. J. Morris and G. Pottinger. Ada-Ariel semantics. Odyssey Research Associates, Inc., 80 pages, July 1990.

60. B. Müller. A Semantics for Hybrid Object–Oriented Prolog Systems. In B. Pehrson and I. Simon (Eds.) *IFIP 13th World Computer Congress 1994*, Volume I: *Technology/Foundations*, Elsevier, Amsterdam, pp. 428–433.

   Extends the rules given in [33] for the user–defined core of Prolog to define the semantics of a hybrid object–oriented Prolog system. The definition covers the central object–oriented features of: object creation and deletion, data encapsulation, inheritance, messages, polymorphism and dynamic binding.

61. A. Poetzsch-Heffter. Interprocedural data flow analysis based on temporal specifications. Technical Report 93-1397, Cornell University, 1993.

   Investigates the specification of data flow problems by temporal logic formulas and proves fixpoint analyses correct. Temporal formulas are interpreted w.r.t. programming language semantics given in the framework of evolving algebras.

62. A. Poetzsch-Heffter. Developing efficient interpreters based on formal language specifications. In P. Fritzson, editor, *Compiler Construction*, 1994. LNCS 786.

Reports on extensions of the MAX system enabling the generation and refinement of interpreters based on formal language specifications. In these specifications, static semantics is defined by an attribution mechanism and dynamic semantics is defined by evolving algebras.

63. A. Poetzsch-Heffter. Comparing action semantics and evolving algebra based specifications with respect to applications. In *Proceedings of the First International Workshop on Action Semantics*, 1994. Appears as technical report of the Aarhus University, Denmark.

Action semantics is compared to evolving algebra based language specifications. In particular, different aspects relevant to language documentation and programming tool development are discussed.

64. A. Poetzsch-Heffter. Deriving Partial Correctness Logics From Evolving Algebras. In B. Pehrson and I. Simon (Eds.) *IFIP 13th World Computer Congress 1994*, Volume I: *Technology/Foundations*, Elsevier, Amsterdam, 434–439.

A proposal for deriving partial correctness logics from simple evolving algebra models of programming languages. A basic axiom (schema) is derived from an evolving algebra and is used to obtain more convenient logics.

65. E. Riccobene. *Modelli matematici per linguaggi logici* (Mathematical models for logic languages). PhD thesis (in Italian), University of Catania, 1992.

Systematic treatment of evolving algebra models for Gödel [24], Parlog [23], Concurrent Prolog [22], GHC, Pandora.

66. D. Rosenzweig. Distributed Computations: Evolving Algebra Approach. In B. Pehrson and I. Simon (Eds.) *IFIP 13th World Computer Congress 1994*, Volume I: *Technology/Foundations*, Elsevier, Amsterdam, 440–441.

Remarks on some evolving algebra models of concurrent and parallel computation.

67. R. Salamone. *Una specifica astratta e modulare della CLAM (An abstract and modular specification of the CLAM)*. Master's thesis (in Italian), Università di Pisa, Pisa, 1993.

   Full version of [34].

68. J. Sauer. *Wissensbasierte Lösen von Ablaufsplanungsproblemen durch explizite Heuristiken*. PhD thesis, 1993. In: Dissertationen zur Künstlichen Intelligenz, Infix-Verlag, Dr. Ekkehardt Hundt, St. Augustin 1993, pp. 204.

   Uses evolving algebras to define the semantics for selection and elaboration of heuristics for computation of goal sets in the language HERA.

69. M. Schrefl and G. Kappel. Cooperation contracts. In T. J. Teorey, editor, *Proc. 10th International Conference on the Entity Relationship Approach*, pages 285–307. E/R Institute, 1991.

   The authors introduce the concept of cooperative message handling and use evolving algebras to give formal semantics.

70. M. Vale. The Evolving Algebra Semantics of COBOL. Part 1: Programs and Control. Research report CSE-TR-162-93, EECS, University of Michigan, Ann Arbor MI, 1993.

71. C. Wallace. The semantics of the C++ Programming Language. In E. Börger, editor, *Specification and Validation Methods*. Oxford University Press, 1994.

   The semantical description in [47] is extended to encompass all of C++.

Part II: Programming Languages

Program Verification and Prolog

Krzysztof R. Apt

Abstract

We show here that verification of Prolog programs can be systematically carried out within a simple framework which comprises syntactic analysis, declarative semantics, modes and types. We apply these techniques to study termination, partial correctness, occur-check freedom, absence of errors and absence of floundering. Finally, we discuss which aspects of these techniques can be automated.
Notes. This research was partly supported by the ESPRIT Basic Research Action 6810 (Compulog 2). A preliminary, shorter, version of this paper appeared as Apt [3].

1 Introduction

1.1 Motivation

Prolog is 20 years old and so is logic programming. However, they were developed separately and these two developments never really merged. The first track is best exemplified by Sterling and Shapiro [36], which puts emphasis on programming style and techniques, and the second by Lloyd [25], which concentrates on the theoretical foundations. As a result of these separate developments, until recently little work was done on verification and development of Prolog programs.

It is natural and almost self-evident to base verification of Prolog programs on the theory of logic programming. However, the choices made in logic programming theory do not necessarily coincide with those made in Prolog (like the choice of a selection rule) and its extensions and modifications. Some new issues (like the occur-check problem) need to be addressed and additional results (like those dealing with termination) need to be established.

The aim of this chapter is to provide an overview of our recent work on verification of Prolog programs. We show that many relevant properties of Prolog programs can be established by means of simple arguments. In particular, we explain how termination and partial correctness can be dealt with by studing declarative interpretation of logic programs. Termination is handled by techniques developed in Apt and Pedreschi [8] and Apt and Pedreschi [9].

We also study here run-time properties. These are properties which refer to the program execution. Examples of such properties include the absence of the occur-check problem, which states that the omission of the occur-check in the unification algorithm does not result in incorrect use of unification, and the absence of run-time errors in the presence of arithmetic operations.

To prove run-time properties of Prolog programs we introduce increasingly more powerful tools. When dealing with the occur-check problem and with the absence of floundering in presence of negation we use syntactic analysis and modes. We follow here the approach of Apt and Pellegrini [10]. Then, when dealing with the absence of run-time errors for Prolog programs with arithmetic, we use directional types, proposed recently by Bronsard, Lakshman and Reddy [14].

1.2 Terminology and Notation

We work here with *queries*, that is sequences of atoms, instead of *goals*, that is constructs of the form $\leftarrow Q$, where Q is a query. We denote by $\square$ the empty query. Throughout the chapter we restrict attention to one selection rule, namely Prolog's leftmost selection rule. We refer to SLD-resolution with the leftmost selection rule as *LD-resolution*. All proof-theoretic notions, such as the computed answer substitution, refer to LD-resolution.

Given two syntactic expressions E and F, we say that E is *more general than* F, and write $E \leq F$, if $E\theta = F$ for some substitution θ. We denote the set of variables occurring in an expression E by $Var(E)$. Given a list $\mathbf{t}$ we write $\mathbf{a} \in \mathbf{t}$ when $\mathbf{a}$ is a member of $\mathbf{t}$ and $\mathbf{a} \notin \mathbf{t}$ when $\mathbf{a}$ is not a member of $\mathbf{t}$. Also, we identify here constants with 0-ary function symbols.

Apart from this we use the standard notation of Lloyd [25] and Apt [2]. In particular, for a program P, B_P stands for its Herband base, M_P stands for its least Herbrand model, $ground(P)$ for the set of all ground instances of clauses of P, and $[A]$ for the set of all ground instances of the atom A.

2 Setting the Stage

2.1 Syntax

We shall deal here with three subsets of Prolog.

2.1.1 Pure Prolog

The syntax of programs written in this subset coincides with the customary syntax of logic programs, though the *ambivalent syntax* and *anonymous variables* are allowed.

Let us explain both concepts. In first-order logic, and consequently in logic programming, it is assumed that function symbols and relation symbols of different arity form mutually disjoint classes of symbols. While this assumption is rarely stated explicitly, it is a folklore postulate in mathematical logic which can be easily tested by exposing a logician to Prolog syntax and waiting for his protests. Namely, in contrast to first-order logic, Prolog allows ambivalent syntax. Thus we can use a binary relation symbol member, unary function symbol member and a binary function symbolmember, and build syntactically legal facts like member(member(a,b), [c, member(a)]). Such expressions can be uniquely parsed once the context is given in which they occur.

The ambivalent syntax at this level is not an issue and it is safe to assume it when studying formally pure Prolog programs. The ambivalent syntax becomes an interesting subject at the moment of considering metainterpreters which use the clause relation – see Kalsbeek [21] and Martens and De Schreye [28] for recent work on this topic. All in all, it is a minor point in this article but still worth mentioning.

Prolog also allows so-called *anonymous variables*, written as "_" (underscore). These variables have a special interpretation, because each occurrence of "_" in a query or in a clause is interpreted as a *different* variable. Thus by definition each anonymous variable occurs in a query or a clause only once. Anonymous variables form a simple and elegant device which sometimes increases the readability of programs in a remarkable way.

2.1.2 Pure Prolog with Arithmetic

This subset extends the previous one by allowing in the bodies of the program clauses the arithmetic comparison operators $<, \leq, =:=, \neq, \geq, >$ and the binary "is" relation of Prolog.

2.1.3 Pure Prolog with Negation

This subset extends the first one by allowing negative literals in the bodies of the program clauses. Thus it coincides with the syntax of general logic programs.

The methods discussed in this chapter can be readily used to deal with the "union" of the last two subsets, that is pure Prolog with arithmetic and negation.

When considering a specific logic program one has to fix a first-order language w.r.t. which it is analyzed. Usually, one associates with the program the language determined by it – its function and relation symbols are the ones occurring in the program (see, e.g., Lloyd [25] and Apt [2]). Another choice was made by Kunen [23] who assumed a universal first-order language with infinitely many function and relation symbols in each arity, in which all programs and queries are written. One can think of this language as the language defined by a Prolog manual.

In this chapter we follow Kunen's choice. In contrast to the other alternative it imposes no syntactic restriction on the queries which may be used for a given program. This better reflects the reality of programming. In Section 2.3 we shall indicate another advantage of this choice. Of course, the sets $ground(P)$ and $[A]$ refer to the ground instances in this universal language. All considered interpretations are interpretations of this universal language.

2.2 Proof Theory

Let us now explain the proof theory for the three subsets introduced above.

2.2.1 *Pure Prolog*

We use, as expected, the LD-resolution. However, in most implementations of Prolog, unification without the occur-check is used. Hence we have to deal with this issue.

Moreover, we assume that, as in Prolog, the clauses of the program are ordered. This ordering will be reflected in the considered LD-trees. It should be added, however, that in our approach to correctness the ordering of the clauses will *never* play any role. In other words, our approach will not be able to distinguish between programs which differ only by the clause ordering. We shall return to this point in Section 3.1, when studying termination.

2.2.2 *Pure Prolog with Arithmetic*

Consider the program QUICKSORT:

```
qs(Xs, Ys) ← Ys is an ordered permutation of the list Xs.
qs([X | Xs], Ys) ←
   part(X, Xs, Littles, Bigs),
   qs(Littles, Ls),
   qs(Bigs, Bs),
   app(Ls, [X | Bs], Ys).
qs([], []).

part(X, Xs, Ls, Bs) ← Ls is a list of elements of Xs which are < X,
                     Bs is a list of elements of Xs which are ≥ X.
part(X, [Y|Xs], [Y|Ls], Bs) ← X > Y, part(X, Xs, Ls, Bs).
part(X, [Y|Xs], Ls, [Y|Bs]) ← X ≤ Y, part(X, Xs, Ls, Bs).
part(_, [], [], []).
```

augmented by the APPEND program **defined by**:

```
app(Xs, Ys, Zs) ← Zs is the concatenation of the lists Xs and Ys.
app([X | Xs], Ys, [X | Zs]) ← app(Xs, Ys, Zs).
app([], Ys, Ys).
```

When studying it formally as a Prolog program we have to decide the status of the built-in's > and ≤. Are they some further unspecified relation symbols whose definitions we can ignore? Well, with this choice we face the following problem. In Prolog the relations > and ≤ are built-in's whose evaluation results in an error when its arguments are not ground arithmetic expressions (in short, gae's). Consequently, the query qs([3,4,X,7], [3,4,7,8]) results in an error at the moment the variable X becomes an argument of >.

Now, logic programming does not have any facilities to deal with runtime errors, but at least one could consider trading them for failure. Unfortunately, this is not possible. Otherwise, for some terms s and t the query s>t would succeed, and then by the Lifting Lemma the query X>Y would succeed as well. So what is the conclusion? The standard theory of logic programming *cannot* be used to capture properly the behaviour of the built-in's > and ≤, and it is not possible to model the fact that the query qs([3,4,X,7], [3,4,7,8]) results in an error.

To model Prolog's interpretation of arithmetic relations within logic programming we follow Kunen [22]. First, we extend the LD-resolution by stipulating that an LD-derivation *ends in an error* when at the moment of evaluation the arguments of the comparison relations are not gae's. In the case of the assignment s is t, an error results when at the moment of evaluation t is not a gae.

Next, we add to each program infinitely many clauses which define the ground instances of the used arithmetic relations. Given a gae n we denote by val(n) its value. For example, val(3+4) equals 7. So for < we add the following set of unit clauses:

$$M_< = \{\text{m} < \text{n} \mid \text{m, n are gae's and val(m)} < \text{val(n)}\},$$

for "is" we add the set

$$M_{\text{is}} = \{\text{val(n) is n} \mid \text{n is a gae}\},$$

etc. So, for example, 7 is $3 + 4 \in M_{\text{is}}$. We also assume that, conforming to the status of built-in's, in the original program arithmetical relations are not used in clause heads.

These added clauses allow us to compute resolvents when the selected atom involves an arithmetic relation. For example, the query X is 3+4, X < 2+3 resolves to only one query, namely 7 < 2+3 (using the clause 7 is 3+4) and the query 7 < 2+3 fails. Thus all LD-derivations of the query X is 3+4, X < 2+3 fail, which agrees with Prolog's interpretation.

Note that thanks to the "ending in an error" provision every query with a selected atom involving an arithmetic relation has at most one descendant in every LD-tree. Consequently, in spite of the fact that the considered programs contain now infinitely many clauses, the resulting LD-trees remain finitely branching.

2.2.3 Pure Prolog with Negation

As expected, to interpret these programs we use the SLDNF-resolution with the leftmost selection rule, further referred to as LDNF-resolution. Less expected is the fact that the usual definition of the SLDNF-resolution given in Lloyd [25] needs to be modified.

We leave to the reader the task of checking that according to the definition of SLDNF-resolution given in Clark [16] and reproduced in Lloyd [24] it is not clear what is the SLDNF-derivation for the program $P = \{p \leftarrow p\}$, and the query $\neg p$, whereas according to the definition given in Lloyd [25] no SLDNF-derivations exist for the program $P = \{p \leftarrow \neg p\}$ and query p. The problem with the first definition is that it is circular and not all cases for forming a resolvent are defined, whereas the latter definition is mathematically correct, but more restrictive than the first one.

It should be pointed out here that the latter definition is *sufficient* for proving soundness and various forms of completeness of SLDNF-resolution. However, when reasoning about termination of Prolog programs we need to have at our disposal a definition of SLDNF-resolution (with the leftmost selection rule) which properly formalizes the computation process and not only correctly predicts the computed results.

Such a definition was proposed by Martelli and Tricomi [27]. In their revision the subsidiary trees used to resolve negative literals are built "inside" the main tree. Another solution was suggested later in Apt and Doets [5] where, as in the original definition, the subsidiary trees are kept "aside" of the "main" tree but their construction is no longer viewed as an atomic step in the resolution process.

Additionally, when studying the LDNF-resolution we need to modify the definition of floundering. It occurs when a negative non-ground literal is selected. We say that $P \cup \{Q\}$ *does not flounder* if no LDNF-derivation of $P \cup \{Q\}$ flounders.

It is perhaps useful to recall here that Prolog ignores floundering. This leads to a number of well-known complications and explains why it is natural to seek conditions which ensure absence of floundering. In fact, our methods for proving termination and partial correctness of general programs do rely on the absence of floundering.

2.3 Semantics

There is no universal agreement as to what is the declarative semantics of a logic program. In this chapter we advocate for a program without negation the use of its least Herband model as its declarative semantics. However, we have to be careful when making this seemingly unique choice.

Consider the proverbial APPEND program. With the first choice of Subsection 2.1 the underlying first-order language has only one constant, viz. [], and one, binary, function symbol [.|.]. Thus the Herbrand universe consists of all ground lists whose flattened form is a list with all elements equal to []. Call such lists *trivial*. It is easy to see that then

$$M_{\text{APPEND}} = \{\text{app}(\text{s}, \text{t}, \text{u}) \mid \text{s}, \text{t}, \text{u} \text{ are trivial lists and } \text{s} * \text{t} = \text{u}\},$$

where "$*$" denotes the operation of concatenating two lists. This is the semantics of the APPEND program given in Sterling and Shapiro [36]. Clearly, it cannot be used to render the meaning of queries in which function symbols other than [] and [.|.] are used.

As soon as the underlying first-order language has another constant than [], and so in particular in our case, the Herbrand universe contains elements which are not lists. Consequently, on the account of the second clause of APPEND, M_{APPEND} contains elements of the form app(s,t,u) where neither t nor u is a list. (On the other hand, it is still the case that whenever app(s,t,u) $\in M_{\text{APPEND}}$, then s is a list.) So the choice of the first-order language affects the structure of the least Herbrand models of the considered programs.

The fact that APPEND and various other well-known programs do admit "ill-typed" atoms in their least Herbrand models complicates matters somewhat. To simplify our presentation we therefore continue our discussion with the "correctly typed" version of APPEND, which we denote by APPEND-T:

```
app([X | Xs], Ys, [X | Zs]) ← app(Xs, Ys, Zs).
app([], Ys, Ys) ← list(Ys).
```

augmented by the LIST program defined by:

```
list(Xs) ← Xs is a list.
list([_ | Ts]) ← list(Ts).
list([]).
```

Note that

$$M_{\text{APPEND-T}} = \{\text{app}(s,t,u) \mid s,t,u \text{ are g. lists}, s * t = u\}$$
$$\cup\ M_{\text{LIST}},$$

where

$$M_{\text{LIST}} = \{\text{list}(s) \mid s \text{ is a g. list}\}.$$

Here and elsewhere "g. list(s)" stands for "ground list(s)".

We shall return to the original program APPEND in Section 6.1. Discussion of the semantics of the other two fragments of Prolog is postponed until Sections 4.2 and 5.3.

3 Pure Prolog

We now discuss correctness of programs written in the three defined subsets of Prolog. We start with pure Prolog.

3.1 Termination

First we consider termination. We present here the approach of Apt and Pedreschi [8]. It is a modification of a method of Bezem [12] which deals with termination w.r.t. all selection rules. For simplicity we restrict our attention here to one atom queries. We recall the relevant concepts.

Definition 3.1 *A program is called left terminating if all its LD-derivations starting with a ground query are finite.* □

To prove that a program is left terminating, and to characterize the queries that terminate w.r.t. such a program, the following notions are introduced.

Definition 3.2

- A *level mapping* for a program P is a function $|\ |: B_P \to N$ from ground atoms to natural numbers. For $A \in B_P$, $|A|$ is the *level* of A.
- An atom A is called *bounded* with respect to a level mapping $|\ |$, if $|\ |$ is bounded on the set $[A]$ of ground instances of A. For A bounded w.r.t. $|\ |$, we define $|A|$, the *level of A w.r.t. $|\ |$*, as the maximum $|\ |$ takes on $[A]$.
- A clause is called *acceptable* with respect to $|\ |$ and an interpretation I, if I is its model and for every ground instance $A \leftarrow \mathbf{A}, B, \mathbf{B}$ of it such that $I \models \mathbf{A}$
$$|A| > |B|.$$

- A program P is called *acceptable* with respect to $|\ |$ and I, if all its clauses are. P is called *acceptable* if it is acceptable with respect to some level mapping and an interpretation. □

The following results link the introduced notions.

Theorem 3.3 *Let P be acceptable w.r.t. $|\ |$ and I. Then, for every atom A bounded w.r.t. $|\ |$, all LD-derivations of $P \cup \{A\}$ are finite. In particular, P is left terminating.* □

Theorem 3.4 *Let P be a left terminating program. Then, for some level mapping $|\ |$ and a Herbrand interpretation I,*

(i) P is acceptable w.r.t. $|\ |$ and I,

(ii) for every atom A, all LD-derivations of $P \cup \{A\}$ are finite iff A is bounded w.r.t. $|\ |$. □

The model I represents the limited declarative knowledge needed to prove termination. Note that using Theorem 3.3 we deal can only establish termination of a query w.r.t. a left terminating program and we use here the notion of so-called "universal" termination, according to which the query terminates irrespectively of the clause ordering. We found that this strong form of termination is satisfied by most pure Prolog programs and queries considered in standard books on Prolog.

To see how this method of proving termination can be applied to specific programs we now consider a couple of examples. When dealing with them we use the following function $|\ |$ from ground terms to natural numbers:

$$|[x|xs]| = |xs| + 1,$$
$$|f(x_1,\ldots,x_n)| = 0 \text{ if } f \neq [.|.].$$

Then for a list xs, $|xs|$ equals its length.

Palindrome

First, let us consider a program whose proof of termination does not involve the choice of the model I. In the following program PALINDROME-T:

```
palindrome(Xs)  ←  the list Xs equals to its reverse.
palindrome(Xs)  ←  reverse(Xs, Xs).

reverse(Xs, Ys)  ←  Ys is the reverse of the list Xs.
reverse(X1s, X2s)  ←  reverse(X1s, [], X2s).

reverse(Xs, Ys, Zs)  ←  Zs is the result of concatenating
                        the reverse of the list Xs and the list Ys.
reverse([X | X1s], X2s, Ys)  ←  reverse(X1s, [X | X2s], Ys).
reverse([], Xs, Xs)  ←  list(Xs).
```

augmented by the LIST program,

the body of each clause has at most one atom. In this case the reduction of the level mapping required in the definition of acceptability has to be achieved irrespective of the choice of the model of the program. The following level mapping | | does the job:

$$\begin{aligned}
|\text{palindrome}(xs)| &= 2 \cdot |xs| + 3, \\
|\text{reverse}(xs, ys)| &= 2 \cdot |xs| + 2, \\
|\text{reverse}(xs, ys, zs)| &= 2 \cdot |xs| + |ys| + 1, \\
|\text{list}(xs)| &= |xs|.
\end{aligned}$$

We leave it to the reader to check that PALINDROME-T is indeed acceptable w.r.t. the level mapping | | and the Herbrand model $B_{\text{PALINDROME-T}}$ (or any other model) of PALINDROME-T. Moreover, for a list xs, the query palindrome(xs) is bounded w.r.t. | | and consequently, by Theorem 3.3, all LD-derivations of PALINDROME-T $\cup$ {palindrome(xs)} are finite.

Sequence

The choice of the level mapping and of the model can affect the class of queries whose termination can be established. To see this consider the following problem from Coelho and Cotta [17] (see page 193) and its formalization in Prolog: arrange three 1's, three 2's, ..., three 9's in sequence so that for all $i \in [1, 9]$ there are exactly i numbers between successive occurrences of i.

```
sublist(Xs, Ys)  ←  Xs is a sublist of the list Ys.
sublist(Xs, Ys)  ←  app(_, Zs, Ys), app(Xs, _, Zs).

sequence(Xs)  ←  Xs is a list of 27 elements.
sequence([_,_,_,_,_,_,_,_,_,_,_,_,_,_,_,_,_,_,_,_,_,_,_,_,_,_,_]).
```

```
question(Ss)  ←  Ss is the desired list of 27 elements.
question(Ss)  ←
  sequence(Ss),
  sublist([1,_,1,_,1], Ss),
  sublist([2,_,_,2,_,_,2], Ss),
  sublist([3,_,_,_,3,_,_,_,3], Ss),
  sublist([4,_,_,_,_,4,_,_,_,_,4], Ss),
  sublist([5,_,_,_,_,_,5,_,_,_,_,_,5], Ss),
  sublist([6,_,_,_,_,_,_,6,_,_,_,_,_,_,6], Ss),
  sublist([7,_,_,_,_,_,_,_,7,_,_,_,_,_,_,_,7], Ss),
  sublist([8,_,_,_,_,_,_,_,_,8,_,_,_,_,_,_,_,_,8], Ss),
  sublist([9,_,_,_,_,_,_,_,_,_,9,_,_,_,_,_,_,_,_,_,9], Ss).
```

augmented by the APPEND-T program.

Call the above program SEQUENCE-T. For those curious to know, there are 6 solutions to this problem, generated by the above program:

```
| ?- question(Ss).

Ss = [7,5,3,8,6,9,3,5,7,4,3,6,8,5,4,9,7,2,6,4,2,8,1,2,1,9,1];

Ss = [3,4,7,9,3,6,4,8,3,5,7,4,6,9,2,5,8,2,7,6,2,5,1,9,1,8,1];

Ss = [3,4,7,8,3,9,4,5,3,6,7,4,8,5,2,9,6,2,7,5,2,8,1,6,1,9,1];

Ss = [1,9,1,6,1,8,2,5,7,2,6,9,2,5,8,4,7,6,3,5,4,9,3,8,7,4,3];

Ss = [1,8,1,9,1,5,2,6,7,2,8,5,2,9,6,4,7,5,3,8,4,6,3,9,7,4,3];

Ss = [1,9,1,2,1,8,2,4,6,2,7,9,4,5,8,6,3,4,7,5,3,9,6,8,3,5,7];

no
```

It is straightforward to verify that SEQUENCE-T is acceptable w.r.t. the level mapping | | defined by:

$$\begin{aligned} |\text{question}(xs)| &= |xs| + 30, \\ |\text{sequence}(xs)| &= 0, \\ |\text{sublist}(xs, ys)| &= |xs| + |ys| + 2, \\ |\text{app}(xs, ys, zs)| &= \min(|xs|, |zs|) + 1, \\ |\text{list}(xs)| &= |xs|, \end{aligned}$$

and the model $B_{\text{SEQUENCE-T}}$. However, with this choice of the level mapping we face the problem that the atom question(Ss) is not bounded. Consequently, we cannot use Theorem 3.3 to prove termination of this query. In fact, using this level mapping we can only prove that for s ground, all LD-derivations of SEQUENCE-T ∪ {question(s)} are finite.

To prove the stronger termination property we change the above level mapping by putting

$$|\text{question}(xs)| = 57,$$

and choose any model I of SEQUENCE-T such that for a ground s

$$I \models \text{sequence}(s) \text{ iff s is a list of 27 elements.}$$

Then SEQUENCE-T is acceptable w.r.t. | | and I. Moreover, the query question(Ss) is now bounded w.r.t. | | and consequently, by Theorem 3.3, all LD-derivations of SEQUENCE-T ∪ {question(Ss)} are finite.

3.1.1 An Improvement

The definition of acceptability requires a strict decrease of the level mapping from the clause head to the atoms of the clause body. Apt and Pedreschi [9] observed that this requirement can be relaxed in the case of non-recursive calls. This leads to an alternative definition of acceptability, that we qualify with the prefix *semi*. This notion is actually equivalent to the original one, but it gives rise to a more flexible proof method.

To describe this modification we need to define first when two relation symbols occurring in a program are mutually recursive.

Definition 3.5 *Let P be a program and p, q relation symbols occurring in it.*

- *We say that p refers to q in P if there is a clause in P that uses p in its head and q in its body.*
- *We say that p depends on q in P, and write $p \sqsupseteq q$, if (p, q) is in the reflexive, transitive closure of the relation refers to.*
- *We say that p and q are mutually recursive, and write $p \simeq q$, if $p \sqsupseteq q$ and $q \sqsupseteq p$. In particular, p and p are mutually recursive.* □

We also write $p \sqsupset q$ when $p \sqsupseteq q$ and $q \not\sqsupseteq p$. The following definition of *semi-acceptability* exploits the introduced orderings over the relation symbols. We denote here by $rel(A)$ the relation symbol occurring in atom A.

Definition 3.6 *Let P be a program, | | a level mapping for P and I an interpretation.*

- *A clause of P is called semi-acceptable with respect to | | and I, if I is its model and for every ground instance $A \leftarrow \mathbf{A}, B, \mathbf{B}$ of it such that $I \models \mathbf{A}$*
  * $|A| > |B|$ *if $rel(A) \simeq rel(B)$,*
  * $|A| \geq |B|$ *if $rel(A) \sqsupset rel(B)$.*

- A program P is called semi-acceptable with respect to $||$ and I, if all its clauses are. P is called semi-acceptable if it is semi-acceptable with respect to some level mapping and an interpretation. □

Thus the level mapping is required to decrease from an atom A in the head of a clause to an atom B in the body of that clause only if the relations of A and B are mutually recursive. Additionally, the level mapping is required not to increase from A to B if the relations of A and B are not mutually recursive.

The following observations are immediate.

Note 3.7 *If a program is acceptable w.r.t. $||$ and I, then it is semi-acceptable w.r.t. $||$ and I.* □

Note 3.8 *If a program is semi-acceptable w.r.t. $||$ and I, then it is acceptable w.r.t. a level mapping $||\ ||$ and the same interpretation I. Moreover, for each atom A, if A is bounded w.r.t. $||$, then A is bounded w.r.t. $||\ ||$.* □

This brings us to the following conclusion.

Corollary 3.9 *A program is acceptable iff it is semi-acceptable.* □

To see how the notion of semi-acceptability leads to more natural level mappings reconsider the programs studied before.

Palindrome

When proving that PALINDROME-T is acceptable, we had to repeatedly use "+1" to ensure the decrease of the level mapping. Now a simpler level mapping $||$ suffices:

$$\begin{aligned}
|\texttt{palindrome}(\texttt{xs})| &= 2 \cdot |\texttt{xs}|, \\
|\texttt{reverse}(\texttt{xs}, \texttt{ys})| &= 2 \cdot |\texttt{xs}|, \\
|\texttt{reverse}(\texttt{xs}, \texttt{ys}, \texttt{zs})| &= 2 \cdot |\texttt{xs}| + |\texttt{ys}|, \\
|\texttt{list}(\texttt{xs})| &= |\texttt{xs}|.
\end{aligned}$$

It is straightforward to check that PALINDROME-T is semi-acceptable w.r.t. the level mapping $||$ and $B_{\texttt{PALINDROME-T}}$.

Sequence

It is easy to see that SEQUENCE-T is semi-acceptable w.r.t. the level mapping $||$ defined by:

$$\begin{aligned}
|\texttt{question}(\texttt{xs})| &= 54, \\
|\texttt{sequence}(\texttt{xs})| &= 0, \\
|\texttt{sublist}(\texttt{xs}, \texttt{ys})| &= |\texttt{xs}| + |\texttt{ys}|, \\
|\texttt{app}(\texttt{xs}, \texttt{ys}, \texttt{zs})| &= \min(|\texttt{xs}|, |\texttt{zs}|), \\
|\texttt{list}(\texttt{xs})| &= |\texttt{xs}|
\end{aligned}$$

and (as before) any model I of SEQUENCE-T such that for a ground s

$I \models$ sequence(s) iff s is a list of 27 elements.

Again, in the above level mapping it was possible to disregard the accumulated use of "+1" 's.

This approach was further generalized in Apt and Pedreschi [9] to a yield a modular method of proving left termination. It was applied there to a number of non-trivial examples including the MAP_COLOR program from Sterling and Shapiro [36] (see page 212) which generates a colouring of a map in such a way that no two neighbours have the same colour.

It should be made clear here that due to Theorems 3.3 and 3.4 it is undecidable whether a program is acceptable. Starting with Ullman and Van Gelder [38] a lot of attention has been devoted to a study of sufficient, decidable conditions for proving left termination, or more generally, left termination of a given query and a program. An interested reader is referred to the recent survey article of De Schreye and Decorte [32] and the last section of this chapter.

3.2 Partial Correctness

Our approach to partial correctness is based on the use of the least Herbrand model M_P. We restrict our attention to left terminating programs. This explains why we treated termination first. The following observation of Apt and Pedreschi [8] explains why for a left terminating program it is easier to verify that a Herbrand interpretation is its least Herbrand model.

Definition 3.10 *We say that a model I of a program P is supported if for every ground atom A such that $I \models A$ there exists $\mathbf{B}$ such that $A \leftarrow \mathbf{B} \in ground(P)$ and $I \models \mathbf{B}$.* □

Intuitively, $\mathbf{B}$ is an explanation (or support) for the truth of A in I.

Lemma 3.11 *For a left terminating program P, M_P is the unique supported Herbrand model of P.* □

Now, for all programs considered here, and for plenty of other "correctly typed" programs, checking that a given Herbrand interpretation is a supported model is straightforward. Consequently, by virtue of the above lemma, for a left terminating program, we omit the proof that a given Herbrand interpretation is its least Herbrand model.

Of course, it is legitimate to ask how one finds a candidate for the least Herbrand model. According to our experience it is usually the "specification" of the program limited to ground queries. We do not consider here the problem of in what language it is most convenient to write this specification.

In the sequel it will be more convenient to work with the instances of the queries instead of with the substitutions. More precisely, we introduce the following definition.

Definition 3.12 *Consider a program P.*

- *We say that Q' is a correct instance of the query Q, if for some correct answer substitution θ for Q, $Q' = Q\theta$; that is, if Q' is an instance of Q and $P \models Q'$.*
- *We say that Q' is a computed instance of the query Q if for some computed answer substitution θ for Q, $Q' = Q\theta$.* □

Clearly, a unique correct (resp. computed) answer substitution can be computed from a query and its correct (resp. computed) instance in a straightforward way. So considering instances instead of substitutions is just a matter of convenience. Using this terminology the usual soundness and strong completeness properties of logic programs, now restricted to the leftmost selection rule, can be formulated as follows.

Theorem 3.13 (**Soundness of LD-resolution**) *Consider a program P and a query Q. Every computed instance of Q is a correct instance of Q.*
□

Theorem 3.14 (**Strong Completeness of LD-resolution**) *Consider a program P and a query Q. For every correct instance Q' of Q there exists a computed instance Q'' of Q such that $Q'' \leq Q'$.* □

Let us now introduce the following notation. For a program P, a query Q and a set of queries $\mathcal{Q}$, we write

$$\{Q\}\ P\ \mathcal{Q}$$

to denote the fact that $\mathcal{Q}$ is the set of computed instances of Q. $\{Q\}\ P\ \mathcal{Q}$ should be read as: "the program P transforms Q into the set of its computed instances $\mathcal{Q}$". In particular, when $\mathcal{Q}$ is a singleton, say $\mathcal{Q} = \{Q'\}$, we have $\{Q\}\ P\ \{Q'\}$ which not accidentally coincides with the syntax of correctness formulas in Hoare style approach to verification of imperative programs (see, e.g., Apt and Olderog [11]). We now present an easy method of establishing constructs of the form $\{Q\}\ P\ \mathcal{Q}$.

Theorem 3.15 *Consider a program P and a query Q. Suppose that the set $\mathcal{Q}$ of ground correct instances of Q is finite. Then*

$$\{Q\}\ P\ \mathcal{Q}.$$

Proof. First note that

$$\text{every correct instance } Q' \text{ of } Q \text{ is ground.} \tag{3.1}$$

Indeed, otherwise, by the fact that the Herbrand universe is infinite, the set $\mathcal{Q}$ would be infinite.

Consider now $Q_1 \in \mathcal{Q}$. By the Strong Completeness Theorem 3.14, there exists a computed instance Q_2 of Q such that $Q_2 \leq Q_1$. By the

Soundness Theorem 3.13, Q_2 is a correct instance of Q, so by (3.1) Q_2 is ground. Consequently $Q_2 = Q_1$, that is Q_1 is a computed instance of Q.

Conversely, take a computed instance Q_1 of Q. By the Soundness Theorem 3.13, Q_1 is a correct instance of Q. By (3.1) Q_1 is ground, so $Q_1 \in \mathcal{Q}$.
□

For a query consisting of just one atom A the set of its ground correct instances equals $[A] \cap M_P$, so the assumption of the above theorem can be rephrased as "the set $[A] \cap M_P$ is finite". This simplifies checking its validity and explains the relevance of M_P in our approach. As the examples below indicate, the above theorem is quite useful.

Append

First consider the APPEND-T program and three of its uses.

(i) Given ground lists s,t,u we have

$$\mathtt{app(s,t,u)} \in M_{\mathtt{APPEND\_T}} \text{ iff } \mathtt{s} * \mathtt{t} = \mathtt{u}.$$

Consequently

- when s*t = u,
$$\{\mathtt{app(s,t,u)}\} \text{ APPEND} - \text{T } \{\mathtt{app(s,t,u)}\};$$

- when s*t ≠ u,
$$\{\mathtt{app(s,t,u)}\} \text{ APPEND} - \text{T } \emptyset.$$

(ii) Given ground lists s,t, the set $[\mathtt{app(s,t,Zs)}] \cap M_{\mathtt{APPEND\_T}}$ consists of just one element: app(s,t,s*t). Thus

$$\{\mathtt{app(s,t,Zs)}\} \text{ APPEND} - \text{T } \{\mathtt{app(s,t,s*t)}\}.$$

(iii) Finally, given a ground list u, we have

$$[\mathtt{app(Xs,Ys,u)}] \cap M_{\mathtt{APPEND\_T}} = \{\mathtt{app(s,t,u)} \mid \mathtt{s,t} \text{ are g. lists, } \mathtt{s} * \mathtt{t} = \mathtt{u}\}.$$

But each list can be split only in finitely many ways, so the set

$$[\mathtt{app(Xs,Ys,u)}] \cap M_{\mathtt{APPEND\_T}}$$

is finite. Thus

$$\{\mathtt{app(Xs,Ys,u)}\} \text{ APPEND} - \text{T } \{\mathtt{app(s,t,u)} \mid \mathtt{s,t} \text{ are g. lists, } \mathtt{s} * \mathtt{t} = \mathtt{u}\}.$$

Palindrome

A slightly less trivial example is the PALINDROME-T program. Given a list s, let rev(s) denote its reverse. It is easy to check that

$$\begin{aligned}M_{\text{PALINDROME-T}} = \ & \{\text{palindrome}(s) \mid s \text{ is a g. list}, \text{rev}(s) = s\} \\ \cup \ & \{\text{reverse}(s,t) \mid s, t \text{ are g. lists}, \text{rev}(s) = t\} \\ \cup \ & \{\text{reverse}(s,t,u) \mid s, t, u \text{ are g.lists}, \text{rev}(s)*t = u\} \\ \cup \ & M_{\text{LIST}},\end{aligned}$$

by noting that for lists x1s, x2s

$$\text{rev}([x|x1s]) * x2s = \text{rev}(x1s) * [x|x2s].$$

Thus for a ground list s

- when rev(s) = s,

$$\{\text{palindrome}(s)\} \ \text{PALINDROME} - \text{T} \ \{\text{palindrome}(s)\};$$

- when rev(s) ≠ s,

$$\{\text{palindrome}(s)\} \ \text{PALINDROME} - \text{T} \ \emptyset.$$

Moreover, for a ground list s, [reverse(s, Ys)] ∩ $M_{\text{PALINDROME-T}}$ = {reverse(s, rev(s))}, so

$$\{\text{reverse}(s, Ys)\} \ \text{PALINDROME} - \text{T} \ \{\text{reverse}(s, \text{rev}(s))\}.$$

Sequence

Finally, consider the SEQUENCE-T program. Call a list of 27 numbers satisfying the description of the sequence a *desired list*. We leave it to the reader to check that

$$\begin{aligned}M_{\text{SEQUENCE-T}} = \ & M_{\text{APPEND-T}} \\ \cup \ & \{\text{sublist}(s,t) \mid s, t \text{ are g. lists}, s \text{ is a sublist of } t\} \\ \cup \ & \{\text{sequence}(s) \mid s \text{ is a g. list of length } 27\} \\ \cup \ & \{\text{question}(s) \mid s \text{ is a desired list}\}.\end{aligned}$$

Thus [question(Ss)]∩$M_{\text{SEQUENCE-T}}$ = {question(s) | s is a desired list}. But the number of desired lists is obviously finite (in fact, as we noted, there are 6 of them). Consequently,

$$\{\text{question}(Ss)\} \ \text{SEQUENCE} - \text{T} \ \{\text{question}(s) \mid s \text{ is a desired list}\}.$$

Clearly, the above approach to partial correctness cannot be used to reason about queries with "non-ground inputs" (or more precisely about queries with non-ground computed instances), like app(s,t,Zs) where s,t are non-ground lists, since [app(s,t,Zs)]∩$M_{\mathrm{APPEND\_T}}$ is infinite. Recently, Apt and Gabbrielli [6] proposed a modification of the above method which allows us to deal properly with such queries.

3.3 Occur-check Freedom

In this section we study the occur-check problem.

3.3.1 *Occur-check Free Programs*

To define this problem we need to recall the unification algorithm due to Martelli and Montanari [26]. Two atoms can unify only if they have the same relation symbol. With two atoms $p(s_1, ..., s_n)$ and $p(t_1, ..., t_n)$ to be unified we associate the set of equations

$$\{s_1 = t_1, ..., s_n = t_n\}.$$

In the sequel we often refer to this set as $p(s_1, ..., s_n) = p(t_1, ..., t_n)$. The algorithm operates on such finite sets of equations. We use below the notions of sets and of systems of equations interchangeably. A substitution θ such that $s_1\theta = t_1\theta, ..., s_n\theta = t_n\theta$ is called a *unifier* of $\{s_1 = t_1, ..., s_n = t_n\}$. Thus the set of equations $\{s_1 = t_1, ..., s_n = t_n\}$ has the same unifiers as the atoms $p(s_1, ..., s_n)$ and $p(t_1, ..., t_n)$.

Two sets of equations are called *equivalent* if they have the same set of unifiers, and a set of equations is called *solved* if it is of the form $\{x_1 = t_1, ..., x_n = t_n\}$, where the x_i's are distinct variables and none of them occurs in a term t_j. If $E = \{x_1 = t_1, ..., x_n = t_n\}$ is solved, then we call $\{x_1/t_1, ..., x_n/t_n\}$ the *unifier determined by* E.

To find a most general unifier (in short, *mgu*) of two atoms it suffices to transform the associated set of equations into an equivalent one which is solved. The following algorithm does it if this is possible and otherwise halts with failure.

MARTELLI-MONTANARI ALGORITHM

Nondeterministically choose from the set of equations an equation of a form below and perform the associated action:

(1) $f(s_1, ..., s_n) = f(t_1, ..., t_n)$ *replace it by the equations* $s_1 = t_1, ..., s_n = t_n,$

(2) $f(s_1, ..., s_n) = g(t_1, ..., t_m)$ where $f \not\equiv g$ *halt with failure,*

(3) $x = x$ *delete it,*

(4) $t = x$ where t is not a variable *replace it by* $x = t,$

(5) $x = t$ where $x \not\equiv t$, x does not occur in t and x occurs elsewhere — *perform the substitution $\{x/t\}$ in every other equation,*

(6) $x = t$ where $x \not\equiv t$ and x occurs in t — *halt with failure.*

The algorithm terminates when no action can be performed or when failure arises. The following theorem holds (see Martelli and Montanari [26]).

Theorem 3.16 (Unification) *The Martelli-Montanari algorithm always terminates. If the original set of equations E has a unifier, then the algorithm successfully terminates and produces a solved set of equations determining an mgu of E, and otherwise it terminates with failure.* □

The test "x does not occur in t" in action (5) is called the *occur-check* and in most Prolog implementations omitted for reasons of efficiency. By omitting the occur-check in (5) and deleting action (6) from the Martelli-Montanari algorithm we are still left with two options depending on whether the substitution $\{x/t\}$ is performed in t itself. If it is, then divergence can result, because x occurs in t implies that x occurs in $t\{x/t\}$. If it is not, then an incorrect result can be produced, as in the case of the single equation $x = f(x)$ which yields the substitution $\{x/f(x)\}$. So in both cases the omission of the occur-check leads to complications. They are usually termed as the *occur-check problem*.

To deal with the occur-check problem we propose simple syntactic conditions which allow us to prove that for a given pure Prolog program and a query the occur-check can be safely omitted. To formally define this property we introduce the following notions.

Definition 3.17
- *A set of equations E is called not subject to occur-check (NSTO in short) if in no execution of the Martelli-Montanari algorithm started with E action (6) can be performed.*
- *Let ξ be an LD-derivation. Let A be an atom selected in ξ and H the head of the input clause selected to resolve A in ξ. Suppose that A and H have the same relation symbol. Then we say that the system $A = H$ is considered in ξ.*
- *Suppose that all systems of equations considered in the LD-derivations of $P \cup \{Q\}$ are NSTO. Then we say that $P \cup \{Q\}$ is occur-check free.*
□

The concept of an NSTO set of equations is due to Deransart, Ferrand and Téguia [19] who studied the conditions under which the occur-check can be safely omitted independently of the selection rule and of the chosen resolution strategy. Note that for an NSTO set of equations it is irrelevant for the purposes of unification whether the occur-check is omitted from the Martelli-Montanari algorithm.

The above definition assumes a specific unification algorithm but allows us to derive precise results. Moreover, the nondeterminism built into the Martelli-Montanari algorithm allows us to model executions of various other unification algorithms. In contrast, no specific unification algorithm in the definition of the LD-derivation is assumed.

Since in the definition of the occur-check freedom *all* LD-derivations of $P \cup \{Q\}$ are considered, all systems of equations that can be considered in a possibly backtracking Prolog execution of a query Q w.r.t. the program P are taken into account.

We now present the approach of Apt and Pellegrini [10] for proving occur-check freedom. To this end we need some preparatory definitions. One of them is the notion of a mode.

3.3.2 Well-moded Queries and Programs

Intuitively, modes indicate how the arguments of a relation should be used. They were first considered in Mellish [29], and more extensively studied in Reddy [31] and Dembinski and Maluszynski [18].

Definition 3.18 *Consider an n-ary relation symbol p. By a mode for p we mean a function m_p from $\{1,\ldots,n\}$ to the set $\{+,-\}$. If $m_p(i) = "+"$, we call i an input position of p, and if $m_p(i) = "-"$, we call i an output position of p (both w.r.t. m_p). By a moding we mean a collection of modes, each for a different relation symbol.* □

We write m_p in a more suggestive form $p(m_p(1),\ldots,m_p(n))$. For example, member(-,+) denotes a binary relation symbol member with the first position moded as output and the second position moded as input.

The definition of moding assumes one mode per relation symbol in a program. Multiple modes may be obtained by simply renaming the relations. In the remainder of this section we assume that *every considered relation symbol* has a fixed mode associated with it. This assumption will allow us to talk about input positions and output positions of an atom.

We now introduce a restriction which constrains the "flow of data" through the query and through the clauses of the programs. To simplify the notation, when writing an atom as $p(\mathbf{u}, \mathbf{v})$, we now assume that $\mathbf{u}$ is a sequence of terms filling in the input positions of p and $\mathbf{v}$ is a sequence of terms filling in the output positions of p.

Definition 3.19
- *A query $p_1(\mathbf{s_1}, \mathbf{t_1}),\ldots, p_n(\mathbf{s_n}, \mathbf{t_n})$ is called well-moded if for $i \in [1, n]$*

$$Var(\mathbf{s_i}) \subseteq \bigcup_{j=1}^{i-1} Var(\mathbf{t_j}).$$

- *A clause*

$$p_0(\mathbf{t_0}, \mathbf{s_{n+1}}) \leftarrow p_1(\mathbf{s_1}, \mathbf{t_1}),\ldots, p_n(\mathbf{s_n}, \mathbf{t_n})$$

is called *well-moded* if for $i \in [1, n+1]$

$$Var(\mathbf{s_i}) \subseteq \bigcup_{j=0}^{i-1} Var(\mathbf{t_j}).$$

- *A program is called well-moded if every clause of it is.* □

In particular, an atomic query $p(\mathbf{s}, \mathbf{t})$ is well-moded if $Var(\mathbf{s}) = \emptyset$, and a unit clause $p(\mathbf{s}, \mathbf{t}) \leftarrow$ is well-moded if $Var(\mathbf{t}) \subseteq Var(\mathbf{s})$.

Thus, a query is well-moded if

- every variable occurring in an input position of an atom ($i \in [1, n]$) occurs in an output position of an earlier ($j \in [1, i-1]$) atom.

And a clause is well-moded if

- ($i \in [1, n]$) every variable occurring in an input position of a body atom occurs either in an input position of the head ($j = 0$), or in an output position of an earlier ($j \in [1, i-1]$) body atom,
- ($i = n + 1$) every variable occurring in an output position of the head occurs in an input position of the head ($j = 0$), or in an output position of a body atom ($j \in [1, n]$).

Finally, we introduce the notion of linearity.

Definition 3.20
- *A family of terms is called* linear *if every variable occurs at most once in it.*
- *An atom is called* input *(resp.* output*)* linear *if the family of terms occurring in its input (resp. output) positions is linear.* □

Thus a family of terms is linear iff no variable has two distinct occurrences in any term and no two terms have a variable in common.

We now state a result allowing us to conclude that $P \cup \{Q\}$ is occur-check free. As we shall see, it can be easily applied to various pure Prolog programs.

Theorem 3.21 *Let P and Q be well-moded. Suppose that*

- *the head of every clause of P is output linear.*

Then $P \cup \{Q\}$ is occur-check free. □

Let us see now how this theorem can be applied to the programs considered in the previous sections.

Append

First, consider the program APPEND with the mode app(+,+,-). It is easy to check that in this mode APPEND is well-moded and the head of every clause is output linear. By Theorem 3.21 we conclude that for s and t ground, APPEND $\cup$ {app(s, t, u)} is occur-check free.

Program Verification and Prolog

Append, again

Also in the mode app(-,-,+) APPEND is well-moded and the head of every clause is output linear. Theorem 3.21 applies and yields that for u ground, APPEND ∪ {app(s, t, u)} is occur-check free.

Palindrome

Finally, consider the program PALINDROME-T. We mode it as follows: palindrome(+), reverse(+,-), reverse(+,+,-), list(+). Clearly, the program PALINDROME-T is then well-moded and the heads of all clauses are output linear, so by Theorem 3.21 for s ground, PALINDROME-T ∪ {palindrome(s)} is occur-check free.

3.3.3 *Nicely Moded Programs*

The above conclusions are still of a restrictive kind, because in each case we had to assume that the input positions of the one atom queries are ground. Moreover, Theorem 3.21 cannot be used to establish that SEQUENCE-T ∪ {question(Ss)} is occur-check free. Indeed, there is no way to mode this program and query so that both of them are well-moded.

To see this, first note that to get the query question(Ss) well-moded we have to use the mode question(-). This implies that to get the clause defining the question relation well-moded, we have to use the mode sequence(-). But then we cannot satisfy the requirement of well-modedness for the unit clause defining the sequence relation.

To deal with these difficulties we introduce the following notion due to Chadha and Plaisted [15] (and independently, though later, rediscovered in Apt and Pellegrini [10]).

Definition 3.22

- *A query* $p_1(\mathbf{s_1}, \mathbf{t_1}), \ldots, p_n(\mathbf{s_n}, \mathbf{t_n})$ *is called nicely moded if* $\mathbf{t_1}, \ldots, \mathbf{t_n}$ *is a linear family of terms and for* $i \in [1, n]$

$$Var(\mathbf{s_i}) \cap (\bigcup_{j=i}^{n} Var(\mathbf{t_j})) = \emptyset.$$

- *A clause*

$$p_0(\mathbf{s_0}, \mathbf{t_0}) \leftarrow p_1(\mathbf{s_1}, \mathbf{t_1}), \ldots, p_n(\mathbf{s_n}, \mathbf{t_n})$$

is called nicely moded if $p_1(\mathbf{s_1}, \mathbf{t_1}), \ldots, p_n(\mathbf{s_n}, \mathbf{t_n})$ *is nicely moded and*

$$Var(\mathbf{s_0}) \cap (\bigcup_{j=1}^{n} Var(\mathbf{t_j})) = \emptyset.$$

In particular, every unit clause is nicely moded.

- *A program is called nicely moded if every clause of it is.* □

Thus, assuming that in every atom the input positions occur first, a query is nicely moded if

- every variable occurring in an output position of an atom does not occur earlier in the query.

And a clause is nicely moded if

- every variable occurring in an output position of a body atom occurs neither earlier in the body nor in an input position of the head.

So, intuitively, the concept of being nicely moded prevents a "speculative binding" of the variables which occur in output positions — these variables are required to be "fresh". The following result of Apt and Pellegrini [10] and Chadha and Plaisted [15] clarifies the importance of this notion.

Theorem 3.23 *Let P and Q be nicely moded. Suppose that*

- *the head of every clause of P is input linear.*

Then $P \cup \{Q\}$ is occur-check free. □

Let us see now how this theorem can be applied to the previously studied programs.

Append

Consider again the program APPEND with the moding app(+,+,-). Then APPEND is nicely moded and the head of every clause is input linear. By Theorem 3.23 we conclude that when u is linear and $Var(s,t) \cap Var(u) = \emptyset$, APPEND $\cup$ { app(s, t, u)} is occur-check free.

Append, again

With the moding app(-,-,+) APPEND is nicely moded as well, and the head of every clause is input linear. Again, by Theorem 3.23 we conclude that when s,t is a linear family of terms and $Var(s,t) \cap Var(u) = \emptyset$, APPEND $\cup$ { app(s, t, u)} is occur-check free.

Sequence

Reconsider now the program SEQUENCE-T. To be able to apply Theorem 3.23 we mode it as follows: sublist(-,+), sequence(+), question(+), app(-,-,+), list(+). Thanks to the use of anonymous variables it is easy to check that then SEQUENCE-T is indeed nicely moded and that the heads of all clauses are input linear. By Theorem 3.23 we now get that when t is linear (and so, for example, a variable), SEQUENCE-T $\cup$ {question(t)} is occur-check free.

Palindrome

So far it seems that Theorem 3.23 allows us to draw more useful conclusions than Theorem 3.21. However, reconsider the program PALINDROME-T. In Chadha and Plaisted [15] it is shown that no moding exists such that PALINDROME-T is nicely moded and the heads of all clauses are input linear.

Thus Theorem 3.23 cannot be applied to this program whereas Theorem 3.21 was applicable.

The last two examples thus show that each of these theorems is applicable to different classes of programs.

4 Pure Prolog with Arithmetic

We now move on to the study of the second subset of Prolog, pure Prolog with arithmetic. The previous approach to termination can be readily applied to this subset – it suffices to use level mappings which assign to ground atoms with arithmetic relations the value 0.

However, some caution has to be exercised. While the base for our approach to termination, Theorem 3.3, remains valid for pure Prolog programs with arithmetic (in fact, the same proof carries through), Theorem 3.4 does not hold anymore. Indeed, consider the program with only one clause: $p \leftarrow x < y, p$. Because the LD-derivations which end in an error are finite, the above program is left terminating. However, it is easy to see that it is not acceptable – just consider the ground instance $p \leftarrow 1 < 2, p$ and recall from Section 2.2 that the clause $1 < 2$ is added to the program, so it is true in every model of it. (In contrast, the program consisting of the clause $p \leftarrow x < x, p$ *is* acceptable.) This shows that the proposed method of proving termination is somewhat less general in the case of programs with arithmetic.

We refer to Apt and Pedreschi [8] for a proof that QUICKSORT is left terminating and that for a list s all LD-derivations of QUICKSORT $\cup$ {qs(s, Ys)} are finite.

The subject of partial correctness is considered after studying the issue of errors.

4.1 Absence of Run-time Errors

To prove absence of errors we use types. We found it convenient to use here an approach recently proposed by Bronsard, Lakshman and Reddy [14] which from the semantic point of view coincides with the method of Bossi and Cocco [13] for proving partial correctness. In our presentation we abstract from the concrete syntax introduced in these papers. Bossi and Cocco [13] use first-order language and concentrate on proofs of partial correctness, whereas Bronsard, Lakshman and Reddy [14] introduce a language which allows us to express in a concise way recursive and polymorphic types which involve incomplete data structures. The idea is to associate with each relation symbol two types: a pre-type and a post-type.

We call an atom a *p-atom* if its relation symbol is p. Recall from Section 3.1 that we denoted by $rel(A)$ the relation symbol occurring in atom A. So an atom A is a $rel(A)$-atom.

The following very general definition of a type is sufficient for our purposes.

Definition 4.1 *Consider a relation symbol p.*

- *A type for p is a set of p-atoms closed under substitution.*
- *A type is a type for a relation symbol p.*
- *A directional type for p is a pair pre_p, $post_p$ of types for p. We call pre_p (resp. $post_p$) a pre-type (resp. a post-type) associated with p.* □

Below we shall often use certain sets of terms in the consider universal language:
$\mathcal{T}$ — the set of all terms,
List — the set of lists,
Gae — the set of of gae's,
ListGae — the set of lists of gae's.

In what follows we write a directional type for a relation symbol p in a more suggestive form used in Pedreschi [30], another recent work on directional types:

$$p : S \to T,$$

where $pre_p = \{p(\mathbf{s}) \mid \mathbf{s} \in S\}$ and $post_p = \{p(\mathbf{t}) \mid \mathbf{t} \in T\}$. For example,

$$\mathbf{app} : (List \times List \times \mathcal{T}) \cup (\mathcal{T} \times \mathcal{T} \times List) \to List \times List \times List$$

is a directional type for a ternary relation symbol **app**.

In the remainder of this section we assume that *every considered relation symbol* has a fixed directional type associated with it. This assumption will allow us to talk about pre- and post-types of a relation symbol.

Definition 4.2 *Given atoms $A_1, \ldots, A_n, A_{n+1}$ and types $T_1, \ldots, T_n, T_{n+1}$, where $n \geq 0$, we write*

$$\models A_1 \in T_1, \ldots, A_n \in T_n \Rightarrow A_{n+1} \in T_{n+1}$$

to denote the fact that for all substitutions θ, if $A_1\theta \in T_1, \ldots, A_n\theta \in T_n$, then $A_{n+1}\theta \in T_{n+1}$. □

We now abbreviate $A \in pre_{rel(A)}$ to $pre(A)$ and analogously for *post*.

Definition 4.3
- *A query $A_1, \ldots, A_n$ is called well-typed if for $j \in [1, n]$*

$$\models post(A_1), \ldots, post(A_{j-1}) \Rightarrow pre(A_j).$$

- *A clause $H \leftarrow B_1, \ldots, B_n$ is called well-typed if for $j \in [1, n+1]$*

$$\models pre(H), post(B_1), \ldots, post(B_{j-1}) \Rightarrow pre(B_j),$$

where $pre(B_{n+1}) := post(H)$.

- *A program is called well-typed if every clause of it is.* □

In particular, an atomic query A is well-typed if $\models pre(A)$, and a unit clause $A \leftarrow$ is well-typed if $\models pre(A) \Rightarrow post(A)$.

The following property of the notion of being well-typed holds (essentially, see Bossi and Cocco [13] or an account of it in Apt and Marchiori [7]).

Lemma 4.4 (Persistence) *An LD-resolvent of a well-typed query, and a well-typed clause that is variable disjoint with it, is well-typed.* □

This brings us to the following important conclusion.

Corollary 4.5 *Let P and Q be well-typed, and let ξ be an LD-derivation of $P \cup \{Q\}$. Then $\models pre(A)$ for every atom A selected in ξ.*

Proof. A variant of a well-typed clause is well-typed and for a well-typed query $A_1, \ldots, A_n$ we have $\models pre(A_1)$. □

In the sequel, we say that an atom A *satisfies its precondition* if $\models pre(A)$.

Quicksort

To see the usefulness of this corollary let us return to the QUICKSORT program. To prove absence of run-time errors we start by typing the relation qs in a way reflecting the following statement: when the first argument is a list of gae's, upon successful termination the second argument is a list a gea's, so:

$$\text{qs} : ListGae \times \mathcal{T} \to \mathcal{T} \times ListGae,$$

and the built-in's $>$ and $\leq$ in such a way that the above corollary can be applied, so:

$$>: Gae \times Gae \to \mathcal{T} \times \mathcal{T},$$

and

$$\leq: Gae \times Gae \to \mathcal{T} \times \mathcal{T}.$$

We now complete the typing in such a way that QUICKSORT is well-typed:

$$\text{part} : Gae \times ListGae \times \mathcal{T} \times \mathcal{T} \to \mathcal{T} \times \mathcal{T} \times ListGae \times ListGae,$$

$$\text{app} : \mathcal{T} \times ListGae \times \mathcal{T} \to \mathcal{T} \times ListGae \times \mathcal{T}.$$

It is worthwhile to note that a trivial directional type, namely

$$\text{app} : \mathcal{T} \times \mathcal{T} \times \mathcal{T} \to \mathcal{T} \times \mathcal{T} \times \mathcal{T}$$

is sufficient here. The reason for using the above directional type will become clear in Section 6.1.

Assume now that s is a list of gae's. By Corollary 4.5 we conclude that all atoms selected in the LD-derivations of QUICKSORT $\cup$ {qs(s,t)} satisfy their preconditions. In particular, when these atoms are of the form u > v or u $\leq$ v, both u and u are gae's. Thus the LD-derivations of QUICKSORT $\cup$ {qs(s,t)} do not end in an error.

Length

The following program LENGTH uses another arithmetic relation, is:

```
length(Xs, N) ← N is the length of the list Xs.
length([_ | Ts], N) ← length(Ts, M), N is M+1.
length([], 0).
```

To prove absence of run-time errors we use the following types:

$$\text{length} : \mathcal{T} \times \mathcal{T} \to \mathcal{T} \times Gae,$$

$$\text{is} : \mathcal{T} \times Gae \to Gae \times \mathcal{T}.$$

It is easy to check that LENGTH is then well-typed. Corollary 4.5 now yields that for arbitrary terms s, t, all atoms selected in the LD-derivations of LENGTH $\cup$ {length(s,t)} satisfy their preconditions. In particular, when these atoms are of the form u is v, v is a gae. So the LD-derivations of LENGTH $\cup$ {length(s,t)} do not end in an error.

4.2 Partial Correctness

When dealing with partial correctness of programs that use arithmetic relations we need to remember (see Section 2.2) that to each program we added infinitely many clauses which define the used arithmetic relations. Both the Soundess Theorem 3.13 and the Strong Completeness Theorem 3.14 remain valid for programs with infinitely many clauses; however, completeness does not hold any more in the presence of arithmetic relations. Indeed, we have $P \models$ X < Y{X/1, Y/2} for any program P that uses <, whereas the LD-derivations of $P \cup$ {X < Y} end in an error. Also Theorem 3.15 does not hold then, as the query X < 2 shows. Still, the following version of this theorem can be used for proofs of partial correctness.

Theorem 4.6 *Consider a program P and a query Q. Assume that the LD-derivations of $P \cup \{Q\}$ do not end in error. Suppose that the set $\mathcal{Q}$ of ground correct instances of Q is finite. Then*

$$\{Q\} \ P \ \mathcal{Q}.$$

Proof. Under the assumptions of the theorem both the Soundness Theorem 3.13 and the Strong Completeness Theorem 3.14 remain valid. For the completeness theorem this is not obvious, since it usually relies on the

Lifting Lemma which does not hold now. Indeed, the query 1 < 2 admits a successful LD-derivation, whereas all the LD-derivations of its more general version X < Y end in an error. However, the admirably short and elegant proof of Stärk [35] does not use the Lifting Lemma and carries through. Consequently, the proof of Theorem 3.15 carries through as well. □

Quicksort

To apply this theorem reconsider the QUICKSORT program. We deal here with its "correctly typed" version QUICKSORT-T, obtained by using APPEND-T instead of APPEND and in which the last clause defining the part relation is replaced by

part(X, [], [], []) ← X ≤ X.

This forces the first argument of part to be a gae. (Without this change the query qs([s],Ys) would succeed for any s.)

Below we use the following terminology. An element a *partitions a list of gae's* s *into* ls, bs if a is a gae, ls is a list of elements of s which are < a and bs is a list of elements of s which are ≥ a.

By extending the previously considered typing with

$$\texttt{list} : ListGae \to ListGae$$

we conclude that for a list of gae's s the LD-derivations of QUICKSORT-T ∪ {qs(s, Ys)} do not end in an error. Moreover, the above-mentioned proof of termination of QUICKSORT ∪ {qs(s, Ys)} can be modified in a straightforward way to the program QUICKSORT-T.

We leave it to the reader to check that

$$M_{\text{QUICKSORT-T}} = M_{\text{APPEND-T}} \cup M_> \cup M_\leq$$
$$\cup \ \{\text{part}(a, s, ls, bs) \mid s, ls, bs \text{ are lists of gae's,}$$
$$\text{a partitions s into ls, bs}\}$$
$$\cup \ \{\text{qs}(s, t) \mid s, t \text{ are lists of gae's and}$$
$$t \text{ is a sorted permutation of s}\}.$$

So for a list of gae's s the set $[\text{qs}(s, \text{Ys})] \cap M_{\text{QUICKSORT-T}}$ consists of just one element: qs(s,t), where t is a sorted permutation of s. Consequently, by Theorem 4.6,

$$\{\text{qs}(s, \text{Ys})\} \ \text{QUICKSORT} - \text{T} \ \{\text{qs}(s, t)\}.$$

Length

In contrast, the LENGTH program can be directly handled without any modification. It is easy to check that

$$M_{\text{LENGTH}} = M_{\text{is}}$$
$$\cup \ \{\text{length}(s,|s|) \mid s \text{ is a g. list}\}.$$

(Recall, that for a list s, |s| is its length.) Such a check involves the use of Lemma 3.11 which is applicable here, since the program LENGTH is easily seen to be acceptable, and so left terminating. So for a ground list s the set $[\text{length}(s, N)] \cap M_{\text{LENGTH}}$ consists of just one element: length(s,|s|). By Theorem 4.6,

$$\{\text{length}(s, N)\} \ \text{LENGTH} \ \{\text{length}(s,|s|)\}.$$

Note that the proof of the above claim for a non-ground list s breaks down because the set $[\text{length}(s, N)] \cap M_{\text{LENGTH}}$ is then infinite.

4.3 Occur-check Freedom

Finally, we deal with the issue of the occur-check. The approach of Section 3.3 is applicable to pure Prolog programs with arithmetic without any modification. The reason is that the unit clauses which define the arithmetic relations are all ground, so they automatically satisfy the conditions of Theorems 3.21 and 3.23. To see how these results apply here reconsider the two running examples of this section.

Quicksort

Consider QUICKSORT with the moding qs(+,-), partition(+,+,-,-), app(+,+,-), >(+, +), ≤(+, +). QUICKSORT is then well-moded and the heads of all clauses are output linear. Theorem 3.21 applies and yields that for s ground, QUICKSORT ∪ {qs(s, t)} is occur-check free.

Moreover, in this moding QUICKSORT is also nicely moded and the head of every clause is input linear. Thus Theorem 3.23 applies as well, and yields that when t is linear and $Var(s) \cap Var(t) = \emptyset$, QUICKSORT ∪ {qs(s, t)} is occur-check free.

Length

Next, consider the LENGTH program with the moding length(+,-), is(-,+). Then LENGTH is well-moded and the heads of all clauses are output linear. By Theorem 3.21 for s ground, LENGTH ∪ {length(s, t)} is occur-check free.

Moreover, in this moding LENGTH is also nicely moded and the head of every clause is input linear. Thus Theorem 3.23 applies here as well, and yields that when t is linear and $Var(s) \cap Var(t) = \emptyset$, LENGTH ∪ {length(s, t)} is occur-check free. In particular, this conclusion holds for any list s and a variable N not appearing in s.

It is well-known that programs with difference-lists easily lead to complications in absence of the occur-check. For example, the program empty

empty(L \ L).

when executed with the goal ← empty([a | X] \ X) leads to the consideration of the system { [a | X] = L, X = L } which is subject to the occur-check. It is worthwhile to note that programs which use difference-lists can be handled by the methods proposed. For example, Theorem 3.23 immediately implies that for s and t linear and variable disjoint, empty ∪ {empty(s, t)} is occur-check free.

However, more complex programs with difference lists like quicksort_dl (program 15.4 on page 244 in Sterling and Shapiro [36]) cannot be handled by the approach discussed here. In Apt and Pellegrini [10] a refinement of this approach is proposed which can be used to deal with such programs.

Of course, there exist programs whose executions for a natural class of queries do result in the occur-check problem. An example is the program that formalizes Curry's system of type assignment for the typed lambda calculus. For such a program and queries a transformation is proposed in Apt and Pellegrini [10] which transforms a program and a query into a program and a query for which only the calls to the built-in unification relation need to be resolved by a unification algorithm with the occur-check.

5 Pure Prolog with Negation

Finally, we deal with the third subset of Prolog, pure Prolog with negation. We call programs written in this subset general programs. Our approach to proving termination and partial correctness of general programs is applicable only under the assumption that floundering does not arise. So we have to deal with this issue first.

5.1 Absence of Floundering

To prove absence of floundering we generalize the notion of a well-moded program (Definition 3.19) to general programs. To this end we simply allow the negation symbol ¬ to occur in front of atoms in queries and clause bodies. More precisely, we introduce the following definition, where ⊙ stands for ¬ or for the empty string.

Definition 5.1
- *A general query* $\odot p_1(\mathbf{s_1}, \mathbf{t_1}), \ldots, \odot p_n(\mathbf{s_n}, \mathbf{t_n})$ *is called well-moded if for* $i \in [1, n]$

$$Var(\mathbf{s_i}) \subseteq \bigcup_{j=1}^{i-1} Var(\mathbf{t_j}).$$

- *A general clause*

$$p_0(\mathbf{t_0}, \mathbf{s_{n+1}}) \leftarrow \odot p_1(\mathbf{s_1}, \mathbf{t_1}), \ldots, \odot p_n(\mathbf{s_n}, \mathbf{t_n})$$

is called well-moded if for $i \in [1, n+1]$

$$Var(\mathbf{s_i}) \subseteq \bigcup_{j=0}^{i-1} Var(\mathbf{t_j}).$$

- *A general program is called well-moded if every general clause of it is.* □

This definition will be useful later.

Definition 5.2 *A general program is called non-floundering if no LDNF-derivation starting in a ground general query flounders.* □

The following result is due to Apt and Pellegrini [10] and, independently, Stroetman [37].

Theorem 5.3 *Consider a well-moded general program P and a well-moded general query Q. Suppose that all relations used in negative literals of P and Q are moded completely input. Then $P \cup \{Q\}$ does not flounder. In particular, P is non-floundering.* □

To see the use of this theorem we now consider two general programs which deal with directed graphs. A directed graph is represented here as a (ground) list of its edges. In turn, an edge from node a to node b is represented by the list $[a, b]$.

Transitive Closure

The first general program, called TRANS-T, computes the transitive closure of a directed graph:

```
trans(X, Y, E, Avoids) ← list(Avoids), member([X, Y], E).
trans(X, Z, E, Avoids) ←
   member([X, Y], E),
   ¬ member(Y, Avoids),
   trans(Y, Z, E, [Y | Avoids]).
```

```
member(Element, List)  ← Element is an element of the list List.
member(X, [Y | Xs])  ← member(X, Xs).
member(X, [X | Xs])  ← list(Xs).
```

augmented by the LIST program.

In a typical use of this program in order to check that [x,y] is in the transitive closure of the directed graph e, one evaluates the query trans(x, y, e, [x]).

With the moding trans(-,-,+,+), list(+), member(+,+) for the occurrence of member in the negative literal ¬ member(Y, Avoids), and member(-,+) for the other occurrences of member, TRANS-T is well-moded. By Theorem 5.3, for e,s ground, TRANS-T ∪ {trans(a, b, e, s)} does not flounder. Moreover, TRANS-T is non-floundering.

Dag

Consider now the problem of testing whether a graph is a dag. Recall that *dag* is the abbreviation for "directed acyclic graph" and that a directed graph is *acyclic* if no path in it exists which forms a cycle. The solution is exceptionally simple, though not very efficient – we add to the general program TRANS-T the general clauses

```
acyclic(E) ← ¬ cyclic(E).
cyclic(E) ← trans(X, X, E, []).
```

Call the resulting general program DAG-T.

We now extend the above moding by cyclic(+), acyclic(+). It is straightforward to check that DAG-T is then well-moded. Thus, by Theorem 5.3, for e ground, DAG-T ∪ {acyclic(e)} does not flounder. Moreover, DAG-T is non-floundering.

5.2 Termination

To deal with termination we use the approach of Apt and Pedreschi [8] which generalizes the method of Section 3.1 to general programs.

Definition 5.4 *A general program is called left terminating if all its LDNF-derivations starting with a ground query are finite.* □

Given a general program P, we now define its "negative part" P^-.

Definition 5.5 *Let P be a general program and p, q relations.*

- *p refers to q iff a general clause in P uses p in its head and q in its body.*
- *p depends on q is the reflexive, transitive closure of refers to.*
- *Neg_P is the set of relations which are used in a negative literal in P.*
- *Neg_P^* is the set of relations on which the relations in Neg_P depend.*
- *P^- is the set of general clauses in P in whose head a relation from Neg_P^* is used.* □

Recall now from Lloyd [25] and Apt [2] that $comp(P)$ stands for Clark's completion of a general program P.

Definition 5.6

- *Given a level mapping $|\ |$, we extend it to ground negative literals by putting $|\neg A| = |A|$. $\neg A$ is bounded with respect to $|\ |$ if A is.*
- *A general clause is called acceptable with respect to $|\ |$ and an interpretation I, if I is its model and for every ground instance $A \leftarrow \mathbf{K}, L, \mathbf{M}$ of it such that $I \models \mathbf{K}$*

$$|A| > |L|.$$

- *A general program P is called acceptable with respect to $|\ |$ and I, if every general clause of it is and if the restriction of I to the relation symbols from Neg_P^* is a model of $comp(P^-)$.* □

The following result relates these notions.

Theorem 5.7 *Let P be a general program acceptable w.r.t. $|\ |$ and I. Then for every literal L bounded w.r.t. $|\ |$ all LDNF-derivations of $P \cup \{L\}$ are finite. In particular, P is left terminating.* □

So to apply the notion of acceptability we need a method for proving that an interpretation I is a model of $comp(P^-)$. For Herbrand interpretations the following observation due to Apt, Blair and Walker [4] comes to our rescue. The notion of a supported model is now extended to general programs in an obvious way.

Note 5.8 *A Herbrand interpretation I is a model of $comp(P)$ iff it is a supported model of P.* □

The following result shows that the restriction to Herbrand models does not result in a limitation of the method.

Theorem 5.9 *Let P be a left terminating, non-floundering general program. Then, for some level mapping $|\ |$ and a Herbrand interpretation I,*

(i) P is acceptable w.r.t. $|\ |$ and I,

(ii) for every literal L all LDNF-derivations of $P \cup \{L\}$ are finite iff L is bounded w.r.t. $|\ |$. □

Apt and Pedreschi [8] showed that `TRANS-T` is acceptable w.r.t. a level mapping $|\ |$ such that $|\text{trans}(a,b,e,s)|$ is a function of e and s, and a Herbrand interpretation I. Thus for e,s ground all LDNF-derivations of `TRANS-T` $\cup$ {`trans(a, b, e, s)`} are finite. In particular, `TRANS-T` is left terminating.

By extending this level mapping to `DAG-T` with

$$|\text{acyclic}(e)| = |\text{cyclic}(e)| + 1,$$
$$|\text{cyclic}(e)| = |\text{trans}(a,a,e,[])| + 1,$$

where a is a constant, and modifying I appropriately, we also conclude that for e ground all LDNF-derivations of `DAG-T` $\cup$ {`acyclic(e)`} are finite and that `DAG-T` is left terminating.

5.3 Partial Correctness

Our approach to partial correctness of general programs is applicable only to general programs which are left terminating and non-floundering. The following result of Apt and Pedreschi [8] is crucial.

Theorem 5.10 *Consider a left terminating, non-floundering general program P. Then,*

(i) P has a unique supported Herbrand model, M_P,

(ii) M_P *is a model of* $comp(P)$,

(iii) for a ground general query Q *such that* $P \cup \{Q\}$ *does not flounder,* $M_P \models Q$ *iff there exists a successful LDNF-derivation of* $P \cup \{Q\}$.

□

We now need to revise Definition 3.12.

Definition 5.11 *Consider a general program* P *and a general query* Q. *We say that* Q' *is a correct instance of* Q, *if* Q' *is an instance of* Q *and* $comp(P) \models Q'$. □

The definition of a computed instance refers now to the LDNF-resolution. The following soundness and completeness results are of help.

Theorem 5.12 **(Soundness of LDNF-resolution)** *Consider a general program* P *and a general query* Q. *Every computed instance of* Q *is a correct instance of* Q. □

Theorem 5.13 **(Limited Completeness of LDNF-resolution)** *Consider a left terminating, non-floundering general program* P *and a general query* Q *such that* $P \cup \{Q\}$ *does not flounder. For every ground correct instance* Q' *of* Q *there exists a computed instance* Q'' *of* Q *such that* $Q'' \leq Q'$.

Proof. $P \cup \{Q'\}$ does not flounder since $P \cup \{Q\}$ does not flounder. By Theorem 5.10(ii), (iii) there exists a successful LDNF-derivation of $P \cup \{Q'\}$. $P \cup \{Q\}$ does not flounder, so we can lift this derivation to a successful LDNF-derivation of $P \cup \{Q\}$ which yields a computed instance Q'' of Q such that $Q'' \leq Q'$. □

These theorems are needed to establish the following result.

Theorem 5.14 *Consider a left terminating, non-floundering general program* P *and a general query* Q *such that* $P \cup \{Q\}$ *does not flounder. Suppose that the set* $\mathcal{Q}$ *of ground correct instances of* Q *is finite. Then*

$$\{Q\} \ P \ \mathcal{Q}.$$

Proof. The proof is analogous to the proof of Theorem 3.15. So first we note that

$$\text{every correct instance } Q' \text{ of } Q \text{ is ground.} \quad (5.1)$$

Consider now $Q_1 \in \mathcal{Q}$. By the Limited Completeness Theorem 5.13, there exists a computed instance Q_2 of Q such that $Q_2 \leq Q_1$. By the Soundness Theorem 5.12, Q_2 is a correct instance of Q, so by (5.1) Q_2 is ground. Consequently, $Q_2 = Q_1$; that is, Q_1 is a computed instance of Q.

Conversely, take a computed instance Q_1 of Q. By the Soundness Theorem 5.12, Q_1 is a correct instance of Q. By (5.1) Q_1 is ground, so $Q_1 \in \mathcal{Q}$.

□

To apply this theorem we need a method to establish the premise "the set $\mathcal{Q}$ of ground correct instances of Q is finite". As in the case of pure Prolog programs, we solve this problem by restricting our attention to the model M_P. Indeed, for an atomic query A the above premise can be rephrased (thanks to Theorems 5.10 and 5.12) as "the set $[A] \cap M_P$ is finite".

As in the case of pure Prolog programs, it is usually straightforward to check that a Herbrand interpretation is a supported model of a general program. So in the examples below we omit the proofs of these facts.

Transitive Closure

We now show how to apply this theorem to the program TRANS-T. In the previous two subsections we proved that TRANS-T is left terminating and non-floundering. Adopt the following terminology. Given a list e, a *path in e from a to b* is a sequence $a_1, \ldots, a_n$ ($n > 1$) such that
- $[a_i, a_{i+1}] \in e$ for $i \in [1, n-1]$,
- $a_1 = a$,
- $a_n = b$.

An *interior* of a path $a_1, \ldots, a_n$ ($n > 1$) is the set $\{a_2, \ldots, a_{n-1}\}$. A path $a_1, \ldots, a_n$ ($n > 1$) is called *acyclic* if the elements of its interior are pairwise different. A path $a_1, \ldots, a_n$ ($n > 1$) *avoids* a list s if no element of its interior is a member of s. In particular, a path consisting of two elements has an empty interior and consequently is acyclic and avoids every s.

It is routine to check that

$$M_{\text{TRANS-T}} = M_{\text{LIST}}$$
$$\cup \ \{\text{trans}(a, b, e, s) \mid e, s \text{ are g. lists, an acyclic path in } e$$
$$\text{from a to b exists which avoids s}\}$$
$$\cup \ \{\text{member}(a, t) \mid t \text{ is a g. list and } a \in t\}.$$

Consider now a directed graph e. We denote its transitive closure by e^*. Then [a,b] $\in e^*$ iff there exists in e an acyclic path from a to b which avoids [a]. By Theorem 5.14 we conclude that

- when [a,b] $\in e^*$,

$$\{\text{trans}(a, b, e, [a])\} \text{ TRANS} - \text{T } \{\text{trans}(a, b, e, [a])\};$$

- when [a,b] $\notin e^*$,

$$\{\text{trans}(a, b, e, [a])\} \text{ TRANS} - \text{T } \emptyset.$$

Note that [a] can be replaced here by [] or by [a,b].

Moreover,

$$[\text{trans}(X, Y, e, [\,])] \cap M_{\text{TRANS-T}} = \{\text{trans}(a, b, e, [\,]) \mid [a, b] \in e^*\},$$

so
$$\{\mathtt{trans(X,Y,e,[\,])}\}\ \mathtt{TRANS-T}\ \{\mathtt{trans(a,b,e,[\,])}\mid [a,b]\in e^*\},$$

since TRANS-T $\cup$ {trans(X, Y, e, [ ])} does not flounder. This, in conjunction with the fact that all LDNF-derivations of TRANS-T $\cup$ {trans(X, Y, e, [ ])} are finite, implies that the query trans(X, Y, e, [ ]) generates all pairs of elements which form the nodes of the transitive closure e^*.

Dag

To deal with the general program DAG-T we extend the above terminology. Given a list e, we call e *cyclic* if for some a a path in e from a to a exists, and we call e *acyclic* if it is not cyclic. We leave it to the reader to check that

$$\begin{aligned}M_{\mathtt{DAG-T}} &= M_{\mathtt{TRANS-T}}\\ &\cup\ \{\mathtt{acyclic(e)}\mid e\text{ is a ground acyclic list}\}\\ &\cup\ \{\mathtt{cyclic(e)}\mid e\text{ is a ground cyclic list}\}.\end{aligned}$$

Now take a directed graph e. By Theorem 5.14 we conclude that:

- when e is acyclic, $\{\mathtt{acyclic(e)}\}$ DAG − T $\{\mathtt{acyclic(e)}\}$;
- when e is cyclic, $\{\mathtt{acyclic(e)}\}$ DAG − T $\emptyset$.

5.4 Occur-check Freedom

When considering the notion of the occur-check freedom for general programs and general queries, we simply reuse the original Definition 3.17 but now apply it to the LDNF-derivations. In this way, we ignore the selection of negative literals, but this does not matter as the choice of a negative literal $\neg A$ either leads to floundering or to the consideration of the query A whose selected literal is positive. In both cases no unification is performed.

Further, we reuse the notion of well-moded general programs and general queries (Definition 5.1) introduced in Section 5.1. Theorem 3.21 easily generalizes to general programs and general queries. More precisely, we have the following result (see Apt and Pellegrini [10]).

Theorem 5.15 *Let P be a general well-moded program and Q a general well-moded query. Suppose that*

- *the head of every general clause of P is output linear.*

Then $P\cup\{Q\}$ is occur-check free. □

Transitive Closure

Let us see now how this result can be applied to TRANS-T. In Section 5.1 we had to introduce two modes for the member relation. Here a simpler moding suffices, namely trans(-,-,+,+), list(+), member(-,+). Then trans is well-moded and the heads of all general clauses are output linear.

So we conclude by Theorem 5.15 that for e,v ground, TRANS-T ∪ {trans(s, t, e, v)} is occur-check free.

Dag

Extending the above moding by cyclic(+), acyclic(+) we can also draw appropriate conclusions for the general program DAG-T: by Theorem 5.15 for e ground, DAG-T ∪ {acyclic(e)} is occur-check free.

It is also possible to generalize the result on nicely moded programs (viz. Theorem 3.23) to the case of general programs. However, the concept of a nicely moded general program does not prevent the use of non-ground input positions in the queries. As a result general programs to which the results on nicely moded general programs can be applied usually flounder. So — in the framework of LDNF-resolution — this generalization is of limited interest and consequently is omitted.

6 Conclusions

6.1 Dealing with "Ill-typed" Programs

In our analysis we only dealt with the "correctly typed" programs, i.e. programs named XXX-T. These programs are easier to handle than their corresponding "ill-typed" XXX versions, but they are much more inefficient due to the added "type checks".

It is possible to deal directly with the "ill-typed" programs, but the study of their partial correctness is quite a nuisance, because it is awkward to describe their unique supported Herbrand models in simple and intuitive terms.

Therefore we propose the following alternative, which we illustrate on the program QUICKSORT. Consider the typing of QUICKSORT defined in Section 4.1. Let qs(s,t) be a well-typed query and let ξ be an LD-derivation of QUICKSORT ∪ {qs(s,t)}. By Corollary 4.5, if the selected atom is of the form part(s_1, s_2, s_3, s_4) then $s_1 \in Gae$, and if the selected atom is of the form app(s_1, s_2, s_3) then $s_2 \in List$.

Thus in both cases in the corresponding LD-derivation of QUICKSORT-T ∪ {qs(s,t)} the inserted "type checks", namely X $\leq$ X and list(Y), succeed with the empty computed answer substitution. Consequently, the computed instances of the query qs(s,t) are the same w.r.t. both programs. In particular, for a list of gae's s we have

$$\{qs(s, Ys)\}\ \text{QUICKSORT}\ \{qs(s, t)\}.$$

The same approach can be applied to other pure Prolog programs and programs with arithmetic.

For general programs we need to extend Definition 4.3. This can be done by simply identifying $pre(\neg A)$ with $pre(A)$ and $post(\neg A)$ with $post(A)$. Then the generalization of Corollary 4.5 to LDNF-derivations holds, so the

above technique is also applicable to general programs, in particular to
TRANS-T and DAG-T.

6.2 Final Remarks

The aim of this chapter was to show that it is possible to reason about correctness of various Prolog programs by means of simple arguments based on syntactic analysis, declarative semantics, modes and types. We hope that this work can form a basis for a similar study of other languages based on the logic programming paradigm. In particular, it would be interesting to carry out such a study for logic programs executed with a dynamic selection rule defined by means of delay declarations. Such dynamic selection rules are for example present in Gödel, a declarative language designed by Hill and Lloyd [20].

In general, all correctness properties studied in this chapter are undecidable. However, certain aspects of the approach discussed here can be automated. We conclude this chapter by discussing this point in some detail and pointing out which issues require further investigation.

6.2.1 Termination

The approach to termination discussed here is based on the use of the notion of acceptability. Apt and Pedreschi [8] noted that some fragments of the proof of accceptability can be automated. In fact, they indicated that in many cases the task of checking the guesses for both the level mapping | | and the model I can be reduced to checking the validity of universal formulas in an extension of Presburger arithmetic by the min and max operators. The validity problem for such formulas is decidable. In fact, Shostak [34] presented for this class a decision algorithm which is exponential. Cinzia Pieramico of the University of Pisa implemented this procedure for checking left termination w.r.t. a level mapping and a Herbrand interpretation which are expressible in the above language and verified mechanically that the quicksort program QS is left terminating.

De Schreye, Verschaetse and Bruynooghe [33] studied the problem of automatic generation of level mappings and Herbrand interpretations w.r.t. which the program is left terminating.

6.2.2 Partial Correctness

The approach to partial correctness reported in this chapter is to our knowledge new and its (partial) automation needs to be further studied. It is worthwhile to point out here that Theorem 5.10 implies that for left terminating (non-floundering general) programs the membership problem for the model M_P is decidable. So given such a (general) program, it is decidable whether a ground (general) query successfully terminates.

However, the complexity of this decision problem is in general forbiddingly high because the results of Bezem [12] imply that every total recursive function can be encoded in a model M_P.

6.2.3 Occur-check Freedom

The methods proposed here can be trivially implemented because they are based on syntactic analysis. However, to use Theorem 3.21 it is necessary to generate modings for which this theorem can be applied. To this end efficient algorithms are needed for generating modings for which a program is well-moded. A test as to whether a query or clause is well-moded w.r.t. a given moding can be efficiently performed by noting that:

- a query Q is well-moded iff every first from the left occurrence of a variable in Q is within an output position;
- a clause $p(\mathbf{s}, \mathbf{t}) \leftarrow \mathbf{B}$ is well-moded iff every first from the left occurrence of a variable in the sequence $\mathbf{s}, \mathbf{B}, \mathbf{t}$ is within the input position of $p(\mathbf{s}, \mathbf{t})$ or within an output position in $\mathbf{B}$.

(We assumed in this description that in every atom the input positions occur first.)

As already mentioned, the concepts of nicely moded program and query and Theorem 3.23 were also introduced in Chadha and Plaisted [15]. They proposed two efficient algorithms for generating modings with the minimal number of input positions, for which the program is nicely moded. These algorithms were implemented and applied to a number of well-known Prolog programs.

6.2.4 Absence of Errors

Our approach to proving absence of errors is based on Corollary 4.5. To apply it one needs to generate typings which include $>: Gae \times Gae \rightarrow \mathcal{T} \times \mathcal{T}$ for which a given program is well-typed. Aiken and Lakshman [1] showed that the problem of whether a program or query is well-typed w.r.t. a given typing is decidable for a large class of types which includes the ones studied here.

6.2.5 Absence of Floundering

Our method of proving absence of floundering is based on the use of the notion of well-modedness, already discussed in the context of the occur-check freedom.

Acknowledgements

Joint research and discussions with Dino Pedreschi on the subject of verification of logic programs helped us to clarify the opinions expressed in this chapter. Also, we thank the referee for helpful comments.

Bibliography

1. A. Aiken and T. K. Lakshman. Automatic type checking for logic programs. Technical report, Department of Computer Science, University of Illinois at Urbana Champaign, 1993.

2. K. R. Apt. Logic programming. In J. van Leeuwen, editor, *Handbook of Theoretical Computer Science*, pages 493–574. Elsevier, 1990. Vol. B.
3. K. R. Apt. Declarative programming in Prolog. In D. Miller, editor, *Proc. International Symposium on Logic Programming*, pages 11–35. MIT Press, 1993.
4. K. R. Apt, H. A. Blair, and A. Walker. Towards a theory of declarative knowledge. In J. Minker, editor, *Foundations of Deductive Databases and Logic Programming*, pages 89–148. Morgan Kaufmann, 1988.
5. K. R. Apt and H. C. Doets. A new definition of SLDNF-resolution. *Journal of Logic Programming*, 18(2):177–190, 1994.
6. K. R. Apt and M. Gabbrielli. Declarative interpretations reconsidered. In P. van Hentenryck, editor, *Proceedings of the 1994 International Conference on Logic Programming*, pages 74–89. MIT Press, 1994.
7. K. R. Apt and E. Marchiori. Reasoning about Prolog programs: from modes through types to assertions. Technical Report CS-R9358, CWI, Amsterdam, The Netherlands, 1993. To appear in Formal Aspects of Computing (FACS).
8. K. R. Apt and D. Pedreschi. Reasoning about termination of pure Prolog programs. *Information and Computation*, 106(1):109–157, 1993.
9. K. R. Apt and D. Pedreschi. Modular termination proofs for logic and pure Prolog programs. In G. Levi, editor, *Advances in logic programming theory*. Oxford University Press, 1994. To appear.
10. K. R. Apt and A. Pellegrini. On the occur-check free Prolog programs. *ACM Toplas*, 16(3):687–726, 1994.
11. K.R. Apt and E.-R. Olderog. *Verification of Sequential and Concurrent Programs*. Texts and Monographs in Computer Science, Springer-Verlag, New York, 1991.
12. M. A. Bezem. Strong termination of logic programs. *Journal of Logic Programming*, 15(1 & 2):79–98, 1993.
13. A. Bossi and N. Cocco. Verifying correctness of logic programs. In *Proceedings of TAPSOFT '89*, Lecture Notes in Computer Science, pages 96–110. Springer-Verlag, 1989.
14. F. Bronsard, T. K. Lakshman, and U. S. Reddy. A directional type system for Prolog: unifying the notions of types and directionality. Technical report, Department of Computer Science, University of Illinois at Urbana Champaign, 1993.
15. R. Chadha and D. A. Plaisted. Correctness of unification without occur check in Prolog. *Journal of Logic Programming*, 18(2):99–122, 1994.
16. K. L. Clark. Predicate logic as a computational formalism. Res. Report

DOC 79/59, Imperial College, Dept. of Computing, London, 1979.
17. H. Coelho and J. C. Cotta. *Prolog by Example*. Springer-Verlag, Berlin, 1988.
18. P. Dembinski and J. Maluszynski. AND-parallelism with intelligent backtracking for annotated logic programs. In *Proceedings of the International Symposium on Logic Programming*, pages 29–38, Boston, 1985.
19. P. Deransart, G. Ferrand, and M. Téguia. NSTO programs (not subject to occur-check). In V. Saraswat and K. Ueda, editors, *Proceedings of the International Logic Symposium*, pages 533–547. The MIT Press, 1991.
20. P. M. Hill and J. W. Lloyd. *The Gödel Programming Language*. The MIT Press, 1994.
21. M. Kalsbeek. The vanilla meta-interpreter for definite logic programs and ambivalent syntax. Technical Report CT-93-01, Department of Mathematics and Computer Science, University of Amsterdam, The Netherlands, 1993.
22. K. Kunen. Some remarks on the completed database. In R. A. Kowalski and K. A. Bowen, editors, *Proceedings of the Fifth International Conference on Logic Programming*, pages 978–992. The MIT Press, 1988.
23. K. Kunen. Signed data depedencies in logic programs. *Journal of Logic Programming*, 7:231–246, 1989.
24. J. W. Lloyd. *Foundations of Logic Programming*. Springer-Verlag, Berlin, 1984.
25. J. W. Lloyd. *Foundations of Logic Programming*. Springer-Verlag, Berlin, second edition, 1987.
26. A. Martelli and U. Montanari. An efficient unification algorithm. *ACM Transactions on Programming Languages and Systems*, 4:258–282, 1982.
27. M. Martelli and C. Tricomi. A new SLDNF-tree. *Information Processing Letters*, 43(2):57–62, 1992.
28. B. Martens and D. De Schreye. Why untyped non-ground meta-programming is not much of a problem. Technical Report CW 159 (Revised November 1993), Department of Computing Science, Katholieke Universiteit Leuven, Belgium, 1993. To appear in Journal of Logic Programming.
29. C. S. Mellish. The Automatic Generation of Mode Declarations for Prolog Programs. DAI Research Paper 163, Department of Artificial Intelligence, Univ. of Edinburgh, August 1981.
30. D. Pedreschi. A proof method for run-time properties of Prolog pro-

grams. In P. van Hentenryck, editor, *Proceedings of the 1994 International Conference on Logic Programming.* MIT Press, 1994. To appear.

31. U. S. Reddy. Transformation of logic programs into functional programs. In *International Symposium on Logic Programming*, pages 187–198, Silver Spring, MD, February 1984. Atlantic City, IEEE Computer Society.

32. D. De Schreye and S. Decorte. Termination of logic programs: the never-ending story. *Journal of Logic Programming*, 19-20:199–260, 1994.

33. D. De Schreye, K. Verschaetse, and M. Bruynooghe. A framework for analyzing the termination of definite logic programs with respect to call patterns. In *Proceedings of the International Conference on Fifth Generation Computer Systems 1992*, pages 481–488. Institute for New Generation Computer Technology, 1992.

34. R. E. Shostak. On the SUP-INF method for proving Presburger formulas. *J. ACM*, 24(4):529–543, 1977.

35. R. Stärk. A direct proof for the completeness of SLD-resolution. In Börger, H. Kleine Büning, and M.M. Richter, editors, *Computer Science Logic 89*, Lecture Notes in Computer Science 440, pages 382–383. Springer-Verlag, 1990.

36. L. Sterling and E. Shapiro. *The Art of Prolog.* MIT Press, 1986.

37. K. Stroetman. A completeness result for SLDNF resolution. *The Journal of Logic Programming*, 15:337–357, 1993.

38. J. D. Ullman and A. van Gelder. Efficient tests for top-down termination of logical rules. *J. ACM*, 35(2):345–373, 1988.

CLAM Specification for Provably Correct Compilation of CLP($\mathcal{R}$) Programs

Egon Börger and Rosario F. Salamone

Abstract

The chapter extends the correctness proof in [4] for compilation of Prolog programs on the WAM to CLP($\mathcal{R}$) programs on the Constraint Logic Arithmetic Machine (CLAM [8, 10]). This serves to illustrate, through a complex case study, how the evolving algebra specification methodology allows us to incorporate modularity and extendability principles in system design.

1 Introduction

This chapter extends, to the Constraint Logic Arithmetic Machine (CLAM) and CLP($\mathcal{R}$) programs, the mathematical analysis of the Warren Abstract Machine (WAM) for executing Prolog and the resulting correctness proof for a general compilation scheme of Prolog to the WAM given in [4]. Starting from an abstract CLP($\mathcal{R}$) model—which paraphrases the primary model for Prolog defined in [5]—we follow the stepwise refinement of Prolog models to the WAM model given in [4] and enrich both the specification and the correctness proofs by what is needed to cover CLP($\mathcal{R}$) constraints and their implementation in the CLAM. Use of Gurevich's evolving algebras [6] as our specification vehicle allows us to couple smoothly the modularity of the WAM specification in [4] to extendibility of unification to handling of CLP($\mathcal{R}$) constraints.

For expository reasons we start (in section 3) from scratch by defining an operational semantics of CLP($\mathcal{R}$) through *CLP($\mathcal{R}$) trees*, close to the usual intuitive picture and to its proof theoretical logical background (resolution-trees). This definition, which serves as our primary mathematical model, is easily shown to be correct w.r.t. resolution (for CLP($\mathcal{R}$) programs without built-in predicates), and can be extended to a transparent rigorous formulation of the full language using the definitions given in [5].

The first major refinement steps are devoted to analysis and implementation of the disjunctive and conjunctive structure of CLP($\mathcal{R}$) programs. These structures correspond to WAM handling of clause selection (predicate structure) and continuations (clause structure) and can be taken unchanged from the WAM as long as the representation of terms and constraints is kept abstract. We then analyze in detail how the WAM representation of terms and substitutions has to be enriched in order to make it work also for constraints (sections 4), the cooperation of unification and contraint solving (section 5) and constraint compilation (section 6). The fine points of the WAM—environment trimming, local and unsafe values, last call optimization, Warren's classification of variables and their on-the-fly initialization—can again be taken almost unchanged from the WAM and enriched by specific CLAM optimizations (section 7).

We thus arrive at a specification of the full CLAM which allows us to prove the following:

Theorem 1.1. (Main Theorem) *Each compiler which satisfies the assumptions for predicate, clause, term compilation listed in [4] and the assumptions for constraint compilation listed in this chapter, compiles CLP($\mathcal{R}$) programs correctly with respect to CLP($\mathcal{R}$) trees and CLAM algebras.*

All we assume of the reader is general understanding of CLP($\mathcal{R}$) and Prolog as programming languages. In order to keep the chapter within reasonable bounds we refer to [4] each time we can take from there without crucial modifications. To help readability we list, however, in section 2 the basic notions from evolving algebras.

2 Prerequisites on Evolving Algebras

The CLAM model constructed in this chapter is an *evolving algebra*, a notion introduced by Gurevich in [7]. Since this notion is a mathematically rigorous form of fundamental operational intuitions of computing, the chapter can be followed without any particular theoretical prerequisites: indeed our rules can be read as "pseudocode over abstract data". For completeness we nevertheless list in this section the basic definitions for evolving algebras.

The abstract data come as elements of sets (domains, *universes*), and the allowed operations as partial *functions*. This determines a class of algebras (in the sense used in logic) or states of an abstract "machine" which we allow to *evolve* in time by executing *function updates* of form $f(t_1, \ldots, t_n) := t$ whose execution is to be understood as *changing* (or defining, if there was none) the value of function f at given arguments.

Definition 2.1 *An* evolving algebra *is a finite set of transition rules of form*

if R? then R!

where R? (condition or guard) is a boolean, the truth of which triggers simultaneous execution of all updates in the finite set R! of function updates.

Simultaneous execution avoids fussing with intermediate storage problems. Since functions may be partial, equality in the guards is to be interpreted as implying that both arguments are defined. The signature of an evolving algebra can always be reconstructed, as the set of function symbols occurring in the rules. An evolving algebra usually comes together with a set of *integrity constraints*, i.e. extralogical axioms and/or rules of inference, specifying the intended domains.

In applications of evolving algebras as here, one usually encounters a *heterogenous* signature with several universes, which may in general grow and shrink in time—update forms are provided to extend a universe:

extend A **by** $t_1, \ldots, t_n$ **with** *updates* **endextend**

where *updates* may (and should) depend on t_i's, setting the values of some functions on *newly created* elements t_i of A. In [6] Gurevich has shown how to reduce such setups to the above basic model of a homogenous signature (with one universe) and function updates only.

The forms obviously reducible to the above basic syntax, which we shall freely use as abbreviations, are **let**, **case** and **if then else**. We shall assume that we have the standard mathematical universes of booleans, integers, lists of whatever etc. (as well as the standard operations on them) at our disposal without further mention. We use usual notations, in particular Prolog notation for lists.

An evolving algebra, as given above, determines the dynamics of a very large transition system. Here we are usually interested only in states reachable from some designated *initial states*, which may be specified in various ways. We use an informal mathematical description, like in model theory; but one could easily devise special initializing evolving algebra rules which, starting from a canonical "empty" state, produce the initial states we need.

As CLP($\mathcal{R}$) is a sequential language, our rules are organized in such a way that at every moment at most one rule is applicable.

3   CLP($\mathcal{R}$) with Predicate and Clause Compilation

In this section we show how one can adapt the Prolog tree model of [5] to CLP($\mathcal{R}$) ([8]) and its refinement with predicate and clause compilation. We suppose the reader to be acquainted with the fundamentals of Prolog and of CLP($\mathcal{R}$).

To obtain a primary model for CLP($\mathcal{R}$), characterized by the programmer's view and close to resolution trees, it suffices to paraphrase the Prolog model of [5] by replacing substitution by constraints and unification by constraint solving, similar to what has been done for the type constraints extension of Prolog in [2].

In the following we define in some detail the primary CLP($\mathcal{R}$) model and then explain shortly how to refine this model to the level where predicates and clauses are no longer abstract but compiled. The reader who is acquainted with [5] or [2] might skip this section.

3.1   CLP Trees

A CLP($\mathcal{R}$) computation can be seen as systematic search of a space of possible solutions to an initially given query. The set of computation states is viewed as carrying a tree structure, with initial state at the root, and *son* relation representing alternative (single) derivation steps. This means to represent *CLP(R) computation states* in a set *NODE* with two distinguished elements *root* and *currnode*, with the latter representing the (dynamically) current state. Each element of *NODE* has to carry all information relevant—at the desired abstraction level—for the computation state it represents. This information consists of *the sequence of goals* still to be executed, the *set of constraints* collected so far, and possibly the *sequence of alternative derivation states* still to be tried, as explained below.

The tree structure over the universe *NODE*, representing the structure of CLP($\mathcal{R}$)'s *backtracking behavior*, is realized by a total function

$$father : NODE - \{root\} \rightarrow NODE$$

such that from each node there is a unique *father* path towards *root*.

When, at a given node n, a user defined atom is selected (as activator *act*) for execution, for each possible immediate derivation state a son of n will be created, to control the alternative computation thread. Each son is determined by a corresponding *candidate clause* of the program, i.e. one of those clauses whose head might unify with *act*. All such *candidate sons* are attached to n as a list $cands(n)$, in the order reflecting the ordering of corresponding candidate clauses in the program. We require of course the *cands* lists to be consistent with *father*, i.e. whenever *Son* is among $cands(Father)$, then $father(Son) = Father$.

This action of augmenting the tree with $cands(n)$ takes place at most once, when n gets first visited (in *Call* mode). The mode then turns to *Select*, and the first unifying son from $cands(n)$ gets visited (i.e. becomes the value of *currnode*), again in *Call* mode. The selected son is simultaneously deleted from the $cands(n)$ list. If control ever returns to n (by *backtracking*, cf. below), it will be in *Select* mode, and the next candidate son will be selected, if any.

If none, that is if in *Select* mode $cands(n) = [\ ]$, all attempts at derivation from the state represented by n will have failed, and n will be *abandoned* by returning control to its *father*. This action is usually called *backtracking*.

The information relevant for determining a computation state will be associated to nodes by appropriate (in general partial) functions on the universe *NODE*. For each state we have to know the sequence of goals still to be executed. In view of the *cut* operator $!$, however, this sequence is not represented linearly, but structured into subsequences—clause bodies decorated with appropriate *cutpoints*, i.e. backtracking states current when the clause was called: a function $decglseq : NODE \rightarrow DECGOAL^*$ for $DECGOAL = (LIT + CONSTRAINT)^* \times NODE$ associates the relevant sequence of (decorated) goals to each node. CONSTRAINT is the universe of constraints coming with functions

$$c : NODE \to CS, \quad solvable : CS \to BOOL$$

where CS is the universe of all sets of constraints.

The above-mentioned switching of *modes* will be represented by a distinguished element $mode \in \{Call, Select\}$ indicating the action to be taken at *currnode*: creating the derivation states, or selecting among them. To be able to speak about *termination* we will use a distinguished element $stop \in \{0, 1, -1\}$, to indicate respectively running of the system, halting with success and final failure. We will use (and consider as part of CLP tree algebras) all the usual CLP($\mathcal{R}$) data structures and *list operations* for which we adopt standard notation. In the same way we shall use hd and bdy to select heads and bodies of clauses, allowing ourselves the freedom to confuse a list of literals and constraints with their iterated conjunction. The codomain of bdy will thus be taken to be $(TERM \cup CONSTRAINT)^*$.

We keep the above-mentioned notion of *candidate clause* (for executing an atom) abstract (regarding it as implementation defined), assuming only the following integrity constraints: every candidate clause for a given atom has the proper predicate (symbol), i.e. the same predicate as the atom (*correctness*); every clause whose head unifies with the given atom is candidate clause for this atom (*completeness*). The reader might think of considering any clause occurrence whose head is formed with the given predicate, or the clause occurrences selected by an indexing scheme, or just all occurrences of unifying clauses.

Having to allow for *dynamic code* and related operations, one has to speak about different occurrences of clauses in a program. We hence introduce an abstract universe $CODE$ of clause occurrences (or pointers), coming with functions

$$clause : CODE \to CLAUSE, \quad cll : NODE \to CODE$$

where $cll(n)$ is the candidate clause occurrence ("clauseline") corresponding to a candidate son n of a computation state, and $clause(p)$ is the clause "pointed at" by p. Note that we do not assume any ordering on $CODE$. We instead assume an abstract function

$$procdef : LIT \times PROGRAM \times CONSTRAINT \to CODE^*,$$

which we assume to yield the (properly ordered) list of the candidate clause occurrences for the given literal in the given program (the constraint parameter will allow us to formalize indexing mechanisms which depend on constraints). The current program is represented by a distinguished element db of $PROGRAM$ (the *database*). Note that existence of $procdef$ is all that we assume of the abstract universe $PROGRAM$.

We assume the following **initialization** for application of the rules given below:

- *root* is supposed to be the nil element—on which no function is defined—and father of *currnode*;
- *currnode* has a one element list [⟨*query*, *root*⟩] as decorated goal sequence, and empty set of constraints;
- the mode is *Call*, *stop* has value 0; *db* has the given program as value;
- the *cands* list is not (yet) defined at *currnode*.

We now define the five basic rules by which the system attempts to reach a state with $stop = 1$ (due to first successful execution of the query) or with $stop = -1$ (due to its final failure by backtracking all the way to *root*). In writing these rules, we suppress the parameter *currnode* by simply writing *father* for *father(currnode)*, *cands* for *cands(currnode)*, *c* for *c(currnode)* and *decglseq* for *decglseq(currnode)*. Components of decorated goal sequence are accessed as $goal \equiv fst(fst(decglseq))$, $cutpt \equiv snd(fst(decglseq))$, $act \equiv fst(goal)^1$, $cont \equiv [\langle rest(goal), cutpt \rangle \mid rest(decglseq)]$, with *act* standing for the selected literal (*activator*), and *cont* for *continuation*. We also use the following abbreviation:

$$backtrack \equiv \textbf{if } father = root \textbf{ then } stop := -1$$
$$\textbf{else } currnode := father$$
$$mode := Select$$

When the *stop* value is 1 or −1, no transition rule will be applicable which is a natural notion of "terminating state". All transition rules will thus be tacitly assumed to stand under the guard

$$OK \equiv stop = 0$$

The following **query success rule**—for successful halt— leads to successful termination when all goals have been executed:

if *all_done* **then** $stop := 1$

where *all_done* abbreviates $decglseq = [\,]$ [2]. The following **goal success rule** describes success of a clause body, when the system continues to execute the rest of its goal sequence:

if $goal = [\,]$ **then** $decglseq := rest(decglseq)$

---

[1] This definition implements the left-to-right computation rule. In general we could have written $act = goal\_select(goal)$, where *goal_select* represents the computation rule. Correspondingly, one has to change the definition of *rest* in *cond*.

[2] Note that we do not describe how output (answer constraints) is given. If the reader wants to view CLP($\mathcal{R}$) as returning all solutions, all he has to do is to modify this rule so as to trigger backtracking.

The existence of *goal*, assumed in the guard, is understood as excluding *all_done*, cf. above abbreviations. Likewise, the existence of *act*, assumed in rules to follow, is understood as excluding both *all_done* and $goal = [\,]$ conditions—we shall, in general, tacitly understand guards, relying on existence of some objects, as excluding all conditions under which these objects could be undefined, suppressing the boolean conditions which would formally ensure such exclusion. In *goal success* rule e.g. the suppressed condition is $NOT(all\_done)$, and in rules mentioning *act* below it is $NOT(all\_done)\ \&\ goal \neq [\,]$.

The crucial derivation step, applicable to a user-defined predicate, is split into *calling* the activator, creating new candidate nodes for alternative derivations from *currnode*, to be followed by *selecting* one of them. We will correspondingly have two rules. The following **call rule**, invoked by having a user-defined activator in *Call* mode, will create as many sons of *currnode* as there are candidate clauses in the procedure definition of its activator, to each of which the corresponding clause(line) will be associated:

> **if** $is\_user\_defined(act)$
> $\&\ mode = Call$
> **then let** $n = length(procdef(act, db))$
>   **extend** $NODE$ **by** $temp_1, \ldots, temp_n$ **with**
> $father(temp_i) := currnode$
> $cll(temp_i) := nth(procdef(act, db), i)$
> $cands := [temp_1, \ldots, temp_n]$
>   **endextend**
> $mode := Select$

where *is_user_defined* is a boolean function recognizing those literals whose predicate symbols are user defined (as opposed to constraints, built-in predicates and language constructs). Note that goals and constraints are undefined for candidate sons, and that the value of *currnode* does not change[3].

The **Selection Rule** is applicable to nodes already visited in *Call* mode. It triggers the visit of the first candidate node or backtracks if the *cands* list is empty. In the former case, the update of the sequence of goals provides for the unification test and the execution of the body. The currently accumulated constraints are copied and the selected node is cancelled from

---

[3] Given database operations of full Prolog this rule formalizes the so-called logical view; see [3].

the *cands* list:

if *is_user_defined(act)* & *mode* = *Select*
then if *cands* = [ ]
    then *backtrack*
    else let *clause* = *rename(clause(cll(fst(cands))), vi)*
        currnode := *fst(cands)*
        c(fst(cands)) := *c*
        decglseq(fst(cands)) :=
            $[\langle append([act \doteq hd(clause)], bdy(clause)), father\rangle \mid cont\,]$
        cands := *rest(cands)*
        mode := *Call*
        vi := *vi* + 1

where $p(t_1,\ldots,t_n) \doteq p(s_1,\ldots,s_n)$ abbreviates the sequence $t_1 = s_1, \ldots, t_n = s_n$. Note that we represent renaming of variables abstractly, without going into details of term and variable representation, by introducing a function

$$rename : TERM \times \mathcal{N} \to TERM$$

renaming all variables in the given term at the given index (renaming level). The current renaming index—the one to be used for the next renaming—is indicated by a 0-ary function *vi*.

The **Add-constraint Rule** fires when the activator is a constraint. In this case the solvability of the current set of constraints put together with the new constraint is tested; if the answer is yes, then the new constraint *act* is added to *c*; otherwise execution backtracks:

        if *is_constraint(act)* **then if** *solvable*($c \bigcup \{act\}$)
                            then $c := c \bigcup \{act\}$
                                succeed
                            else *backtrack*

where *succeed* stands for *decglseq* := *cont*. This concludes the description of the primary CLP($\mathcal{R}$) model as far as user-defined predicates are concerned. For built-in predicates one can now proceed as in Prolog; we refer for this to the full description given in [5] and show here only the example of the cut. It suffices to update *father* to *cutpt*:

        if *act* = ! **then** *father* := *cutpt*
                      succeed

It is easy to show that this model of CLP($\mathcal{R}$) is correct for CLP($\mathcal{R}$) programs without built-in predicates with respect to the usual resolution based definition of procedural semantics.

3.2 Compilation of Predicates and Clauses

For compilation of predicate and clause structure by WAM instructions, CLP($\mathcal{R}$) constraints behave in the same way as unification equations $s = t$ as long as terms and constraints remain abstract. Therefore the primary (tree based) model for CLP($\mathcal{R}$) of the preceding section can easily be refined to reflect WAM code for creation, reuse and discarding of choicepoints (including switching) and for (de-)allocation of environments (representing clause structure): just apply to the primary CLP($\mathcal{R}$) tree model the same refinement steps as defined (and proved to be correct) for Prolog in [4]. This goes through embedding of the tree into a stack, reuse of choicepoints, determinacy detection, *try- retry- trust-* and *switching*-code (where switching will be canonically extended to arithmetical terms) and environment handling code (where to instructions $call(G)$ also instructions $resolve(C)$ for constraints C will be added). Thus the modularity of the WAM specification in [4] allows us to naturally embed that specification into the CLP($\mathcal{R}$) context and to proceed directly to compilation of terms and constraints.

4 Representation of Constraints

When passing to the level of term representation, the CLAM requires to properly extend all corresponding WAM data structures and to introduce new data areas for representation and construction of arithmetic constraints.

CLAM data area locations may contain, in addition to Prolog objects, numeric constants (tagged *Numb*) and "solver variables", i.e. variables appearing in the current collection of arithmetic constraints. Solver variable locations, tagged *S_var*, contain a reference, called the (solver) identifier of that solver variable, to another memory area (*SVAR_AREA*) in which information regarding solver variables becomes accessible. Different solver variables may have the same identifier. Therefore, as in the WAM, we have *DATAAREA*, a set of "locations" with mutually inverse successor and predecessor functions $(+, -)$, and with a "content" function

$$val\ :\ DATAAREA \rightarrow CLPO + MEMORY$$

where, as in the WAM, *MEMORY* is a universe that contains *DATAAREA*, to enable storage of pure pointers, to be elaborated and used below. The set *CLPO* extends the set *PO* of Prolog objects by *SVAR_AREA + NUMBER*, coupled with an extension of the WAM encoding scheme

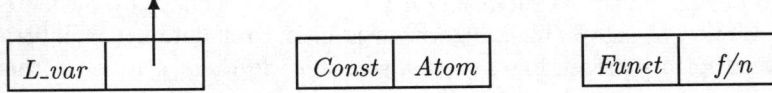

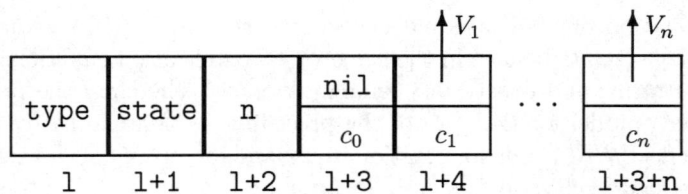

FIG. 1. Inequality $c_0 + c_1 V_1 + \ldots + C_n V_n \Delta\, 0$, $\Delta \in \{>, \geq\}$.

using functions

$$\begin{array}{rcl}
tag & : & CLPO \to \{L\_var, S\_var, Numb, Const, List, Struct, Funct\} \\
ref & : & CLPO \to DATAAREA + SVAR\_AREA + NUMBER + \\
& & ATOM + ATOM \times ARITY
\end{array}$$

where for uniformity the type label *ref*, used in the WAM to denote logical variables, is replaced by *L_var*.

For arithmetic constraints we use a stack[4] (*PF_AREA,PFO;pftop,pfbottom*;+, −) to store "parametric forms" via a function *pfval* : *PF_AREA* → *PFO* as follows.

We call terms of form $c_0 + c_1 V_1 + \ldots + c_n V_n$ "linear parametric forms", where c_i is a numeric constant and V_i (called parametric variables) are distinct solver variables with $n \geq 1$. Linear equations or inequalities are of the form $V = lpf$ or $lpf\, \Delta\, 0$, where *lpf* is linear parametric form, $\Delta \in \{\geq, >\}$ and V (called nonparametric variable) is different from the variables in *lpf*. A linear inequality is stored (in consecutive locations starting from l) as shown in Fig. 1, where type $\in \{\geq, >\}$; state $\in \{active, dormant\}$ indicates whether the linear form refers to a constraint which is actually contained in the current collection of constraints (active linear form), or whether it has been abandoned (in which case it may be restored during backtracking and is called dormant); pointers to the parametric variables V_i are pointers to locations in *SVAR_AREA* (i.e. the identifiers of the V_i). Linear equations (type is =) have one more cell (coming after the arity cell) containing the identifier of the nonparametric variable.

The 0-ary functions $top_=$, $top_\geq$ and $top_>$ represent the (addresses of the) topmost linear equation, nonstrict inequality and strict inequality, respectively. Equations are solved with the Gaussian elimination method. In order to determine the solvability of a set of linear inequalities, an incremental version of the Simplex algorithm is used to maintain inequalities in a solved form representing a certain solution. So there will be another

---

[4] A stack is used because arithmetic constraints are subject to backtracking.

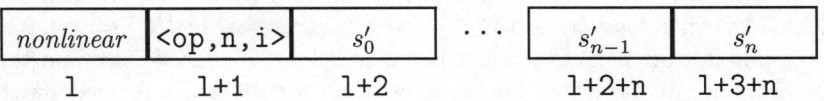

FIG. 2. Nonlinear constraint.

area to store the solved form of each inequality (it is actually a Simplex tableau). In addition, the "inequality solver" also has to determine the equalities implied by a consistent collection of linear inequalities. At this level of abstraction we specify the inequality solver only through abstract updates on which conditions are imposed to ensure correctness.

Nonlinear constraints are stored in nonlinear form, $s_0 = op(s_1, \ldots, s_n)$ where s_j is either a numeric constant or a variable, $0 \leq j \leq n$. A nonlinear constraint stored at location l is represented in Fig. 2, where $\langle op, n, i \rangle \in (ATOM \times ARITY \times \mathcal{N})$ and, if s_j is a constant then $s'_j = s_j$, otherwise s'_j is the identifier of variable s_j. The index i codifies the *wakeup degree*. CLAM delays the satisfiability of nonlinear constraints until they become linear. In order to detect when a nonlinear constraint becomes linear, it is assigned wakeup degrees representing the information currently known about variables appearing in the constraint. As variables become ground, a particular instance of a nonlinear constraint changes degree until it can be awoken.

Nonlinear equations are kept in normal form, in the sense that when a solver identifier gets instantiated to a ground value, it is substituted out in all its "nonlinear" occurrences. The 0-ary function top_{nl} keeps the address of the topmost nonlinear equation.

When a solver variable gets instantiated to an arithmetic term, its value must be substituted in every linear form where it appears and, if the value is ground, also in every nonlinear form. Therefore for each solver variable we need the address of its occurrences and the address of the linear parametric form the variable is possibly bound to. When a solver variable is instantiated to a ground value, this value has to be kept accessible through $SVAR\_AREA$ because other S_var locations in $DATAAREA$ may point to the same identifier. Therefore $SVAR\_AREA$ is realized as a stack ($SVAR\_AREA; svtop, sbottom; +, -$) to store those 3 kinds of objects (accessed using a content function $sval$ into $SVARO$):

$$svar\_occ \ : \ SVARO \ \to \ (PF\_AREA \times \mathcal{N})^*$$
$$svar\_lpf \ : \ SVARO \ \to \ PF\_AREA \ + \ \{nil\}$$
$$svar\_value \ : \ SVARO \ \to \ NUMBER \ + \ \{nil\}$$

Formally we therefore assume that nonparametric variables correspond to identifiers l with $svar\_lpf(sval(l)) \neq nil$ and parametric variables to identifiers with $svar\_lpf(sval(l)) = nil$ & $svar\_value(sval(l)) = nil$ (this corresponds to linear constraints being in solved form). We assume that the elements of the list of occurrences of an identifier are formed by the address of a linear or nonlinear form in which the identifier appears, and its relative position within this form (a sort of offset with respect to the address of the form, for details see [11]).

Notationally, we often suppress the value functions and write $tag(l)$ for $tag(val(l))$, $ref(l)$ for $ref(val(l))$, $svar\_lpf(l)$ for $svar\_lpf(sval(l))$ etc. We borrow from [4] the following abbreviations:

$$l_1 \leftarrow l_2 \equiv val(l_1) := val(l_2),\ l \leftarrow \langle T, R \rangle \equiv tag(l) := T,\ ref(l) := R$$
$$l\_unbound(l) \equiv (tag(l) = L\_var\ \&\ ref(l) = l)$$
$$mk\_l\_unbound(l) \equiv l \leftarrow \langle L\_var, l \rangle$$

and define their solver variable analogues by:

$$\begin{aligned} s\_unbound(l) &\equiv tag(l) = S\_var\ \&\ svar\_lpf(ref(l)) = nil \\ & \quad\ svar\_value(ref(l)) = nil \\ s\_unfree(l) &\equiv tag(l) = S\_var\ \&\ svar\_lpf(ref(l)) \neq nil \\ s\_ground(l) &\equiv tag(l) = S\_var\ \&\ svar\_value(ref(l)) \neq nil \\ mk\_id\_unbound(l) &\equiv svar\_lpf(l) := nil, svar\_occ(l) := [],\\ & \quad\ svar\_value(l) := nil \\ mk\_s\_unbound(l) &\equiv l \leftarrow \langle S\_var, svtop \rangle, mk\_id\_unbound(svtop),\\ & \quad\ svtop := svtop + \end{aligned}$$

We extend the WAM dereferencing and term reconstructing functions $deref : DATAAREA \rightarrow DATAAREA$ and $term : DATAAREA \rightarrow TERM$ from [4] to include solver variables. We add the analogues for reconstructing linear parametric forms $lpf : PF\_AREA \rightarrow TERM$ and solver variable values $svar : SVAR\_AREA \rightarrow TERM$. The usual WAM layout for the term represented at location l is thus extended to solver variables and linear parametric forms by the following requirements, assuming that mk_var associates a unique $CLP(\mathcal{R})$ variable (without any type annotation about variables being logical or arithmetic) to an arbitrary location in $DATAAREA$ or $SVAR\_AREA$:

$$\begin{aligned} deref(l) &= \begin{cases} deref(ref(l)) & \text{if } tag(l) = L\_var\ \&\ NOT(l\_unbound(l)) \\ l & \text{otherwise} \end{cases} \\ lpf(l) &= c_0 + c_1 * svar(l_1) + \ldots + c_n * svar(l_n) \end{aligned}$$

CLAM Specification and Compiler Correctness

$$term(l) = \begin{cases} mk\_var(l) & \text{if } l\_unbound(l) \\ mk\_var(ref(l)) & \text{if } s\_unbound(l) \\ term(deref(l)) & \text{if } tag(l) = L\_var \ \& \\ & \quad NOT(L\_unbound(l)) \\ ref(l) & \text{if } tag(l) \in \{Const, Numb\} \\ svar(ref(l)) & \text{if } NOT(s\_unbound(l)) \ \& \\ & \quad tag(l) = S\_var \\ [term(ref(l)) \mid & \\ \quad term(ref(l)+)] & \text{if } tag(l) = List \\ f(a_1,\ldots,a_n) & \text{if } tag(l) = Struct \ \& \\ & \quad ref(ref(l)) = \langle f, n \rangle \ \& \\ & \quad term(ref(l)+i) = a_i \end{cases}$$

where $pfval(l)$ type is "=", $pfval(l+2) = n$, $pfval(l+4) = \langle c_0, nil \rangle$, $pfval(l+4+i) = \langle c_i, l_i \rangle$ for $1 \leq i \leq n$.

$$svar(l) = \begin{cases} mk\_var(l) & if\ s\_unbound(l) \\ lpf(svar\_lpf(ref(l))) & \text{if } s\_unfree(l) \\ svar\_value(ref(l)) & \text{if } s\_ground(l) \end{cases}$$

From these functions one can reconstruct arithmetic constraints by means of functions $eq, ineq, nlpf : PF\_AREA \rightarrow CONSTRAINT$ defined on locations l when the type of $pfval(l)$ is $=, \geq$ or $>$ and *nonlinear* respectively.

5 Unification

The "arithmetic part" of the current constraint system consists of all active equations, active inequalities and nonlinear constraints; the "logical part" is defined by the bindings in *DATAAREA*. The structures occurring during unification are represented as in Prolog on the stack usually called $(HEAP; h, boh)$, which is contained in *DATAAREA* and contains a 0-ary function *str*, a subterm (or structure) pointer to be used for navigating through substructures. The active part of *HEAP* will be abbreviated as $heap \equiv \{l \in HEAP \mid boh \leq l < h\}$ (its finiteness follows from *boh* being the initial value of h).

For unification we use the standard *pushdown list* stack

$$(PDL; pdl, nil; +, -)$$

with content function *pval* into *DATAAREA*. In the unification algorithm we add to the abstract update $bind(l_1, l_2)$ (to bind the "logical" variable stored at l_1 to $term(l_2)$) an update $equate(l_1, l_2)$ to call the equality solver for the two arithmetic terms stored at l_1 and l_2; see below. $bind(l_1, l_2)$, a "logical operation", is always consistent with the current collection of arithmetic constraints.

To the assumptions for *bind* in [4] we add an assumption for *equate*:

Bind Assumption Let $l_1, l_2 \in DATAAREA$ and cs be the current constraint system. If $l\_unbound(l_1)$ holds and $mk\_var(l_1)$ does not occur in $term(l_2)$, then, after execution of $bind(l_1, l_2)$, the new constraint system is equal to

$$cs \bigcup \{mk\_var(l_1) = term(l_2)\}$$

If the new constraint system is unsolvable, then execution backtracks.

Equate Assumption Let $l_1, l_2 \in DATAAREA$ such that $term(l_1)$ and $term(l_2)$ are "arithmetic terms", and cs be the current constraint system. After the execution of $equate(l_1, l_2)$, the new constraint system is the normalization[5] of

$$cs \bigcup \{term(l_1) = term(l_2)\}$$

If the new constraint system is unsolvable, then execution backtracks.

Unification will be triggered by setting a 0-ary function *What_to_do* with values in $\{Run, Unify\}$, given that the terms to be unified have already been pushed to *PDL*. The rules which control unification considerably extend the rules known for Prolog and can be obtained from Tables 1, 2 and 3.

The mathematical unification fails on an attempt to bind a variable to a term in which it occurs. To model such unification with "occur-check" it suffices to require of $bind(l_1, l_2)$ to trigger backtracking whenever $mk\_var(l_1)$ occurs in $term(l_2)$. In accordance with usual practice in logic programming, we do not specify the behavior of the system when the occur check fails.

The abbreviations in the unification tables are defined as follows; the contents of the empty slots can be obtained by the symmetric cases (with *dl* and *dr* exchanged):

$$
\begin{aligned}
left &\equiv pval(pdl), right \equiv pval(pdl-), dl \equiv deref(left),\\
&\quad dr \equiv deref(right)\\
failure &\equiv What\_to\_do := Run, backtrack\\
top\_check &\equiv \textbf{if } value(dl) \neq value(dr) \textbf{ then } failure \textbf{ else } pdl := pdl - -
\end{aligned}
$$

where $value(l)$ gives $ref(l)$ if l is a *Numb* cell; otherwise $svar\_value(ref(l))$. *list_check* denotes the updates for unification with lists $[l \mid l']$:

$$
\begin{aligned}
list\_check \equiv\ &pval(pdl-) := ref(dr),\\
&pval(pdl) := ref(dl),\\
&pval(pdl+) := ref(dr)+,\\
&pval(pdl++) := ref(dl)+,\\
&pdl := pdl++
\end{aligned}
$$

---

[5] See next section.

Table 1 Unification Table I.

	$L\_unbound$(dl)	$s\_unbound$(dl)	$tag(dl) =$ **Numb** or $s\_ground(dl)$
$L\_unbound(\mathrm{dr})$	$bind(dl, dr)$ $pdl := pdl - -$		
$s\_unbound(\mathrm{dr})$	$bind(dl, dr)$ $pdl := pdl - -$	$equate(dl, dr)$ $pdl := pdl - -$	
$tag(\mathrm{dr}) =$ **Numb** or $s\_ground(dr)$	$bind(dl, dr)$ $pdl := pdl - -$	$equate(dl, dr)$ $pdl := pdl - -$	top_check
$tag(\mathrm{dr}) =$ **Struct**	$bind(dl, dr)$ $pdl := pdl - -$	$failure$	$failure$
$s\_unfree(\mathrm{dr})$	$bind(dl, dr)$ $pdl := pdl - -$	$equate(dl, dr)$ $pdl := pdl - -$	$equate(dl, dr)$ $pdl := pdl - -$
$tag(\mathrm{dr}) =$ **Const**	$bind(dl, dr)$ $pdl := pdl - -$	$failure$	$failure$
$tag(\mathrm{dr}) =$ **List**	$bind(dl, dr)$ $pdl := pdl - -$	$failure$	$failure$

Table 2 Unification Table II.

	$tag(dl) =$ **Struct**	$s\_unfree(dl)$
$tag(dr) =$ **Struct**	$func\_check$	
$s\_unfree(dr)$	$failure$	$equate(dl, dr)$ $pdl := pdl - -$
$tag(dr) =$ **Const**	$failure$	$failure$
$tag(dr) =$ **List**	$failure$	$failure$

$func\_check$ describes the updates for unification with terms $f(t_1, \ldots, t_n)$:

$$
\begin{aligned}
func\_check \quad \equiv \quad & \textbf{if } ref(ref(dl)) = ref(ref(dr)) \\
& \textbf{then seq } pdl := pdl - - \\
& \qquad \textbf{seq } i = 1 \ldots arity(ref(dl)) \\
& \qquad\qquad pval(pdl+) := ref(dr) + i \\
& \qquad\qquad pval(pdl++) := ref(dl) + i \\
& \qquad\qquad pdl := pdl + + \\
& \qquad \textbf{endseq} \\
& \textbf{endseq} \\
& \textbf{else } failure
\end{aligned}
$$

The crucial update *equate*, which we keep abstract here, has to re-

Table 3 Unification Table III.

	$tag(dl) =$ **Const**	$tag(dl) =$ **List**
$tag(dr) =$ **Const**	top_check	
$tag(dr) =$ **List**	failure	list_check

flect the complex interaction between solver modules for linear equations, inequalities and nonlinear equations (see Fig. 3). In particular *equate* is assumed to:

(1) Rewrite the equation $term(l_1) = term(l_2)$ in such a way that exactly one variable (called the subject) appears on the left-hand side[6]; the result is stored in *PF_AREA* and occurrences lists are updated.

(2) "Propagate" the rewritten equation to other constraints so that occurrences lists are updated and constraints are mantained in solved form.

(3) Invoke the Simplex algorithm if the subject of the new equation is contained in inequalities; the set of implied equalities is calculated and each of them is handled by *equate*.

(4) Calculate the wakeup degrees of all modified nonlinear constraints for each grounding equation which affects nonlinear equalities; if a nonlinear constraint is awoken[7], then an *equate* update is invoked.

It is further assumed that whenever a linear form must be changed, it is put to sleep and rewritten on top of *PF_AREA*. From the above assumptions one can prove the following:

Lemma 5.1. (Unification Lemma) *Let l_1, l_2 be in DATAAREA such that $term(l_1), term(l_2) \in TERM$ and let cs be the current constraint system. After execution of $unify(l_1, l_2)$, the new constraint system is the normalization of*

$$cs \bigcup \{term(l_1) = term(l_2)\}$$

If the new constraint system is unsolvable, then execution backtracks.

6 Compilation of Constraints

In this section we show how the formal description of WAM compilation of terms can be naturally extended to constraints. For simplicity we assume here that all variables are permanent and get initialized to *unbound* as soon as they are allocated[8].

---

[6] The choice of the subject variable is ruled by efficiency criteria.

[7] An awoken nonlinear constraint gives rise to a linear equation.

[8] This assumption can be eliminated later by a refined variable classification.

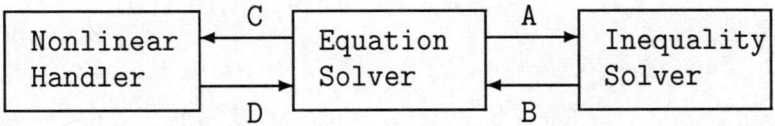

A: Equation affecting inequalities;
B: Inferred equality;
C: Equation affecting nonlinear equalities;
D: Awoken nonlinear constraint.

FIG. 3. Interactions between solver modules.

Term arguments occurring during term compilation will be represented in a register subdomain $AREGS$ of $DATAAREA$, disjoint from the heap. Registers are numbered by a function $x : \mathcal{N} \to AREGS$ for which we write $x_i \equiv x(i)$.

The CLAM code for compiled body subgoals is accessed from a subset $CODEAREA$ of $MEMORY$ through a content function $code$ into the universe $INSTR$ of instructions which is assumed to contain all WAM instructions and the following instructions for handling of constraints:

$$
\begin{array}{lll}
unify\_number(c) & put\_number(c, x_j) & get\_number(c, x_j) \\
initpf(c) & addpf\_val(c, x_j) & addpf\_val(c, y_n) \\
addpf\_var(c, x_j) & get\_lpf(x_j) & set\_svariable(x_j) \\
solve\_eq0 & solve\_ge0 & solve\_gt0 \\
put\_lpf(x_j) & &
\end{array}
$$

with $n, j \in \mathcal{N}$, $y_n \in DATAAREA$, $c \in NUMBER$, $x_j \in AREGS$ ($INSTR$ will be tacitly extended with further instructions occurring below).

For compilation of arithmetic constraints, coming as streams of simple token patterns, we need a concept of constraint normal form which is an analogue of the logical notion of term normal form. An arithmetic equation, inequality or nonlinear constraint is said to be in normal form if it is of form $lpf = 0$, $lpf \geq 0$, $lpf > 0$, $nlpf$, respectively, where lpf is a linear parametric form and $nlpf$ is a nonlinear form.

We extend the usual normalization procedures nf_s and nf_a —corresponding to the analysis (for putting instructions) and synthesis (for getting instructions) of terms—from logical term equations to constraints as follows:

$$
\begin{array}{ll}
nf(X_i = Y_n) = [X_i = Y_n], & nf(X_i = c) = [X_i = c] \\
nf(Y_i = Y_n) = nf(X_i = X_i) = & nf(c = c) = [\,]
\end{array}
$$

$$nf_s(X_i = c_0 + c_1 s_1 + \ldots + c_n s_n) = \mathit{flatten}([\, nf_s(Z_1 = s_1), \ldots,$$
$$nf_s(Z_n = s_n),$$
$$X_i = c_0 + c_1 Z_1 + \ldots + c_n Z_n \,])$$

The same applies for linear inequalities replacing $X_i =$ by $0 <, 0 \leq$ respectively:

$$nf_s(s_0 = op(s_1, \ldots, s_m)) = \mathit{flatten}([\, nf_s(Z_0 = s_0),$$
$$nf_s(Z_1 = s_1), \ldots, nf_s(Z_m = s_m),$$
$$Z_0 = op(Z_1, \ldots, Z_m) \,])$$

$$nf_a(X_i = op(s_1, \ldots, s_m)) = \mathit{flatten}([X_i = op(Z_1, \ldots, Z_m),$$
$$nf_a(Z_1 = s_1), \ldots nf_a(Z_m = s_m)])$$

$$nf_a(X_i = c_0 + c_1 s_1 + \ldots + c_n s_n) = \mathit{flatten}([X_i = c_0 + c_1 Z_1 + \ldots +$$
$$c_n Z_n,$$
$$nf_a(Z_1 = s_1), \ldots, nf_a(Z_n = s_n)])$$

where nf stands for both nf_s and nf_a; Z_i is equal to s_i if s_i is a constant or a variable, otherwise it is a fresh X variable.

Use of normalization is justified by the well known fact that the constraint $s \Delta t$ is equivalent to the set of constraints $nf(s \Delta t)$; computationally this is reflected by the CLP($\mathcal{R}$) effect of executing $s \Delta t$ being the same as executing all members of $nf(s \Delta t)$.

For each nonlinear operation, instructions are provided for creating a nonlinear constraint of any degree. For example, we could define five instructions for pow, corresponding to the various wakeup degrees (see [10]):

- $pow\_vvv(V_i, V_j, V_k)$ for $V_i = pow(V_j, V_k)$, $pow\_cvv(c, V_j, V_k)$ for $c = pow(V_j, V_k)$
- $pow\_vcv(V_i, c, V_k)$ for $V_i = pow(c, V_k)$, $pow\_vvc(V_i, V_j, c)$ for $V_i = pow(V_j, c)$
- $pow\_cvc(c_0, V_j, c_1)$ for $c_0 = pow(V_j, c_1)$

We suppose that we have an auxiliary function nl_instr that takes a normalized nonlinear constraint and returns the appropriate instruction. For example,

$$nl\_instr(X = pow(3, Y)) = pow\_vcv(X, 3, Y)$$

6.1 Putting Instructions (Body Subgoals Compilation)

We extend the WAM function put_instr, yielding the sequence of instructions which compiles by a normalized equation, to provide also compiled code for constraints. The extension is defined according to the following table, where j stands for an arbitrary "top level" index (corresponding to input $X_j = t$ for term normalization), k for a "non top level" index (corresponding to an auxiliary variable introduced by normalization itself) and i

for any index:
$$X_j = c \rightarrow [\mathit{put\_number}(c, x_j)]$$
$$X_i = c_0 + c_1 Z_1 + \ldots + c_n Z_n \rightarrow [\mathit{initpf}(c_0), \mathit{addpf}(c_1, z_1), \ldots,$$
$$\mathit{addpf}(c_n, z_n), \mathit{put\_lpf}(x_i)]$$

where $\mathit{addpf}(c, z_i)$ is $\mathit{addpf\_val}(c, y_n)$ if $Z_i = Y_n$ and $\mathit{addpf\_val}(c, x_i)$ if $Z_i = X_i$. The same applies for $c_0 + c_1 Z_1 + \ldots + c_n Z_n \; \Delta \; 0$ replacing $\mathit{put\_lpf}(x_i)$ by $\mathit{instr}(\Delta)$, where

$$\mathit{instr}(\Delta) = \begin{cases} \mathit{solve\_eq0} & \text{if } \Delta = \text{"="} \\ \mathit{solve\_ge0} & \text{if } \Delta = \text{"}\geq\text{"} \\ \mathit{solve\_gt0} & \text{if } \Delta = \text{">"} \end{cases}$$

Next we consider the case of nonlinear constraint. Note the use of the *set_svariable* instruction because nonlinear instructions are supposed to handle variables which are already initialized:

$$X_i = op(Z_1, \ldots, Z_m) \rightarrow [\mathit{set\_svariable}(x_i), \mathit{nl\_instr}(X_i = op(Z_1, \ldots, Z_m))]$$
$$V = op(Z_1, \ldots, Z_m) \rightarrow [\mathit{nl\_instr}(V = op(Z_1, \ldots, Z_m))]$$
$$\text{where } V = c \text{ or } V = Y_n$$

Moreover, a numeric constant c appearing inside a structure or a list is compiled into the instruction $\mathit{unify\_number}(c)$, with $y_n \in \mathit{DATAAREA}$, $x_i \in \mathit{AREGS}$.

The function *put_seq*—defining the compilation of a body goal, see [4]—is here extended to specify how constraints are to be compiled. The definition uses the auxiliary function *put_code*, defined by flattening the result of mapping *put_instr* along $\mathit{nf}_s(X_i = t)$, $\mathit{nf}_s(c_0 + c_1 s_1 + \ldots + c_n s_n \; \Delta \; 0)$ and $\mathit{nf}_s(s_0 = op(s_1, \ldots, s_m))$, where $\Delta \in \{=, >, \geq\}$. For terms s_i where the outermost function symbol is not arithmetic, we set as for body goals in the WAM:

$$\mathit{put\_seq}(s_1 = s_2) = \mathit{flatten}([\mathit{put\_code}(X_1 = s_1), \mathit{put\_code}(X_2 = s_2)])$$
$$\text{with top level } j = 1, 2$$

For nonlinear constraints *put_seq* coincides with *put_code*:

$$\mathit{put\_seq}(s_0 = op(s_1, \ldots, s_m)) = \mathit{put\_code}(s_0 = op(s_1, \ldots, s_m))$$

On arithmetic constraints, *put_seq* applies *put_code* to a simplified constraint version where all terms with the same variable are collected and all constants are added:

$$\mathit{put\_seq}(t_1 = t_2) = \mathit{put\_code}(\mathit{simplify}(t_1 - t_2 = 0))$$
$$\mathit{put\_seq}(t_1 > t_2) = \mathit{put\_code}(\mathit{simplify}(t_1 - t_2 > 0))$$
$$\mathit{put\_seq}(t_1 \geq t_2) = \mathit{put\_code}(\mathit{simplify}(t_1 - t_2 \geq 0))$$

$$put\_seq(t_1 < t_2) = put\_code(simplify(t_2 - t_1 > 0))$$
$$put\_seq(t_1 \leq t_2) = put\_code(simplify(t_2 - t_1 \geq 0))$$

In the following rules which describe the execution of code generated by putting, an auxiliary stack ($ACCUMULATOR$; $acctop$, $accbottom$) is needed which allows us to construct linear forms to build arithmetic constraints. Its content function $accval$ has to yield constants or pairs (constant, solver identifier).

Also a 0-ary function $add\_counter$ is added containing the number of parametric variables which have appeared so far in the linear form being read.

For the WAM putting instructions the rules defined in [4] are taken. For the CLAM instructions the rules are defined now. The rules for put_number and $unify\_number$ are like those for WAM instructions $put\_constant$ and $unify\_constant$:

if $code(p) = put\_number(c, x_j)$
then $x_j \leftarrow \langle Numb, c \rangle$
   $succeed$

if $code(p) = unify\_number(c)$
   & $mode = Write$
then $h \leftarrow \langle Numb, c \rangle$
   $h := h+$
   $succeed$

The rule for $set\_svariable(x_i)$ is used for initializing a fresh free solver variable pointed at by x_i. It is similar to the instruction $set\_variable$ used in [1]:

if $code(p) = set\_svariable(x_i)$
then $mk\_s\_unbound(x_i)$
   $succeed$

The instruction $set\_svariable$ will be optimized away in the sequel.

The rule that begins the construction of a linear parametric form[9] puts the constant on top of the accumulator and sets $add\_counter$ to zero (there are still no parametric variables):

if $code(p) = initpf(c)$
then $accval(acctop) := c$
   $acctop := acctop+$
   $add\_counter := 0$
   $succeed$

The instruction $addpf\_var(c, l)$ enriches the linear form being built in

---

[9] Note that the arithmetic term which is "accumulated" will not necessarily result in a linear form: it may be simply a numerical constant.

the accumulator with a variable to be initialized:

if $code(p) = addpf\_var(c, x_i)$
then $mk\_s\_unbound(x_i)$
$\quad accval(acctop) \leftarrow \langle c, svtop \rangle$
$\quad acctop := acctop+$
$\quad add\_counter := add\_counter + 1$
$\quad succeed$

The instruction $addpf\_val(c, l)$ enriches the linear form being built in the accumulator with a new component. We have the following cases:

(1) $deref(l)$ gives the address of a *Numb* cell or a ground solver variable: the constant so obtained is multiplied by c and then the result is added to the constant already stored at the bottom of the accumulator.

(2) $deref(l)$ gives the address of a free logical variable: the logical variable is transformed into a solver variable; its identifier is put onto the accumulator (along with the constant c) and $add\_counter$ is incremented by 1.

(3) $deref(l)$ gives the address of a free solver variable: if the solver variable is a parametric variable already appearing in the linear form being built with coefficient c', then c is added to c'; otherwise the element $\langle c, ref(deref(l)) \rangle$ is put onto the accumulator and $add\_counter$ is incremented by 1.

(4) $deref(l)$ gives the address of an unfree solver variable pointing to a linear form lpf: the term to be added is $c * lpf$.

Note that the linear form is built so as to be in solved form when it has to be copied in PF_AREA. In the $addpf\_val$ rule we make use of an abstract binary update add, for which we assume that it does what is described in (3) and (4):

$$add(c') \equiv accval(accbottom) := accval(accbottom) + c * c'$$

and of the trail update discussed below:

if $code(p) = addpf\_val(c, l)$ **then case** $tag(deref(l))$ **of**
$\quad Numb \quad : \quad add(ref(deref(l)))$
$\qquad\qquad\qquad succeed$
$\quad L\_var \quad : \quad mk\_s\_unbound(deref(l))$
$\qquad\qquad\qquad trail(deref(l))$
$\qquad\qquad\qquad accval(acctop) \leftarrow \langle c, svtop \rangle$
$\qquad\qquad\qquad acctop := acctop +$
$\qquad\qquad\qquad add\_counter := add\_counter + 1$
$\qquad\qquad\qquad succeed$
$\quad S\_var \quad : \quad$ **if** $s\_ground(deref(l))$
$\qquad\qquad\qquad$ **then** $add(svar\_value(ref(deref(l))))$
$\qquad\qquad\qquad\qquad succeed$
$\qquad\qquad\qquad$ **else** $add(c, deref(l))$
$\qquad\qquad\qquad\qquad succeed$
$\quad other \quad : \quad backtrack$

The instruction $put\_lpf(x_i)$ concludes the construction of a linear form by storing the equation in memory. We have two possible cases:

(1) $add\_counter = 0$. The arithmetical term built on the accumulator is a numerical constant: in this case register x_i is instantiated to that constant.

(2) $add\_counter > 0$: the arithmetic term built on the accumulator is actually a linear form that has to be stored on top of PF_AREA. A new free solver identifier is initialized and then the equality solver is called:

if $code(p) = put\_lpf(x_i)$
then $succeed$
$\quad$ **if** $add\_counter = 0$ **then** $x_i \leftarrow \langle NUMB, accval(accbottom) \rangle$
$\qquad\qquad\qquad\qquad\qquad$ **else** $mk\_s\_unbound(x_i)$
$\qquad\qquad\qquad\qquad\qquad\qquad trigger\_equate(x_i, accbottom)$

In the following we make use of an abbreviation to store linear inequalities:

$\quad store(type) \quad \equiv \quad pfval(pftop) := type$
$\qquad\qquad\qquad\qquad pfval(pftop+) := active$
$\qquad\qquad\qquad\qquad pfval(pftop + 2) := add\_counter$
$\qquad\qquad\qquad\qquad pfval(pftop + 3) := \langle accval(accbottom), nil \rangle$
$\qquad\qquad\qquad\qquad$ **seq** $j = 1, \ldots, add\_counter$
$\qquad\qquad\qquad\qquad\quad pfval(pftop + 3 + j) := accval(accbottom + j)$
$\qquad\qquad\qquad\qquad$ **endseq**
$\qquad\qquad\qquad\qquad pftop := pftop + add\_counter + 4$

where *trigger_equate* is an abstract update which triggers *equate*[10]. The instruction *put_lpf* will become superfluous in the sequel.

The instruction *solve_ge0* concludes the construction of an arithmetic term in the accumulator; this term must be compared with zero if it is ground, otherwise it must be stored as a nonstrict inequality in *PF_AREA*. We have two cases:

(1) *add_counter* = 0: the contructed arithmetic term is a numeric constant, so the test can be done;

(2) *add_counter* > 0: the contructed arithmetic term is a linear form, so it has to be copied onto *PF_AREA* with type $\geq$; Lists of occurrences are updated (using an abstract update *update_occ*) and the inequality solver is called.

The call to the inequality solver is represented by an abstract update *inequality*(*l*), which yields *backtrack* if the Simplex tableau becomes unsolvable. Eventual equalities are inferred and for each of them the equality solver is called.

The same also holds for *solve_gt0* which generates a strict inequality:

$\quad$ **if** $code(p) = solve\_ge0 \mid solve\_gt0$
$\quad$ **then if** *add_counter* $= 0$
$\qquad$ **then if** $accval(accbottom) \geq 0 \mid > 0$
$\qquad\quad$ **then** *succeed*
$\qquad\quad$ **else** *backtrack*
$\qquad$ **else** $store(\geq) \mid store(>)$
$\qquad\quad$ *update_occ*
$\qquad\quad$ $top_\geq := pftop \mid top_> := pftop$
$\qquad\quad$ *succeed*
$\qquad\quad$ *trigger_inequality*(*pftop*)

where *trigger_inequality* is an abstract update which triggers the update *inequality*.

The rule for *solve_eq0* is quite similar to the previous one:

$\quad$ **if** $code(p) = solve\_eq0$
$\quad$ **then if** *add_counter* $= 0$
$\qquad$ **then if** $accval(accbottom) = 0$
$\qquad\quad$ **then** *succeed*
$\qquad\quad$ **else** *backtrack*
$\qquad$ **else** *succeed*
$\qquad\quad$ *trigger_equate*(*accbottom*, 0)

For instructions for nonlinear constraints, we consider as a typical ex-

---

[10] Note that the equality solver is called after the creation of the linear form and the solver variable.

ample the real operator *sin*, defined for any real number (so it is not invertible). Sleeping nonlinear constraints involving this function have only one wakeup degree, call it *ind*, and are awoken when the argument gets instantiated to a ground term. *sin* has two instructions $sin\_vv(l_1, l_2)$ and $sin\_cv(c, l)$. Using the abbreviation

$$\begin{aligned}
store\_nlpf(l) \quad &\equiv \quad pfval(pftop) := nonlinear \\
&\quad pfval(pftop+) := \langle sin, ind, 1 \rangle \\
&\quad pfval(pftop + 2) := c \\
&\quad pfval(pftop + 3) := l \\
&\quad nleq := pftop \\
&\quad pftop := pftop + 4 \\
&\quad update\_occ
\end{aligned}$$

we have the rule for *sin_cv*, using *dl* instead of *deref(l)*:

```
if code(p) = sin_cv(c, l)
then case tag(dl) of
   Numb  :  if c = sin(ref(dl))
            then succeed
            else backtrack
   L_var :  if −1 ≤ c ≤ 1
            then trail(dl)
                 mk_s_unbound(dl)
                 store_nlpf(svtop)
                 succeed
            else backtrack
   S_var :  if s_ground(dl)
            then if c = sin(svar_value(ref(dl)))
                 then succeed
                 else backtrack
            else if −1 ≤ c ≤ 1
                 then store_nlpf(ref(dl))
                      succeed
                 else backtrack
   other :  backtrack
```

From the assumptions made for the abstract updates introduced above one can prove:

Lemma 6.1. (Putting Lemma I) Let $\{Y_1, \ldots Y_l\}$ be the set of variables occurring in the $CLP(\mathcal{R})$ literal $g(t_1, \ldots, t_n)$, $y_n \in DATAAREA$ with $term(y_n) \in TERM$ $(n = 1, \ldots, l)$, cs be the current constraint system associating every Y_n with $term(y_n)$ and X_i be fresh pairwise distinct variables, $i = 1, \ldots, m$. The effect of executing (setting p to a value where unload yields) $put\_seq(g(t_1, \ldots, t_n))$ is that the new constraint system is the

normalization of
$$cs \bigcup \{X_i = t_i\}$$

Lemma 6.2. (Putting Lemma II) *Let $\{Y_1, \ldots, Y_l\}$ be all the variables occurring in the CLP($\mathcal{R}$) constraint c, $y_n \in DATAAREA$ with $term(y_n) \in TERM$ $(n = 1, \ldots, l)$ and let cs be the current constraint system associating Y_n with $term(y_n)$. The effect of executing put_seq(c) is that if $cs \bigcup \{c\}$ is solvable then it will be equal (up to normalization) to the new constraint system; otherwise execution backtracks.*

6.2 Getting Instructions (Clause Head Compilation)

The compilation of clause heads is defined in the same way as clause body compilation where only the function *get_instr* is different.

For $X_j = c$ and $X_i = c_0 + c_1 Z_1 + \ldots + c_n Z_n$ it suffices to replace *put* by *get*, whereas for nonlinear forms we set

$$X_i = op(Z_1, \ldots, Z_m) \quad \rightarrow \quad \textit{flatten}([\textit{set\_seq}([Z_1, \ldots, Z_m]),\\ \textit{nl\_instr}(X_i = op(Z_1, \ldots, Z_m))])$$

The *set_seq* ensure that when a variable X_i first occurs in a nonlinear constraint, it is initialized before executing the appropriate "nonlinear" instruction[11]:

$$\begin{aligned}
\textit{set\_seq}([]) &= [] \\
\textit{set\_seq}([X_i \mid T]) &= [\textit{set\_svariable}(x_i) \mid \textit{set\_seq}(T)] \\
\textit{set\_seq}([c \mid T]) &= \textit{set\_seq}(T) \\
\textit{set\_seq}([Y_n \mid T]) &= \textit{set\_seq}(T)
\end{aligned}$$

In addition to the rules for WAM's getting instructions (see [4]), we define now the rules for new CLAM instructions. The *get_number* rule is

---

[11] Use of *set_seq* could been avoided by introducing variants of nonlinear instructions which allow a variable to be initialized. For example, for a constraint $c = sin(Y_n)$ where Y_n appears in its first occurrence, the instruction sin_cV can be used with execution rule:

$$\text{if } code(p) = sin\_cV(c,l) \text{ then if } -1 \leq c \leq 1 \text{ then } \begin{array}{l} mk\_s\_unbound(l) \\ store\_nlpf(svtop) \\ succeed \end{array}$$
$$\text{else backtrack}$$

It is easy to see that the sequence $\textit{set\_svariable}(y_n)$, $sin\_cv(c, y_n)$ is equivalent to $sin\_cV(c, y_n)$.

analogous to the *get_constant* rule:

if $code(p) = get\_number(c, x_i)$
then case $tag(deref(x_i))$ **of**
  Numb : **if** $c = ref(deref(x_i))$
           then *succeed*
           else *backtrack*
  L_var : $deref(x_i) := \langle Numb, c \rangle$
           $trail(deref(x_i))$
           succeed
  S_var : **if** $s\_ground(deref(x_i))$
           then if $c = svar\_value(ref(deref(x_i)))$
               then *succeed*
               else *backtrack*
           else *succeed*
               $trigger\_equate(deref(x_i), c)$
  other : *backtrack*

The rule for *unify_number* is analogous to the rule for *unify_constant*:

if $code(p) = unify\_number(c)$ & $mode = Read$
then case $tag(deref(str))$ **of**
  Numb : **if** $c = ref(deref(str))$
           then $str := str+$
               succeed
           else *backtrack*
  L_var : $deref(str) := \langle Numb, c \rangle$
           $trail(deref(str))$
           $str := str+$
           succeed
  S_var : **if** $s\_ground(deref(str))$
           then if $c = svar\_value(ref(deref(str)))$
               then $str := str+$
                   succeed
               else *backtrack*
           else $str := str+$
               succeed
               $trigger\_equate(deref(str), c)$
  other : *backtrack*

The instruction $get\_lpf(x_i)$ unifies the arithmetic term built in the accumulator with $term(x_i)$. In order to make updates more readable we split the rule into two. The first regards the case in which the term constructed in the accumulator is a constant:

if $code(p) = get\_lpf(x_i)$ & $add\_counter = 0$
then case $tag(deref(x_i))$ **of**
  $Numb$:   **if** $ref(deref(x_i)) = accval(accbottom)$
              then *succeed*
              else *backtrack*
  L_var : $deref(x_i) \leftarrow \langle Numb, accval(accbottom)\rangle$
              $trail(deref(x_i))$
              succeed
  S_var :   **if** $s\_ground(deref(x_i))$
              then if $accval(accbottom) = svar\_value(ref(deref(x_i)))$
                  then *succeed*
                  else *backtrack*
              else *succeed*
                  $trigger\_equate(deref(x_i), accbottom)$
  $other$:   *backtrack*

The second rule regards the case in which a linear form has been built:

if $code(p) = get\_lpf(x_i)$ & $add\_counter > 0$
then case $tag(deref(x_i))$ **of**
  $Numb, S\_var$:   *succeed*
                        $trigger\_equate(deref(x_i), accbottom)$
        L_var : $mk\_s\_unbound(deref(x_i))$
                        $trail(deref(x_i))$
                        succeed
                        $trigger\_equate(deref(x_i), accbottom)$
        $other$:   *backtrack*

The instruction *get_lpf* will be optimized away in the sequel. For the getting code described above one can prove:

Lemma 6.3. (Getting Lemma) *Let all variables occurring in the literal* $g(t_1, \ldots, t_m)$ *be among* $\{Y_1, \ldots, Y_l\}$, *and let further* $y_n \in DATAAREA$ *with* $l\_unbound(y_n)$, $n = 1, \ldots, l$, X_i *fresh pairwise distinct variables with* $x_i \in DATAAREA$ *and* $term(x_i) \in TERM$, $1 \leq i \leq m$. *Let cs be the current constraint system. If*

$$cs \bigcup \{term(x_i) = t_i\}$$

is solvable, then, after executing (setting p to) $get\_seq(g(t_1, \ldots, t_m))$, *it will be equal (up to normalization) to the new constraint system; otherwise execution backtracks.*

Modifying *put-* and *get-code* (to generate *unify_local_value* instead of *unify_value* for all occurrences of local variables), as in the WAM one can preserve the *Heap Variable Constraint* (that no heap variable points outside

b:	n	(number of arguments)
b+1:	x_1	(argument register 1)
⋮		
b+n:	x_n	(argument register n)
b+n+1:	e	(continuation environment)
b+n+2:	cp	(continuation pointer)
b+n+3:	b	(previous choicepoint)
b+n+4:	p	(next clause)
b+n+5:	$ttop$	(trail pointer)
b+n+6:	h	(heap pointer)
b+n+7:	$svtop$	($SVAR\_AREA$ pointer)
b+n+8:	$top_\geq$	(topmost nonstrict inequality)
b+n+9:	$top_>$	(topmost strict inequality)
b+n+10:	top_{nl}	(topmost nonlinear equation)
b+n+11:	$top_=$	(topmost linear equation)

FIG. 4. Choicepoint frame.

the heap); see [4].

7 CLAM

In this section we obtain a description of the CLAM by embedding the compilation of terms and constraints into the CLP($\mathcal{R}$) model with predicate and clause compilation (outlined in section 3).

7.1 Stack and Trail

The first step is, as in the WAM, to refine the choicepoint and environment stack to become a subalgebra $(STACK; tos(b, e), bos; +, -; val)$ of $DATAAREA$ disjoint from $HEAP$ and $AREGS$. The distinguished elements b and e stand for the (address of the) topmost choicepoint and environment, respectively. The environment frame is taken unchanged from the WAM (see [4]), while the choicepoint frame gets extended by information on constraints as described in Fig. 4. Formally:

$$svtop(l) \equiv l + n + 7 \quad top_\geq(l) \equiv l + n + 8 \quad top_>(l) \equiv l + n + 9$$
$$top_{nl}(l) \equiv l + n + 10 \quad top_=(l) \equiv l + n + 11 \quad hb \equiv val(h(b))$$
$$n(l) \equiv l$$

Thus we have the same form of environment (de-)allocation and choicepoint handling rules as for the WAM (including the conditions on binding and $HEAP < STACK < AREGS$; see [4]). We have to refine in particular the *trail* update, which allows to undo, on backtracking, all the modifications to the constraint system made after creation of the choicepoint where the system backtracks to. The stack ($TRAIL, TO; ttop, tbottom; +, -$) is thus extended to contain (via a function *tval*) not only $DATAAREA$ locations, but *trail objects* which are tagged and refer to the items to be stored:

$$ttag \;:\; TO \to \{FREE\_L, FREE\_S, S\_var, LPF, ID, NLPF\}$$
$$tref \;:\; TO \to \; DATAAREA + PF\_AREA +$$
$$(PF\_AREA \times SVAR\_AREA) +$$
$$+ SVAR\_AREA + (PF\_AREA \times \mathcal{N})$$

under the following conditions (writing $ttag(l)$ for $ttag(tval(l))$, $tref(l)$ for $tref(tval(l))$):

case	$ttag(l)$	**of**
$FREE\_L$	:	$tref(l) \in DATAAREA$
$FREE\_S$	:	$tref(l) \in SVAR\_AREA$
ID, S_var	:	$tref(l) \in (PF\_AREA \times SVAR\_AREA)$
LPF	:	$tref(l) \in PF\_AREA$
$NLPF$	:	$tref(l) \in (PF\_AREA \times \mathcal{N})$

According to the location to be trailed the update $trail(l)$, assumed to be executed at each invocation of *bind* or *equate* concerning l, can be:

- $trail\_lf(l)$ if $l\_unbound(l)$; l is an unbound logical variable;
- $trail\_sf(l)$ if $id\_unbound(l)$; l is an unbound solver identifier;
- $trail\_sid(l)$ if $id\_unfree(l)$; l is a solver identifier equated to a linear form;
- $trail\_lpf(l)$ if $pfval(l) \in \{=, \geq, >\}$; l is the initial address of a linear form which is going to be put to sleep;
- $trail\_nlpf(l)$ if $pfval(l) = nonlinear$; l is the address of a nonlinear constraint whose wakeup degree is going to be modified[12];
- $trail\_id(l)$ if $pfval(l) \in SVAR\_AREA$; l contains the address of a non-constant parameter of a nonlinear constraint.

$$
\begin{aligned}
trail\_lf(l) \;\equiv\;& ttag(ttop) := FREE\_L, \\
& tref(ttop) := l, \\
& ttop := ttop + \\
trail\_sf(l) \;\equiv\;& ttag(ttop) := FREE\_S, \\
& tref(ttop) := l, \\
& ttop := ttop +
\end{aligned}
$$

---

[12] Alternatively, the wakeup degree of all nonlinear constraints affected by trailing operations could be calculated as part of the *backtrack* update.

$$trail\_sid(l) \equiv ttag(ttop) := S\_var,$$
$$fst(ttref(ttop)) := svar\_lpf(l),$$
$$snd(tref(ttop)) := l,$$
$$ttop := ttop+$$

$$trail\_lpf(l) \equiv ttag(ttop) := LPF,$$
$$tref(ttop) := l,$$
$$ttop := ttop+$$

$$trail\_nlpf(l) \equiv ttag(ttop) := NLPF,$$
$$fst(tref(ttop)) := l,$$
$$snd(tref(ttop)) := third(pfval(l+)),$$
$$ttop := ttop+$$

$$trail\_id(l) \equiv ttag(ttop) := ID,$$
$$fst(tref(ttop)) := l,$$
$$snd(tref(ttop)) := pfval(l),$$
$$ttop := ttop+$$

Accordingly, the WAM backtrack update must be refined to undo all constraints trailed after the current choicepoint was pushed. In the following definition $ttop(b)$ yields the value $ttop$ had when the choicepoint b was created. Here is the definition:

$$backtrack \equiv \textbf{if } b = bos \textbf{ then } stop := -1$$
$$\textbf{else } p := val(p(b))$$
$$\textbf{seq } l = ttop - \ldots tr(b)$$
$$\textbf{case } ttag(l) \textbf{ of}$$
$$FREE\_L \; : \; mk\_l\_unbound(tref(l))$$
$$FREE\_S \; : \; mk\_id\_unbound(tref(l))$$
$$S\_var \; : \; svar\_lpf(snd(tref(l))) :=$$
$$fst(tref(l))$$
$$update\_occ$$
$$LPF \; : \; pfval(tref(l)+) := active$$
$$update\_occ$$
$$NLPF \; : \; third(pfval(fst(tref(l)))) :=$$
$$snd(tref(l))$$
$$ID \; : \; pfval(fst(tref(l))) :=$$
$$snd(tref(l))$$
$$update\_occ$$
$$\textbf{endcase}$$
$$\textbf{endseq}$$

(Recall that we assume that $update\_occ$ adjusts occurrence lists.)

Trailing operations (and backtracking) also have to take into account the result of the inequality solver. Since we keep the latter unspecified, we assume that trailing records the inequality solver data structures (for example the Simplex tableau) which are relevant for the currently "active" inequalities stored in *PF_AREA*.

Putting together all the assumptions made for compilation of predicates, clauses, terms and constraints one can prove the main theorem stated in the introduction; see [11].

7.2 Optimizations

In this section we outline some of the major optimizations for the CLAM.

The classification of variables—which is crucial for environment trimming and last call optimization—can be taken together with all the proofs almost literally from the WAM model of [4] thanks to the modularity of the specification introduced here. We state here only the adaptation, to clauses with constraints, of the definition of permanent and temporary variables:

Definition 7.1 *A variable occurring before or in a body subgoal α_i of a clause $H : -\alpha_1, \ldots, \alpha_n$, is needed at α_i, $1 \leq i < n$, if either (a) it occurs in some α_j, $j > i$, and there exists k with $i \leq k < j$ such that α_k is an atom or (b) α_i is an atom (not the last one) and the first occurrence of the variable in the clause is an argument position of α_i.*

Definition 7.2 *A variable appearing in a clause is said to be permanent if it is needed at some body subgoal; otherwise it is temporary.*

The environment allocation is superfluous when the clause body is empty or contains only constraints or contains only constraints followed by one atom: in all these cases no variable is needed at any subgoal.

Trailing operations on variables can be optimized by executing the update *trail_lf(l)* only if $(l \in heap\ \&\ l < hb)$ or $(l \in STACK\ \&\ l < b)$ just as in the WAM. An optimization for linear parametric forms can be obtained by executing *trail_lpf(l)* only if one of the following conditions holds:

$$pfval(l) = eq\quad \&\quad val(leq(b)) \geq l$$
$$pfval(l) = ge\quad \&\quad val(nsineq(b)) \geq l$$
$$pfval(l) = gt\quad \&\quad val(sineq(b)) \geq l$$

Also *trail_sf(l)* and *trail_sid(l)* can be optimized, executing them only if $l < val(svtop(b))$. For nonlinear constraints *trail_nlpf(l)* and *trail_id(l)* can be optimized by executing them only if $val(nleq(b)) \geq l$.

One of the principal mechanisms for enhancing efficiency is to avoid invoking the full solver when constraints are simple. As we have seen in section 5, the process of solving a linear constraint consists first of building a linear form in the accumulator[13] and then handling the constraint by means of *solve_eq0*, *solve_ge0* or *solve_gt0* instructions. Solving an equation amounts to:

---

[13] A linear form built on the accumulator contains only parametric and new variables.

(1) finding a parameter V to become nonparametric;
(2) writing the equation with subject V, i.e. in the form $V = lpf$;
(3) substituting out V using lpf in all other linear constraints;
(4) adding the new constraint $V = lpf$.

Suppose that a new variable appears in the equation to be compiled; then it will certainly appear in the linear form built at run time. So it may be chosen in step 1 at compile time. Much of the work in step 2 can also be compiled away. Step 3 is not needed because the variable is new. Only step 4 must be executed at runtime, so a new instruction is needed, which executes it and always succeeds. Similar simplifications can be made for the compilation of inequalities which contain a new variable. The presence of a new unconstrained variable in an inequality can in fact significantly simplify the work made by the inequality solver. The new instructions are:

$$solve\_no\_fail\_eq(l),\ solve\_no\_fail\_ge(l),\ solve\_no\_fail\_gt(l)$$

The instruction $solve\_no\_fail\_eq$ contains a special call to the equality solver containing the terms to be equated and the variable that shall become nonparametric:

if $code(p) = solve\_no\_fail\_eq(l)$
then $succeed$
    if $add\_counter = 0$
    then $l \leftarrow \langle Numb, accval(accbottom) \rangle$
    else $mk\_s\_unfree(l)$
          $equate\_no\_fail(svtop, accbottom)$

where

$$mk\_s\_unfree(l) \equiv\ l \leftarrow \langle S\_var, svtop \rangle$$
$$svar\_lpf(svtop) := pftop$$
$$svar\_occ(svtop) := []$$
$$svar\_value(svtop) := nil$$
$$svtop := svtop +$$

The update $equate\_no\_fail(l, a)$ has the same effect as a call to the solver in order to equate the identifier l, chosen to become nonparametric, with the linear form built in the accumulator.

The instructions for inequalities are quite similar:

if $code(p) = solve\_no\_fail\_ge(l)\ |\ solve\_no\_fail\_gt(l)$
then $mk\_s\_unbound(l)$
    $store\_v(\geq, svtop)\ |\ store\_v(>, svtop)$
    $top_\geq := pftop\ |\ top_> := pftop$
    $inequality\_no\_fail(pftop, svtop)$
    $succeed$

where

$$store\_v(type, l) \equiv \begin{aligned} &pfval(pftop) := type \\ &pfval(pftop+) := active \\ &pfval(pftop + 2) := add\_counter \\ &pfval(pftop + 3) := \langle accval(accbottom), nil \rangle \\ &\textbf{seq } j = 1, \ldots, add\_counter \\ &\quad pfval(pftop + 3 + j) := accval(accbottom + j) \\ &\textbf{endseq} \\ &pfval(pftop + add\_counter + 4) := \langle 1, l \rangle \\ &pftop := pftop + add\_counter + 5 \end{aligned}$$

$inequality\_no\_fail(l_{pf}, l_{id})$ has the same effect as $inequality(l_{pf})$, except that the inequality solver can exploit the presence of the new identifier l_{id}.

Since put_lpf is used only for the first occurrence of a variable, a similar optimization can be made for the instruction $put\_lpf(x_i)$, which assigns x_i to a new identifier. This comes up to replace in the put_lpf-rule

$mk\_s\_unbound(x_i)$ by $mk\_s\_unfree(x_i)$
$trigger\_equate(x_i, accbottom)$ $equate\_no\_fail(svtop, accbottom)$

By this transformation rules $put\_lpf(x_i)$ and $solve\_no\_fail\_eq(x_i)$ become identical, so that put_lpf can be eliminated.

When building a linear form in the accumulator, the cases where the constant is zero or the coefficient is 1 or -1 occur in the majority of instances. Special instructions can be introduced to cater for these commonly occurring cases in order to keep down the code size and cut down on decode time. The new instructions are:

- $initpf\_0$
  start a new linear form with constant 0;
- $addpf\_va\{lr\}\_\{+-\}^{14}(x_i)$
  add a term consisting of a temporary variable with coefficient 1 or -1;
- $addpf\_va\{lr\}\_\{+-\}(y_n)$
  add a term consisting of a permanent variable with coefficient 1 or -1.

We omit to spell out the simple rules for these new instructions.

Note also that $get\_lpf(x_i)$ can be replaced by

$$addpf\_val\_-(x_i), \; solve\_eq0$$

The instruction get_lpf may then be entirely dispensed with. Through elimination of $set\_svariable$, put_lpf and get_lpf we obtain the same instruction

---

[14] The brace notation stands for the instructions $addpf\_var\_+$, $addpf\_var\_-$, $addpf\_val\_+$ and $addpf\_val\_-$.

set as described in [10].

Bibliography

1. H.Aït-Kaci, *Warren's Abstract Machine. A tutorial reconstruction*, MIT Press, 1991.
2. C.Beierle & E.Börger, *Correctness proof for the WAM with types.* In: Computer Science Logic (Eds. E. Börger, G. Jäger, H. Kleine Büning, M. Richter), Springer LNCS 626, 1992, 15–34.
3. E.Börger & D.Rosenzweig, *An analysis of Prolog Database Views and their Uniform Implementation*, In: Prolog. Paris Papers-2. ISO/IEC JTC1 SC22 WG17 Prolog Standardization Report no. 80, July 1991, pp. 87–130.
 = CSE-TR-89-91, University of Michigan, Ann Arbor, Michigan 1991.
4. E.Börger & D.Rosenzweig, *The WAM—Definition and Compiler Correctness*, to appear in Logic Programming: Formal Methods and Practical Applications (Eds. C.Beierle, L.Plümer), Studies in Computer Science and Artificial Intelligence, North-Holland, 1994.
5. E.Börger & D.Rosenzweig, *Mathematical Definition of Full Prolog*, to appear in Science of Computer Programming, 1994.
6. Y.Gurevich, *Evolving Algebras. A Tutorial Introduction* in: Bulletin of the European Association for Theoretical Computer Science, no.43, February 1991, pp. 264–284.
7. Y.Gurevich, *Logic and the Challenge of Computer Science*, in: E.Börger (Ed.), Trends in Theoretical Computer Science. Computer Science Press, Rockville MA 1988, pp. 1–57.
8. J.Jaffar, S.Michaylov, P.J.Stuckey & R.H.C.Yap, *The CLP(R) Language and System*, ACM Transactions on Programming Languages and Systems, July 1992, pp 339–395.
9. Nevin C.Heintze, Joxan Jaffar, Spiro Michaylov, Peter J.Stuckey & Roland H.C.Yap, *The CLP(R) Programming Manual, Version 1.2*, September 1992.
10. J.Jaffar, S.Michaylov, P.J.Stuckey & R.H.C.Yap, *An Abstract Machine for CLP(R)*, November 1992.
11. R.F.Salamone, *An Abstract Modular Specification of the CLAM*, Tesi di Laurea, Dipartimento di Informatica, Università di Pisa, July 1993.

The Semantics of the C++ Programming Language

Charles Wallace[*]

1 Introduction

In this chapter we extend the evolving algebra presented in [GH] to give formal operational semantics for the C++ programming language. The evolving algebra of [GH] is a specification for the C programming language; here we propose modifications to it to accommodate the features of C++. We refer the reader to [GH] for a description of the C algebra, and to [Gu] for an introduction to evolving algebras. [KR] describes the ANSI standard for the C language, on which the algebra of [GH] is based. We assume the informal specification for C++ in [ES] as guidelines for our semantics. Knowledge of C++ will ease comprehension but is not necessary, as we shall explain the new features of C++ and illustrate their use with examples as we proceed.

The C++ programming language is designed to be an "extension" of C, retaining all of C's language facilities and adding new ones. On a syntactic level, the differences between C and C++ consist entirely of language constructs allowable in C++ but not in C. Our algebra for C++ will alter the rules for C in [GH], maintaining their functionality while extending them to capture the new features of C++. Many of the extensions we shall consider do not require any changes at all to the rules. Some extensions, such as derived classes, affect only static information about the program, determined when the program is compiled and never changed during the running of the program. Other extensions, such as the keyword `class`, simply constitute syntactic alternatives to constructs present in C. In addition to proposing changes to the rules, we shall discuss the extensions which do not require any rule changes and explain how we can handle them.

1.1 Outline

The new features of C++ support the "object-oriented" programming paradigm. The term "object" can be defined simply as the instantiation of a type. This approach to programming is a synthesis of several principles, which we summarize as follows. First, object-oriented programming supports the inclusion of *operations* performed on an object within the defi-

---

[*]Partially supported by NSF grant #029862 and ONR grant #028355. The author's address is: EECS Department, University of Michigan, Ann Arbor, MI 48109-2122. Electronic mail address: wallace@eecs.umich.edu.

nition of the object's type. New types can be defined in terms of preexisting types through *inheritance*. Finally, access to an object's data is localized through *encapsulation*.

The features required to implement encapsulation and inheritance are presented in section 2, while those required to combine type and operation definitions are presented in section 3. Section 4 deals with the features supporting creation and destruction of objects. In sections 5 and 6 we discuss extensions that are not object-oriented in nature; section 5 concerns overloading and parameterized type definitions, and section 6 covers the remaining extensions.

For the sake of readability, we define a set of macros for commonly used rule expressions. The definitions of these macros appear in Appendix A.

1.2 Acknowledgments

I would like to thank Yuri Gurevich for inspiring me to write this chapter and guiding me during its development. I would also like to thank Jim Huggins and Solomon Foster for their many helpful comments.

2 Class structure and encapsulation

The central notion of the object-oriented programming paradigm is the encapsulation of data types and operations associated with them. Encapsulation ensures that the data stored within an object is accessed only by the operations associated with the object's type. This localization of access is conducive both to data security and to good programming style. Encapsulation is achieved in C++ through the `class` construct, which defines aggregate types similar to `struct` types in C. A `class` type combines the components of a programmer-defined data type with the functions and operators to manipulate it. The notion of a class is introduced in section 2.1. The level of localization of access is achieved by specifying access status for the components of the type; access status is discussed in section 2.4.

In object-oriented programming, redundant code may be eliminated by allowing one type to "inherit" the data structure and operations of another. The inherited structure and operations may then be modified or extended to suit the new type. Inheritance is called "derivation" in C++; the features supporting class derivation are discussed in sections 2.2 and 2.3.

2.1 Classes

C++ introduces a new keyword `class` which indicates the definition of a new type. This is almost identical in functionality to the C keyword `struct`. Both define types whose instantiations are contiguous sequences of ordered fields (or "members") in memory; in C++, both may have operations, or "member functions," associated with them. The only difference between the two is in the default "access status" assigned to their fields.[1] As we shall see in section 2.4, access status is itself a C++ extension of a purely syntactic nature; thus we can treat `class` types in the same way we treat `struct` types in the C algebra, with no rule modifications necessary. We hereby adopt C++ terminology: we shall use the term "class" to refer to both `struct` and `class` types and the term "member" as a synonym for "field." In addition, we shall use the term "object" to refer to a contiguous area of memory serving as an instantiation of a particular type; in particular, the term "class object" refers to an area allocated as an instantiation of a `class` or `struct` type.

2.2 Derived classes

In addition to the members defined explicitly in its declaration, a class may inherit the members of a set of other classes. A class that inherits members is said to be "derived"; the classes whose members it inherits are its "base" classes. The base classes of a derived class are specified in its declaration. For example, given the class `person` containing the members `name` and `age`:[2]

```
// declaration of (nonderived) class "person"
class person                    // (no members inherited)
{ char name[25];                // person's name (string)
  int age;                      // person's age (integer)
  void printPerson(); };        // function to print person's name and age
```

we can add the derived classes `professor` and `student`:

```
// declaration of derived class "professor"
class professor: person      // (inherits members of class "person")
{ int salary;                // professor's salary (integer)
  void printProfessor(); };  // function to print professor's info
// declaration of derived class "student"
class student: person        // (inherits members of class "person")
{ int year;                  // student's year (integer)
  float GPA;                 // student's GPA (decimal)
  void printStudent(); };    // function to print student's info
```

Professors and students in the real world are individuals with names and ages, as well as professor- and student-specific attributes. The classes `professor` and `student` represent this by inheriting the members of the class `person`. Both derived classes contain `name`, `age` and `printPerson`, the members of their base class; in addition, the class `professor` contains the members `salary` and `printProfessor`, while the class `student` contains `year`, `GPA` and `printStudent`.

---

[1] The default access status is "public" for a `struct` and "private" for a `class` type. The default status is assigned to a field if no status is specified.

[2] In C++, a pair of slash characters (//) indicates the beginning of a one-line comment. Our C++ examples include comments for clarificational purposes; the text of these comments should not be confused with C++ code.

From these two derived classes we can create another derived class, `teachingAssistant`:

```
// declaration of derived class "teachingAssistant"
class teachingAssistant: professor, student
// (inherits members of classes "professor" and "student")
{ professor* worksFor;            // professor that TA works for
                                   // (ptr to "professor" object)
  int section;                     // section that TA teaches (integer)
  void printTA(); };               // function to print TA's info
```

In the real world, a teaching assistant is a single individual with attributes of both a professor and a student. We represent this via "multiple inheritance": class `teachingAssistant` contains the members of both `professor` and `student`, as well as the members `worksFor`, `section` and `printTA`.

An object of a nonderived class consists of a sequence of members arranged contiguously in memory; the members are arranged according to the order in which they appear in the class declaration. An object of a derived class also consists of a sequence of members; some members are inherited from the base classes, and some are declared in the derived class itself. Unlike nonderived classes, there is no way of determining the ordering of a derived class' members from the class declaration. In particular, the relative order of base- and derived-class members is implementation-dependent; base members may precede derived members, or *vice versa*.

Regardless of the relative ordering chosen by a given implementation, a derived class shares with a nonderived class the property of a fixed ordering of members over all objects of its class. That is, given a derived class D with a set of derived members and a set of underived members, each object of class D will order these members in the same sequence $m_1..m_n$. Thus given a nonderived class ND which declares the same members of D in the order $m_1..m_n$, objects of type ND will be structurally equivalent to those of type D. We shall therefore treat derived classes as if they were declared in a nonderived form; given a base class B and a class D derived from it, we simply add B and D as distinct elements in the types universe.

2.3 Virtual base classes

A class may be designated as "virtual"; the virtual status of a class affects the way in which its members are inherited by other classes. Consider our class `teachingAssistant`: this class inherits members from both `professor` and `student` classes. Since both `professor` and `student` classes in turn inherit members from the class `person`, `teachingAssistant` inherits `person`'s members from two bases. For the class `teachingAssistant` as it is currently defined, this means that the class contains two disjoint sets of `person` members. Each object of this class will have two `name` members and two `age` members, conceivably with different values. For certain applications this is desirable,[3] but if we wish to constrain objects of type `teachingAssistant` to a single `name` and `age` value, our definition of `teachingAssistant` as it stands is unsatisfactory.

To remedy this problem, we declare class `person` as a virtual class. Declaring a class as virtual ensures that any class derived from it will contain only one set of its members. We modify our declaration of class `person`, prefixing it with the keyword `virtual`:

```
// modified declaration of class "person," making class virtual
virtual class person
{ char name[25];
  int age;
  void printPerson(); };
```

With `person` declared as a virtual class, the class `teachingAssistant` still inherits the members of `person` from two bases, but objects of class `teachingAssistant` will contain only a single `name` member and a single `age` member.

Virtual base classes do not require any changes to the algebra. The virtual status of a base class affects only static information about a class subsequently derived from it: namely, the sequence of members it contains. Following our example, if we were to declare `person` nonvirtual, the members contained in `teachingAssistant` may be arranged as the sequence {name, age, S, name, age, P, TA}, where S, P and TA are sequences of the members defined in classes `student`, `professor` and `teachingAssistant`, respectively.[4] Declaring `person` virtual would simply truncate this sequence to {name, age, S, P, TA}. As the number and types of a class' members are statically determined, and the effect of a class' virtual status extends only to this static information, the introduction of virtual base classes does not require any changes to the algebra rules.

---

[3]For an example in which duplication of inherited members is desirable, consider a derived class representing a research project between a professor and a student:

```
// declaration of class "researchProject"
class researchProject: professor, student
{ char topic[25];                        // research topic
  int funding; };                        // amount of funding for research
```

This class contains information representing a professor and a student, two distinct people. Here it is necessary to inherit separate copies of the `person` members; the `name` and `age` members corresponding to the professor and student will have distinct values. Thus the class `person` should be declared as nonvirtual in this case.

[4]This is only one possible ordering of members; as noted in section 2.2, the relative ordering of derived and underived members is implementation-dependent.

2.4 Access control

Class members may be specified as "public," "private" or "protected." These specifications restrict the "accessibility" of the members, *i.e.*, the set of functions which may access them. A "private" member may only be accessed by a member function of the class in which it is declared; a function that is not a member of any class or is the member of a different class, even a derived class which inherits the private member, may not refer to it. A "protected" member is less restricted: it may be accessed by a member function of any class in which it is declared or inherited. A "public" member may be accessed by any function, regardless of the function's class membership. For example, let us assign private status to the name and age members of class person:

```
// modified declaration of class "person," specifying access status
virtual class person
{ private:
  char name[25];
  int age;
  public:
  void printPerson(); };
```

Since name, age and printPerson are declared in the class person, the private status of name and age does not prevent printPerson from accessing these members:[5]

```
// definition of "printPerson" function for class "person"
person::printPerson()
// print the "name" and "age" members of the "person" object
{ output("name:", name);            // note reference to "name"
  output("age:", age); }            // note reference to "age"
```

On the other hand, printProfessor is not declared in the same class as name or age. Therefore, name and age cannot be accessed by printProfessor. If we had assigned name and age protected status, printProfessor would have been able to access these members, as printProfessor's class professor is a derived class containing name and age members.

Access to a class' private members may be granted to nonmember functions by giving them "friend" status within the class declaration. For example, we can define a global version of our printPerson function that is not a member of the person class:

```
// definition of global function "globalPrintPerson"
void globalPrintPerson(person p)
{ output("name:", p.name);                    // reference to "name"
```

---

[5] In this and following examples, we assume that the function output simply takes a sequence of arguments, of any number, and sends their values to an output device. We do not define the function explicitly.

```
   output("age:", p.age); }                    // reference to "age"
```

For the nonmember function `globalPrintPerson` to access the private members `name` and `age`, we must declare it as a friend to `person` within the class declaration:

```
// modified declaration of class "person,"
// allowing function "globalPrintPerson" to access private members
virtual class person
{ private:
   char name[25];
   int age;
   public:
   void printPerson();                         // member function
   friend void globalPrintPerson(person); };   // global function
```

Access status is a purely syntactic feature; since each member's status is assigned in the declaration of the class and cannot be changed, access restrictions can be enforced before the program is run and need not be enforced later. A member's status has no further effect on either the member itself or the functions which access it. Therefore, no algebra rules need to be changed to accommodate this feature.

2.5   Scope resolution operator

In both C and C++, names may differ in their scope. In C, a name may be either global or local; in C++, the situation is more complex, as a nonglobal name may have scope over any of a number of nested classes. The possibility of overlapping scopes leads to potential ambiguity. For example, let us add a member `course` to the class `professor`; `course` will itself be a class, containing the members `name`, `studentsEnrolled` and `print`:

```
// modified declaration of class "professor," with member "course"
class professor:   private person
{ private:
   int salary;
   class course                       // course that professor teaches
   { private:
      char name[25];                  // name of course (string)
      int studentsEnrolled;           // number of students (integer)
      public:
        void print(); };              // function to print info about course
   public:
   void nonvirtualPrint();
   void virtualPrint(); };
```

The class `professor` contains two instances of the member name `name`: one inherited from the base class `person`, and one nested inside the class `course`. Both instances have scope over the nested class `course`. If we introduce a global variable `name`,

```
// declaration of global variable "name"
char name[25];                                          // name of university
```

we now have three identical names with scope over the class course.[6] The member function print of class course refers to name:

```
// definition of "print" function for class "course"
void professor::course::print()
{ output("course name:", name);                         // reference to "name"
  output("students enrolled:", studentsEnrolled); }
```

The identifier name here could conceivably refer to two possible variables: the member name defined inside course or the global variable name. In the event of such a reference, the more local referent of name, *i.e.*, the member of course, is selected. The global variable name is said to be "hidden." Note that the member name defined inside professor is not a possible referent; within a member function body, only members of the function's class may be referred to by a simple identifier. Thus there are two problems in our example: given the set of C++ features we have considered so far, there is no way to refer to either the global variable or the member of professor from within the class course.

The scope resolution operator :: solves both of these problems. Its unary form allows for references to hidden global variables; the single operand is the name of a global variable, and the expression refers to the global variable of that name. Its binary form allows for references to members of enclosing classes. The left-hand operand is the name of an enclosing class, and the right-hand operand is the name of a member of the enclosing class; the expression refers to the member of the given name within the enclosing class of the given name. For example, the function print within course can refer to the global variable name using the unary form of the scope resolution operator, and to the name member of person via the binary form:

```
// modified definition of "print" function for class "course,"
// using scope resolution operator
professor::course::print()
{ output("university:", ::name);                        // global variable
  output("professor:", professor::name);                // "professor" member
  output("course name:", name);                         // "course" member
  output("students enrolled:", studentsEnrolled); }
```

Neither form of the scope resolution operator requires changes to the algebra. An expression consisting of an variable name preceded by the unary operator is simply a reference to the global variable of that name; such an expression corresponds to a simple identifier task. An expression

---

[6]Of course, this is bad programming practice; the confusion here could be easily eliminated by choosing more descriptive labels for the three name variables.

involving the binary form of the operator corresponds to a "data-member" task, which we discuss in sections 3.1 and 3.2. We treat such expressions as class-reference tasks, referring to a member within an object and involving a statically determined offset to the member, provided by the *ConstVal* function. The assumptions made in section 3.2 to handle data-member tasks will also handle binary scope resolution expressions.

3 Programmer-defined class operations

In object-oriented programming, the operations that access a given data type are included as part of the definition of the type. As C does not allow functions to be included as part of a type definition, C++ introduces this possibility for class types; this is discussed in sections 3.1 and 3.2. Functions associated with a class may be declared as "virtual." If a function is so declared, references to it will rely on dynamic rather than static type resolution. The features supporting virtual functions are presented in sections 3.3 and 3.4.

3.1 Member functions

The first extension requiring a change in the algebra is the ability of classes to have functions as members. This is not allowed in C; inclusion of a function field in a C `struct` type is illegal. This extension involves changes to the algebra because the way in which member functions are accessed does not parallel the way in which other members are accessed. Unlike members of other types, referred to as "data members," a member function does not occupy a memory area at some predetermined offset from the starting location of its class; thus our rule for member references as it stands is incapable of handling a reference to a member function.

The value returned by a reference to a member function must be the starting address of the function. For nonvirtual functions,[7] this address is statically determined and cannot be changed. Thus a given nonvirtual member function reference refers to a particular, unchangeable function address; in other words, a particular memory address is associated with each such reference task. We therefore define a partial function *FunLoc: tasks* → *addresses* which maps a member function reference to the corresponding starting address of the member function. To distinguish between member functions and data members, we add the values *data* and *nonvirtual-function* to the *tags* universe, and a function *MemberStatus: tasks* → *tags* to determine whether a given member reference is a reference to a member function or to a data member. We change the task-type tag *struct-reference* to *class-reference*, in keeping with our new terminology. Our new rule for class references is shown in Fig. 1.

---

[7]The situation is somewhat more complicated for "virtual" functions, which we discuss in section 3.4.

```
if TaskType (CT) = class-reference then
    if ValueMode (CT) = lvalue then
        ReportValue (OVal (CT, ST) + ConstVal (CT))
    elseif ValueMode (CT) = rvalue then
        if MemberStatus (CT) = data then
            ReportValue (ObjValue (OVal (CT, ST) + ConstVal (CT)))
        elseif MemberStatus (CT) = nonvirtual-function then
            ReportValue (FunLoc (CT))
        endif
    endif
    Moveto (NextTask (CT))
endif
```

FIG. 1. TRANSITION RULE FOR CLASS REFERENCE EXPRESSIONS.

Allowing functions as members means that members may in some cases be accessed without an explicit class reference. In particular, inside the body of a member function a reference to a member of the function's class may be made simply by an expression consisting of the member's name; no class name or class-reference operator need appear. Consider our example in section 2.4: within the body of the member function printPerson, the class' name and age members are referred to simply as "name" and "age." This is possible because name, age and printPerson are members of the same class.

To handle such references within member functions, we shall treat them in the same way as explicit class references; an expression of this form will correspond to a class-reference task. As the left operand is missing from these implicit class-reference expressions, the question arises as to what the left-operand value as defined by *OVal* should be. As this requires consideration of certain issues that we have not yet addressed, we shall wait until the next section before answering this question.

3.2 Implicit this parameters

Every member function has a hidden argument that is not included explicitly in either the function's list of parameter declarations or the list of argument expressions in a call to the function. This hidden argument's value is always the address of the class object of which the function is a member. Thus in our example in section 2.4, the function person::printPerson is explicitly defined as a nullary function, and no arguments are supplied when it is called; nevertheless, it is in fact a one-place function whose sole argument is a pointer to the class object.

To support this in our algebra, we assume that each member function does indeed take a class-pointer argument in addition to the arguments explicitly defined by the programmer: in particular, we assume the existence of an implicit parameter declaration in the function body. We wish to be able to distinguish this parameter as the implicit class-pointer parameter; we do this by adding the partial function *IsImplicitParm: tasks* → {*true, false*}, which determines whether a given declaration task is the declaration of an implicit parameter. We also add the partial function *ImplicitParm: stack* → *tasks*, which returns the declaration task of the implicit class pointer for a given level of the stack. When the parameter declaration task for the implicit parameter is encountered, we change the *ImplicitParm* function to return this declaration task. Our new rule for parameter declarations is shown in Fig. 2.

---

if TaskType (CT) = *parameter-declaration* then
   DoAssign (NewMemory (CT), ParamValue (CT, ST), VType (CT))
   OVal (CT, ST) := *NewMemory (CT)*
   if IsImplicitParm (CT) = *true* then
      ImplicitParm (ST) := *CT*
ENDIF

FIG. 2. TRANSITION RULE FOR PARAMETER DECLARATIONS.

We also assume the existence of an expression task returning the address of the function's class in each call to a member function. We introduce the macro *ThisPtr* to express the value of the implicit class-pointer parameter. Within a member function, the value of the implicit parameter can be accessed via an expression consisting of the keyword **this**. To handle this new type of expression, we introduce a tag, *this*, and a corresponding rule. The definition of *ThisPtr* and the rule for **this** expressions are shown in Fig. 3.

---

macro ThisPtr: MemoryValue (OVal (ImplicitParm (ST), ST),
                            VType (ImplicitParm (ST)))

if TaskType (CT) = *this* then
   ReportValue (ThisPtr)
   Moveto (NextTask (CT))
endif

FIG. 3. MACRO *ThisPtr*; TRANSITION RULE FOR **this** EXPRESSIONS.

With the *ThisPtr* macro returning the implicit class pointer parameter value, we are now able to handle a member function's references to members of its own class. For a nonfunction member, the value to return for such a reference is the memory address value of the implicit parameter, offset by some value determined by *ConstVal*. For a reference to a function member, the value to return is the function's memory location, determined via *FunLoc* with either the static or object type of the implicit parameter. Assuming that we treat member references within a member function as class-reference tasks, we simply define the task's left-operand value to be the value *ThisPtr*. Thus the implicit class-reference name in our example in section 2.4 will be equivalent to the explicit class reference this->name.

3.3 Object type

In C++, each class object has a particular type associated with it. If the object has been allocated as the memory location for a variable of a certain class type, the object's type will simply be the predetermined "static type" of the variable. In the simple case, a class object's type also corresponds to the static type of a pointer variable pointing to it; the variable is declared as a pointer to a particular class, and the object that it points to is of that class. However, this is not necessarily true; under certain conditions an object's type may differ from the static type of a variable pointing to it.

First, a pointer with a given static type, say A*, may be assigned the address of an object of a different static type, say B, by explicitly casting the address as type A*. In this case, the static type of A* would dictate that the static type of its dereferencing is A; however, the type of the object it points to is B. Second, given a hierarchy of a base class and one or more classes derived from it, and a variable declared as a pointer to an object of the base class, the pointer may be assigned to point to an object of either the base class or any of the classes derived from it, without any casting. For example, let us assume the following variable declarations, using our predefined person, professor and student classes:

```
// declaration of "personObject," "profObject" and "studentObject"
person personObject;
professor profObject;
student studentObject;
```

We shall also assume the declaration of personPtr,[8] defined as a pointer to an object of class person:

```
// declaration of variable "personPtr"
person* personPtr;
```

The object type of personObject, profObject and studentObject is fixed at the time of their declaration: the object type of personObject is person, the object type of profObject is professor, and the object type of studentObject is student. The value of personPtr can be changed to point to any of the objects defined by personObject, profObject or studentObject,[9] without having to cast the new values as type person*:

---

[8] In general, given a type name T the type name T* is a pointer type that points to an object of type T. Thus the type name person* in personPtr's declaration denotes a pointer type that points to an object of class person.

[9] The unary operator & returns the memory location of its operand; thus in our example, we set personPtr to the address of personObject, profObject, and so on.

```
personPtr = &personObject;        // object type is "person"
personPtr = &profObject;          // object type is "professor"
personPtr = &studentObject;       // object type is "student"
```

Furthermore, the object type of each object pointed to by `personPtr` will remain the same; it will not be affected by the assignment expressions.

An object's type is information stored in the object itself and determined at the time of initialization of the object. Thus while a variable can point to objects of different types, the type of an object *per se*, as a sequence of fields at a particular memory location, cannot change.

To keep track of an object's type, we simply associate a type with the object's location in memory. We define a partial function *ObjType: addresses → types*, which returns the type of the object at the given memory location. When a new object is initialized, either by a variable declaration or by use of the `new` operator,[10] the *ObjType* function is changed to reflect the type of the object at the new address.

We must alter the rules for both automatic and static variable declarations. As the changes required for the two rules are identical, we show only the automatic variable case, in Fig. 4.

---

if TaskType (CT) = declaration and DecType ≠ static then
   if Defined (Initializer (CT)) and Undefined (RVal (CT, ST)) then
      Moveto (Initializer (CT))
   else
      OVal (CT, ST) := NewMemory (CT)
      ObjType (NewMemory (CT)) := VType (CT)
      if Defined (Initializer (CT)) then
         DoAssign (NewMemory (CT), RVal (CT, ST), VType (CT))
      else
         Moveto (NextTask (CT))
ENDIF

FIG. 4. TRANSITION RULE FOR AUTOMATIC VARIABLE DECLARATIONS.

3.4 Virtual functions

The importance of object type is manifested in its interaction with "virtual functions." A member function may be labeled "virtual" by placing the keyword `virtual` before the definition of the function. A function defined as virtual for a base class is also virtual for all classes derived from the base class, even if the function is redefined in a derived class. The virtual nature of a member function manifests itself in the case where the function is originally defined in a base class and redefined in a derived class. In such a case, an access of the member name may refer to either the base-class

---

[10] The `new` operator is discussed in section 4.1.

version or the derived-class version of the function; the difference between a virtual and a nonvirtual function is in the way in which the correct version is chosen. For a nonvirtual function, the choice is based on the static type associated with the function's class; for a virtual function, the choice is based on the type associated with the class object.

As an example, let us add member functions to the classes person and professor. In place of the functions printPerson, globalPrintPerson and printProfessor, we add the functions virtualPrint and nonvirtualPrint to person and the function virtualPrint to professor:

```
// modified declaration of class "person," with new members
virtual class person
{ private:
    char name[25];
    int age;
  public:
    virtual void virtualPrint();           // virtual print function
    void nonvirtualPrint(); };              // nonvirtual print function
// modified declaration of class "professor," with new members
class professor: person
{ private:
    int salary;
  public:
    virtual void virtualPrint(); };         // virtual print function
```

These functions simply print the member values of the class:

```
// definition of nonvirtual print function for class "person"
void person::nonvirtualPrint()
{ output("Nonvirtual print function for 'person' object");
  output("name:", name);                  // print "name" member
  output("age:", age); }                  // print "age" member
// definition of virtual print function for class "person"
void person::virtualPrint()
{ output("Virtual print function for 'person' object");
  output("name:", name);                  // print "name" member
  output("age:", age); }                  // print "age" member
// definition of virtual print function for class "professor"
void professor::virtualPrint()
{ output("Virtual print function for 'professor' object");
  person::nonvirtualPrint();              // print function for class "person"
  output("salary:", salary); }            // print "salary" member
```

Let us assume the declaration of a variable profObject, of type professor. This will initialize an object of type professor. A variable of type person* may then be assigned to point to this object:

```
// declaration of variables "profObject" and "personPtr"
person* personPtr = &profObject;          // points to "profObject"
```

Thus according to the static type of the variable personPtr, the type of the object it points to is `person`; however, the object type of `personPtr`'s dereferencing is `professor`. The member functions `personPtr->nonvirtualPrint` and `personPtr->virtualPrint` will now exhibit different behaviors.[11] Since `nonvirtualPrint` is a nonvirtual function, a function call of the form `personPtr->nonvirtualPrint()` will call the version of `nonvirtualPrint` as defined by the static type of `personPtr`'s dereferencing, namely `person`. The resulting output will be

```
Nonvirtual print function for "person" object
name:  Hazel Motes     age:  45
```

On the other hand, `virtualPrint` is a virtual function, so a function call of the form `personPtr->virtualPrint()` will call the version of `virtualPrint` as defined by the object type of `personPtr`'s dereferencing, namely `professor`. The output will be

```
Virtual print function for "professor" object
name:  Hazel Motes     age:  45     salary:  50000
```

Virtual functions require a change to the rule for class references. The rules for accessing virtual member functions will be different from that for accessing data members; while accessing a data member merely requires the address of the class object and an offset to the correct member, accessing a virtual function member involves the type of the object. To determine the correct address of a virtual function reference, we redefine *FunLoc* as a binary function: $tasks \times types \rightarrow addresses$, which determines the address for a given member function identifier and class type. In the case of a nonvirtual function, the type argument provided will be the static type associated with the member's class, as determined by the *VType* function; in the case of a virtual function, the argument will be the class object's type, as determined by *ObjType*. We also introduce a new element *virtualfunction* to the *tags* universe, to signify a reference to a virtual function member. Our new rule for class references is shown in Fig. 5.

4 Object creation and destruction

C++ introduces convenient mechanisms for creating and destroying objects. The operator `new` allocates memory for a new object, while the operator `delete` deallocates memory already associated with an object. These operators are covered in sections 4.1 and 4.2 respectively. In addition, the programmer may define functions to be invoked implicitly when an object is created or destroyed. Discussion of these "constructor" and "destructor" functions appears in sections 4.3 and 4.4 respectively.

---

[11]The class member access operator `->` returns the value of the field specified by its right-hand operand, in the class object that its left-hand operand points to. In other words, it performs a member access on the dereferencing of its left-hand operand. Thus the expressions `personPtr->nonvirtualPrint` and `(*personPtr).nonvirtualPrint` are equivalent.

if TaskType (CT) = class-reference then
   if ValueMode (CT) = lvalue then
      ReportValue (OVal (CT, ST) + ConstVal (CT))
   elseif ValueMode (CT) = rvalue then
      if MemberStatus (CT) = data then
         ReportValue (ObjValue (OVal (CT, ST) + ConstVal (CT)))
      elseif MemberStatus (CT) = nonvirtual-function then
         ReportValue (FunLoc (CT, VType (CT)))
      elseif MemberStatus (CT) = virtual-function then
         ReportValue (FunLoc (CT, ObjType (OVal (CT, ST))))
      endif
   endif
   Moveto (NextTask (CT))
endif

FIG. 5. TRANSITION RULE FOR CLASS REFERENCE EXPRESSIONS.

4.1 The new operator

C++ introduces an operator `new` for dynamic object creation. This operator takes a type name as an operand; it allocates a region of memory whose size corresponds to that of the indicated type and then returns the memory location of this newly allocated memory. In other words, it creates an object of a given type and returns a pointer value to it. For example, the expression `new person` allocates enough space for the `name` and `age` members of a `person` object and returns a pointer value to this newly allocated space. Memory allocation is accomplished by a call to the global function `operator new`; if the object being allocated contains a member function `operator new`, the member function is called instead.

The `new` operator introduces a new task type tag, *new-object*, to the universe of tags. As with variable declarations, an initializing expression, if one exists, is evaluated; the evaluation task for this initializer is determined by the function *Initializer*. We introduce a partial function *Allocator: tasks → tasks*, which maps each expression involving the `new` operator to a task which calls the appropriate version of `operator new`. This function call changes the *OVal* function, setting the `new` expression's value to a new memory location. In addition, we modify the *ObjType* function to indicate that a new object of a particular type has been initialized at the new memory location. Once a location has been established for the new object, it is returned as the value of the `new` expression; if an initializer is provided, the object is assigned its value. Our new rule is shown in Fig. 6.

4.2 The delete operator

The `delete` operator reverses the effects of the `new` operator: given the address of an object as an operand, it deallocates the memory allocated for the object, allowing subsequent memory allocations to use the object's

```
if TaskType (CT) = new-object then
    if Defined (Initializer (CT)) and Undefined (RVal (CT, ST)) then
        Moveto (Initializer (CT))
    elseif Undefined (OVal (CT, ST)) then
        Moveto (Allocator (CT))
    else
        ObjType (OVal (CT, ST)) := PointsToType (CT)
        ReportValue (OVal (CT, ST))
        if Defined (Initializer (CT)) then
            DoAssign (OVal (CT), RVal (CT, ST),
                        PointsToType (CT))
        else
            Moveto (NextTask (CT))
ENDIF
```

FIG. 6. TRANSITION RULE FOR new-OPERATOR EXPRESSIONS.

space. For example, given the declaration

```
// declaration of pointer variable "personPtr"
person* personPtr = new person;
```

the expression `delete person` deallocates the memory allocated by the `new` operator; the pointer `personPtr` no longer points to an object. Memory deallocation is accomplished by calling the global function `operator delete`; if the deallocated object contains a member function of this name, its member function will be called. An expression with the `delete` operator returns a value of type `void`.

We add a new task type tag *delete-object* to the universe of tags. We add a partial function *Destructor: tasks → tasks*, which maps each expression involving the `delete` operator to a task which calls the appropriate version of `operator delete`. The rule for the `delete` operator, shown in Fig. 7, returns the operator expression's `void` value, sets the object type of the operand's memory location to an undefined value, and passes control to the task invoking the function `operator delete`.

```
if TaskType (CT) = delete-object then
    ReportValue (Void)
    ObjType (RVal (CT, ST)) := undef
    Moveto (Destructor (CT))
endif
```

FIG. 7. TRANSITION RULE FOR delete-OPERATOR EXPRESSIONS.

4.3 Constructors

When defining a class, the programmer may define special member functions to be invoked when an object of the class is created; these functions are called "constructor functions." Constructors are commonly used to initialize newly created objects with default values. It is important to note that a constructor function does not actually create a new object, in the sense of allocating new memory to be used as a class object. The name of a constructor function member within a class is simply the name of the class itself; like other function names, it may be overloaded. To illustrate, we add two constructor functions to our class **person**:

```
// modified declaration of class "person" with constructor functions
virtual class person
{ private:
    char name[25];
    int age;
  public:
    person();              // "default" constructor: requires no argument
    person(const char*, int);    // constructor taking string and int
    virtual void virtualPrint();
    void nonvirtualPrint(); };
```

The first constructor function takes no arguments; an invocation of this function fills in the **name** and **age** members with default values:[12]

```
// definition of default constructor for class "person"
person::person()
{ strcpy(name, "");        // set "name" member to null string
  age = -1; }              // set "age" member to invalid value
```

The second constructor function takes two arguments and fills in the **name** and **age** members with these argument values:

```
// definition of binary constructor function for class "person"
person::person(const char* n, int a)
{ strcpy(name, n);  // copies contents of string "n" to "name" member
  age = a; }
```

A constructor may be invoked when an automatic or static variable is declared; in the case of a static variable, it is invoked only the first time the declaration is encountered. For example, the declarations

---

[12] We assume the definition of the function **strcpy** from the **<string.h>** library. The **strcpy** function takes two string pointers as arguments and copies the first argument's string to that of the second argument.

```
// declaration of "person" variables "p1" and "p2"
person p1(), p2("Lily Hawks", 30);
```

initialize variable `p1` with the first constructor function and variable `p2` with the second constructor function. When a constructor function with no arguments, a so-called "default constructor," is defined, it may be invoked without the use of argument parentheses; thus the declaration of `p1` above is equivalent to

```
// alternate, equivalent declaration of p1
person p1;
```

Alternatively, the declaration of a variable may initialize the variable's new object in the standard C fashion, via direct assignment; in this case, the constructor function is not called.

A constructor function may also be called when a new object is allocated using the **new** operator. For example, the expression `new person("Hoover Shoats", 68)` allocates memory for a new object of class `person` and initializes it by calling the binary constructor function for `person`. Finally, a constructor may be called explicitly in the standard form for functions. Given the declaration of `p1` above, the subsequent expression `p1.person()` calls the appropriate constructor function, reinitializing `p1`'s members.

Programmer-defined constructor functions require changes to our rules for tasks which create new objects: namely, variable declarations and expressions involving the operator **new**. We add a partial function *Constructor: tasks → tasks* which maps a class-variable declaration task to a task calling the class' constructor function. After memory is allocated for the variable, the constructor function is called to initialize the new object. The modified rule for automatic variable declarations is shown in Fig. 8. As before, we must also change the rule for static variable declarations, but as the change required is identical to that for the automatic variable declaration case, we do not show the modified rule.

We make a similar change to our rule for the operator **new**. The *Constructor* function maps an instance of the operator to a constructor-function call; this function-call task is performed after allocation of memory for a new object. The modified rule is shown in Fig. 9.

4.4 Destructors

Just as constructor functions can be defined to handle initialization of new class objects, special member functions may also be defined to perform certain actions when a class object is destroyed. These functions, called "destructor functions," are invoked implicitly by a variable going out of scope or by use of the **delete** operator, or explicitly by a simple function call to the destructor. As an example, let us add a destructor function to

if TaskType (CT) = declaration and DecType ≠ static then
   if Defined (Initializer (CT)) and Undefined (RVal (CT, ST)) then
      Moveto (Initializer (CT))
   else
      OVal (CT, ST) := NewMemory (CT)
      ObjType (NewMemory (CT)) := VType (CT)
      if Defined (Initializer (CT)) then
         DoAssign (NewMemory (CT), RVal (CT, ST), VType (CT))
      elseif Defined (Constructor (CT)) then
         Moveto (Constructor (CT))
      else
         Moveto (NextTask (CT))
ENDIF

FIG. 8. TRANSITION RULE FOR AUTOMATIC VARIABLE DECLARATIONS.

if TaskType (CT) = new-object then
   if Defined (Initializer (CT)) and Undefined (RVal (CT, ST)) then
      Moveto (Initializer (CT))
   elseif Undefined (OVal (CT, ST)) then
      Moveto (Allocator (CT))
   else
      ObjType (OVal (CT, ST)) := PointsToType (CT)
      ReportValue (OVal (CT, ST))
      if Defined (Initializer (CT)) then
         DoAssign (NewMemory (CT), RVal (CT, ST), PointsToType (CT))
      elseif Defined (Constructor (CT)) then
         Moveto (Constructor (CT))
      else
         Moveto (NextTask (CT))
ENDIF

FIG. 9. TRANSITION RULE FOR new-OPERATOR EXPRESSIONS.

the class **person**:

```
// modified declaration of class "person," with destructor function
virtual class person
{ private:
  char name[25];
  int age;
  public:
  person();
  person(const char*, int);
  ~person();                                    // destructor function
  virtual void virtualPrint();
  void nonvirtualPrint(); };
```

We also add a global variable `totalPeople` to keep track of the number of allocated `person` objects:

```
// declaration of global counter variable "totalPeople"
int totalPeople = 0;
```

This global variable can be incremented and decremented in the class' constructor and destructor functions; then once the class is defined, the programmer need not perform any explicit incrementing or decrementing outside the class. We modify our constructor functions, adding a statement incrementing `totalPeople`:

```
// modified definition of default constructor for class "person,"
// including increment of global object counter
person::person()
{ strcpy(name, "");
  age = -1;
  totalPeople++; }                        // counter incremented
// modified definition of binary constructor function
// for class "person," including increment of global object counter
person::person(const char* n, int a)
{ strcpy(name, n);
  age = a;
  totalPeople++; }                        // counter incremented
```

Now each time a new object of class `person` is created, the counter `totalPeople` is incremented. The opposite action is performed by the destructor function: when an object is destroyed, the counter is decremented:

```
// definition of destructor function for class "person"
person::~person() { totalPeople--; }      // counter decremented
```

As mentioned above, the destructor function is called implicitly when a variable goes out of scope. For a local automatic variable, this is the point at which the function in which it is declared ends. For a static or global automatic variable, it is the end of the program. The destructor is also called implicitly when the `delete` operator is used to deallocate a class object. Finally, the programmer may call the destructor member function explicitly: the function name is simply the class name preceded by a tilde (~). Thus the expression `p1.~person()` will call the destructor function and decrement the global counter.

Explicit calls to destructor functions are handled by the existing rule for function invocations. However, as not all destructor-function calls are explicit in the program code, we must make them so in the representation of the program. We simply add a destructor function call task at each point where a class variable with a destructor function defined goes out of scope: this will be either at the end of a function or the end of the program, depending on the variable type. We shall refer to the sequence of implicit destructor function calls followed by a `return` task at the end of a function or program as a "return sequence."

The `delete` operator may also invoke a destructor function. To handle this, we alter our definition of the *Destructor* function: in `delete`-expression tasks involving an object of a class with a destructor function defined, the *Destructor* function maps to a task that calls the destructor function. The task following this function call, as defined in *NextTask*, is a task calling the appropriate `operator delete` function.

5 Overloading and parameterized types

C++ allows function names and operators to be "overloaded." Overloading is a loosening of the restrictions on associating names with functions. While in C a particular function name may refer to at most one function, in C++ a name may refer to a family of functions. The particular function referred to by an instance of a name is determined by the types of the arguments and return type associated with the name instance. Overloading allows the programmer to refer to conceptually similar functions with the same name. We discuss overloading in sections 5.1 and 5.2.

In a similar vein, the template mechanism allows the programmer to define a family of conceptually similar types through a parameterized type definition. An instantiation of a type from the family is attained by supplying values for the parameters. As with overloading of functions and operators, this allows the programmer to refer to similarly defined types with a single name. Template definitions are discussed in section 5.3.

5.1 Function overloading and default arguments

In C++, function names may be "overloaded": a function name may refer to more than one function declaration within the same scope. When an overloaded name is used in an expression, it refers to a particular function; the function it refers to is determined by matching the actual arguments of the function reference with the formal arguments of a function declaration.[13] As an example, let us add an overloaded function, `monthlySalary`, as a friend to the `professor` class defined in section 2.2. Within the class definition, we declare two functions, both named `monthlySalary`: the first `monthlySalary` function takes a single `int` argument, while the second `monthlySalary` function takes two `int` arguments. The first `monthlySalary` function calculates a monthly salary for the `professor` object by dividing its `yearlySalary` argument by 12:

```
// definition of unary "monthlySalary" function
int monthlySalary(int yearlySalary) { return yearlySalary / 12; }
```

---

[13]There need not be an exact match between actual and formal arguments. [ES] lays out a set of rules to determine the best match when no exact match exists. For the sake of simplicity, we shall only consider examples where formal and actual arguments match exactly.

The second `monthlySalary` function divides its integer `yearlySalary` argument by its integer `months` argument:

```
// definition of binary "monthlySalary" function
int monthlySalary(int yearlySalary, months)
{ return yearlySalary / months; }
```

A subsequent function call using the name `monthlySalary` is disambiguated by considering the arguments supplied in the function call. An expression `monthlySalary(40000)` is a call to the first function declaration, as its arguments match the formal arguments of the first declaration exactly. An expression `monthlySalary(30000, 9)` is likewise a call to the function defined in the second declaration.

Function overloading does not require any changes to the algebra because the mapping between function references and function declarations is static. When an overloaded function name is used, the function it refers to is determined by the types of its arguments; since these types are statically determined, the referent of the overloaded name is as well. For any expression task T consisting of an overloaded function name, we simply determine the best match for the function reference and assign $Decl(T)$ the declaration task of the best-match function.

Another C++ addition, related to function overloading, is the ability to supply default values for the formal arguments of a function. A function with a default value specified for one of its arguments may be called either with or without a value for that argument; if no actual argument is supplied, the default value is used. For instance, rather than defining separate unary and binary `monthlySalary` functions, we can define the function once as a binary function and give the `months` argument a default value of 12:

```
// modified definition of binary "monthlySalary" function,
// with default value for "months" argument
int monthlySalary(int yearlySalary, months = 12)
{ return yearlySalary / months; }
```

The result is identical to that of defining unary and binary `monthlySalary` functions. The function may be called with two arguments, in which case the formal argument `months` receives the value of the second argument; it may also be called with one argument, in which case `months` receives the default value 12.

There is no standard method for implementing default argument values; however, none of the different possible approaches require changes to the algebra. Functions with default argument values can be thought of as special cases of function overloading. The definition of a function with formal arguments $a_1..a_n$ and a_n assigned a default value is then essentially a definition of two functions: one with formal arguments $a_1..a_n$, and another with formal arguments $a_1..a_{n-1}$ and a local variable a_n set to the default value. Thus the above definition of `monthlySalary` would be equivalent to the following definitions:

```
// binary "monthlySalary" function
int monthlySalary(int yearlySalary, months)
{ return yearlySalary / months; }
// unary "monthlySalary" function
int monthlySalary(int yearlySalary)
{ int months = 12;
  return yearlySalary / months; }
```

An alternate approach to implementing default arguments is to define a single function and modify calls to the function, supplying default values as actual arguments if need be. For instance, our definition of `monthlySalary` above would instantiate a single binary function, and a unary function call like `monthlySalary(40000)` would be changed to `monthlySalary(40000, 12)`.

The overloaded-function approach requires no changes to the algebra, as we have seen that function overloading is a purely syntactic feature. The single-function approach does not even require function overloading; it simply involves calls to a nonoverloaded function. Thus our algebra as it stands is able to handle default argument values, regardless of their implementation.

5.2 Operator overloading

Operators may also be overloaded: in particular, they may be extended to have special meanings when applied to class objects. The user may define an "operator function" for a particular operator, taking at least one class object as an argument. When an operator is used with no class objects as operands, the result is the standard action for the operator as defined in C; when used with a class object as one of its operands, the result is a call to the operator function defined for that class. Operator functions taking different argument types may be defined for the same operator. As with overloaded functions, the operator function for a given occurrence of an operator is determined by matching the actual operands with the formal arguments of the operator functions.

As an example, we shall overload the relational operator > to accommodate our class `student`. Within the class definition, we declare two friend functions, both denoted by `operator>`:

```
// modified declaration of class "student,"
// allowing operator functions to access private members
class student:  private person
{ private:
   int year;
   float GPA;
```

```
public:
  void printStudent();
  friend int operator>(student, student);          // operator >
  friend int operator>(student, int); };           // operator >
```

Both operator functions take a **student** class object as a left operand; the first declaration defines a function taking a **student** object as a right operand, while the second defines a function taking an **int** object as a right operand. We define the first version of **operator>** so as to return a "true" value if the **year** member of the left operand is greater than that of the right operand:[14]

```
// definition of operator function > for (student, student) operands
int operator>(student s1, s2) { return s1.year > s2.year; }
```

We define the second version of the operator function so as to return a "true" value if the **year** member of the left operand is greater than the second operand:

```
// definition of operator function > for (student, int) operands
int operator>(student s, int p) { return s.year > p; }
```

When the operator **>** is used with a **student** object as its left operand, the appropriate version of the operator function is chosen based on the type of the right operand. Thus given the **student** variables **s1** and **s2**,

```
// declaration of variables "s1" and "s2"
student s1, s2;
```

the expression **s1 > s2** will result in a call to the first function, since the type of the actual argument **s2** matches that of the first function's formal argument. The expression **s1 > 5** will result in a call to the second member function, for similar reasons.

Any programmer-defined operator function can also be invoked by an explicit function call. In our example, we declared two operator functions with the name **operator>**; a function call using this name is equivalent to using the operator **>**. Thus the function calls **operator>(s1, s2)** and **operator>(s1, 5)** are equivalent to the two operator expressions above.

Operator overloading, like function overloading, does not require any changes to the algebra rules as it uses only statically determined information. The use of a given operator requires one or more operand expressions

---

[14]It should be noted that this definition is somewhat problematic. The values of the **year** members is not the only possible basis for a "greater-than" ordering of **student** objects; they could just as easily be ordered by the values of their **age** members, for instance. It may not be clear to a programmer using the **operator>** function what the basis for the ordering is. This is a common problem with defining operators for classes; one way of avoiding this confusion would be to define a function with a meaningful name, like **atSchoolLonger**, rather than an overloaded operator.

of a given type: this static type information is all that is needed to determine the correct meaning of the operator. Using a programmer-defined operator function corresponds to a function-invocation task, with the function to invoke determined statically by the types of the actual arguments. For each task T involving an overloaded operator function name, we determine the best match for the function reference and assign to $Decl(T)$ the result of this best match, as with overloaded nonoperator functions.

5.3 Templates

The template mechanism in C++ allows the programmer to define "container classes," classes containing members whose types are specified outside the class definition. A container class defines a family of classes differing in the types of some of their members but sharing common structure. "Abstract data types" such as stacks and queues can be represented as container classes. For example, the notion of a list defines the way in which list items, or nodes, are linked to one another and methods of manipulating the items but leaves undefined the type of information stored in a node. A family of list types can be defined simply by specifying different values for this type information. A template separates the structure common to all members of the family from the type information specifying a particular member of the family. A list of type arguments is supplied first, followed by a declaration; the specific type information is supplied as arguments, while the common structure is defined in the declaration.

A common example of a container class is the "singly-linked list." This abstract data type consists of two data items and a set of manipulation functions. The data items are the information contained in a node of the list and a pointer to the next node in the list, and typical manipulation functions include a print function and a node-addition function. The term "singly-linked list" denotes a family of data types all sharing the above characteristics but differing in the type of information stored in each node. We define the common characteristics within the template's declaration:

```
// definition of template "listNode" for singly-linked list node
template <class T>
class listNode
{ private:
    T data;                         // data contained in node
    listNode* next;        // ptr to node following this node in list
  public:
    void print();                 // print data for all nodes in list
    void addNode(); };                              // add node to list
```

The only information not specified in the declaration, the type of T, is supplied as an argument whenever the template is used. For example, to create a singly-linked list of person objects, we declare a variable using the listNode template:

```
listNode<person>* personList;
```

Nodes in this list have `data` members of type `person`. A linked list of nodes with data members of type `int` can be created in a similar way:

```
listNode<int>* intList;
```

A template's declaration need not be a type declaration; a family of functions can be defined by a function declaration within a template. For instance, we can create a function template `max` which, given two objects of the same type as arguments, returns the greater of the two. The function declaration within the template specifies everything except the return type of the function and the type of its arguments:

```
// definition of function template "max"
template<class T>
T max (T a, b) { return (a > b) ? a : b; }
```

The type information is supplied in a particular invocation of the template; for instance, the function call `max<int>(1, 2)` will compare the two `int` objects and return the `int` value 2. The function call `max<student>(s1, s2)` will compare two `student` objects, using our definition of > in section 5.2, and return a `student` value.

The template feature is another language facility that affects only the static information associated with a program. As stated earlier, a template defines a family of types; in terms of static type information, defining a template is equivalent to defining each type in its associated family separately. Thus we may treat types like `listNode<int>` and `listNode<person>` as entirely distinct types and functions like `max<int>` and `max<student>` as distinct functions; the fact that they are generated by the same template has no effect on the operation of the program. As templates affect only the way in which a program's static information is determined, we do not need to alter our algebra to accommodate them.

6 Other extensions

Apart from the extensions we have considered so far, C++ introduces several language features which do not fit well into any category. The extensions discussed here round out the set of C++ extensions.

6.1 Constant objects

When an object is created, it may be specified as "constant." An object so specified may be given an initial value, but this value may not be subsequently modified. Constant status is assigned by prefixing the keyword `const` to the object's type. For example, once a constant `person` object has been created from the declaration of variable `p1`,

```
const person p1 ("Leora Watts", 26);
```

an expression that simply accesses a member of the object, such as
`p1.age`, is valid, but an expression that would modify the value of a member,
such as `p1.age++`, results in an error at compile time.[15]

Apart from special considerations during compile time, constant objects
are treated no differently from nonconstant objects. Expressions and statements that would alter the value of a constant object are simply rejected
during compilation; once a program is compiled, constant and nonconstant
objects are equivalent. Thus our algebra need not be changed to accommodate constant objects.

6.2 Inline functions

A function may be declared as "inline" by prefixing the keyword `inline` to
its declaration; this indicates to the compiler that it should try to handle
calls to this function without using the standard function-call mechanism.
Rather than creating a single memory location for the function and subsequently passing control to this location each time it is called, the compiler
will try to replace each call to the function with the sequence of code contained within the function. The function name then acts much like a macro.
For example, let us declare our `monthlySalary` function as inline:

```
// modified definition of function "monthlySalary" as "inline"
inline int monthlySalary(int yearlySalary, months = 12)
{ return yearlySalary / months; }
```

If the compiler accepts the request to treat `monthlySalary` as an inline function, it will transform an expression like `monthlySalary(30000, 9)`
into an expression not involving a function call. Replacing the formal arguments of the inline function with actual arguments results in the expression
`30000 / 9`, which may then be simplified to `3333`.

The inline option affects only the static structure of a program's code;
it may modify expressions within the code, but it has no effect on the code
once it is compiled. Our algebra applies only to the compiled version of a
program; thus changes to the code made by inlining are assumed. As the
inline status of a function has no further effect on the program, we need
not change our algebra to accommodate inlining.

6.3 References

C++ introduces the "reference" as a means of attaching a name to an
object. A reference is declared in a way similar to the declaration of a
variable: a declaration contains a name for the reference and a type specification followed by the symbol `&`. A reference declaration must also contain
an initializing expression determining the object that the reference refers

---

[15]The postfix operator `++` takes a variable reference as its sole operand, returns the variable's value, and increments that value by 1. It is this last step that violates the `const` constraint on `p1`.

to. For instance, given the declaration of `personObject` in section 3.3, we may subsequently declare a reference `personReference`:

```
// declaration of reference "personReference"
person& personReference = personObject;
```

This creates a reference which returns the value of the object referred to by `personObject` each time it is used. Note that the declaration does not create a new object of type `person`; `personReference` simply refers to the existing object `personObject`. Thus a modification to `personReference`'s object is a modification to `personObject`'s object; after the assignment

`personReference.age = 22;`

the expressions `personObject.age` and `personReference.age` will both return the value 22.

Our existing rules for declarations can accommodate references, with one additional stipulation. In a reference declaration, the reference is assigned the address, *i.e.*, the "lvalue," of an object specified in the required initializer expression. We therefore stipulate that the initializer-expression task associated with a reference via the function *Initializer* returns the lvalue of its expression. In addition, we must alter the rules for identifiers and class references. The use of a reference as an identifier or class-reference expression should return the lvalue or rvalue of the reference's object. This is determined indirectly by the address stored when the reference is declared. Thus an lvalue access returns the address stored in the reference, while an rvalue access returns the value of the object stored at this address. We add a partial function *IsReference: tasks* → {*true, false*} to determine whether a given expression task is a reference expression. If the value of this function is *true*, we simply follow an extra level of indirection in accessing the identifier's value. The modified versions of the identifier and class-reference rules are shown in Fig. 10 and Fig. 11, respectively.

6.4 Exception handling

C++ adds exception handling as a means of recovering from run-time errors. A set of "exception catchers" may be associated with a block of code, a "try block." These catchers are themselves blocks of code, intended to be used as a means of recovering smoothly from run-time errors occurring within the try block. A catcher is invoked by "throwing an exception"; this results in control being passed to an exception catcher associated with an enclosing try block. An "exception" is an object, and different exception catchers are associated with different object types; thus the catcher invoked for a given exception is determined by matching the exception object's type and the type associated with a catcher. If an exception is thrown within a function and no catcher is defined for the exception within the function, the function invocation is popped off the stack, destructor functions are called for any objects local to the function, control returns to the next function

```
if TaskType (CT) = identifier then
   if ValueMode (CT) = lvalue then
      if GlobalVar (CT) = true then
         if IsReference (CT) = true then
            ReportValue (ObjValue (GlobalVarLoc))
         else
            ReportValue (GlobalVarLoc)
         endif
      elseif GlobalVar (CT) = false then
         if IsReference (CT) = true then
            ReportValue (ObjValue (LocalVarLoc))
         else
            ReportValue (LocalVarLoc)
         endif
      endif
   elseif ValueMode (CT) = rvalue then
      if GlobalVar (CT) = true then
         if IsReference (CT) = true then
            ReportValue (Deref (ObjValue (GlobalVarLoc)))
         else
            ReportValue (ObjValue (GlobalVarLoc))
         endif
      elseif GlobalVar (CT) = false then
         if IsReference (CT) = true then
            ReportValue (Deref (ObjValue (LocalVarLoc)))
         else
            ReportValue (ObjValue (LocalVarLoc))
         endif
      endif
   endif
   Moveto (NextTask (CT))
endif
```

FIG. 10. TRANSITION RULE FOR IDENTIFIER EXPRESSIONS.

invocation on the stack, and a catcher is searched for there.

To illustrate, we add exception handling to the member functions of our `person` class. As this class contains a string member, `name`, it harbors a potential run-time error common to all types containing strings: namely, the possibility of string overflow. Consider adding a member function `inputPerson` which accepts name and age values from the user and then calls the constructor function with these values. A user could enter a string longer than 25 characters, exceeding the bounds of the name member. In this case, we would like to issue a warning to the user and truncate the string to the 25-character limit. We first add a new member `nameTooLong` to serve as an "exception class"; this is the type of object to be thrown when a string overflow exception is encountered:

`// modified declaration of class "person,"`

if *TaskType (CT) = class-reference* **then**
   if *ValueMode (CT) = lvalue* **then**
     if *IsReference (CT) = true* **then**
        ReportValue (ObjValue (OVal (CT, ST) + ConstVal (CT)))
     else
        ReportValue (OVal (CT, ST) + ConstVal (CT))
     endif
   elseif *ValueMode (CT) = rvalue* **then**
     if *MemberStatus (CT) = data* **then**
       if *IsReference (CT) = true* **then**
          ReportValue (Deref (ObjValue (OVal (CT, ST)
                                       + ConstVal (CT))))
       else
          ReportValue (ObjValue (OVal (CT, ST) + ConstVal (CT)))
       endif
     elseif *MemberStatus (CT) = nonvirtual-function* **then**
       ReportValue (FunLoc (CT, VType (CT)))
     elseif *MemberStatus (CT) = virtual-function* **then**
       ReportValue (FunLoc (CT, ObjType (OVal (CT, ST))))
     endif
   endif
   Moveto (NextTask (CT))
endif

FIG. 11. TRANSITION RULE FOR CLASS REFERENCE EXPRESSIONS.

```
// with exception class "nameTooLong"
virtual class person
{ private:
  char name[25];
  int age;
  public:
  class nameTooLong { } ;       // exception class for string overflow
  person();
  person(const char*, int);
  ~person();
  void inputPerson();           // new member function "inputPerson"
  virtual void virtualPrint();
  void nonvirtualPrint();
  friend void birthday(person); };
```

Next, we modify the `person` constructor function so as to throw a nameTooLong exception if it encounters a string of length greater than 25:

```
// modified definition of binary constructor function
// for class "person," with exception "nameTooLong"
person::person(const char* n, int a)
{ if (strlen(n) > 25) throw nameTooLong;
  strcpy(name, n);
  age = a; }
```

Finally, we add the `inputPerson` function; we enclose the call to the constructor function within a `try` block and add a catcher for a `nameTooLong` exception:[16]

```
// definition of function "inputPerson," with catcher for exception
person::inputPerson()
{ char n[80];
  int a;
  try {
    input(n);
    input(a);
    person(n, a);}
  catch(nameTooLong)
  { output("Warning:   truncating name to 25 characters");
    n[24] ='\0';        // set end-of-string marker after character 25
    person(n, a); } } // call constructor again with truncated string
```

Exception handling is now in place for the `inputPerson` function. If the function is invoked and the user enters an overly long string, the `nameTooLong` exception will be thrown when the constructor function is invoked. At this point, memory is allocated for a temporary `nameTooLong` exception object. As the constructor function has no `nameTooLong` exception catcher, the function terminates and control returns to `inputPerson`. This function does contain a `nameTooLong` catcher, so control passes directly to the catcher; the warning is displayed, the name member truncated, and the constructor function invoked again.

In extending the algebra to include exception handling, we add a new task type to handle `throw` statements and a corresponding tag name *throw*. In the rule for such statements, shown in Fig. 12, we check to see whether memory has been allocated for the exception object; if no space has been allocated, we move to a task calling the `operator new` function. Once memory has been allocated, we assign to it the exception object's value; in addition, we set the value of two new nullary functions. *Unwinding*: {*true, false*}, which determines whether the stack is being unwound as the result of an exception, is set to *true*; *Exception: tasks*, which returns the `throw`-statement task that has been executed, is set to the current task:

With the introduction of exception handling, a program can be in one of two states: an exception may have been thrown and not yet handled, in which case the stack must be unwound and control passed to the nearest catcher, or it may be that no unhandled exception has been thrown, in which case control passes from one task to another as already defined. We add a new rule to be executed when a program is in the former state, *i.e.*, when the value of *Unwinding* is *true*. We also add two new functions.

---

[16] We assume that the function `input` reads input from a device and sets the value of its argument to this input value. As with the function `output`, we do not define the function explicitly.

```
if TaskType (CT) = throw then
   if Undefined (OVal (CT, StackRoot)) then
      Moveto (Allocator (CT))
   else
      Unwinding := true
      Exception := CT
      DoAssign (OVal (CT, StackRoot), RVal (CT, ST), VType (CT))
ENDIF
```

FIG. 12. TRANSITION RULE FOR **throw** STATEMENTS.

Catcher: tasks × types → tasks maps each task to the catcher associated with it for the given exception-object type. If no catcher with a given exception-object type is defined for a given task, the value of *Catcher* is *undef* for that task and type. *Return: tasks → types* maps each task to the first task of the return sequence, *i.e.*, the sequence of destructor function calls followed by a **return** statement at the end of the task's function.[17] Our rule for the "unwinding" state, shown in Fig. 13, will pass control to an exception catcher if one of the appropriate type is defined for the current task and will pass control to the return sequence at the end of the function if no catcher is defined:

```
if Unwinding = true then
   if Defined (Catcher (CT, VType (Exception))) then
      Unwinding := false
      Moveto (Catcher (CT, VType (Exception)))
   else
      Moveto (Return (CT))
ENDIF
```

FIG. 13. TRANSITION RULE FOR UNWINDING STATE.

This is the only rule that should be executed when in the unwinding state; thus we must place an extra constraint on all our other rules so that they are not executed. We make the following changes: for each rule of the form *"if G then [rule body]"* where *G* is a truth-functional guard condition, we change the rule to: *"if Unwinding = false and G then [rule body]."*

Finally, we make an assumption about the tasks within an exception catcher. As the exception object is eliminated when the catcher terminates, the destructor function for this object must be called. Thus at the end of the catcher we add a function-invocation task which calls the destructor of the exception object.

---

[17]See section 4.4 for a discussion of "return sequences."

7 Conclusion

Our algebra as it stands represents all the features of C++ as described in [ES]. Unfortunately, we cannot claim that our specification constitutes a standard version of C++, as no standard has been established for the language. [ES] has been chosen as a "starting point" for an ANSI standard; thus it seems likely that our specification will closely approximate any eventual standard.

Appendix A Macro definitions

We assume the macro definitions shown in Fig. 14. *CT*, *ST*, *OVal*, *RVal* and *VType* are simply abbreviations of functions defined in [GH]. *Defined* and *Undefined* test whether a given value is defined or undefined. The macros *GlobalVarLoc* and *LocalVarLoc* are used to determine the memory locations of global and local variables. *ObjValue* returns the value of an object, given the object's memory location. Finally, *Deref* takes a pointer value and returns the value of the object pointed to by the pointer.

---

macro CT: CurTask
macro ST: StackTop
macro OVal: OnlyValue
macro RVal: RightValue
macro VType: ValueType
macro Defined(Value): Value $\neq$ undef
macro Undefined(Value): Value $=$ undef
macro GlobalVarLoc: OVal (Decl (CT), StackRoot)
macro LocalVarLoc: OVal (Decl (CT), ST)
macro ObjValue(MemLoc): MemoryValue (MemLoc, VType (CT))
macro Deref(Value): MemoryValue (Value, PointsToType (CT))

FIG. 14. INITIAL MACRO DEFINITIONS.

Bibliography

[ES] Ellis, M. and B. Stroustrup. (1990). *The Annotated C++ Reference Manual.* Addison-Wesley.

[Gu] Gurevich, Y. (1992). "Evolving Algebras: An Attempt to Discover Semantics," in *Current Trends in Theoretical Computer Science* (ed. G. Rozenberg and A. Salomaa), World Scientific, 266-292.

[GH] Gurevich, Y. and J. Huggins. (1993). "The Semantics of the C Programming Language," in *Lecture Notes in Computer Science*, **702** (ed. E. Börger et al.), Springer-Verlag, 274-308.

[KR] Kernighan, B. and D. Ritchie. (1988). *The C Programming Language.* Prentice-Hall.

Part III: Parallel and Distributed Programs

Verification of Parameterized Programs

Zohar Manna and Amir Pnueli

1 Introduction

In this chapter we present an approach to the verification of parameterized reactive programs, using temporal logic[1].

A parameterized program consists of several similar processes whose number is determined by an input parameter. A challenging problem is to provide methods for the *uniform* verification of such programs, i.e., proving correctness of the program for *any* number of processes. The ability to conduct a uniform verification of a parameterized program is one of the striking advantages of the deductive method for temporal verification over model-checking techniques such as [2] and [1].

Let M denote the input parameter which determines the number of processes in the considered system. We can use model-checking to verify the desired properties of the system for specific values of M, such as $M = 3, 4, 5$. Usually, the model checker's memory capacity is exceeded for values of M smaller than 100. Furthermore, in the general case, nothing can be concluded about the property holding for any value of M from the fact that it holds for some finite set of values. In comparison, the deductive method establishes in one fell swoop the validity of the property for any value of M.

The verification approach presented here extends the methodology introduced in [5] to the case of parameterized programs. Preliminary examples of verification of parameterized programs were presented in [4] and [7]. Verification of safety properties of parameterized programs is discussed in [9].

We start by introducing in Section 2 our general computational model for fair transition systems, the simple concurrent programming language SPL, and the specification language of temporal logic. We then introduce parameterized programs (Section 3), and show how to verify their safety properties (Section 4) and their response properties (Section 5). In Sec-

---

[1]This research was supported in part by the National Science Foundation under grant CCR-92-23226, by the Defense Advanced Research Projects Agency under contracts NAG2-892, by the United States Air Force Office of Scientific Research under contract F49620-93-1-0139, and by the European Community ESPRIT Basic Research Action Project 6021 (REACT).

tion 6, we present verification diagrams and illustrate their use for presenting proofs of response properties. Finally, in Section 7, we present a set of examples of parameterized programs that communicate by "add-and-store" statements.

2 Preliminaries

We assume a universal set of variables $\mathcal{V}$, called the *vocabulary*. Variables in $\mathcal{V}$ are typed, where the type of a variable, such as *boolean*, *integer*, etc., indicates the domain over which the variable ranges.

We define a *state* s to be a type-consistent interpretation of $\mathcal{V}$, assigning to each variable $u \in \mathcal{V}$ a value $s[u]$ over its domain. We denote by Σ the set of all states.

2.1 Computational Model: Fair Transition System

As a computational model for reactive systems we take *fair transition systems*. Such a system consists of the following components:

- $V = \{u_1, ..., u_n\}$: A finite set of *system variables*. Some of these variables represent *data* variables, which are explicitly manipulated by the program text. Other variables are *control* variables, which represent, for example, the location of control in each of the processes in a concurrent program.
- Θ: The *initial condition*. This is an assertion characterizing all the initial states, i.e., states at which a computation of the program can start. A state is defined to be *initial* if it satisfies Θ. It is required that Θ be satisfiable, i.e., there exists at least one state satisfying Θ.
- $\mathcal{T}$: A finite set of *transitions*. Each transition $\tau \in \mathcal{T}$ is a function $\tau : \Sigma \mapsto 2^\Sigma$, mapping each state $s \in \Sigma$ into a (possibly empty) set of τ-successor states $\tau(s) \subseteq \Sigma$. A transition τ is said to be *enabled* on s iff $\tau(s) \neq \emptyset$. Otherwise τ is *disabled* on s.
- $\mathcal{J} \subseteq \mathcal{T}$: A set of *just* transitions (also called *weakly fair* transitions). The requirement of justice for $\tau \in \mathcal{J}$ disallows a computation in which τ is continually enabled beyond a certain point but taken only finitely many times.
- $\mathcal{C} \subseteq \mathcal{T}$: A set of *compassionate* transitions (also called *strongly fair* transitions). The requirement of compassion for $\tau \in \mathcal{C}$ disallows a computation in which τ is enabled infinitely many times but taken only finitely many times.

The function associated with a transition τ is represented by an assertion $\rho_\tau(V, V')$, called the *transition relation*, which relates a state $s \in \Sigma$ to its τ-successor $s' \in \tau(s)$ by referring to both unprimed and primed versions of the system variables. An unprimed version of a system variable refers to its value in s, while a primed version of the same variable refers to its value in s'. For example, the assertion $x' = x + 1$ states that the value of x in s' is greater by 1 than its value in s.

The transition relation $\rho_\tau(V, V')$ identifies state s' as a τ-*successor* of state s if
$$\langle s, s' \rangle \vDash \rho_\tau(V, V'),$$
where $\langle s, s' \rangle$ is the joint interpretation which interprets $x \in V$ as $s[x]$, and x' as $s'[x]$.

The enabledness of a transition τ can be expressed by the formula
$$En(\tau) : (\exists V')\rho_\tau(V, V'),$$
which is true in s iff s has some τ-successor.

We require that every state $s \in \Sigma$ has at least one transition enabled on it. This is often ensured by including in $\mathcal{T}$ the *idling* transition τ_I (also called the *stuttering* transition), whose transition relation is $\rho_I : (V = V')$. Thus, s' is a τ_I-successor of s iff s agrees with s' on the values of all system variables.

Let $\mathcal{S}$ be a transition system for which the above components have been identified. We define a *computation* of $\mathcal{S}$ to be an infinite sequence of states $\sigma : s_0, s_1, s_2, ...$, satisfying the following requirements:

- *Initiation:* s_0 is initial, i.e., $s_0 \vDash \Theta$.
- *Consecution:* For each $j = 0, 1, ...$, the state s_{j+1} is a τ-successor of the state s_j, i.e., $s_{j+1} \in \tau(s_j)$ for some $\tau \in \mathcal{T}$. In this case, we say that the transition τ is *taken* at position j in σ.
- *Justice:* For each $\tau \in \mathcal{J}$, it is not the case that τ is continually enabled beyond some position in σ but taken at only finitely many positions in σ.
- *Compassion:* For each $\tau \in \mathcal{C}$, it is not the case that τ is enabled on infinitely many states of σ but taken at only finitely many positions in σ.

2.2 A Simple Programming Language: Syntax

To present programs, we introduce a simple concurrent programming language (SPL) in which processes communicate by shared variables. A program is constructed out of statements which may be labeled. Labels serve as unique names for the statements and also as possible sites of control.

The following is a list of some SPL statements together with an explanation of their intended meaning. We present only the statements that are used in this chapter; the reader is referred to [6] for a description of the full language.

- *Assignment*: For a list of variables $u_1, \ldots, u_k$ and a list of expressions of corresponding types $e_1, \ldots, e_k$,
  $$(u_1, \ldots, u_k) := (e_1, \ldots, e_k)$$
  is an *assignment* statement. For the case that $k = 1$, we write simply $u := e$.

- *Await*: For a boolean expression c,
    await c

  is an *await* statement. We refer to condition c as the *guard* of the statement. Execution of **await** c changes no data variables. Its sole purpose is to wait until c becomes true, at which point it terminates.

- *Request*: For an integer variable r,
    request r

  is a *request* statement. This statement can be executed only when r has a positive value. When executed, it decrements r by 1.

- *Release*: For an integer variable r,
    release r

  is a *release* statement. Execution of this statement increments r by 1.

- *Conditional*: For statement S and a boolean expression c,
    if c **then** S

  is a (one-branch) *conditional* statement. Its execution begins by evaluating c. If c evaluates to F, execution of the statement terminates. Otherwise, subsequent steps proceed to execute S.

- *While*: For a boolean expression c and a statement S,
    while c **do** S

  is a *while* statement. Its execution begins by evaluating c. If c evaluates to F, execution of the statement terminates. Otherwise, subsequent steps proceed to execute S. When S terminates, c is tested again.

  We introduce the notation
    loop forever do S

  as an abbreviation for
    while T **do** S.

- *Concatenation*: For statements $S_1, \ldots, S_k$,
    $S_1; \cdots; S_k$

  is a *concatenation* statement. Its intended meaning is sequential composition. The first step in an execution of $S_1; \cdots; S_k$ is the first step in an execution of S_1. Subsequent steps continue to execute the rest of S_1, and when S_1 terminates, proceed to execute $S_2, S_3, \ldots, S_k$. In a program presented as a multi-line text, we often omit the separator ";" at the end of a line.

- *Selection*: For statements $S_1, \ldots, S_k$,
    S_1 **or** $\cdots$ **or** S_k

  is a *selection* statement. Its intended meaning is a non-deterministic selection of a statement S_i and its execution. The first step in the execution of the selection statement selects a statement S_i, $i = 1, \ldots, k$, that is currently enabled and performs the first step in the execution of S_i. Subsequent steps proceed to execute the rest of the selected substatement, ignoring the other S_j's. If more than one of $S_1, \ldots, S_k$ is enabled, the selection is non-deterministic.

- *Cooperation*: For statements $S_1, \ldots, S_k$,
  $$\ell: [\ell_1: S_1; \widehat{\ell_1}:] \parallel \cdots \parallel [\ell_k: S_k; \widehat{\ell_k}:]; \widehat{\ell}:$$
  is a *cooperation* statement. Its intended meaning is the parallel execution of $S_1, \ldots, S_k$. The first step in the execution of a cooperation statement is referred to as the *entry* step. It can be conceived as setting the stage for the parallel execution of $S_1, \ldots, S_k$ while moving from ℓ to $\ell_1, \ldots, \ell_k$. Subsequent steps proceed to perform steps from $S_1, \ldots, S_k$. When all $S_1, \ldots, S_k$ have terminated, there is an additional *exit* step that closes the parallel execution, and moves from $\widehat{\ell_1}, \ldots, \widehat{\ell_k}$ to $\widehat{\ell}$. Each parallel component is assigned an *entry label* ℓ_i and an *exit label* $\widehat{\ell_i}$, which is the location of control after execution of S_i terminates. Label $\widehat{\ell_i}$ can be viewed as labeling an empty statement following S_i. We refer to component $[\ell_i: S_i; \widehat{\ell_i}:]$ as a *process* of the cooperation statement, and say that statements $S_1, \ldots, S_k$ are parallel to one another.

  It is important to note that in the combination
  $$([\ell_1: S_1; \widehat{\ell_1}:] \parallel [\ell_2: S_2; \widehat{\ell_2}:]); S_3,$$
  execution of S_3 cannot start until both S_1 and S_2 have terminated.

  Execution of the cooperation statement, once it has been initialized, proceeds by *interleaving*. That is, transitions from the various processes $S_1, \ldots, S_k$ are nondeterministically chosen and executed, one at a time. The two fairness requirements, justice and compassion, ensure that a computation does not consistently ignore one of the processes forever.

Schematic Statements

The following statements provide a schematic representation of segments of code that appear in programs for solving the mutual exclusion problem. Typically, we are not interested in the internal details of this code but only in its behavior with respect to termination.

- *Noncritical*: The statement
  noncritical
  is used to represent the noncritical activity in programs for mutual exclusion, where coordination between the processes is required. It is not required that this statement terminate.
- *Critical*: The statement
  critical
  represents the critical activity in programs for mutual exclusion. It is required that this statement terminates.

It is assumed that none of these statements modify any program variables.

Programs

A program P has the form

$P ::\ \big[\text{declaration};\ [P_1 ::\ [\ell_1\colon S_1;\ \widehat{\ell}_1 :]\ \|\ \cdots\ \|\ P_m ::\ [\ell_m\colon S_m;\ \widehat{\ell}_m :]]\big],$

where $P_1 ::\ [\ell_1\colon S_1;\ \widehat{\ell}_1 :], \ldots, P_m ::\ [\ell_m\colon S_m;\ \widehat{\ell}_m :]$ are *named processes*. The names of the program and of the processes are optional, and may be omitted. The *body* $[\ell_i\colon S_i;\ \widehat{\ell}_i :]$ of process P_i consists of a (possibly labeled) statement $\ell_i : S_i$ and an exit label $\widehat{\ell}_i$, which is where control resides after execution of S_i terminates. Label $\widehat{\ell}_i$ can be viewed as labeling an empty statement following S_i.

A declaration consists of a sequence of *declaration statements* of the form

$$\text{variable}, \ldots, \text{variable}: \text{type }\textbf{where }\varphi.$$

Each declaration statement lists several variables that share a common type, i.e., the domain over which the variables range, and identifies their type. We use *basic types* such as **integer**, **character**, etc., as well as *structured types*, such as **array**, **list**, and **set**.

The optional assertion φ imposes constraints on the initial values of the variables declared in this statement.

Let $\varphi_1, \ldots, \varphi_n$ be the assertions appearing in the declaration statements of a program. We refer to the conjunction $\varphi : \varphi_1 \wedge \cdots \wedge \varphi_n$ as the *data-precondition* of the program.

Example (Program ANY-Y) Fig. 1 presents a simple program consisting of two processes communicating by the shared variable x, initially set to 0. Process P_1 keeps incrementing variable y as long as $x = 0$. Process P_2 has only one statement, which sets x to 1. Obviously, once x is set to 1, process P_2 terminates and some time later so does P_1, as soon as it observes that $x \neq 0$. ⌐

$$x, y: \textbf{integer where } x = y = 0$$

$$P_1 ::\ \begin{bmatrix} \ell_0: & \textbf{while } x = 0 \textbf{ do} \\ & [\ell_1 : y := y + 1] \\ \ell_2: & \end{bmatrix}\ \Big\|\ P_2 ::\ \begin{bmatrix} m_0: & x := 1 \\ m_1: & \end{bmatrix}$$

FIG. 1. Program ANY-Y: a simple concurrent program.

2.3 Semantics of the Programming Language

The semantics of the simple programming language is defined by a translation of programs into fair transition systems. This is done by showing how to construct the five components of a fair transition system for a given program.

Consider a program P given by
$$\left[\text{declaration};\ [P_1 :: [\ell_1: S_1;\ \widehat{\ell}_1 :] \| \cdots \| P_m :: [\ell_m: S_m;\ \widehat{\ell}_m :]]\right].$$
Let L_i denote the set of *locations* (labels) of process P_i, $i = 1, \ldots, m$, and $L_P = L_1 \cup \cdots \cup L_m$.

We will show how to define a fair transition system $\mathcal{S}_P$ corresponding to program P.

System Variables and States

The *system variables* V for system $\mathcal{S}_P$ consist of the *data variables* Y : $\{y_1, \ldots, y_n\}$ that are declared at the head of the program, and a single *control variable* π. The data variables Y range over their respectively declared data domains. The control variable π ranges over subsets of L_P, i.e., sets of locations. The value of π in a state denotes all the locations of the program in which control currently resides.

For example, the system variables for program ANY-Y are $V : \{\pi, x, y\}$, where x and y range over the integers, and π ranges over subsets of the location set $\{\ell_0, \ell_1, \ell_2, m_0, m_1\}$.

As states we take all possible interpretations that assign to the system variables values over their respective domains. For example, the initial state of program ANY-Y is

$$\langle \pi : \{\ell_0, m_0\},\ x : 0,\ y : 0 \rangle.$$

For a statement $\ell : S$ belonging to process P_i, we use the abbreviation
$$at\_\ell :\quad \pi \cap L_i = \{\ell\}.$$
Variable π satisfying at_ℓ implies that $\ell \in \pi$ and that no other location $\tilde{\ell} \in L_i$, $\tilde{\ell} \neq \ell$, satisfies $\tilde{\ell} \in \pi$. For example, for program ANY-Y, $\pi = \{\ell_0, m_0\}$ satisfies at_ℓ_0 and at_m_0 but does not satisfy at_ℓ_1 or at_m_1.

The Initial Condition

Let φ denote the *data-precondition* of program P. We define the *initial condition* Θ for $\mathcal{S}_P$ as
$$\Theta:\quad \pi = \{\ell_1, \ldots, \ell_m\} \wedge \varphi.$$
This implies that the first state in an execution of the program begins with the control variable set to the initial locations of the processes, and the data variables satisfying the data precondition.

For example, the initial condition for program ANY-Y is given by
$$\Theta:\quad \pi = \{\ell_0, m_0\} \wedge x = 0 \wedge y = 0.$$

Transitions

To facilitate the expression of transition relations, we introduce several abbreviations. Let L and $\widehat{L}$ be two sets of locations. The abbreviation
$$move(L, \widehat{L}):\quad \bigwedge_{[\ell] \in L} at\_\ell\ \wedge\ \pi' = (\pi - L) \cup \widehat{L}$$

expresses a simultaneous move of control from all the locations in L to the new locations in $\widehat{L}$. For the simple case that $L = \{\ell\}$ and $\widehat{L} = \{\widehat{\ell}\}$, we write $move(\{\ell\}, \{\widehat{\ell}\})$ simply as $move(\ell, \widehat{\ell})$.

We also use the abbreviation
$$pres(U): \bigwedge_{u \in U} (u' = u),$$
to denote that all variables in the set U are preserved by the transition.

To ensure that every state has some transition enabled on it, we uniformly include the idling transition τ_I in the transition system corresponding to each program. The transition relation for τ_I is
$$\rho_I: \; pres(V).$$

We proceed to define the transition relations for the transitions associated with each of the previously introduced statements.

- *Assignment*:   Consider the statement
  $$\ell: (u_1, \ldots, u_k) := (e_1, \ldots, e_k); \; \widehat{\ell}:$$
  where $\widehat{\ell}$ is the location to which control moves after the statement terminates. We refer to $\widehat{\ell}$ as the *post-location* of statement ℓ. With this statement we associate a transition τ_ℓ, with the transition relation
  $$\rho_\ell: \quad move(\ell, \widehat{\ell}) \wedge y'_1 = e_1 \wedge \cdots \wedge y'_k = e_k \wedge pres(Y - \{y_1, \ldots, y_k\}).$$
  The last conjunct claims that all data variables Y, excluding $y_1, \ldots, y_k$, retain their values over the transition τ_ℓ.

- *Await*:   With the statement $\ell:$ **await** c; $\widehat{\ell}:$, we associate a transition τ_ℓ, with the transition relation
  $$\rho_\ell: \quad move(\ell, \widehat{\ell}) \wedge c \wedge pres(Y).$$
  The transition τ_ℓ is enabled only when control is at ℓ and the condition c holds. When taken, it moves from ℓ to location $\widehat{\ell}$.

- *Request*:   With the statement $\ell:$ **request**(r); $\widehat{\ell}:$, we associate a transition τ_ℓ, with the transition relation
  $$\rho_\ell: \quad move(\ell, \widehat{\ell}) \wedge r > 0 \wedge r' = r - 1 \wedge pres(Y - \{r\}).$$
  Thus, this statement is enabled when control is at ℓ and r is positive. When executed it decrements r by 1.

- *Release*:   With the statement $\ell:$ **release**(r); $\widehat{\ell}:$, we associate a transition τ_ℓ, with the transition relation
  $$\rho_\ell: \quad move(\ell, \widehat{\ell}) \wedge r' = r + 1 \wedge pres(Y - \{r\}).$$
  This statement increments r by 1.

- *Conditional*:   With the statement $\ell:$ [**if** c **then** $\widetilde{\ell}: S$]; $\widehat{\ell}:$, we associate a transition τ_ℓ, with the transition relation
  $$\rho_\ell: \quad \begin{pmatrix} c \wedge move(\ell, \widetilde{\ell}) \\ \vee \\ \neg c \wedge move(\ell, \widehat{\ell}) \end{pmatrix} \wedge pres(Y).$$

  According to ρ_ℓ, when c evaluates to T control moves from ℓ to $\widetilde{\ell}$, and when c evaluates to F control moves from ℓ to $\widehat{\ell}$.

- *While:* With the statement ℓ: [**while** c **do** $[\widetilde{\ell}\!:\!\widetilde{S}]]$; $\widehat{\ell}\!:$, we associate a transition τ_ℓ, with the transition relation
$$\rho_\ell: \quad \begin{pmatrix} c \wedge \mathit{move}(\ell, \widetilde{\ell}) \\ \vee \\ \neg c \wedge \mathit{move}(\ell, \widehat{\ell}) \end{pmatrix} \wedge \mathit{pres}(Y).$$
According to ρ_ℓ, when c evaluates to T control moves from ℓ to $\widetilde{\ell}$, and when c evaluates to F control moves from ℓ to $\widehat{\ell}$. Note that, in this context, the post-location of $\widetilde{S}$ is ℓ. Note also that the enabling condition of τ_ℓ is $\mathit{at\_\ell}$, which does not depend on the value of c.

- *Cooperation* Excluding the body of the program, we associate with each *cooperation* statement,
$$\ell: \ [[\ell_1\!:\!S_1;\ \widehat{\ell}_1]\ \|\ \cdots\ \|\ [\ell_k\!:\!S_k;\ \widehat{\ell}_k]];\ \widehat{\ell}\!:$$
an *entry transition* τ_ℓ^{E} and an *exit transition* τ_ℓ^{X}. The corresponding transition relations are given, respectively, by
$$\rho_\ell^{\mathrm{E}}: \quad \mathit{move}(\{\ell\}, \{\ell_1, \ldots, \ell_k\}) \wedge \mathit{pres}(Y)$$
$$\rho_\ell^{\mathrm{X}}: \quad \mathit{move}(\{\widehat{\ell}_1, \ldots, \widehat{\ell}_k\}, \{\widehat{\ell}\}) \wedge \mathit{pres}(Y).$$
The entry transition begins execution of the cooperation statement by placing in π the set of locations that are just in front of the parallel statements $S_1, \ldots, S_k$. The exit transition can be taken only if all the parallel statements have terminated, which is detectable by observing that π satisfies
$$\mathit{at\_\widehat{\ell}_1} \wedge \cdots \wedge \mathit{at\_\widehat{\ell}_k}.$$
Note that the absence of entry or exit transitions associated with the body of the program is consistent with the fact that, according to the initial condition, execution starts with π set to the entry locations of the top-level processes.

- *Noncritical:* With the statement ℓ: **noncritical**; $\widehat{\ell}\!:$, we associate a transition τ_ℓ, with transition relation
$$\rho_\ell: \quad \mathit{move}(\ell, \widehat{\ell}) \wedge \mathit{pres}(Y).$$
Thus, the only observable action of this statement is to terminate. The situation that execution of the noncritical section does not terminate is modeled by a computation that does not take transition τ_ℓ. This is allowed by excluding τ_ℓ from the justice set.

- *Critical:* With the statement ℓ: **critical**; $\widehat{\ell}\!:$, we associate a transition τ_ℓ, with transition relation
$$\rho_\ell: \quad \mathit{move}(\ell, \widehat{\ell}) \wedge \mathit{pres}(Y).$$
The only observable action of the critical statement is to terminate.

The discerning reader may have observed that no transitions are directly associated with the concatenation statement. This is because each transition occurring in the execution of a concatenation statement can be attributed to one of its substatements.

When there is no danger of confusion, we will refer to the transition τ_ℓ simply as ℓ.

For example, the fair transition system corresponding to program ANY-Y has the transitions
$$\tau_I, \tau_{\ell_0}, \tau_{\ell_1}, \tau_{m_0},$$
which can also be presented as $\tau_I, \ell_0, \ell_1, m_0$. Transition τ_{ℓ_1}, for example, has the transition relation
$$\rho_{\ell_1}: \quad move(\ell_1, \ell_0) \wedge y' = y + 1 \wedge x' = x.$$

Justice and Compassion

For the simplistic programming language we have presented, the justice and compassion requirements are straightforward:

- *Justice*: As the *justice* set, we take the set of all transitions, excluding the idling transition τ_I and transitions associated with the **noncritical** statement.
- *Compassion*: As the *compassion* set, we take the set of all semaphore **request** transitions in the program. This will suffice for the examples presented in this chapter. The programs presented in [6] use additional statements, such as communication statements, that give rise to additional compassionate transitions.

Note that the transitions associated with **request** statements are both just and compassionate.

This concludes the definition of the transition system $\mathcal{S}_P$ corresponding to a program P. We refer to computations of $\mathcal{S}_P$ also as computations of P.

2.4 Requirement Specification Language: Temporal Logic

As a requirement specification language for reactive systems we take *temporal logic*.

We assume an underlying first-order assertion language $\mathcal{L}$ over interpreted symbols for expressing functions and relations over some concrete domains, such as the integers, arrays, and lists of integers. Easy reference to the location of control is provided by the predicate at_ℓ_i. We also use the expression $at\_\ell_{i,j}$ as an abbreviation for the disjunction $at\_\ell_i \vee at\_\ell_j$.

We refer to a formula in the assertion language $\mathcal{L}$ as a *state formula*, or simply as an *assertion*.

A *temporal formula* is constructed out of state formulas by applying the boolean operators $\neg$ and $\vee$ (the other boolean operators can be defined from these), and temporal operators. There are two classes of temporal operators, future and past; in this presentation we refer only to the future operators. The basic future temporal operators are:

$$\bigcirc - \text{Next} \qquad \mathcal{U} - \text{Until}$$

A *model* for a temporal formula p is an infinite sequence of states σ : $s_0, s_1, ...$, where each state s_j provides an interpretation for the vocabulary of p, i.e., the variables occurring in p.

For a given state s_j and state formula q, we write
$$s_j \models q,$$
to denote that q yields T when evaluated over s_j.

Given a model σ, we present an inductive definition for the notion of a temporal formula p holding at a position $j \geq 0$ in σ, denoted by $(\sigma, j) \models p$:

- For a state formula p,
  $(\sigma, j) \models p \quad \iff \quad s_j \models p$
  That is, we evaluate p locally, using the interpretation provided by s_j.
- $(\sigma, j) \models \neg p \quad \iff \quad (\sigma, j) \not\models p$
- $(\sigma, j) \models p \vee q \quad \iff \quad (\sigma, j) \models p$ or $(\sigma, j) \models q$
- $(\sigma, j) \models \bigcirc p \quad \iff \quad (\sigma, j+1) \models p$
- $(\sigma, j) \models p \mathcal{U} q \quad \iff \quad$ for some $k \geq j, (\sigma, k) \models q$,
  and $(\sigma, i) \models p$ for every i such that $j \leq i < k$

Additional temporal operators can be defined as follows:

$\diamondsuit p = \text{T} \, \mathcal{U} \, p$ – Eventually
$\square p = \neg \diamondsuit \neg p$ – Henceforth
$p \, \mathcal{W} \, q = \square p \vee (p \, \mathcal{U} \, q)$ – Wait-for (Unless, Weak Until)

Another useful derived operator is the *entailment* operator, defined by:
$$p \Rightarrow q \quad \iff \quad \square(p \to q).$$

Validity, Congruence, and P-Validity

For a state formula p and a state s such that p holds on s, we say that s is a p-*state*. A state formula that holds on all states is called *state valid*.

For a temporal formula p and a position $j \geq 0$ such that $(\sigma, j) \models p$, we say that j is a p-*position* (in σ).

If $(\sigma, 0) \models p$, we say that p *holds* on σ, and denote it by $\sigma \models p$. A formula p is called *satisfiable* if it holds on some model. A formula is called (*temporally*) *valid* if it holds on all models.

In the sequel, we adopt the convention by which a formula p that is claimed to be valid is state valid if p is an assertion, and is temporally valid if p contains at least one temporal operator.

Two formulas p and q are defined to be *equivalent*, denoted $p \sim q$, if the formula $p \leftrightarrow q$ is valid, i.e., $\sigma \models p$ iff $\sigma \models q$, for all models σ.

The formulas p and q are defined to be *congruent*, denoted $p \approx q$, if the formula $\square(p \leftrightarrow q)$ is valid, i.e., $(\sigma, j) \models p$ iff $(\sigma, j) \models q$, for all models σ and all positions $j \geq 0$. If $p \approx q$ then p can be replaced by q in any context, i.e., $\varphi(p) \approx \varphi(q)$ for any formula $\varphi(p)$ containing occurrences of p.

The notion of (temporal) validity requires that the formula holds over *all* models. Given a program P, we can restrict our attention to the set of models which correspond to computations of P, i.e., $\mathcal{C}omp(P)$. This leads to the notion of P-validity, by which a temporal formula p is P-*valid* (valid over program P) if it holds over all the computations of P. Obviously, any formula that is temporally valid is also P-valid for any program P. In a similar way, we obtain the notions of P-satisfiability and P-equivalence.

A state s that appears in some computation of P is called a *P-accessible* state. A state formula is called *P-state valid* if it holds over all P-accessible states. Obviously, any state formula that is state valid is also P-state valid for any program P.

Again, we adopt the convention by which we may refer to a P-state valid formula simply as P-valid.

2.5 Specification of Properties

A temporal formula φ that is valid over a program P specifies a property of P, i.e., states a condition that is satisfied by all computations of P. The properties expressible by temporal logic can be arranged in a hierarchy that identifies different classes of properties according to the form of formulas expressing them.

Here we will consider only properties falling into the two most important classes: *safety* and *response*.

Safety Properties

Safety properties are those that can be expressed by a formula generated from state formulas, the boolean operators $\vee$ and $\wedge$, and the temporal operators $\Box$ and $\mathcal{W}$. We refer to a formula of this form as a *canonical safety formula*.

The only safety properties we consider in this presentation are those that can be expressed by the *invariance* formula $\Box \varphi$, where φ is a state formula.

The following are several safety formulas that are valid over program ANY-Y and therefore specify properties of this program:

- $\Box(x = 0 \vee x = 1)$
  This formula claims that x has the values 0 or 1 in all states appearing in computations of ANY-Y.
- $\Box(x = 1 \leftrightarrow at\_m_1)$
  This formula claims that x equals 1 if and only if control of process P_2 is at location m_1.
- $at\_\ell_1 \Rightarrow at\_m_1$
  This formula claims that P_1 can be at location ℓ_1 only if control of process P_2 is at location m_1.

Response Properties

We also consider response properties that can be expressed by a formula
$$p \Rightarrow \Diamond q,$$
for state formulas p and q.

For example, the response formula

$$at\_\ell_0 \wedge at\_m_0 \Rightarrow \Diamond(at\_\ell_2 \wedge at\_m_1)$$

states the property of *termination* of program ANY-Y. This property ensures that the program eventually reaches a state in which P_1 is at ℓ_2 while P_2 is at m_1.

Verification Conditions

For a transition τ and state formulas p and q, we define the *verification condition* of τ relative to p and q, denoted $\{p\}\tau\{q\}$, to be the implication

$$(\rho_\tau \wedge p) \to q',$$

where ρ_τ is the transition relation corresponding to τ, and q', the *primed version* of the assertion q, is obtained from q by replacing each variable occurring in q by its primed version. Since ρ_τ holds for two states s and s' iff s' is a τ-successor of s, and q' states that q holds on s', it is not difficult to see that

> if the verification condition $\{p\}\tau\{q\}$ is P-state valid, then every τ-successor of a p-state is a q-state.

For a set of transitions $T \subseteq \mathcal{T}$, we denote by $\{p\}T\{q\}$ the conjunction of verification conditions $\{p\}\tau\{q\}$ for each $\tau \in T$.

In the context of program ANY-Y, consider for example the verification condition of transition ℓ_1 with respect to assertions $p = q : y \geq 0$.

$$\{y \geq 0\} \ \ell_1 \ \{y \geq 0\}.$$

Expanding the definition of the verification condition, this yields

$$\underbrace{\cdots \wedge y' = y+1 \wedge \cdots}_{\rho_{\ell_1}} \wedge \underbrace{y \geq 0}_{p} \to \underbrace{y' \geq 0}_{q'}.$$

which is state valid. This shows that every ℓ_1-successor of a state satisfying $y \geq 0$ also satisfies $y \geq 0$.

3 Parameterized Programs

Many distributed programs, in particular those that control communication and synchronization of networks, have as their body a parallel composition of many identical processes.

For example, we may consider the simple case of many processes coordinating mutual exclusion by a single semaphore. In this case, the body S of each process may have the form

$$\ell_0: \textbf{loop forever do} \begin{bmatrix} \ell_1: \textbf{noncritical} \\ \ell_2: \textbf{request } y \\ \ell_3: \textbf{critical} \\ \ell_4: \textbf{release } y \end{bmatrix}$$

The complete program, for the special case of three processes, is given by

$$\boxed{\begin{array}{l}\textbf{in}\quad M\colon \textbf{integer where } M \geq 1\\ \phantom{\textbf{in}\quad}x\,:\,\textbf{array } [1..M] \textbf{ of integer}\\ \textbf{out } z\,:\,\textbf{integer where } z=0\\[4pt] \overset{M}{\underset{j=1}{\|}}\ P[j]\,::\,\begin{bmatrix}\text{local } y\colon \text{integer}\\ \ell_0\colon\ y:=x[j]\\ \ell_1\colon\ z:=z+y\cdot y\\ \ell_2\colon\end{bmatrix}\end{array}}$$

FIG. 2. Program PAR-SUM (parallel sum of squares).

$$P^3\,::\,\Big[\textbf{local } y\colon \textbf{integer where } y=1;\ \big[S \,\|\, S \,\|\, S\big]\Big]$$

Some renaming of locations will be needed to distinguish between the three copies of S.

However, establishing the correctness of this three-process program, i.e., showing that mutual exclusion is maintained, does not formally guarantee anything about the following similar program, which has four copies of the statement S as its processes:

$$P^4\,::\,\Big[\textbf{local } y\colon \textbf{integer where } y=1;\ \big[S \,\|\, S \,\|\, S \,\|\, S\big]\Big]$$

In some cases, it is possible to treat the whole (infinite) family of programs $P^1, P^2, P^3, P^4, \ldots$ in a *uniform* way, providing a single proof that guarantees correctness of P^n for any $n \geq 1$. The key to such a uniform treatment is *parameterization*, i.e., presenting a single syntactic object that actually represents a family of objects. There are three areas that we have to parameterize: the programs, their specifications, and the corresponding verification process.

3.1 Parameterizing the Syntax of Programs

Programs may be parameterized by using compound statements of variable size. Here we only consider a variable-size *cooperation* statement, which has the following form:
$$\overset{M}{\underset{j=1}{\|}}\ S[j].$$

The *parameterized* statement $S[j]$ may contain explicit occurrences of the parameter j as a variable in expressions and as a subscript in array references. In addition, the parameter j is considered to implicitly subscript all the variables that are declared local to $S[j]$ and all the labels occurring within $S[j]$.

Example Consider program PAR-SUM of Fig. 2 that computes in z the sum of the squares of the elements of the array $x[1..M]$.

$$\boxed{\begin{array}{l}\textbf{in}\quad M\colon \textbf{integer where } M \geq 1\\ \quad x\ \colon \textbf{array } [1..M] \textbf{ of integer}\\ \textbf{out } z\ \colon \textbf{integer where } z = 0\\[4pt] \displaystyle\mathop{\|}_{j=1}^{M}\ P[j]\ ::\ \begin{bmatrix}\textbf{local } y[j]\colon \textbf{ integer}\\ \ell_0[j]\colon\ y[j] := x[j]\\ \ell_1[j]\colon\ z := z + y[j]\cdot y[j]\\ \ell_2[j]\colon\end{bmatrix}\end{array}}$$

FIG. 3. Program PAR-SUM — explicitly subscripted version.

The body of this program is a variable-size *cooperation* statement. The cooperation statement consists of a parallel composition of processes $P[1], \ldots, P[M]$. As we see in this program, the parameter j appears explicitly in the reference to $x[j]$. It is also assumed to implicitly subscript all the labels appearing in $P[j]$, as well as the variable y which is locally declared in $P[j]$. In Fig. 3 we present the same program with the subscripting by j made explicit.

Usually, we prefer to present program PAR-SUM as in Fig. 2, but to reason about its behavior in terms of the fully subscripted version as in Fig. 3.

3.2 Parameterized Transition Systems

Several extensions are necessary for the convenient representation of parameterized programs as transition systems. The main extension is the need to replace the notion of *finiteness* by that of *finite representability*.

For example, all the transition systems we have considered so far had a fixed number of transitions. This is no longer true in the case of parameterized programs. Consider, for example, statement ℓ_0 in the program of Fig. 2. This statement copies the value of $x[j]$ to the variable y, which is local to $P[j]$. Associating transitions with statements, we must have a separate transition $\tau_0[j]$ for each $j = 1, \ldots, M$. Since M is not fixed, there are unboundedly many transitions associated with the statement ℓ_0. On the other hand, we can represent all these transitions by a single *transition relation scheme* that uses j as a parameter. This transition scheme is given by

$$\rho_0[j]\colon\quad move\bigl(\ell_0[j],\ \ell_1[j]\bigr)\ \wedge\ y'[j] = x[j].$$

Consider a fully subscripted program, such as the one presented in Fig. 3; it is quite straightforward to define the transition system associated with it. Let us point out the main constituents of this transition system.

- *System Variables*
  These consist of

π M x z y.

The variable π ranges over sets of locations, some of which may be subscripted, e.g., of the form $\ell_1[j]$ for various j's. Arrays, whether explicit (e.g., x) or implicit (e.g., y in Fig. 2), are treated as variables that range over functions. Thus, x and y are considered as functions from the (subscript) domain $[1..M]$ to the integers.

- *Initial Condition*

  $\Theta:$ $\pi = \{\ell_0[1], \ldots, \ell_0[M]\} \land M \geq 1 \land z = 0.$

- *Transitions*

  The transitions of the program consist of

  $\ell_0[j]$:   place $x[j]$ in $y[j]$.
  $\ell_1[j]$:   add $y[j] \cdot y[j]$ to z.

We present below a computation of program PAR-SUM for the case that $M = 2$ and $x = \langle 1, 2 \rangle$. For each state, we list the current values of π, z, and y.

$$\langle\{\ell_0[1],\ \ell_0[2]\},\ 0,\ \langle -,\ -\rangle\rangle \xrightarrow{\ell_0[2]}$$
$$\langle\{\ell_0[1],\ \ell_1[2]\},\ 0,\ \langle -,\ 2\rangle\rangle \xrightarrow{\ell_1[2]} \langle\{\ell_0[1],\ \ell_2[2]\},\ 4,\ \langle -,\ 2\rangle\rangle \xrightarrow{\ell_0[1]}$$
$$\langle\{\ell_1[1],\ \ell_2[2]\},\ 4,\ \langle 1,\ 2\rangle\rangle \xrightarrow{\ell_1[1]} \langle\{\ell_2[1],\ \ell_2[2]\},\ 5,\ \langle 1,\ 2\rangle\rangle$$

To retrieve the value of the kth element of any array y, we use the notation $y[k]$ that can be viewed as applying the function y to the argument k. To represent the modification of an array x, we use the notation

$$update(x,\ k,\ e).$$

The value of this expression is an array that agrees with x on all subscript values $i \neq k$, and has as its kth element the value of e.

The main properties of the *update* function are

$update(x,\ k,\ e)[k] = e$
$j \neq k \rightarrow update(x,\ k,\ e)[j] = x[j].$

Thus, the proper representation of the transition relation for $\ell_0[j]$ is

$\rho_0[j]$: $move(\ell_0[j],\ \ell_1[j]) \land y' = update(y,\ j,\ x[j]).$

When there is no danger of confusion, we will abbreviate equalities of the form $y' = update(y, k, e)$, to $y'[k] := e$. Note that even if the transition modifies k, the value to be used is that of k rather than k'.

3.3   Examples

We present two examples that illustrate the structure of parameterized programs. In later discussions, we will specify and verify these two examples.

Example (multiple mutual exclusion by semaphores)

To illustrate the succinct way in which a parameterized program represents an infinite family of programs, consider the parameterized program MPX-SEM (Fig. 4) that achieves mutual exclusion by semaphores.

In this program we use incrementation modulo M, defined by

```
in     M: integer where M ≥ 2
local y : array [1..M] of integer
        where y[1] = 1, y[j] = 0 for 2 ≤ j ≤ M

  M         ⎡ℓ_0: loop forever do                      ⎤
  ∥  P[j] ::⎢    ⎡ℓ_1: noncritical        ⎤            ⎥
 j=1        ⎢    ⎢ℓ_2: request y[j]       ⎥            ⎥
            ⎢    ⎢ℓ_3: critical           ⎥            ⎥
            ⎣    ⎣ℓ_4: release y[j ⊕_M 1] ⎦            ⎦
```

FIG. 4. Program MPX-SEM (multiple mutual exclusion by semaphores).

```
local y: array [1..2] of integer where y[1] = 1, y[2] = 0

          ⎡ℓ_0[1]: loop forever do              ⎤
          ⎢       ⎡ℓ_1[1]: noncritical  ⎤       ⎥
  P[1] :: ⎢       ⎢ℓ_2[1]: request y[1] ⎥       ⎥
          ⎢       ⎢ℓ_3[1]: critical     ⎥       ⎥
          ⎣       ⎣ℓ_4[1]: release y[2] ⎦       ⎦

            ∥

          ⎡ℓ_0[2]: loop forever do              ⎤
          ⎢       ⎡ℓ_1[2]: noncritical  ⎤       ⎥
  P[2] :: ⎢       ⎢ℓ_2[2]: request y[2] ⎥       ⎥
          ⎢       ⎢ℓ_3[2]: critical     ⎥       ⎥
          ⎣       ⎣ℓ_4[2]: release y[1] ⎦       ⎦
```

FIG. 5. Program MPX-SEM — elaboration for $M = 2$.

$$j \oplus_M 1 = (j \bmod M) + 1 = \begin{cases} j+1 & \text{if } j < M \\ 1 & \text{if } j = M \end{cases}$$

In Fig. 5 we present one member of the family, corresponding to $M = 2$, in which we explicitly represent the dependence of the locations on the process' subscript. ∎

Example (finding the maximum of an array)

As another illustrative example, consider program MAX-ARRAY given in Fig. 6. This program places in the output variable z the maximum ele-

```
┌─────────────────────────────────────────────────────────────────┐
│        in    M: integer where M ≥ 1                             │
│              x : array [1..M] of integer                        │
│        local y : array [1..M] of boolean where y = T            │
│        out   z : integer                                        │
│                                                                 │
│        ℓ₀:    ||      P[i,j] ::  ⎡ℓ₁: if x[i] < x[j] then ℓ₂: y[i] := F⎤ │
│            i,j∈[1..M]             ⎣ℓ₃:                              ⎦ │
│                                                                 │
│                 M                                               │
│        ℓ₄:    ||   Q[i] ::   ⎡ℓ₅: if y[i] then ℓ₆: z := x[i]⎤   │
│                i=1            ⎣ℓ₇:                          ⎦   │
│        ℓ₈:                                                      │
└─────────────────────────────────────────────────────────────────┘
```

FIG. 6. Program MAX-ARRAY (finding maximum of an array).

ment of the integer array x. A unique feature of this program is that the maximum value is computed in a highly parallel fashion.

The initial value of array y is specified to be $y[j] = \text{T}$ for all $j = 1, \ldots, M$.

The first statement spawns into M^2 processes. Each process $P[i,j]$ sets the boolean variable $y[i]$ to F if the array element $x[i]$ is smaller than the element $x[j]$. After all the processes in the cooperation statement ℓ_0 have terminated, we are guaranteed that, for every i such that $x[i]$ is not maximal in x, $y[i] = \text{F}$. It follows that $y[i] = \text{T}$ iff $x[i]$ is maximal.

The parallel processes spawned in ℓ_4 set z to $x[i]$ if $x[i]$ is maximal. Note that, since there may be more than one i such that $x[i]$ is maximal, more than one process may assign a value to z, but all the assigned values are the same.

The statement comprising the body of the MAX-ARRAY program may be inserted anywhere in a larger program, where we have an array $x[1..M]$ and need to efficiently compute its maximum[2]. The variable M may assume different values in different entries to this statement. On each entry, the appropriate number of processes is spawned.

3.4 Specifying Parameterized Programs

To specify and reason about parameterized programs, we introduce some conventions and special notation.

Subscripted Locations

An important requirement for the specification of parameterized programs is the ability to refer to parameterized locations. We use integer variables

---

[2] Program MAX-ARRAY is very efficient in terms of time, but may be considered wasteful in terms of space requirements.

to subscript locations, and allow the general integer operations, predicates, and quantifiers to be applied to these variables.

Thus, to specify the property of mutual exclusion for program MPX-SEM (Fig. 4) for an arbitrary M, $M \geq 2$, we may use the formula
$$\forall i,j \in [1..M]\colon i \neq j\colon \quad \Box \underbrace{\neg\bigl(at\_\ell_3[i] \wedge at\_\ell_3[j]\bigr)}_{\psi[i,j]} \ .$$
This formula states that for every two distinct processes $P[i]$ and $P[j]$, $i, j \in [1..M]$, $i \neq j$, it is never the case that control is at $\ell_3[i]$ and $\ell_3[j]$ at the same time.

Notations

Several notational conventions are useful for reasoning about parameterized programs. For a location ℓ_i in a parameterized process we define the set L_i by
$$L_i \;=\; \{j \mid \ell_i[j] \in \pi\},$$
that is, the set of indices of the processes (a subset of $\{1..M\}$) that currently reside at location ℓ_i. We define a corresponding integer
$$N_i \;=\; |L_i|,$$
that represents the *number* of processes currently residing at location ℓ_i.

This notation is easily extended to refer to *location sets* rather than to individual locations. Thus,
$$\begin{aligned}
L_{i_1,i_2,\ldots,i_k} &= L_{i_1} \cup L_{i_2} \cup \ldots \cup L_{i_k} \\
L_{i..j} &= L_i \cup L_{i+1} \cup \ldots \cup L_j \\
N_{i_1,i_2,\ldots,i_k} &= |L_{i_1,i_2,\ldots,i_k}| \\
N_{i..j} &= |L_{i..j}|.
\end{aligned}$$

4 Verifying Invariance Properties

Now that we have discussed the transition semantics of parameterized programs and introduced a sufficiently expressive assertion language, we can proceed with the verification of properties of parameterized programs, starting with *state-invariance* properties.

4.1 A Rule for State Invariance

For an assertion (state formula) p, the formula $\Box p$ is called a (*state*) *invariance formula*. If $\Box p$ is valid over program P, we say that p is an invariant of P, implying that all P-accessible states satisfy p.

Rule INV, presented in Fig. 7, is a complete rule for proving that assertion p is an invariant of program P.

Premise I1 of rule INV requires that Θ, the initial condition of P, implies the auxiliary assertion φ. Premise I2 of the rule implies that the auxiliary assertion φ implies assertion p, whose invariance we wish to prove. Premise I3 requires that all transitions in P preserve φ. The premise contains

$$
\begin{array}{|ll|}
\hline
\multicolumn{2}{|l|}{\text{For assertions } \varphi \text{ and } p,} \\
& \\
\text{I1.} & \Theta \to \varphi \\
\text{I2.} & \varphi \to p \\
\text{I3.} & \rho_\tau \land \varphi \to \varphi' \quad \text{for every } \tau \in \mathcal{T} \\
\hline
& \Box\, p \\
\hline
\end{array}
$$

FIG. 7. Rule INV (invariance).

φ', the *primed version* of the assertion φ, which is obtained by replacing each variable occurring in φ by its primed version. Since $\rho_\tau(V, V')$ holds whenever V characterizes one state and V' characterizes its τ-successor, the P-state validity of premise I3 implies that every τ-successor of a φ-state is also a φ-state.

Premises I1 and I3 state that φ holds at the initial state of every computation and that it propagates from any state to its τ-successor, for every transition τ of the system. Thus, every state in each computation of P satisfies φ. Due to the implication I2, every such state also satisfies p. It follows that p is an invariant of system P.

Example Let us illustrate the application of rule INV to prove that assertion
$$p: \quad y \geq 0$$
is an invariant of program ANY-Y. We take $\varphi = p : y \geq 0$ in the rule.

Premise I1 requires showing
$$\underbrace{\cdots \land y = 0 \land \cdots}_{\Theta} \to \underbrace{y \geq 0}_{\varphi}$$
This implication is state-valid and, therefore, also P-state valid.

Premise I2 is trivially valid since $\varphi = p$.

Premise I3 has to be checked for the 3 transitions of program ANY-Y, which are $\{\tau_I, \ell_0, \ell_1, m_0\}$.

We find it sufficient to check two kinds of transitions:

- The verification condition for transition ℓ_1 is:
$$\underbrace{\cdots \land y' = y + 1 \land \cdots}_{\rho_{\ell_2}} \land \underbrace{y \geq 0}_{\varphi} \to \underbrace{y' \geq 0}_{\varphi'}$$

- All other transitions $\tau \in \{\tau_I, \ell_0, m_0\}$ preserve the value of y. Therefore, their verification condition is:
$$\underbrace{\cdots \land y' = y \land \cdots}_{\rho_\tau} \land \underbrace{y \geq 0}_{\varphi} \to \underbrace{y' \geq 0}_{\varphi'}$$

Obviously, all these implications are state-valid. ∎

An assertion φ that satisfies premises I1 and I3 is called *inductive*. If φ is an inductive assertion, then we can apply rule INV, taking $p = \varphi$ and conclude that any assertion which is inductive over P is P-invariant. Rule INV can be viewed as suggesting a proof strategy that can be summarized as follows:

To prove $\Box\, p$, find an inductive assertion φ that is stronger than p. We refer to this as the *strengthening strategy*.

4.2 Application to Parameterized Programs

The transitions of parameterized programs can be characterized by a fixed number of transition relation schemes. Therefore, premise I3 has to be established for each of the transition schemes by a proof that treats the parameter j as any other logical variable. We say that premise I3 is established by a *uniform proof* (uniform in j).

We present several examples of uniform proofs of invariance properties of parameterized programs.

Example (multiple mutual exclusion by semaphores)

The invariance property of program MPX-SEM (Fig. 4) is mutual exclusion, which is specified by

$$p: \quad \forall i, j \in [1..M]\colon\ i \neq j\colon\ \Box \underbrace{\neg(at\_\ell_3[i] \wedge at\_\ell_3[j])}_{\psi[i,j]}\ .$$

To prove this statement, we have to establish, for arbitrary i and j, where $i, j \in [1..M]$ and $i \neq j$, the invariance of the assertion $\psi[i,j]$.

To establish the invariance of $\psi[i,j]$, we have to find an assertion φ stronger than p, i.e., implying p, which is *inductive*, i.e., satisfies premises I1 and I2. Such an assertion can be given by the conjunction $\varphi_1 \wedge \varphi_2$ of the following two assertions:

$$\varphi_1: \quad \forall j\colon y[j] \geq 0$$

$$\varphi_2: \quad N_{3,4} + \sum_{j=1}^{M} y[j] = 1.$$

Recall that $N_{3,4}$ is the number of processes which currently execute at locations $\ell_{3,4}$.

To show that the conjunction $\varphi_1 \wedge \varphi_2$ is inductive, i.e., satisfies premises I1 and I3, it is sufficient to show that each of φ_1, φ_2 satisfies these two premises separately.

There are two transitions that may affect φ_1 or φ_2. They are $\ell_2[i]$ and $\ell_4[i]$. We observe that $\rho_2[i]$ implies

$$at\_\ell_2[i] \wedge at'\_\ell_3[i] \wedge y[i] > 0 \wedge y'[i] = y[i] - 1 \wedge \forall j\colon j \neq i\colon y'[j] = y[j]$$

and $\rho_4[i]$ implies

$$at\_\ell_4[i] \wedge at'\_\ell_0[i] \wedge y'[i \oplus_M 1] = y[i \oplus_M 1] + 1 \wedge \forall j(j \neq i \oplus_M 1)\colon y'[j] = y[j].$$

- φ_1 *is Inductive*

  Clearly $\Theta \to \varphi_1$, that is
  $$\underbrace{M \geq 2 \wedge \pi = \{\ell_0[1], \ldots, \ell_0[M]\} \wedge y[1] = 1 \wedge y[2] = \cdots = y[M] = 0}_{\Theta} \to \underbrace{\forall j\colon y[j] \geq 0}_{\varphi_1}.$$

  It is easy to establish, for every $i \in [1..M]$,
  $$\ell_2[i]\colon \underbrace{\cdots \wedge y[i] > 0 \wedge y'[i] = y[i] - 1 \wedge \forall j\colon j \neq i\colon y'[j] = y[j]}_{\rho_2[i]} \wedge$$
  $$\underbrace{\forall j\colon y[j] \geq 0}_{\varphi_1} \to \underbrace{\forall j\colon y'[j] \geq 0}_{\varphi_1'}$$

  $$\ell_4[i]\colon \underbrace{\cdots \wedge y'[i \oplus_M 1] = y[i \oplus_M 1] + 1 \wedge \forall j\colon j \neq i \oplus_M 1\colon y'[j] = y[j]}_{\rho_4[i]} \wedge$$
  $$\underbrace{\forall j\colon y[j] \geq 0}_{\varphi_1} \to \underbrace{\forall j\colon y'[j] \geq 0}_{\varphi_1'}.$$

  This establishes the preservation of φ_1 over all transitions. Consequently, φ_1 is inductive.

- φ_2 *is Inductive*

  Clearly $\Theta \to \varphi_2$, that is
  $$\underbrace{M \geq 2 \wedge \pi = \{\ell_0[1], \ldots, \ell_0[M]\} \wedge y[1] = 1 \wedge y[2] = \cdots = y[M] = 0}_{\Theta} \to$$
  $$\underbrace{N_{3,4} + \sum_{j=1}^{M} y[j] = 1}_{\varphi_2}.$$

  The implication holds since $\pi = \{\ell_0[1], \ldots, \ell_0[M]\}$ implies $N_{3,4} = 0$ and $y[1] = 1 \wedge y[2] = \cdots = y[M] = 0$ implies $\sum_{j=1}^{M} y[j] = 1$.

  The effects of $\ell_2[i]$ and $\ell_4[i]$ on φ_2 can be expressed respectively by
  $$\ell_2[i]\colon \quad N'_{3,4} = N_{3,4} + 1 \quad \wedge \quad \sum_{j=1}^{M} y'[j] = \left(\sum_{j=1}^{M} y[j]\right) - 1$$
  $$\ell_4[i]\colon \quad N'_{3,4} = N_{3,4} - 1 \quad \wedge \quad \sum_{j=1}^{M} y'[j] = \left(\sum_{j=1}^{M} y[j]\right) + 1.$$

  Consequently, φ_2 is also inductive.

  Clearly, $\varphi_1 \wedge \varphi_2$ implies

$$N_3 \leq N_{3,4} = 1 - \sum_{j=1}^{M} y[j] \leq 1,$$

showing that there can be at most one process at ℓ_3. Thus, $\varphi_1 \wedge \varphi_2$ implies p which claims mutual exclusion, confirming premise I2.

This establishes mutual exclusion for program MPX-SEM for an arbitrary parameter M, $M \geq 2$. ∎

Example (finding the maximum of an array)

Consider program MAX-ARRAY of Fig. 6. The initial condition of the program is given by

$$\Theta: \quad \pi = \{\ell_0\} \wedge \bigwedge_{i=1}^{M} (y[i] = \mathrm{T})$$

We wish to prove the partial correctness of program MAX-ARRAY, which is given by the invariance of the assertion

$$\psi: \quad at\_\ell_8 \to maximal(z,x),$$

where $maximal(z,x)$ states that z is the maximal element of the array $x[1..M]$ and is an abbreviation for the formula:

$$maximal(z, x): \quad \exists k \in [1..M]: z = x[k] \wedge \forall j \in [1..M]: x[j] \leq z.$$

We base our proof on the property that, in any array, one of the elements is maximal. Let $a \in [1..M]$ be the index of an element which is maximal in x. Thus,

$$\forall j \in [1..M]: x[j] \leq x[a].$$

We formulate several assertions whose conjunction can be shown to be inductive, and hence invariant:

$$\varphi_1[i,j]: \quad at\_\ell_2[i,j] \to x[i] < x[j]$$
$$\varphi_2[i]: \quad at\_\ell_6[i] \to y[i]$$
$$\varphi_3: \quad y[a]$$
$$\varphi_4[i]: \quad x[i] = x[a] \vee at\_\ell_0 \vee at\_\ell_{1,2}[i,a] \vee \neg y[i]$$
$$\varphi_5: \quad N_{0..4} > 0 \vee at\_\ell_{5,6}[a] \vee z = x[a]$$

where $N_{0..4}$ is the number of processes which currently reside at locations $\ell_0, \ldots, \ell_4$. The indices i and j range over $1, \ldots, M$.

Assertion $\varphi_1[i,j]$ claims that process $P[i,j]$ can reach location ℓ_2 only if $x[i] < x[j]$.

Assertion $\varphi_2[i]$ claims that process $Q[i]$ can reach location ℓ_6 only if $y[i]$ is true.

Assertion φ_3 claims that $y[a]$ remains true throughout the computation.

Assertion $\varphi_4[i]$ claims that if $x[i] \neq x[a]$ (and hence $x[i] < x[a]$), then either the program is still at ℓ_0, or process $P[i,a]$ is still comparing $x[i]$ with $x[a]$ at $\ell_1[i,a]$, or is at the assignment $\ell_2[i,a]$ that will eventually set $y[i]$ to F, or $y[i]$ has already been set to F. For the program to function correctly we must ensure that, by the time execution reaches ℓ_4, $y[i]$ is false for all i such that $x[i] \neq x[a]$ (and therefore $x[i] < x[a]$). Assertion $\varphi_4[i]$ guarantees this by stating that if $x[i] \neq x[a]$ and $y[i]$ is true then the execution of process $P[i,a]$ has not terminated yet. Note that process $P[i,a]$ is expected to set $y[i]$ to false.

Assertion φ_5 claims that either process $Q[a]$, which will eventually set z to $x[a]$, has not terminated yet, or z has already been set to $x[a]$ (and will retain this value).

To conclude the partial correctness of the program, we observe that at_ℓ_8 contradicts each of the disjuncts $N_{0..4} > 0$ and $at\_\ell_{5,6}[a]$, appearing in φ_5, leading to
$$at\_\ell_8 \to z = x[a],$$
which by the assumed maximality of $x[a]$ implies the invariance of
$$at\_\ell_8 \to maximal(z, x).$$

5 Verifying Response Properties

In this and the succeeding sections, we present rules for proving response properties of parameterized programs. The main rule for verifying response properties relies on the notion of a *well-founded domain* for measuring progress towards the goal.

5.1 Well-founded Domains

We define a *well-founded domain* $(\mathcal{A}, \succ)$ to consist of a set $\mathcal{A}$ and a *well-founded order* relation $\succ$ on $\mathcal{A}$. A binary relation $\succ$ is called an *order* if it is

- transitive: $a \succ b$ and $b \succ c$ imply $a \succ c$, and
- irreflexive: $a \succ a$ for no $a \in \mathcal{A}$.

The relation $\succ$ is called *well-founded* if there does not exist an infinitely descending sequence $a_0, a_1, \ldots$ of elements of $\mathcal{A}$ such that
$$a_0 \succ a_1 \succ \cdots.$$

A typical example of a well-founded domain is $(\mathbb{N}, >)$, where $\mathbb{N}$ are the natural numbers (including 0) and $>$ is the greater-than relation. Clearly, $>$ is well-founded over the natural numbers, because there cannot exist an infinitely descending sequence of natural numbers
$$n_0 > n_1 > n_2 > \cdots.$$

For $\succ$, an arbitrary order relation on $\mathcal{A}$, we define its *reflexive extension* $\succeq$ to hold between $a, a' \in \mathcal{A}$ if either $a \succ a'$ or $a = a'$.

The Lexicographic Product

Given two well-founded domains, $(\mathcal{A}_1, \succ_1)$ and $(\mathcal{A}_2, \succ_2)$, we can form their *lexicographical product* $(\mathcal{A}, \succ)$, defined as follows:

$\mathcal{A}$ is defined as $\mathcal{A}_1 \times \mathcal{A}_2$, i.e., the set of all pairs (a_1, a_2), such that $a_1 \in \mathcal{A}_1$ and $a_2 \in \mathcal{A}_2$.

$\succ$ is an order defined to hold between $(a_1, a_2) \in \mathcal{A}$ and $(a'_1, a'_2) \in \mathcal{A}$ iff
$$a_1 \succ_1 b_1 \quad \text{or} \quad a_1 = b_1 \wedge a_2 \succ_2 b_2.$$
Thus, in comparing the two pairs (a_1, a_2) and (b_1, b_2), we first compare a_1 against b_1. If $a_1 \succ_1 b_1$, then this determines the relation between the pairs to be $(a_1, a_2) \succ (b_1, b_2)$. If $a_1 = b_1$, we compare a_2 with b_2, and the result of this comparison determines the relation between the pairs.

The order $\succ$ is called *lexicographic*, which implies that, as when searching in a dictionary, we locate the position of a word by checking the first letter first, and only after locating the place where the first letter matches do we continue matching the subsequent letters.

The importance of the lexicographic product follows from the following claim:

Claim (lexicographic product)
If the domains $(\mathcal{A}_1, \succ_1)$ and $(\mathcal{A}_2, \succ_2)$ are well-founded, then so is their lexicographic product $(\mathcal{A}, \succ)$.

Clearly, by the above, the domain $(\mathbb{N}^2, \succ)$, where $\succ$ is the lexicographic order between pairs of natural numbers, is well-founded. This order is defined by

$$(n_1, n_2) \succ (m_1, m_2) \quad \text{iff} \quad (n_1 > m_1) \text{ or } (n_1 = m_1 \text{ and } n_2 > m_2).$$

According to this definition
$$(10, 20) \succ (5, 15) \quad (1, 0) \succ (0, 100) \quad (1, 5) \succ (1, 3).$$

New well-founded domains can be constructed by taking lexicographic products of more than two well-founded domains. Applying this construction to the domain $(\mathbb{N}, >)$ of natural numbers, we obtain the domain $(\mathbb{N}^k, \succ)$, for $k \geq 2$, where $\succ$ is the lexicographic order between k-tuples of natural numbers. The order $\succ$ is defined by
$$(n_1, \ldots, n_k) \succ (m_1, \ldots, m_k) \quad \text{iff} \quad n_1 = m_1, \ldots, n_{i-1} = m_{i-1}, n_i > m_i$$
$$\text{for some } i,\ 1 \leq i \leq k.$$

For example, for $k = 3$
$$(7, 2, 1) \succ (7, 0, 45).$$
It is easy to show that the domain $(\mathbb{N}^k, \succ)$ is well-founded.

It is possible to make lexicographic comparisons between tuples of integers of different lengths. The convention is that the relation holding between $(a_1, \ldots, a_i)$ and $(b_1, \ldots, b_k)$ for $i < k$ is determined by lexicographically comparing $(a_1, \ldots, a_i, 0, \ldots, 0)$ to $(b_1, \ldots, b_i, b_{i+1}, \ldots, b_k)$. That is, we pad the shorter tuple by zeros on the right until it assumes the length of the longer tuple.

According to this definition, $(0, 2) \succ 0$, since $(0, 2) \succ (0, 0)$. In a similar way, $1 \succ (0, 2)$.

For assertions p, q, and $\varphi_1, \ldots, \varphi_m$,
a well-founded domain $(\mathcal{A}, \succ)$,
ranking functions $\delta_1, \ldots, \delta_m \colon \Sigma \mapsto \mathcal{A}$, and
helpful sets $h_1, \ldots, h_m \subseteq \mathcal{J}$

JH1. $\quad p \;\to\; q \vee \bigvee_{j=1}^{m} \varphi_j$

The following three premises hold for $i = 1, \ldots, m$

JH2. $\quad \rho_\tau \wedge \varphi_i \;\to\; \left[\begin{array}{l} q' \vee \bigvee_{j=1}^{m} (\varphi'_j \wedge \delta_i \succ \delta'_j) \\ \vee \begin{pmatrix} \varphi'_i \wedge \delta_i = \delta'_i \wedge \\ \mathcal{E}(h_i) \subseteq \mathcal{E}'(h_i) \end{pmatrix} \end{array} \right]$

for every $\tau \in \mathcal{T}$

JH3. $\quad \rho_\tau \wedge \tau \in h_i \wedge \varphi_i \;\to\; q' \vee \bigvee_{j=1}^{m} (\varphi'_j \wedge \delta_i \succ \delta'_j)$

for every $\tau \in \mathcal{T}$

JH4. $\quad \varphi_i \;\to\; \exists \tau \in h_i \colon En(\tau)$

$p \;\Rightarrow\; \Diamond q$

FIG. 8. Rule JH-WELL (well-founded response with helpful sets).

5.2 The Rule

In Fig. 8, we present rule JH-WELL for proving response properties of parameterized programs. The rule uses a fixed number of assertions $\varphi_1, \ldots, \varphi_m$, and associated *sets* of helpful transitions $h_1, \ldots, h_m$, $h_i \subseteq \mathcal{J}$ for $i = 1, \ldots, m$. We refer to h_i as the *helpful set* for assertion φ_i, $i = 1, \ldots, m$. The notation $\mathcal{E}(h_i)$ denotes the set of transitions belonging to h_i that are enabled. Both h_i and $\mathcal{E}(h_i)$ may depend on the state. The inclusion $\mathcal{E}(h_i) \subseteq \mathcal{E}'(h_i)$ is an abbreviation for the formula

$$\forall \tau \in h_i \colon \quad En(\tau) \to En'(\tau),$$

implying that any helpful transition that was enabled before the transition is still enabled after the transition.

The rule uses a well-founded domain $(\mathcal{A}, \succ)$, and ranking functions $\delta_i \colon \Sigma \mapsto \mathcal{A}$, mapping states of the system to elements of $\mathcal{A}$. The ranking functions measure progress of the computation towards the goal q.

Premise JH1 requires that every p-position either satisfies q or satisfies one of $\varphi_1, \ldots, \varphi_m$.

Premise JH2 requires that the application of an arbitrary transition τ to a φ_i-position k leads to a successor position $k' = k+1$ satisfying one of the following:
- k' satisfies q, or
- k' satisfies some φ_j with a rank $\delta_j(k')$ smaller than $\delta_i(k)$, or
- k' satisfies φ_i with a rank $\delta_i(k')$ equal to $\delta_i(k)$, and with a set of enabled helpful transitions $\mathcal{E}'(h_i)$ containing $\mathcal{E}(h_i)$.

Note that in the case of no observable progress, described by the third clause above, we require the persistence of enabled helpful transitions. That is, any helpful transition that is enabled at k is also enabled at k'. Position k' may have some additional enabled helpful transitions.

Premise JH3 requires that the application of a helpful transition $\tau \in h_i$, to a φ_i-position k, leads to a successor position k' which either satisfies q or satisfies some φ_j with a rank lower than that of k.

Since premise JH3 covers the cases of $\tau \in h_i$, it is sufficient to establish premise JH2 only for $\tau \notin h_i$.

Premise JH4 requires that every φ_i-position has at least one helpful transition which is enabled.

Justification To justify the rule, assume a computation such that p holds at position k and no later position $i \geq k$ satisfies q. By JH1 some φ_j must hold at position k. Let φ_{i_1} be the formula holding at k, and denote the rank δ_{i_1} at k by u_1. By JH4, there exists some helpful transition $\tau_{i_1} \in h_{i_1}$ which is enabled at position k.

Consider the transition τ taken at position k, leading into position $k+1$. By JH2, either position $k+1$ has a lower rank $u_2 \prec u_1$, or it has an equal rank $u_2 = u_1$, but then τ_{i_1} is still helpful and enabled at $k+1$. In the case of equal ranks, we can continue the argument from $k+1$ to $k+2$, $k+3$, etc. However, we cannot have all positions $i > k$ with the same rank. To see this, assume that all positions beyond k do have the same rank. By JH2, this implies that τ_{i_1} is continuously helpful and enabled. By JH3, τ_{i_1} is not taken beyond k because taking it would have led to a state with a rank lower than u_1. Thus, our assumption that all positions beyond k have the same rank leads to the situation that τ_{i_1} is continuously enabled and not taken, violating the justice requirement for τ_{i_1}.

Thus, eventually, we must reach a position k_2, $k_2 > k$, with rank u_2, where $u_2 \prec u_1$. In a similar way we can establish the existence of a position $k_3 > k_2$, with rank u_3, where $u_3 \prec u_2$. Continuing in this manner, we construct an infinitely descending sequence $u_1 \succ u_2 \succ u_3 \succ \cdots$ of elements of $\mathcal{A}$. This is impossible, due to the well-foundedness of $\succ$ on $\mathcal{A}$.

We conclude that every p-position must be followed by a q-position, establishing the consequence of the rule.

Example Consider the parameterized program TRIVIAL of Fig. 9. This program satisfies the response property
$$\underbrace{N_0 > 0}_{p} \;\Rightarrow\; \Diamond\underbrace{N_1 > 0}_{q},$$
which states that if some process is at ℓ_0, then eventually some process will be at ℓ_1.

$$\boxed{\begin{array}{l} \textbf{in}\quad M\quad:\textbf{integer where }M>0 \\[4pt] \displaystyle\|_{i=1}^{M}\; P[i] ::\quad [\ell_0:\ \textbf{skip};\ \ell_1:\ \textbf{skip};\ell_2:\ ] \end{array}}$$

FIG. 9. Program TRIVIAL.

To prove this property, we use a simple case of the rule for $m = 1$. As intermediate assertion we take
$$\varphi = p:\quad N_0 > 0.$$
As ranking function we take $\delta = 1$. The helpful set is
$$h:\quad \{\ell_0[1],\ \ldots,\ \ell_0[M]\}$$

For this simple example, the goal $q: N_1 > 0$ is achieved after taking a single helpful transition. Therefore, we do not have to consider helpful steps that decrease the ranking function δ, which can be chosen to be a constant.

We consider the premises of rule JH-WELL.

- Premise JH1

  This premise requires showing
  $$p \;\to\; q \vee \varphi.$$
  Since $\varphi = p$, this implication is trivially valid.

- Premise JH2

  This premise requires showing for each $\tau \in \mathcal{T}$
  $$\rho_\tau \wedge \underbrace{N_0 > 0}_{\varphi} \;\to\; \begin{bmatrix} \cdots \vee \cdots \\ \vee \\ \underbrace{N_0' > 0}_{\varphi'} \wedge \underbrace{1=1}_{\delta=\delta'} \wedge \mathcal{E}(h) \subseteq \mathcal{E}'(h) \end{bmatrix}.$$

  As previously observed, it is sufficient to consider transitions $\tau \not\in h$, i.e., $\tau \ne \ell_0[k]$ for any $k \in [1..m]$. These transitions do not change the set of j's for which $at\_\ell_0[j]$ holds. Consequently, these transitions preserve the value of N_0 and the set $\mathcal{E}(h)$.

- Premise JH3

  This premise requires showing for each $\tau \in \mathcal{T}$

$$\rho_\tau \wedge \tau \in h \wedge N_0 > 0 \rightarrow \underbrace{N_1' > 0}_{q'} \vee \cdots,$$

that is, we have to show that for each $i \in [1..M]$
$$\rho_{\ell_0[i]} \wedge N_0 > 0 \rightarrow N_1' > 0 \vee \cdots.$$
Clearly, $\rho_{\ell_0[i]}$ implies $at'\_\ell_1[i]$ from which $N_1' > 0$ follows.

- Premise JH4
  This premise requires showing
  $$\underbrace{N_0 > 0}_{\varphi} \rightarrow \underbrace{\exists i \in [1..M]\colon\ En(\ell_0[i])}_{En(h)}.$$
  By $N_0 > 0$, there is at least some i for which $at\_\ell_0[i]$ is true, implying that $\ell_0[i]$ is enabled. ◢

A Notation for Helpful Sets

Let $\|_{p \in R} S[p]$ be a parallel statement, where the parameter p ranges over some set R (e.g., $[1..M]$). Let ℓ_k be a location within statement S. We write T_k to denote the set of transitions of the form $L_k[p]$, i.e.,
$$T_k\colon\ \ \{\ell_k[p] \mid p \in R\}.$$
For example, in program MAX-ARRAY of Fig. 10 (also Fig. 6), T_2 denotes the set of transitions $\{\ell_2[i,j] \mid i,j \in [1..M]\}$, while T_5 denotes the set $\{\ell_5[i] \mid i \in [1..M]\}$.

This notation is extended to denote sets of transitions over a set of labels such as $T_{2,3}$ and sets of transitions over ranges of labels such as $T_{5..7}$. For example, $T_{0..7}$ denotes the set of all just transitions of program MAX-ARRAY.

Example (program MAX-ARRAY)

As a second example, reconsider program MAX-ARRAY (Fig. 10) for parallel computation of the maximum of an integer array.

In Section 4, dealing with safety, we proved the partial correctness of MAX-ARRAY, expressed by
$$at\_\ell_8 \Rightarrow maximal(z, x).$$
To complete the verification of this program, we have to prove its termination, expressed by the response property
$$\underbrace{at\_\ell_0}_{p} \Rightarrow \Diamond \underbrace{at\_\ell_8}_{q}.$$
Intuitively, termination is obvious, since each process is a sequential program with no loops. To prove it formally, using rule JH-WELL, we identify a well-founded domain
$$(\mathcal{A}, \succ)\colon\ \ ([1..8], >) \times ([0..M^2], >).$$
The parameterized intermediate assertions, helpful transitions, and the ranking functions are given in the table of Fig. 11.

Note that we refer to the exit transitions from the cooperation statements ℓ_0 and ℓ_4 by the names ℓ_3 and ℓ_7, respectively. These are *single*

```
in    M: integer where M ≥ 1
      x : array [1..M] of integer
local y : array [1..M] of boolean where y = T
out   z : integer
```

$$\ell_0: \underset{i,j \in [1..M]}{\|} P[i,j] :: \begin{bmatrix} \ell_1: \text{ if } x[i] < x[j] \text{ then } \ell_2: y[i] := \text{F} \\ \ell_3: \end{bmatrix}$$

$$\ell_4: \underset{i=1}{\overset{M}{\|}} Q[i] :: \begin{bmatrix} \ell_5: \text{ if } y[i] \text{ then } \ell_6: z := x[i] \\ \ell_7: \end{bmatrix}$$

$\ell_8:$

FIG. 10. Program MAX-ARRAY (finding the maximum of an array).

$\varphi_8:$	at_ℓ_0	$h_8:$	$\{\ell_0\}$	$\delta_8:$	8
$\varphi_7:$	$N_1 > 0 \wedge N_{1..3} = M^2$	$h_7:$	T_1	$\delta_7:$	$(7, N_1)$
$\varphi_6:$	$N_2 > 0 \wedge N_{2,3} = M^2$	$h_6:$	T_2	$\delta_6:$	$(6, N_2)$
$\varphi_5:$	$N_3 = M^2$	$h_5:$	$\{\ell_3\}$	$\delta_5:$	5
$\varphi_4:$	at_ℓ_4	$h_4:$	$\{\ell_4\}$	$\delta_4:$	4
$\varphi_3:$	$N_5 > 0 \wedge N_{5..7} = M$	$h_3:$	T_5	$\delta_3:$	$(3, N_5)$
$\varphi_2:$	$N_6 > 0 \wedge N_{6,7} = M$	$h_2:$	T_6	$\delta_2:$	$(2, N_6)$
$\varphi_1:$	$N_7 = M$	$h_1:$	$\{\ell_7\}$	$\delta_1:$	1

FIG. 11. Assertions, transitions and rankings for program MAX-ARRAY.

transitions that are enabled only when all processes within the cooperation statement have reached their terminal locations ℓ_3 and ℓ_7.

As we see, the table refers to eight parameterized assertions and helpful transition sets. Assertions φ_6 and φ_7 are associated with helpful sets of size M^2. Assertions φ_2 and φ_3 are associated with helpful sets of size M. The remaining assertions are associated with helpful sets of size 1. Note that the ranking of the assertions with singleton helpful sets consist of a single positive integer $\delta \in \{1, 4, 5, 8\}$ which should be interpreted as abbreviation for the pair $(\delta, 0)$.

The proof uses the following invariant which can be established by rule INV:

$$\psi: \begin{pmatrix} (N_{0,4,8} = 1 & \wedge & N_{1..3,5..7} = 0) & \vee \\ (N_{1..3} = M^2 & \wedge & N_{0,4..8} = 0\ ) & \vee \\ (N_{5..7} = M & \wedge & N_{0..4,8} = 0\ ) \end{pmatrix}$$

It is not difficult to check the premises of rule JH-WELL and verify that they are all satisfied.

For example, let us check premise JH3 for assertion φ_2. We show that the following implication is state valid:

$$\underbrace{\rho_{\ell_6[i]} \wedge N_6 > 0 \wedge N_{6,7} = M}_{\varphi_2} \to \cdots \vee \underbrace{N_7' = M \wedge (2, N_6) \succ (1, 0)}_{\varphi_1' \wedge \delta_2 \succ \delta_1'}$$
$$\vee \underbrace{N_6' > 0 \wedge N_{6,7}' = M \wedge (2, N_6) \succ (2, N_6')}_{\varphi_2' \wedge \delta_2 \succ \delta_2'}.$$

Assertion φ_2: $N_6 > 0 \wedge N_{6,7} = M$ implies $N_7 \leq M - 1$. To show the validity of the implication, we consider two cases. If $N_7 = M - 1$, then transition $\ell_6[i]$ leads to a successor state in which $N_7 = M$, establishing φ_1'. If $N_7 < M - 1$, there exists another index $k \neq i$ such that $at\_\ell_6[k]$ holds at the state before the transition and therefore also at the successor state. This establishes φ_2' and a rank decrease at the successor state. ∎

6   Representation by Verification Diagrams

The main task of constructing a proof by rule JH-WELL involves the identification of the constructs required by the rule, which consist of the auxiliary assertions, their associated helpful sets, and ranking functions. These constructs can be conveniently and effectively presented by a diagram that summarizes the assertions with their associated helpful transitions and ranking functions, and displays the possible transitions between the assertions.

We define a *verification diagram* to be a directed labeled graph constructed as follows:

- *Nodes* in the graph are labeled by assertions and their corresponding ranking functions. We will often refer to the node by the assertion labeling it.
- *Edges* in the graph represent transitions between assertions. Each edge connects one assertion to another and is labeled by an expression denoting a set of transitions in the program. We distinguish two types of edges. Double-lined edges represent helpful transitions, while single-lined edges represent unhelpful transitions.
- One of the nodes is designated as a *terminal node* ("goal" node). In the graphical representation, this node is distinguished by having a boldface boundary. No edges depart from a terminal node.

It is required that every node except the goal node has a double edge departing from it. It is also required that, if a node has a departing edge labeled by set expression S_1 and another departing edge labeled by S_2, then either $S_1 = S_2$ or $S_1 \cap S_2 = \emptyset$. Furthermore, the same set expression S cannot label both a single and a double edge departing from the same node.

Verification and Enabling Requirements for Verification Diagrams

Consider a nonterminal node labeled by assertion φ and ranking function δ, and S, a set-valued expression specifying a set of transitions. Let $\varphi_1, \ldots, \varphi_k$, $k \geq 0$, be the successors of φ by edges labeled with S, and $\delta_1, \ldots, \delta_k$ be the ranking functions of these successors.

- If S labels a single (-lined) edge, then the following verification condition is implied for every $\tau \in S$:

$$\rho_\tau \wedge \varphi \;\to\; \left(\begin{array}{l} (\varphi \wedge \delta = \delta' \wedge \mathcal{E}(h) \subseteq \mathcal{E}'(h)) \vee (\varphi \wedge \delta \succ \delta') \\ \vee \\ (\varphi_1 \wedge \delta \succ \delta'_1) \vee \cdots \vee (\varphi_k \wedge \delta \succ \delta'_k) \end{array} \right),$$

where h is the helpful set for assertion φ, i.e., the set labeling double edges departing from φ's node. If $k = 0$, i.e., S denotes the set of transitions which do not label any edge departing from φ, then the second disjunct is omitted.

- If $S = h$ labels a double edge identifying S as the helpful set for φ, then the following verification condition is implied for every $\tau \in \mathcal{T}$:
  $\rho_\tau \wedge \tau \in h \wedge \varphi \;\to\; (\varphi_1 \wedge \delta \succ \delta'_1) \vee \cdots \vee (\varphi_k \wedge \delta \succ \delta'_k).$
- If h labels a double edge departing from φ, we require
  $\varphi \;\to\; \exists \tau \in h\colon En(\tau).$

Note that in the case of an unhelpful transition, we allow a τ-successor with a rank equal to that of φ, provided it satisfies the same assertion φ. To make the treatment uniform, the preceding definitions require a ranking δ_0 for the terminal node and that transitions entering this node cause a rank decrease.

Valid Verification Diagrams

A verification diagram is said to be *valid over program P* (*P-valid* for short) if all the verification conditions and enabling requirements associated with the diagram are P-state valid.

The consequences of having a valid verification diagram are stated in the following claim:

Claim R A P-valid verification diagram establishes that the response formula

$$\bigvee_{j=0}^{m} \varphi_j \;\Rightarrow\; \Diamond \varphi_0$$

is P-valid. If, in addition, we can establish the P-state validity of the following implications:

(R1) $\quad p \rightarrow \bigvee_{j=0}^{m} \varphi_j \quad$ and $\quad$ (R2) $\quad \varphi_0 \rightarrow q,$

then we can conclude the validity of
$$p \Rightarrow \Diamond q.$$

The type of verification diagram defined here is specialized for the presentation of proofs by rule JH-WELL. We refer the reader to [8] for a general description of other types of verification diagrams.

Example (program TRIVIAL)

In Fig. 12 we present a verification diagram establishing the response property
$$\underbrace{N_0 > 0}_{p} \Rightarrow \Diamond \underbrace{N_1 > 0}_{q},$$
for program TRIVIAL of Fig. 9.

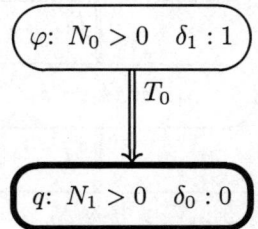

FIG. 12. A verification diagram for program TRIVIAL.

Example (program MAX-ARRAY)

We return to the example of program MAX-ARRAY (Fig. 10), for which we wish to prove termination, specified by
$$\underbrace{at\_\ell_0}_{p} \Rightarrow \Diamond \underbrace{at\_\ell_8}_{q}.$$

We present two proofs of this property using rule JH-WELL. In Fig. 13 we present a verification diagram which represents in a graphical form the previous proof of this property that appeared in the table of Fig. 11.

The second proof illustrates the power of rule JH-WELL, by using only a single intermediate assertion and single ranking function and helpful set:

$\varphi: \quad \begin{pmatrix} at\_\ell_0 \land N_{1..7} = 0 & \lor & N_{1..3} = M^2 \land N_{0,4..7} = 0 & \lor \\ at\_\ell_4 \land N_{0..3,5..7} = 0 & \lor & N_{0..4} = 0 \land N_{5..7} = M & \end{pmatrix}$

$\delta: \quad (N_0, N_1, N_2, N_3, N_4, N_5, N_6, N_7)$

$h: \quad T_{0..7}$

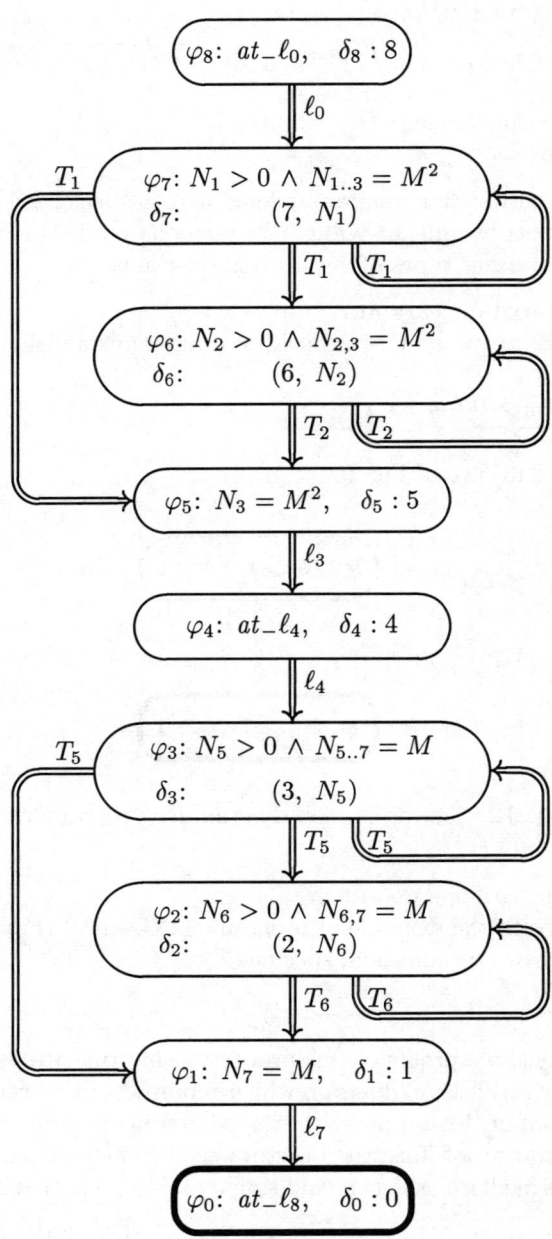

FIG. 13. A verification diagram for program MAX-ARRAY.

Thus, the well-founded domain used is N^8, consisting of 8-tuples of natural numbers. It is not difficult to see that each of the transitions in $T_{0..7}$ causes δ to decrease, and that at leat one of these transitions is enabled on every φ-state. ∎

6.1 Structured Verification Diagrams

We introduce some encapsulation conventions, inspired by the Statecharts formalism of Harel [3]. These conventions lead to more structured and hierarchical diagrams and improve the readability and manageability of large complex diagrams.

The basic construct of encapsulation is the introduction of a *compound node* containing internal nodes. We refer to the contained nodes as the *descendants* of the compound node. Nodes that are not compound are called *basic nodes*.

- *Departing edges*
  An edge departing from a compound node is interpreted as though it departed from each of its descendants. We thus have the graphical equivalence presented in Fig. 14.

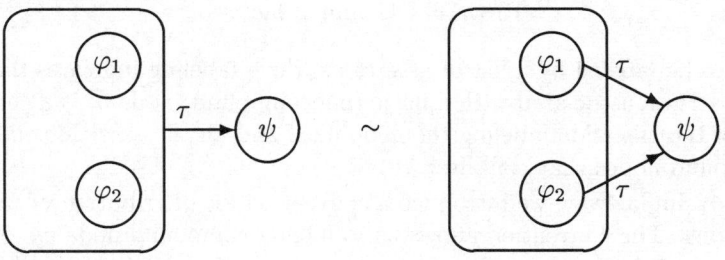

FIG. 14. Departing edges.

- *Arriving edges*
  In a similar way, an edge arriving at a compound node is interpreted as though it arrived at each of its descendants. Thus, we have the graphical equivalence presented in Fig. 15.
- *Common factors*
  An assertion φ labeling a compound node is interpreted as though it were a conjunct added to each of its descendants. This is described by the graphical equivalence presented in Fig. 16.

6.2 Distributing the Ranking Functions

To make verification diagrams more readable, we introduce an additional encapsulation convention. The previous convention allowed a compound

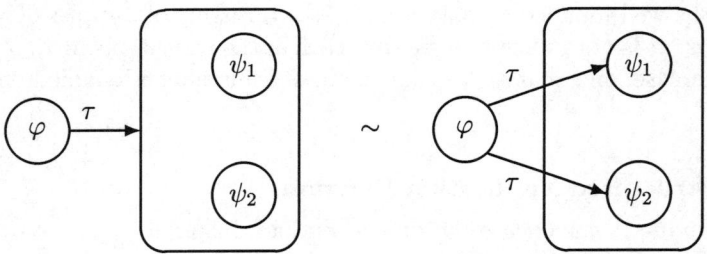

FIG. 15. Arriving edges.

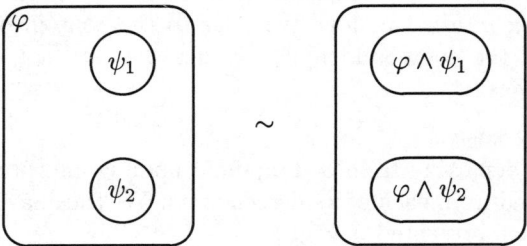

FIG. 16. Common factors.

node to be labeled by a list of assertions. Such labeling indicates that the full assertion associated with a basic (noncompound) node n_i is a conjunction of the assertion labeling the node itself and all the assertions labeling compound nodes that contain n_i.

In a similar way, we introduce a convention for distribution of ranking functions. The convention allows us to label a compound node by

$$\delta: f,$$

where f is some ranking function mapping states into a well-founded domain $\mathcal{A}$.

Consider a basic node n_i labeled by assertion φ_i and local ranking function f_b. Assume that node n_i is contained in a nested sequence of compound nodes that are labeled by ranking labels $\delta: f_1, \ldots, \delta: f_m$, as we go from the outermost compound node towards n_i. This situation is depicted in Fig. 17. Then the full ranking function associated with the node φ_i is given by the tuple

$$\delta_i = (f_1, \ldots, f_m, f_b).$$

That is, we consider the outermost ranking f_1 to be the most significant component in δ_i, and the local ranking f_b to be the least significant component.

Another part of the rank distribution convention allows us to omit the local rank labeling a node φ_i altogether. This is interpreted as though the

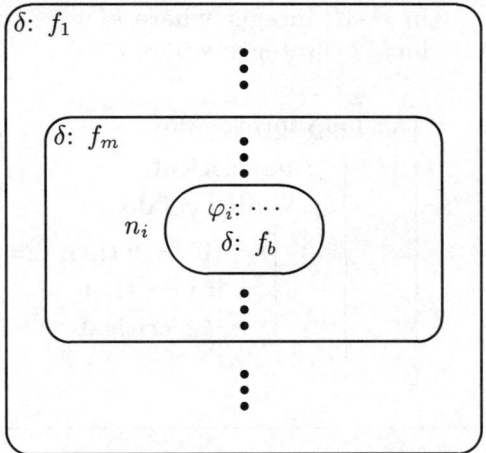

FIG. 17. Encapsulated sequence of nodes.

node was labeled with the ranking function $\delta: i$, where i is the index of the node (and the assertion labeling it).

Example (mutual exclusion by turn setting)

Consider program TURN of Fig. 18 which manages mutual exclusion between an arbitrary number of processes by turn setting. The program uses a shared variable t, which is initially 0. Each process $P[i]$, interested in entering its critical section, loops in $\ell_{2..5}$ trying to change t to the identity number of $P[i]$, namely i. The grouped statement at ℓ_3 is such that it sets t to i only if it finds $t = 0$. If $P[i]$ finds $t \neq 0$ it does not modify t but still moves to ℓ_4. The angular brackets around the statement imply that the complete statement is executed as one transition in a single step. At ℓ_4 the process checks whether its execution of ℓ_3 succeeded in setting t to i. Finding a value $t = i$ at ℓ_4, $P[i]$ enters its critical section ℓ_5. Otherwise it returns to ℓ_2 and then to ℓ_3 to try again.

Mutual exclusion is ensured by the invariant
$$\chi: \quad i \in L_{5,6} \quad \to \quad t = i.$$
We wish to show a weak-accessibility property, formulated by
$$\psi: \quad \underbrace{N_2 > 0 \wedge t = 0}_{p} \quad \Rightarrow \quad \Diamond \underbrace{N_5 > 0}_{q}\ .$$
This formula states that if some process is at ℓ_2 with $t = 0$, then eventually some process will get to ℓ_5. We refer to it as *weak accessibility* (sometimes also as *communal accessibility*), since it does not guarantee that the same process detected at ℓ_2 with $t = 0$ will be the one to enter ℓ_5. The stronger property of accessibility, claiming that any individual process visiting ℓ_2 with $t = 0$ will eventually reach ℓ_5, which can be expressed by the formula

$$\boxed{\begin{array}{l} \textbf{in} \quad M\text{: integer where } M > 1 \\ \textbf{local } t \ : \text{integer where } t = 0 \\ \\ \displaystyle\mathop{\|}_{i=1}^{M} P[i] :: \begin{bmatrix} \ell_0\text{: } \textbf{loop forever do} \\ \quad \begin{bmatrix} \ell_1\text{: } \textbf{noncritical} \\ \ell_2\text{: } \textbf{while } t \neq i \textbf{ do} \\ \quad \begin{bmatrix} \ell_3\text{: } \langle \textbf{if } t = 0 \textbf{ then } t := i \rangle \end{bmatrix} \\ \ell_4\text{: } \textbf{if } t = i \textbf{ then} \\ \quad \ell_5\text{: } \textbf{critical} \\ \ell_6\text{: } t := 0 \end{bmatrix} \end{bmatrix} \end{array}}$$

FIG. 18. Program TURN (mutual exclusion by turn setting).

$$at\_\ell_2[i] \wedge t = 0 \;\Rightarrow\; \Diamond\, at\_\ell_5[i],$$

is not valid for this program.

To verify the weak-accessibility property expressed by ψ, we use the following in rule JH-WELL:

φ_3:	$N_2 > 0 \wedge N_3 = 0 \wedge t = 0$		δ_3: 3		h_3: T_2
φ_2:	$N_3 > 0 \wedge t = 0$		δ_2: 2		h_2: T_3
φ_1:	$at\_\ell_4[t] \wedge t \neq 0$		δ_1: 1		h_1: $\ell_4[t]$

We proceed to check the premises of rule JH-WELL.

- Premise JH1 requires showing $p \to \cdots \vee \varphi_2 \vee \varphi_3$. Since $N_3 \geq 0$ is an obvious invariant of program TURN, it follows that p: $N_2 > 0 \wedge t = 0$ implies φ_2: $N_3 > 0 \wedge t = 0$ or φ_3: $N_2 > 0 \wedge N_3 = 0 \wedge t = 0$.
- Premise JH2 will be checked for each $i = 1, 2, 3$.
  - φ_3: $N_2 > 0 \wedge N_3 = 0 \wedge t = 0$

  Most of the transitions satisfy JH2 for φ_3 by preserving φ_3 and $\mathcal{E}(h_3)$. The only transitions that may falsify φ_3 or disable transitions in h_3: T_2 are transitions of the form $\ell_2[i]$. Transition $\ell_2[i]$ leads to a state satisfying φ_2: $N_3 > 0 \wedge t = 0$.
  - φ_2: $N_3 > 0 \wedge t = 0$

  The only transitions that can falsify φ_2 or disable a transition belonging to h_2: T_3 are of the form $\ell_3[i]$. However, this transition leads to a state satisfying φ_1: $at\_\ell_4[t] \wedge t \neq 0$.
  - φ_1: $at\_\ell_4[t] \wedge t \neq 0$

  The only transition that can falsify φ_1 is $\ell_4[t]$, which leads to a state satisfying the goal assertion q: $N_5 > 0$.
- Premise JH3 will be checked for each $i = 1, 2, 3$.

- φ_3: $N_2 > 0 \land N_3 = 0 \land t = 0$

Here we show for each $\tau \in h_3 \colon T_2$
$$\rho_\tau \land \varphi_3 \;\to\; \varphi_2' \land \delta_3 \succ \delta_2'.$$
That is,
$$\rho_{\ell_2[i]} \land \underbrace{\cdots \land t = 0}_{\varphi_3} \;\to\; \underbrace{N_3' > 0 \land t' = 0}_{\varphi_2'} \land \; 3 > 2.$$
Since $\rho_{\ell_2[i]}$ implies $at'\_\ell_3[i]$ and $t' = t$, the implication is valid.

- φ_2: $N_3 > 0 \land t = 0$

Here we show for each $\tau \in h_2 \colon T_3$
$$\rho_\tau \land \varphi_2 \;\to\; \varphi_1' \land \delta_2 \succ \delta_1'.$$
That is,
$$\rho_{\ell_3[i]} \land \underbrace{N_3 > 0 \land t = 0}_{\varphi_2} \;\to\; \underbrace{at'\_\ell_4[t'] \land t' \neq 0}_{\varphi_1'} \land \; 2 > 1.$$
Since $\rho_{\ell_3[i]}$ under $t = 0$ implies $at'\_\ell_4[i]$ and $t' \neq 0$, the right-hand side follows.

- φ_1: $at\_\ell_4[t] \land t \neq 0$

We will show
$$\rho_{\ell_4[t]} \land \underbrace{at\_\ell_4[t] \land t \neq 0}_{\varphi_1} \;\to\; \underbrace{N_5' > 0}_{q'}.$$
Since $\rho_{\ell_4[t]}$ and $t \neq 0$ imply $at'\_\ell_5[i]$, the right-hand side follows.

- Premise JH4 is obviously satisfied, since φ_i implies $\mathcal{E}(h_i) \neq \emptyset$ for $i = 1, 2, 3$.

We can summarize this JH-WELL proof in the verification diagram presented in Fig. 19. Note the assertion $t = 0$ that has been factored out of φ_3 and φ_2. ∎

6.3 State-dependent Helpful Sets

In all the preceding examples, the helpful sets h_i, $i = 1, \ldots, m$, depended on the index i but not on the state (or position) at which they were evaluated. This is not always sufficient and, in more complicated examples, we encounter cases where state-dependent helpful sets are necessary.

Consider program RACE, presented in Fig. 20. This program consists of M competing processes. The first process $P[k_1]$ to perform statement ℓ_1 will set its local variable $t[k_1]$ to 1, while incrementing the shared variable y to 2. This process eventually gets back to location ℓ_0 and, on finding $t[k_1] = 1$, will proceed to ℓ_2. All processes performing statement ℓ_1 later than $P[k_1]$ will obtain values of $t[k]$ greater than 1, and cannot exit the while loop at ℓ_0.

The property we wish to establish for this program is that eventually some process reaches ℓ_2. This property is stated by the following response formula:

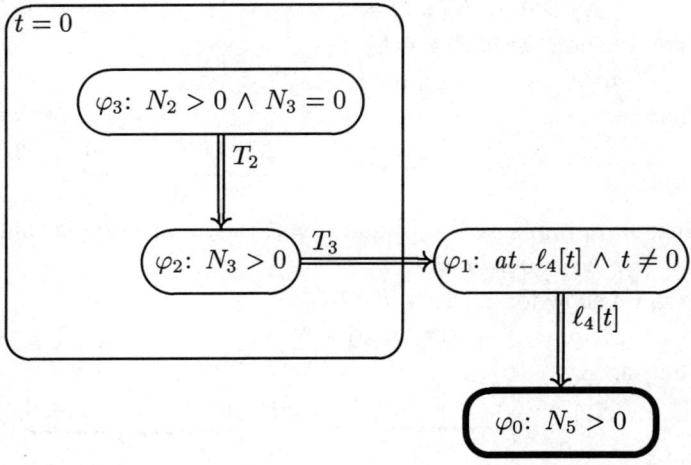

FIG. 19. Verification diagram for program TURN.

$$
\prod_{k=1}^{M} P[k] :: \begin{bmatrix} \textbf{in} & M: \textbf{integer where } M > 0 \\ \textbf{local } y : \textbf{integer where } y = 1 \\ \textbf{local } t: \textbf{integer where } t = 0 \\ \ell_0: \textbf{while } t \neq 1 \textbf{ do} \\ \quad \ell_1: (t, y) := (y, y+1) \\ \ell_2: \end{bmatrix}
$$

FIG. 20. Program RACE.

$$\underbrace{N_0 > 0 \wedge y = 1}_{p} \Rightarrow \underbrace{\Diamond N_2 > 0}_{q}.$$

It is easy to trace the progress of the computation towards the goal $N_2 > 0$ through the stages

$\varphi_3: \quad N_0 > 0 \wedge y = 1$

(initial) and

$\varphi_2: \quad N_1 > 0 \wedge y = 1,$

up to

$\varphi_1: \quad \exists k: at\_\ell_0[k] \wedge t[k] = 1.$

The question is how to justify the last helpful step from φ_1 to

$\varphi_0: \quad N_2 > 0.$

More specifically, the problem is the identification of the set h_1 of transitions that are helpful for φ_1.

A natural candidate for h_1 is T_0: $\{\ell_0[k] \mid k \in [1..M]\}$. Unfortunately, this does not work since not all $\ell_0[k]$-transitions are helpful. A transition $\ell[k]$ such that $t[k] \neq 1$ does not lead from φ_1 to φ_0 but is only guaranteed to preserve φ_1.

The right choice for the helpful set of φ_1 is
$$h_1: \quad \{\ell_0[k] \mid k \in [1..M] \wedge at\_\ell_0[k] \wedge t[k] = 1\}$$
This set is not fixed and may contain different transitions in different states. We say that h_1 is a *state-dependent* helpful set. However, as required by premise JH4 of rule JH-WELL, the set h_1 contains at least one enabled transition in each state satisfying φ_1: $\exists k \in [1..M]: at\_\ell_0[k] \wedge t[k] = 1$.

Consequently, we choose assertions, helpful sets, and ranking functions as follows:

φ_3: $\quad N_0 > 0$ $\qquad\qquad h_3$: T_0 $\qquad\qquad \delta_2$: 3

φ_2: $\quad N_1 > 0$ $\qquad\qquad h_2$: T_1 $\qquad\qquad \delta_2$: 2

φ_1: $\quad \exists k \in [1..M]:$ $\qquad h_1$: $\{\ell_0[k] \mid k \in [1..M] \wedge$ $\qquad \delta_1$: 1
$\qquad at\_\ell_0[k] \wedge t[k] = 1 \qquad\qquad at\_\ell_0[k] \wedge t[k] = 1\}$

φ_0: $\quad N_2 > 0.$

Note that φ_1 can also be written as $h_1 \neq \emptyset$.

It is straightforward to check that premise JH1 and premises JH2–JH4 for $i = 2, 3$ are all P-state valid. Let us dwell a while longer on premises JH2–JH4 for $i = 1$.

- Premise JH2 for $i = 1$ can be established by showing
$$\rho_\tau \wedge \underbrace{\exists k \in [1..M]: at\_\ell_0[k] \wedge t[k] = 1}_{\varphi_1} \rightarrow$$
$$\cdots \vee \cdots \vee \left(\varphi_1' \wedge 1 = 1 \wedge \mathcal{E}(h_1) \subseteq \mathcal{E}'(h_1)\right).$$

As previously observed, it is sufficient to establish JH2 only for $\tau \notin h_1$. Obviously, no transition $\tau \notin h_1$ can change the local state (location and value of t) of any process $P[k]$ satisfying $at\_\ell_0[k] \wedge t[k] = 1$. Consequently φ_1 will also hold after the transition, and $\mathcal{E}(h_1) = h_1 \subseteq h_1' = \mathcal{E}'(h_1)$.

- Premise JH3 for $i = 1$ can be established by showing
$$\rho_{\ell_0[k]} \wedge \underbrace{at\_\ell_0[k] \wedge t[k] = 1}_{\tau \in h_1} \wedge \cdots \rightarrow \underbrace{N_2' > 0}_{q'} \vee \cdots.$$
Clearly, taking $\ell_0[k]$ when $t[k] = 1$ establishes, by $\rho_{\ell_0[k]}$, $at'\_\ell_2[k]$ from which $N_2' > 0$ follows.

- Consider premise JH4 for $i = 1$. Observe that

$\exists \tau \in h_1: En(\tau) = \exists \tau \in \{\ell_0[k] \mid k \in [1..M] \wedge at\_\ell_0[k] \wedge t[k] = 1\}: En(\tau)$

can be simplified to

$$\exists k \in [1..M]: at\_\ell_0[k] \land t[k] = 1 \land En(\ell_0[k])$$
which is equivalent to
$$\underbrace{\exists k \in [1..M]: at\_\ell_0[k] \land t[k] = 1}_{\varphi_1} .$$

Thus, premise JH4 reduces to the trivial implication

$$\underbrace{\exists k \in [1..M]: at\_\ell_0[k] \land t[k] = 1}_{\varphi_1} \;\to\; \underbrace{\exists k \in [1..M]: at\_\ell_0[k] \land t[k] = 1}_{\exists \tau \in h_1:\; En(\tau)} .$$

This concludes the proof that property $N_0 > 0 \land y = 1 \Rightarrow \Diamond(N_2 > 0)$ is valid over program RACE. In Fig. 21, we present a verification diagram representing this proof.

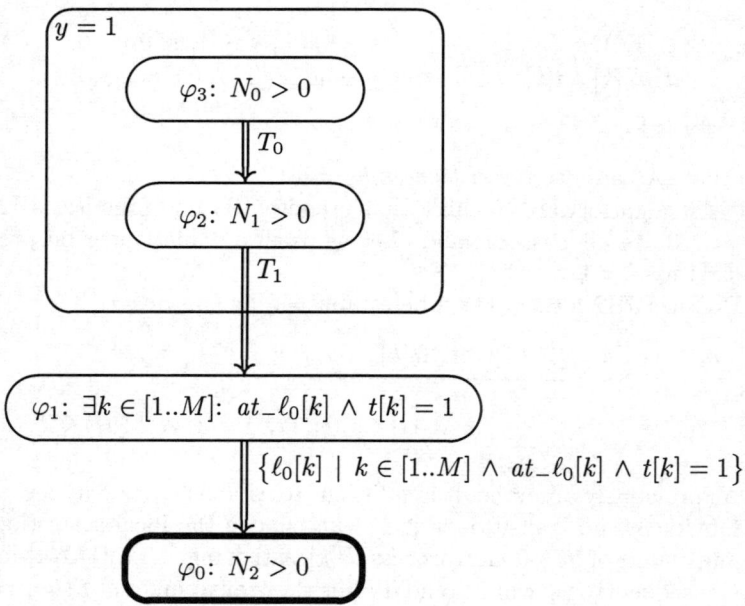

FIG. 21. Verification diagram for program RACE.

Let ℓ_r be (the label of) a statement within a process $P[k]$, $k \in [1..M]$. We introduce the following notations:
$$T_r^{t=1}: \quad \{\ell_r[k] \mid k \in [1..M] \land at\_\ell_r[k] \land t[k] = 1\}$$
Thus, $T_r^{t=1}$ denotes in a given state s the set of all transitions $\ell_r[k]$, $k \in [1..M]$, such that $at\_\ell_r[k] \land t[k] = 1$ holds at s. These notations often simplify the identification of state-dependent helpful sets.

In the example of program RACE, the helpful set h_1 can be replaced by $T_0^{t=1}$, and assertion φ_1 can be written as $T_0^{t=1} \neq \emptyset$. Consequently, we can rewrite the verification diagram of Fig. 21 as the verification diagram of Fig. 22.

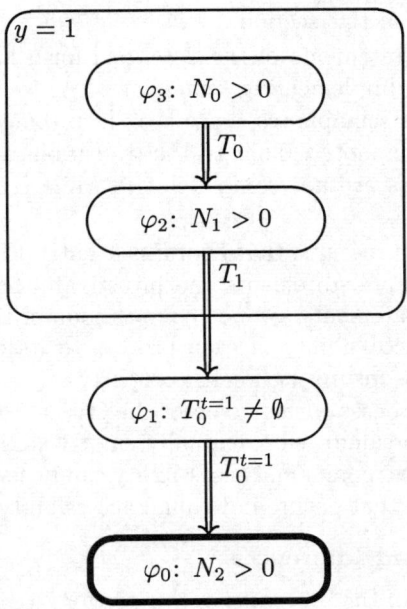

FIG. 22.   Simplified verification diagram for program RACE.

7   Coordination by Add-and-store

As our final set of examples, illustrating the techniques for proving response properties of parameterized programs, we present a family of algorithms based on a special synchronization instruction.

Some computers have special "add-and-store" instructions that fetch a value from a location in memory, add to it a number and store the result in the same location, all within one execution cycle. If several processors are connected to a common shared memory then, while one of them performs such an add-and-store instruction, no other processor can interfere with the value being fetched and stored at this location. This provides a natural implementation of the atomic instruction $y := y + e$ for a shared variable y and a *local expression* e. A local expression is an expression that depends only on variables local to the process. Usually, the value which is stored is also retained in an internal register. This enables a single transition implementation of the multiple assignment statement

$$(t, y) := (y + e, y + e),$$

where y is a shared variable, e is a local expression, and t is a variable local to the process that is executing this instruction.

To emphasize the special role of this statement, it is written in the form

$$t := y := y + e,$$

in all the programs in this section.

Add-and-store statements of the described form have often been suggested as means for implementing semaphores. As we will see below, they are not as strong as semaphores, since they lack the compassion property associated with semaphores. That is, the transitions associated with add-and-store statements are not compassionate while semaphore transitions are.

We present two programs that coordinate entry to critical sections by means of add-and-store statements and investigate their response properties. Since these statements are not compassionate, they cannot directly ensure individual accessibility of each process to its critical section. Instead, they can only ensure the weaker property of communal accessibility by which, if some process wishes to enter the critical section, some process (not necessarily the same) will eventually enter its critical section. However, as will be shown, communal accessibility can be used to program more involved algorithms that ensure individual accessibility.

7.1 Notations and Inferences

To facilitate proofs of the programs in this section, we introduce some special notations that rely on the special structure of the considered programs. All programs considered here consist of a parallel composition of M processes $P[1], \ldots, P[M]$, where M is an input to the program. Each process has a local variable t. Let ℓ_a and ℓ_b, $a \leq b$, be two locations in the program. We define the following notations:

$$L_{a..b}^{t\sim c}: \quad \{i \in [1..M] \mid at\_\ell_{a..b}[i] \land t[i] \sim c\},$$
$$N_{a..b}^{t\sim c}: \quad |L_{a..b}^{t\sim c}|$$

where $\sim$ is one of the six binary relations $\{<, \leq, =, \neq, \geq, >\}$.

Thus, $L_{3..4}^{t>0}$ denotes the set of all process indices $i \in [1..M]$, such that $P[i]$ is currently at ℓ_3 or at ℓ_4 and $t[i] > 0$, and $L_{3..4}^{t>c}$ denotes the total number of such processes.

For the case that $b = a$, we write $L_{a..b}^{t\sim c}$ and $N_{a..b}^{t\sim c}$ simply as $L_a^{t\sim c}$ and $N_a^{t\sim c}$. For the case that $b = a + 1$, we write $L_{a..b}^{t\sim c}$ and $N_{a..b}^{t\sim c}$ simply as $L_{a,b}^{t\sim c}$ and $N_{a,b}^{t\sim c}$.

As in the previous section, we define

$$T_a^{t\sim c}: \quad \{\ell_r[k] \mid k \in [1..M] \land at\_\ell_a[k] \land t[k] \sim c\}.$$

There is an obvious connection between assertions referring to expressions such as $N_{a..b}^{t\sim c}$ and assertions that use existential quantification over

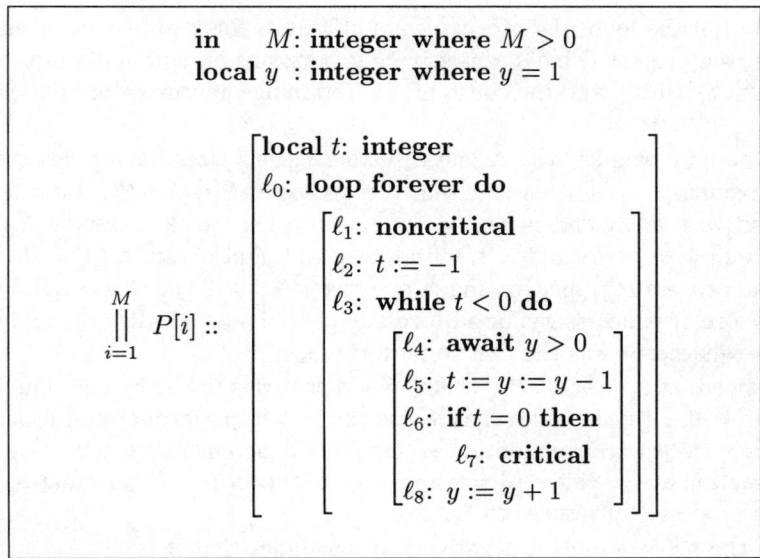

FIG. 23. Program MUX-AST (mutual exclusion by add-and-store).

the index i. For example, the following equivalence is a direct consequence of the definitions:

$$N_{a..b}^{t>0} > 0 \leftrightarrow \exists i: \left(at\_\ell_{a..b}[i] \land t[i] > 0 \right)$$

All quantified variables in this section are rigid variables denoting process indices which range over $[1..M]$. We therefore omit their range specifications from the formulas.

7.2 Mutual Exclusion by Add-and-store

We first consider program MUX-AST presented in Fig. 23, which implements mutual exclusion by add-and-store instructions.

The program consists of $M > 0$ processes that coordinate their entry to their critical sections via the shared variable y. In addition, each process $P[i]$ has a local variable t which is used in the program. The program for each process is an endless loop, in which the process alternates between the execution of its noncritical section at ℓ_1 and the attempt to enter its critical section at ℓ_7.

The process may elect to stay forever in its noncritical section.

If the process exits its noncritical section, the protocol for trying to enter the critical section starts at ℓ_2, where the variable t is set to -1. Then, the process enters a loop at ℓ_3 which is terminated only when t becomes nonnegative. A nonnegative value of t (actually 0) signals that the process managed to enter its critical section, and may therefore return to ℓ_1.

Within the loop, the process waits first at ℓ_4 for y to become positive. When the process detects a positive y it performs an add-and-store statement at ℓ_5 with y and the constant -1, retaining the value stored in y also in t.

One may wonder why we need further checks after having detected a positive y at ℓ_4. The answer is that two processes $P[i]$ and $P[j]$ may detect a positive y at ℓ_4 and move, one after the other, to ℓ_5. Assume $P[i]$ to be the first to perform ℓ_5. It will lower y to 0 and obtain a $t[i] = 0$. The second process $P[j]$, performing ℓ_5 one step later, will get to $y = t[j] = -1$. Therefore, it is necessary for a process to check its own t after the addition to see whether it was the first to perform ℓ_5.

Indeed, at ℓ_6 process $P[i]$ checks whether it was the lucky one. On finding $t[i] = 0$, $P[i]$ concludes that it was the first to perform ℓ_5 and proceeds to enter the critical section at ℓ_7. On exit it increments y, offsetting the subtraction at ℓ_5. Since $t[i] = 0$ in this case, the loop of ℓ_3 terminates, and lucky process $P[i]$ returns to ℓ_1.

If the process finds a negative t, it concludes that it is not its turn to enter, and proceeds to ℓ_8. Here it increments y to offset the subtraction at ℓ_5. Since $t < 0$, the loop of ℓ_3 does not terminate, and the process returns to ℓ_4 to try its luck once more.

Proving Safety Properties: Mutual Exclusion

As a first step in the verification of program MUX-AST, let us prove the safety property of mutual exclusion. This property states that at most one process may be at ℓ_7, and is expressible by:

$$N_7 \leq 1.$$

We prove several invariants that lead to the desired conclusion.

The first invariant is given by

$$at\_\ell_7[i] \;\rightarrow\; t[i] = 0.$$

Observe that the assertions refer to the instance of variable t that belongs to process $P[i]$ as $t[i]$. This invariant can be verified by checking the relevant transitions. They are $\ell_6[i]$ which proceeds to ℓ_7 only if $t[i] = 0$, and transitions $\ell_2[i]$ and $\ell_5[i]$ which modify $t[i]$ but do not end up at $\ell_7[i]$.

We can obviously rewrite this invariant as

$$at\_\ell_7[i] \;\rightarrow\; at\_\ell_{6..8}[i] \,\wedge\, t[i] = 0,$$

due to the trivial observation that $at\_\ell_7[i]$ implies $at\_\ell_{6..8}[i]$.

Another way of expressing this invariant is by the inequality

$$I_1: \quad N_7 \leq N_{6..8}^{t=0}.$$

This inequality states that the number of processes $P[i]$ such that $at\_\ell_7[i]$ is true is smaller or equal to the number of processes $P[i]$ such that $at\_\ell_{6..8}[i] \wedge t[i] = 0$ is true.

A second invariant is given by

$$I_2: \quad N_{6..8} + y = 1.$$

This is easily verifiable by observing that initially $N_{6..8} = 0$ and $y = 1$. Then we check the relevant transitions and find that $\ell_5[i]$ decrements y by 1 but increments $N_{6..8}$ by 1. The latter is because process $P[i]$ has just joined the set $L_{6..8}$ by entering ℓ_6. Similarly, transition ℓ_8 increments y by 1 but decrements $N_{6..8}$ by 1. Thus, both preserve the sum $N_{6..8} + y$.

From this invariant it follows that $y \leq 1$ is also invariant.

The last invariant we consider is:
$$I_3: \quad N_{6..8}^{t=0} \leq 1.$$

The only transition which may endanger the validity of this invariant is $\ell_5[i]$, and then only if $N_{6..8}^{t=0} = 1$ before the transition. However, in this case $N_{6..8} > 0$ which, in view of I_2, implies $y \leq 0$. Since transition $\ell_5[i]$ leads to $t'[i] = y - 1$, it follows that $t'[i] < 0$. Therefore, i does not satisfy $at'\_\ell_{6..8}[i] \wedge t'[i] = 0$ and will not join $L_{6..8}^{t=0}$ as a result of taking $\ell_5[i]$.

This leads to $\left(N_{6..8}^{t=0}\right)' = 1$, which preserves assertion I_3.

From I_1 and I_3 we conclude
$$N_7 \leq 1.$$

Proving Response Property: Communal Accessibility

As we have already commented, the add-and-store instructions are not strong enough to guarantee individual accessibility, i.e., that *each* process wishing to enter its critical section will eventually do so. Instead, we prove the weaker property of *communal accessibility*. This can be expressed by:
$$N_2 > 0 \quad \Rightarrow \quad \Diamond(N_7 > 0).$$
Let us prove this property.

Consider the progress of a process from ℓ_2 to ℓ_7. It can certainly advance unhindered until it reaches ℓ_4. At ℓ_4 it has to wait until y becomes positive. Due to I_2, y becomes positive only when the range $\ell_{6..8}$ is evacuated of all processes currently residing there. When y becomes positive, one or more processes will reach ℓ_5. The first process to execute ℓ_5 while y is positive will get a zero value of t and will eventually get to ℓ_7.

Thus, we can partition the description of progress into phases, identified as follows:
1. Some process gets to ℓ_4.
2. While some process is at ℓ_4 and $y \leq 0$, the range $\ell_{6..8}$ is evacuated until y becomes 1.
3. Some process executes ℓ_5 while y is still 1, gets a zero t, and proceeds to ℓ_7.

Consequently, we prove these stages in the progress towards entry to the critical section as separate lemmas.

Lemma A $\quad N_2 > 0 \quad \Rightarrow \quad \Diamond(N_4 > 0)$

In Fig. 24 we present a verification diagram proof of this response formula.

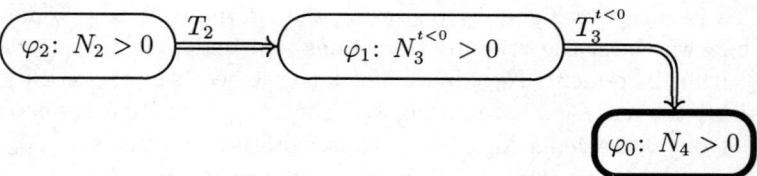

FIG. 24. A verification diagram for Lemma A.

Once we know that some process is at ℓ_4, there are two cases to consider, depending on whether y is positive. Consider first the more difficult one, in which $y \leq 0$.

Lemma B $N_4 > 0 \land y \leq 0 \;\Rightarrow\; \Diamond(N_4 > 0 \land y = 1)$

We prove this lemma by rule JH-WELL. The proof is presented by the verification diagram of Fig. 25.

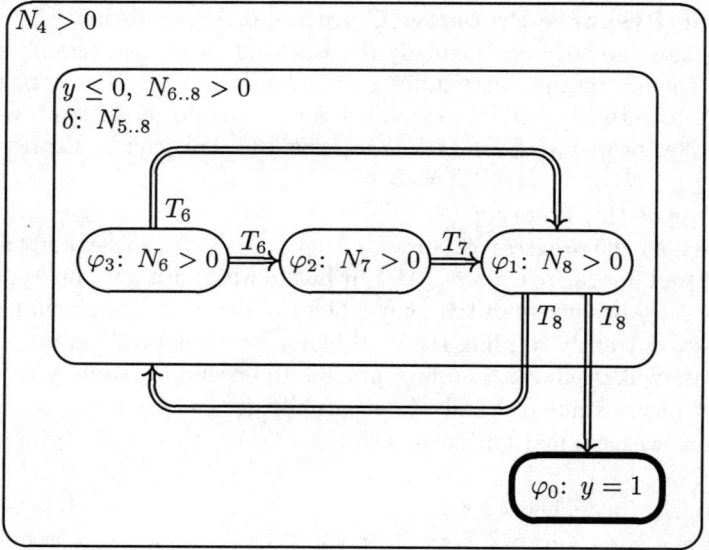

FIG. 25. A verification diagram for Lemma B.

Note that any transition that causes $N_{6..8}$ to become 0 leads, according to I_2, to $y = 1$.

The reason we use the ranking $N_{5..8}$ instead of $N_{6..8}$, which is mentioned in I_2, is that $N_{6..8}$ can increase by execution of ℓ_5. The rank $N_{5..8}$ cannot increase while $y \leq 0$, because no process can pass ℓ_4 if $y \leq 0$.

Lemma C $N_4 > 0 \land y = 1 \;\Rightarrow\; \Diamond(N_7 > 0)$

This lemma is also proven by rule JH-WELL, tracing the progress from ℓ_4 to ℓ_7. The proof is presented in the verification diagram of Fig. 26.

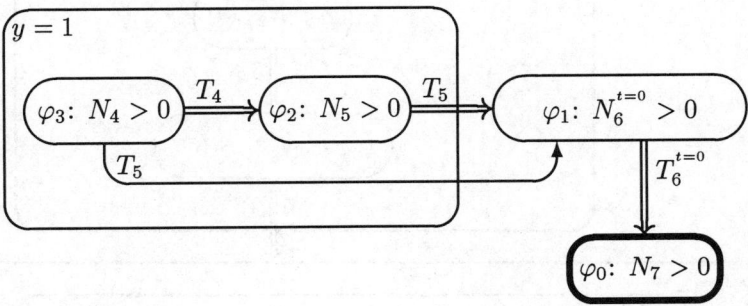

FIG. 26. A verification diagram for Lemma C.

The three lemmas can be combined into a single verification diagram, presented in Fig. 27. Note that when N_4 becomes positive, there are two possibilities: either $y \leq 0$, or $y > 0$ which by I_2: $N_{6..8} + y = 1$ implies $y = 1$.

It is possible to omit most of the internal details of this diagram, and retain just the top-level structure, identifying the lemmas which lead from one phase to the next. This leads to the diagram of Fig. 28.

This schematic diagram identifies the partition of the proof into three lemmas. Each lemma is represented as a box, with double-edge exits that lead to subsequent boxes. The box represents the response property, guaranteeing that eventually the computation will exit to one of the successors of this box along one of the exits labeled by the lemma's name.

7.3   From Communal to Individual Accessibility

Program MUX-AST for mutual exclusion by add-and-store instructions does not fully satisfy our expectations for a satisfactory solution to the mutual exclusion problem. It falls short by guaranteeing communal accessibility rather than individual accessibility. However, once some process is admitted to the critical section we can appoint it as an arbitrator for the next round. This is because while being in the critical section it can perform activities such as determining which process will be the next to be admitted without having to worry about possible interference from other processes.

In Fig. 29 we present program IMUX-AST, which implements individual accessibility. This program extends program MUX-AST in several ways. It contains an additional variable *next* ranging over $1..M$, and whose value represents the index of a process that has been given high priority in the

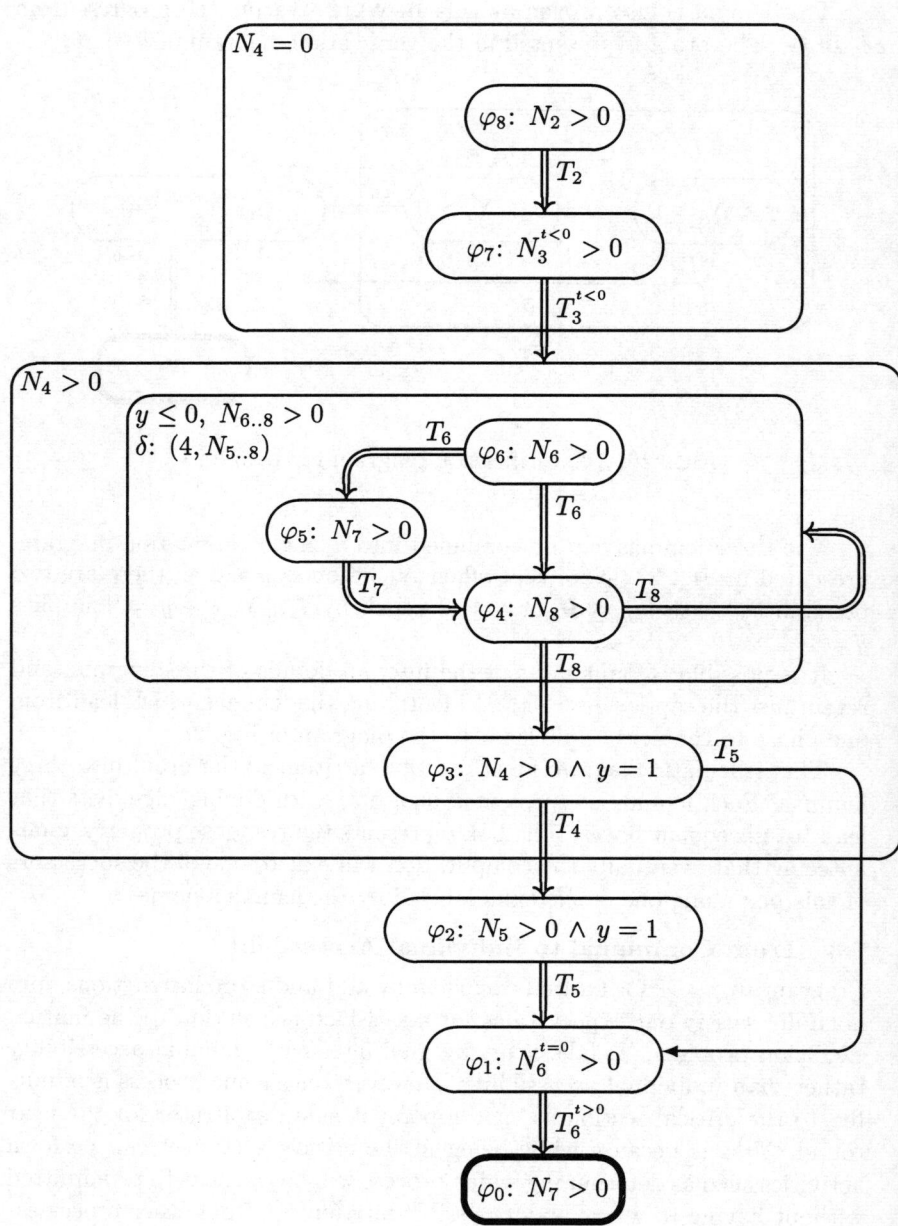

FIG. 27. A verification diagram for $N_2 > 0 \Rightarrow \Diamond(N_7 > 0)$.

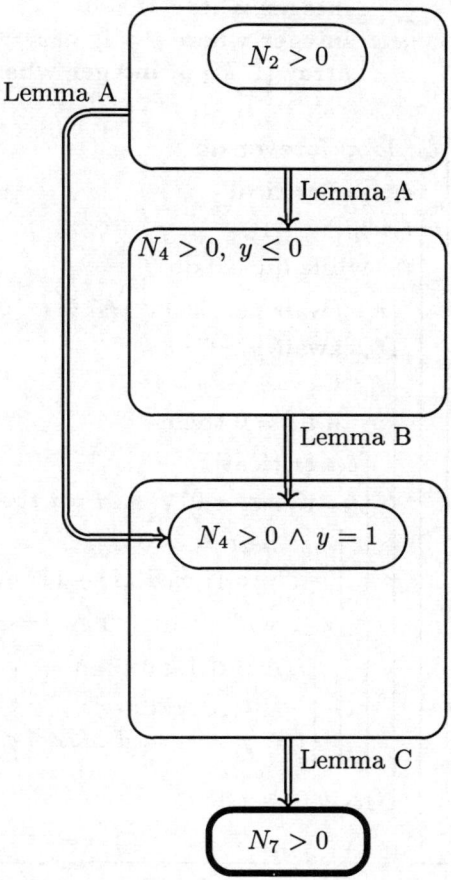

FIG. 28. The top-level structure of the proof.

last arbitration round. The local variable t of MUX-AST is transformed in IMUX-AST into an array $t[1..M]$ that can be inspected by each of the processes. Initially $next = 0$.

The protocol proceeds very much as before, except that at ℓ_4 we introduced a new gate. The function of the gate at ℓ_4 is to hold all processes except the one that has been given high priority. Note that if no process has been given priority, $next = 0$ and all processes can pass the gate at ℓ_4. From there on, the protocol proceeds as before, except that there is an additional code performing an arbitration round at $\ell_{9..15}$. Since this code follows immediately after the critical section it is guaranteed to be performed in exclusion, by a single process $P[i]$.

The first question asked at ℓ_9 is whether a new round of arbitration

$$
\begin{array}{l}
\textbf{in} \quad M \quad\quad\quad : \textbf{integer where } M = 0 \\
\textbf{local } j,\ y,\ next: \textbf{integer where } y = 1,\ next = 0 \\
\quad\quad\quad t \quad\quad\quad : \textbf{array } [1..M] \textbf{ of integer where } t = 0
\end{array}
$$

$$
\|_{i=1}^{M} P[i] ::
\left[
\begin{array}{l}
\ell_0: \textbf{ loop forever do} \\
\left[
\begin{array}{l}
\ell_1: \textbf{noncritical} \\
\ell_2: t[i] := -1 \\
\ell_3: \textbf{while } t[i] < 0 \textbf{ do} \\
\left[
\begin{array}{l}
\ell_4: \textbf{await } next = 0 \vee next = i \\
\ell_5: \textbf{await } y > 0 \\
\ell_6: t[i] := y := y - 1 \\
\ell_7: \textbf{if } t[i] = 0 \textbf{ then}
\end{array}
\right] \\
\left[
\begin{array}{l}
\ell_8: \textbf{critical} \\
\ell_9: \textbf{if } next = 0\ \vee\ next = i \textbf{ then} \\
\left[
\begin{array}{l}
\ell_{10}: next := 0 \\
\ell_{11}: j := (i \bmod M) + 1 \\
\ell_{12}: \textbf{while } next = 0\ \wedge\ j \neq i \textbf{ do} \\
\left[
\begin{array}{l}
\ell_{13}: \textbf{if } t[j] < 0 \textbf{ then} \\
\quad\quad \ell_{14}: next := j \\
\ell_{15}: j := (j \bmod M) + 1
\end{array}
\right]
\end{array}
\right] \\
\ell_{16}: y := y + 1
\end{array}
\right]
\end{array}
\right]
\end{array}
\right]
$$

FIG. 29. Program IMUX-AST — guaranteeing individual accessibility.

is needed. A new round is needed if no process has been assigned a high priority, i.e., $next = 0$, or if the process with the high priority is $P[i]$ itself.

The other case is that some other process, $P[k]$, for $k \neq i$, has been assigned a high priority, but $P[i]$ entered the critical section ahead of $P[k]$. The algorithm is such that some overtaking is possible. In this case, $P[k]$ is still attempting entry to its critical section and we should not modify its priority. Hence, in such a case, $P[i]$ proceeds directly to ℓ_{16} and no arbitration takes place.

On entering the arbitration section, variable $next$ is reset to 0 for the case that its previous value was i. Process $P[i]$ then sets variable j to the index following i in cyclic order, and enters the *while* loop at ℓ_{12}. The loop searches for the first j in cyclic order such that $t[j] < 0$. Note that $t[j] < 0$ is a reliable indicator that $P[j]$ is interested in entering the critical section but has not done so yet. If such a j is found, $P[i]$ sets *next* to j, thus declaring j to have a high priority, and then exits the loop. Another possibility is that no such j has been found, and then j will close a full cycle and return to the value i. The loop terminates in both of these cases.

The reader is invited to verify that this program guarantees individual accessibility, i.e., that it satisfies the requirement

$$at\_\ell_2[k] \;\;\Rightarrow\;\; \Diamond\, at\_\ell_7[k].$$

7.4 Readers-Writers with Add-and-store Instructions

An interesting extension of the mutual exclusion problem is the readers-writers problem. In this problem we distinguish two types of critical sections, called a *reading section* and a *writing section*. The required exclusion property is that

while some process resides in a writing section, no other process may reside in either a reading or a writing section.

Note that this allows several processes to cohabit a reading section.

The Program

Program READ-WRITE for solving the readers-writers problem, using add-and-store instructions, is presented in Fig. 30. After the statement *noncritical* at ℓ_1, which represents the noncritical activity of the processes, each process branches nondeterministically to either the *read protocol R*, at location $\ell_{2..7}$, or to the *write protocol W*, at $\ell_{8..14}$.

In the *read protocol*, each reader tries to decrement y and achieve a nonnegative value in t (and in y). Since the initial value of y is M, up to M readers may decrement y by 1, and still obtain a nonnegative value. If a reader succeeds in obtainining a nonnegative value for t, it proceeds to the *read section* at ℓ_6. If it does not, it increments y at ℓ_7 (compensating for the subtraction at ℓ_4) and continues to loop.

The *write protocol* is similar, except that a writer subtracts M from y, attempting to obtain a nonnegative value. This is possible only if that particular writer is the only one currently subtracting from y. Even if one reader has subtracted and lowered y to $M-1$, the writer, subtracting a further M, will already obtain -1, and be barred from entering the writing section.

Another special feature of the write protocol is the wait at ℓ_{10} for y to become M. This is similar to the **await** $y > 0$ we had in the mutual exclusion program MUX-AST (Fig. 23). This is necessary, because otherwise we can construct a computation in which two writers chase one another around the ℓ_9 loop, keeping y always negative, without any of them or a reader being able to enter any of the critical sections. With the *await* gate at ℓ_{10}, this cannot happen, as we will prove below.

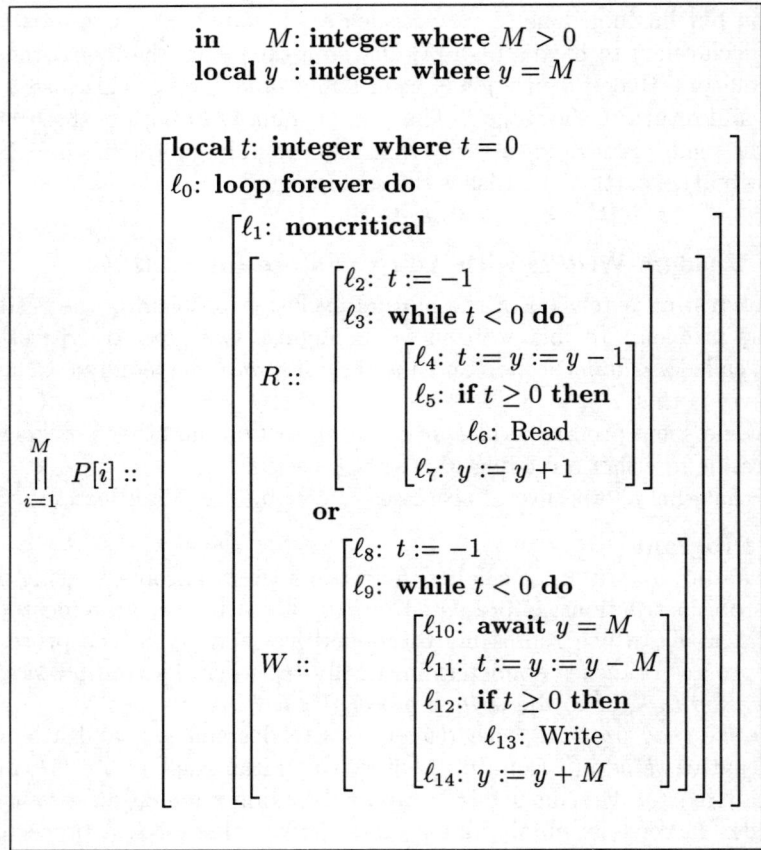

FIG. 30. Program READ-WRITE (readers-writers).

Proving Mutual Exclusion

The first property we prove is that of exclusion, as required by the problem. This is established by several invariants.

- *Invariant I_1*

  $N_{5..7} + M \cdot N_{12..14} + y = M.$

  This equality holds initially, since $y = M$ and $N_{5..7} = N_{12..14} = 0$. It is preserved by transitions, such as ℓ_4 which increments $N_{5..7}$ by 1 and decrements y by 1, or ℓ_{11} which increments $N_{12..14}$ by 1 and decrements y by M. Similarly, it is preserved by ℓ_7 and ℓ_{14}.

- *Invariant I_2*

  $N_{5..7}^{t \geq 0} + M \cdot N_{12..14}^{t \geq 0} \leq M.$

  There are two transitions that may endanger the invariance of this assertion.

  - $\ell_4[i]$ while $N_{5..7}^{t \geq 0} + M \cdot N_{12..14}^{t \geq 0} = M$

However, due to I_1,
$$y = M - N_{5..7} - M \cdot N_{12..14}$$
$$\leq M - N_{5..7}^{t \geq 0} - M \cdot N_{12..14}^{t \geq 0} = 0.$$
So the execution of $\ell_4[i]$ will produce $t'[i] < 0$, and hence $N_{5..7}^{t \geq 0}$ does not increase.

- $\ell_{11}[i]$ while $N_{5..7}^{t \geq 0} + M \cdot N_{12..14}^{t \geq 0} > 0$

This is a dangerous situation since by adding one more element to $N_{12..14}^{t \geq 0}$ the sum will increase beyond M. However due to I_1, and a calculation identical to the one before, we obtain
$$y \leq M - N_{5..7}^{t \geq 0} - M \cdot N_{12..14}^{t \geq 0} < M.$$
Consequently, the execution of $\ell_{11}[i]$ produces $t'[i] < 0$, and does not increase $N_{12..14}^{t \geq 0}$.

- Invariant I_3
$$L_6 \subseteq L_{5..7}^{t \geq 0}.$$
This is equivalent to the implication
$$at\_\ell_6[i] \rightarrow t[i] \geq 0,$$
claimed for every $i = 1, \ldots, M$. The invariant can be verified by considering the transitions that enter ℓ_6. Since a process $P[i]$ can enter ℓ_6 only if $t[i] \geq 0$, it follows that $i \in L_{5..7}^{t \geq 0}$, after the transition.

- Invariant I_4
Similarly to the above invariant, we can also prove
$$L_{13} \subseteq L_{12..14}^{t \geq 0},$$
which is equivalent to
$$at\_\ell_{13}[i] \rightarrow t[i] \geq 0.$$
From I_3 and I_4 we can conclude
$$N_6 + M \cdot N_{13} \leq N_{5..7}^{t \geq 0} + M \cdot N_{12..14}^{t \geq 0}.$$
Using I_2 we conclude
$$N_6 + M \cdot N_{13} \leq M.$$
From this it is easy to infer
$$N_{13} > 0 \rightarrow N_6 = 0 \wedge N_{13} = 1,$$
which is precisely the exclusion property required. It states that if some process is at ℓ_{13}, then it is the only one there, and no process is at ℓ_6.

Proving Accessibility

The response property we prove for this program is again that of *communal accessibility*. Since this program has two types of critical sections, a *read* and a *write* section, communal accessibility has an even broader interpretation. It states that if some process is interested in entering *one* of the critical sections, then some process will eventually enter *one* of the critical sections. We cannot even guarantee, for example, that if some process wants to read (write) then some process will eventually read (write). This property is expressible by

$$N_2 + N_8 > 0 \;\Rightarrow\; \Diamond(N_6 + N_{13} > 0).$$

We prove this property by two lemmas, concentrating first on the *writers*.

Lemma A $\quad N_8 > 0 \;\Rightarrow\; \Diamond(N_6 + N_{13} > 0)$

This lemma states that if a process is interested in writing, then eventually some process will either read (visit ℓ_6) or write (visit ℓ_{13}).

The proof of the lemma is established by a sequence of simpler lemmas, identifying important intermediate stages in getting from $N_8 > 0$ to $N_6 + N_{13} > 0$. We refer the reader to Fig. 31, which presents a high-level verification diagram showing the structure of the proof.

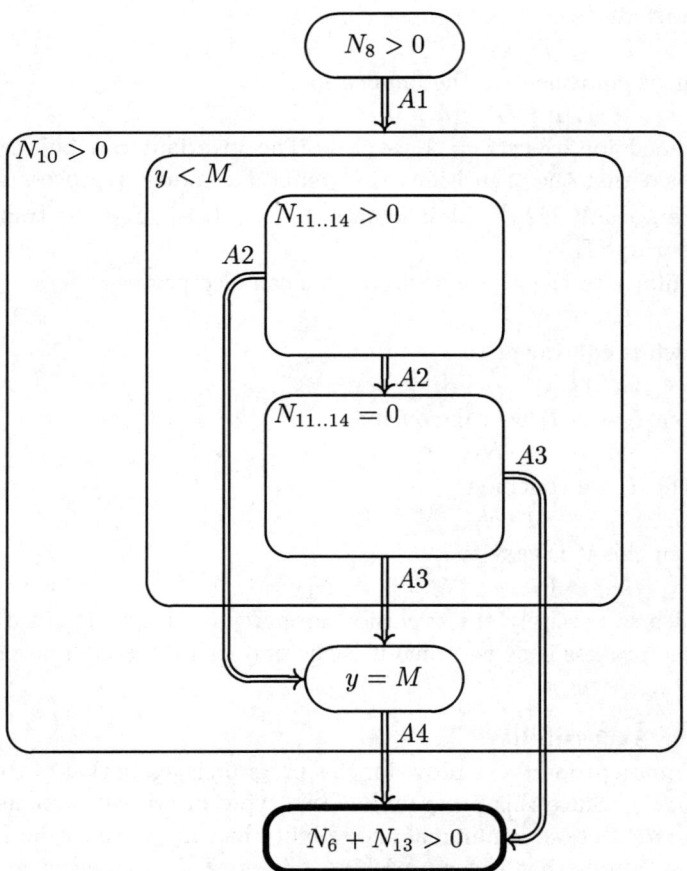

FIG. 31. Structure of the proof of Lemma A.

Lemma A1 $N_8 > 0 \Rightarrow \Diamond(N_{10} > 0)$

This lemma ensures that if some process is currently at ℓ_8 then eventually some process will arrive at ℓ_{10}.

This simple property is proven by the verification diagram of Fig. 32.

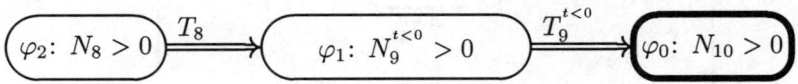

FIG. 32.   A verification diagram for Lemma A1.

Arriving at a state satisfying $N_{10} > 0$, there are two cases to be considered. The easier one is that $y = M$, and Lemma A4 below shows how to get from this situation to the goal $N_6 + N_{13} > 0$. The more complicated situation is when $y < M$ (in view of the invariant I1: $y \leq M$, $y \neq M$ implies $y < M$). The two lemmas, A2 and A3, show that being at $N_{10} > 0 \wedge y < M$ we eventually get to the easier case of $N_{10} > 0 \wedge y = M$, unless we reach first a state which already satisfies the goal assertion $N_6 + N_{13} > 0$. The lemmas split the case $N_{10} > 0 \wedge y < M$ into two sub-cases, according to whether $N_{11..14}$ is positive or zero, and show that from both we eventually arrive to $N_{10} > 0 \wedge y = M$ or to $N_6 + N_{13} > 0$.

Lemma A2 $N_{10} > 0 \wedge y < M \wedge N_{11..14} > 0 \Rightarrow$

$$\Diamond(N_{10} > 0 \wedge (N_{11..14} = 0 \vee y = M))$$

The proof of this lemma can be based on rule JH-WELL, and is presented in the verification diagram of Fig. 33.

Note that transitions from ℓ_{14} may either retain $N_{11..14} > 0$ and $y < M$, or evacuate $L_{11..14}$ completely, or increase y to become M. It is possible for y to equal M, while some processes are still at ℓ_{11}.

Note that we also have to consider the possibility that a transition ℓ_7 increases y to become M.

In the proof we rely on the fact that while $y < M$, all transitions of the form $\ell_{10}[i]$ are disabled.

Lemma A3 $N_{10} > 0 \wedge y < M \wedge N_{11..14} = 0 \Rightarrow$

$$\Diamond((N_{10} > 0 \wedge y = M) \vee N_6 + N_{13} > 0)$$

The proof of the lemma is presented in the verification diagram of Fig. 34.

We observe that, due to I_1, the antecedent implies that $0 < N_{4..7} < M$ and $0 < y < M$. This situation is split in the diagram into several sub-cases:

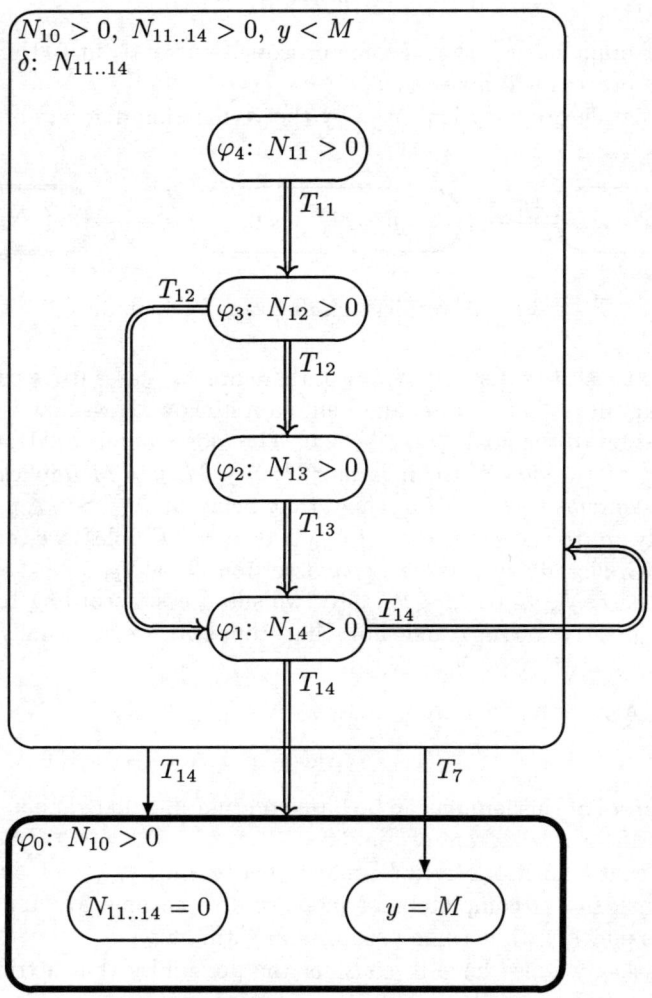

FIG. 33. A verification diagram for Lemma A2.

- $N_4 = N_6 = 0 \land N_5^{t<0} + N_7 > 0$ is covered by φ_3 and φ_4
- $N_4 > 0$ is covered by φ_2
- $N_5^{t\geq 0} > 0$ is covered by φ_1
- $N_6 > 0$ is covered by the disjunct $N_6 + N_{13} > 0$ of φ_0.

The sum $N_5^{t<0} + N_7$ decreases on each ℓ_7 transition. It must eventually drop to zero, ensuring $y = M$, unless N_4 becomes positive before.

Combining Lemmas A2 and A3 together, we obtain

$$N_{10} > 0 \land y < M \Rightarrow \Diamond((N_{10} > 0 \land y = M) \lor N_6 + N_{13} > 0).$$

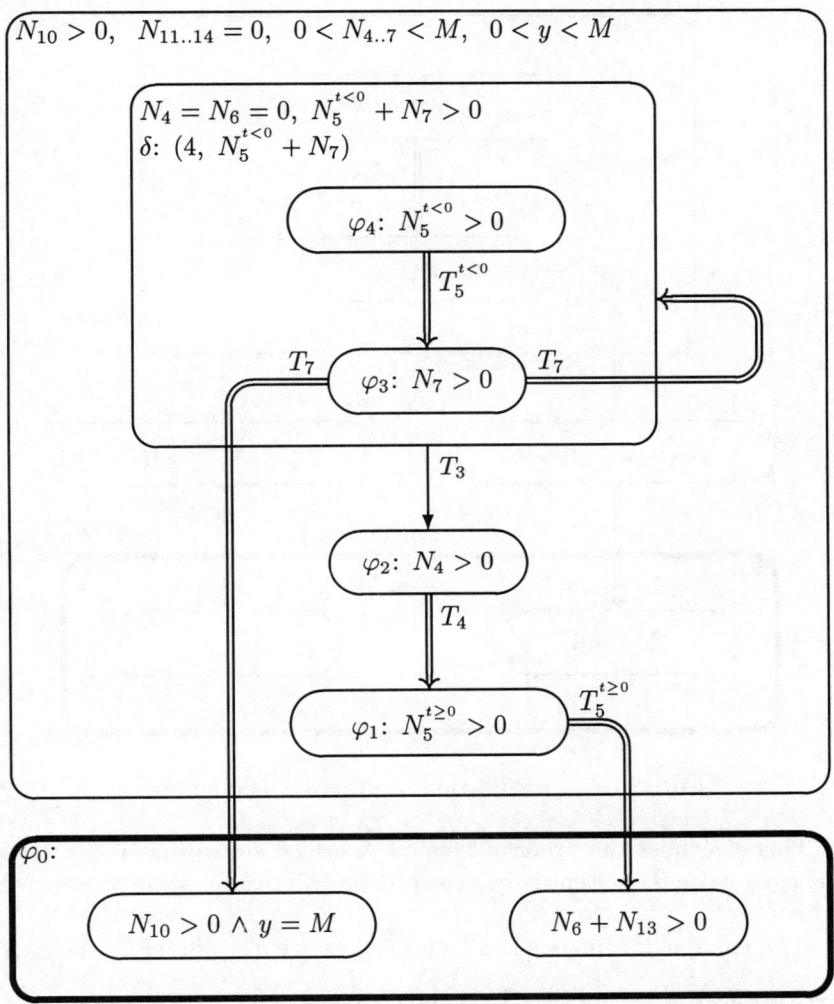

FIG. 34. A verification diagram for Lemma A3.

It remains to show that from $(N_{10} > 0) \land (y = M)$ we are also guaranteed to reach $N_{13} + N_6 > 0$. This is claimed by the next lemma.

Lemma A4 $\quad N_{10} > 0 \land y = M \;\Rightarrow\; \Diamond(N_6 + N_{13} > 0)$

The proof of this lemma is presented in verification diagram of Fig. 35. We split the initial situation into two cases:

- $N_{10} > 0$, $N_{11} = 0$ ⠀⠀covered by φ_4
- $N_{11} > 0$, ⠀⠀⠀⠀⠀⠀⠀⠀⠀covered by φ_3.

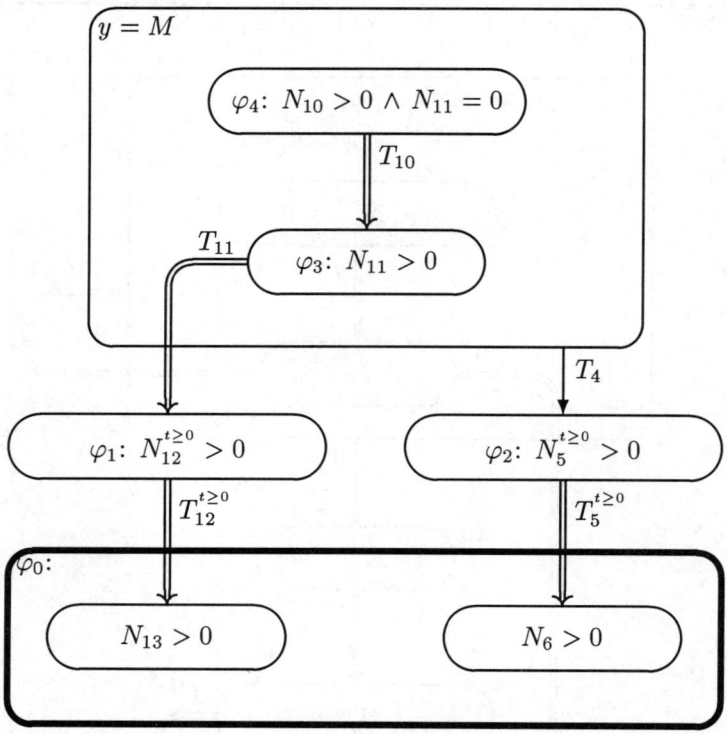

FIG. 35. A verification diagram for Lemma A4.

This concludes the proof of Lemma A, which states that if a process wishes to write then eventually some process will read or some process will write.

By combining Lemmas A1, A2, and A3, we can also obtain Corollary A.

Corollary A $\quad N_{10} > 0 \ \Rightarrow \ \Diamond(N_6 + N_{13} > 0)$

The second case we have to handle is the possibility that a process wishes to read. This is covered by the following lemma:

Lemma B $\quad N_2 > 0 \ \Rightarrow \ \Diamond(N_6 + N_{13} > 0)$

The proof of Lemma B is also split into several intermediate stages. In Fig. 36 we present these stages and the lemmas that lead from one stage to the next.

Lemma B1 $\quad N_2 > 0 \ \Rightarrow \ \Diamond\left(N_{3..7}^{t<0} > 0\right)$

This simple lemma follows a process, that wishes to read, from location ℓ_2 to location ℓ_3, where it arrives with $t[i] < 0$. The lemma is so simple that we skip its proof.

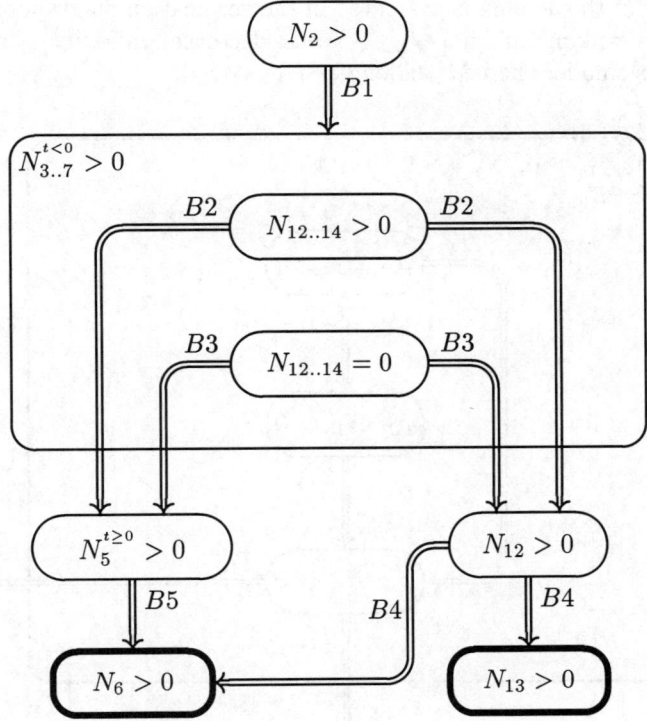

FIG. 36. Structure of the proof of Lemma B.

Arriving at ℓ_3, it is important to distinguish between the case that $y > 0$ and the case $y \leq 0$. Due to the invariant I_1, if $y \leq 0$ then either $N_{12..14} > 0$ or $N_{5..7} = M$. Since $N_3 > 0$, it is impossible for all processes to be at $\ell_{5..7}$, and therefore we conclude that $N_{12..14} > 0$. The next lemma shows that this case must develop to the simpler case in which $N_{12..14} = 0$. However, we cannot hope that while this happens, the process which is currently at ℓ_3 will stand still. What can it do? It can loop around $\ell_{3..7}$ and perhaps even get to ℓ_5 with a nonnegative $t[i]$. If this happens then we are close to our goal $N_6 > 0$. If it does not happen, we should at least make sure that this process does not escape the loop $\ell_{3..7}$ without visiting ℓ_6 first. To contain some processes in the loop we use the set $L_{3..7}^{t<0}$, observing that the only way a process can leave this set is by moving to $L_5^{t \geq 0}$.

Consequently, we have the following:

Lemma B2

$$N_{3..7}^{t<0} > 0 \wedge N_{12..14} > 0 \;\Rightarrow\; \Diamond \left[\begin{array}{l} (N_{3..7}^{t<0} > 0 \wedge N_{12..14} = 0) \vee \\ N_5^{t \geq 0} > 0 \vee N_{12} > 0 \end{array} \right]$$

The proof of this lemma is presented in the verification diagram of Fig. 37. It uses the ranking function $N_{12..14}$, which decreases on each ℓ_{14} transition. By I1, y is smaller than M, as long as $N_{12..14} > 0$.

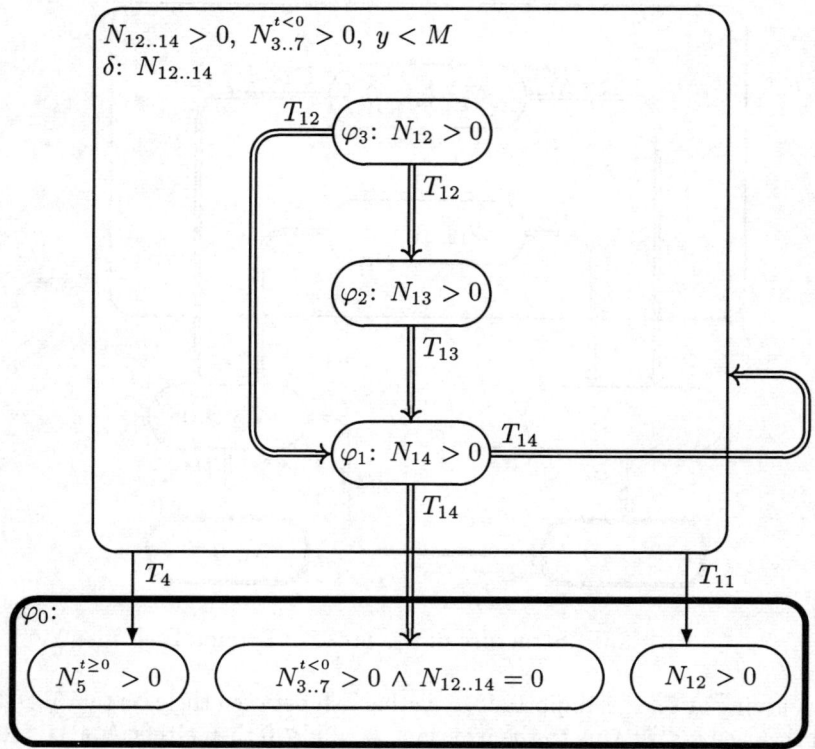

FIG. 37. A verification diagram for Lemma B2.

In a more general situation we would have to worry about the possibility of $N_{12..14}$ increasing due to an ℓ_{11} transition. Here, however, any ℓ_{11} transition makes L_{12} nonempty, which is one of the goals of this lemma.

Similarly, the only transition that can violate $N_{3..7}^{t<0} > 0$ is ℓ_4, taken in a state with a positive y. This, however, makes $L_5^{t \geq 0}$ nonempty, which is another goal.

The next lemma considers a situation in which there is still some unsatisfied process (i.e., $t[i] < 0$) in the $\ell_{3..7}$ loop, while $N_{12..14} = 0$. It shows that eventually one of the sets $L_5^{t \geq 0}$ or L_{12} must become nonempty.

Lemma B3 $\quad N_{3..7}^{t<0} > 0 \wedge N_{12..14} = 0 \;\Rightarrow\; \Diamond\!\left(N_5^{t \geq 0} > 0 \vee N_{12} > 0\right)$

The lemma is proved in the verification diagram of Fig. 38. Note that while being at ℓ_6, $t[i] \geq 0$, so that $L_6^{t<0}$ is always empty. Therefore, having $N_{3..7}^{t<0} > 0$ implies that we must have a nonempty $L_{3..5,7}$. If L_4 is nonempty, then due to $N_{12..14} = 0$ and to I1, we are guaranteed to have a positive y. Therefore, any ℓ_4 transition from such a state leads to a nonempty $L_5^{t\geq 0}$.

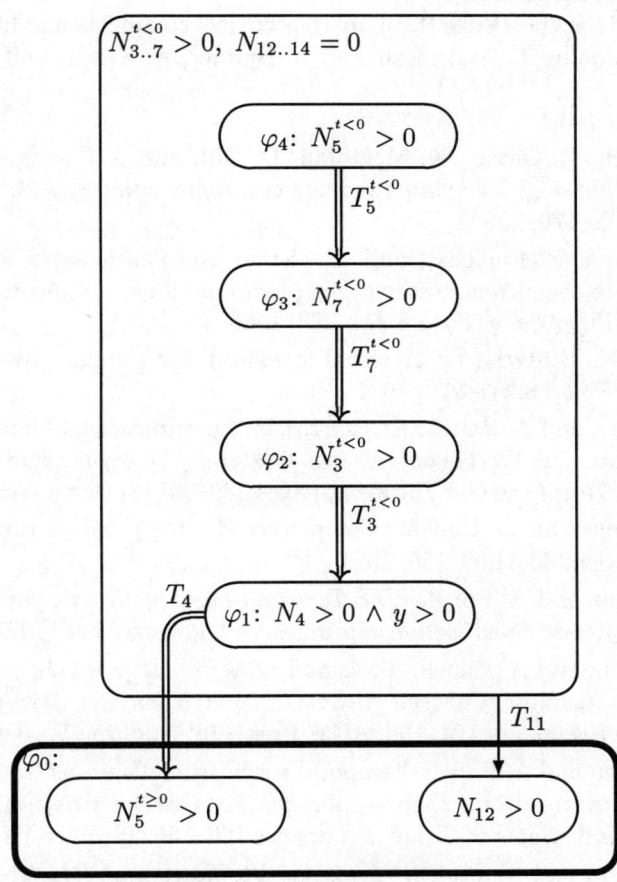

FIG. 38. A verification diagram for Lemma B3.

Lemma B4 $\quad N_{12} > 0 \;\Rightarrow\; \Diamond(N_6 + N_{13} > 0)$

This lemma starts from a situation in which we identify a writer at ℓ_{12}. If $t[i] \geq 0$ for this process, then we can easily prove that eventually $N_{13} > 0$. Otherwise, $t[i] < 0$, and we can easily trace the progress of this process from ℓ_{12}, through ℓ_{14}, ℓ_9 until it reaches ℓ_{10}. We now use Lemma A to show that if L_{10} is nonempty, then eventually some process will reach ℓ_6 or ℓ_{13}.

Lemma B5 $N_5^{t \geq 0} > 0 \;\Rightarrow\; \Diamond(N_6 > 0)$

This lemma requires one helpful step, performed by any of the processes in $L_5^{t \geq 0}$, to achieve a nonempty L_6.

Acknowledgement

We gratefuly acknolwedge the numerous critical comments and helpful suggestions made by A. Anuchitanukul, N. Bjørner, A. Kapur, and T. Uribe.

Bibliography

1. J. Burch, E. Clarke, K. McMillan, D. Dill, and J. Hwang. Symbolic model checking: 10^{20} states and beyond. *Information and Computation*, 98(2):142–170, 1992.
2. E. Clarke, E. Emerson, and A. Sistla. Automatic verification of finite state concurrent systems using temporal logic specifications. *ACM Trans. Prog. Lang. Sys.*, 8:244–263, 1986.
3. D. Harel. Statecharts: A visual formalism for complex systems. *Sci. Comp. Prog.*, 8:231–274, 1987.
4. Z. Manna and A. Pnueli. An exercise in the verification of multi-process programs. In W. Feijen, A. van Gasteren, D. Gries, and J. Misra, editors, *Beauty is Our Business*, pages 289–301. Springer-Verlag, 1990.
5. Z. Manna and A. Pnueli. Completing the temporal picture. *Theor. Comp. Sci.*, 83(1):97–130, 1991.
6. Z. Manna and A. Pnueli. *The Temporal Logic of Reactive and Concurrent Systems: Specification*. Springer-Verlag, New York, 1991.
7. Z. Manna and A. Pnueli. Tools and rules for the practicing verifier. In R. Rashid, editor, *Carnegie Mellon Computer Science: A 25-year Commemorative*, pages 121–156. ACM Press and Addison–Wesley, 1991.
8. Z. Manna and A. Pnueli. Temporal verification diagrams. In T. Ito and A. R. Meyer, editors, *Theoretical Aspects of Computer Software*, volume 789 of *Lect. Notes in Comp. Sci.*, pages 726–765. Springer-Verlag, 1994.
9. Z. Manna and A. Pnueli. *Temporal Verification of Reactive Systems: Safety*. Springer-Verlag, New York, 1995.

The Bakery Algorithm: Yet Another Specification and Verification

Egon Börger,[*]   Yuri Gurevich[†]   and

Dean Rosenzweig[‡]

Abstract

In a meeting at Schloss Dagstuhl in June 1993, Uri Abraham and Menachem Magidor have challenged the thesis that an evolving algebra can be tailored to any algorithm at its own abstraction level. As an example they gave an instructive proof which uses lower and higher views to show correctness of Lamport's Bakery Algorithm. We construct two evolving algebras capturing lower and higher view respectively, enabling a simple and concise proof of correctness for the Bakery Algorithm.

Uri Abraham [Abraham93] has devised an instructive correctness proof for various variants of Lamport's Bakery Algorithm, relying on a distinction between a lower view and a higher view of the algorithms. Actions at the higher level represent complex lower level computations. He formulates abstract conditions on higher level actions which are then shown to suffice for correctness and fairness (in the form of a 'first-come-first-served' property and deadlock-freedom) and to be satisfied by the corresponding lower level computations.

At a seminar at Schloss Dagstuhl in June 1993, Uri Abraham and Menachem Magidor have expressed doubts that such a proof could be naturally carried out in the evolving algebra framework of [Gurevich91], since the latter uses a notion of atomic instantaneous action.

We construct, in Section 1, two evolving algebras, reflecting the lower and higher views of Lamport's improved version of the Bakery Algorithm (see [Lamport79]).

In Section 2 we display abstract conditions on higher level actions, in terms of atomic-action semantics, enabling a simple and concise proof of the first-come-first-served property (FCFS) and deadlock-freedom. The conditions are easily seen to be satisfied by corresponding lower level computations. Since actions of an evolving algebra are assumed there to be atomic, that proof treats the case of atomic reads and writes to shared registers.

---

[*]Partially supported by MURST 91.

[†]Partially supported by NSF Grant CCR 92-04742 and ONR grant N00014-91-J-11861.

[‡]Partially supported by CNR/Gnasaga grant 2.94.

In Section 3 we explain the semantics of evolving algebras assuming *durative actions*, actions taking time, and allowing overlapping of reads and writes to shared registers. Refining the abstract conditions for the case of *regular* reads (see [Lamport86]), we show that the proof of the previous section goes through with only slight modifications. For the more general case of *safe* registers, correctness of the algorithm from [Lamport74] is then easily proved by a slight adaptation of the present argument—the improved algorithm from [Lamport79] is not correct for safe registers, as shown by a simple counterexample.

Thus the two interpretations of evolving algebra dynamics reflect two disciplines for accessing shared registers—by atomic and non-overlapping reads and writes, or by durative and possibly overlapping ones. What really changes is the notion of state: for atomic actions we have global states, whereas for durative actions we have instead local states of agents (see the concept of external and internal locations in section 3.1). The correctness proof, however, remains essentially the same.

In order to make the chapter technically self-contained, except for basic notions about evolving algebras of [Gurevich91, Gurevich94], we start Section 1 with a review of Lamport's 1979 algorithm and give full details of proofs also in those places where we borrow from [Abraham93].

1 The algorithms

This section presents Lamport's algorithm (taken in a form which is adapted from [Abraham93]), the corresponding 'lower level' evolving algebra, and the more abstract evolving algebra reflecting the 'higher level view'.

1.1 Lamport's algorithm

For arbitrary but fixed N let $P_1, \ldots, P_N$ be processes that may want from time to time to access a 'critical section' CS of code. Any mutual exclusion protocol—which each P_i is supposed to execute in order to enter the critical section—has to prevent two processes from being in the critical section simultaneously. The Bakery Algorithm provides each P_i with a (shared) register R_i and a (private) array $n[1], \ldots, n[N]$ holding natural numbers. Only P_i is allowed to write to R_i but every process can read the register. We assume each register to be initialized with value 0.

The Bakery Algorithm is divided into six consecutive phases: *start*, *doorway*, *ticket* assignment, *wait* section, *critical section* and *finale*. A process P_i starts by declaring its interest in accessing the critical section through writing 1 into its register recording the value written also in its corresponding array variable. In the doorway section, P_i copies all the other registers into its array. It then writes a *ticket*, greater than each number in its array, into its register and into $n[i]$. During the subsequent wait section, process P_i keeps reading, into its array, the registers of each other process P_j, until the resulting array value $n[j] = 0$ or $n[j] > n[i]$ or

$n[j] = n[i] \wedge j > i$. Then P_i enters the critical section. Upon leaving CS, as finale, P_i sets its register to 0:

Start
```
    n[i] := 1
    write(R_i,n[i])
```
Doorway
```
    for all j≠i, read(R_j,n[j])
```
Ticket
```
    n[i] := 1 + max_j n[j]
    write(R_i,n[i])
```
Wait
```
    for all j≠i, repeat
        read(R_j,n[j]) until
        n[j]=0 or n[j]>n[i] or (n[j]=n[i] and j>i)
```
Critical Section

Finale
```
    write(R_i,0)
```

Note that by ordering pairs of positive integers lexicographically:

$$(i,j) < (k,l) \longleftrightarrow [i < k \text{ or } (i = k \text{ and } j < l)]$$

one can write the until condition as follows: n[j]=0 or (n[j],j)>(n[i],i). The condition assures that, in case two processes get the same 'ticket', the one with the smaller identifier gets the priority.

Note also that the for-all commands in the doorway and the wait section may be executed in many ways: in various sequences, all at once, concurrently etc.

1.2 The lower level algebra $\mathcal{B}_1$

As the basis for the subsequent analysis and 'higher level' abstraction, we reformulate here the above Bakery Algorithm as an evolving algebra $\mathcal{B}_1$. It contains, for each process, a *customer-agent*. The customers execute the module with rules Start, Ticket, Entry, Exit, Finale—corresponding to the homonymous Bakery Algorithm phases. In order to preserve the freedom of choosing an ordering of reads, in Doorway and Wait, $\mathcal{B}_1$ contains also *reader-agents* $r(X,Y)$, where X,Y are customers. Each reader-agent $r(X,Y)$ reads, during the doorway and the wait section of X, the register $R(Y)$ of process Y into X's array component $A(X,Y)$, doing the work of the *Doorway* and *Wait* phases. The module of a reader-agent has two rules, Read and Check.

Each customer X can execute the rules Start, Ticket, Entry, Exit, Finale only sequentially, in that order; this is assured by the function *mode* which for each X assumes cyclically the values *satisfied, doorway, wait, CS, done* and *satisfied*. The *mode* function also assures that Ticket and Entry can be executed by X only after all readers have executed their Read and Check rules respectively. Thus the following rules faithfully represent the corresponding phases of the Bakery Algorithm (given that initially all registers $R(X)$ have value 0 and all customers are satisfied):

Customer X
Start

    if mode(X)=satisfied then
        A(X,X) := 1, R(X) := 1, mode(X) := doorway

Ticket

    if mode(X)=doorway and $(\forall Y \neq X)$ mode(r(X,Y))=wait then
        A(X,X) := $1 + \max_Y$ A(X,Y), R(X) := $1 + \max_Y$ A(X,Y)
        mode(X) := wait

Entry

    if mode(X) = wait and $(\forall Y \neq X)$ mode(r(X,Y)) = doorway then
        mode(X) := CS

Exit

    if mode(X) = CS then
        mode(X) := done

Finale

    if mode(X) = done then
        R(X) := 0, mode(X) := satisfied

Reader $r(X,Y)$
Read

    if mode(r(X,Y)) = mode(X) then
        A(X,Y) := R(Y)
        if mode(r(X,Y))=doorway then mode(r(X,Y)) := wait
        if mode(r(X,Y))=wait then mode(r(X,Y)) := check

Check

```
if mode(r(X,Y)) = check then
    if A(X,Y)=0 or (A(X,Y),id(Y)) > (A(X,X),id(X)) then
        mode(r(X,Y)) := doorway
    else mode(r(X,Y)) := wait
```

The modules of rules are written as templates, i.e. there is a module for each customer X and a module for each reader $r(X,Y)$.

1.3 The higher level algebra B_2

In this subsection we define an evolving algebra expressing a 'higher level' view of the Bakery Algorithm. The relevant datum to be described abstractly is the *ticket* assigned to a customer X (and written into its register $R(X)$) when X leaves the doorway and enters the wait section. We introduce for this purpose an external function T whose values are determined dynamically by the outside world, cf. [Gurevich91].

The relevant moment to be analyzed is the moment at which a process which has received a ticket is allowed to enter the critical section. This 'permission to go' will also be represented by an external function, Go.

In subsequent sections we will impose conditions upon T and Go which will be shown to guarantee the correctness of the higher level Bakery Algebra.

The higher level algebra has only one module, parametric in a customer X, which has five rules. Again, we assume that initially all registers have value 0 and all customers are satisfied:

Start

```
if mode(X) = satisfied then
    R(X) := 1, mode(X) := doorway
```

Ticket

```
if mode(X) = doorway then
    R(X) := T(X), mode(X) := wait
```

Entry

```
if mode(X) = wait and Go(X) then
    mode(X) := CS
```

Exit

```
if mode(X) = CS then
    mode(X) := done
```

Finale

```
if mode(X) = done then
    mode(X) := satisfied, R(X) := 0
```

2 Atomic actions interpretation
2.1 Semantics of $\mathcal{B}_1$

We rely on the notion of run of [Gurervich94], specialized to *real time*.

This means that we shall speak of a move (rule execution) taking place at moment a. Since we consider atomic actions here, we assume moves to take zero time. Each move is performed by an agent (a customer or a reader) and, since agents are sequential, two moves by the same agent cannot take place at the same moment. For any moment a the set of all moves taking place no later than a is finite (let us call this property 'cofiniteness'). The state (static algebra) $\mathcal{S}_b$ at time b is the one resulting from all moves taking place before b. We shall denote the value a term t takes (in the state) at time b by t_b.

If a move is executed at time b, $\mathcal{S}_b$ is the state in which the move is executed; for some sufficiently small ϵ, $\mathcal{S}_{b+\epsilon}$ is the state resulting from the move. We do not allow (in this section) to read from and write to the same location at the same time. We assume that no module stalls forever; eventually it makes a move (provided a move is enabled all the time). There is one exception: customers are allowed to remain in mode *satisfied* forever.

We now define intervals of (real) time characterized by the moments of successive executions, by a process X, of its rules Start, Ticket, Entry and Exit.

Definition 2.1 Suppose X executes Start and Ticket rules at moments a and b and does not execute anything in between. Then the open interval $x = (a, b)$ is a *doorway* of X. If b is the last execution of X then the *wait interval* $W(x) = (b, \infty)$ and the *CS interval* $CS(x)$ is undefined. Suppose that the execution of Ticket rule at b is followed by executions of Entry rule at c and Exit rule at d. Then $W(x) = (b, c)$ and $CS(x) = (c, d)$.

By the assumption that no module stalls forever, every doorway is finite. This is in accordance with the fact that in the low-level Bakery Algebra, $T(x)$ is always defined when interpreted as $1 + \max_Y A(X, Y)$.

2.2 Semantics of $\mathcal{B}_2$

The semantics of $\mathcal{B}_2$ is similar to that of $\mathcal{B}_1$. There are no readers around. The definition of doorways and related periods applies also to $\mathcal{B}_2$.

Contrary to $\mathcal{B}_1$, $\mathcal{B}_2$ has external functions, namely T and Go. We are going to impose some constraints on them. To avoid repetitive case distinctions for processes which (being satisfied) have register 0, and of processes which happen to receive the same ticket, we introduce the following notation. If f is a function from the original processes to natural numbers, let

$$f'(X) = \begin{cases} N \cdot f(X) + \text{id}(X), & \text{if } f(X) > 0; \\ \infty, & \text{otherwise.} \end{cases}$$

We assume that the identifiers of the N processes are natural numbers $< N$.

For real intervals I, J we define $I < J$ to mean that $a < b$ for all $a \in I$, $b \in J$. This ordering will help us to formalize the idea that tickets increase together with doorways (see C1 below). This should also apply in a way to overlapping doorways; these are ordered by the following relation $\triangleleft$, borrowed from [Abraham93].

Let $X \neq Y$, x ranges over doorways of X, y ranges over doorways of Y.

Definition 2.2 $x \triangleleft y$ if $x \cap y \neq \emptyset$ and $T'(x) < T'(y)$. Further, $x \prec y$ if $x \triangleleft y$ or $x < y$.

Lemma 2.3 $x \prec y$ or $y \prec x$.

Proof Note that $T'(y) \neq T'(x)$ for $X \neq Y$. □

Constraints on T and Go

C0 $T(x)$ is a positive integer > 1.
C1 If $y < x$ then either $\mathrm{CS}(y) < \sup(x)$ or $T'(y) < T'(x)$.
C2 If $Go(X)$ holds at moment $t > \sup(x)$ then, for every $Y \neq X$, there exists a moment $b \in W(x)$ such that $T'(x) < R'_b(Y)$.
C3 If $W(y)$ is finite for all $y \prec x$, then $W(x)$ is finite.

Intuitively, C1 says that tickets respect the temporal precedence of doorways with overlapping wait periods, C3 is an induction principle, and C2 expresses that permission to go is obtained by checking the ticket against competitors' registers.

2.3 $\mathcal{B}_1$ implements $\mathcal{B}_2$ correctly

We check that the constraints are satisfied in the first algebra, where $T(X) = 1 + \max_Y A(X, Y)$, and $Go_t(X)$ means that the condition of the rule Entry is satisfied at moment t.

C0 is satisfied since the maximum in the rule Ticket is taken over each Y, including X which at that moment has register value $R(X) = 1$.

C1. Let t be the time of the Read move by $r(X, Y)$ during x. If there exists a Finale move by Y during $(\sup(y), t)$, then $\mathrm{CS}(y) < \sup(x)$. Otherwise $R_t(Y) = T(y)$ and therefore $T(x) \geq 1 + R_t(Y) > T(y) > 0$. Hence $T'(x) > T'(y)$.

C2. $Go(X)$ becomes true in $\mathcal{B}_1$ when all readers $r(X, Y)$ finish their wait-section readings. Fix a $Y \neq X$ and consider the last Read move by $r(X, Y)$ during $W(x)$. In view of the corresponding Check move, the time of that Read move is the desired b.

C3. By contradiction, suppose that the premise is satisfied but the conclusion is false, i.e. $W(x)$ is infinite.

Claim: There is a moment $b \in W(x)$ so late that the following two properties hold for each y:

(i) if $y \prec x$ then $b > \sup(CS(y))$; (ii) if $x \prec y$ then $b > \sup(y)$.

Given the claim, it suffices to prove that any $r(X, Y)$ finishes its reading during $W(x)$ (in contradiction to the assumption that $W(x)$ is infinite). If $r(X, Y)$ finishes its reading before b, we are done since $b \in W(x)$. Otherwise, by definition of b, no $Y \neq X$ can be in mode doorway at or after b. Thus, at or after b, $r(X, Y)$ can read either 0 or $T(y)$ for some $y \succ x$. In the first case the next Check of $r(X, Y)$ will succeed; in the second case it will also succeed, since $T'(y) > T'(x)$ (by C1 if $x < y$, and by definition of $\triangleleft$ if $x \triangleleft y$). Thus, the very first reading at or after b will be the last reading of $r(X, Y)$.

To prove the claim, note that, by the cofiniteness condition of runs, there are only finitely many doorways y coming earlier than or overlapping with x. Note that, for $y \prec x$, $\sup(CS(y)) < \infty$ by the assumption that $W(y)$ is finite and that no module stalls forever. It suffices to prove that, for each Y, there is at most one $y > x$. Suppose $x < y$. Then, by C1, $T'(x) < T'(y)$ (since $W(x)$ is infinite), and Y remains waiting forever, i.e. $r(Y, X)$ keeps forever executing waiting section Reads.

2.4 Correctness and fairness of $\mathcal{B}_2$

Lemma 2.4 (FCFS) *If $y \prec x$ and $W(x)$ is finite, then $W(y)$ is finite and $CS(y) < CS(x)$.*

Proof Assume the premise is satisfied and the conclusion is false. Take b as given by C2.

Claim 1 : $T'(y) < T'(x)$.

Claim 2 : $\sup(y) < b$.

Given the claims, we have $T'(y) < T'(x) < R'_b(Y)$ and thus Y must be writing to $R(Y)$ at some time in $(\sup(y), b)$. But the first such write after $\sup(y)$ must be a Finale move, which contradicts the assumption that the conclusion of the lemma is false.

Claim 1 follows immediately from the definition of $\prec$ in case of overlap, and from C1 otherwise.

To prove Claim 2, we first note that $b > \inf(y)$, in view of $y \prec x$. It is impossible that $inf(y) < b \leq \sup(y)$, since then $R_b(Y) = 1$. □

Lemma 2.5 $\prec$ *is transitive.*

Proof By contradiction. Suppose $x \prec y \prec z \prec x$. Count the number n of <'s in the above sequence of $\prec$ signs. In case $n = 0$ the statement follows from the fact that the order of integers (tickets) is transitive, and in cases $n = 2, 3$ the statement follows from the fact that the order < of real intervals is transitive. In case $n = 1$, without loss of generality, we have $x \triangleleft y \triangleleft z < x$ and therefore $T'(x) < T'(y) < T'(z)$. By Lemma 2.4, the assumption $x \prec y \prec z \prec x$ implies that $W(x), W(y)$ and $W(z)$ are all infinite. Thus we can apply C1 to obtain also $T'(z) < T'(x)$, which is impossible. □

Lemma 2.6 (Deadlock-freedom) *Every $W(x)$ is finite.*

Proof By the cofiniteness condition on runs, $\prec$ is well-founded. Then C3 is precisely the induction principle required to establish the claim. □

This section is summarized in the following:

Theorem 2.7 *Doorways are linearly ordered by $\prec$. All waiting sections are finite, and $x \prec y$ implies $CS(x) < CS(y)$.*

3 Durative actions interpretation

3.1 Semantics of $\mathcal{B}_1$

Let S be an initial state where all customers are in mode *satisfied*, all readers are in mode *doorway*, and all registers $R(X)$ have value 0—the values of A don't matter. We consider runs from S.

A run of $\mathcal{B}_1$ consists of the following:

- A collection M of elements, called *moves*.
- A function $\mathcal{A}$ from M to the set of agents. $\mathcal{A}(\mu)$ is the agent that makes the move μ.
- A function P that associates a nonempty finite open time interval with each move. $P(\mu)$ is the execution period of μ. No move can last forever.

However, not every triple $(M, \mathcal{A}, P)$ is a run. The following conditions 1–6 should be satisfied. The first condition reflects the fact that our agents are sequential:

1 For each agent X, $\{P(\mu) : \mathcal{A}(\mu) = X\}$ is linearly ordered by $<$. Moreover, this ordered set is isomorphic to an initial segment of positive integers, and if it is infinite then $\sup_\mu P(\mu) = \infty$.

We say that an agent Z is passive at moment t (resp. in interval I) if t does not belong to (resp. I does not intersect) the period $P(\mu)$ of any move of Z. We would like to insure that X has a well defined state $\mathcal{S}_t(X)$ at every passive moment t of X.

2 If $[a, b]$ is a passive interval of an agent X then $\mathcal{S}_b(X) = \mathcal{S}_a(X)$.

To insure that condition 2 is satisfied, we stipulate the following.

A customer X. Locations of dynamic functions internal to X: mode(X), $A(X, X)$ and $R(X)$. Locations of dynamic functions external to X: mode$(r(X, Y))$ and $A(X, Y)$ where $Y \neq X$.

A reader $r(X, Y)$. Internal locations: mode$(r(X, Y))$ and $A(X, Y)$. External locations: mode(X), $A(X, X)$ and $R(Y)$.

States of an agent reflect only the values of internal locations. Notice that every location of any function is internal to some agent.

Call a move μ of an agent X *atomic* with respect to an external location ℓ if ℓ is not updated during $P(\mu)$. A move μ is *atomic* if it is atomic with respect to all its external locations. An agent is *atomic* if all its moves are so.

3 If an agent X makes an atomic move μ and $P(\mu) = (a, b)$, then $\mathcal{S}_b(X)$ is the result of executing one step of X at $\mathcal{S}_a(X)$. (See [Gurervich94] for the definition of the result of a one-step execution of a sequential evolving algebra at a given state.)

4 All customers are atomic. All Check moves of readers are atomic. All Read moves of any $r(X, Y)$ are atomic with respect to mode(X).

Read moves of a reader $R(X, Y)$ may be nonatomic with respect to $R(Y)$. We adopt Lamport's notion of regular reads (with a different but equivalent definition):

5 Suppose that (a, b) is the period of a Read move μ by a reader $Q = r(X, Y)$. The value of $A(X, Y)$ in state $\mathcal{S}_b(Q)$, at passive moment b of Q, is nondeterministically chosen among the values of $R(Y)$ at moments t satisfying at least one of the following conditions:
- t is Y's last passive moment $\leq a$,
- t is one of Y's passive moments in (a, b),
- t is Y's first passive moment $\geq b$.

Let $\xi(\mu)$ be the chosen moment t.

6 If an agent Z has an infinite passive interval during which it is enabled in its final state then Z is an original agent and its mode is *satisfied*.

In other words, we assume again that no agent stalls forever except if it is an original agent in mode satisfied. We will use the following refined definition of doorway, wait and CS sections.

Definition 3.1

- Suppose X executes Start during (a_1, a_2) and then executes Ticket during (b_1, b_2), so that the interval $[a_2, b_1]$ is passive for X. Then $x = (a_2, b_2)$ is a *doorway* of X.
- Suppose that X executes Ticket during (b_1, b_2). If the execution of Ticket is not followed by an execution of Entry then the *wait period* $W(x)$ is (b_2, ∞). Suppose that the execution of Ticket is followed by an execution of Entry during some period (c_1, c_2), so that the interval $[b_2, c_1]$ is passive for X. Then $W(x) = (b_2, c_1)$.
- Suppose that X executes Entry during (c_1, c_2) and then executes Exit during (d_1, d_2), so that the interval $[c_2, d_1]$ is passive for X. Then the *critical section period* $CS(x)$ is (c_1, d_2).

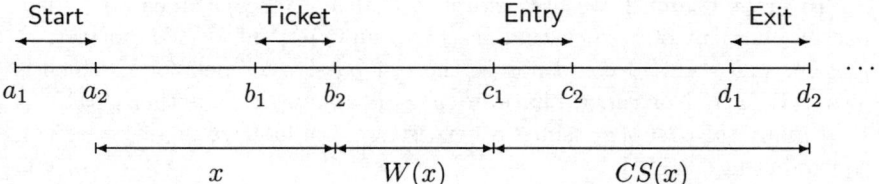

3.2 Semantics of B_2

The semantics of B_2 is similar to that of B_1. The constraints C0, C1 and C3 of the previous section remain the same, while C2 is refined for regular registers as follows:

C2 If $Go(X)$ holds at moment $t > \sup(x)$ then, for every $Y \neq X$, there exists a passive moments b for Y such that $T'(x) < R'_b(Y)$ and one of the following holds:
$b \in W(x)$, or
b is the last passive moment of Y which is $\leq \inf(W(x))$, or
b is the first passive moment of Y which is $\geq \sup(W(x))$.

3.3 B_1 implements B_2 correctly

The proofs that C0 and C3 hold of B_1 remain the same; the proofs for C1 and C2 are modified as follows:

C1. Let μ be the Read move by $r(X,Y)$ during x and $t = \xi(\mu)$. If there exists a Finale move ν by Y such that $P(\nu)$ intersects $P(\mu)$, then $CS(y) < \sup(x)$. Otherwise $R_t(Y) = T(y)$ and therefore $T(x) \geq 1 + R_t(Y) > T(y) > 0$. Hence $T'(x) > T'(y)$.

C2. $Go(X)$ becomes true in B_1 when all readers $r(X,Y)$ finish their wait-section readings. Fix a $Y \neq X$ and consider the last Read move ν by $r(X,Y)$ during $W(x)$. The desired b is $\xi(\nu)$.

3.4 Correctness and fairness of B_2

All proofs of the previous section remain, except for the proof of Lemma 2.4, which is modified as follows.

Proof Assume that the premise is satisfied and that the conclusion is false. Take b as given by C2.

Claim 1 : $T'(y) < T'(x)$.

Claim 2 : $\sup(y) < b$.

Given the claims, we have $R'_{\sup(y)}(Y) = T'(y) < T'(x) < R'_b(Y)$ and thus Y must be writing to $R(Y)$ somewhere in $(\sup(y), b)$ so that this write starts before $\sup(W(x))$. But the first such write after $\sup(y)$ must be a Finale move, which contradicts the assumption that the conclusion of the lemma is false.

Claim 1 follows immediately from the definition of $\prec$ in case of overlap, and from C1 otherwise.

To prove Claim 2, we first establish that $b \geq \inf(y)$. Since $\inf(y)$ is a passive moment of Y such that $\inf(y) < \sup(x) = \inf(W(x))$ (in view of $y \prec x$), so $b < \inf(y)$ could not be the last passive moment of Y which is $\leq inf(W(x))$. Nor can we have $\inf(y) \leq b < \sup(y)$, since then $R_b(Y) = 1$. Finally, $b \neq \sup(y)$, since otherwise we would have $R_b(Y) = T(y)$, contradicting Claim 1. □

3.5 Counterexample for safe registers

The following example shows that the algorithm of [Lamport79] is not correct for the more general case of *safe* registers (see [Lamport86])—where a read overlapping with a write may get any admissible value whatsoever.

There are two customers X and Y which act at the indicated times as follows:

12.00–12.05:	X and Y both write 1 into their registers and the array
12.05–12.10:	Y reads 1 from $R[X]$
12.10–12.40:	Y writes ticket 2 into $R[Y]$ and the array
12.15–12.20:	X reads from $R[Y]$ getting (by overlap) 17
12.25–12.30:	X writes ticket 18 to $R[X]$ and the array
12.30–12.35:	X reads $R[Y]$ getting 117 (by overlap)
12.45–12.50:	Y reads 18 from $R[X]$
13.00:	X and Y both go to CS

It is, however, easy to adapt the present proof to show correctness of the algorithm of [Lamport74] for safe registers, rephrased as an appropriate evolving algebra, using the same abstract conditions C0–C3.

Acknowledgment. We thank Uri Abraham for useful discussions.

Bibliography

[Abraham93] Abraham, U. *Bakery Algorithms*. In: "Proc. of the Concurrency, Specification and Programming Workshop, Niewbortow 1993", Eds. H.-D. Burkhard, L. Czaja, and P. Starke, Wydawnictwa Uniw. Warszawskiego, Warsaw 1994, 1–40. Manuscript. 1993, pp.35

[Gurevich91] Gurevich, Y., *Evolving Algebras. A Tutorial Introduction*, EATCS Bulletin 43, February 1991, pp. 264–284. A slightly revised version appeared in "Current Trends in Theoretical Computer Science", Eds. G. Rozenberg and A. Salomaa, World Scientific, 1993, 266–292.

[Gurevich94] Gurevich, Y., *Evolving Algebra 1993: Lipari Guide*, this volume

[Lamport74] Lamport, L., *A new solution of Dijkstra concurrent programming problem*. In: *Comm. ACM*, vol. 17, 8, 453–455.

[Lamport79] Lamport, L., *A New Approach to Proving the Correctness of Multiprocess Programs*. In: *ACM Transaction on Programming Languages and Systems*, vol.1, 1, July 1979, 84–97.

[Lamport86] Lamport, L., *On Interprocess Communication*. In: *Distributed Computing*, vol.1, 77–101.

Part IV: Protocols

Kermit: Specification and Verification

James K. Huggins*

Kermit is a popular communication protocol. We formally specify Kermit and verify it. As far as we know, this has not been done yet, though the alternating bit and sliding window protocols, used by Kermit, have been specified and verified by many authors [Kr, SL, LM]. Our main goal is a faithful readable specification which allows one to formalize the intuitive verification proof without much overhead.

In his foreword to [DaC], Donald Knuth writes "I hope that many readers of this book will be challenged to find high-level concepts and invariant relations by which various versions of the Kermit protocol can be proved correct in a mathematical sense." We believe our specification and verification meets this challenge.

We use the evolving algebra approach. A full definition of evolving algebras may be found in [Gur]. We use the term "ealgebra" (read e-algebra) as an abbreviation for "evolving algebra". We begin with ealgebra specifications and verifications of two more abstract communications protocols used by various versions of Kermit: the alternating bit protocol and the sliding window protocol. The nice feature of the ealgebra approach is that the road from an intuitive proof to a precise one is very short; there is little overhead. Then we will present a series of ealgebras for the Kermit protocol, filling in the pieces where necessary to show how Kermit uses the abstract protocols.

As usual with protocols, we prove theorems dealing with properties of safety ("bad things don't happen") and liveness ("good things do happen"). Our safety theorems are of the form "Every state reachable in any relevant run satisfies property Φ" and are proved by induction on relevant runs. It is usually obvious that relevant initial states satisfy Φ; more work is required to show that the transition rules preserve Φ. The liveness theorems have the form "Every fair run has such and such property."

Acknowledgments. Yuri Gurevich directed this study; his comments throughout its development were numerous and extremely helpful. Frank da Cruz made useful comments on a later draft.

1 The Alternating Bit Protocol (ABP)

The alternating bit protocol (ABP), first proposed in [BSW], is a simple protocol at the heart of many communication protocols currently in use. Each agent participating in the protocol (we will call them "sender" and

---

*Partially supported by ONR grant N00014-91-J-1861 and NSF grant CCR-92-04742.

"receiver", though both agents send and receive messages) has a private synchronization bit. The sender has data which she sends to the receiver. The receiver sends an acknowledgment message for each datum received. Messages are marked with a synchronization bit to distinguish between data which has and has not been received by the receiver.

We present a generalized version of the ABP which sends an infinite sequence of data between the two agents and prove its correctness, using sequential runs throughout. An ABP which sends a finite sequence of data and terminates can easily be developed from our more general version.

As an aid to comprehension, we use feminine pronouns to refer to the sender and masculine pronouns to refer to the receiver.

1.1 Function Descriptions

1.1.1 Common Functions

Our agents send messages, each comprising a datum and a synchronization bit, through a network. This leads to universes of *messages*, *data*, and *bits*. We represent each communication path between agents as a queue of messages; this leads to a universe of *queues*. (Note that by "queue" we mean the abstract datatype and not a particular physical device.) We also make use of the universe of *integers*.

We use the functions $Msg: data \times bits \to messages$, $Bit: messages \to bits$ and $Data: messages \to data$ to compose and decompose messages, respectively. (That is, if $Msg(d,b) = m$, then $Bit(m) = b$ and $Data(m) = d$.) The distinguished element *Null: data* is a datum used as a placeholder for acknowledgment messages (in which the only important information is the bit, not the datum). The function $Flip: bits \to bits$ flips a bit to its opposite value. That is, $Flip(0) = 1$ and $Flip(1) = 0$.

For *queues*, we use the functions $Append: queues \times messages \to queues$, $Head: queues \to messages$, and $Tail: queues \to queues$ with the obvious meanings. The distinguished element $EmptyQueue: queues$ is a queue containing no messages. We denote $Append(a,b)$ by $a \mathrel{+\!+} b$. We define a partial ordering $\leq$ on queues as follows: for queues a and b, $a \leq b$ if a can be obtained from b by deleting zero or more messages from b while maintaining the relative ordering of the remaining messages. If either a or b is not a queue, $a \not\leq b$.

For *integers*, we use the standard infix addition function $+$, as well as the constant 1.

The function *Timeout: Bool* is used to generate re-transmissions of messages.

1.1.2 Private Functions

Each agent has a distinguished element *SenderInMsg, ReceiverInMsg: messages* which holds the current message being processed by the agent, and a distinguished element *SenderBit, ReceiverBit: bits* which holds the agent's synchronization bit. Distinguished elements *SenderQueue, ReceiverQueue: queues* store messages waiting to be processed.

The data that the sender sends is stored in a function *SenderFile: integers* → *data*; the receiver stores all data received in a corresponding function *ReceiverFile: integers* → *data*. The distinguished functions *SenderNo, ReceiverNo: integers* indicate the current datum being sent or received.

1.2 Module Specifications

We use abbreviations *Defined(t), Undefined(t), Clear(t)* for $t \neq undef$, $t = undef$ and $t := undef$ respectively; here t is a term.

The sender examines each acknowledgment message sent to her by the receiver. If the sender receives an acknowledgment whose bit matches her synchronization bit, she knows that her last message arrived successfully, and she can now send a new message (with a new bit). Any messages received whose bit does not match her synchronization bit are discarded.

To insure against message loss due to an unreliable network, the sender also re-sends her last message when a timeout signal occurs. We also use this behavior to begin the communication process; during any run, no transition rules will fire until a timeout signal occurs, at which point the sender will send her first message.

The receiver acknowledges every message he receives from the sender by re-transmitting the bit from the received message. Additionally, if the bit received matches his synchronization bit, the receiver records the datum from the message in his output file, and updates his file marker and synchronization bit to be ready to accept the next datum from the sender. The sender and receiver modules are given in Fig. 1.

Agents communicate by placing messages into queues (*SenderQueue, ReceiverQueue*) and by reading messages placed into reception variables (*SenderInMsg, ReceiverInMsg*). Two communications modules, shown in Fig. 2, transfer messages between these queues and reception variables.

If the communications network were reliable, no further modules would be needed. However, messages may be lost, although not corrupted or reordered. As a result, we need to generate timeout signals to enable the sender to re-transmit messages. We present three modules which describe this behavior in Fig. 3.

1.3 Run Definitions

We now wish to prove the correctness of the ABP. We cannot prove that any of the protocols to be discussed here are correct for all runs; most protocols assume, for example, that both agents satisfy some initial conditions. Consequently, we restrict our attention to certain types of runs. Call a run ρ *regular* if its initial state satisfies a specified set of initial conditions. The initial conditions for the ABP are shown in Fig. 4. Our safety properties will be proved over regular runs.

Module: Sender
Rule: ReTransmit
if *Timeout* **then**
    ReceiverQueue :=
        ReceiverQueue ++ *Msg(SenderFile(SenderNo),SenderBit)*
    Timeout := *false*
endif

Rule: ProcessAck
if *Defined(SenderInMsg)* **and** *Bit(SenderInMsg)* = *SenderBit* **then**
    ReceiverQueue :=
        ReceiverQueue ++ *Msg(SenderFile(SenderNo+1),Flip(SenderBit))*
    SenderBit := *Flip(SenderBit)*, *SenderNo* := *SenderNo + 1*
endif

Rule: ClearMessage
if *Defined(SenderInMsg)* **then** *Clear(SenderInMsg)* **endif**

Module: Receiver
Rule: AcceptDatum
if *Defined(ReceiverInMsg)* **and** *Bit(ReceiverInMsg)* = *ReceiverBit* **then**
    ReceiverFile(ReceiverNo) := *Data(ReceiverInMsg)*
    ReceiverNo := *ReceiverNo + 1*, *ReceiverBit* := *Flip(ReceiverBit)*
endif

Rule: AcknowledgeMessage
if *Defined(ReceiverInMsg)* **then**
    SenderQueue := *SenderQueue* ++ *Msg(Null,Bit(ReceiverInMsg))*
    Clear(ReceiverInMsg)
endif

FIG. 1. ABP SENDER AND RECEIVER MODULES.

Communication may not be possible even in a regular run. The sender might never receive a timeout when one is needed, or a communications module might be too active, throwing away all messages sent by one agent. The latter corresponds to the real-world situation where the underlying communications medium breaks down; obviously, no protocol can succeed under those conditions. Thus, we must make certain minimal assumptions about the underlying medium in order to complete our proofs. Essentially, we wish to exclude the "unfair" conditions described above.

Module: SenderCommunicate
if $Undefined(SenderInMsg)$ **and** $SenderQueue \neq EmptyQueue$ **then**
  $SenderInMsg := Head(SenderQueue)$
  $SenderQueue := Tail(SenderQueue)$
endif

Module: ReceiverCommunicate
if $Undefined(ReceiverInMsg)$ **and** $ReceiverQueue \neq EmptyQueue$ **then**
  $ReceiverInMsg := Head(ReceiverQueue)$
  $ReceiverQueue := Tail(ReceiverQueue)$
endif

FIG. 2. ABP SENDER AND RECEIVER COMMUNICATION MODULES.

Module: SenderLoseMessage
if $v \leq SenderQueue$ **then** $SenderQueue := v$ **endif**

Module: ReceiverLoseMessage
if $v \leq ReceiverQueue$ **then** $ReceiverQueue := v$ **endif**

Module: Timeout
if $SenderQueue = ReceiverQueue = EmptyQueue$
    and $SenderInMsg = ReceiverInMsg = undef$ **then**
  $Timeout := true$
endif

FIG. 3. NETWORK LOSS AND TIMEOUT MODULES.

For our purposes, it seems sufficient to require only that certain agents (which we will call *positive* agents) cannot be prohibited from making a move indefinitely. We consequently define an infinite sequential run ρ to be *fair* if for every positive agent X and every tail ρ' of ρ, if X is enabled infinitely often in ρ', then X must make a move in ρ'. For the ABP, the only agents which are not positive are SenderLoseMessage and ReceiverLoseMessage. Our liveness properties will be proved for fair runs.

1.4 Proof of Correctness

We begin with a few notational definitions:

$\forall x \geq 0$ $ReceiverFile(x) = undef$	$SenderNo = ReceiverNo = 0$
$SenderInMsg = ReceiverInMsg = undef$	$SenderBit = ReceiverBit$
$ReceiverQueue = SenderQueue = EmptyQueue$	

FIG. 4. INITIAL CONDITIONS FOR THE ABP.

- *SQ* (respectively, *RQ*) is the sequence of messages in *SenderQueue* (*ReceiverQueue*).
- *SIM* (respectively, *RIM*) is *SenderInMsg* (*ReceiverInMsg*) except when the latter is undefined, when it is the empty sequence.
- *Bit(S)*, where S is a message sequence, is the natural extension of the *Bit* function from messages to sequences of messages.
- + denotes concatenation of message sequences.

Most of our invariant conditions are proved by induction over the number of moves in a run; we will simply say "by induction" in such cases.

Lemma 1.1 *In any reachable state, $Bit(SIM + SQ + RIM + RQ)$ has the form $(Flip(SenderBit))^*(SenderBit)^*$.*

Proof. By induction. Initially, the specified bit sequence is empty. We consider all moves that affect functions present in the invariant.

ClearMessage empties *SenderInMsg*, eliminating the first bit in the bit sequence. This does not affect the truth of the invariant.

ReTransmit appends a copy of *SenderBit* to *ReceiverQueue*, maintaining the invariant.

ProcessAck flips *SenderBit* and appends a copy of the new value of *SenderBit* to *ReceiverQueue*. Since $Bit(SenderInMsg) = SenderBit$ when ProcessAck fires, we know (by the inductive hypothesis) that all bits of the bit sequence must be copies of *SenderBit*. Thus, after ProcessAck completes, the bit sequence will have the form $((Flip(SenderBit))^x SenderBit)$ for some x, satisfying the invariant.

AcknowledgeMessage, SenderCommunicate, ReceiverCommunicate, SenderLoseMessage, and ReceiverLoseMessage transfer bits between or remove bits from various functions but do not alter the order of any of the bits in the bit sequence, preserving the invariant. □

Lemma 1.2 *In any reachable state in which SenderInMsg or SenderQueue contains a message μ such that $Bit(\mu) = SenderBit$, $SenderBit = Flip(ReceiverBit)$.*

Proof. By induction. Initially, both *SenderInMsg* and *SenderQueue* are empty. We consider all moves that affect functions present in the invariant.

ProcessAck flips *SenderBit*. Lemma 1.1 shows that all bits in *SenderQueue* will be copies of $Flip(SenderBit)$ after ProcessAck fires.

AcknowledgeMessage places a copy of *Bit(ReceiverInMsg)* into *SenderQueue*. If this new bit is *Flip(SenderBit)*, then (by Lemma 1.1) the bit sequence of *SenderQueue* has the form *Flip(SenderBit)** and the invariant is maintained.

If not, then *Bit(ReceiverInMsg)* = *SenderBit*. If *SenderBit* = *ReceiverBit* at this time, then rule AcceptDatum must also fire, flipping *ReceiverBit* and yielding *SenderBit* = *Flip(ReceiverBit)*. Otherwise, we have *SenderBit* = *Flip(ReceiverBit)* both before and after AcknowledgeMessage fires, maintaining the invariant.

ClearMessage, SenderCommunicate, and SenderLoseMessage remove messages from or transfer messages between *SenderQueue* and *SenderInMsg*, which does not affect the invariant. □

Lemma 1.3 *In any reachable state, if either ReceiverInMsg or ReceiverQueue contains a message μ such that $Bit(\mu) = Flip(SenderBit)$, then SenderBit = ReceiverBit.*

Proof. By induction. Initially, both *ReceiverInMsg* and *ReceiverQueue* are empty. We consider all moves that affect functions present in the invariant.

ProcessAck flips *SenderBit*. ProcessAck implies that *Bit(SenderInMsg)* = *SenderBit*. By Lemma 1.2, *SenderBit* = *Flip(ReceiverBit)*. Thus, flipping *SenderBit* yields *SenderBit* = *ReceiverBit*, maintaining the invariant.

ReTransmit appends a message with a copy of *SenderBit* to *ReceiverQueue*, which does not affect the truth of the invariant.

AcceptDatum flips *ReceiverBit*. AcceptDatum implies that *Bit (ReceiverInMsg)* = *ReceiverBit*. If *Bit(ReceiverInMsg)* = *SenderBit*, all of the messages in *ReceiverQueue* have copies of *SenderBit* (by Lemma 1.1), and flipping *ReceiverBit* does not affect the invariant.

Otherwise, *Bit(ReceiverInMsg)* = *Flip(SenderBit)*, which implies that *Flip(SenderBit)* = *ReceiverBit*. But this cannot occur: the induction hypothesis implies that *SenderBit* = *ReceiverBit*.

Modules AcknowledgeMessage, ReceiverCommunicate, and ReceiverLoseMessage remove messages from or transfer messages between *ReceiverQueue* and *ReceiverInMsg*, which does not affect the invariant. □

Lemma 1.4 *In any reachable state, the following are true:*

$$SenderBit = ReceiverBit \rightarrow SenderNo = ReceiverNo,$$

$$SenderBit = Flip(ReceiverBit) \rightarrow SenderNo + 1 = ReceiverNo.$$

Proof. By induction. Initially, *SenderBit* = *ReceiverBit* and *SenderNo* = *ReceiverNo=0*. We consider all moves affecting functions in the invariant.

ProcessAck flips *SenderBit* and increments *SenderNo*. By Lemma 1.2, ProcessAck only fires when *SenderBit* = *Flip(ReceiverBit)*; by the induction hypothesis, *SenderNo + 1* = *ReceiverNo*. Flipping *SenderBit* and incrementing *SenderNo* yields the other condition.

AcceptDatum flips *ReceiverBit* and increments *ReceiverNo*. By Lemma 1.3, AcceptDatum only fires when *SenderBit* = *ReceiverBit*; by the induction hypothesis, *SenderNo* = *ReceiverNo*. Flipping *ReceiverBit* and incrementing *ReceiverNo* yields to the other condition. □

Lemma 1.5 *In any reachable state, for any message μ contained in either ReceiverInMsg or ReceiverQueue, $Bit(\mu) = SenderBit \to Data(\mu) = SenderFile(SenderNo)$, and $Bit(\mu) = Flip(SenderBit) \to Data(\mu) = SenderFile(SenderNo-1)$.*

Proof. By induction. Initially, no messages exist in *ReceiverInMsg* or *ReceiverQueue*. We consider all moves that affect functions present in the invariant.

ProcessAck flips *SenderBit* and increments *SenderNo*. We must have $Bit(SenderInMsg) = SenderBit$ in order for ProcessAck to fire; by Lemma 1.1, all messages μ under consideration have $Bit(\mu) = SenderBit$. By the induction hypothesis, we also have $Data(\mu) = SenderFile(SenderNo)$. Incrementing *SenderNo* and flipping *SenderBit* thus results in $Bit(\mu) = Flip(SenderBit)$ and $Data(\mu) = SenderFile(SenderNo-1)$, as desired.

Additionally, a new message μ' is appended to *ReceiverQueue*. After ProcessAck fires, we will have $Bit(\mu') = SenderBit$ and $Data(\mu') = SenderFile(SenderNo)$, as desired.

ReTransmit appends a message containing *SenderFile(SenderNo)* and *SenderBit* to *ReceiverQueue*, maintaining the invariant.

AcknowledgeMessage, SenderCommunicate, and ReceiverLoseMessage remove messages from or transfer messages between *ReceiverInMsg* or *ReceiverQueue*, which does not affect the invariant. □

Theorem 1.6 *In any reachable state, $Defined(ReceiverFile(x)) \to ReceiverFile(x) = SenderFile(x)$. That is, any data that has been accepted by the receiver is stored in the correct order.*

Proof. By induction. Fix an x. Initially, $ReceiverFile(x) = undef$.

Only AcceptDatum may change *ReceiverFile(x)*. By Lemma 1.3, we know that $SenderBit = ReceiverBit$ in this state; Lemma 1.4 tells us further that $SenderNo = ReceiverNo$.

Since $Bit(ReceiverInMsg) = SenderBit$, we know that $Data(ReceiverInMsg) = SenderFile(SenderNo)$ (by Lemma 1.5). AcceptDatum will thus assign $ReceiverFile(ReceiverNo) := SenderFile(SenderNo)$. □

Lemma 1.7 *In any reachable state, $ReceiverNo > 0 \to Defined(ReceiverFile(ReceiverNo-1))$.*

Proof. By induction. Initially $ReceiverNo = 0$; *ReceiverNo* is incremented precisely when *ReceiverFile (ReceiverNo)* is modified by AcceptDatum. □

Lemma 1.8 *In the future of any state of a fair run, the first message of SIM+SQ (or RIM+RQ) will eventually be removed.*

Proof. The proof is similar for both cases; we present the case of *SenderInMsg* and *SenderQueue* here.

Suppose we have a state in a fair run where *SenderInMsg* or *SenderQueue* (or both) is not empty. If *SenderInMsg* is not empty, rule ClearMessage is enabled. ClearMessage must eventually fire (by fairness), emptying *SenderInMsg* (which satisfies the lemma).

If *SenderQueue* is not empty, two modules are enabled: SenderCommunicate and SenderLoseMessage. If SenderLoseMessage fires, it may remove the first message in *SenderQueue*, satisfying the lemma. If not, SenderCommunicate will be continuously enabled, and by fairness must eventually fire, transferring the first message of *SenderQueue* into *SenderInMsg*, where it will eventually be emptied (as shown above). □

Theorem 1.9 *In any fair run, any data sent is eventually received.*

Proof. For any fair run, consider a particular datum being sent by the sender; the item corresponds to a particular value of *SenderNo* (say x). Consider the states in this run where $SenderNo = x$. If at least one of those states also has $SenderBit = Flip(ReceiverBit)$, by Lemmas 1.4, 1.7, and Theorem 1.6, $SenderFile(x)$ has already been stored in $ReceiverFile(x)$. Thus, it remains to show that from any state in a fair run where $SenderBit = ReceiverBit$ and $SenderNo = x$, we eventually arrive at a state where $SenderBit = Flip(ReceiverBit)$ and $SenderNo = x$.

By contradiction, assume that we have $SenderBit = ReceiverBit$ for every state in which $SenderNo = x$. Since *SenderNo* is incremented (by rule ProcessAck) only when $Bit(SenderInMsg) = SenderBit$, Lemma 1.2 tells us that rule ProcessAck will never fire, leaving *SenderNo* and *SenderBit* unchanged for the rest of the run.

Consider *SIM+SQ*. By Lemma 1.8, the first message in the non-empty sequence $SIM + SQ + RIM + RQ$ will be removed infinitely often. Since *SenderBit* never changes, and rule ReTransmit only sends messages with copies of *SenderBit*, eventually all messages with $Flip(SenderBit)$ in the system will be removed, leaving only messages with *SenderBit*. By Lemma 1.2, all copies of *SenderBit* must lie in *ReceiverInMsg* or *ReceiverQueue*, so *SenderInMsg* and *SenderQueue* will be empty for the duration of the run.

The only rule which can now create new messages is ReTransmit, which requires $Timeout = true$. Since messages are always being removed from $RIM + RQ$, if no copy of the desired message reaches the receiver, eventually *ReceiverInMsg* and *ReceiverQueue* will be empty, continuously enabling module Timeout. By fairness, Timeout will eventually fire, enabling rule ReTransmit. ReTransmit will eventually fire (by fairness), placing another copy of *SenderBit* into *ReceiverQueue*. If this new copy of *SenderBit* is discarded, Timeout will be re-enabled and by fairness will re-transmit the message. A repetition of the previous argument shows that if this message is repeatedly discarded, it will be re-transmitted infinitely often.

Thus, rule SenderCommunicate is enabled infinitely often, and by fairness must fire. So, eventually $Bit(ReceiverInMsg) = SenderBit = ReceiverBit$, and rule AcceptDatum will accept the datum and flip *ReceiverBit*, yielding $SenderBit = Flip(ReceiverBit)$ as desired. □

Theorem 1.10 *In any fair run, for any data sent, a corresponding acknowledgment arrives at the sender.*

Proof. The proof is similar to that for Theorem 1.9, with the focus of attention on *ReceiverQueue* instead of *SenderQueue*. The major difference is that the receiver does not re-transmit acknowledgment messages when signaled by *Timeout*, as the sender does, but must wait for another message from the sender. A simple extension of the proof in Theorem 1.9 shows that the sender will transmit infinitely many copies of a given message until an acknowledgment is received, and thus infinitely many copies of that message will be received by the receiver, who will thus be enabled to send the corresponding acknowledgment message infinitely often. □

Theorem 1.11 *In any fair run, all data is eventually sent and acknowledged.*

Proof. By induction over the number of data sent and acknowledged, represented by *SenderNo*. If $SenderNo = 0$, Theorem 1.10 shows that this datum is eventually sent and acknowledged.

Suppose *SenderFile(n)* has been sent. When an acknowledgment for *SenderFile(n)* arrives at the sender (assured by the induction hypothesis), ProcessAck is enabled and (by fairness) will eventually fire, incrementing *SenderNo* and sending a copy of *SenderFile(n+1)* to the receiver. Theorem 1.10 shows that this datum will eventually be accepted and successfully acknowledged as well. □

2 Symmetric ABP

Our version of the ABP is designed for two agents, each of which is described by a different module. In most real communication protocols, such as Kermit, the roles of sender and receiver may be interchanged by two agents during the course of a communication session. (That is, Alice may send a file to Bob, but Bob may send a file to Alice afterwards.)

We present another version of the ABP in which both agents are represented by module templates containing identical transition rules. Our rules for Kermit contain modules which are similar to this symmetric ABP; we present this version as a transition between the classic ABP presented earlier and the full Kermit descriptions to come.

2.1 Function Descriptions

As before, we use the universes of *messages*, *queues*, *data*, and *integers*. We use *integers* instead of *bits* as the second component of each message; we thus define static functions $Data: messages \rightarrow data$, $Num: messages$

$\to$ *integers*, and *Msg: data* $\times$ *integers* $\to$ *messages* in a similar manner to that shown previously. The static functions *Null*, *EmptyQueue*, *Append*, *Head*, and *Tail* are unchanged.

A universe of *ids* contains two elements corresponding to the sender and receiver. The static functions *Sender: ids* and *Receiver: ids* indicate which agent corresponds to which identifier; the private static functions *Me: ids* and *You: ids* identify to each module/agent his or her own identifier, with the obvious requirements on their values.

Each module has a private function *File: integers* $\to$ *data*, used to store data being sent or received, and a private function *MyNum: integers*, used to denote the current location within *File*. A private function *LastMsg: messages* is used to store the last message sent by each agent. A function *Timeout: ids* $\to$ *Bool* holds the timeout signal location for each agent.

Common functions *Q: ids* $\to$ *queues* and *InMsg: ids* $\to$ *message* represent the two message queues and incoming message variables, respectively.

It proves convenient for later purposes to separate the input and output activities of each agent; we thus define a universe *tags* = {*Get*, *Put*} and a private function *Mode: tags* to distinguish between these activities.

2.2 Module Specifications

The sender and receiver module is given in Fig. 5. The communications modules, shown in Fig. 6, are similar to those given earlier. The only unfair modules are those produced by the **LoseMessage** template.

The initial state for the symmetric ABP satisfies the conditions shown in Fig. 7, where *Sender.X* and *Receiver.X* refer to the values of the private function X as seen by the sender and receiver, respectively.

2.3 Correctness

The proof of correctness for the symmetric ABP is similar to that of the non-symmetric ABP presented earlier. Rather than repeat the proof, we instead explain the similarities between the two protocols. The reader should be able to reconstruct our proof of correctness without difficulty.

Many expressions have different names in the two protocols; we present a table of equivalent expressions below. It is easy to verify that each pair of expressions yield elements of the same universe (or are of the same "type"):

SenderQueue/*ReceiverQueue*	$\equiv$	*Q*(*Sender*)/*Q*(*Receiver*)
SenderInMsg	$\equiv$	*InMsg*(*Sender*)
ReceiverInMsg	$\equiv$	*InMsg*(*Receiver*)
SenderFile/*ReceiverFile*	$\equiv$	*File*
SenderNo/*ReceiverNo*	$\equiv$	*MyNum*
SenderBit/*ReceiverBit*	$\equiv$	*MyNum* mod 2

We have replaced *SenderBit* and *ReceiverBit* by references to *MyNum* mod 2. In the old ABP, *SenderBit* is flipped precisely when *SenderNo* is

---
Module: Sender/Receiver Template

if $Mode = Put$ **then**
  if $Me = Sender$ **then**
    $Q(You) :=$
      $Q(You) \mathbin{++} Msg(File(MyNum+1), (MyNum+1) \bmod 2)$
    $LastMsg := Msg(File(MyNum+1), (MyNum+1) \bmod 2)$
  else
    $Q(You) := Q(You) \mathbin{++} Msg(Null, (MyNum \bmod 2))$
    $LastMsg := Msg(Null, (MyNum \bmod 2))$
  endif
  $MyNum := MyNum + 1$, $Mode := Get$
endif

if $Mode = Get$ **then**
  if $Defined(InMsg(Me))$
      and $Num(InMsg(Me)) = (MyNum \bmod 2)$ **then**
    if $Me = Receiver$ **then**
      $File(MyNum) := Data(InMsg(Me))$
    endif
    $Mode := Put$
  endif
  if ($Defined(InMsg(Me))$ **and** $Num(InMsg(Me)) \neq (MyNum \bmod 2)$)
      or $Timeout(Me)$ **then**
    $Q(You) := Q(You) \mathbin{++} LastMsg$ **endif**
    $Timeout(Me) := false$
  endif
  if $Defined(InMsg(Me))$ **then** $Clear(InMsg)$ **endif**
endif

FIG. 5. SYMMETRIC SENDER/RECEIVER MODULE.

incremented; thus, if initially we have $SenderBit = SenderNo = 0$, *SenderBit* will always be equal to $SenderNo \bmod 2$. A similar argument holds for *ReceiverBit* and *ReceiverNo*.

LastMsg stores the last message sent by an agent to be used later in re-transmission. *LastMsg* does not appear in the old ABP; thus, we must show that whenever the sender of the symmetric ABP sends a copy of *LastMsg*, the sender of the old ABP sends an identical message.

For the sender agent, $Num(LastMsg) = MyNum \bmod 2$ is an invariant; This is easily proved: *MyNum* is incremented precisely when *LastMsg* is

Module: Communicate Template
if $Undefined(InMsg(Me))$ **and** $Q(Me) \neq EmptyQueue$ **then**
    $InMsg(Me) := Head(Q(Me)), Q(Me) := Tail(Q(Me))$
endif

Module: LoseMessage Template
if $v \leq Q(Me)$ **then** $Q(Me) := v$ **endif**

Module: Timeout Template
if $Undefined(InMsg(Me))$ **and** $Q(Me) = EmptyQueue$
        and $Undefined(InMsg(You))$ **and** $Q(You) = EmptyQueue$ **then**
    $Timeout(Me) := true$
endif

FIG. 6. SYMMETRIC COMMUNICATIONS MODULES.

$Sender.Me = Sender$ $Receiver.Me = Receiver$
$Sender.Mode = Put$ $Receiver.Mode = Get$
$Sender.MyNum = 0$ $Receiver.MyNum = 0$
$\forall x\ Receiver.File(x) = undef$ $Receiver.LastMsg = Msg(Null,-1)$
$Q(Sender) = Q(Receiver) = EmptyQueue$
$InMsg(Sender) = InMsg(Receiver) = undef$
$Timeout(Sender) = Timeout(Receiver) = false$

FIG. 7. NEW INITIAL CONDITIONS.

updated, and the updates for *LastMsg* yield the invariant condition immediately. Similarly, it can be seen that $Data(LastMsg) = File(MyNum)$ is an invariant for the sender agent. The sender of the symmetric ABP sends a copy of *LastMsg* precisely when the sender of the old ABP sends a copy of *Msg(SenderFile(SenderNo),SenderBit)*; our argument shows that these messages are identical.

The reader can easily verify that each move of the old ABP is duplicated by one or two moves of the symmetric ABP. The symmetric ABP differs in that the receiver has the capability of re-transmitting when a timeout occurs (which only the sender does in the old ABP); this difference means that the receiver may re-transmit a lost acknowledgment more often than in the old ABP, but that does no harm to the correctness of the protocol.

3 Sliding Windows

The sliding window protocol (SWP) is an extension of the ABP. In a communications medium where two-way simultaneous communication is possible, it can be wasteful to have only one datum in transition between the agents, since the capacity of the underlying network may be grossly underutilized. In such situations, it is desirable to have a number of distinct data currently in transit between the two agents, providing for a continual stream of data rather than the sporadic activity characteristic of "stop and wait" protocols like the ABP.

In the case where the size of the window being used is 1, the behavior of the sliding window protocol is similar to that of the ABP. Other than the use of unbounded message numbers in the sliding window protocol, each agent in either protocol makes similar moves.

One should probably not speak of a single SWP; many sliding window algorithms use that window in different ways. We base our SWP upon one given in [DaC] for Kermit's implementation of sliding windows.

3.1 Function Descriptions

We use the *Msg*, *Data*, *Num*, and *Null* functions defined in the symmetric ABP to compose and decompose messages. We still represent our communication network with queues, using the *Append*, *Head*, *Tail*, and *EmptyQueue* functions as defined previously. The data storage functions *SenderFile* and *ReceiverFile* remain as in the ABP, as does *Timeout*.

Each agent uses *SenderInMsg* and *ReceiverInMsg* as in the ABP to hold the current message being processed. Private distinguished elements *SenderLo*, *SenderHi*, *ReceiverLo*, *ReceiverHi: integers* denote the boundaries of each agent's current window. Additionally, the sender has a function *ReceivedAck: integers* → *Bool* which notes which messages have been successfully acknowledged. The distinguished element *WinSize: integers* denotes the maximum window size for both agents.

3.2 Module Specifications

We define *SenderWindowFull* as an abbreviation for *SenderHi* − *SenderLo* + 1 = *WinSize*. Thus, *SenderWindowFull* is true exactly when there are exactly *WinSize* messages between *SenderLo* and *SenderHi*, inclusive.

As before, the sender examines each acknowledgment message sent to her by the receiver. If the acknowledgment number is within the current window, the sender marks that message as acknowledged. At any time, if the sender's window is not full, the sender sends another message to the receiver, increasing the size of her window accordingly. Also, if the oldest entry in her window has been successfully acknowledged, she slides up the lower edge of her window, thus decreasing the size of the window.

The receiver's action upon receipt of a message depends upon the message number. If the number is within his current window, he acknowledges the message and records the data in his data storage area. If the number follows his current window, the receiver slides his window up until the message falls within his window.

The sender and receiver modules are given in Fig. 8. The observant reader may note that no rule is given for the case when the receiver receives a message with a message number preceding the current window; we will prove that this situation never occurs.

We use the same communications modules (SenderCommunicate, ReceiverCommunicate, SenderLoseMessage, and ReceiverLoseMessage) used in the ABP.

We use the same definitions of regular and fair run as in the ABP. The initial state of the SWP satisfies the conditions shown in Fig. 9. The only modules which are not positive are SenderLoseMessage and ReceiverLoseMessage.

3.3 Proof of Correctness

Lemma 3.1 *In any reachable state, for any message μ sent by the sender and present within the state, $Num(\mu) \leq SenderHi$.*

Proof. By induction. Initially the sender has sent no messages.

SendMessage is the only rule which may affect the invariant. If the sender's window is not full, $SenderHi$ is incremented (which maintains the invariant for any messages previously sent), and a new message μ is sent with $Num(\mu) = SenderHi$. If the sender's window is full, any message μ that is sent will have $Num(\mu) = SenderLo$, and $SenderWindowFull$ implies that $SenderLo \leq SenderHi$. □

Lemma 3.2 *In any reachable state, $(SenderHi - SenderLo + 1 \leq WinSize)$ and $(ReceiverHi - ReceiverLo + 1 \leq WinSize)$. That is, the size of both the sender's and receiver's windows is $\leq WinSize$.*

Proof. By induction. Initially $SenderHi - SenderLo + 1 = 0$, and $ReceiverHi - ReceiverLo + 1 = 0$. We consider all moves that affect functions present in the invariant.

SlideSenderWin increments $SenderLo$, which maintains the invariant.

SendMessage may increment $SenderHi$ if $SenderHi - SenderLo + 1 < WinSize$; after incrementing $SenderHi$, the invariant still holds.

SlideReceiverWin increments $ReceiverHi$ and may also increment $ReceiverLo$; the rule insures that the invariant is maintained. □

Lemma 3.3 *In any reachable state, $(0 \leq x < SenderLo \rightarrow ReceivedAck(x))$.*

Proof. By induction. Initially, $SenderLo = 0$. Only SlideSenderWin may change $SenderLo$; its guard ensures that the invariant is preserved. □

Lemma 3.4 *In any reachable state, for any message μ which exists in SenderInMsg or SenderQueue, Defined$(ReceiverFile(Num(\mu)))$ is true.*

Module: Sender
Rule: SendMessage
if *Not(SenderWindowFull)* **then**
   ReceiverQueue :=
      ReceiverQueue ++ Msg(SenderFile(SenderHi+1),SenderHi+1)
   SenderHi := SenderHi+1
elseif *Timeout* **then**
   ReceiverQueue :=
      ReceiverQueue ++ Msg(SenderFile(SenderLo),SenderLo)
   Timeout := false
endif

Rule: ProcessAck
if *Defined(SenderInMsg)* **then**
   if $SenderLo \leq Num(SenderInMsg) \leq SenderHi$ **then**
      ReceivedAck(Num(SenderInMsg)) := true
   endif
   Clear(SenderInMsg)
endif

Rule: SlideSenderWin
if *ReceivedAck(SenderLo)* **then** *SenderLo := SenderLo + 1* **endif**

Module: Receiver
Rule: AcceptMessage
if *Defined(ReceiverInMsg)* **and**
      $ReceiverLo \leq Num(ReceiverInMsg) \leq ReceiverHi$ **then**
   SenderQueue := SenderQueue ++ Msg(Null,Num(ReceiverInMsg))
   ReceiverFile(Num(ReceiverInMsg)) := Data(ReceiverInMsg)
   Clear(ReceiverInMsg)
endif

Rule: SlideReceiverWin
if *Defined(ReceiverInMsg)* **and** *Num(ReceiverInMsg) > ReceiverHi* **then**
   ReceiverHi := Num(ReceiverInMsg)
   ReceiverLo := Max(0,Num(ReceiverInMsg)−WinSize+1)
endif

FIG. 8. SLIDING WINDOW SENDER AND RECEIVER MODULES.

$\forall x \geq 0$ $ReceiverFile(x) = undef$
$\forall x \geq 0$ $ReceivedAck(x) = false$
$SenderLo = ReceiverLo = 0$
$SenderHi = ReceiverHi = -1$
$SenderInMsg = ReceiverInMsg = undef$
$ReceiverQueue = SenderQueue = EmptyQueue$

FIG. 9. SWP INITIAL CONDITIONS.

Proof. By induction. Initially, both *SenderInMsg* and *SenderQueue* are empty. We consider all moves that affect functions present in the invariant.

AcceptMessage appends a new message to *SenderQueue*. Its guard shows that when $Msg(Null,x)$ is appended to *SenderQueue*, $ReceiverFile(x)$ is being defined at the same moment.

ProcessAck, SenderCommunicate, and SenderLoseMessage discard messages from or transfer messages between *SenderQueue* and *SenderInMsg*, which does not affect the invariant. □

Lemma 3.5 *In any reachable state, $ReceivedAck(x) \rightarrow Defined(ReceiverFile(x))$.*

Proof. By induction. Fix an x. Initially, $ReceivedAck(x) = false$. The only rule which modifies *ReceivedAck* is ProcessAck, which sets $ReceivedAck(x)$ to true if $Num(SenderInMsg) = x$ and x is within the sender's current window. By Lemma 3.4, we know that $ReceiverFile(x)$ is defined. □

Lemma 3.6 *In any reachable state, $(ReceiverHi \leq SenderHi)$.*

Proof. By induction. Initially, $ReceiverHi = SenderHi = -1$. We consider all moves that affect functions present in the invariant.

SendMessage increments *SenderHi*, maintaining the invariant.

SlideReceiverWin updates *ReceiverHi* to the current value of $Num(ReceiverInMsg)$, which by Lemma 3.1 is bounded above by *SenderHi*, maintaining the invariant. □

Lemma 3.7 *In any reachable state, $(ReceiverLo \leq SenderLo)$.*

Proof. By induction. The invariant is true initially, since $SenderLo = ReceiverLo = 0$. We consider all moves that affect functions present in the invariant.

SlideSenderWin increments *SenderLo*, maintaining the invariant.

SlideReceiverWin updates *ReceiverLo*. If *ReceiverLo* is changed to a non-zero value, the guard for SlideReceiverWin assures us that $ReceiverLo = ReceiverHi - WinSize + 1$. Lemmas 3.2 and 3.6 yield the result. □

Lemma 3.8 *In any reachable state, $(0 \leq x < ReceiverLo \rightarrow Defined(ReceiverFile(x)))$.*

Proof. Immediate from Lemmas 3.7, 3.3, and 3.5. □

Lemma 3.9 *In any reachable state, consider the sequence of messages $RIM+RQ$. For any two messages α and β in that sequence, if α precedes β, then $(Num(\alpha) - Num(\beta))$ is at most $WinSize - 1$.*

Proof. By induction. Initially, no messages exist in $RIM+RQ$. We consider all moves that affect functions present in the invariant.

SendMessage appends a message β to *ReceiverQueue*. If $Num(\beta) = SenderHi+1$ (before *SenderHi* is updated), we know from Lemma 3.1 that all other messages α in *ReceiverInMsg* or *ReceiverQueue* have $Num(\alpha) \leq SenderHi < Num(\beta)$, and the invariant is preserved.

Otherwise, $Num(\beta) = SenderLo$. Lemma 3.1 tells us that that the largest message number present in *ReceiverInMsg* or *ReceiverQueue* is *SenderHi*; Lemma 3.2 shows that $SenderHi - SenderLo$ is at most $WinSize - 1$.

ReceiverCommunicate, ReceiverLoseMessage, and AcceptMessage remove messages from or transfer messages between *ReceiverQueue* and *ReceiverInMsg*, which does not affect the invariant. □

Theorem 3.10 *In any reachable state, for any message μ in ReceiverInMsg or ReceiverQueue, $Num(\mu) \geq ReceiverLo$. That is, the receiver module will never receive a message whose number precedes the current window.*

Proof. By induction. Initially, no messages exist. We consider all moves that affect functions present in the invariant.

SendMessage creates a new message μ. SendMessage implies $Num(\mu) \geq SenderLo$; Lemma 3.7 asserts that $SenderLo \geq ReceiverLo$.

SlideReceiverWin increments *ReceiverLo*. If $Num(ReceiverInMsg) = x$, SlideReceiverWin sets *ReceiverLo* to $(x - WinSize + 1)$. Lemma 3.9 implies that all messages in *ReceiverQueue* have numbers in the desired range.

ReceiverCommunicate, ReceiverLoseMessage, and AcceptMessage remove messages from or transfer messages between *ReceiverQueue* and *ReceiverInMsg*, which does not affect the invariant. □

Theorem 3.11 *In any reachable state $Defined(ReceiverFile(x)) \rightarrow ReceiverFile(x) = SenderFile(x)$.*

Proof. Fix an x. Initially, $ReceiverFile(x) = undef$.

Only rule AcceptMessage can change $ReceiverFile(x)$. Rule SendMessage shows that every message from the sender to the receiver has the form $Message(SenderFile(n), n)$ for some n; thus, the receiver's assignment to *ReceiverFile* must set $ReceiverFile(x)$ to the value of $SenderFile(x)$. □

Theorem 3.12 *In any fair run, any datum is eventually sent, received, and acknowledged.*

Proof. The proof generally follows that of Theorems 1.9 and 1.10. Lemma 3.8 and Theorem 3.11 assure us that once the receiver's window moves past position x, message x will have been correctly received and stored. The proof that the receiver's and sender's windows continue to move forward is similar to those shown before.

An important difference involves the loss of messages within the current sender's window which are not at the bottom of the window. Since the sender only re-transmits messages at the bottom of the window, we must assure ourselves that a lost message which is not at the bottom of the window will eventually be re-transmitted. But this is easy to show; since the message at the bottom of the window is being re-transmitted, eventually the message at the bottom of the window will be received by the receiver and its acknowledgment received by the sender. The sender will then move her window forward, thus moving the lost message one position closer to the bottom of the window. A short inductive argument shows that eventually this message will reach the bottom of the window and be successfully transmitted. □

4 Bounded Sliding Windows

The SWP presented in the previous section uses arbitrary integers as message numbers. In real-world settings, one cannot use an arbitrarily increasing integer as a unique message identifier. Thus, most sliding window protocols (including the one implemented in Kermit) use a fixed set of message numbers, and restrict the size of the sliding window to one half of the total number of message numbers allowed.

We present modified rules for the SWP which use only finitely many message numbers and prove that the behavior of this protocol is identical to that of the one presented previously. Our version has different rules for the sender and receiver; a symmetric version could be produced (as with the ABP) but is unnecessary for our purposes, since Kermit's sliding window protocol description is not symmetric.

Remark. The use of finitely many message numbers, as well as the bounds which we will prove, are well known (see for example [Wal]). We do not claim that our proof of this bound is unique; rather, we intend to show that this bound can be easily proven within our framework.

4.1 Function Descriptions

All functions previously defined will be used. We will also use the infix functions $*$, $/$, and mod operators, representing integer multiplication, division, and remainder (or modulus).

Additionally, we define two functions *SenderNum*, *ReceiverNum*: *messages* → *integers* as follows: *SenderNum* is the largest integer less than or equal to *SenderHi* and equivalent to $Num(\mu) \bmod (2*WinSize)$. *ReceiverNum* is the smallest integer greater than or equal to *ReceiverLo* and equivalent to $Num(\mu) \bmod (2*WinSize)$. We will see that *SenderNum* and

ReceiverNum represent the "true" message number; that is, the number which was used by the agent who created that message.

4.2 Module Specifications

Our communications modules remain unchanged. We need to change the sender and receiver modules to use message numbers modulo $2*WinSize$ instead of an unbounded set of numbers. The revised transition rules are given in Fig. 10, where changes to the previous rules are written in **bold**.

4.3 Proof of Correctness

Our intention here is to show that *SenderNum* and *ReceiverNum* perform the same function that *Num* did in the unbounded SWP. Having done this, the proofs presented in the previous section will still be valid for the bounded SWP. All of our proofs use the unbounded SWP.

Lemma 4.1 *In any reachable state, for any message μ which exists in SenderInMsg or SenderQueue, $Num(\mu) \leq ReceiverHi$.*

Proof. By induction. Initially, *SenderInMsg* and *SenderQueue* contain no messages. We consider all moves that affect functions present in the invariant.

AcceptMessage appends a new message to *SenderQueue*; the rule assures that the number of the message is bounded above by *ReceiverHi*.

SlideReceiverWin increments *ReceiverHi*, maintaining the invariant.

ProcessAck, SenderLoseMessage, and SenderCommunicate transfer messages between or remove messages from *SenderInMsg* and *SenderQueue*, which does not affect the invariant. □

Lemma 4.2 *In any reachable state, ReceivedAck(x) $\rightarrow$ ReceiverHi $\geq x$.*

Proof. By induction. Initially, $ReceivedAck(x) = false$ for all x. We consider all moves that affect functions present in the invariant.

ProcessAck sets $ReceivedAck(Num(SenderInMsg)) := true$. By Lemma 4.1, we know that $Num(SenderInMsg) \leq ReceiverHi$, so the invariant is maintained.

SlideReceiverWin increments *ReceiverHi*, maintaining the invariant. □

Lemma 4.3 *In any reachable state, SenderLo $-$ ReceiverHi ≤ 1.*

Proof. By induction. Initially, $SenderLo - ReceiverHi = 0 - (-1) = 1$. We consider all moves that affect functions present in the invariant.

SlideSenderWin increments *SenderLo*. The rule implies that *ReceivedAck(SenderLo)* is true; by Lemma 4.2, we know that $SenderLo - ReceiverHi \leq 0$. Incrementing *SenderLo* then gives us the desired result.

SlideSenderWin increments *ReceiverHi*, maintaining the invariant. □

Lemma 4.4 *In any reachable state, SenderHi $-$ ReceiverLo $\leq 2*WinSize - 1$. That is, there are at most $2*WinSize$ messages between the bottom of the receiver's window and the top of the sender's window.*

Module: Sender
Rule: SendMessage
if *Not(SenderWindowFull)* **then**
   ReceiverQueue :=
      ReceiverQueue ++ *Msg(SenderFile(SenderHi+1),*
          (SenderHi+1) mod (2∗WinSize)*)*
   SenderHi := *SenderHi+1*
elseif *Timeout* **then**
   ReceiverQueue :=
      ReceiverQueue ++ *Msg(SenderFile(SenderLo),*
                    SenderLo mod (2∗WinSize)*)*
endif

Rule: ProcessAck
if *Defined(SenderInMsg)* **then**
   if $SenderLo \leq$ **SenderNum(SenderInMsg)** $\leq SenderHi$ **then**
      *ReceivedAck(***SenderNum(SenderInMsg)***)* := *true*
   endif
   Clear(SenderInMsg)
endif

Rule: SlideSenderWin
if *ReceivedAck(SenderLo)* **then** *SenderLo* := *SenderLo + 1* **endif**

Module: Receiver
Rule: AcceptMessage
if *Defined(ReceiverInMsg)* **and**
      $ReceiverLo \leq$ **ReceiverNum(ReceiverInMsg)** $\leq ReceiverHi$ **then**
   SenderQueue := *SenderQueue* ++ *Msg(Null,Num(ReceiverInMsg))*
   *ReceiverFile(***ReceiverNum(ReceiverInMsg)***)* := *Data(ReceiverInMsg)*
   Clear(ReceiverInMsg)
endif

Rule: SlideReceiverWin
if *Defined(ReceiverInMsg)* **and**
      ReceiverNum(ReceiverInMsg) $> ReceiverHi$ **then**
   ReceiverHi := **ReceiverNum(ReceiverInMsg)**
   ReceiverLo := *Max(0,***ReceiverNum(ReceiverInMsg)** $- WinSize + 1)$
endif

FIG. 10. REVISED SLIDING WINDOW MODULES.

Proof. Immediate from Lemmas 3.2 and 4.3. □

Theorem 4.5 *In any reachable state, for any message μ, $SenderNum(\mu)$ = $ReceiverNum(\mu)$.*

Proof. By the definitions of *SenderNum* and *ReceiverNum*, we know that $SenderNum(\mu)$ and $ReceiverNum(\mu)$ are congruent modulo $2 * WinSize$. The definitions also tell us that the following are invariants:

$$ReceiverLo \leq ReceiverNum(\mu) \leq ReceiverLo + 2 * WinSize - 1,$$

$$SenderHi - 2 * WinSize + 1 \leq SenderNum(\mu) \leq SenderHi.$$

If $SenderNum(\mu) \neq ReceiverNum(\mu)$, we must have $SenderNum(\mu) = ReceiverNum(\mu) + d$, where d is some non-zero multiple of $2*WinSize$. If d is positive, we have $ReceiverLo \leq SenderNum + d \leq SenderHi$, which implies that $SenderHi - ReceiverLo \geq 2*WinSize$, contradicting Lemma 4.4. If d is negative, a similar argument also creates a contradiction. □

Remark. It turns out that $2 * WinSize$ message numbers are not only sufficient for the sliding window protocol, but also necessary [Wal]. Suppose that both agents are using only $2*WinSize$ - 1 message numbers and consider the following run. The sender sends *WinSize* messages to the receiver, numbered 0 through $WinSize - 1$. The receiver receives all of the messages and sends acknowledgments numbered 0 through $WinSize - 1$ to the sender.

The next message the receiver receives has a message numbered 0. What should he do with this message?

- If the sender received all of the receiver's acknowledgments, the sender would have moved her window forward by *WinSize*, thus enabling her to send messages numbered *WinSize* through $2*WinSize-1$. In that case, the message numbered $2*WinSize-1$ would have arrived at the receiver as message 0 (since we are counting modulo $2*WinSize-1$), and this message should be accepted and stored.
- If the sender didn't receive the receiver's acknowledgment for message 0, the sender would have re-sent her message 0. In that case, this message should be acknowledged, but not stored.

The receiver cannot determine whether this message is an old, retransmitted message or a new message which should be stored. Thus, at least $2 * WinSize$ message numbers are necessary.

5 Alternating Bit Kermit: The Session Layer

We consider Kermit, as specified by [DaC], at three different layers of abstraction: the session, transport, and datalink layers. The session layer controls sending and receiving files; the network connection is assumed to be reliable, delivering messages intact and in the proper order. The task of the transport layer is to provide a reliable connection even though the actual connection may lose or alter messages during transmission. The datalink layer controls message representation, transforming abstract messages into strings which can be sent through typical communication networks.

Kermit also uses a presentation layer, which transforms a file (seen here as a finite string of arbitrary length) into a sequence of shorter strings which are to be sent through the network. These transformations are fairly mechanical, and we present without comment a couple of static functions which perform this transformation.

The names given to these layers are similar to those used in the ISO Open Systems Interconnection Reference Model (or OSI model) [Tan]. However, since Kermit was developed before the OSI model, the layer names do not always have the same connotations.

From the session layer, Kermit is driven by a finite state automaton. Two agents generate and accept strings of the form $S(FD^*Z)^*B$, where each letter represents a different type of message being sent:

- S represents the *start* of a communications session.
- B represents the end (or *break*) of a communications session.
- F represents the name of a *file*.
- Z represents the end of a file. (Most likely the Z is due to the widespread use of the control-Z character as an end-of-file marker in many operating systems. Alternatively, the last letter of the English alphabet may be appropriate to signal the last datum of a file.)
- D represents *data*.

A few other message types are used: Y indicates a positive acknowledgment (*"yes"*), N indicates a negative acknowledgment (*"no"*), and E indicates the occurrence of an unrecoverable *error*.

The finite state automata used by the sender and receiver agents are shown in Fig. 11. The labels on the transitions should be read in this manner: if an arc from state S to state T is labeled A/B, then in state S, if the agent receives a message labeled A, the agent may send a message labeled B and enter state T.

Most of the names of the states used in the automata are used in the original specification [DaC] and may be read as follows: *ssini* is the sender's initial state, *ssfil* is the sender's state for receiving new files, *ssdat* is the sender's state for receiving data, and *sseot* is the sender's state for ending a transaction. The states of the receiver's automaton are similar.

5.1 Function Descriptions

As with the symmetric ABP, each agent participating in a Kermit file transfer has both the capability of sending and receiving. Our descriptions assume that the external world (*i.e.* the persons using the Kermit program)

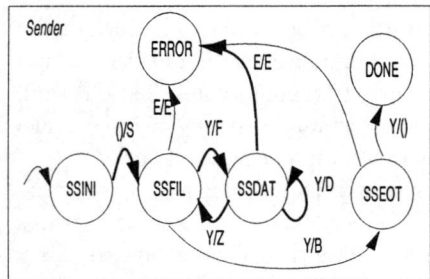 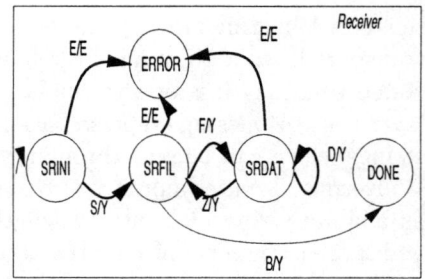

Fig. 11. Kermit session layer finite automata.

determine which agent will act as the sender and which as the receiver for a given transmission session. We describe a single module which contains the rules for any Kermit agent, as well as additional modules which describe the communications medium.

5.1.1 *Common Functions*

The states of the finite state machines shown above are represented by a universe of *modes*. A universe of *symbols* contains the symbols "S", "F", *etc.* that are transmitted between agents as described above. These symbols are used in messages which contain other textual data; this leads us to universes of *messages* and *strings*. We use the universe of *integers* to count files. Finally, to distinguish between the sender and receiver, we use a universe of *ids*.

Messages are composed of a symbol (the type of the message) and a string (the data content of the message). We thus use functions *Msg: symbols* × *strings* → *messages*, *Type: messages* → *symbols*, and *Data: messages* → *strings* in the usual manner: if $Msg(t,d) = m$, then $Type(m) = t$ and $Data(m) = d$. The function *InMsg: ids* → *messages* indicates the current incoming message for each agent.

The function *Concat: strings* × *strings* → *strings* is the usual string concatenation, which we denote with the infix operator +. The distinguished element ϵ: *strings* is the empty string.

For historical reasons, the data transmitted by Kermit is usually translated at the presentation layer into printable ASCII characters before transmission. (This avoids the transmission of non-printable characters which the communications medium might interpret as commands.) We represent this encoding by a pair of functions *EncodePrefix: strings* × *strings* → *strings* and *Remainder: strings* × *strings* → *strings*. The input to both of these functions is a pair *(source, params)*, where *source* is the string to be encoded, and *params* is a string containing various encoding parameters, such as the maximum length of any encoding, the prefix character to be used for non-printable characters, and so on. *EncodePrefix (source, params)* returns the encoding of an initial segment of *source*; *Remainder (source, params)* returns the segment of *source* not translated by *Encode-Prefix*. A function *Decode: strings × strings → strings* decodes any input string, using a similar string of decoding parameters.

We require that applying *Decode* to an encoded datum with the same parameter string used in its encoding should yield the original datum; that is, if *Decode (Encode (source, params))* = x, then x + *Remainder (source, params)* = *source*. Further, we require that the length of *Remainder(source, params)* should be less than the length of *source* as long as *source* $\neq \epsilon$.

5.1.2 Private Functions

Each agent has a private function *Mode: modes* which indicates the current state of its finite automata. A private function *Layer: {session, transport}* indicates whether control is currently focused in the session or transport layer. Initially, *Layer = session* for both agents. As in the symmetric ABP, each agent has private functions *Me: ids* and *You: ids*.

The private functions *RecvdType: symbols* and *RecvdData: strings* indicate the type and datum of the last message received from the other agent. The private functions *SendType: symbols* and *SendData: strings* indicate the type and datum of the next message to be sent to the other agent. The private function *TransportCommand: {send, receive}* indicates the latest command given to the transport layer.

Kermit allows for more than one file to be sent between the sender and the receiver in a single communications session; thus, we need to store the list of files being sent and received, as well as the list of corresponding file names. We do this with the private functions *FileText: integers → strings* and *FileName: integers → strings*, where the integer argument to each function denotes the position within the list of the appropriate file and file name. The private function *FileNo: integers* indicates which file is currently being sent; the private function *TextToSend: strings* indicates (for the sender) what data in the current file remains to be sent.

Finally, each agent has a private function *MyParams: strings* which provides local parameters used during the initialization of the transaction.

5.2 Transition Rules

5.2.1 Sending Rules

The sender agent begins in state *ssini* by sending an "*S*" to the receiver, along with her initialization parameters, and entering state *ssfil*. The transition rule for this state is shown in Fig. 12. Later we will present transition rules which perform the actual transmission of data implied by *TSEND*.

Automata state *ssini* is the only state in which an agent acts without first receiving a message. Fig. 13 presents a transition rule which performs the action of receiving input for all other automata states. As with *TSEND*, we will present transition rules which perform this action later.

Rule: SSINI
if *Layer* = *session* **and** *Mode* = *ssini* **then**
   TSEND("S",MyParams)
   GOTO(ssfil)
endif

Abbreviation: GOTO(x)
   Clear(RecvdType)
   Mode := *x*

Abbreviation: TSEND(type,datum)
   TransportCommand := *send*, *Layer* := *transport*
   SendType := *type*, *SendData* := *datum*

FIG. 12. TRANSITION RULE FOR STATE *ssini*.

Rule: GetInput
if *Layer* = *session* **and** *Undefined(RecvdType)* **and** *Mode* $\neq$ *ssini* **then**
   Layer := *transport*
   TransportCommand := *receive*
endif

FIG. 13. TRANSITION RULE FOR RECEIVING INPUT.

In automata state *ssfil*, the sender can either begin transmission of a new file (if one remains to be sent) or end the transaction. To begin sending a file, the sender sends the file name in an *"F"* message to the receiver and moves to state *ssdat*, initializing the local *TextToSend* variable with the data contained in that file. To end the transaction, the sender sends a *"B"* message to the receiver. The transition rule for this automata state is shown in Fig. 14. (Note that here and elsewhere, "**ENDIF**" abbreviates a series of "**endif**"s).

HANDLE-INITS is an abbreviation for a set of transition rules which handles the initialization parameters sent between agents (which occurs only on the first exchange of messages). See Appendix A for a fuller explanation of *HANDLE-INITS*. *EINFO* is a string containing information needed to encode text properly in order to be decoded by the receiver.

In automata state *ssdat*, the sender either sends the next segment of the file being transmitted, or signals the end of transmission of this file. To send a new file segment, the sender sends the text in a *"D"* message to the receiver, and updates the local *TextToSend* variable accordingly. To end transmission of a file, the sender sends a *"Z"* message to the receiver. The transition rule for this automata state is shown in Fig. 15.

Rule: SSFIL
if *Layer* = *session* **and** *Mode* = *ssfil* **and** *Defined(RecvdType)* **then**
    if *RecvdType* ≠ *"Y"* **then** *ERROR* **endif**
    if *RecvdType* = *"Y"* **then**
        if *FileNo* = 0 **then** *HANDLE-INITS* **endif**
        if *Defined(FileName(FileNo))* **then**
            TSEND("F",EncodePrefix(FileName(FileNo),EINFO))
            TextToSend := FileText(FileNo), GOTO(ssdat)
        else
            TSEND("B",ϵ), GOTO(sseot)
ENDIF

Abbreviation: ERROR
    TSEND("E", "Unexpected Message"), GOTO(error)

Fig. 14. Transition rule for state *ssfil*.

Rule: SSDAT
if *Layer* = *session* **and** *Mode* = *ssdat* **and** *Defined(RecvdType)* **then**
    if *RecvdType* ≠ *"Y"* **then** *ERROR* **endif**
    if *RecvdType* = *"Y"* **then**
        if *TextToSend* ≠ ϵ **then**
            TSEND("D",EncodePrefix(TextToSend,EINFO))
            TextToSend := Remainder(TextToSend,EINFO)
            GOTO(ssdat)
    else
        TSEND("Z",ϵ), FileNo := FileNo + 1, GOTO(ssfil)
ENDIF

Fig. 15. Transition rule for state *ssdat*.

In automata state *sseot*, the sender waits for an acknowledgment of its last message to the receiver, which was a "*B*" message. Upon receipt, the sender terminates. The transition rule for this state is shown in Fig. 16.

5.2.2 *Receiver Rules*

The receiver agent starts in a state with *Mode* = *srini*, where he waits for the initial "*S*" message from the sender. After receipt, the receiver processes the sender's initialization parameters, sends his own parameters to the sender in an acknowledgment message ("*Y*"), and moves to state

Rule: SSEOT
if Layer = session **and** Mode = sseot **and** Defined(RecvdType) **then**
    if RecvdType = "Y" **then** GOTO(done) **endif**
    if RecvdType $\neq$ "Y" **then** ERROR **endif**
endif

FIG. 16. TRANSITION RULE FOR STATE *sseot*.

srfil to prepare to receive files. The transition rule for this state is shown in Fig. 17.

Rule: SRINI
if Layer = session **and** Mode = srini **and** Defined(RecvdType) **then**
    if RecvdType $\neq$ "S" **then** ERROR **endif**
    if RecvdType = "S" **then**
        HANDLE-INITS, TSEND("Y",MyParams), GOTO(srfil)
ENDIF

FIG. 17. TRANSITION RULE FOR STATE *srini*.

In automata state *srfil*, the receiver receives either an "*F*" message or a "*B*" message from the sender, indicating whether another file is about to be sent. The receiver moves to the appropriate state, storing any file name sent. The transition rule for this automata state is shown in Fig. 18.

Rule: SRFIL
if Layer = session **and** Mode = srfil **and** Defined(RecvdType) **then**
    if RecvdType $\neq$ "F" **and** RecvdType $\neq$ "B" **then** ERROR **endif**
    if RecvdType = "F" **then**
        FileName(FileNo) := Decode(RecvdData,DINFO)
        TSEND("Y",ϵ), GOTO(srdat)
    endif
    if RecvdType = "B" **then**
        TSEND("Y",ϵ), GOTO(done)
ENDIF

FIG. 18. TRANSITIONS RULE FOR STATE *srfil*.

In automata state *srdat*, the receiver either stores the next file segment transmitted in a "D" message, or ends file reception when a "Z" message is received. The transition rule for this automata state is shown in Fig. 19.

Rule: SRDAT
if *Layer* = *session* **and** *Mode* = *srdat* **and** *Defined(RecvdType)* **then**
   if *RecvdType* ≠ "D" **and** *RecvdType* ≠ "Z" **then** ERROR **endif**
   if *RecvdType* = "D" **then**
      FileText(FileNo) :=
         FileText(FileNo) + *Decode(RecvdData,DINFO)*
      TSEND("Y",ϵ), GOTO(srdat)
   endif
   if *RecvdType* = "Z" **then**
      FileNo := *FileNo* + 1, *TSEND("Y",ϵ), GOTO(srfil)*
ENDIF

FIG. 19. TRANSITION RULE FOR STATE *srdat*.

5.2.3 Interim Transport Layer Module

In our proofs of correctness, we intend to prove the correctness of each layer separately, assuming the correctness of any lower layers on which that layer depends. Through this separation of concerns, our proofs become smaller and more manageable. Consequently, at each layer, we present transition rules which act as a correct implementation of the succeeding layers. These rules will be replaced with more detailed rules later.

The session layer of Kermit calls upon the transport layer to perform the actual task of transferring messages between the two agents. We present a simple module template in Fig. 20 which describes a reliable communications medium from one agent to the other.

5.2.4 Regular Run

The initial state of our Kermit algebra satisfies the conditions shown in Fig. 21.

5.3 Proof of Correctness

Throughout our proofs, we use $S.X$ and $R.X$ to refer to the private function X of the sender and receiver, respectively.

Module: InterimTransport
Rule: TSEND
if $Layer = transport$ **and** $TransportCommand = send$ **then**
   $InMsg(You) := Msg(SendType, SendData)$
   $Clear(SendType), Clear(SendData), Layer := session$
endif

Rule: TGET
if $Layer = transport$ **and** $TransportCommand = receive$
     and $Defined(InMsg(Me))$ **then**
   $RecvdType := Type(InMsg(Me)), RecvdData := Data(InMsg(Me))$
   $Clear(InMsg(Me)), Layer := session$
endif

FIG. 20. INTERIM TRANSPORT LAYER RULES.

$S.Mode = ssini$	$R.Mode = srini$
$S.Layer = session$	$R.Layer = session$
$S.RecvdType = undef$	$R.RecvdType = undef$
$S.FileNo = 0$	$R.FileNo = 0$

FIG. 21. INITIAL CONDITIONS FOR KERMIT.

Lemma 5.1 *Define*

$$R.Next = \begin{cases} R.RecvdType & \text{if } Defined(RecvdType) \\ Type(InMsg(Receiver)) & \text{if } Undefined(RecvdType) \wedge \\ & Defined(InMsg(Receiver)) \\ S.SendType & \text{otherwise} \end{cases}$$

and define S.Next similarly. Then in any reachable global state, the values of S.Mode, S.Next, R.Mode, and R.Next match one of the lines of the following table:

Kermit: Specification and Verification

	S.Mode	S.Next	R.Mode	R.Next
(a)	ssini	undef	srini	undef
(b)	ssfil	undef	srini	"S"
(c)	ssfil	"Y"	srfil	undef
(d)	ssdat	undef	srfil	"F"
(e)	ssdat	"Y"	srdat	undef
(f)	ssdat	undef	srdat	"D"
(g)	ssfil	undef	srdat	"Z"
(h)	sseot	undef	srfil	"B"
(i)	sseot	"Y"	done	undef
(j)	done	undef	done	undef

Proof. By induction. The initial state satisfies condition (a) of the table.

- GetInput, TSEND, and TGET do not affect any condition in the table.
- Rule SSINI transforms condition (a) to (b).
- Rule SRINI transforms condition (b) to (c).
- Rule SSFIL transforms condition (c) to (d) or (h).
- Rule SRFIL transforms condition (d) to (e) and transforms condition (h) to (i).
- Rule SSDAT transforms condition (e) to (f) or (g).
- Rule SRDAT transforms condition (f) to (e) and transforms condition (g) to (c).
- Rule SSEOT transforms condition (i) to (j). □

Lemma 5.2 *In any reachable state, the ERROR macro is never executed.*

Proof. It is observable from the table in Lemma 5.1 and the transition rules that in any state where $S.RecvdType$ or $R.RecvdType$ is defined, its value will not allow the $ERROR$ macro to be executed. □

Lemma 5.3 *In any regular run, any message sent by the sender is acknowledged by the receiver.*

Proof. By Lemma 5.1, we know that any message sent by the sender is expected by the receiver; *i.e.* the receiver will not execute the $ERROR$ macro, but execute some other transition rules. The message will not be discarded by the reliable network; thus, the receiver will accept the message. An examination of the receiver's rules shows that every message which does not generate an error (as these messages will not) is acknowledged. □

Lemma 5.4 *In any reachable state, if $R.Mode = srdat$, then $R.FileText(x) = \epsilon$ for every $x > R.FileNo$; if $R.Mode \neq srdat$, then $R.FileText(x) = \epsilon$ for every $x \geq R.FileNo$.*

Proof. By induction. Initially, $R.FileText(x) = \epsilon$ for every $x \geq 0$. We consider all moves that affect functions present in the invariant.

SRFIL may set $R.Mode$ to $srdat$, but will leave $R.FileNo$ and $R.FileText$ unchanged; thus, the truth of the invariant is unaffected.

SRDAT has different effects on the functions named in the invariant, depending upon the value of $R.RecvdType$. Before SRDAT fires, the invariant asserts that $R.FileText(x) = \epsilon$ for all $x > R.FileNo$. If $R.RecvdType$ = "Z", SRDAT updates $R.Mode$ to $srfil$ and increments $R.FileNo$; afterwards, we will have $R.FileText(x) = \epsilon$ for all $x \geq R.FileNo$. Otherwise, $FileText(FileNo)$ may be modified, but this does not affect the invariant. □

Lemma 5.5 *In any reachable state, the following conditions are true:*

$$S.Mode = ssfil \land R.Mode = srdat \rightarrow S.FileNo = R.FileNo + 1,$$

$$\neg(S.Mode = ssfil \land R.Mode = srdat) \rightarrow S.FileNo = R.FileNo.$$

Proof. By induction. Initially, $S.Mode = ssini$, $R.Mode = srini$, and $S.FileNo = R.FileNo = 0$.

From Lemma 5.1, we see that we may enter a state where $S.Mode = ssfil$ and $R.Mode = srdat$ (condition (g)) only when $S.Mode = ssdat$ and $R.Mode = srdat$ (condition (e)), by rule SSDAT. By the induction hypothesis, $S.FileNo = R.FileNo$ before SSDAT fires, and we will have $S.FileNo = R.FileNo+1$ after SSDAT fires, since SSDAT increments $S.FileNo$.

Similarly, we may only leave a state where $S.Mode = ssfil$ and $R.Mode = srdat$ (condition (g)) by rule SRDAT. SRDAT increments $R.FileNo$; thus, we will have $S.FileNo = R.FileNo$ as desired after SRDAT fires. □

Lemma 5.6 *Define*

$$code = \begin{cases} R.RecvdData & \text{if } Defined(R.RecvdData) \\ Data(InMsg(Receiver)) & \text{if } Undefined(R.RecvdData) \\ & \land\ Defined(InMsg(Receiver)) \\ \epsilon & \text{otherwise} \end{cases}$$

Then in any reachable state, if $S.Mode = ssdat$, then $S.FileText(S.FileNo) = R.FileText(R.FileNo) + Decode(code, DINFO) + S.TextToSend$.

Proof. By induction. Initially, $S.Mode = ssini$, making the premise of the invariant false, thus satisfying the invariant. We consider all moves that affect functions present in the invariant.

SSFIL may update $S.Mode$ to $ssdat$; if it does, we will have $S.TextToSend = S.FileText(S.FileNo)$ and $code = \epsilon$. Applying Lemmas 5.1 and 5.4 shows that $R.FileText(R.FileNo) = \epsilon$. If firing SSFIL does not update $S.Mode$ to $ssdat$, the invariant is not affected.

SSDAT may update $S.Mode$ to $ssfil$; in that case, the premise of the invariant becomes false, making the invariant true. Otherwise, text may be transferred from *S.TextToSend* into *code*, which does not affect the invariant.

TGET may move text from *InMsg(Receiver)* into *R.RecvdData*, which does not affect the invariant (since both are part of the definition of *code*).

SRDAT may move text from *code* into *R.FileText(R.FileNo)*, which maintains the truth of the invariant. Otherwise, R.FileNo may be incremented; but Lemma 5.1 shows that $S.Mode \neq ssdat$ in this case, violating our premise. □

Theorem 5.7 *In any regular run, assuming finite input both sides will terminate with Mode = done, and for all x, $S.FileText(x) = R.FileText(x)$ and $S.FileName(x) = R.FileName(x)$.*

Proof. We consider a regular run from the sender's perspective, since the receiver acknowledges every message sent by the sender (Lemma 5.3). By Lemma 5.2, we know the regular run will never enter an error state.

The sender starts by sending an *"S"* and enters mode *ssfil*, which is also entered any time a file has been successfully sent. If there are more files to send, a new *"F"* message is sent with the new file name and the sender enters mode *ssdat*. In a moment, we will show that the sender eventually returns to *ssfil* with *FileNo* incremented by one. Thus, if only finitely many files have been specified for sending, eventually no more files will be available and the sender proceeds to mode *sseot* where a *"B"* message is sent. After its acknowledgment, both sides move to mode *done*.

It remains to show that from mode *ssdat*, the sender eventually returns to mode *ssfil*. In mode *ssdat*, the length of *TextToSend* decreases each time a *"D"* message is sent, which is eventually acknowledged. Thus, eventually the entire file will be sent, *FileNo* will be incremented, and control will be returned back to *ssfil*.

How do we know that file names and texts are transmitted correctly? Lemma 5.5 shows that $S.FileNo = R.FileNo$ when file names and file texts are transmitted; thus, file names sent from the sender to the receiver will be placed in corresponding places in the private function *FileName*. Lemma 5.6 shows that when the sender is about to send the end-of-file *"Z"* marker, $S.TextToSend = code = \epsilon$. Thus, *S.FileText* and *R.FileText* will match with respect to the current value of *FileNo*. □

6 Alternating Bit Kermit: The Transport Layer

The goal of the transport layer is to transform a possibly unreliable connection into a reliable one. In Alternating Bit Kermit, the transport layer is a variant on the ABP, described in section 2. This similarity allows us to rely on the proofs of correctness for the ABP for the correctness of the transport layer.

A couple of new message types are used by the transport layer. Q indicates that a message has been corrupted (altered) during transmission through the network. T indicates that a timeout signal has occurred while waiting for a message to arrive.

6.1 New Function Descriptions

6.1.1 *Common Functions*

Messages will now be composed of three parts: a symbol indicating the type of the message, a string indicating the data content of the message, and an integer used to maintain proper sequencing of messages. We thus re-define *Msg: symbols × strings × integers → messages*, and define a new function *Num: messages → integers*. We will only number messages with the integers $\{0, \ldots, 63\}$; consequently, we will use the modulus function over the integers to compute message numbers.

The communications paths between agents are represented by *queues*, as in the ABP. Functions *EmptyQueue: queues*, *Append: queues × messages → queues*, *Head: queues → messages*, and *Tail: queues → messages* perform the usual operations. In addition, we define a partial ordering $\preceq$ on queues as follows: for queues a and b, $a \preceq b$ if a can be obtained from b by replacing zero or more messages in b with messages of type "Q". If either a or b is not a queue, $a \not\preceq b$.

The function *Q: ids → queues* represents the queues between the pair of agents. For a given agent, $Q(Me)$ is the queue of messages to be received by that agent, and $Q(You)$ is the queue of messages sent by that agent but not yet received by the other agent.

6.1.2 *Private Functions*

Each agent has a private function *SeqNo: integers* which holds the message number it expects to receive in the next message from the other agent. Private functions *FetchType: symbols*, *FetchNo: integers*, and *FetchData: strings* hold the message symbol, number, and datum from the most recently retrieved message.

The private function *Retry: integers* indicates the number of times the transport layer has attempted to send the current message. The private function *RetryLimit: integers* indicates the maximum number of times retransmission of a particular message should occur. The private function *LastMsg: messages* holds a copy of the last message sent to the other agent.

6.2 Transition Rules

We replace the interim module template presented in the last section with the rules presented in this section.

The transport layer module has two transition rules (shown in Fig. 22) which implement the sending and receiving of messages; they are essentially those of the symmetric ABP. Rule *TSEND* uses a couple of abbreviations; these are defined in Fig. 23. Finally, we need to define the *SEND* and *GET* abbreviations used throughout these rules; they are shown in Fig. 24.

Rule: TSEND
if Layer = transport **and** TransportCommand = send **then**
   if Sender = Me **then**
      SEND(SendType, SendData, (SeqNo + 1) mod 64)
   else SEND(SendType, SendData, SeqNo)
   endif
   SeqNo := (SeqNo + 1) mod 64
   Clear(SendType), Clear(SendData), Layer := session
endif

Rule: TGET
if Layer = transport **and** TransportCommand = receive **then**
   if Undefined(FetchType) **then** GET **endif**
   if Defined(FetchType) **then**
      if (FetchNo = SeqNo) **and** (FetchType $\notin$ { "N", "Q", "T"}) **then**
         RETURN(FetchType, FetchData)
      elseif FetchType = "N" **and** FetchNo = (SeqNo+1) mod 64 **then**
         RETURN("Y", FetchData)
      else RESEND
ENDIF

FIG. 22. TRANSITION RULES FOR TRANSPORT-LEVEL SENDING AND RECEIVING.

Abbreviation: RESEND
   if Retry > RetryLimit **then**
      SEND("E", ϵ), RETURN("E", ϵ)
   elseif LastMsg $\neq$ undef **then** Q(You) := Q(You) ++ LastMsg
   else SEND("N", ϵ, SeqNo)
   endif
   Clear(FetchType), Clear(FetchData)

Abbreviation: RETURN (type, datum)
   Retry := 0, RecvdType := type, RecvdData := datum
   Clear(FetchType), Clear(FetchData), Layer := session

FIG. 23. DEFINITIONS FOR RESEND AND RETURN.

Abbreviation: SEND (type, datum, num)
    $LastMsg := Msg(type, datum, num)$
    $Q(You) := Q(You) \mathbin{++} Msg(type, datum, num)$

Abbreviation: GET
    if $Defined(InMsg(Me))$ **then**
        $FetchType := Type(InMsg(Me))$, $FetchNo := Num(InMsg(Me))$
        $FetchData := Data(InMsg(Me))$, $Clear(InMsg(Me))$
    elseif $Timeout(Me)$ **then**
        $FetchType :=$ "T", $FetchNo := SeqNo$
        $Timeout(Me) := false$
    endif

FIG. 24. DEFINITIONS FOR *SEND* AND *GET*.

The network modules for Kermit, which allow for corruption of messages as well as discarding of messages, are a simple extension of those for the ABP and are shown in Fig. 25.

Module: Transfer Template
if $Undefined(InMsg(Me))$ **and** $Q(Me) \neq EmptyQueue$ **then**
    $InMsg(Me) := Head(Q(Me))$, $Q(Me) := Tail(Q(Me))$
endif

Module: Shrink Template
if $v \leq Q(Me)$ **then** $Q(Me) := v$ **endif**

Module: Corrupt Template
if $v \preceq Q(Me)$ **then** $Q(Me) := v$ **endif**

FIG. 25. NETWORK MODULE TEMPLATES FOR KERMIT.

6.3 Correctness

The transition rules presented in the last section are functionally equivalent to those of the symmetric ABP. *TSEND* corresponds to the transition rules of the symmetric ABP invoked when *Mode = Put*, and *TGET* corresponds to the rules invoked when *Mode = Get*. The alternation between modes *Get* and *Put* which appears naturally in the symmetric ABP is assured by the session-layer rules, which alternate calls to *TSEND* and *TGET*.

The symmetric ABP used 0 and 1 as message numbers, while Kermit uses the entire set $\{0, \ldots, 63\}$. It can easily be shown, as in the ABP, that only two distinct message numbers exist in the various queues and message holders in the Kermit protocol at any one moment. Furthermore, these two message numbers are consecutive mod 64; thus, they can be seen to correspond to the ABP's 0 and 1 bits, where a message number is mapped to 0 if it is even and 1 if it is odd. Thus, using this larger set of message numbers does not affect the correctness of the protocol.

Kermit also detects that an *"N"* message numbered x is equivalent to a *"Y"* message numbered $x - 1$, since an *"N"* message numbered x cannot be sent before a *"Y"* message numbered $x - 1$. This feature can improve efficiency slightly but has no affect on correctness.

Kermit does not re-transmit messages infinitely often, as our version of the ABP does; otherwise, Kermit would never terminate if a network failure prohibited all messages from reaching their destinations. Since such a failure may not be detectable, Kermit "gives up" after a fixed number of re-transmissions without receiving a response. This number may be changed by the user.

The network modules for Kermit may corrupt messages as well as discarding them; Kermit treats corrupted messages similarly to timeout signals by requesting re-transmission of the last message sent.

Thus, the transport layer of Alternating Bit Kermit is correct if and only if the ABP is correct. Immediately we have the following theorem:

Theorem 6.1 *Any message sent by the transport layer of one agent, if it is not lost or corrupted more than RetryLimit times, eventually is received by the transport layer of the other agent.*

In addition, if all rules involving *RetryLimit* were to be removed from our description of Kermit, it can be proved that the only regular Kermit runs which do not terminate are "unfair" runs; that is, runs in which the modules which discard or corrupt messages interfere do not allow the other network modules to transmit messages.

7 Alternating Bit Kermit: The Datalink Layer

The datalink layer of Kermit translates the abstract domain of "messages" into strings which may be transmitted across the network. The string corresponding to a Kermit message is the concatenation of the following:

- A fixed number of padding characters, needed by some implementations to allow an agent to detect the beginning of a message. The number of padding characters, as well as the characters themselves, are determined during the initial negotiations.
- A special "mark" character, denoting the true start of the message.

- The length of the "true" message (consisting of the length, message number, message type, and datum), encoded as a single printable character.
- The message number, encoded as a single printable character.
- The message type symbol.
- The datum being sent.
- A checksum computed on the whole string produced so far, excluding the padding and mark characters, encoded as a few printable characters (dependent on the checksum algorithm selected during the initial negotiations).
- A special end-of-line character.

Thus, all that is required to modify for the datalink layer of Kermit is to provide more specific definitions for the *Msg*, *Type*, *Data*, and *Num* functions specified earlier. We show their definitions in Fig. 26, where + denotes string concatenation and the behavior of previously unspecified functions should be clear from the above descriptions.

Msg(type, data, num) = *Pad(PadChar,PadLen)* + *Mark* + *BODY*
    + *ToChar(ChkSum(BODY))* + *Eol*
(where *BODY* = *ToChar(Length(data)+3)* + *ToChar(num)*
    + *type* + *data*)

Type(msg) =
  if *Chksum(Substr(DATA,2,LEN))* ≠ *UnChar(Substr(DATA,LEN+2,1))*
  then "Q" **else** *Substr(DATA,4,1)*
Data(msg) = *Substr(DATA,5,LEN-3)*
Num(msg) = *UnChar(Substr(DATA,3,1))*
        (where *DATA* = *FindStr(msg, Mark)*
        and *LEN* = *UnChar(Substr(DATA,2,1))*))

FIG. 26. DEFINITIONS OF DATALINK FUNCTIONS.

We also modify the *Corrupt* function (which corrupts messages in transit) to modify messages in such a manner that the alteration is detectable by the *Chksum* function as defined here. Certainly a message could be altered and still pass this type of test; however, there is no way in general to be certain that a given message has been unaltered by transmission through an unreliable medium. Many checksum functions have been developed which can detect most types of errors common in network transmissions; [DaC] specifies three different checksum functions which may be used in Kermit.

7.1 Correctness

Since the only changes we have made in the datalink layer are to the functions *Msg*, *Type*, *Data*, and *Msg*, the correctness of the datalink layer is directly related to the relationships between these functions:

Theorem 7.1 *For any symbol t, datum d, and message number n, Type (Msg (t,d,n)) = t, Data(Msg(t,d,n)) = d, and Num(Msg(T,d,n)) = n.*

Proof. Immediate from the definitions given above. □

8 Sliding Windows Kermit

Since the basic Kermit protocol was standardized, a number of optional extensions to Kermit have been developed. A Kermit agent can be instructed to act as a file server, both sending and receiving files from the other agent at her request. A protocol extension is defined for encoding 8-bit data for transmission over 7-bit networks. Most of these extensions can be modeled easily using evolving algebras, but do not provide much of a challenge. We describe here an optional extension of greater interest: the use of a sliding window protocol.

If both sides agree to the use of sliding windows, each agent may use Kermit's version of the sliding window protocol while file data is being transmitted in states *ssdat* and *srdat*. The standard ABP is used in all other states. The specification given in [DaC] is a combination of the session and transport layers, with the sliding window protocol used in place of the ABP. Consequently, we present transition rules for Kermit's use of sliding windows which are a combination of the session and transport layer rules.

8.1 New Functions

The sender agent has a private function *WinMsg: integers → messages* which is used to store messages that have been sent; the receiver agent has a corresponding function *WinData: integers → data* used to store data that has been received. Both agents have a private function *WinAck: integers → Bool* which indicates which messages have been acknowledged.

Both agents have private functions *WinLo, WinHi: integers* which indicate the current window boundaries. A global static function *WinMax: integers* indicates the largest window size permitted; as shown in section 4, at least $2 * WinMax$ distinct messages are needed to use a window of size *WinMax*. Consequently, we assume that all our arithmetic with respect to message numbers is done modulo $2 * WinMax$.

A function *Windows: Bool* indicates whether or not the sliding windows protocol is to be used during data transmission. Its value is determined during the initial protocol negotiations.

8.2 Transition Rules

Rule GetInput, presented in Fig. 13, attempts to get a new input message whenever there is no message available (except in the initial state of the sender, since the sender must send the first message). In Sliding Windows Kermit, we only wish to obtain messages at specific moments; in particular, we need to disable this automatic retrieval of messages when our sliding window is in operation. Thus, we need to disable GetInput for certain values of *Mode*. The modified transition rule is shown in Fig. 27. Further, we add the Boolean condition ($Windows = false$) to the outermost guard of rules *SSDAT* and *SRDAT* presented in section 5.2.

Rule: GetInput
if $Layer = session$ **and** $Undefined(RecvdType)$ **and** $(Mode \neq ssini$ **or**
 $(Windows = true$ **and** $Mode \notin \{ssdat, ssdatrotate, srdat, ssini,$
  $srdatnak, srdatrotate\}))$ **then**
  $Layer := transport, TransportCommand := receive$
endif

FIG. 27. MODIFIED TRANSITION RULE FOR RECEIVING INPUT.

Once the sender arrives in state *ssdat* during a sliding window file transfer, she repeatedly sends messages until an acknowledgment arrives, the window of unacknowledged messages fills, or the entire file has been sent. The transition rule for sending messages in state *ssdat* is shown in Fig. 28, and corresponds to rule SendMessage of the SWP shown in Fig. 8.

Rule: SSDAT:Windows:1
if $Mode = ssdat$ **and** $Windows = true$ **and** $Undefined(FetchType)$ **then**
  if $SeqNo - WinLo + 1 \leq WinMax$ **and** $TextToSend \neq \epsilon$ **then**
    $WinMsg(SeqNo) :=$
      $Msg(\text{``D''}, EncodePrefix(TextToSend, EINFO), SeqNo)$
    $SEND(\text{``D''}, EncodePrefix(TextToSend, EINFO), SeqNo)$
    $TextToSend := Remainder(TextToSend, EINFO)$
    $SeqNo := SeqNo + 1$
  else GET
ENDIF

FIG. 28. TRANSITION RULE FOR SENDING DATA USING SLIDING WINDOWS.

If acknowledgments within the sender's window are waiting to be processed, the appropriate window slots are marked as acknowledged and control passes to *ssdatrotate*, which rotates the window forward as far as possible. Otherwise, a retry mechanism is used to re-transmit certain messages a limited number of times. The transition rule for processing acknowledgments in state *ssdat* is shown in Fig. 29, and corresponds to rule **ProcessAck** of the SWP shown in Fig. 8.

Rule: SSDAT:Windows:2
if $Mode = ssdat$ **and** $Windows$ **and** $Defined(FetchType)$ **then**
   if $WinLo \leq FetchNo \leq SeqNo$ **then**
      if $FetchType =$ "Y" **then**
         $WinAck(FetchNo) := true$, $Retry(FetchNo) := 0$
         $Clear(FetchType)$
         if $FetchNo = WinLo$ **then** $Mode := ssdatrotate$ **endif**
      endif
      if $FetchType =$ "N" **then** $RETRY(FetchNo)$ **endif**
      if $FetchType =$ "T" **then** $RETRY(WinLo)$ **endif**
      if $FetchType \notin \{$ "Y", "N", "T", "Q"$\}$ **then** $ERROR$ **endif**
   endif
endif

Abbreviation: RETRY(num)
if $Retry(num) > RetryLimit$ **then** $ERROR$
else
   $Q(You) := Q(You) \mathrel{++} WinMsg(num)$
   $Retry(num) := Retry(num) + 1$, $Clear(FetchType)$
endif

FIG. 29. TRANSITION RULE FOR RECEIVING ACKNOWLEDGMENTS USING SLIDING WINDOWS.

The rules for *ssdatrotate* slide the sender's window forward as far as possible. Additionally, if all acknowledgments have been received for a particular file, we send the end-of-file Z indicator and resume normal Kermit operations. The transition rule for *ssdatrotate* is shown in Fig. 30, and corresponds to rule **SlideSenderWin** of the SWP shown in Fig. 8.

In state *srdat*, the receiver using sliding windows processes data (D) messages within the current window by storing the received data and sending an acknowledgment message. When the end-of-file Z message arrives, the receiver clears his window of all data which has been received but not

```
Rule: SSDATROTATE
if Mode = ssdatrotate then
    if WinAck(WinLo) = true then
        WinAck(WinLo) := false, WinLo := WinLo + 1
    elseif WinLo = SeqNo and TextToSend = ε then
        TSEND("Z",ε), GOTO(ssfil)
    else GOTO(ssdat)
    endif
endif
```

FIG. 30. TRANSITION RULE FOR STATE *ssdatrotate*.

yet shifted out of the window. Finally, if a timeout or corrupted message arrives, a negative acknowledgment (NAK) message is generated for the oldest message in the current window not yet received. The transition rule for state *srdat* is given in Fig. 31; it corresponds to rule AcceptMessage of the SWP shown in Fig. 8.

In state *srdatnak*, the receiver generates a NAK message for the unacknowledged message within his window with the lowest message number. If there are no such messages, the receiver generates a NAK message for the first message outside of the window (*i.e.* the next message expected by the receiver) only if this NAK was generated by a timeout condition. The transition rule for state *srdatnak* is given in Fig. 32; it has no corresponding rule in the SWP.

Messages arriving outside of the current window require that the receiver's window be shifted forward; control passes to state *srdatrotate* to accomplish this. State *srdatrotate* rotates the receiver's window forward until the just-received datum can be placed into the message. At the same time, all the data which is shifted out of the window is stored in the output file. The transition rule is shown in Fig. 33; it corresponds to rule SlideReceiverWin of the SWP shown in Fig. 8.

8.3 Correctness

The proof of correctness for this extension to Kermit is similar to that for the bounded SWP presented in section 4. We point out here the main similarities and differences between the protocols.

The principal difference between the two protocols is that Kermit runs for a finite amount of time. The Kermit sender must wait to send the Z message until every message containing data from the current file has been successfully acknowledged. In addition, the Kermit receiver must rotate all messages in the current window out of the window (and into the output file) once the end-of-file (Z) message has been received.

Rule: SRDAT:Windows
if $Mode = srdat$ and $Windows$ and $Defined(FetchType)$ then
   if $FetchType =$ "D" then
      $DSEND($"Y", ϵ, $FetchNo)$
      if $WinLo \leq FetchNo \leq WinHi$ then
         $WinData(FetchNo) := FetchData$, $WinAck(FetchNo) := true$
         $GOTO(srdat)$
      else $GOTO(srdatrotate)$
      endif
   endif
   if $FetchType =$ "Z" then
      if $WinLo \leq WinHi$ then
         $FileText(FileNo) := FileText(FileNo) +$
                            $Decode(WinData(WinLo), DINFO)$
         $WinLo := WinLo + 1$, $WinAck(WinLo) := false$
      else
         $SeqNo := FetchNo+1$, $FileNo := FileNo + 1$
         $DSEND($"Y", ϵ, $FetchNo)$, $GOTO(srfil)$
      endif
   endif
   if $FetchType =$ "Q" or $FetchType =$ "T" then
      $Mode := srdatnak$, $Counter := WinLo$
   endif
   if $FetchType \notin \{$"D", "Z", "Q", "T"$\}$ then $ERROR$ endif
endif

FIG. 31. TRANSITION RULE FOR STATE *srdat* USING SLIDING WINDOWS.

Agents may re-transmit lost messages more often in the Kermit protocol than in the SWP, since the receiver can generate NAKs for missing messages at certain times. This does not affect the correctness of the protocol; it may, however, improve performance as the server may not wait as long in order to re-transmit a lost or garbled message.

The way in which the agents slide their windows is different in the two protocols. In the SWP, the sender may slide her window in parallel with the sending of new messages; in Kermit, the sender must slide her window separately from sending new messages. In the SWP, the receiver may slide his window by large amounts; in Kermit, the receiver slides his window only by single messages. The net result is the same in each case.

The size of the agents' windows is determined during the initial protocol negotiation, but is at most 32 (since Kermit uses only 64 message numbers).

Rule: SRDATNAK
if Mode = srdatnak **then**
  if Counter ≤ WinHi **then**
    if WinAck(Counter) = false **then**
      DSEND("N",ϵ, Counter), GOTO(srdat)
    else Counter := Counter + 1
    endif
  else
    if FetchType = "T" **then** DSEND("N",ϵ, WinHi+1) **endif**
    GOTO(srdat)
  endif
endif

FIG. 32. TRANSITION RULE FOR STATE *srdatnak*.

Rule: SRDATROTATE
if Mode = srdatrotate **then**
  if WinHi+1 ≤ FetchNo **then**
    DSEND("N",ϵ, WinHi)
    if WinHi − WinLo + 1 = WinMax **then**
      FileText(FileNo) := FileText(FileNo) +
                          Decode(WinData(WinLo),DINFO)
      WinLo := WinLo + 1, WinAck(WinLo) := false
    endif
    WinHi := WinHi + 1
  else
    WinData(FetchNo) := FetchData, WinAck(FetchNo) := true
    GOTO(srdat)
ENDIF

FIG. 33. TRANSITION RULE FOR STATE *srdatrotate*.

Immediately we have the following theorem:

Theorem 8.1 *Every message sent by Sliding Windows Kermit is eventually received and successfully acknowledged.*

Appendix A   Kermit Initialization

The first messages sent by each agent in a Kermit file transfer (that is, the sender's "S" message and the receiver's first "Y" message) contain initialization parameters. The combination of these two sets of parameters uniquely determine information of importance to the protocol (for example, the maximum message length to be used).

The *HANDLE-INITS* transition rules handle the setting of these parameters. We present some of these rules in Fig. 34, leaving the reader to deduce the behavior of previously unspecified functions. Rules for handling other parameter initializations are similar.

---

if $Length(RecvdData) \geq 1$ *then*
   if $MAXL \geq 10$ *then* $MaxMsgLen := MAXL$
   else $MaxMsgLen := 80$ *endif*
endif
if $Length(RecvdData) \geq 2$ *then*
   if $TIME > 0$ *then* $TimeoutLen := TIME$
   else $TimeoutLen := 5$ *endif*
endif
if $Length(RecvdData) \geq 3$ *then*
   if $NPAD > 0$ *then* $PadLen := NPAD$ *else* $PadLen := 0$ *endif*
endif
if $Length(RecvdData) \geq 4$ *then* $PadChar := PADC$ *endif*
if $Length(RecvdData) \geq 5$ *then*
   if $2 \leq EOL \leq 31$ *then* $Eol := EOL$
   else $Eol := CarriageReturn$ *endif*
endif
if $Length(RecvdData) \geq 6$ *then*
   if $32 \leq QCTL \leq 63$ *or* $95 \leq QCTL \leq 127$ *then* $CtlPrefix := QCTL$
   else $CtlPrefix := \text{``\#''}$ *endif*
endif

where $MAXL = UnChar(Substr(RecvdData, 1, 1))$
      $TIME = UnChar(Substr(RecvdData, 2, 1))$
      $NPAD = UnChar(Substr(RecvdData, 3, 1))$
      $PADC = Ctl(Substr(RecvdData, 4, 1))$
      $EOL = Unchar(Substr(RecvdData, 5, 1))$
      $QCTL = Substr(RecvdData, 6, 1)$

FIG. 34. SOME TRANSITION RULES OF THE *HANDLE-INITS* ABBREVIATION.

Appendix B Partially Ordered Runs of Kermit

In all our protocol proofs presented above, we used sequential runs. In distributed computations such as those of Kermit, sequential runs are too restrictive; *e.g.* moves of the sender and receiver may certainly overlap in time. Fortunately, our theorems survive when we consider partial runs (defined in [Gur]).

Our safety properties are of the form "Every state reachable in a regular run satisfies property Φ" and are proved by induction over regular sequential runs. Recall that a sequential run is *regular* if it satisfies a specified set of initial conditions. Call a partial run *regular* if its initial state satisfies the same set of initial conditions. It is shown in [Gur] that a property Φ holds in every reachable state of a partially ordered run ρ if it holds in every reachable state of every linearization of ρ; each of these linearizations is a sequential run of the program in question. Thus, every safety result for regular sequential runs gives the same result for regular partial runs.

Our liveness properties have the form "Every fair run satisfies such and such property." Our definition of sequential fair runs relies implicitly on the total ordering of steps in a run; consequently, we need a different definition of fairness for partially ordered runs. Recall that a sequential run is *fair* if for every positive agent X and every tail ρ' of ρ, if X is enabled infinitely often in ρ', then X must make a move in ρ'. We call a partially ordered run ρ *fair* if some linearization of ρ is fair.

With this new definition, it can be seen that any of our fairness properties of sequential runs can be proved over partially ordered runs as well. As an example, consider Theorem 1.9, which asserts that in any sequential fair run of the ABP, any datum sent is eventually received.

Theorem Appendix B.1 *In every fair run ρ, every datum sent is eventually received. That is, if the sender sends a datum d during a move μ, there exists a move ν during which the receiver accepts d and where $\nu > \mu$. Moreover, there is a constant N such that every initial segment of ρ containing more than N moves contains ν.*

Proof. We show first that ρ contains a move ν of the receiver accepting d, where $\mu < \nu$. Since ρ is fair, let ρ' be a linearization of ρ which is fair. Theorem 1.9 shows that ρ' must contain the desired ν.

Let $I = \{\mu' : \mu' \not> \nu\}$. Since ρ is a partial run, I is finite. Let $N = \|I\|$. By the definition of I, if an initial segment σ of ρ contains more than N moves, σ either contains ν or a move ν' such that $\nu < \nu'$. But since σ is downward closed, σ must contain ν as well. □

All other proofs of fairness can be applied to partially ordered runs in a similar manner.

Bibliography

[BSW] K. A. Bartlett, R. A. Scantlebury, and P. T. Wilkinson, "A note on reliable full-duplex transmission over half-duplex links", *Communications of the ACM*, volume 12 (1969), no. 5, pp. 260–261, 265.

[DaC] F. DaCruz, *Kermit: A File Transfer Protocol*, Digital Press, 1987.

[Gur] Y. Gurevich, "Evolving Algebras 1993: Lipari Guide", this volume.

[Kr] F. Kröger, *Temporal Logic of Programs*, Springer-Verlag, 1987.

[LM] K. G. Larsen and R. Milner, "A Compositional Protocol Verification Using Relativized Bisimulation," *Information and Computation*, volume 99 (1992), no. 1, pp. 80–108.

[SL] A. U. Shankar and S. S. Lam, "A Stepwise Refinement Heuristic for Protocol Construction," *ACM Transactions on Programming Languages and Systems*, volume 14 (1992), no. 3, pp. 417–461.

[Tan] A. S. Tanenbaum, *Computer Networks*, Prentice-Hall, 1981.

[Wal] J. Walrand, *Communication Networks: A First Course*, Aksen Associates, 1991.

Group Membership Protocol: Specification and Verification

Yuri Gurevich* and Raghu Mani[†]

1 Introduction

According to the Evolving Algebra thesis [3], evolving algebras should allow one to specify any algorithm succinctly. There exists substantial evidence confirming this thesis in the case of sequential algorithms (see the annotated bibliography in [3]). In other chapters, e.g., [1, 5], evolving algebras are used to specify distributed algorithms. For this chapter, we wanted to look at a time-constrained algorithm that does something useful and poses some challenge to specify and verify. Our colleague Farnam Jahanian brought Cristian's article on group membership protocols [2] to our attention. In this chapter, we specify and verify one of the protocols presented in that article. It is an interesting protocol to verify as we need to specify and prove both timing as well as functional properties.

Group membership protocols [2, 6, 7] are used mainly to provide fault tolerance for distributed computing services. One possible way of ensuring service availability in a distributed system despite processor failures is to have several servers *cooperate* to provide the service (each such set of servers is termed a *server group*) and to *replicate* information relevant to the service (this is termed *service state information*) at all the sites in the network. For example, if the service in question is a C compiler then the state information may include a list of servers offering this service that are currently alive and information regarding how heavily loaded each of these servers is. The purpose of group membership and other related protocols is to ensure that the state information stored at each group member remains up-to-date and that, in the steady state, all group members see the same state information – despite information propagation delays and server failures.

Central to the problem of server-group membership is *processor-group membership* which, to put it briefly, is the problem of achieving global agreement about the set of all correctly functioning processors in the system. Given a solution for the processor group membership problem, it is possible to use it to construct a solution to the server-group membership problem. The protocol we consider in this chapter is a solution to the processor-group membership problem in synchronous systems.

---

*Partially supported by ONR grant N00014-91-J-1861 and NSF grant CCR-92-04742.
[†]Partially supported by NSF grant CCR-92-04742.

2 Overview of the Protocol

In this section, we describe the assumptions about the system, the protocol itself and finally the goals that the protocol is supposed to achieve. In an attempt to simplify the exposition and make this chapter self-contained, we allow ourselves slight changes of terminology.

In the following two subsections, we describe our interpretation of the assumptions made by Cristian about the system. It turns out that not all his assumptions are necessary.

2.1 Synchronous Communication Network

There is a fixed finite collection of processors p, each with its own clock $Clock(p)$ or $Clock_p$. You may think about $Clock_p$ as a real-valued function of real time. Cristian assumes that every $Clock_p$ is strictly monotone ("successive readings yield strictly increasing values") and there is a bound on the deviations $\mid Clock_p(t) - t \mid$. It follows that there is a bound on the skew between any pair of clocks. In our specification, we do not make any assumption about the connection between the clocks and real time. We do not assume directly the existence of a skew bound, though a weaker form of that assumption will follow from one of our later assumptions.

Each processor hosts various processes, and processes handle tasks. Processors can be interrupted but a task is run until completion. Typically, a task has a *start deadline* (henceforth, simply *deadline*). Scheduling is assumed to be *earliest deadline first*. A task may not be scheduled well in advance of its deadline – more precisely, if the deadline of the task is d then it may not be scheduled until time $d - d_u$, where d_u is a constant called the *scheduling uncertainty*. A task may, however, be scheduled after its deadline has passed – this can happen when tasks with earlier deadlines take too long to complete, thus preventing the task in question from being scheduled in timely fashion. d_u is one of a series of system-related bounds and constants we will be describing in this section. When we say that such and such bound exists we mean that it exists and is known.

Cristian speaks about correct and incorrect processors. The following abstraction seems appropriate. A processor can be *crashed*, *recovering* or *sober*. It is assumed that there is a minimum delay of d_r time units (the *recovery* bound) between the time a processor crashes and the time it next becomes sober. A processor is *correct* at a particular instant of time if it is sober and it has no pending tasks whose deadlines have been exceeded. This latter situation is termed a *performance failure*.

A reliable broadcast mechanism is assumed. It guarantees that every message m broadcast by a correct processor p will be delivered to every processor on the network. The only reason for a scheduled broadcast not reaching all the processors on the network is if the sender crashes or suffers a performance failure. It is also assumed that performance failures can be detected and turned into crashes. We make the same assumptions here.

Moreover, there is a bound on the time taken to carry m over from p to any processor q. The time can be "measured on any processor clock" [2]. It seems a little more natural to measure the time of sending on $Clock(p)$ and the time of delivery on $Clock(q)$. We will assume that there is a carry-over bound d_c with the following property: If the sending time of m is t_1 with respect to $Clock(p)$ and the delivery time is t_2 with respect to $Clock(q)$ then $0 < Clock(q) - Clock(p) \leq d_c$. This, in fact, is the only assumption we make relating the clocks of two different processors and follows from Cristian's assumptions related to time; of course a natural way to satisfy our assumption is to satisfy the time-related assumptions of Cristian. Cristian assumes also that messages are seen in order of their deadlines and that two messages with the same deadline are seen in the same order by all correct processors. The latter assumption turns out to be unnecessary.

In this protocol, the only type of message sent is a broadcast – therefore, in this document, the terms "sent" and "broadcast" will be synonymous.

2.2 Informal Description of the Protocol

Each processor p hosts a *membership server* $MS(p)$ that handles the entry of the processor into a processor-group and helps maintain state information while the processor is alive, and a *broadcast server* $BS(p)$ that periodically sends a broadcast to all the other processors in the system. In addition to these, there may be other processes running on the processor. The only way these can affect the protocol are by using up time and hence delaying protocol-related tasks. Tasks relevant to the protocol are – recovering from a crash, processing an incoming message (both handled by the $MS(p)$) and sending a broadcast (handled by the $BS(p)$).

$MS(p)$ maintains the state information stored at p and processes incoming messages. The state information stored at p consists of:

- The *group identifier* of p's group – new groups are created each time a processor fails or recovers. In this protocol, a group identifier is a timestamp that indicates when the group was formed.
- Identifiers of the processors in p's current group – the *membership view* of p.

In [2] the state information includes a flag that indicates whether or not p is currently part of a group. We can do away with this as the desired property can be determined from whether or not the group id (or the membership view) is defined.

$BS(p)$ sends broadcasts at periodic intervals – these *heartbeats* inform other processors that p is alive. If p misses a heartbeat then the other processors conclude that p has failed. The interval between two successive heartbeats is a system-wide constant and is denoted by d_h in this document. When $BS(p)$ is scheduled, one of the following two situations can arise:

- *Clock*(p) is greater than the deadline of the currently scheduled heartbeat – this means that p has missed a deadline and therefore is, in some sense, not functioning correctly. In such a case, $BS(p)$ concludes that p has failed and removes p from its current group.
- *Clock*(p) is less than or equal to the deadline t of the currently scheduled heartbeat – in this case, when scheduled, $BS(p)$ sends a present message with timestamp t and sets the time of the next heartbeat to $t + d_h$.

$MS(p)$ operates as follows:

- When recovering from a failure, $MS(p)$ initializes the state variables, and broadcasts a new_gp message – this message indicates to all other processors that p is rejoining the system and attempting to form a new group. The timestamp t of this message is equal to the sum of *Clock*(p) and a constant d_n which is larger than the maximum network propagation delay – the idea being to ensure that the message is seen by every correctly functioning processor q before *Clock*(q) $= t$.
- If $MS(p)$ sees a new_gp message then one of the following two situations can arise:
  - *Clock*(p) is greater than the timestamp of the new_gp message – in such a case, $MS(p)$ assumes that p has failed and removes p from its current group.
  - *Clock*(p) is not greater than the timestamp t of the new_gp message – in such a case, $MS(p)$ cancels any pending heartbeat, sets the time for the next heartbeat to $t+d_h$ and broadcasts a present message with timestamp t. This present message indicates to all other processors that p is going to join the new group. $MS(p)$ sends no further present messages until the next new_gp message arrives. All other present messages from p are sent by $BS(p)$.
- If $MS(p)$ sees a present message m then it does the following:
  - It checks its box of incoming messages for present messages from other processors with the same timestamp as m, removes all of them (including m) and computes the union v of their sender processor ids.
  - If v is identical to the membership view of p then it does nothing else.
  - If v is different from the membership view of p then it makes v the new membership view and sets the group id of p to the timestamp of m.

2.3 Summary of Bounds and Constants

d_u: an upper bound on the uncertainty in scheduling.

d_c: an upper bound on the time taken to carry a message over the network.
d_h: the heartbeat interval.
d_n: the new_gp timestamp increment.
d_r: a lower bound on the time between a crash and a subsequent recovery.

It is assumed that $d_h > d_u$, $d_n > d_c + d_u$ and $d_r > d_h + d_u$.

2.4 Goals of the Protocol

Whenever we mention a time value in the context of a processor p, it will mean the time as recorded by Clock(p).

G1. *Stability of local views:* Once a processor joins a group, it stays in that group until either a processor fails or one recovers and attempts to rejoin.

G2. *Agreement on history:* If p and q are joined to a common group g during a run of the system, then if the next groups joined by p and q after leaving g are g^p and g^q respectively, and neither processor crashes in the interval between the time it joined g and the time it joined its next group, then $g^p = g^q$.

G3. *Agreement on group membership:* If p and q are joined to the same group and are both alive then their membership views are identical.

G4. *Reflexivity:* If p is alive and joined to a group then its id will be included in its membership view.

G5. *Bounded join delays:* There exists a time constant d_j such that if a processor becomes sober at time t then, by time $t + d_j$, it will join a new group g along with every other processor q that stays correct in the interval $[t, t + d_j]$.

G6. *Bounded failure detection delays:* There exists a time constant d_f such that if a processor p belonging to group g fails at time t then, by time $t + d_f$, all the members of g that that stay correct in the interval $[t, t + d_f]$ will join a group g' that does not contain p.

3 The Program

The semantics of evolving algebras are described in [4]. In order to understand the material in this chapter, the reader need only read about ground distributed evolving algebras. We use variables in this chapter only to make the rules easier to read. Variables are, in fact, not needed and can easily be eliminated.

The algebra is modeled as five module templates. MembershipServer and BroadcastServer model the membership and broadcast servers of the protocol respectively. Scheduler handles recovery from crashes and scheduling of processes, MessageCarrier handles transmission of messages across the network and Custodian handles orderly delivery of messages to the membership server.

The transition rules are all named. We have also named the clauses in these transition rules that we shall be referring to often.

In this section we will observe the following conventions. Variables p and q range over processors; variable m ranges over messages. Abbreviations are written in SMALL CAPS and external functions are written in *Slanted Sans Serif*.

3.1 Vocabulary

We do not describe the vocabulary explicitly since most of it is quite obvious from the program, but we explain here some of the less obvious functions and abbreviations.

If t is a term then DEFINED(t) is an abbreviation for $t \neq$ undef.

We define MessageType to be the universe containing two objects present and new_gp. Real is the universe of real numbers; Processor is the universe of processor ids. A message m is a triple $(x, y, z) \in$ MessageType $\times$ Real $\times 2^{\text{Processor}}$; x is $MesType(m)$, y is $Timestamp(m)$ and z is $View(m)$. Let Message be the universe of messages.

Messages have deadlines associated with them. The deadline of a message m (written $Deadline(m)$) is defined as follows:

1. If m is a new_gp message then $Deadline(m) = Timestamp(m)$.
2. If m is a present message then $Deadline(m) = Timestamp(m) + d_n$.

We define the following dynamic functions. $InBox(p) \in 2^{\text{Message}}$ is the set of messages that have been delivered to p but have not been seen by the membership server. $CurMes(p)$ stores the message currently being seen by the membership server. It turns out that this message has the earliest deadline among all current messages. $BCastTime(p)$ gives the time for which the next broadcast is scheduled.

The deadline for a process x (written DLINE(x)) is the minimum among the deadlines of the tasks waiting to be handled by x. The two processes we are concerned with here are the membership and broadcast servers. The relevant tasks handled by the membership server are (i) initializing the internal functions of the processor after recovering from a crash and (ii) handling incoming messages. Each incoming message corresponds to a separate task. The dynamic function $CurMes(p)$ should always store a message with the earliest deadline. DLINE$(MS(p))$ abbreviates, therefore, $Deadline(CurMes(p))$. The tasks handled by the broadcast server are broadcast sends. In this protocol, there is at most one broadcast scheduled at a given processor at any given time. DLINE$(BS(p))$ abbreviates, therefore, $BCastTime(p)$.

ENABLED$(MS(p))$ abbreviates

$$\text{DEFINED}(CurMes(p)) \land (\text{DLINE}(MS(p)) \geq \textsf{Clock}(p) - d_u)$$

and ENABLED$(BS(p))$ abbreviates

$(\text{DLINE}(BS(p)) \geq \textit{Clock}(p) - d_u)$.

Informally, $\text{APTPART}(p)$ is the set of messages m in $InBox(p)$ such that $Deadline(m) \geq \textit{Clock}(p) - d_u$. More formally, define the static function Apt as follows. Given an element $I \in 2^{\textsf{Message}}$ and two reals t_1 and t_2, it computes an element $J \in 2^{\textsf{Message}}$ which (viewed as a set) comprises all messages $m \in I$ such that $(Deadline(m) \geq t_1 - d_u) \wedge (Timestamp(m) \geq t_2)$. $\text{APTPART}(p)$ abbreviates $Apt(InBox(p), \textit{Clock}(p), StartUpTime(p))$. Here $StartUpTime(p)$ is the time at which p recovered from its last crash.

3.2 Scheduler(p)

Each processor hosts a number of processes. The Scheduler agent for a processor p handles recovery from crashes and scheduling of processes on the processor. The two processes on p that we are concerned with in this specification are the membership server process $MS(p)$ and the broadcast server process $BS(p)$. These are the two processes that implement the protocol – we assume that the other processes running on the processor do not affect the protocol in any way other than using up time.

<u>Transition Recover</u>
if $Status(p) = $ crashed **then**
    $Status(p) := $ recovered, $CurProc(p) := MS(p)$
endif

When a processor has recovered from a crash, the only process ready to execute is the membership server. Scheduling a process on p is modeled by setting $CurProc(p)$ (the process currently running on p) to the appropriate value.

<u>Transition Schedule</u>
if $(CurProc(p) = $ undef$) \wedge (Status(p) = $ sober$) \wedge$
    $((\text{APTPART}(p) = \emptyset) \vee \text{DEFINED}(CurMes(p))) \wedge$
    $[((x = MS(p)) \wedge (y = BS(p))) \vee ((x = BS(p)) \wedge (y = MS(p)))]$ **then**
    if $\text{ENABLED}(x) \wedge \neg \text{ENABLED}(y)$ **then** $CurProc(p) := x$
    elseif $\text{ENABLED}(x) \wedge \text{ENABLED}(y)$ **then**
        if $\text{DLINE}(x) < \text{DLINE}(y)$ **then** $CurProc(p) := x$
        else $CurProc(p) := y$
        endif
    endif
endif

Scheduling is earliest-deadline-first and nonpreemptive. To ensure nonpreemption, we add the term $CurProc(p) = $ undef to the guard of transition Schedule and $CurProc(p) = MS(p)$ and $CurProc(p) = BS(p)$ to the guards of the transitions of the MembershipServer and BroadcastServer modules respectively. When the membership server or broadcast server of p completes its current task, it sets $CurProc(p)$ to undef – which enables the scheduler to run. The scheduler then schedules the next process by setting $CurProc(p)$ to the appropriate value.

APTPART(p) is the set of messages from which $CurMes(p)$ is chosen. If APTPART(p) = $\emptyset$ then there are currently no messages available for the membership server to see; hence the scheduler goes ahead. If APTPART(p) is not empty then there are messages available; the scheduler therefore waits till one of these messages has been selected (in other words, till $CurMes(p)$ becomes defined).

In addition to the membership and broadcast servers there may be other processes running tasks unrelated to our protocol. These tasks need to be taken into account because they can affect our protocol by taking too much time to execute and causing the protocol-related tasks to miss their deadlines. We can model this situation using the nondeterminism of transition rules. To put it another way, a transition rule need not fire the instant it is enabled. The time between the instant the transition rule was enabled to the instant it fired can be considered to be time utilized by some other process.

3.3 MembershipServer(p)

<u>Transition Initialize</u>
if $(Status(p) = \text{recovered}) \wedge (CurProc(p) = MS(p))$ **then**
$\quad BCastTime(p) := \text{undef}, CurMes(p) := \text{undef}$
$\quad GroupId(p) := \text{undef}, Members(p) := \text{undef}$
$\quad StartUpTime(p) := Clock(p) + d_n$
$\quad InTransit((\text{new\_gp}, Clock(p) + d_n, \{p\})) := \text{true}$
$\quad Status(p) := \text{sober}, CurProc(p) := \text{undef}$
endif

The above rule initializes the state information and broadcasts a new_gp message. The state information stored by the membership server of a processor p consists of the group identifier of p's current group ($GroupId(p)$), a set containing the members of p's group ($Members(p)$) and the time at which the processor recovered from its last crash ($StartUpTime(p)$).

Sending a broadcast m is modeled by setting $InTransit(m)$ to true – this signifies that m is currently being propagated on the network.

Add $(Status(p) = \text{sober}) \wedge (CurProc(p) = MS(p))$ as a conjunct to the guards of the following two transitions.

Transition HandleNewGpMes

if $(MesType(CurMes(p)) = \text{new\_gp})$ **then**
    if $(Clock(p) > Timestamp(CurMes(p)))$ **then**   Crash_MS
        $Status(p) := \text{crashed}$
    else   PrMesSend_MS
        $InTransit((\text{present}, Timestamp(CurMes(p)), \{p\})) := \text{true}$
        $BCastTime(p) := Timestamp(CurMes(p)) + d_h$
        $CurMes(p) := \text{undef}, CurProc(p) := \text{undef}$
    endif
endif

If the membership server of p gets scheduled after the deadline of the message has been exceeded, it removes itself from the group it is currently a member. This "removal" is modeled by setting $Status(p)$ to crashed.

Transition HandlePresentMes

if $(MesType(CurMes(p)) = \text{present})$ **then**
    if $(Members(p) \neq View(CurMes(p)))$ **then**   ChangeGp
        $Members(p) := View(CurrMes(p))$
        $GroupId(p) := Timestamp(CurMes(p))$
    endif
    $CurMes(p) := \text{undef}, CurProc(p) := \text{undef}$
endif

3.4 BroadcastServer(p)

Transition HandleBCast

if $(Status(p) = \text{sober}) \wedge (CurProc(p) = BS(p))$ **then**
    if $(Clock(p) > BCastTime(p))$ **then**   Crash_BS
        $Status(p) := \text{crashed}$
    else   PrMesSend_BS
        $InTransit((\text{present}, BCastTime(p), \{p\})) := \text{true}$
        $BCastTime(p) := BCastTime(p) + d_h, CurProc(p) := \text{undef}$
    endif
endif

3.5 MessageCarrier(p)

To model the transmission of a message from one processor to another, we introduce a MessageCarrier agent for each processor p; this agent delivers messages intended for p to p. The "delivery" is done by incorporating the message into $InBox(p)$ which is an element of 2^{Message} – the set of finite sets of messages. We view $InBox(p)$ both as an element as well as a set.

An incoming message m of type new_gp is simply added to the $InBox(p)$. Messages of type present with identical timestamps are, however, bunched together into one message. If m is an incoming message (to p) of type present and there is no present message in $InBox(p)$ with the same timestamp as m, then m is simply added to $InBox(p)$. If there exists a single present message m' with the same timestamp as m, then m' is deleted from $InBox(p)$ and the message (present, $Timestamp(m), View(m) \cup View(m')$) is added in its place. It is easy to see that there can never be more than one present message with the same timestamp in $InBox(p)$. The message to be incorporated into $InBox(p)$ is given by the external function InMes(p). More will be said about this function in section 4.

Transition DeliverIncomingMes

if (InMes(p) = (a, b, c)) **then**
    if (a = new_gp) **then** $InBox(p) := InBox(p) \cup \{$InMes($p$)$\}$
    elseif ($Present(InBox(p), b)$ = undef) **then**
        $InBox(p) := InBox(p) \cup $ InMes(p)$\}$
    elseif ($Present(InBox(p), b) = m$) **then**
        $InBox(p) := (InBox(p) - \{m\}) \cup \{(a, b, View(m) \cup c)\}$
    endif
endif

The static function $Present$ is defined as follows. Given $I \in 2^{\text{Message}}$ and a real t, if there exists a unique present message $m \in I$ with timestamp t, then $Present(I, t) = m$; otherwise $Present(I, t) =$ undef.

Note that transition DeliverIncomingMes never removes any message from $InTransit$, thus allowing $InTransit$ to grow in an unbounded manner. If we wish to keep the size of $InTransit$ bounded, we can modify the program as follows. Currently, if we wish to broadcast a message m, we set $InTransit(m)$ to true, thus sending a single copy of m to the entire group. Instead of doing this we can send a separate copy of m to each processor q, by making $InTransit$ a binary function – the first argument being the message sent and the second being its target – and replacing all updates of the form $InTransit(m) :=$ true with $InTransit(m, q) :=$ true. Then, the message carrier of each processor can remove its copy of m from $InTransit$ when it incorporates m into its $InBox$.

3.6 Custodian(p)

The protocol requires that all the membership servers see the messages in order of their deadlines. Since the message carrier need not deliver the messages in this order, we have an agent Custodian for every processor p, which delivers a message with the minimal timestamp to the membership server.

Transition SelectCurMes

if ($Status(p)$ = sober) $\wedge$ ($CurMes(p)$ = undef)$\wedge$
    ($\text{AptPart}(p) \neq \emptyset$) $\wedge$ $MinDl(m, \text{AptPart}(p))$) **then**
    $CurMes(p) := m, InBox(p) := InBox(p) - m$
endif

Given a message m and a set I, $MinDl(m, I)$ is true if $m \in I$ and there is no message $m' \in I$ whose deadline is less than that of m.

Note that the custodian of p removes those messages that have been seen by the membership server from $InBox(p)$. However, the messages that arrive while the processor is crashed may never be seen by the membership server and hence are never removed. Thus, $InBox(p)$ can grow in an unbounded manner. To keep the number of messages in $InBox(p)$ bounded, we can have the custodian periodically remove from $InBox(p)$ those messages that can never be selected by transition SelectCurMes. For example, when the processor is crashed, we could remove all those messages whose timestamp is less than $Clock(p)$ and when the processor is alive, we could remove all those messages whose timestamp is less than $StartUpTime(p)$. Removal of these "unselectable" messages, however, does not relate to the protocol we are specifying; therefore, we do not deal with it in our specification.

4 Semantics: Definitions and Discussion

In subsection 4.1, we describe our "official" semantics. Real-time versions of that semantics and various other issues are discussed in subsection 4.2.

4.1 Definitions

For each processor p, let $\mathcal{E}(p)$ be the restriction of our evolving algebra $\mathcal{E}$ that involves only the five agents related to p: the scheduler, membership server, broadcast server, message carrier and custodian of p. For simplicity, we drop the processor name from the arguments of functions if it is clear from the context which processor we are referring to.

Semantics of $\mathcal{E}(p)$:

Vocabulary: Let $\sigma(p)$ be the vocabulary of $\mathcal{E}(p)$ excluding function $InTransit$.

Internal and external functions: Functions $Clock$ and $InMes$ are external input functions of $\mathcal{E}(p)$. From the point of view of $\mathcal{E}(p)$, their values are provided by the environment. Function $InTransit$ is an output external function; that is why it does not belong to $\sigma(p)$. The other functions in the vocabulary $\sigma(p)$ of $\mathcal{E}(p)$ are internal. Let $\sigma^-(p)$ be the internal vocabulary of $\mathcal{E}(p)$.

States: For brevity, we speak about states and runs of p rather than $\mathcal{E}(p)$. A *state* of p is a static $\sigma(p)$-algebra. An *internal state* of p is a static $\sigma^-(p)$-algebra. If S is a state, let S^- be the corresponding internal state.

Runs: Let I range over initial segments of natural numbers. A *(sequential) run* of p is a sequence $\rho_p = \langle S_n : n \in I \rangle$ of states of p such that, for each positive n, S_n^- is obtained from S_{n-1} by executing one rule $r(n)$ of $\mathcal{E}(p)$ at S_n. Notice that ρ_p uniquely determines rules $r(n)$ and each rule uniquely determines the agent whose program contains the rule. Call run ρ_p *monotone* if it satisfies the following condition:

R1. *Monotonicity of the clock:* The values of Clock at states S_0, S_1, S_2, etc. form a strictly increasing sequence. If there is a final state then Clock $= \infty$ in the final state.

Restrict attention to monotone runs. States S_n are *stages* of p in $\rho_p = \langle S_n : n \in I \rangle$. If $n \neq \max(I)$ then rule $r(n+1)$ *fires* at stage S_n. Notice that all stages have the same superuniverse. An *extended* $\sigma(p)$-*term* (relative to a run) is an expression built from elements of the superuniverse by means of functions in $\sigma(p)$.

Abbreviations: Let $\rho_p = \langle S_n : n \in I \rangle$ be a run of p and $a = S_n$. If k is a (possibly negative) integer and $n + k \in I$, then $a + k = S_{n+k}$. If τ is an extended $\sigma(p)$-term, then τ_a is the value of τ at stage a. Suppose that $n \neq \max(I)$ so that some rule $r = r(n+1)$ fires at a. If r assigns value x to a $\sigma(p)$-term τ, we say that p *sets* τ to x at stage a or τ *gets* value x at stage $a+1$. If $r(n+1)$ assigns value true to $InTransit(m)$, we say that p *sends* message m at stage a. Call a monotone run $\rho_p = \langle S_n : n \in I \rangle$ of p *regular* if it satisfies the following two conditions:

R2. *Lower bound on recovery time:* If $Status_a =$ crashed and $Status_{a+k} =$ recovered and $k > 0$, then $Clock_{a+k} - Clock_a \geq d_r$.

R3. *Initial state:* If a is the initial state, then $Status_a =$ crashed and $InBox_a = \emptyset$, and $CurMes_a$, $GroupId_a$, $Members_a$, $StartUpTime_a$, $BCastTime_a$ are all undef.

We define a *run* ρ of the whole evolving algebra $\mathcal{E}$ to be simply a collection of runs ρ_p of p where p ranges over the processors. ρ is *regular* if all constituent runs ρ_p are regular and ρ satisfies the following condition:

R4. *Carry time bound:* If p sends message $m = (x, y, z)$ to q at some stage a, then there is a unique stage b of q such that:
1. $InMes(q)_b = m$ and
2. There exists $m' = (x, y, z')$ in $InBox(q)_{b+1}$ where $z' \supseteq z$ and
3. $0 < Clock(q)_b - Clock(p)_a \leq d_c$.

4.2 Discussion

We could use real-time semantics with either zero-time or prolonged actions, as in [1], but the material lends itself to simpler semantics which is more general in a sense.

Sequential Runs: According to [4], a sequential run is a sequence of states together with the agent-witness function. Since the sequence of states uniquely determines the agent-witness function in our case, we have simplified the definition. Also, we took advantage of the fact that agents of $\mathcal{E}(p)$ can fire only one rule a time and further simplified the definition.

Partially Ordered Runs: We restrict attention to sequential runs only to simplify the exposition. There are no significant changes in the correctness proof if one uses partially ordered runs as defined in [4].

Stages: Usually stages of a run $\rho_p = \langle S_n : n \in I \rangle$ are pairs (n, S_n). The first component ensures the distinctness of stages and is not needed in the case of our monotone runs.

Initial states: Condition R3 can be generalized.

InMes Function: We don't care about the value of *InMes*(p) at stage a unless the message carrier of p acts at a; it may be **undef**. It is probably more honest to remove *InMes* from the vocabularies of those stages where the message carrier is passive, but this would complicate the definition of run a little.

InMes and $InTransit$ Functions: The only connection between *InMes* (p) and $InTransit$ is the condition R4. It is assumed that the environment-supplied *InMes* satisfies R4. Actually, we do not really need the environment to supply *InMes*. Instead, we can add a nondeterministic rule to choose an incoming message from $InTransit$. Alternatively, we can eliminate nondeterminism altogether by turning every message into an agent.

4.3 More Abbreviations and Definitions

Definition 1. *The predicate $Correct(p)$ is true for processor p at stage s if the following conditions are met:*

1. $Clock(p)_s \geq StartUpTime(p)_s$.
2. For all $m \in InBox(p)_s$, if $TimeStamp(m) \geq StartUpTime(p)_s$ then $Deadline(m) \geq Clock(p)_s$.
3. $BCastTime(p)_s \geq Clock(p)_s$.

Definition 2. *We define correctness in intervals as follows:*

1. If $a \leq b$ are stages of p, then p is correct in $[a, b]$ if it is correct at any stage c with $a \leq c \leq b$.
2. Let I be a real interval and $t_1 = \inf(I)$, $t_2 = \sup(I)$. Then, p is correct in I if it is correct in the stage interval $[a, b]$, where $C(p)_a \leq t_1 < C(p)_{a+1}$ and $C(p)_{b-1} < t_2 \leq C(p)_b$.

For brevity, we shorten the names of some functions – *Clock* is now C, $Timestamp$ is $TStamp$, $StartUpTime$ is $UpTime$, $CurMes$ is Mes, Mes $Type$ is $Type$, $GroupId$ is $GpId$ and the abbreviation DEFINED is DEF. For readability, we give the following definitions:

D1. p joins group g: there is a stage s of p such that $GpId(p)_s = g$.

D2. A message (a, b, c) is added to $InBox(p)$ at stage s by time $t - C(p)_s \leq t$ and there exists a message $(a, b, c') \in InBox(p)_{s+1}$ such that $(a = \textsf{present}) \to (c' \supseteq c)$ and $(a = \textsf{new\_gp}) \to (c' = c)$.

D3. A message from q with timestamp t is in $InBox(p)$ at stage s: $\exists m = (a, t, c) \in InBox(p)_s$ such that $q \in c$.

D4. p sees a message with timestamp t at stage s: $Status(p)_s = \textsf{sober}$ and $CurProc(p)_s = MS(p)$ and $TStamp(Mes(p))_s = t$.

D5. p fails at stage s: At least one of the following conditions is true at stage s and none is true at stage $s - 1$:
   a. $BCastTime(p)_s < C(p)_s$;
   b. $(Type(Mes(p))_s = \textsf{new\_gp}$ and $(TStamp(Mes(p))_s < C(p)_s)$;
   c. $\exists m \in InBox(p)_s$ such that $(Type(m) = \textsf{new\_gp}$ and $(UpTime(p)_s \leq TStamp(m) < C(p)_s)$.

4.4 What We Shall Be Proving

The following are the properties that we will be proving about every regular run of $\mathcal{E}$. These correspond to goals G1 through G6 described in section 2.4.

Theorem 4: *Stability of local views*
   For every p and all stages $a < b$ of p, the following holds. If undef $\neq GpId_a \neq GpId_b$ then there is a stage $c < b$ such that either
   1. $c \geq a$ and $Status_c = \textsf{crashed}$ or
   2. $c \geq a$ and $Type(Mes)_c = \textsf{present}$ and
      $Members_c - View(Mes)_c \neq \emptyset$ or
   3. p sees a new_gp message m at c from some processor $q \neq p$ and
      $TStamp(m) \in (GpId(p)_a, GpId(p)_b]$.

Theorem 2: *Agreement on history*
   Suppose that
   1. $GpId(p)_a = GpId(q)_c \neq$ undef and
   2. b is the first stage $> a$ such that undef $\neq GpId(p)_b \neq GpId(p)_a$ and
   3. d is the first stage $> c$ such that undef $\neq GpId(q)_d \neq GpId(q)_c$ and
   then, if $GpId(p)_b$ and $GpId(q)_d$ are not undef, they are equal.

Theorem 1: *Agreement on group membership*
   If $GpId(p)_a = GpId(q)_b \neq$ undef then $Members(p)_a = Members(q)_b$.

Theorem 3: *Reflexivity*
   For every p and stage a of p if $GpId_a \neq$ undef then $p \in Members_a$.

Theorem 5: *Bounded join delays*
   There exists a positive real d_j satisfying the following condition. If
   1. $Status(p)$ is set to sober at stage a and
   2. p is correct in the interval $I = (C(p)_a, C(p)_a + d_j]$,
   then there exists a group $g > C(p)_a$ such that for every q correct in I
      $GpId(q)$ is set to g at some stage b of q with $C(q)_b \in I$.

Theorem 6: *Bounded failure detection delays*
There exists a positive real d_f satisfying the following condition. If
1. p fails at stage a and
2. $I = (C(p)_a, C(p)_a + d_f]$ and $GpId(p)_a = g \neq$ undef

then there exists $g' > g$ such that
1. p never joins group g' and
2. for every q that joins group g and is correct in I
   $GpId(q)_b = g'$ for some stage b of q with $C(q)_b \in I$.

5 Proof of Protocol

Fix any regular run ρ. In some of the proofs, we will be considering sums of stages. We define the sum of two stages a and b as follows. If a is the ith stage of p and b is the jth stage of q, then $a + b$ is the number $i + j$. The initial state of any processor p is stage number 0.

5.1 Propositions Dealing With Message Sends and Receives

Proposition 1. *If p sends a message m to q at stage a, then m is added to $InBox(q)$ at some stage b such that $C(q)_b < Deadline(m) - d_u$.*

Proof: Recall that $TStamp(m) = C(p)_a + d_n$ if m is a new_gp message. Examining rules HandleNewGpMes and HandleBCast (which are the only rules which can send a present message) we see that $TStamp(m) \geq C(p)_a$ if m is a present message. Also recall that $Deadline(m) = TStamp(m)$ if m is a new_gp message and $= TStamp(m) + d_n$ if m is a present message. Therefore $Deadline(m) \geq C(p)_a + d_n$ in either case. By the carry time bound constraint, $C(q)_b \leq C(p)_a + d_c \leq Deadline(m) - d_n + d_c$. But $d_n > d_c + d_u$ (see section 2.3). Therefore $C(q)_b < Deadline(m) - d_u$. □

Proposition 2. *If $Mes(p)_a = (x, y, z)$ and $q \in z$ then there exists a stage b of q at which q sends the message $(x, y, \{q\})$.*

Proof: Straightforward. □

5.2 Properties Satisfied at any Stage of any Processor

Proposition 3. *If $Status(p)_a = $ sober and $\text{DEF}(BCastTime(p)_a)$ then $BCastTime(p)_a \geq UpTime(p)_a$.*

Proof: By induction on ρ.
Basis Case: At the initial stage a_0 of p, $Status(p)_{a_0} = $ crashed; hence the claim is vacuously true.
Induction Step: Assume that the statement is true at stage $a-1$. The only interesting case is if $Status(p)_a = $ sober and $\text{DEF}(BCastTime(p)_a)$. If the value of $BCastTime(p)$ does not change between $a - 1$ and a, we know by the induction hypothesis that the claim holds at a. The only transitions that can change $BCastTime(p)$ or $UpTime(p)$ are Initialize, PrMesSend_MS and PrMesSend_BS.

Initialize sets $BCastTime(p)$ to undef so it cannot violate the claim. PrMesSend_BS just increments $BCastTime(p)$ so it cannot violate the claim. PrMesSend_MS sets $BCastTime(p)$ to $TStamp(Mes(p))+d_h$. From examination of the custodian we can see that $TStamp(Mes(p))$ has to be $\geq UpTime(p)$ – therefore, firing PrMesSend_MS cannot violate the claim. □

Proposition 4. *If p sends a present message with timestamp t in a stage a then the $UpTime(p)_a \leq t$.*

Proof: By induction on ρ.
Basis Case: At the initial stage a_0 of p, $Status(p)_{a_0}$ = crashed; hence the claim is vacuously true.
Induction Step: Assume that the statement is true at stage $a - 1$. There are two ways a present message can be sent at stage a.
Case 1: PrMesSend_BS fires at a. The timestamp of the message sent is equal to $BCastTime(p)_a$ which, by Proposition 3, is $\geq UpTime(p)_a$.
Case 2: PrMesSend_MS fires at a. The timestamp of the message sent is equal to $TStamp(Mes(p))_a$. From examination of the custodian, we can see that this is $\geq UpTime(p)_a$. □

5.3 Relationships Between Different Stages of the Same Processor

Proposition 5. *If $a < b$ then $UpTime(p)_a \leq UpTime(p)_b$.*

Proof: Observe that $UpTime(p)$ is set only when Initialize is fired and, moreover, the new value is $C(p) + d_n$. Since $C(p)$ monotonically increases, we can say the same about $UpTime(p)$. □

Proposition 6. *If $GpId(p)_c = g \neq$ undef then there exists a stage $a < c$ such that:*
1. *$GpId(p)$ was set to g at a by the firing of ChangeGp and*
2. *ChangeGp was not fired at any stage $b \in (a, c)$.*

Proof: Observe that ChangeGp is the only clause that sets $GpId(p)$ to a value $\neq$ undef. If $GpId(p)_c = g \neq$ undef, the value must have been set by the last firing of ChangeGp. □

Proposition 7. *If $q \in Members(p)_c$ then there is a stage $a < c$ and message m such that:*
1. *$q \in View(m)$ and p sees m at a but not at $a + 1$ and*
2. *For all stages $b \in (a, c)$,*
   either $Mes(p)_b = Mes(p)_c$ or $Mes(p)_b =$ undef and
   neither Initialize nor HandlePresentMes is fired at b.

Proof: Since $\text{DEF}(Members(p)_c)$, we can see that this value is set by some firing of ChangeGp before c. Therefore HandlePresentMes fires at some state $s < c$ and Initialize is not fired in $[s, c)$. Let a be the latest stage $< c$ at which HandlePresentMes fires. Examining the rules, we can see that $Mes(p)_{a+1} = \text{undef}$.

If p sees a present message $m' \neq Mes(p)_c$ at some $b \in (a+1, c)$, then from examination of the rules we can see that HandlePresentMes fires at some stage $b' \in [b, s)$. This is impossible since we have assumed that a is the latest stage before c at which HandlePresentMes fires. We can see from examining HandlePresentMes that $Members(p)_{a+1} = View(m)$ and since ChangeGp does not fire in (a, c), $Members(p)_c = Members(p)_{a+1}$. Therefore if $q \in Members(p)_c$, $q \in View(m)$. □

Proposition 8. *Suppose $GpId(p)_a = g$ and c is the first stage $> a$ such that p sees a* present *message m at c and $View(m) \neq Members(p)_c$ and p stays* sober *in the interval $[a, c]$. Then, for all stages $b \in [a, c]$, $GpId(p)_a = g$.*

Proof: Observe that while p stays sober, the only way that $GpId(p)$ can change is if p sees a present message m such that $View(m) \neq Members(p)_c$ at some stage $c > a$. □

Proposition 9. *If $Mes(p)_b = m$ and $\text{DEF}(m)$ then*
1. $C(p)_{b-1} \geq Deadline(m) - d_u$ *and*
2. *there exists an $a < b$ such that $m \in InBox(p)_a$ and $C(p)_{a-1} < Deadline(m) - d_u$.*

Proof: Without loss of generality, let us assume that b is the first stage where $Mes(p) = m$. This implies that $Mes(p)$ is set to m at $b - 1$. From examination of the custodian, we can see that $C(p)_{b-1} \geq Deadline(m) - d_u$ – this proves the first part of the claim. Consider any $q \in View(m)$. By Proposition 2, this implies that q sent a message m' to p with timestamp equal to $TStamp(m)$. By Proposition 1, m' is added to $InBox(p)$ by time $Deadline(m) - d_u$. This proves the second part of the claim. □

Proposition 10. *If p sees a* present *message m at stage a but not at $a+1$ and a* present *message m' at stage $b > a$, then $TStamp(m) \neq TStamp(m')$.*

Proof: By contradiction. Assume that $TStamp(m) = TStamp(m')$. By Proposition 9, there exists a stage a' such that $C(p)_{a'-1} < Deadline(m) - d_u$ and $m \in InBox(p)_{a'}$. There exists a similar stage b' for m'. Proposition 9 also tells us that if, at any stage c, $Mes(p)_c = m$ or $Mes(p)_c = m'$ then $C(p)_{c-1} \geq Deadline(m) - d_u$. This implies that there exists a stage d such that $C(p)_{d-1} < Deadline(m) - d_u$ and $m, m' \in InBox(p)_d$. From examination of the message carrier, we can see that this is impossible. Therefore $TStamp(m) \neq TStamp(m')$. □

Proposition 11. *If $m = Mes(p)_s \neq \text{undef}$ and $m' = Mes(p)_{s'} \neq \text{undef}$ and $Deadline(m) < Deadline(m')$, then $s < s'$.*

Proof: By contradiction. By Proposition 9, there exists an $a < s$ such that $C(p)_{a-1} < Deadline(m) - d_u$ and $m \in InBox(p)_a$ and that there exists an $a' < s'$ such that $C(p)_{a'-1} < Deadline(m') - d_u$ and $m' \in InBox(p)_{a'}$. Assume that $s' < s$. We know from examination of the custodian that $Mes(p)$ cannot be set to m' until time $Deadline(m') - d_u$.

Let $b' < s'$ be a stage such that $Mes(p)$ is set to m' at b' and $Mes(p)$ stays unchanged in $[b'+1, s']$. Therefore, $C(p)_{b'} \geq Deadline(m') - d_u > Deadline(m) - d_u$. Since $C(p)_{a-1} < Deadline(m) - d_u$, $a \leq b' < s'$.

Let b be the stage at which $Mes(p)$ is set to m. We know that setting $Mes(p)$ to m will also cause m to be removed from $InBox(p)$. Since p sees m at stage s and since $s' < s$, we conclude that $b' < b$. Since $a \leq b'$, we can conclude that $m \in InBox(p)_{b'}$ – this implies that there is a message with an earlier deadline than that of m' in $InBox(p)$ when $Mes(p)$ is set to m'.

The only way this can happen is if m is ineligible for selection – in this case, that implies $UpTime(p)_{b'} > TStamp(m)$. But we know that $Mes(p)$ is set to m at stage $b > b'$. By Proposition 5, $UpTime(p)_{b'} \leq UpTime(p)_b$ which implies m is *not* ineligible at b' – a contradiction. □

Proposition 12. *If* $a < b$, $\text{DEF}(GpId(p)_a)$ *and* $\text{DEF}(GpId(p)_b)$, *then* $GpId(p)_a \leq GpId(p)_b$.

Proof: By contradiction. The only interesting case is when $GpId(p)_a \neq GpId(p)_b$. By Proposition 6, if $GpId(p)_a = g$ and $GpId(p)_b = g'$, then there exists $a' < a$ such that $Type(Mes(p))_{a'} = \textsf{present}$, $TStamp(Mes(p))_{a'} = g$, ChangeGp is fired in stage a', ChangeGp is not fired at any stage in (a', a) and there exists a stage $b' < b$ such that $Type(Mes(p))_{b'} = \textsf{present}$, $TStamp(Mes(p))_{b'} = g'$, ChangeGp is fired in stage b' and ChangeGp is not fired at any stage in (b', b). Since we are considering the case where $GpId(p)_a \neq GpId(p)_b$, $a' \neq b'$.

Assume the claim is false – in other words, that $GpId(p)_a > GpId(p)_b$. This implies that $TStamp(Mes(p))_{a'} > TStamp(Mes(p))_{b'}$. By Proposition 11, that implies $a' > b'$. But we know that $a < b$ and that ChangeGp does not fire in (a', a). This implies $a' \leq b'$ – a contradiction. □

Proposition 13. *If* $a < c$, $m_1 = Mes(p)_a \neq \textsf{undef}$, $m_2 = Mes(p)_c \neq \textsf{undef}$, p *stays* sober *in the interval* $[a, c]$ *and there exists a message* $m_3 = (x, y, z)$ *and stage* s *such that* $m_3 \in InBox(p)_s$ *and* $Deadline(m_1) < Deadline(m_3) < Deadline(m_2)$, *then there exists a stage* $b \in (a, c)$ *at which* p *sees a message* $m_4 = (x, y, z')$ *where* $z' \supseteq z$.

Proof: Argument similar to Proposition 11. □

Proposition 14. *If* $m_1 = Mes(p)_b \neq \textsf{undef}$, $UpTime(p)_b = t$, *and there exists a stage* s *and message* $m_2 = (x, y, z)$ *such that* $m_2 \in InBox(p)_s$ *and* $t \leq Deadline(m_2) < Deadline(m_1)$, *then there exists a stage* $a < b$ *at which* p *sees a message* $m_3 = (x, y, z')$ *where* $z' \supseteq z$.

Proof: Argument similar to Proposition 11. □

Proposition 15. *If p gets* sober *at stage a then there exists a $b > a$ such that:*
1. p stays sober *in $[a, b]$ and*
2. p sees a new_gp *message m' at b such that $TStamp(m) = UpTime(p)_b$ and*
3. p does not see any message in $[a, b)$.

Proof: Since p gets sober at stage a, transition Initialize must have been fired at stage $a - 1$, sending a new_gp message (call it m) to p. By Proposition 1, m is added to $InBox(p)$ at some stage $c > a$. Examining the rules, we can see that the two ways p can crash are by the firing of transition Crash_MS or Crash_BS. In the first case, p sees a new_gp message before crashing. In the second case, $BCastTime(p)$ has to be defined. $BCastTime(p)$ becomes defined only when a new_gp message is seen by p. In both cases, p will see *some* message before crashing.

Let the first stage $> a$ in which p sees a message be b and let the message seen be m'. Since p sends new_gp message m in a, $UpTime(p)_{a+1} = TStamp(m)$. Since p does not crash in $[a+1, b]$, $UpTime(p)$ remains $TStamp(m)$ in $[a+1, b]$. Examining the custodian therefore, we can see that $TStamp(m') \geq TStamp(m)$. Since m is a new_gp message, $Deadline(m) = TStamp(m)$. Therefore, $Deadline(m') \geq Deadline(m)$. If $Deadline(m') > Deadline(m)$ then, by Proposition 14, p sees m at some stage $d \in (a, b)$ – which contradicts our earlier assumption that m' is the first message seen by p since a. Therefore $Deadline(m') = Deadline(m)$.

We know $TStamp(m') \geq TStamp(m)$. $TStamp(m')$ cannot be greater than $TStamp(m)$ since that would mean that $Deadline(m') > Deadline(m)$. Therefore, $TStamp(m') = TStamp(m)$. Since the timestamps and deadlines of m' and m are the same and since m is a new_gp message, so is m'. This proves the claim. □

Proposition 16. *If p gets* sober *at stage a and there exists an b such that*
1. p stays sober *in $[a, b]$ and*
2. p sees a present *message at b and*
3. p does not see any present *messages in $[a, b)$*
then $TStamp(Mes(p))_b = UpTime(p)_b$

Proof: Argument similar to Proposition 15. □

Proposition 17. *If p sends a* present *message with timestamp t at stage a and there exists a stage $b > a$ such that $Status(p)_b =$* sober *and $Type(Mes(p))_b =$* present *and $TStamp(Mes(p))_b = t$, then p stays* sober *in (a, b).*

Proof: By contradiction. Let m be $Mes(p)_b$. From examining the custodian, we know that $UpTime(p)_b \leq TStamp(m) = t$. From examination of rules PrMesSend_MS and PrMesSend_BS we can see that $C(p)_a \geq t - d_u$. If there is some stage $c \in (a, b)$ such that $Status(p)_c =$ crashed, we know, from our premise, that there must be some other stage $d \in (c, b]$ such that $Status(p)_d =$ sober.

Without loss of generality, assume that d is the first such stage since c. By our failure and recovery constraints, $UpTime(p)_d > t$. Since $d \leq b$, by Proposition 5, $UpTime(p)_d \leq UpTime(p)_b$ and therefore $UpTime(p)_b > t$. This contradicts our earlier conclusion that $UpTime(p)_b \leq t$. □

Proposition 18. Let $x = CurProc(p)_s$ and $x' = CurProc(p)_{s'}$. If $\text{DEF}(x)$, $\text{DEF}(x')$, $x \neq x'$ and $\text{DLINE}(x)_s < \text{DLINE}(x')_{s'}$ then $s < s'$.

Proof: By contradiction. There are two cases.
Case 1: $x = MS(p)$ and $x' = BS(p)$. Let m denote $Mes(p)_s$. Let t denote $Deadline(m)$ and t' denote $BCastTime(p)_{s'}$. From the premise, we know $t < t'$. Assume that $s' < s$. Let $a' < s'$ be the stage such that $CurProc(p)$ is set to $BS(p)$ at a' and $BCastTime(p)_{a'} = t'$. Examining the scheduler, we know that $C(p)_{a'} \geq t' - d_u > t - d_u$. From Proposition 9, there exists a stage $a < s$ such that $m \in InBox(p)_a$ and $C(p)_a < t - d_u$. Since $C(p)_{a'} > t - d_u$, $a < a'$.

Since p sees m at s, there is some stage $c < s$ such that $Mes(p)$ is set to m at c and $Mes(p)$ stays unchanged in $[c+1, s]$. We consider two cases.

First, assume $c < a'$. In that case, $Mes(p)_{a'} = m$. This means that at a', the broadcast server is scheduled when there exists a message with an earlier deadline – a contradiction.

The other case is $c \geq a'$. If $\text{DEF}(Mes(p)_{a'})$ then by Proposition 11, $Deadline(Mes(p))_{a'} \leq t$. This once again means that at a', the broadcast server is scheduled when there exists a message with an earlier deadline – a contradiction. Therefore, $Mes(p)_{a'} =$ undef.

We know from Proposition 10 that there cannot be a state $d < a'$ such that $Type(Mes(p))_d = Type(m)$ and $TStamp(Mes(p))_d = TStamp(m)$. We also know that there is a stage $a < a'$ such that $m \in InBox(p)_a$. Since the only transition that removes a message from $InBox(p)$ is SelectCurMes, $m \in InBox(p)_{a'}$. Since $C(p) > t - d_u$, $m \in \text{APTPART}(p)_{a'}$. This, however, means that transition Schedule cannot fire at a' – a contradiction.

Case 2: $x = BS(p)$ and $x' = MS(p)$. Let m' denote $Mes(p)_{s'}$. Let $t = BCastTime(p)_s$ and $t' = Deadline(m')$. Let a be the latest stage $< s$ such that $BCastTime(p)_a \neq t$. Therefore, $BCastTime(p)_{a+1} = t$ and it stays unchanged in $(a+1, s]$. $BCastTime(p)$ can be set by either PrMesSend_MS or by PsMesSend_BS. In either case, we can see by examining the scheduler that $C(p)_a \geq t - d_h - d_u$.

Examining rules HandleNewGpMes and HandleBCast, we can see that $C(p)_a \leq t - d_h$. Assume $s' < s$. Let a' be the latest stage $< s'$ such that $CurProc(p)_{a'} \neq MS(p)$. By examining the scheduler, we can see that $Mes(p)_{a'} = m'$. From examination of the custodian, we can see that

$Mes(p)$ can be set to m' only when $C(p) \geq t' - d_u$. Therefore, $C(p)_{a'} \geq t' - d_u$. We know that $C(p)_a \leq t - d_h$. Since $t < t'$ and $d_u < d_h$, $a < a'$. Since $a' < s' < s$, $BCastTime(p)'_a = t$. But this means that the broadcast task had an earlier deadline than the membership server task that was scheduled at a' – a contradiction. □

Proposition 19. *If p sees a* new_gp *message at stage a then $BCastTime(p)_a \leq TStamp(Mes(p))_a + d_h$.*

Proof: By induction on ρ.
Basis Case: At the initial stage a_0 of p, $Status(p)_{a_0}$ = crashed and therefore p cannot see any message at a_0; hence the claim is vacuously true.
Induction Step: Assume that the statement is true for all stages $< a$. Let m be $Mes(p)_a$. Let $Type(m)$ = new_gp and let t denote $TStamp(m)$. Assume that $BCastTime(p)_a > t + d_h$. This value is not set by the previous firing of PrMesSend_MS since, by Proposition 11, the timestamp of the last new_gp message seen by p is $\leq t$. So, the value is set by the last execution of the broadcast server. This implies that there exists a stage $b < a$ such that $(CurProc(p)_b = BS(p)) \wedge (BCastTime(p)_b > t)$. But this is impossible since it violates Proposition 18. □

Proposition 20. *If* DEF$(BCastTime(p)_a)$ *then* $BCastTime(p)_a \leq C(p)_{a-1} + d_h + d_u$.

Proof: By induction on ρ.
Basis Case: At the initial stage a_0 of p, $BCastTime(p)_{a_0}$ = undef; hence the claim is vacuously true.
Induction Step: Assume that the statement is true for all stages $< a$. The difference between $BCastTime(p)_a$ and $C(p)_{a-1}$ will be greatest if $BCastTime(p)$ is changed at $a-1$. Thereafter, the difference shrinks until we get to the next stage at which $BCastTime(p)$ is changed. There are two possible ways at which $BCastTime(p)$ can be changed.
Case 1: PrMesSend_MS fires at $a-1$. From examination of the scheduler we can see that $C(p)_{a-1} \geq TStamp(Mes(p))_{a-1} - d_u$ and from examination of HandleNewGpMes, we can see that $C(p)_{a-1} \leq TStamp(Mes(p))_{a-1}$. Since $BCastTime(p)_a = TStamp(Mes(p))_{a-1} + d_h$, the claim is true.
Case 2: PrMesSend_BS fires at $a-1$. Examining the scheduler rules, we can see that $C(p)_{a-1} \geq BCastTime(p)_{a-1} - d_u$ and examining HandleBCast, we can see that $C(p)_{a-1} \leq BCastTime(p)_{a-1}$. Since $BCastTime(p)_a = BCastTime(p)_{a-1} + d_h$, the claim is true. □

Proposition 21. *If $a < b$,* DEF$(BCastTime(p)_a)$ *and* DEF$(BCastTime(p)_b)$, *then $BCastTime(p)_a \leq BCastTime(p)_b$.*

Proof: Let $t = BCastTime(p)_a$ and $t' = BCastTime(p)_b$. Without loss of generality, we can restrict our attention to the following two cases.

Case 1: A transition fired at a causes the processor to crash and b is the first stage after the crash where $\text{DEF}(BCastTime(p))$. By Proposition 20, $t \leq C(p)_{a-1} + d_h + d_u$. From our failure and recovery constraints, we can see that $UpTime(p)_b > t$. Let $t'' = UpTime(p)_b$. We can also see from examination of the algebra that $BCastTime(p)$ is set by the first new_gp message seen by p after the crash. By Proposition 15, the timestamp of that message is equal to t''. Examining transition HandlePresentMes, we can see that $t' = t'' + d_h > t + d_h$. Therefore the claim cannot be violated in this case.

Case 2: p stays alive between a and b and b is the first stage $> a$ at which the value of $BCastTime(p)$ is different from $BCastTime(p)_a$. The value of $BCastTime(p)$ can be changed by two transitions – PrMesSend_MS and PrMesSend_BS. If the value is changed by transition PrMesSend_BS, the new value will obviously be greater than the previous one. Consider the case when the value is changed by PrMesSend_MS. We know that $BCastTime(p)_{b-1} = t$. By Proposition 19, $TStamp(Mes(p))_{b-1} + d_h \geq t$. Therefore $t' > t$. □

Proposition 22. *If $a < c$, $v_1 = CurProc(p)_a$, $v_2 = CurProc(p)_c$, p stays* sober *in $[a, c]$ and there exists stage s of p and message $m = (x, y, z)$ such that*
1. $m \in InBox(p)_s$ *and*
2. $\text{DLINE}(v_1) < Deadline(m) < \text{DLINE}(v_2)$,

then there exists a stage $b \in (a, c)$ at which p sees a message $m' = (x, y, z')$ where $z' \supseteq z$.

Proof: Argument similar to that for Proposition 18. □

Proposition 23. *If $a < c$, $v_1 = CurProc(p)_a$, $v_2 = CurProc(p)_c$, p stays* sober *in $[a, c]$ and there exists stage s of p such that $\text{DLINE}(v_1) < BCastTime(p)_s < \text{DLINE}(v_2)$, then there exists a stage $b \in (a, c)$ such that $BCastTime(p)_s = BCastTime(p)_b$ and $CurProc(p)_b = BS(p)$.*

Proof: Argument similar to that for Proposition 18. □

Proposition 24. *Let $m = Mes(p)_a$ and $m' = Mes(p)_{a'}$. Then, if $a' < a$, and*
1. $Type(m') = Type(m) =$ present *and*
2. $p \in View(m')$ *and*
3. p *stays* sober *and does not see any* present *messages other than m and m' in $[a', a]$,*

then $0 \leq TStamp(m) - TStamp(m') \leq d_h$.

Proof: By contradiction. Let $t = TStamp(m)$ and $t' = TStamp(m')$. Assume that $t - t' > d_h$. If $m = m'$ then the claim is trivially true, so assume $m \neq m'$. By Propositions 10 and 11, $t - t' > 0$. Since $p \in View(m')$, by Proposition 2, p sends a present message with timestamp t' at some stage $b' < a'$. Examining the membership and broadcast servers, we can see that $BCastTime(p)_{b'+1} = t' + d_h$.

By Proposition 17, p stays sober in (b', a'). From the premise, p stays sober in $[a', a]$. Therefore, p stays sober in $(b', a]$. By Propositions 22 and 23, either this broadcast is sent or is preempted by the arrival of a new_gp message. In either case, p sends a present message with timestamp $t_1 \in (t', t' + d_h]$.

By Propositions 1 and 13, p sees a present message with timestamp t_1 at some stage $a_1 \in (a', a)$. This is a contradiction since, by our premise, p does not see any present messages other than m and m' in (a', a). □

5.4 Relationships Between Stages of Two Processors

Proposition 25. *If $Mes(p)_s = (x, y, z)$ then, for any processor q:*
1. *There exists a stage a such that $(x, y, z) \in InBox(q)_a$ and*
2. *There is no stage b such that $(x, y, z') \in InBox(q)_b$, where $z' - z \neq \emptyset$.*

Proof: By examining the custodian, we can see that there exists an $s' < s$ such that $(x, y, z) \in InBox(p)_{s'}$. By Propositions 2 and 1, for every $r \in z$, a message $(x, y, \{r\})$ is added to $InBox(q)$ by time $Deadline((x, y, z)) - d_u$.

We can see from examination of the message carrier that any incoming new_gp messages are simply added to $InBox$ and not "bunched" together as present messages are. Therefore, for any new_gp message m, $View(m)$ always contains exactly one processor id. Therefore, if $x = $ new_gp, z contains exactly one processor id – which means that (x, y, z) is added to $InBox(q)$ at some stage a, then $(x, y, z) \in InBox(q)_{a+1}$. This proves the claim.

If $x = $ present, we can see from examining the message carrier that all present messages with the same timestamp are "compressed" into one message. By examining the custodian, we can see that this message cannot be removed from $InBox(q)$ until time $y + d_n - d_u$. We know that for every $r \in z$, $(x, y, \{r\})$ is added to $InBox(q)$ by time $y + d_n - d_u$. Therefore, there exists a stage a such that $(x, y, z') \in InBox(q)_a$ where $z' \supseteq z$. By symmetry, any message $(x, y, \{r\})$ that is added to $InBox(p)$ is also added to $InBox(q)$; hence $z \supseteq z'$. This means that $z' = z$. □

Proposition 26. *If $Type(Mes(p))_a = Type(Mes(q))_b = $ present and $TStamp(Mes(p))_a = TStamp(Mes(q))_b$, then $Mes(p)_a = Mes(q)_b$.*

Proof: By contradiction. Let $m_1 = Mes(p)_a$ and $m_2 = Mes(q)_b$. We have to show that $View(m_1) = View(m_2)$. Assume the converse. By examining the custodian, we know that there exists an $a' < a$ such that $m_1 \in InBox(p)_{a'}$ and there exists a $b' < b$ such that $m_2 \in InBox(p)_{b'}$. But, by Proposition 25, such a situation is impossible. □

5.5 The First Group of Theorems

Lemma 1. If $x = CurProc(p)_a$, $y = CurProc(p)_b$, $\text{DEF}(x)$, $\text{DEF}(y)$ and $\text{DLINE}(x)_a < \text{DLINE}(y)_b$, then $a < b$.

Proof: Recall that the deadline for a membership server task is $Deadline(Mes(p))$ and the deadline for a broadcast is $BCastTime(p)$. There are three cases.
Case 1: $x = y = MS(p)$. The claim follows from Proposition 11.
Case 2: $x = y = BS(p)$. The claim follows from Proposition 21.
Case 3: $x \neq y$. The claim follows from Proposition 18. □

Theorem 1. If $GpId(p)_a = GpId(q)_b \neq \text{undef}$ then $Members(p)_a = Members(q)_b$.

Proof: By induction on $a + b$.
Basis Case: $a + b = 0$. In that case $GpId(p)_a = GpId(q)_b = \text{undef}$; hence the claim is vacuously true.
Induction Step: Assume that the statement is true for $a + b < k$. There are three cases.
Case 1: $GpId(p)_{a-1} = GpId(p)_a = g$. All we have to show is that $Members(p)_{a-1} = Members(p)_a$ and the claim follows from the induction hypothesis. Assume that $Members(p)_{a-1} \neq Members(p)_a$. The only way that this can happen is if p sees a present message with timestamp g at stage $a - 1$ and transition ChangeGp is fired. Since $GpId(p)_{a-1} = g$, we know from Proposition 6 that there exists a stage $c < a - 1$ at which p sees a present message and ChangeGp is fired. From examination of rule Handle-PresentMes, we can see that $Mes(p)_{c+1} = \text{undef}$. This implies that p sees two present messages with the same timestamp. This violates Proposition 10 – a contradiction.
Case 2: $GpId(q)_{b-1} = GpId(q)_b = g$. Argument similar to Case 1.
Case 3: $GpId(p)_{a-1} \neq GpId(p)_a$ and $GpId(q)_{b-1} \neq GpId(q)_b$. This implies that transition ChangeGp is fired at both $a-1$ and $b-1$ which implies that $Members(p)_a = View(Mes(p))_{a-1}$ and $Members(q)_b = View(Mes(q))_{b-1}$. Since $GpId(p)_a = GpId(q)_b$, we know that $TStamp(Mes(p))_{a-1} = TStamp(Mes(q))_{b-1}$. This implies, by Proposition 26, that $View(Mes(p))_{a-1} = View(Mes(q))_{b-1}$ which implies $Members(p)_a = Members(q)_b$. □

Theorem 2. Suppose that
1. $GpId(p)_a = GpId(q)_b \neq \text{undef}$ and
2. a' is the first stage $> a$ such that $GpId(p)_{a'} \neq GpId(p)_a$ and
3. b' is the first stage $> b$ such that $GpId(q)_{b'} \neq GpId(q)_b$.

Then, if $GpId(p)_{a'}$ and $GpId(q)_{b'}$ are not undef, they are equal.

Proof: By contradiction. Without loss of generality assume that $a' = a+1$ and $b' = b + 1$. Let $g = GpId(p)_a = GpId(q)_b$ and let $g_a = GpId(p)_{a'}$ and

$g_b = GpId(q)_{b'}$. By Proposition 12, $g < g_a$ and $g < g_b$. Assume the claim is false. Assume without loss of generality that $g_b < g_a$.

By Proposition 6, there exists a stage $c < a$ at which p sees a present message with timestamp g and at which ChangeGp fires and for all $c' \in (c, a]$, $GpId(p)_{c'} = g$. Since $Status(p)_a =$ sober and since $GpId(p)$ does not change in $(c, a]$, we can conclude that p stays sober in $(c, a]$.

Since $GpId(p)$ changes at a and $GpId(q)$ changes at b we know that ChangeGp fires in both stages. Let $m = (x, y, z) = Mes(q)_b$. By Proposition 25, there exists stage d of p such that $m \in InBox(p)_d$ and there is no stage d' and message $m' = (x, y, z')$ such that $m' \in InBox(p)_{d'}$ and $z' - z \neq \emptyset$.

Comparing group Ids, we can see that $Deadline(Mes(p)_c) < Deadline(m) < Deadline(Mes(p)_a)$. By Proposition 13 therefore, there exists a stage $e \in (c, a)$ and message $m' = (x, y, z')$ such that p sees m' at e and $z' \supseteq z$. We already know that $z' - z = \emptyset$; therefore $z' = z$ which implies $m' = m$. Since $e \in (c, a)$, $GpId(p)_e = g$. Since $GpId(p)$ doesn't change at stage $e + 1$, we know that $Members(p)_e = View(m)$. Since $GpId(q)$ does change at b, we know that $Members(q)_b \neq View(m)$. But $GpId(p)_e = GpId(q)_b = g$. Therefore, by Theorem 1, $Members(p)_e = Members(q)_b$ – a contradiction. □

Lemma 2. Let $m = Mes(p)_a$, $t = TStamp(m)$, $m' = Mes(p)_{a'}$ and $t' = TStamp(m')$. Suppose that $p \neq q$, $a' < a$ and
1. q sends a present message with timestamp t at stage b by firing PrMesSend_BS. and
2. $Type(m') = Type(m) =$ present and
3. for all $s < a$, if $Type(Mes(p))_s =$ present then $p \in View(Mes(p))_s$ and
4. p stays sober and does not see any present messages other than m' and m in $[a', a]$.
Then, $t - t' = d_h$.

Proof: By contradiction. Assume that $t' \neq t - d_h$. By our premise, $p \in View(m')$. This implies by Proposition 2 that p sends a present message at some stage $a_1 < a'$ and the message sent has timestamp equal to t'. This implies that either PrMesSend_MS or PrMesSend_BS is fired at a_1. In either case, $BCastTime(p)_{a_1+1} = t' + d_h$. There are two possible cases.
Case 1: $t' < t - d_h$. We know from Proposition 24 that this cannot occur.
Case 2: $t' > t - d_h$. Since PrMesSend_BS is fired, we know a broadcast is sent. We can see from examination of the membership and broadcast servers that $BCastTime(q)$ is set to t at some stage $b' < b$ where a present message m_1 with timestamp equal to $t - d_h$ is sent.

We first show that $q \notin View(m')$ by contradiction. Assume that $q \in View(m')$. This implies, by Proposition 2, that q sends a present message with timestamp t' at some stage b_1. From Lemma 1, $b_1 < b$. Examining the broadcast and membership servers, we can see that $BCastTime(q)_{b_1+1} > t$.

By Proposition 21, the value $BCastTime(a)_b > t$. This, however, means that PrMesSend_MS is fired at b and not PrMesSend_BS – which contradicts our premise.

We have established that $q \notin View(m')$ and that q sends a present message m_1 with timestamp equal to $t - d_h$. There are two possible subcases.

Subcase 2.1: There is a stage a_2 of p at which p sees a present message with timestamp equal to $TStamp(m_1)$.

By Proposition 11, $a_2 < a'$. By our premise, $p \in View(Mes(p))_{a_2}$. Therefore, by Proposition 2, there exists an $a_3 < a_2$ at which a present message with timestamp equal to $TStamp(m_1)$ is sent. By Lemma 1, $a_3 < a_1$. This implies that $BCastTime(p)_{a_3+1} = TStamp(m_1) + d_h$. Since $t-t' < d_h$ and $TStamp(m_1) = t-d_h$, p sends a message with timestamp less than $TStamp(m_1) + d_h$. The only way this can happen is if PrMesSend_MS is fired at stage a_1. This implies that $Type(Mes(p))_{a_1}$ = new_gp and $TStamp(Mes(p))_{a_1} = t'$.

Subcase 2.2: There is no stage of p at which p sees a present message with timestamp equal to $TStamp(m_1)$. By Proposition 1, there exists a stage a_2 of p and present message m_2 such that $m_2 \in InBox(p)_{a_2}$ and $TStamp(m_2) = TStamp(m_1)$. Since p *does* see m' we know from examination of the custodian that $UpTime(p)_{a'} \leq t'$. We also know that $UpTime(p)_{a'} > TStamp(m_1)$ since, otherwise, Proposition 14 will be violated. Therefore, $TStamp(m_1) = t - d_h < UpTime(p)_{a'} \leq t'$. Since p is sober at a', there exists a stage a_3 such that p gets sober at a_3, $UpTime(p)_{a_3} = UpTime(p)_{a'}$ and a new_gp message with timestamp equal to $UpTime(p)_{a'}$ is sent and p stays sober in $(a_3, a']$.

By Proposition 14, this new_gp message is seen by p at some stage $a_4 \in (a_3, a')$. Since p stays sober in $(a_3, a]$, we know that p sends a present message with timestamp equal to $UpTime(p)_{a'}$ at some stage $a_5 \geq a_4$. Since the timestamp of the new_gp message seen at a_4 is in $(t - d_h, t']$ and since $t - t' < d_h$, we can see from examination of HandleNewGpMes that $BCastTime(p)_{a_5+1} > t'$. Therefore, PrMesSend_MS is fired at a_1. This implies that $Type(Mes(p))_{a_1}$ = new_gp and $TStamp(Mes(p))_{a_1} = t'$.

In both subcases, we can see from Proposition 2 that some processor r sends a new_gp message with timestamp t'. Call this message m_2. By Proposition 1, m_2 is added to $InBox(q)$. From our failure and recovery constraints, we can see that q stays sober in (b', b). Therefore, by Proposition 22, q sees m_2 at some stage $b_1 \in (b', b)$. Since q stays sober in (b', b), we know that q sends a present message with timestamp t' in reply to this new_gp message. This, however, implies that $q \in View(m')$ – a contradiction. □

Lemma 3. *If* $Type(Mes(p))_a$ = present *then* $p \in View(Mes(p))_a$.

Proof: We prove this by induction.
Basis Case: At the initial stage a_0 of p, $Mes(p)_{a_0}$ = undef; hence the claim

is vacuously true.

Induction Step: Assume that the statement is true for all stages $< a$. Let $m = Mes(p)_a$. We need concern ourselves only with the case where $Type(m) =$ present and $p \notin View(m)$. Consider a processor $q \in View(m)$. By Proposition 2, there exists a stage b at which a present message with timestamp equal to $TStamp(m)$ is sent. This implies that either PrMesSend_MS or PrMesSend_BS is fired at b.

Case 1: PrMesSend_MS is fired at b. By Proposition 2, there exists a processor r and stage c of r such that a new_gp message m_r with timestamp equal to $TStamp(m)$ is sent. We know from examination of the custodian that $UpTime(p)_a \leq TStamp(m)$. Therefore, by Propositions 1 and 14, p sees message m_r at some stage a'.

Examining the custodian, we can see that $C(p)_{a'-1} \geq TStamp(m) - d_u$. Therefore, if p crashes in the interval (a', a), we know from our failure and recovery constraints that $UpTime(p)_a > TStamp(m)$ — therefore, p stays sober in (a', a). This implies that at some stage $a_1 > a'$ PrMesSend_MS is fired. From this, Proposition 1 and examination of the custodian, we can conclude that $p \in View(m)$ — a contradiction.

Case 2: PrMesSend_BS is fired at b. Since HandleBCast sends a broadcast, $BCastTime(q)$ has been set at some stage $b' < b$ where a present message with timestamp equal to $TStamp(m) - d_h$ was sent. There are two subcases to consider.

Subcase 2.1: p sees a present message at stage $a' < a$ and stays sober in (a', a). Let $m' = Mes(p)_{a'}$. Without loss of generality, assume that p does not see any present messages other than m in (a', a).

By Lemma 2, $TStamp(m) - TStamp(m') = d_h$. By the induction hypothesis, $p \in View(m')$. Therefore, by Proposition 2, p sends a present message with timestamp equal to $TStamp(m')$ at stage $a_1 < a'$. We can see that $BCastTime(p)_{a_1+1} = TStamp(m)$. There are only two ways this scheduled broadcast can be preempted.

The first is if there exists $a_2 > a_1$ at which PrMesSend_MS fires and the timestamp of the present message sent is between $TStamp(m) - d_h$ and $TStamp(m)$. In that case, by Propositions 1 and 13, there exists an $a_3 \in (a', a)$ at which p sees a present message and $TStamp(m) - d_h < TStamp(Mes(p))_{a_3} < TStamp(m))$. This is impossible since m' is the last present message seen by p before m.

The other way in which the broadcast can be preempted is if there exists a stage in (a_1, a) at which p gets crashed. In that case, by our our failure and recovery constraints, $UpTime(p)_a > TStamp(m)$. Let $a_4 \leq a$ be the first stage such that $Mes(p)_{a_4} = m$. Examining the custodian, we can see that $UpTime(p)_{a_4-1} \leq TStamp(m)$ and since p stays sober in $[a_4, a]$, we know that $UpTime(p)_a \leq TStamp(m)$ — a contradiction. Therefore, a present message with timestamp equal to $TStamp(m)$ *is* sent by p. This implies, from Proposition 1 and examination of the custodian, that $p \in View(m)$.

Subcase 2.2: Between stage a and its immediately previous crash, p sees no present messages. By Proposition 16, $UpTime(p)_a = TStamp(m)$. Let a' be a stage such that $Status(p)$ gets sober at a' and p stays sober in $[a', a]$. We know that p sends a new_gp message (call it m_1) with timestamp equal to $TStamp(m)$ in $a' - 1$. By Proposition 15, p sees m_1 at some stage $a_1 \in (a', a)$. Since p stays sober in $[a', a]$, we know that there exists a stage $a_2 \in [a_1, a)$ such that p sees m_1 at a_2 and PrMesSend_MS is fired at a_2, thus sending a present message with timestamp equal to $TStamp(m)$. This, however, implies that $p \in View(m)$. □

Theorem 3. If $\text{DEF}(GpId(p)_a)$, $p \in Members(p)_a$.

Proof: By induction on ρ.
Basis Case: Let s_0 be the initial stage of p. We know that $GpId(p)_{s_0} =$ undef – hence the claim is vacuously true.
Induction Step: Assume that the claim is true for all stages $\leq a$. The only interesting case is if ChangeGp is fired at a. Otherwise, $Members(p)$ remains unchanged, and by the induction hypothesis, the claim is true. Let $V = View(Mes(p))_a$. We can see from examining rule HandlePresentMes that $Members(p)_{a+1} = V$. By Lemma 3, $p \in V$. Therefore $p \in Members(p)_{a+1}$ – which proves the claim. □

5.6 The Second Group of Theorems

Lemma 4. *If p sees a present message m at stage a and b is the first stage $> a$ such that*
1. p sees a present message $m' \neq m$ at b and
2. p stays sober in (a, b),
then $0 \leq TStamp(m') - TStamp(m) \leq d_h$.

Proof: By Lemma 3, $p \in View(m)$. The claim then follows from Proposition 24. □

Lemma 5. *If p sees present messages $m \neq m'$ at stages $a < b$, p stays sober in (a, b) and $TStamp(m') - TStamp(m) < d_h$ then there exists a processor $q \neq p$ and stage s of q such that q sends a new_gp message with timestamp equal to $TStamp(m')$ in s.*

Proof: Without loss of generality, assume that m' is the first present message seen by p after m. By Lemma 3, $p \in View(m)$ and $p \in View(m')$. Since $p \in View(m)$ we know, by Proposition 2, that there is a stage $a' < a$ at which p sends a present message with timestamp equal to $TStamp(m)$. Similarly, there exists a stage $b' < b$ at which p sends a present message with timestamp equal to $TStamp(m')$. We can see from Lemma 1 that $a' < b'$.

We can show that there exists no $c' \in (a', b')$ at which a present message with timestamp in $(TStamp(m), TStamp(m'))$ is sent. We proceed as follows. If there is such a stage then, by Proposition 1, a present message with timestamp in $(TStamp(m), TStamp(m'))$ is added to $InBox(p)$. Since p stays sober in $[a, b]$, we have by Proposition 13 that p sees a present message with timestamp in $(TStamp(m), TStamp(m'))$ at some stage $c \in (a, b)$. This contradicts our assumption that m' is the first present message seen by p since m.

We know, from examination of the rules, that at stage $a'+1$, $BCastTime$ $(p)_{a'+1} = TStamp(m) + d_h$. If this broadcast is sent then $TStamp(m') = TStamp(m) + d_h$, which is not true. Therefore, the broadcast is preempted by a firing of PrMesSend_MS and the message sent has timestamp equal to $TStamp(m')$. This, however, implies that there exists a q and stage s at which q sends a new_gp message. □

Theorem 4. *For all stages $a < b$ of p, the following holds. If* undef $\neq GpId(p)_a \neq GpId(p)_b$ *then there is a stage $c < b$ such that:*
1. $c \geq a$ and $Status(p)_c \neq$ sober or
2. $c \geq a$ and $Type(Mes(p))_c =$ present and $Members(p)_c - View(Mes(p))_c \neq \emptyset$ or
3. p sees a new_gp message m at c from some processor $q \neq p$ and $TStamp(m) \in (GpId(p)_a, GpId(p)_b]$.

Proof: We have to show that whenever $GpId(p)$ changes, one of the above three scenarios will hold. Without loss of generality assume b is the first stage $> a$ such that $GpId(p)_b \neq GpId(p)_a$. This implies that the value of $GpId(p)$ changes at stage $b - 1$. There are only two transitions that can change the value of $GpId(p)$.

Case 1: Initialize. This implies that $Status(p)_{b-1} =$ recovered – which corresponds to the first scenario.

Case 2: ChangeGp. For the rest of the proof, we use abbreviations t_{b-1} for $TStamp(Mes(p))_{b-1}$, V_{b-1} for $View(Mes(p))_{b-1}$ and M_{b-1} for $Members$ $(p)_{b-1}$. If ChangeGp fires, $M_{b-1} \neq V_{b-1}$. If $M_{b-1} - V_{b-1} \neq \emptyset$, we have our second scenario. Therefore assume that $V_{b-1} - M_{b-1} \neq \emptyset$. We prove by contradiction that, in this case, the third scenario holds.

By Proposition 6, there is a stage $a' < a$ such that ChangeGp fires at a', $TStamp(Mes(p))_{a'} = GpId(p)_a$ and neither ChangeGp nor Initialize fire in (a', a). Since ChangeGp fires in a' and $TStamp(Mes(p))_{a'} = GpId(p)_a$, we know that $GpId(p)_{a'+1} = GpId(p)_a$. Since neither Initialize nor ChangeGp fire in (a', a), we know that $GpId(p)$ does not change in (a', a). Therefore b is the first state $> a' + 1$ in which the value of $GpId(p)$ is different from $GpId(p)_a$. Therefore, p stays sober in $[a', b]$.

By Proposition 4, $UpTime(p)_{a'} \leq GpId(p)_a$. Since p stays sober in $[a', b]$, $Uptime(p)_b \leq GpId(p)_a$. If p sent a new_gp message with timestamp in $(GpId_a, GpId(p)_b]$, we know by Lemma 1 that it would have been sent before b, which implies by Proposition 5 that $UpTime(p)_b > GpId(p)_a$ – which contradicts our earlier conclusion that $UpTime(p)_b \leq$

$GpId(p)_a$. Therefore, p does not send a new_gp message with timestamp in $(GpId(p)_a, GpId(p)_b]$.

If p sees a new_gp message with timestamp in $(GpId(p)_a, GpId(p)_b]$ from some processor other than p, we have our third scenario. Therefore, assume that there is no stage $c < b$ and processor r that satisfies the third scenario.

Since ChangeGp fires at $b-1$, we know that p sees a present message with timestamp equal to $GpId(p)_b$ at $b-1$. Since $\text{DEF}(GpId(p)_a)$ and since $GpId(p)_a = GpId(p)_{b-1}$, we know by Proposition 6 that there exists a stage $d < a < b-1$ at which p sees a present message and that p stays sober in (d, a). Let s be latest stage $< b-1$ such that p sees a present message at s and $Mes(p)_s \neq Mes(p)_{b-1}$.

Since we have assumed that p does not see any new_gp messages with timestamps in $(GpId(p)_a, GpId(p)_b]$, we have by Lemma 5 that $TStamp$ $(Mes(p))_s = t_{b-1} - d_h$. Consider any $q \in V_{b-1} - M_{b-1}$. By Theorem 3, $p \in M_{b-1}$, therefore, $q \neq p$. All we have to show is that there exists a stage $c < b$ such that p sees a new_gp message m from q at c and $TStamp(m) \in (GpId(p)_a, GpId(p)_b]$ and we have a contradiction.

Since $q \notin M_{b-1}$, we have by Proposition 7 that $q \notin View(Mes(p))_s$. Since $q \in V_{b-1}$ we know by Proposition 2 that there exists a stage e of q at which q sends a present message with timestamp equal to t_{b-1}. Let e' be a stage of q such that q gets sober at e' and stays sober in $[e', e]$.

It easy to see that q cannot send a present message in (e', e) that has timestamp less than t_{b-1}. We proceed as follows. If there were such a message (call it m_1) then we can see from examination of the algebra that $t_{b-1} - d_h \leq TStamp(m_1) < t_{b-1}$. Since q sends m_1, by Proposition 1, it is added to $InBox(p)$. $TStamp(m_1) \neq t_{b-1} - d_h$ since $q \notin View(Mes(p))_s$. $TStamp(m_1) \not> t_{b-1} - d_h$ implies, by Proposition 13, that p will see a present message in $(s, b-1)$ with timestamp equal to $TStamp(m_1)$. But we know that p does *not* see any present messages in $(s, b-1)$ other than $Mes(p)_s$ and $Mes(p)_{b-1}$.

Therefore the first present message sent by q since e' has timestamp equal to t_{b-1}. This, however, implies that $UpTime(q)_e = t_{b-1}$ which in turn implies that q sends a new_gp message with timestamp t_{b-1} at stage $e' - 1$. By Propositions 1 and 14, it follows that p sees this message – a contradiction. □

Lemma 6. *If p sees a* new_gp *message from q with timestamp t at stage a and a* present *message with timestamp t at stage $b > a$ and* $\text{DEF}(Members$ $(p)_b)$, *then $q \notin Members(p)_b$.*

Proof: There are two cases.

Case 1: p has seen no present messages between the time $Status(p)$ last became sober and stage b. From examination of the algebra we can see that this implies that $Members(p)_b = \text{undef}$ – which proves the claim.

Case 2: p has received at least one present message between the time $Status$

(p) last became sober and stage b. Assume the claim to be false. In other words, assume that $q \in Members(p)_b$. Let $m = Mes(p)_b$. Let b' be the latest stage before b at which p sees a present message $m' \neq m$.

By Lemma 4, $TStamp(m) - TStamp(m') \leq d_h$. By Proposition 7, $q \in View(m')$. This implies, by Proposition 2, that q sends a present message at some stage c with timestamp equal to $TStamp(m')$. By Proposition 2, q sent a new_gp message at some stage d with timestamp equal to t. By Proposition 4, $UpTime(q)_c \leq TStamp(m') < t$. Since sending a present message does not change the value of $UpTime(p)$ we have $UpTime(q)_{c+1} < t$. Since q sends a new_gp message with timestamp t, we can see that $UpTime(q)_{d+1} = t$. Therefore, by Proposition 5, $c+1 < d+1$; hence $c < d$.

This implies that q crashes somewhere in the interval (c, d). Examining the scheduler, we can see that $C(q)_c \geq TStamp(m') - d_u$ which implies, by our failure and recovery constraints, that $C(q)_d > TStamp(m') + d_h > t$, which implies that $UpTime(q)_{d+1} > TStamp(m)$ – a contradiction. □

Theorem 5. *There exists a positive real d_j satisfying the following conditions. If*
1. *$Status(p)$ is set to sober at stage a and*
2. *p is correct in the interval $I = (C(p)_a, C(p)_a + d_j]$,*
then there exists a group id $g > C(p)_a$ such that for every q correct in I
$GpId(q)$ is set to g at some stage b of q with $C(q)_b \in I$.

Proof: Let $t = C(p)_a$. Let d_j be any constant $> 2d_n$. If $Status(p)$ is set to sober at stage a, then it sends a new_gp message m with timestamp $t + d_n$.

Since p is correct in the interval $[t + d_n - d_u, t + d_j]$, we can conclude that there exists a stage $b > a$ such that p sees m at b and PrMesSend_MS is fired at b. This causes a present message with timestamp $t + d_n$ to be sent.

Consider any q that is correct in the interval $[t + d_n - d_u, t + d_j]$. Since q is correct in the interval $[t + d_n - d_u, t + d_j]$, q sees m and q sees a present message with timestamp $t + d_n$. Let c be a stage of q at which q sees a present message with timestamp $t + d_n$. Since p sends a present message with timestamp $t + d_n$, $p \in View(Mes(p))_c$.

By Lemma 6, either $Members(q)_c =$ undef or $p \notin Members(q)_c$. In either case, $Members(q)_c \neq View(Mes(q))_c$. This implies that at some stage $d > c$, $GpId(q)$ is set to $t + d_n$. Since q stays correct in $[t + d_n - d_u, t + d_j]$, we can conclude that $C(q)_d \leq t + d_j$. □

Lemma 7. *If p sees present message m at stage a and q sees m at stage a' then $GpId(p)_a = GpId(q)_{a'}$.*

Proof: By induction on $a + a'$.
Basis Case: $a + a' = 0$. This means that both p and q are at their initial

stages. Since $Mes(p)_0 = Mes(q)_0 =$ undef, the claim is vacuously true.
Induction Step: Assume that the statement is true for $a+a' < k$. Consider $a+a' = k$. Let $g = GpId(p)_a$ and $g' = GpId(q)_{a'}$. Assume $g \neq g'$. Without loss of generality, let $g' > g$. The only interesting case is if p sees a present message m at a and q sees the same message m at a'.

By Propositions 6 and 11, $g < TStamp(m)$ and $g' < TStamp(m)$. By Proposition 6, there exists stage $b' < a'$ at which q sees a present message with timestamp equal to g', $GpId(q)_{b'+1} = g'$ and there exists stage $b < a$ at which p sees a present message with timestamp equal to g and that p stays alive in the interval (b, a).

Therefore, by Propositions 25 and 13 and the fact that $g < g' < TStamp(m)$, there exists a stage $c \in (b, a)$ at which p sees a present message with timestamp equal to g'. By Proposition 26, $View(Mes(p))_c = View(Mes(q))_{b'}$. Therefore, $Mes(p)_c = Mes(q)_{b'}$.

By the induction hypothesis, therefore, $GpId(p)_c = GpId(q)_{b'}$. This implies by Theorem 1 that $Members(p)_c = Members(q)_{b'}$ which implies that $GpId(p)_{c+1} = GpId(q)_{b'+1} = g'$. But $c+1 \leq a$ and $GpId(p)_{c+1} > GpId(p)_a$. This contradicts Proposition 12. Therefore $GpId(p)_a = GpId(q)_{a'}$. □

Lemma 8. Let I be the interval $(t, t+\delta)$, where $\delta > d_h + d_n + d_u$. Then, if q is correct in I, q sends a present message with timestamp $t' \in (t, t+d_h+d_u]$.

Proof: Consider any q correct in I. Let s be the latest stage of q such that $C(q)_s \leq t$. Consider the value of $BCastTime(p)_s$. Since q is correct in I, we know that $UpTime(q)_s \leq t$. We also know that $Status(q)_s =$ sober.

Let $s' < s$ be a stage such that q becomes sober at s' and stays sober in $(s', s]$. This implies that q sends new_gp message m_1 with timestamp equal to $UpTime(q)_s$ at s' and stays sober at all stages in $(s', s]$.

By Proposition 1, m_1 is added to $InBox(q)$ at some stage in (s', s) and from the definition of correctness, there exists a stage $s_1 \in (s', s]$ such that q sees m_1 at s_1 and PrMesSend_MS is fired at s_1. If this were not the case, q would not be correct at s.

The firing of PrMesSend_MS sets $BCastTime(q)$ to some value that is not undef. Since q does not crash in $[s_1, s]$, we know that $\text{DEF}(BCastTime(p)_s)$. Since q is correct at s, we know that $BCastTime(q)_s \geq C(q)_s$. By Proposition 20, $BCastTime(q)_s \leq C(q)_s + d_h + d_u$. By our initial assumption, $C(q)_s \leq t$.

We can also deduce that $C(q)_s \geq t - d_h - d_u$. We proceed as follows. Assume that $C(p)_s < t - d_h - d_u$. This means that $BCastTime(q)_s < t$. Consider the value of $BCastTime(q)$ at $s+1$. If it does not change at s, then $BCastTime(q)_{s+1} < t$. Since $C(q)_{s+1} > t$, this implies that q is incorrect at $s+1$ – a contradiction. Now consider the case where $BCastTime(q)$ does change at s. There are two clauses that can change $BCastTime(q)$ – PrMesSend_MS and PrMesSend_BS. If PrMesSend_BS fires at s, then we can see by examining the scheduler that $BCastTime(q)_s < t - d_h$. This means that $BCastTime(q)_{s+1} < t$ — which makes q incorrect at $s + 1$ — a contradiction. If PrMesSend_MS fires at s then $BCastTime(q)_{s+1} = TStamp(Mes(q))_s + d_h$. We can see by examining the scheduler that $TStamp(Mes(q))_s < t - d_h$. Therefore $BCastTime(q)_{s+1} < t$ — which makes q incorrect at $s + 1$ — a contradiction. By a similar argument, we can show that $BCastTime(p)_s > t - d_h$.

What is the value of $BCastTime(p)$ at $s+1$? The highest possible value of $C(q)_s$ is t. Hence, by Proposition 20, $BCastTime(q)_s \leq t + d_h + d_u$. Since q is correct at $s+1$, $BCastTime(q)_{s+1} > t$. Using an argument similar to the one in the previous paragraph, we can show that $BCastTime(q)_{s+1} \leq t + d_h + d_u$. Therefore $BCastTime(q)_{s+1} \in (t, t + d_h + d_u]$.

Since q stays correct in this interval, this broadcast will either be sent or will be preempted by the arrival of a new_gp message whose timestamp is less than $BCastTime(p)_{s+1}$. Since q stays correct in $(t, t + d_h + d_u]$, the timestamp of this new_gp message is $> t$. Therefore, q sends a present message with timestamp $t' \in (t, t + d_h + d_u]$. □

Theorem 6. *There exists a positive real d_f satisfying the following conditions. If*
1. p fails at stage a and
2. $I = (C(p)_a, C(p)_a + d_f]$ and $GpId(p)_a = g \neq$ undef,
then there exists $g' > g$ such that
1. p never joins group g' and
2. for every q that joins group g and is correct in I
   $GpId(q)$ is set to g' at some stage b of q with $C(q)_b \in I$.

Proof: Let $t = C(p)_a$. Let d_f be any real constant $> d_h + d_u + d_n$. Since p fails at time t, we have by Lemma 1 and our failure and recovery constraints that p cannot send a present message with timestamp in $(t, t + d_h + d_u]$.

Consider any q correct in I. By Lemma 8, q sends a present message with timestamp $t' \in (t, t + d_h + d_u]$. By Proposition 1 and the definition of correctness, every processor that is correct in I sees a present message with timestamp t'. By Proposition 26, all processors correct in I will see the same present message m with timestamp t'.

Consider any $r \neq q$ that stays correct in I. Since both q and r stay correct in I, both of them see m. We know that since p does not send a present message with timestamp t', $p \notin View(m)$. Since q is correct in I, there will be a stage b_q in which q sees m, $C(q)_{b_q} \in I$ and HandlePresentMes fires. There is a similar stage b_r of r. By Lemma 7, we know that $GpId(q)_{b_q} = GpId(r)_{b_r}$. Therefore, by Theorem 1, $Members(q)_{b_q} = Members(r)_{b_r}$. We also know that $p \notin View(m)$. Therefore, $GpId(q)_{b_q+1} = GpId(r)_{b_r+1}$ and p is not contained in either $Members$ set. □

Bibliography

1. E. Börger, Y. Gurevich and D. Rosenzweig. The Bakery Algorithm: Yet Another Specification and Verification. *This Volume*.
2. F. Cristian. Reaching Agreement on Processor-Group Membership in Synchronous Distributed Systems. *Distributed Computing*, 6:175–187, April 1991.
3. Y. Gurevich. Evolving Algebras: An Attempt to Discover Semantics. In G. Rozenberg and A. Salomaa, editors, *Current Trends in Theoretical Computer Science*, pages 266–292. World-Scientific, 1993.
4. Y. Gurevich. Evolving Algebras 1993: Lipari Guide. *This Volume*.
5. J. Huggins. Kermit: Specification and Verification. *This Volume*.
6. F. Jahanian, R. Rajkumar and S. Fakhouri. Processor Group Membership Protocols: Specification, Design and Implementation. In *Symposium on Reliable Distributed Systems*, 1993.
7. A. M. Ricciardi and K. P. Birman. Using Process Groups to Implement Failure Detection in Asynchronous Environments. In *11th ACM Symposium on Principles of Distributed Computing*, pages 341–353, 1991.

Part V: Architecture Design

Specification and Verification of VHDL-based System-level Hardware Designs

Werner Damm, Bernhard Josko and Rainer Schlör

Abstract

This chapter provides the semantic foundation of a formal verification environment for VHDL. The envisaged tool supports *specification* of system-level hardware designs using an extension of the classical concepts of timing diagrams allowing us to express first-order properties and causality relations between events. A formal semantics of such *symbolic timing diagrams* is given in terms of a linear time first-order temporal logic. System-level designs expressed in VHDL — an IEEE standard hardware description language — can be verified against temporal logic specifications using a *compositional proof system* presented in this chapter. This proof-system is proved correct with respect to a *formal semantics* for VHDL in the style of *structural operational semantics* based on *transition systems*. For the special case of VHDL designs using finite data types only, the semantics provides a link to *model-checking* tools allowing *automatic verification* of VHDL designs against a temporal logic specification. Such a verification environment is currently under development within the ESPRIT project FORMAT.

Keywords: VHDL, hardware verification, temporal logic, specification languages, formal semantics, visual formalisms

1 Introduction

Hardware verification can be carried out at any of the typical levels of hardware-design: transistor-level, switch-level, gate-level, register-transfer-level, or system-level. The design level addressed primarily in this chapter is the system-level. Whereas primitives at the gate-level are just gates and hence consist of only a handful of transistors, components at system-level typically consist of a couple of thousand to 100 000 transistors. The *raison d'être* of hardware description languages like VHDL is to allow behavioural descriptions of such design objects without being forced to elaborate the designs in terms of primitives at RT- or even gate-level. When describing system-level components, the aim is to provide an *abstract* view of a piece of hardware, showing only just enough detail to verify the interplay of the components and to understand the basic functionality of the component in its relation to the "surrounding world". In its physical realization, system-level designs talk about gluing together complex macro-cells in on-chip design or find their counterpart in PCB design, or even designs distributed over many PCBs or even many cabinets (think, e.g., of a multiprocessor-system). Hence typical components might be a RISC cpu, a memory management unit, a floating-point chip, a cache with its controller, a switch in an interconnection network, a serial I/O-interface, a memory system, etc.

This chapter provides the semantical foundation of a verification environment for VHDL based system-level designs. In doing so, it develops a *formal semantics for VHDL*, provides a *correctness logic* to reason about VHDL designs, and shows how to hide the logic from the designer using *symbolic timing diagrams* as graphical specification front-end. To understand the design decisions taken in setting up this verification environment, we survey the current state of the art of verification approaches supporting VHDL. The focus on VHDL can be motivated easily: it is *the* (IEEE-) standard hardware description language supported by all major CAD tool suppliers. Readers not familiar with VHDL are urged to consult the introductory Section 2 before picking up on the survey of verification tools supporting VHDL.

Whenever design steps are inherently interactive, but are carried out in an intricate design space with many potential pitfalls, the question of *design verification* pops up. Hardware designers have always been conscious about *validating* their design. There is a rich body of methods aiming at the detection of *faults arising in the production process* of integrated circuits, including algorithms to automatically generate *test-patterns* from gate-level designs. A second equally important issue is that of the *logical correctness* of the design. Traditional design-flow tries to detect *logical design faults* through extensive simulations, were in addition to test-vectors representing the *desired behaviour* also higher-level testing concepts are employed, such as the simulation of instruction sequences to check for the correctness of a processor design. Apart from the obvious observation, that simulation can only establish the presence of logical errors, the growing complexity of ICs has motivated growing industrial interest in *formal verification approaches* to establish freedom from logical errors. Out of these, methods allowing us to *symbolically represent the state-space* of a design have found highest acceptance. Such symbolic methods typically code the current valuation of the system's state in a formula in some *formal logic* and allow a *complete* analysis of the state-space on the basis of such a symbolic representation. Two examples of this approach have found their way into commercially available tools and are used in some companies within the standard design flow.

The first examples aim to support optimization techniques when passing from gate-level to transistor-level designs. While today's design tools free the user from carrying out transistor-level designs at all, manual designs can be required in high-volume ICs to optimize critical paths. Assuming that the gate-level design has been validated, the transistor-level design is *verified* against the gate-level description. For *combinatorial* designs, *propositional logic* suffices to characterize the input–output behaviour of the gate-level design; similarly, the transistor-level behaviour can be abstracted to a gate-level behaviour characterized by formula in propositional logic. Clearly this fact alone cannot explain why suddenly formal verification should be feasible while testing would be prohibitive. However, observe that the testing approach in its naive way has to consult for each output pin all entries of the truth table of the boolean function associated with this pin, hence has to exercise on exponential number of tests. By not evaluating the circuit for each input individually but rather for a *class* of inputs represented by a *formula*, the symbolic approach has an edge over the explicit enumeration approach. It is successful if the classes expressed by a formula can remain *large*, i.e. if verification does not too often force splitting of a formula into subcases. The implementation of this idea uses *reduced ordered binary decision diagrams* as introduced by [14] as a symbolic representation of boolean functions. This approach assumes the existence of a linear ordering of the involved boolean variables. Each node in such a DAG corresponds to a boolean variable, which are consulted in the given linear order. Each node has outdegree two; picking, e.g., the "left" successor node will give the behaviour of the function under the assumption that the variable represented by the node takes value **true**. "Common parts" of the function under different variable valuations are *shared* by pointing to the same subgraph; the "reduced order" property requires that the DAG does not contain isomorphic subdags. Together with the requirement of the fixed order of variables, they constitute a canonical form for boolean functions. The underlying NP-completeness of the equivalence check of these behaviours is thus hidden in the potentially exponential size of the BDDs. The practical relevance of this approach rests in the fact that often variable orderings can be found which keep the BDDs small. Thus, good orderings require little splitting, or — expressed in BDD terminology — few nodes until reaching a leave. While this heuristic approach has been successfully used to verify large industrial designs, it is well known that many functions resist compact representations [15]. A key to further enhance the practicality of this method is the development of heuristics for automatic construction of good variable orderings. Much research has also been directed to find non-canonical variants of BDDs with good average complexity [6]. Various compilers taking a gate-level combinatorial design represented by a net list or as a program in a hardware description language and producing an RoBDD are available today [21, 22, 30].

A key observation of [17, 60] based on [14] helped to lift these symbolic methods to the level of *sequential circuits*. Still exploiting the *finiteness* of the design, they represent the underlying (deterministic) Mealy automata *symbolically* by coding the transition and output functions as BDDs and lift algorithms to analyse or compare Mealy automata to this symbolic representation. The compilers cited above typically also support finite-state machines; e.g. [30] defines a subset of VHDL equivalent to Mealy automata and shows how to compile this into a symbolic representation of transition systems. The V-formal tool supports equivalent checks of deterministic Mealy automata expressed in VHDL. Both tools require the compared automata to have essentially the same state encoding.

Alternatively, rather than using state machines both as specification and implementation, a large body of research has been devoted to using variants of *temporal logic* [32, 55, 59] to specify the behaviour of hardware components. Early work by Clarke et al. [19, 20] developed a linear time algorithm for model-checking of propositional *branching time* temporal logic and used this to verify simply sequential circuits with models explicitly enumerating the state space. Later research by this group has lifted these model-checking algorithms to *symbolic representations* and has demonstrated the application potential of this approach in verifying (system-level) designs with up to 10^{100} states [16]. As in the simpler combinatorial case, the success of such methods strongly hinges on finding good variable ordering and the required amount of splitting of symbolic states; failing to find a good ordering renders even the construction of the symbolic representation impossible. But even once a model is constructed, the verification of a given formula may well cause exponential splitting. Recent research in this area is thus directed to directly reducing the size of the state-space, e.g. by *abstracting* from aspects irrelevant to establish a given property (as in [18, 29, 77]), or exploiting symmetries in the model [49]. These approaches try to cope with the complexity of models stemming from the underlying state-space. A second source of potential exponential growth results from the representation of systems running in *parallel*. If represented in *one global* model, a naive approach will make the model grow exponentially w.r.t. to the number of parallel components, since it is has to represent all possible interactions of its components. A rich body of research addresses this issue. The lines of attack include approaches to representing only *equivalence classes* of interleavings rather than all interleavings [74, 75, 76]. Other approaches, including the one presented in this chapter, use *compositional proof systems* to reason about the interaction of parallel subsystems and employ model-checking only for individual components; knowledge about the behaviour of other components can be explicitly stated as assumptions again expressed in temporal logic or directly as a finite state machine. Examples of this line of research are [1, 27, 40, 50, 51, 56, 65].

All approaches discussed so far exploit the *finiteness* of hardware designs allowing a complete (symbolic) evaluation and thus work with *propositional* logics. While the complexity of both model-checking and decidability procedures vary, all approaches benefit from the at least potential support of *fully automatic* verification tools. The price to be paid is the restrictive expressiveness of this logic and the always present risk of exponential blow-up. In contrast, choosing *first-order* or even *higher-order* logics provides increased expressiveness allowing us to for example cope with inductively defined designs or providing room for more detailed timing models as for example required for transistor level designs. The price to be paid is given by the inherent undecidability of these logics. But also in this realm of *theorem-proving*, a rich body of heuristics has been developed over the past years, allowing for example successful application to hardware verification. We discuss three representative examples of this approach to hardware verification.

The HOL system [37, 38] has been extensively used in the context of hardware-verification. The HOL system is a *tactical theorem prover* supporting a higher order logic. Verification of a piece of hardware requires the generation of an HOL description of the hardware together with a specification of the hardware expressed in HOL. Using the axioms and rules of the system, it is shown that the formula representing the hardware implies the formula serving as specification.

To use the system in a VHDL context, [69, 70, 71] sets out to define the semantics of VHDL in HOL. A piece of hardware described in VHDL thus possesses via the VHDL semantics an HOL representation. Either an HOL formula explicitly entered or an HOL formula generated from a "more abstract" VHDL description can then be used as specification. A subset of VHDL called Femto-VHDL has been embedded in the HOL system. Femto-VHDL retains enough features to claim that the approach is extendible to full VHDL. It covers arbitrary delay expressions in signal assignments and supports processes with sensitivity lists. Not handled are the wait statement (except for the version corresponding to sensitivity lists) and resolution functions (to solve conflicting accesses to shared signals). The limitation to objects of boolean type serves only to simplify the representation and is not inherent to the approach. For practical applications, forcing a hardware engineer to reason about his design explicitly using its representation in higher order logic seems prohibitive. However, from a theoretical point of view, such an embedding of VHDL into HOL is an attractive solution to VHDL verification with a rigid semantical basis.

It is worthwhile to point out that a variant of the HOL system, the *LAMBDA system* [34], has attacked the problem of user acceptance by hiding the logical representation of hardware objects and deductions in this logic using a graphical interface, similarly to a schematic entry tool. For gate-level applications, a component library is delivered together with the system. While such libraries in traditional simulation tools provide simulation models of the components, the LAMBDA library contains an HOL axiomatization of the behaviour of the components. This allows us to express rule instantiations (of rules characterizing a component) by entering a schematic representation of the component, which then automatically induces a simplification of the current goal. In some cases, this can reduce direct user-interaction with the logic to providing a top level specification (in HOL) of the design. The LAMBDA system has also been used in work carried out by Siemens [73] to embed VHDL into a tactical theorem prover. Essentially all of VHDL is given a semantics by translation into the functional language ML. There exists a compiler generating input to the LAMBDA system from VHDL. Again, the applicability suffers from the need to reason on the level of the semantic representation of VHDL rather in terms of VHDL's language constructs. The use of the LAMBDA system for hardware verification is also the topic of a companion chapter in this volume.

The *Boyer-Moore prover* [12, 13] supports a completely different style of theorem proving. Its logic allows us to express equality of inductively defined total functions or to prove properties of such functions based on automatically generated induction schemes. While the HOL system supports interactive reasoning, the Boyer-Moore prover is an automatic theorem prover trying to establish goals using powerful internal heuristics. If the prover fails to establish a goal, the user has to enter lemmata, hoping that it will enable the prover to find the proof. In practice this process requires expertise of the user about the heuristics employed by the system: a cleverly formulated lemma may significantly cut down the search space of the prover. This has stimulated ongoing work providing an *interactive* version of the system.

The system has been successfully employed in applications ranging from security models to hardware verification, including the verification of a microprocessor [46, 47]. The approach to verification is similar to the scenario described for HOL, with the Boyer-Moore logic taking over the role of HOL. To apply the Boyer-Moore prover to VHDL verification, [11] axiomatise the semantics of VHDL in the Boyer-Moore logic. The verification scenario then resembles that in the HOL environment, i.e. either a formula in the supported logic can serve as specification, or a formula derived from a more abstract view plays the role of specification. However, there is a key difference induced by the different underlying theorem-proving paradigms. In "good" cases, the Boyer-Moore prover could find the proof automatically; in such a situation, the designer will never have to see the logical representation of his design. Unfortunately, this will not be the typical situation; experience shows that non-trivial applications do require user assistance. The approach then suffers from the same drawbacks as described in the HOL scenario: the designer is forced to suggest "good" lemmata for proving automatically generated formula representing his design. Again, in practical applications, this will not be acceptable. At CLI research is under way to embed VHDL into the interactive version of the Boyer-Moore system. A comparative case-study on the use of the Boyer-Moore and the HOL system in the verification of combinatorial circuits is reported in [4].

The *state delta verification system* [33, 57] uses as internal logic an extension of first-order *pre/poststyle specifications* called state-deltas allowing nesting of such specifications. The system defines an operational transition-system style semantics of state-deltas, taking a valuation of what is called *places* satisfying the precondition of a state-delta in an evaluation satisfying its postcondition, thus allowing symbolic simulation of state-delta specifications. As verification support, rewriting techniques for dedicated theories are supplied. The operational view is similar in style to actions in the architecture description language AADL [26] and corresponds also to the deterministic variant of evolving algebras [36]. The system provides compilers from various languages to state-delta specifications, including a representative kernel of VHDL [33], thus allowing verification of VHDL designs against state-delta specifications. The considered subset is similar to Femto-VHDL discussed above, also disallowing resolved signals. The state delta verification system has been employed in numerous correctness proofs [23]; its VHDL interface is comparatively new, and hence only minor verification examples involving it have been reported. In principle, the verification task proceeds interactively, being supported by automatic provers for dedicated theories. Again the user has to reason about the semantic representation of the VHDL design.

The above survey of current research on VHDL verification shows a clear separation of automatic finite state methods and essentially interactive prover environments providing a powerful meta-logic. The results reported in this chapter form the semantics basis of verification-environment for VHDL developed within the FORMAT project [9, 43, 53, 63, 72]. FORMAT strives for a *marriage* of these two lines of attack to verify VHDL designs, delegating verification tasks to fully automatic finite-state tools whenever possible, but exploiting the power of higher order logic in order to support for example inductive reasoning. This is achieved by integrating into one verification environment symbolic model-checking tools, symbolic simulation provers, and the LAMBDA system. The FORMAT project supports *declarative* as well as *operational* specification styles, and provides for both styles both a *textual* and a *graphical* specification entry tool. Fig. 1 shows the supported languages, which are all integrated into an extension of VHDL called VHDL/S [43]. This chapter concentrates on *declarative specifications*, providing the semantic foundation to verify properties of the type

$$\underline{des} \models \Phi$$

for a VHDL design $\underline{des}$ and a declarative specification Φ written in either the graphical or textual declarative specification style. The semantics is given for a *kernel language* which is rich enough to express full VHDL 1076. Indeed, the transformation from full VHDL to the kernel language is given in the language reference manual [48] and there called elaboration.

	operational	declarative
textural	VHDL	Temporal Logic
visual	VHDL/S Statecharts	Symbolic Timing Diagrams

FIG. 1. Specification styles.

While the implementation in FORMAT covers function and procedure calls and the package mechanisms, we restrict our attention in this chapter to the *peculiar features* of VHDL, i.e. its timing-model, its ability to express structure and behaviour, its powerful configuration concepts, the concept of processes, and typical statements such as the *signal assignment statement* and the *wait statement*. In order to provide a link to model-checking tools, we give a *transition-system* based semantics, in a style close to *structural operational semantics* [64]. From this we derive the *observational semantics* of VHDL designs by considering all infinite runs of the transition system and restricting their observation to objects derived from a designs entity declaration.

The resulting transition system is in general infinite; imposing the following restrictions will allow the use of the symbolic finite state verification tools developed within FORMAT:

- procedures and functions must be non-recursive;
- time expressions have to be computable at elaboration time;
- all employed types must be finite.

While this chapter provides a direct semantics in terms of transition systems, the compilation process into symbolic transition systems is for complexity reasons structured in two phases, a generation of an intermediate Petri-net representation, and a subsequent compilation of this net into a symbolic representation of its transition system. To this end Petri-net based semantics have been developed in [25, 62], out of which the second covers full VHDL whereas the emphasis of the first is the support for compositional reasoning. The compilation of this intermediate representation into BDDs is discussed in [45]. The application of abstraction techniques in this model generation process preserving properties of a given specification is covered in [28].

A *compositional proof-system* for correctness formula $\underline{des} \models \Phi$, where Φ is an assumption commitment style first-order linear time temporal logic formula, is provided allowing us to reason about composite designs. Since global time is observable, the logic can be used not only to specify unbounded liveness properties but also real-time properties of VHDL designs. A weakening calculus for the logic is currently embedded in the LAMBDA system, which in its turn relies on an axiomatisation of VHDL's data types within the LAMBDA system. In this chapter, we provide only the core rules of the correctness logic and disregard implementation aspects.

While the verification tools employed in the system indeed see specifications as temporal logic formulae, we consider it unrealistic for practical applications to demand hardware designers to provide such specifications directly. Instead, the graphical specification language of *symbolic timing diagrams* [54, 67, 68] is provided as user interface. Timing diagrams are a well known specification style to hardware designers. At the same time, they can be given a formal semantics in terms of temporal logic, thus providing a path to all verification tools and methods based on temporal logic. This chapter provides the semantic link between symbolic timing diagrams and the supported temporal logic.

The remainder of this chapter has the following structure. Section 2 is of an introductory nature. Its first subsection gives a simple example VHDL design subsequently used to illustrate the correctness logic. Its second subsection develops the abstract syntax of the kernel language. Symbolic timing diagrams are introduced by giving a specification of the VHDL design example. The formal semantics of the VHDL kernel is provided in Section 3. Section 4 goes on to develop the correctness logic and prove its soundness. The final Section 5 gives a formal semantics of symbolic timing diagrams in terms of temporal logic.

2 Ingredients of VHDL-based system-level design: a short introduction

The aim of this section is to familiarize the reader with the concepts occurring in VHDL-based system-level design. We introduce as an example to be used throughout the chapter a simple bus protocol, formalize the features of VHDL covered in the formal semantics, and introduce timing diagrams as graphical specification language. The chapter assumes familiarity with VHDL on the level of for example the tutorial [7]; for a more detailed understanding of the subtleties of VHDL, we refer the reader to [58].

2.1 An example

To illustrate the specification and verification method for VHDL designs we consider an architecture consisting of a master unit and two slave units as shown in Fig. 2. Every slave component controls a memory unit. The master component may request read and write operations and the slave

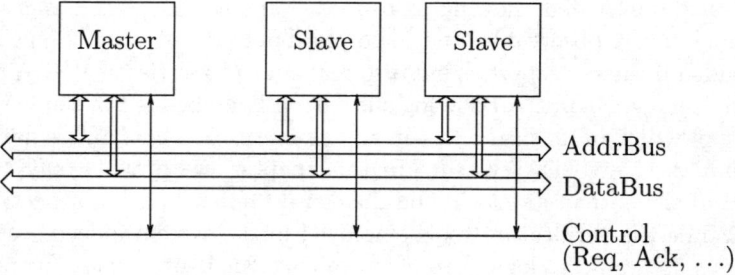

FIG. 2. Master/slave architecture.

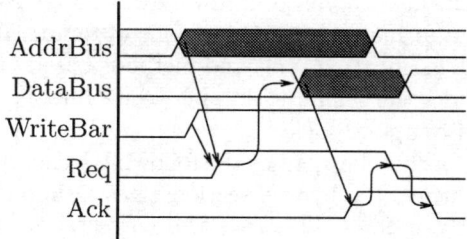

FIG. 3. Read cycle.

which is responsible for the given address has to respond to the request in an appropriate manner. Figure 3 shows a timing diagram for a read cycle. The master module initiates the read cycle by putting the address on the address bus, setting the signal $\overline{write}$ to high (read request) and sending a request signal to the slaves. The slave responsible for the requested data responds to the request by writing the data on the data bus and acknowledging the completion by raising the acknowledge signal. The protocol will be closed by resetting the request and acknowledge signals.

To demonstrate the verification method we use a simplified version of the architecture (cf. Fig. 4). We do not distinguish between read and write operations and hence also omit the data bus. The address bus is reduced to the bits defining the relevant address block, i.e. identifying the responsible slave. In our case this is modelled by one bit. Usually the operations of the master component are controlled by a program running on the system. This is modelled by a demand signal in conjunction with an instruction signal which consists only of the value indicating the next address range.

The following VHDL code describes the simplified slave module and the master component:

```
entity Slave is
    generic (id : bit := '0');
```

Specification and verification of VHDL-based Hardware Designs

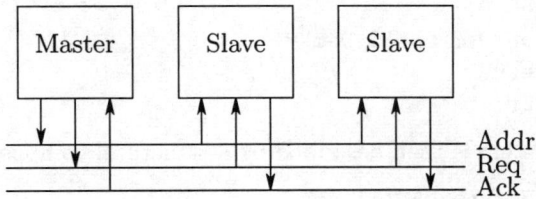

FIG. 4. Simplified master/slave architecture.

```
   port (Addr : in bit;
         Req  : in bit;
         Ack  : out bit);
end Slave;

architecture behaviour of Slave is
begin
   process
   begin
      wait on Req until Req = '1';
      if (Addr = id) then
         Ack <= '1';
         wait on Req until Req = '0';
         Ack <= '0';
      end if;
   end process;
end behaviour;

entity Master is
   port (Dem  : in bit;
         Instr: in bit;
         Addr : out bit;
         Req  : out bit;
         Ack  : in bit);
end Master;

architecture behaviour of Master is
begin
   process
   begin
      wait on Dem,Ack until Dem = '1' and Ack = '0';
      Addr <= Instr;
      Req <= '1';
      wait on Ack until Ack = '1';
```

```
      Req <= '0';
      wait on Dem until Dem = '0';
   end process;
end behaviour;
```

The whole system is then described by a structural composition:

```
use work.ROM_types.all;
entity System is
   port (Dem   : in bit;
         Instr : in bit );
   signal Addr, Req : bit;
   signal Ack : resolve_level;
end System;

architecture structure of System is
   component Master
      port(Dem : in bit; Instr : in bit;
           Addr : out bit; Req : out bit; Ack : in bit);
   end component;
   component Slave
      generic (id : bit := '0');
      port (Addr : in bit; Req : in bit; Ack : out bit);
   end component;
begin
   M : Master
      port map (Dem => Dem, Instr => Instr,
                Addr => Addr, Req => Req, Ack => Ack);
   S1 : Slave
      generic map (id => '1')
      port map (Addr => Addr, Req => Req, Ack => Ack);
   S2 : Slave
      generic map (id => '0')
      port map (Addr => Addr, Req => Req, Ack => Ack);
end structure;
```

The package ROM_types defines the resolution function for the acknowledge signal:

```
package ROM_types is
  function resolve_ack(drivers : in bit_vector) return bit;
  subtype resolve_level is resolve_ack bit;
end ROM_types;

package body ROM_types is
  function resolve_ack(drivers : in bit_vector) return bit is
```

```
begin
   for index in drivers'range loop
      if drivers(index) = '1' then return '1';
      end if;
   end loop;
   return '0';
end resolve_ack;
end ROM_types;
```

2.2 The covered VHDL subset and its formal definition

VHDL is an extremely rich language providing powerful modularization concepts. It inherits from ADA the package concept allowing modular specification of the employed data-types, and uses the concept of components and configurations to support an evolutionary design approach. Within the scope of a publication, it is impossible to cover the complete range of VHDL. Instead, we focus our attention on a *kernel language* which is rich enough to express all of VHDL, and *disregard all issues related to scoping* since these are not particular to VHDL.

The VHDL language reference manual explicates the relation of full VHDL to the considered kernel language. A process called *elaboration* maps every VHDL design into a flat parallel composition of *sequential processes*, which communicate over signals. It thus "safe" to restrict our VHDL subset to architectures, which describe the design either purely in *behavioural style* (i.e. as a VHDL sequential process), or purely in terms of *structure*, i.e. by declaring the components of the design and their interconnection. A VHDL *design entity* consists of two parts:

- the first, called *entity declaration*, defines the components' interface and initial values;
- the second, called *architecture body*, defines the components behaviour as visible at the interface. According to the employed description style, we classify these into *behavioural* and *structural* bodies.

We do formalize VHDL's concept of *configurations* which allows us to bind component instances to design entities. Our semantics does not detail handling of expressions (cf., e.g., [44, 62, 71] for a formal treatment a VHDL expression semantics). For the purpose of this chapter we simply assume a collection of *types Types* with typical element τ. Example types are **bool, bit, integer, time, bitvector, arrays**, and enumeration types. Of these, the only type deserving attention in this chapter is the type **time**. VHDL assumes a *discrete* time model. The minimal considered time-unit is 1 femto-second; the user can choose to observe the design with a coarser time granularity by redefining the length of the unit time. For the purpose of this chapter, the time domain is isomorphic to the integers. VHDL is a strongly typed language; in particular all variables v and signals s are typed.

We use $VVar_\tau$ resp. Sig_τ to denote the set of VHDL variables and signals of type τ. Among the variables of type **time** there is a predefined variable *now* giving the current "simulation" time. VHDL expressions are built up from variables, signals, constants, a set of base functions and relations, and user defined functions in a standard way not discussed in this chapter; we simply assume a syntactic category $<\exp>_\tau$ of expressions of type τ. All variables in VHDL are initialized with a default value d_τ^0 required to exist in the semantic domain D_τ for expressions of type τ.

A VHDL design entity is a *reactive system* in the sense of [42]: it is a conceptually non-terminating process which maintains an ongoing interaction with its environment. The *entity declaration* of a design entity determines what aspects of a design entity are *observable* (and thus corresponds to a *hiding-operator*): only those signals declared there are visible to other design entities. Visible signals of a design entity are referred to as *ports*. The entity declaration specifies for each port its *direction* (in this chapter we consider only **in** and **out**) and for each outport its *initial value*. Variables are *always* local to the design entity except for a special subset defined as (read-only) parameters in the entity declaration of so-called *generics*, which must be computable at elaboration time. Generics serve to parameterize the design by e.g. allowing us to talk about n instances of a component or signal assignments with delay n. In elaborated designs, generics behave like constants w.r.t. the formal semantics.

Formally, an *entity declaration* is a tuple

$$(I, O, V_{gen}, init)$$

where I and O are disjoint finite sets of (in- resp. out-) ports (in Sig), V_{gen} is a set of generics (in $VVar$), and *init* is a function assigning to each outport an expression of matching type. We denote the set of entity declarations by ED with typical element *ed*, and refer to its ports (resp. inports, outports, generics, initialization function) by *ports(ed)* (resp. *inports(ed)*, *outports(ed)*, *generics(ed)*, *init(ed)*).

A *behavioural* design entity for an entity declaration *ed* is a tuple

$$\langle ed, proc \rangle \in \underline{BB(ed)}$$

where $proc \in \underline{PR}$. $\underline{PR}$ is the class of sequential VHDL processes defined according to the following "macro"-syntax:

```
< process-statement >  ::=  process < process-declarative-part >
                            begin{< sequential-statement >}
                            end process;
```

Each process allows us to declare local variables and functions in its declarative part. Its body is given by a so-called *sequential statement*, which is executed continuously as if enclosed in a *do forever* loop. VHDL's sequential statement contains standard statements such as *variable assignments*, *if-*, *case-*, and *while-* statements, and *assert* statements. VHDL's ability to describe hardware designs rests on two "dedicated" classes of statements, *signal assignments* and *wait-statements*, to be discussed extensively in this chapter. Formally, a sequential statement is defined by

$$
\begin{aligned}
<\text{sequential-statement}> &::= \\
&\quad <\text{variable-assignment-statement}> \\
&\mid\ <\text{if-statement}> \\
&\mid\ <\text{case-statement}> \\
&\mid\ <\text{loop-statement}> \\
&\mid\ <\text{signal-assignment-statement}> \\
&\mid\ <\text{wait-statement}> \\
&\mid\ <\text{sequential-statement}> \{;<\text{sequential-statement}>\}*
\end{aligned}
$$

A signal assignment statement takes one of the following forms:
- inertial delay signal assignment

$$s_\tau <= \textbf{inertial } e_\tau \textbf{ after } e_{time};$$

- transport delay signal assignment

$$s_\tau <= \textbf{transport } e_\tau \textbf{ after } e_{time};$$

Informally, it schedules the event that s takes value e_τ to occur after e_{time} time units. Subsequent signal assignments may **cancel** the occurrence of this event in a way depending on the *mode* of the signal assignment:
- in *transport* mode, all events scheduled to occur *after the newly scheduled event* are cancelled;
- in *inertial* mode, *additionally* all *previous* events are cancelled, if the value of the event differs from the newly scheduled value. The default mode is inertial.

VHDL's wait statement serves to *synchronize* all processes, to *advance time*, and to *propagate events* on signals if scheduled for the newly computed time. We defer a more detailed discussion of the semantics of this overloaded construct to the next section and only elaborate on its syntax. It comes in variants allowing a process to wait for:
- *time to elapse* for e_{time} time units, as in **wait for** e_{time};
- a *signal s* to *change its value*, as in **wait on** s;
- a *condition* e_{bool} to become true, as in **wait until** e_{bool};

Any combination of the variants is allowed.

The syntax employed in this chapter uses the non-terminals defined in the standard [48], which the reader may consult to expend the undefined syntactic categories.

Intuitively, a *structural design* is like an unmounted printed circuit board; the type of the employed sockets is given by so-called *component declarations*, they are "placed" on the PCB using *component instantiation statements*, and are "electrically" connected via *signals* (the "wires"); for each component instance a *port map* "glues" the ports of a component instance to a wire or a port of the PCB. The description also specifies what happens if multiple outports are connected to one wire using so-called *resolution functions*: they determine the value of a signal representing a wire in terms of the values of the outports "driving" the wire. Finally, generics also allowed in component declarations must be instantiated.

Syntactically, component declarations are identical to entity declarations. To emphasize their difference in usage we introduce CD as new names for the class of component declarations, with typical element C.

Formally, a structural design for an entity declaration ed is a tuple

$$sb = \langle ed, \|_{\underline{sig},\underline{vis}}(id_1 : C_1, \ldots, id_n : C_n), \underline{gmap}, \underline{res}\rangle$$

such that

- $n \geq 2$ the number of created component instances
- id_i, $i = 1, \ldots, n$,   are unique local *component instance names* taken from a set $\underline{CompNames}$
- $C_i \in \underline{CD}$ are (not necessarily distinct) local component declarations; we use $comp(sb)(id_i)$ to refer to the component declaration C_i of the component instance id_i in structural body sb
- $\underline{sig} : \left\{(id_i, p) \mid 1 \leq i \leq n, p \in ports(C_i)\right\} \longrightarrow Sig$ is the component of the *port map* which connects ports of component instances to *local* signals declared in the design entities body
- $\underline{gmap} : \left\{(id_i, v) \mid 1 \leq i \leq n, v \in generics(comp(id_i))\right\} \longrightarrow <\exp>$ assigns to each generic of the component instance an expression of matching type instantiating the generic. The expression must be computable at elaboration time; thus all variables occurring in $<\exp>$ must be contained in $generics(ed)$
- $\underline{vis} : range(\underline{sig}) \longrightarrow ports(ed)$ a partial mapping modelling the component of the port map which connects those signals of the structural design which shall be visible to ports of its entity declaration ed[1]

---

[1]Here we slightly deviate from VHDL by enforcing local signals between ports of components and ports of the structural design entity. This allows a more uniform two-stage approach in the formal semantics, evaluating first the semantics of signals and then propagating the value to ports. The adaption to standard VHDL is straightforward.

In the concrete syntax of VHDL, ports of components may directly be bound to ports of the design entity using the components' port maps; internal signals can only be propagated to outports using e.g. concurrent signal assignments, which after elaboration

- $\underline{res} : range(\underline{sig}) \longrightarrow\, <\exp>$ for a signal s of type τ, $res(s)$ denotes a function of type $\tau-\mathbf{list} \to \tau$. $\underline{res}$ defines for some (so-called *resolved*) signals a so-called *resolution function*, which must be associative, commutative, and reflexive[2]. The expression defining the resolution function for a signal s may only depend on generics of ed and those outports of component instances, which are "glued" via $\underline{sig}$ with s, i.e. on $generics(ed) \cup \underline{sig}^{-1}(s)$.

We denote the class of structural design entities matching an entity declaration ed by $\underline{SB}(ed)$, with typical element sb. We refer to the constituents of a structural design entity sb by $ed(sb)$; we also have $cd(sb)$ — the set of component declarations occurring in sb, $compnames(sb)$ — the set of component instance names occurring in sb, $comp(sb)$, and $Sig(sb)$ — the set of signals occurring in sb, $sig(sb)$, $vis(sb)$, and $res(sb)$.

VHDL puts restrictions on the bindings of ports and signals which will be captured through the following well-formedness condition. Intuitively, these ensure that all "wires" have a well-defined value. Problems may arise if no "pin" drives a wire (in this case the wire is called *open*) or if many pins drive a wire (which then is called *multiple-driven*). In the latter case, a resolution function must be defined for the wire. Moreover, the direction of ports of the structural design entity must match the thus defined status of wires: inports may only be connected to open wires; outports require driven wires.

Definition 2.1 (driven and open signals, well-formedness) *Let* $sb \in \underline{SB}(ed)$ *be given as above.*

1. *Signals* s *in* $range(\underline{sig})$ *are either driven or open depending on the value of* $\underline{sig}^{-1}(s)$:

   - *if* $\underline{sig}^{-1}(s)$ *contains only inports, then* s *is open;*
   - *if* $\underline{sig}^{-1}(s)$ *contains exactly one outport, then* s *is single-driven;*
   - *if* $\underline{sig}^{-1}(s)$ *for some* $s \in range(\underline{sig})$ *contains more than one outport, then* s *is multiple-driven;*
   - s *is called driven iff it is single-driven or multiple-driven.*

2. sb *is called* well-formed *(notation:* $\underline{wf}(sb)$*) iff the following conditions are satisfied:*

   - *for all multiple-driven signals* s, $\underline{res}(s)$ *is defined;*
   - *for all open signals* s, $\underline{vis}(s)$ *is defined*[3];

---

would constitute another design component bound via a configuration to a behavioural design entity. In VHDL it is not possible to associate a component port to both a local signal and an port of the design entity.

[2] A function $f : D_\tau^* \to d_\tau$ is called *reflexive* iff, for all $d \in D_\tau$, $f(d) = d$.

[3] This condition ensures that all signals have a defined value: signals which are not driven by components must be connected to an inport.

- *vis induces an association of signals with ports of the associated entity declarations ed which is compatible with the direction of ports:*
  * $inports(ed) = \{\underline{vis}(s) \mid s \text{ is open }\}$[4]
  * $outports(ed) = \{\underline{vis}(s) \mid s \text{ is driven }\}$

The binding of component instances to entity declarations and architectures is achieved using configurations. To simplify the exposition, we assume that association of component and entity ports and generics is given by positional specification (e.g. the i-th port of a component will be bound to the i-th port of the entity). We assume compatibility of the direction of ports and of initial values. The verification approach does not depend on this restriction.

Formally, a *configuration* is a pair $\underline{conf} = \langle \underline{ed}, \underline{ab} \rangle$ of partial mappings

$$\underline{ed} : \underline{SB} \times \underline{CompNames} \times \underline{CD} \longrightarrow \underline{ED}$$
$$\underline{ab} : \underline{SB} \times \underline{CompNames} \times \underline{CD} \longrightarrow \underline{SB} \cup \underline{BB}$$

such that for all $id \in \underline{CompNames}$, for all $sb \in \underline{SB}$, for all $C \in \underline{CD}$:

- if $\underline{ed}(sb, id, C)$ is defined then $comp(sb)(id) = C$
- $\underline{ed}(sb, id, C)$ is defined iff $\underline{ab}(sb, id, C)$ is defined
- $(sb, id, C) \in dom(\underline{ab}) \Rightarrow$
  $\underline{ab}(sb, id, C) \in \underline{SB}(\underline{ed}(sb, id, C)) \cup \underline{BB}(\underline{ed}(sb, id, C))$
- $(sb, id, C) \in dom(ed) \Rightarrow \underline{ed}(sb, id, C) = C$

The first condition only enforces what could otherwise be expressed using dependent types: the configuration only binds labels of component instances together with "their" component declaration. Semantic restrictions are only imposed by the last conditions, which require that the body of the design entity must match the entity declaration required by the configuration which in its turn must match the configured component declaration.

The separation of structural designs and configurations allows us to manipulate partial designs, a mandatory feature when managing complex designs. In carrying out structural design, the designer can postpone the decision of how to realize the functionality of a component and concentrate on the purely structural aspects. It is only when the design is completed that all component instances must be configured. A pair of a design entity and a configuration satisfying this property is called a *complete VHDL design*.

---

[4] At this point we slightly deviate from VHDL by making all signals visible. This separation of the definition of parallel definition and a separate so-called hiding operator only serves to simplify the definition of proof rules and is thus only a technical issue.

A configuration $\underline{conf} = \langle \underline{ed}, \underline{ab} \rangle$ is called *complete* relative to $sb \in SB(ed)$ iff

- $\forall id \in CompNames(sb) : (sb, id, comp(sb)(id)) \in dom(\underline{ab})$
- $\forall id \in CompNames(sb) : \underline{ab}(sb, id, comp(sb)(id)) \in SB \Rightarrow \underline{conf}$ is complete relative to $\underline{ab}(sb, id, comp(sb)(id))$

A *complete design* is a triple $\underline{des} = \langle \underline{ed}, \underline{ab}, \underline{conf} \rangle$ s.t.

- $ab \in \underline{SB(ed)} \cup \underline{BB(ed)}$
- $ab \in \underline{SB(ed)} \Rightarrow \underline{conf}$ is complete relative to ab

The class of all designs with entity declaration ed is denoted by $\underline{DS(ed)}$. The depth of a design $\underline{des} = \langle \underline{ed}, \underline{ab}, \langle \underline{ed}, \underline{ab} \rangle \rangle$ is defined by

$$depth(\underline{des}) = \begin{cases} 0 & \text{if } ab \in \underline{BB(ed)} \\ 1+ \max \left\{ \begin{array}{l} depth(\langle \underline{ed}(sb, id, comp(sb)(id)), \\ \underline{ab}(sb, id, comp(sb)(id)), \langle \underline{ed}, \underline{ab} \rangle \rangle) \\ id \in CompNames(sb) \end{array} \right\} & \\ & \text{if } ab = sb \in \underline{SB(ed)} \end{cases}$$

2.3 Introduction to Symbolic Timing Diagrams

In order to specify requirements we use a graphical formalism called Symbolic Timing Diagrams (STD's), which is derived from the notion of classical timing diagrams as used by hardware designers. In contrast to these diagrams, which are often used informally or with an ad-hoc semantics in mind, STD's have a precise semantics, which is defined by translation into a characterizing temporal-logic formula (as introduced in [67]). STD's are intended to be used for a declarative specification of the behaviour of individual system components as observable at their interface. While in the realm of hardware design specifications often take the form of protocols with concrete timing constraints, STD's are directed towards the early steps of a complex hardware design (i.e. the system or even more abstract level), where requirements are abstract system properties wherein only the *order* of events and their (under given premises) guaranteed occurrence matters.

In the following we give a short introduction to STD's; a detailed exposition is given in Section 5. An STD consists of a number of *symbolic waveforms*. Each waveform has several *regions* which are separated by *edges*. The regions are labelled by predicates (denoted by boolean expressions over the variables observable at the components' interface). Between any two edges on different waveforms there may be *constraints* (denoted by respective arrow shapes) used to express a required temporal ordering of these edges. Figure 5 shows different forms of constraints. A *causality constraint* (denoted by an emphasized arrow) expresses that (1) an event matched by edge $e2$ must not occur before an event matched by edge $e1$ and (2) if an event matched by edge $e1$ occurs, then an event matched by edge $e2$ will occur eventually. A *precedence constraint* is weaker than a causality constraint and expresses only condition (1). A *simultaneous constraint* expresses that an event matched by edge $e1$ and an event matched by edge $e2$ must occur simultaneously (Fig. 5).

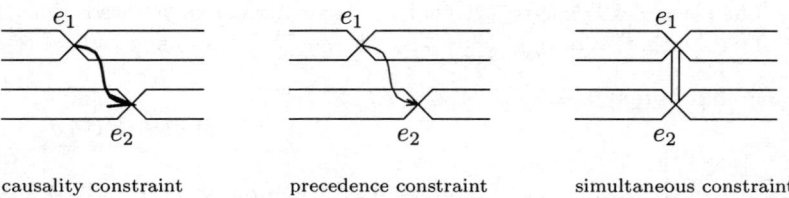

FIG. 5. Basic types of constraints and their graphical denotation.

An STD can be regarded as a dynamic pattern called into effect whenever the values of the interface variables conform to the conjunction of the initial predicates on each symbolic waveform of the diagram (called the activation condition for the diagram). In the following part of the run of the system the constraints have to be obeyed. Note that each constraint also has a *weak* form (denoted by dashed arrow shapes). The weak form expresses a *premise* rather than a requirement: If the premise is violated, the STD becomes deactivated, i.e. it does not restrict the run of the system any longer.

We pick up the example STD given in Fig. 2 of Section 2.1 and focus on the protocol running on the control lines *Req* and *Ack*. Note that in a modular specification of the component *Slave*, the environment of *Slave* (i.e. the component *Master*) may set and reset *Req* at any time due to the asynchronous mode of communication. Hence the protocol is captured by Fig. 6: the emphasized solid arrows state a requirement about the behaviour of the module *Slave* (whenever module *Master* raises *Req*, then module *Slave* will eventually raise *Ack*, but not earlier). In contrast, the dashed arrows state an *expectation* about the behaviour of the module *Master*: in order to guarantee correct function, the module *Slave* will assume that whenever module *Master* raises *Req*, then it will keep the line stable unless module *Slave* has raised *Ack*. This distinction between required and expected behaviour is the key solution to modular specification and verification, which is explained in detail in Section 4.

```
┌─────────────────────────────────────────────────────────┐
│  TD_{Req,Ack}()                                         │
├─────────────────────────────────────────────────────────┤
│                                                         │
│   Req = '0'  Req = '1'     Req = '0'     Req = '1'      │
│                                                         │
│   Ack = '0'      Ack = '1'       Ack = '0'              │
│                                                         │
└─────────────────────────────────────────────────────────┘
```

FIG. 6. STD specifying a 4-cycle handshake.

3 A formal semantics for VHDL

This section provides a formal semantics for VHDL designs as formalised in Section 2. We define a *linear-time* (sometimes also called *stream-based*) semantics to VHDL: we associate with a design *a set of observations*. Each observation is an infinite sequence of valuations of *observables* of the design entity. It is the entity declaration of a design which determines the degree of observability by defining its ports: VHDL allows us to observe the *current* and the *last* value of a port (and thus whether the port has changed its value), whether the design entity is willing to engage in a synchronization (i.e. whether control has reached a wait statement), and the current simulation time. The temporal logic defined in Section 4 will contain atomic formula corresponding to these observables.

To develop this *observational semantics* of VHDL designs we use transition systems as intermediate representations of VHDL designs. States of the transition system carry control-flow information and valuations of variables and signals. The choice of the transition-system based semantics (rather than a denotational semantics) is only motivated by the close link to model-checking techniques: if all data types are finite and all time-expressions are computable at elaboration time, the resulting transition system is finite and can be used in symbolic model-checking tools. This line of development as well as the use of Petri-nets as an intermediate level of compilation to cope with the complexity of full VHDL is emphasized in companion papers [25, 28, 31, 45]. In this chapter, we disregard finite-state aspects and only use the transition system semantics as a basis for defining a correctness logic for VHDL w.r.t. temporal logic specifications. Since the logic only supports compositional reasoning for structural designs, we will provide a global definition of the transition system associated with a behavioural design and provide a parallel composition operator on transition systems capturing VHDL's notion of structural designs. The observational semantics of a VHDL design is then defined as the projection of the set of runs of the constructed transition system $T[\![\underline{des}]\!]$ to the set of observables.

The section is structured as follows. We pick up the sequential VHDL statements peculiar to this language in separate subsections. One subsection gives sufficient hints on how to extent the semantics to all sequential statements. A more involved subsection handles structural designs, and wraps up the translation into transition systems by defining semantics of complete VHDL designs.

3.1 The semantics of signal assignment statements

VHDL distinguishes between two types of carriers for state-information. *Variables* are used as "scratchpad memory" inside sequential processes in order to facilitate the computation of new values for signals. In particular, processes cannot communicate via shared variables[5]. The second type of carriers of state-information are *signals*. Whereas variable assignments become immediately visible, signal assignments *serve only to schedule events* and *do not immediately change the value of a signal*. This distinction of carrier types is closely related to VHDL's view of time; hence a short digression on this topic is in order before expanding on the signal assignment. Consider an elaborated VHDL design. As mentioned before, such a design can be seen as a flat parallel composition of, say, n sequential processes. Technically, using the notations developed in the previous section, this would be described by one structural design entity whose components are configured with behavioural design entities. For the sake of this discussion, assume that all wait statements in processes are uniquely labelled. Call a *wait configuration* of an elaborated design an n-vector of labels of wait-statements; its i-th component has label L iff the i-th process is currently willing to execute the wait-statement labelled L. The execution of such a design can be pictured as moving from one wait configuration to a successor wait configuration. All processes can be seen as performing these moves *concurrently*, working only on their private variables, and scheduling events to occur. Now recall that VHDL assumes a discrete global time scale. It is important to understand that all computations between wait-statements occur *"instantaneously"*, i.e. they *do not affect* global time. Note that (due to potentially infinite loops), it is thus possible for an infinite number of computation steps to occur in zero time, a decision shared with the family of *synchronous languages* (like [8]) and e.g. corresponding to the micro-steps of the original statechart semantics [41]. If (and only if!) all processes have moved to a new wait-statement, the collection of scheduled events and timeout conditions is analysed to determine the increase in global time as the next point in discrete time, where either an

---

[5]Unfortunately the recent balloted new version of VHDL is moving towards the introduction of shared variables. This chapter is based on the original VHDL standard [48]

event is scheduled to occur or a timeout happens; due to what VHDL calls δ-*delays*, i.e. signal assignments with delay 0, the increase in global time may be 0. It is at this stage, that events scheduled for this point in time become visible: the value of the signal is updated with the value associated with the event, thus becoming accessible to other processes. These new signal values may in their turn cause reactivation of processes, starting a new sweep of local computation steps. To summarize, we have identified two types of communication steps: *local steps* proceed in zero-time and work on "frozen" copies of signal values and private variables, and additionally only *scheduling* events; *environment steps* are executed only if all processes have reached a wait, and induce an increase in time and process communication using possibly updated signal values.

We now pick up on the formal semantics of the signal assignment, and discuss first the transport delay model. The data-structure memorizing the events scheduled for a signal s (say, of type τ) is called s'*projected waveform* (in the terminology of [48]). Its entries represent events of type

$$\underline{events}_\tau = \tau \times \mathbf{int}.$$

The first component of an event e, $e.val$, represents the scheduled value, and its second component $e.del$ the number of time-units which have to elapse until the event becomes visible. With each signal s of type τ we associate a "shadow variable" s_{wv} of type

$$\underline{prvw}_\tau = \underline{events}_\tau^*.$$

Note that in general projected waveforms can grow arbitrarily (consider a loop with a signal assignment in its body, whose delay expression is incremented every iteration). We use standard list functions to manipulate projected waveforms.

It is now time to introduce some semantic domains. For each type τ we assume a semantic domain D_τ. This association is lifted canonically to derived types such as $\underline{prvw}_\tau$. For technical reasons we split the classical denotational concept of a *state*, i.e. a valuation of variables by their current value, into separate valuations for inports, outports, and local variables (including shadow variables introduced to give the semantics such as those representing projected waveforms). Clearly all variants of states are *type-preserving*.

Consider a design entity with entity declaration $ed = (I, O, V_{gen}, init)$ and a set of local variables Vloc. We associate with each signal s occurring as an in- or outport of type τ a shadow variable $s'last\_value$ in the set Ilv_τ (resp. Olv_τ) and with each outport o of type a shadow variable o_{wv} in the set of waveform variables Owv_τ. We redefine $VVar$ to contain also all shadow variables and generics:

$$VVar_\tau = \text{V}loc_\tau \cup \text{V}gen_\tau \cup \text{I}lv_\tau \cup \text{O}lv_\tau \cup \text{O}wv_\tau$$

- The set of *input-valuations* $inputs(I)$ with typical element inp is defined by $inputs(I) = (I \to D)$.
- The set of *output-valuations* $outputs(O)$ with typical element out is defined by $outputs(O) = (O \to D)$.
- The set of *local states* $states(VVar)$ with typical element σ is defined by $states(VVar) = (VVar \to D)$.

The valuations are type-preserving, e.g. for $i : \tau$ we must have $inp(i) \in D_\tau$. Note that we explicitly memorize in these denotations the syntactical objects. This will become important in defining the formal semantics of structural bodies.

We assume the semantics of a VHDL expression $e : \tau$ relative to an input valuation inp and a local state σ, $[\![e]\!]\, inp\, \sigma \in D_\tau$ as given. We restrict ourselves to expressions whose evaluation is free of side-effects. Note that the valuation does not depend on the current value of an outport.

Now consider the execution of a transport delay signal assignment

$$s <= \textbf{transport}\ e_\tau\ \textbf{after}\ e_{time};$$

for a signal s of type τ in local state σ and input valuation inp. Let

- $d = [\![e_\tau]\!]\, inp\, \sigma \in D_\tau$
- $t = [\![e_{time}]\!]\, inp\, \sigma \in \mathbf{N}$
- $pw = \sigma(s_{wv})$.

For each timing model, we define a function on the domain of projected waveforms, capturing the effect of the timing model. For the transport delay model, we simply insert the new event $\langle d, t \rangle$ in pw and purge pw from all other entries with a greater (or equal) delay component.

The following function *transport* on projected waveforms captures the transport-delay model:

$$transport : \underline{events}_\tau \times \underline{prvw}_\tau \longrightarrow \underline{prvw}_\tau$$

is defined using an auxiliary function *purge* by

$$transport(\langle d,t \rangle, pw) = \langle d,t \rangle :: purge(\langle d,t \rangle, pw),$$

where *purge* is defined by induction on the list-structure of projected waveforms:

$$purge(\langle d,t \rangle, \mathbf{nil}) = \mathbf{nil},$$
$$purge(\langle d,t \rangle, \langle d',t' \rangle :: pw') =$$
$$\begin{cases} purge(\langle d,t \rangle, pw') & \text{if } t' \geq t \\ \langle d',t' \rangle :: purge(\langle d,t \rangle, pw') & \text{otherwise.} \end{cases}$$

It is now straightforward to define the semantics of the above signal assignment statement as a function transforming the valuations of inports and local variables:

$$[\![s <= \text{transport } e_\tau \text{ after } e_{time}]\!] \, inp \, \sigma =$$
$$\sigma[s/transport(\langle [\![e_\tau]\!] inp \, \sigma, [\![e_{time}]\!] inp \, \sigma\rangle, \sigma(s_{wv}))].$$

where we use the standard notation $\sigma[v/d]$ to denote the *variant* of the function σ, which only differs from σ, in the redefined value d for its argument v.

We now consider the inertial delay signal assignment

$$s_\tau <= \textbf{inertial } e_\tau \textbf{ after } e_{time};$$

We again use d, t, pw to stand for the result of evaluating the value and time components and the current state of s' projected waveform in a given local state σ and input valuation inp. Apart from cancelling events as in the transport timing model, also all events scheduled prior to t are analysed. If there is one event whose value component differs from d, then all events up to last one with a different value are cancelled. We capture this timing model in the following function, inserting an event according to the inertial delay model into a projected waveform:

$$inertial : \underline{events}_\tau \times \underline{prvw}_\tau \longrightarrow \underline{prvw}_\tau$$

is defined using an auxiliary function *ipurge* by

$$inertial(\langle d, t\rangle, pw) = \langle d, t\rangle :: ipurge(\langle d, t\rangle, pw),$$

where *ipurge* is defined by induction on the list-structure of projected waveforms:

$$ipurge(\langle d, t\rangle, \textbf{nil}) = \textbf{nil},$$
$$ipurge(\langle d, t\rangle, \langle d', t'\rangle :: pw') =$$
$$\begin{cases} ipurge(\langle d,t\rangle, pw') & \text{if } t' \geq t \\ \textbf{nil} & \text{if } t' < t \text{ and } d \neq d' \\ \langle d', t'\rangle :: ipurge(\langle d, t\rangle, pw') & \text{otherwise.} \end{cases}$$

This allows us to define the semantics of inertial delay signal assignments w.r.t. an input valuation inp and a local state σ:

$$[\![s <= \textbf{inertial } e_\tau \textbf{ after } e_{time}]\!] \, inp \, \sigma =$$
$$\sigma[s/inertial(\langle [\![e_\tau]\!] \, inp \, \sigma, [\![e_{time}]\!] \, inp \, \sigma\rangle, \sigma(s_{wv}))].$$

3.2 Transition systems for VHDL designs

We will define the semantics of VHDL designs *operationally* using the well-known concept of transition systems. For the sake of completeness, we recall the following:

Definition 3.1 (transition system)

1. Let Σ denote some finite set of states. A transition-system T over Σ is a triple
$$T = (\Sigma, \rightarrow, \Sigma_0)$$
with $\rightarrow \subseteq \Sigma \times \Sigma$ (the transition relation) and $\Sigma_0 \subseteq \Sigma$ (the set of initial states).

2. The set of runs of T, $run(T)$, is defined to be
$$\underline{run}(T) = \{ \ w \in \Sigma^*\{\delta\} \cup \Sigma^\infty \ | \ w\langle 0\rangle \in \Sigma_0 \wedge \forall j \in \mathbf{N}: \\ (w\langle j\rangle \rightarrow w\langle j+1\rangle) \vee \\ [\neg(\exists \sigma \in \Sigma: w\langle j\rangle \rightarrow \sigma) \wedge w\langle j+1\rangle = \delta]) \ \} \ .$$

Note that δ is used as a marker to recognize stuck computations.

States of transition systems associated with VHDL designs consist of valuations of signals and variables, as well as *control-information*. For simplicity we assume each statement to possess a unique label and refer to the statement belonging to label l by $stat(l)$. We code the control-flow in lists of sequential statements using $next(l)$.

Note that the valuation of inports is determined purely by the environment of the design entity. To express in a modular fashion the global synchronization required when executing wait-statements, we include in the transition system a flag $ENV'at\_wait$ which is controlled by the environment. Similarly, we need information from the environment to determine the increase global time: the shadow variable $ENV'delay$ of type integer carries the increase of time allowed by the environment. We collect these into a state component $ENV = \mathbf{B} \times \mathbf{N}_\infty$ with selectors at_wait resp. $delay$. Similarly, we represent the synchronization status of the design under consideration in a state-component MOD. We combine these in one state-component $SYNCH\_STATE = MOD \times ENV$.

Generics are required to be instantiated at elaboration time. Their value is then fixed throughout the execution of the design. We model this by parameterizing the transition system w.r.t. a (type-preserving) valuation $genval: V_{gen} \rightarrow D$ of generics. To simplify the notation, this parameterization *is not explicitly indicated*.

More formally, we will now define the set of states of the transition system associated with a design entity $\underline{des}$. Let its entity declaration be given by $ed = (I, O, V_{gen}, init)$ and
$$VVar_\tau \ = \ Vloc_\tau \cup Vgen_\tau \cup Ilv_\tau \cup Olv_\tau \cup Owv_\tau$$
as above. For the time being, let $control(\underline{des})$ denote some finite set with a designated element $start$.

The set $\Sigma(\underline{des})$ of states of the transition system associated with $\underline{des}$ is given by
$$\Sigma(\underline{des}) = control(\underline{des}) \times SYNCH\_STATE \times \\ inputs(I) \times states(VVar) \times outputs(O).$$

The set of initial states is determined as follows. The control component has a unique starting point. All components set by the environment have an arbitrary value. All local variables of type τ up to generics are initialized with d_τ^0. For the type $\underline{prvw}_\tau$ of projected waveforms taking values in D_τ this is the *empty list*. The valuation of outports is given by the init function in the entity declaration. We use σ_Σ as typical element of $\Sigma(\underline{des})$.

Formally, we define the set of *initial states* of the transition system associated with $\underline{des}$, $\Sigma(\underline{des})_0$, by

$$\Sigma(\underline{des})_0 = \Big\{ \langle start, \langle \langle \textbf{false} \rangle, env \rangle, inp, \sigma, out \rangle \in \Sigma(\underline{des}) \,\Big|\, \\ (\forall v \in VVar_\tau \setminus V_{gen} : \sigma(v) = d_\tau^0) \quad \wedge \\ (\forall v \in V_{gen} : \sigma(v) = genval(v)) \quad \wedge \\ (\forall o \in O : out(o) = [\![init(o)]\!]\sigma) \Big\}$$

We now consider a *behavioural* design and assume that each statement owns a unique label. Assuming n labels (identified with natural numbers) and 1 to be the label of the body of the process, we let $control(\underline{des}) = \{1, \ldots, n\}$ and $start = 1$. The *transition-relation* is defined by inspecting the control information to find the statement to be executed and update the local state and output evaluation according to the statement and advancing the "program counter" according to the VHDL code. We omit the trivial inductive definition of a function $next(\underline{des})$, which gives the label of the successor statement in lists of sequential statements. The cyclic behaviour of processes is captured by setting the next-pointer of leaves of the VHDL code (viewed as its syntax-tree) to the **start**-label.

The following examples illustrate the definition of the transition relation $\longrightarrow_{\underline{des}}$. The rules follow the standard pattern of structural operational semantics [64]. The allowed transitions are exactly those generated by the rules for all sequential statements:

- *signal assignment statements*:
  if $stat(j) = "s <= \textbf{transport } e_\tau \textbf{ after } e_{time}"$ then
  $$\langle j, ss, inp, \sigma, out \rangle \longrightarrow_{\underline{des}} \langle next(\underline{des})(j), ss, inp, \\ [\![s <= \textbf{transport } e_\tau \textbf{ after } e_{time}]\!]inp\,\sigma, out \rangle$$

- *if statement*:
  if $stat(j) = "\textbf{if } e \textbf{ then } j_{true} : S_1 \textbf{ else } j_{false} : S_2 \textbf{ fi}"$ then
  $$\langle j, ss, inp, \sigma, out \rangle \longrightarrow_{\underline{des}} \langle j_{[\![e]\!]_{inp\,\sigma}}, ss, inp, \sigma, out \rangle$$

It is a standard exercise to give the remaining rules for loop-, case-, assert- and variable assignment statements in a similar fashion. The remaining typical VHDL construct, the wait-statement, is covered in the next subsection.

We close this section by introducing $TS(ed)$ as notation for the class of transition systems belonging to a design entity with entity declaration ed.

3.3 The wait statement

We now turn to the wait statement. In VHDL's simulation semantics, the wait statement captures four key ingredients:

1. Wait statements constitute synchronization barriers which can only be passed if **all** processes in the design have arrived with their control at a wait statement; in particular, if **one** process runs into an infinite loop not containing a wait statement then the complete system diverges.
2. It is only when executing wait statements that simulation time increases.
3. It is only when executing wait statements that the effect of signal assignments becomes visible as a change of the value of an outport.
4. The design entities control may only pass the wait statement if the specified conditions (timeout, signal-changes of signals specified in **on**-clauses, or conditions to be awaited as specified in **until**-clauses) is satisfied.

To handle 1 in a compositional fashion, we have introduced the boolean shadow variable $ENV'at\_wait$. If it is set, then at least the environment is willing to engage in a synchronization. If additionally also the considered design entity's control component points to a wait statement, then synchronization takes place and aspects 2 and 3 are addressed.

Now suppose that a synchronization takes place. How do we determine the increase in simulation time? In principle, global time is advanced to the next point in time with a pending event. The maximal possible advance of time allowed by the *environment* is represented in the integer-valued shadow-variable $ENV'delay$. The maximal increase in simulation time allowed by the design entity under consideration is computed by consulting its projected waveforms as well as an auxiliary variable *timeout* used to handle wait statements with a timeout condition. Note that *advancing time* not only updates the auxiliary variable *now* (keeping track of the current simulation time), but also the delay components of all projected waveforms and *timeout*. Since these keep track of the time still to wait[6], they have to

---

[6] We choose in the semantics to work with relative time components in projected waveforms to ensure a finite representation when all delay expression are compile-time computable. In [48], time components contain the point in simulation time when events are expected to become visible.

be decremented by the amount time gets advanced. Note that this amount is determined in such a way that no negative delay components appear. Indeed, we have to ensure that no event is simply "forgotten" because no one cared to look for it. Similarly, *timeout* is decremented according to the number of elapsed time units.

Once delay components in projected waveforms are decremented, we can check what events are to become visible *now*: these are exactly those whose delay component is now zero. For all those events, the following actions have to carried out:

- The valuation of the corresponding outports is updated with the value component of the visible event. This corresponds in language like CSP to sending a message over a channel, updating all inports attached (in a structural body via some signal) to this outport. In our transition system this is reflected by allowing the valuation of inports to change. Since the environment of the module and thus the new values of inports are not known, they change to an arbitrary value.

- Prior to this message exchange we save the old values of signals in the corresponding *last_value* shadow variable.

Finally we check whether the process's control will have to stay at this wait statement or is allowed to proceed to the next instruction. For timeout conditions, this is a simple check as to whether the timeout variable has now become zero. For sensitivity lists, we compare all listed signals with their *last-value*. If for at least one we observe a change, the process is allowed to proceed. For until conditions, we check whether at least one signal occurring in the condition has changed its value. If so, we check for the validity of the until condition. If this has become valid, the process is allowed to proceed. Until conditions thus carry an implicit oncondition. To simplify the exposition of the semantics, we require this to be explicit; thus all waits with an until-clause must have an on-clause listing all signals occurring in the until condition. To handle these uniformly, we consider all waits with only on-clauses to be extended with a until clause with wait condition **true**, reducing the variants of the wait to three cases. In case the wait possesses both a timeout clause and an on- and untilclause, satisfaction of either condition allows the process to pass the wait statement.

There is a peculiar situation easily overlooked for wait statements with an on-clause and an *empty* sensitivity list. VHDL requires at *least one* signal in the sensitivity list to have changed; if there is none, the passcondition will never be satisfied. This entails that the innocent looking statement **wait until true** will cause the process to suspend forever: an implicit on-clause with an empty sensitivity list is added. By the same token, wait conditions which do not depend on a signal will cause the process to suspend forever, unless an on-condition with non-empty sensitivity list or a timeout clause saves it from this boring situation.

We now turn this informal discussion of the semantics of the wait statement into a formal semantics. To this end we derive, for each of the four stages, auxiliary functions and state-transformations carrying out the desired computations and then combine all these to formally define the transition-relation induced by the wait statement. All this is a rather straightforward exercise in denotational semantics.

We first handle the computation of the maximal possible advancement of time as viewed by the design entity. To this end, we define a function *delay* from state-valuations to integers:

$$delay : states(VVar) \longrightarrow \mathbf{N}$$

is given by

$$delay(\sigma) = \min(\sigma(timeout), \min\{e.del \mid e \in \sigma(s_{wv}) \land s \in O\})$$

The validity of this definition hinges on the stipulation that the newly introduced variable timeout ranges over the integers extended with infinity, and that *timeout* is initialized with ∞, the default value for this type. All integer-operations are extended strictly to this domain (e.g. $\infty - n = \infty$ for all integers n). This value gets overwritten whenever a wait with timeout-clause is evaluated by the value of its time-expression.

Now that we have determined the local increase in time, we formalize the side effects resulting from updating time with this amount. This affects the global simulation time, the variable *timeout*, and all delay components of all projected waveforms. For the latter objects we define an auxiliary function *countdown*, decrementing all delay components by a specified amount:

$$countdown : \underline{prvw} \times \mathbf{N} \longrightarrow \underline{prwv}$$

$$countdown(\mathbf{nil}, n) = \mathbf{nil}$$
$$countdown(\langle d, t \rangle :: pw, n) = \langle d, t - n \rangle :: countdown(pw, n)$$

All side effects from advancing time are captured in the function

$$advance : \mathbf{N} \longrightarrow states(VVar) \longrightarrow states(VVar)$$

$$advance(n)(\sigma) = \sigma'$$

where

$$\begin{aligned}
\sigma'(now) &= \sigma(now) + n \\
\sigma'(timeout) &= \sigma(timeout) - n \\
\sigma'(s_{wv}) &= countdown(\sigma(s_{wv}), n) \quad \text{for all } s \in O \\
\sigma'(v) &= \sigma(v) \quad \text{otherwise.}
\end{aligned}$$

Specification and verification of VHDL-based Hardware Designs

We now "program" the update of signals. Given a state of the transition system, we copy all current values of inports and those outport values which are about to change into the corresponding *last-value* variable while concurrently deleting the visible events from the projected waveforms and updating the outports. To manipulate projected waveforms, we define an auxiliary function *active* which checks whether a projected waveform has a visible event. For active waveforms, we use the function *get_new_value* to pick out the value component of the visible event and to delete the event from the projected waveform:

$$active: \underline{prwv} \longrightarrow \mathbf{B}$$

$$active(\mathbf{nil}) = \mathbf{false}$$
$$active(\langle d, t \rangle :: pw) = t = 0 \text{ or } active(pw)$$

$$get\_new\_value: \underline{prwv} \longrightarrow D \times \underline{prwv}$$

$$get\_new\_value(\mathbf{nil}) = \langle d^0, \mathbf{nil} \rangle$$
$$get\_new\_value(\langle d, t \rangle :: pw) = \begin{cases} \langle d, pw \rangle & \text{if } t = 0 \\ get\_new\_value(pw) & \text{otherwise.} \end{cases}$$

Note that VHDL's timing model guarantees that each projected waveform contains at most one event with zero delay component.

All activities related to updating signals are combined into

$$update\_signals : inputs(I) \times states(VVar) \times outputs(O)$$
$$\longrightarrow states(VVar) \times outputs(O)$$

$$update\_signals(\langle inp, \sigma, out \rangle) = \langle \sigma', out' \rangle$$

where

$$out'(o) = \begin{cases} get\_new\_value(\sigma(o_{wv})).val & \text{if } active(\sigma(o_{wv})) \\ out(o) & \text{otherwise} \end{cases}$$
$$\text{for all } o \in O$$

$$\sigma'(i'last\_value) = inp(i) \quad \text{for all } i \in I$$

$$\sigma'(o'last\_value) = \begin{cases} out(o) & \text{if } active(\sigma(o_{wv})) \\ \sigma(o'last\_value) & \text{otherwise} \end{cases}$$
$$\text{for all } o \in O$$

$$\sigma'(o_{wv}) = \begin{cases} get\_new\_value(\sigma(o_{wv})).pw & \text{if } active(\sigma(o_{wv})) \\ \sigma'(o_{wv}) & \text{otherwise} \end{cases}$$
$$\text{for all } o \in O$$

$$\sigma'(v) = \sigma(v) \quad \text{otherwise.}$$

We now embed these computations into the transition relation. Each wait statement first passes through a prelude, which establishes the willingness to synchronize and computes the local delay. The subsequent step is only possible if the environment is also willing to synchronize. It is then that the advance in time is negotiated and performed and signals are exchanged as well as conditions for passing the wait being evaluated:

- *the prelude step*
  if $stat(j) = $ "**wait** ... " then

$$\langle j, \langle mod, env \rangle, inp, \sigma, out \rangle \longrightarrow_{des}$$
$$\langle j, \langle \mathbf{true}, delay(\sigma) \rangle, env' \rangle, inp, \sigma, out \rangle$$

Note that we provide room for the environment to update its synchronization status by not restricting env'. Now consider a wait statement

$$\textbf{wait for } e_{time}.$$

To check for the timeout condition, we initialize *timeout* with the value of the timeout expression. Now consider the situation, where several synchronizations take place while the process waits for the timeout event to happen. Clearly we don't want to reinitialize the counter *timeout* at every synchronization. In order to avoid introducing yet another control-state in our transition system, we "precompile" our VHDL code by introducing a variable assignment

$$timeout := e_{time};$$

prior to each such wait statement. Its evaluation will cause the counter to be initialized. Once control reaches the wait statement, we only have to check for the timeout event to happen.

A final trick helps to reduce the remaining three variants of the wait statement to one form: by extending VHDL's time expressions with the constant **ever** (interpreted by ∞), we can add to each wait statement without timeout clause the timeout clause **for ever**. The generic form of the wait statement is thus given by

$$\textbf{wait for } e_{time} \textbf{ on } sensitivity\_set \textbf{ until } e_{bool}.$$

In the subsequent rule, inports may change arbitrarily, since each module may potentially update its outports. The new state is computed by first advancing time with the minimum of the delays tolerable by the module itself and the environment and then performing side-effects in connection with the update of signals. This new state is then used to evaluate whether control can pass the wait statement. If the condition to pass the wait is satisfied, the module withdraws its willingness to engage in synchronization. Otherwise, the module retains its willingness to engage in synchronization and only updates its delay component. Accordingly, the environment part of the synchronization status may change:

- the *wait-step*:
  if $stat(j) = $ "**wait for** e_{time} **on** $sensitivity\_set$ **until** e_{bool}" then

$$\langle j, \langle \langle \mathbf{true}, n \rangle, \langle \mathbf{true}, m \rangle \rangle, inp, \sigma, out \rangle \longrightarrow_{des} \langle k, \langle mod, env \rangle, inp', \sigma', out' \rangle$$

where
  * $\sigma' = update\_signals(inp, advance(\min(n,m))(\sigma), out).state$
  * $out' = update\_signals(inp, advance(\min(n,m))(\sigma), out).out$
  * $k = next(\underline{des})(j)$ and $mod = \langle \mathbf{false}, n \rangle$ if
       $[\![e_{time}]\!]\, inp'\, \sigma' = 0$
    or $\exists s \in sensitivity\_set:$
       $inp'(s) \neq \sigma'(s'last\_value) \land [\![e_{bool}]\!]\, inp'\, \sigma'$
    $k = j$ and $mod = \langle \mathbf{true}, delay(\sigma') \rangle$ otherwise.

3.4 Structural design entities and configurations

Structural bodies in VHDL can intuitively be viewed as non-packed PCBs: all information regarding component types, placement of component instances, and their interconnection are known; all that remains to be done to complete the design is to mount the ICs. In our context, configuration specifications will tell what design entity to bind to what component instance. Once such a configuration specification is given, we can compute inductively for each design entity the associated transition system. Hence the semantics of a structural body must be an operator on transition systems, telling how to combine transition systems representing the semantics of component instances into a transition system representing the configured structural body.

For the remainder of this section, we assume a fixed structural body

$$sb = \langle ed, \|_{sig,vis}(id_1 : C_1, \ldots, id_n : C_n), gmap, \underline{res} \rangle \in \underline{SB(ed)}$$

After configuring the design and generating transition systems representing the semantics of component instances, we will be in a situation where we have transition systems

$$T_1, \ldots, T_n$$

matching entity declarations $comp(sb)(id_j)$. We will define the parallel composition operator

$$\|_{sig,\underline{vis},\underline{res},\underline{gmap}}: TS(comp(sb)(id_1)) \times \cdots \times TS(comp(sb)(id_n)) \longrightarrow TS(ed)$$

by defining the transition system

$$T = \|_{sig,\underline{vis},\underline{res},\underline{gmap}}(T_1, \ldots, T_n) = (\Sigma, \rightarrow, \Sigma_0).$$

We first discuss informally how to construct T. As a first approximation, T has n parallel components, which are allowed to run independently, operating on their own state space, as long as no synchronization is required. In well behaved VHDL code, all parallel components will eventually arrive at a state whose local component of the synch-state indicates its willingness to engage in synchronization. It is at such states where the *guessed* environment components in the T_i's have to match the information generated by the now known part of the environment. Let us elaborate on this point, taking the perspective of some fixed T_i. For T_i, the environment consists of the other parallel components T_j and the environment of sb.

Consider first the environment component of T_i's synch-state. T_i's environment is willing to synchronize iff all T_j are willing to synchronize and sb's environment is willing to synchronize. We can formalize this as an invariance condition for T_i's $ENV'at\_wait$ flag: it must always be the conjunction of the T_j's at_wait flags and the $ENV'at\_wait$ flag for sb's environment.

A similar invariant condition holds for the environment-delay component in T_i's synch-state. Here the maximal allowed time increases possible for the T_j's as well as for the environment of sb have to be taken into account. Of all the possible runs for T_i, in the given context only those will be possible where the environment delay component was *guessed* "correctly" to be the minimum of the delays allowed by the T_j's and by sb's environment.

We now pick up the last guessed component of T_i's state, the valuation of inports. Again, T_i provides runs for all possible valuations of inports, out of which the given context will only allow that subset where the assumed input matches the value of the signal to which the input is connected. This value, in turn, is determined by the *outport(s)* driving the signal or, if the signal is open, by the environment of sb. In case the signal is multiple-driven, s' resolution function has to be consulted to determine the value of s from the value of its drivers. This again can be formalized as an invariant condition of the corresponding objects.

Before entering the formal treatment, a word about generics. As discussed in Section 3.2 of this chapter, T_i's transition-relation (and states) is actually parameterized w.r.t. a given valuation of the generics occurring in its entity declaration. sb now determines the value of generics for its component instances in terms of the generics in ed's entity declaration. Assuming their valuation to be given (as an implicit parameter in the construction of T), we can determine the "version" of T_i we need: it is with respect to that valuation of T_i's generics, which can be computed by evaluating the expression provided by *gmap* for each generic w.r.t. the given valuation for sb's generics.

As usual, to run components in parallel we essentially want T's states to be the cross-product of the states of the T_i's. Since transition systems derived from VHDL designs have a structured state space, a bit more work is required. Let us pick up the components of the state space one at a time and in doing so define Σ formally. Let $T_i = (\Sigma_i, \rightarrow_i, \Sigma_{i,0})$, and let $ed = (I, O, V_{gen}, init)$.

control This part is simple and indeed the cross-product of the control components of the T_is:

$$\Sigma.control := \Sigma_1.control \times \cdots \times \Sigma_n.control$$

Control is initialized with $start := (start_1, \ldots, start_n)$.

SYNCH_STATE is a predefined component of T. We will represent the component's synch-state within the valuations of variables, by turning them into local variables of sb.

inputs(I) is again predefined from sb's entity declaration.

outputs(O) is again predefined from sb's entity declaration. We will represent the component's outports as *local* variables of sb.

states(VVar) This is determined by the definition of the set V of local variables of sb.

Recall that different component instances may be configured to the same design entity; thus the component transition systems might operate on common variables. To ensure the intended invisibility of local variables w.r.t. other design entities we rename all local variables by prefixing them with the (unique!) label of the component instance. Note that this includes all timeouts, projected waveforms and last-value variables. The only exception is the variable *now* keeping track of global time; clearly one version of *now* suffices to do so.

In order to be able to construct a state of a component system from a global state, we include as well outports and local synch-state information of the components as local variables. Note that due to resolution functions it is in general **not** possible to reconstruct the value of a component outport from the value of an attached signal. The local synch-state information could be recovered from the embedded projected waveforms and timeout variables; here it is only a matter of technical convenience to retain these as local variables of sb.

This set is extended by including sb's signals as local variables. Indeed, also for structural bodies only ports of the entity declaration are visible; hence signals one wants to observe have to be explicitly connected to ports (using *vis*). A question requiring a bit more reflection relates to the auxiliary variables for signals: do or do we not need last-values and projected waveforms for sb's signals? Given the strict separation of behaviour and structure enforced in this chapter, the answer is "no": only the sequential processes resulting from elaboration retain drivers and last values, since the values of signals are determined uniquely from these projected waveforms (and resolution functions) and sensitivity on signals is only tested within the sequential processes. Once we ensure that signal values are propagated down through all levels of the structural hierarchy to the appropriate ports of sequential processes, we can safely do sensitivity tests using the last values for these ports only.

We cast this into the following formal definition of the set V of sb's *local variables*:

$$\begin{aligned} V \quad := \quad & \{ \langle id_i, v \rangle \mid 1 \leq i \leq n \wedge v \in var(T_i) \backslash \{now\} \} \\ \cup \ & range(\underline{sig}) \\ \cup \ & \{ \langle id_i, o \rangle \mid 1 \leq i \leq n \wedge o \in outports(T_i) \} \\ \cup \ & \{ \langle id_i, at\_wait \rangle, \langle id_i, delay \rangle \} \\ \cup \ & \{ p'last\_value \mid p \in ports(sb) \} \end{aligned}$$

We now collect the invariants relating the different components of the state space. Rather than expressing the invariance properties semantically, we collect them in a first-order formula Φ_{sb} for later reuse in developing the proof-theory for VHDL, anticipating from the next chapter the standard notion $\sigma_\Sigma \models \Phi_{sb}$ of validity of a formula w.r.t. a valuation of its free variables. Note that this formula also "sees" local variables of sb in order to be able to express the invariants:

$$\Phi_{sb} \equiv \Phi_{wait} \wedge \Phi_{delay} \wedge \Phi_{sig} \wedge \Phi_{vis}$$

where

- $\Phi_{wait} \equiv at\_wait \leftrightarrow \bigwedge \{ id_i'at\_wait \mid 1 \leq i \leq n \}$
  sb is willing to engage in a synchronization iff all its component instances are willing to do so;
- $\Phi_{delay} \equiv delay = \min\{ id_i'delay \mid 1 \leq i \leq n \}$
  the maximal time increase allowed by sb is determined from the maximal time increase allowed by the component instances;
- $\Phi_{sig} \equiv \Phi_{open} \wedge \Phi_{single\_driven} \wedge \Phi_{multiple\_driven}$ where
  * $\Phi_{open} \equiv \bigwedge \{ s = i \mid s \text{ is open and } \underline{vis}(s) = i \}$
    the value of an open signal is determined by the value of its associated inport;
  * $\Phi_{single\_driven} \equiv \bigwedge \{ s = id_i'o \mid \underline{sig}^{-1}(s) = id_i'o \}$
    the value of a single driven signal is determined by the value of its driving outport;
  * $\Phi_{multiple\_driven} \equiv \bigwedge \{ s = \underline{res}(s)(id_{i_1}'o_1, \ldots, id_{i_r}'o_r) \mid \underline{sig}^{-1}(s) = \{id_{i_1}'o_1, \ldots, id_{i_r}'o_r\} \text{ and } r > 1 \}$
    the value of a multiple driven signal is determined by applying its resolution function to the driving outports;

- $\Phi_{vis} \equiv \bigwedge \{ s = o \mid \underline{vis}(s) = o \in O \}$
  the value of sb's outports is determined by its corresponding signal.

In the following we fix a valuation $genval$ of sb's generics. The valuation $id_i.genval$ of generics of component instances is determined by the valuation of sb's generics by

$$id_i.genval(id_i, v) = [\![gmap(id_i, v)]\!] \, genval.$$

We are now in a position to define the set of *initial states* of sb's transition system:

$$\begin{aligned}
\Sigma_0 = \{ \, \sigma_\Sigma = \langle start, ss, inp, \sigma, out \rangle \in \Sigma \mid \\
(\forall v \in V_{gen}: \sigma(v) = genval(v)) \land \\
(\forall o \in O: out(o) = [\![init(o)]\!]\sigma) \land \\
(\forall v \in generics(comp(id_i)): \sigma(id_i, v) = id_i.genval(id_i, v)) \land \\
\sigma(now) = 0 \land \sigma_\Sigma \models \Phi_{sb} \quad \}
\end{aligned}$$

Note that the set of initial states is empty if the initial valuation of an outport of sb is not compatible with the initial valuation of component outports driving via some signal (and resolution function) this outport.

To determine sb's transition relation, we have to be able to let a component of sb "run" on "its part" of sb's state. Because of the structure of the state-space, we need a little bit of work to determine the *projection of sb's state* onto the state-space of a component. The following definition of such a projection function constructs the environment components of the local transition system taking into account the now known part of its environment. It is at this point where out of the set of all possible runs of the component transition system we pick those runs which match the known parts of the environment:

$$proj_r : \Sigma \longrightarrow \Sigma_r$$

$$proj_r(\langle \langle c_1, \ldots, c_n \rangle, \langle mod, \langle b, t \rangle \rangle, inp, \sigma, out \rangle) = \\
\langle c_r, \langle mod', env' \rangle, inp', \sigma', out' \rangle$$

where

- $mod' = \langle \sigma(\langle id_r, at\_wait \rangle), \sigma(\langle id_r, delay \rangle) \rangle$
- $env'.at\_wait = \mathbf{true}$ iff $b = \mathbf{true}$
  and for all $1 \leq j \leq n$ with $r \neq j$ $\sigma(\langle id_j, at\_wait \rangle) = \mathbf{true}$
- $env'.delay = \min(t, \min\{\sigma(\langle id_j, delay \rangle) \mid 1 \leq j \leq n \land r \neq j\})$
- $inp'(i) = \sigma(\underline{sig}(\langle id_r, i \rangle))$ for all $i \in inports(comp(sb)(id_r))$
- $\sigma'(v) = \sigma(\langle id_r, v \rangle)$ for all local variables of T_r
- $\sigma'(now) = \sigma(now)$
- $out'(o) = \sigma(\langle id_r, o \rangle)$ for all $i \in inports(comp(sb)(id_r))$

Transitions of sb consist of *synchronization steps* taken jointly by all components if both sb and sb's environment are willing to synchronize, and *local steps*, which are only allowed when a component has not arrived at the synchronization barrier. Since local steps of components are completely independent (recall that they work on independent parts of the state-space), their execution can be carried out in an *arbitrary* order, e.g. by running first the first component, then the second, etc. In this semantics, we take an *interleaving approach*.

The definition of the *local* part is straightforward: project the global state onto the state of a component, let it run one step, and lift the result back into the global state. In doing so, we have to possibly update sb's synch-state component. When taking a synchronization step, we also have to guarantee the subformulae of Φ_{sb} relating to signals:

$$\sigma_\Sigma = \langle \langle c_1, \ldots, c_n \rangle, \langle \langle b, t \rangle, env \rangle, inp, \sigma, out \rangle \longrightarrow$$
$$\langle \langle c'_1, \ldots, c'_n \rangle, \langle \langle b', t' \rangle, env' \rangle, inp', \sigma', out' \rangle = \sigma'_\Sigma$$

iff

- *synchronization step*:
  $b = $ **true** and $env.at_wait = $ **true** $\wedge$
  $\forall\, 1 \leq r \leq n : \exists \sigma_{\Sigma,r} \in \Sigma_r$: such that the following properties hold:
  1. $proj_r(\sigma_\Sigma) \longrightarrow_r \sigma_{\Sigma,r}$
  2. $proj_r(\sigma'_\Sigma) = \sigma_{\Sigma,r}$
  3. $\sigma'(s) = \sigma_{\Sigma,r}.state(o)$ if s is single driven from $\langle id_r, o \rangle$
  4. $\sigma'(s) = [\![res(s)]\!]\ \sigma[\langle id_{r,j}, o_j \rangle / \sigma_{\Sigma,r,j}.state(o_j)\ |$
                           $\langle id_{r,j}, o_j \rangle \in \underline{sig}^{-1}(s)]$ if s is multiple-driven
  5. $\sigma'(s) = inp'(s)$ if s is open
  6. $out'(o) = \sigma'(s)$ if $o = \underline{vis}(s)$
  7. $b' = \bigwedge \{ \sigma_{\Sigma,r}.ss.mod.at\_wait\,|\,1 \leq r \leq n \}$
  8. $t' = \min \{ \sigma_{\Sigma,r}.ss.mod.delay\,|\,1 \leq r \leq n \}$
  9. $\sigma'(now) = \sigma(now) + \min(t, env.delay)$
  10. $\sigma'(i'last\_value) = inp(i)$ for all $i \in inports(sb)$
  11. $\sigma'(o'last\_value) = out(o)$ for all $o \in outports(sb)$

or

- *local step* (possibly combined with an environment step):
  $b = $ **false** $\wedge$
  $\exists\, 1 \leq r \leq n : \exists\, \sigma_{\Sigma,r} \in \Sigma_r$: such that the following properties hold:
  1'. $proj_r(\sigma_\Sigma) \longrightarrow \sigma_{\Sigma,r}$
  2'. $proj_r(\sigma'_\Sigma) = \sigma_{\Sigma,r}$
  3'. $proj_r(\sigma_\Sigma).ss.mod.at_wait = $ **false**
  4'. $b' = \bigwedge \{ \sigma_{\Sigma,r}.ss.mod.at\_wait\,|\,1 \leq r \leq n \}$
  5'. $t' = \min \{ \sigma_{\Sigma,r}.ss.mod.delay\,|\,1 \leq r \leq n \}$

or

- *environment step*:
  $b = \textbf{true}$ and $env.at\_wait = \textbf{false} \land$
  1". $inp' = inp$
  2". $\sigma' = \sigma$
  3". $out' = out$
  4". $\langle b', t' \rangle = \langle b, t \rangle$
  5". $\langle c'_1, \ldots, c'_n \rangle = \langle c_1, \ldots, c_n \rangle$

In the *synchronization step* (1) and (2) together assure that the global computation step corresponds to a parallel execution of a synchronization step in each component. In particular, (2) ensures that the *correct guess* of the otherwise unrestricted *inp*- and *env*-components is assumed in the successor state of the local computations. It is through this condition and (5) that signal changes of *sb*'s environment are propagated to become signal changes in the component's inports. (3) and (4) guarantee propagation of driver values up to the level of signals. Again by condition (2) they are propagated down to those inports of components, which are connected to the driven signal. Condition (6) propagates the produced valuation of visible signals to the corresponding outport. (2) also guarantees that new valuations of the component's outports, local variables, and local synch-control are correctly represented in the global successor state. Clauses (7) and (8) guarantee the invariants for *wait* and *delay*. Clause (9) guarantees that global time is advanced correctly. Note that condition (1) and the delay invariant together guarantee that all components will advance time with the same amount, entailing that the evaluation of *now* in *any* of the local successor states yields the value enforced in clause (9). The last clauses simply remember the last value of *sb*'s ports in the corresponding local variables.

A *local step* is only possible if there exists a component which is not yet willing to synchronize (captured by (3')). The interleaving semantics allows any such component to take a step. Again the first two conditions ensure that the local step is lifted to the global level; (2') guarantees that all values of local variables are correctly reflected in the successor state of *sb*'s transition system. Note that neither outports nor inports of the component nor global time will change in such a local step; hence clauses (3)—(6) and (9) have no counterpart in a local step. However, local computation may *enter* a wait-state (through a *prelude step*). If so, the willingness to engage in synchronization as well as the new tolerated increase in global time must be propagated, as done by clauses (4') resp. (5').

It is a trivial consequence of the above construction that *sb*'s transition relation takes states satisfying *sb*'s invariant into states again satisfying the formula. Since initial states satisfy Φ_{sb} by definition, it is thus justified to employ the term "invariant" for Φ_{sb}.

Lemma 3.2

$$\forall \sigma_\Sigma \in \Sigma: \ \sigma_\Sigma \models \Phi_{sb} \land \sigma_\Sigma \rightarrow \sigma'_\Sigma \ \text{implies} \ \sigma'_\Sigma \models \Phi_{sb}$$

Having completed the definition of the parallel composition operator for transition systems, it is now straightforward to extend the semantics to all VHDL designs. We define by induction on the depth of a VHDL design the transition system inducing its observational semantics.

Definition 3.3 (transition system semantics of VHDL designs)

1. Let sb be as above. The semantics of sb is defined to be

$$[\![sb]\!] := \|_{sig,vis,res,gmap} : \\ TS(comp(sb)(id_1)) \times \cdots \times TS(comp(sb)(id_n)) \longrightarrow TS(ed)$$

2. Let $\underline{des} = \langle ed, ab, \langle \underline{ed}, \underline{ab} \rangle \rangle$ be a VHDL design.
   We define the transition system semantics of $\underline{des}$, $\mathcal{T}[\![\underline{des}]\!]$ by induction on the depth of $\underline{des}$:
   - If $\underline{depth}(\underline{des}) = 0$, then $ab \in \underline{BB}(ed)$ and $\mathcal{T}[\![\underline{des}]\!] := \mathcal{T}[\![ab]\!]$ as defined in Section 3.2.
   - If $\underline{depth}(\underline{des}) > 0$, then $ab = sb \in \underline{SB}(ed)$.
     Let $sb = \langle ed, \|_{sig,vis}(id_1 : C_1, \ldots, id_n : C_n), gmap, res \rangle$.
     Then both $\underline{ab}(sb, id, C)$ and $\underline{ed}(sb, id, C)$ are defined for all component instances occurring in sb. By induction we can construct

$$T_j \ = \ \mathcal{T}[\![\langle \underline{ed}(sb, id_j, C_j), \underline{ab}(sb, id_j, C_j), \langle \underline{ed}, \underline{ab} \rangle \rangle]\!]$$

We define the transition system semantics of des, $\mathcal{T}[\![\underline{des}]\!]$, by

$$\mathcal{T}[\![\underline{des}]\!] \ = \ [\![sb]\!](T_1, \ldots, T_n).$$

We close this section by defining the observational semantics of VHDL designs. At this point we simply hide all information in runs not pertinent to our set of observables.

Recall that it is the entity declaration of a design which determines the degree of observability by defining its ports: VHDL allows us to observe the *current* and the *last* value of a port (and thus whether the port has changed its value), whether the design entity is willing to engage in a synchronization (i.e. whether control has reached a wait statement), and the current simulation time. Now consider an run w of $\mathcal{T}[\![\underline{des}]\!]$. Each element of this infinite sequence gives the complete information of the current state of $\mathcal{T}[\![\underline{des}]\!]$. We project this to retain only the current value of the following entities:

- I the valuation of all inports
- Ilv the "last" valuation of all inport (i.e. the valuation at the last synchronization point)

Specification and verification of VHDL-based Hardware Designs 371

- O the valuation of all outports
- Olv the last valuation of all outports
- now the global time
- at_wait the design entity is willing to engage in a synchronization (i.e. its control points to a wait statement)
- $delay$ at synchronization points the maximal advance in time possible for the design entity
- $ENV'\,at\_wait$ the environment of the design entity is willing to engage in a synchronization
- $ENV'\,delay$ at synchronization points the maximal advance in time possible for the environment

Let $Observables(\underline{des})$ denote the union of these sets.

The only possibility for a run of a transition system induced from VHDL designs to get stuck is at synchronization points. In the observational semantics we simply extend such stuck computations to infinite computations by iterating the last valuation. Since wait-states are observable, we can still exclude stuck computations by e.g. requiring at_wait to become true infinitely often.

Formally, an *observation* of $\underline{des}$ is an infinite sequence π of valuations of observables s.t. there exists a run w of the transition system associated with $\underline{des}$ whose projection after extending it to an infinite sequence w_∞ yields π. The *observation semantics* of $\underline{des}$, $[\![\underline{des}]\!]$, is the set of all such observations.

Definition 3.4

1. For $w \in \underline{run}(\mathcal{T}[\![\underline{des}]\!])$, we define its infinite extension w_∞ by

$$w_\infty := \begin{cases} w \cdot w(n)^\infty & \text{if } |w| = n \in \mathbf{N} \\ w & \text{otherwise} \end{cases}$$

2. The observation semantics *of $\underline{des}$ is defined by*

$$[\![\underline{des}]\!] = \{\, \pi : \mathbf{N} \longrightarrow (Observables(\underline{des}) \to D) \mid$$
$$\exists\, w \in \underline{run}(\mathcal{T}[\![\underline{des}]\!])\ \forall\, n \in \mathbf{N}$$

- $\pi(n)(i) = w_\infty(n).inp(i)$
  for all $i \in inports(\underline{des})$
- $\pi(n)(i'last\_value) = w_\infty(n).state(i'last\_value)$
  for all $i \in inports(\underline{des})$
- $\pi(n)(o) = w_\infty(n).out(o)$
  for all $o \in outports(\underline{des})$
- $\pi(n)(o'last\_value) = w_\infty(n).state(i'last\_value)$
  for all $o \in outports(\underline{des})$
- $\pi(n)(now) = w_\infty(n).state(now)$
- $\pi(n)(at\_wait) = w_\infty(n).ss.mod.at\_wait$

- $\pi(n)(delay) = w_\infty(n).ss.mod.delay$
- $\pi(n)(ENV'at\_wait) = w_\infty(n).ss.env.at\_wait$
- $\pi(n)(ENV'delay) = w_\infty(n).ss.env.delay$ }

This completes the formal definition of VHDL's observation semantics. The next section is devoted to the development of a proof-theory allowing us to compositionally verify the correctness of a VHDL design w.r.t. a first-order linear time temporal logic. The logic reduces the correctness of complete designs to that of each basic building blocks, i.e. behavioural designs. If only finite types are employed and all time expressions are computable at elaboration time, the transition system associated with a VHDL design is *finite*; hence in principle their correctness w.r.t. a temporal logic specification can be checked via model-checking [20]. Companion papers [45] discuss how to generate a symbolic transition system out of behavioural design entities, thus providing the link to symbolic model-checking tools. There and in the implementation of this approach within the FORMAT project the translation is factored for complexity reasons into two stages, using *Petri-Nets* as intermediate compilation steps. The implementation also exploits the fact that the resulting transition systems are *input deterministic*, i.e. for each state and each input valuation the successor state is uniquely determined.

4 A correctness logic for VHDL

In this section we introduce the correctness logic used to describe properties of VHDL designs. As the semantics of a hardware system is given by its ongoing behaviour over time we use a first-order temporal logic as specification language. Considering a simple architecture we discuss the ingredients of that logic. The semantics of temporal logic formulae is given in Section 4.1.1. Section 4.1.2 treats some properties concerning the structural composition of architectures and thus prepares the ground for Section 4.2, which gives a proof system to derive a correctness property of a composed architecture from the correctness assertions of its components. In Section 4.3 we apply the proof system to deduce a correctness assertion of the example architecture introduced in Section 2.1.

4.1 Specification language

Properties of a state can be expressed by first-order formulae as usual. These formulae are built up from VHDL expressions over the variables and signals used in the architecture. To illustrate the specification language we consider a 4-bit adder. Its entity declaration is given by

```
entity Adder_4Bit is
   port( in1, in2 : in bit_4; cin : in bit;
         result : out bit_4; cout : out bit);
end Adder_4Bit;
```

To express that an architecture of such an entity declaration implements the addition operation we could specify its behaviour by a formula like

$$cout * 32 + result = in1 + in2 + cin .^7 \qquad (4.1)$$

But the result is usually not available at the same time instant as the inputs are supplied to the component. Hence we use temporal operators to compare different time instants. The $\Diamond$ operator is used to express that a formula is valid sometimes in the future. Furthermore, as the inputs may change in the meantime we have to remember their values in some auxiliary variables. Whereas VHDL variables and signals may change their values along a computation, auxiliary variables are rigid. Hence the specification 4.1 is modified to

$$\Box \, (in1 = y1 \wedge in2 = y2 \wedge cin = y3 \; \Rightarrow$$
$$\Diamond \, (cout * 32 + result = y1 + y2 + y3)) \qquad (4.2)$$

where y_1, y_2, y_3 are rigid variables. The temporal operator $\Box$ is used to indicate that the component should act as an adder *at all time instants*. Delays of hardware components can also be incorporated into the specification. On the one hand we could annotate the temporal operators with delays, e.g.

$$\Diamond_{4ns} \phi$$

to express that ϕ will hold after $4\,ns$. On the other hand we could also use the VHDL time variable **now** to refer to the elapsed time:

$$now = y \; \Rightarrow \; \Diamond \, (now = (y + 4\,ns) \wedge \phi)$$

Progress of a system and of its components is only guaranteed if all processes of a system reach a wait statement[8]. Due to this global synchronization the specification of an adder given above can only be guaranteed provided the environment, in which the adder will be inserted, will not prevent the progress. To describe this dependency of the behaviour of a component from its environment we use an assumption/commitment style for specifications. An assumption/commitment specification is given by a pair of formulae

$$(assm, \; comm)$$

where *assm* describes the expected behaviour of the environment and *comm* denotes the specification of a component provided the environment guarantees *assm*. As progress is only achieved by a global synchronization

---

[7] To be more precise we should convert the bit vectors to integers using a function bit2int: $bit2int(cout) * 32 + bit2int(result) = bit2int(in1) + bit2int(in2) + bit2int(cin)$.

[8] Typically, combinatorial circuits are expressed using concurrent signal assignments. However, elaboration will convert these into processes waiting on changes of the involved signals. The following discussion refers to the elaborated VHDL code.

step which is executed if all processes are at a wait statement, it should be expressible that a component has reached a wait statement. Hence we use the predicates *at_wait*, ENV' *at_wait*, and I' *at_wait* to denote that the component under consideration, its environment, resp. the instance I of a subarchitecture, is at a wait statement. Hence, adding the assumption that the environment will reach a wait statement again and again, the specification 4.2 changes to:

$$(\ \Box \Diamond \text{ENV'} \ at\_wait, \quad \Box \ (in1 = y1 \land in2 = y2 \land cin = y3 \Rightarrow \\ \Diamond \ (cout * 32 + result \ = \ y1 + y2 + y3)) \ ) \quad (4.3)$$

But reaching a synchronization point infinitely often does not guarantee progress of time due to possible delta delays. If e.g. the adder will put the result on the output ports with a delay of 4 ns, but on the other hand the environment will do infinitely many micro-steps, i.e. delta delay steps, time does not proceed. Hence to guarantee progress of time we should be able to refer to the delays of the next scheduled events. Hence we use variables of type Time, *delay*, ENV' *delay*, and I' *delay*, to denote the delay of the next scheduled event of the component under consideration, its environment, resp. the instance I. Adding constraints on delays, the specification (4.3) is changed to:

$$(\ \Box \Diamond \ (\text{ENV'} \ at\_wait \land \text{ENV'} \ delay > 0 \, ns), \\ \Box \ (at\_wait \land (now = y) \land in1 = y1 \land in2 = y2 \land cin = y3 \Rightarrow \\ \Diamond \ (now = y + 4 \, ns) \land (cout * 32 + result \ = \ y1 + y2 + y3)) \ ) \quad (4.4)$$

The assumption that the delay of the next scheduled event of the environment is non-zero again and again ensures that eventually any given amount of time will have elapsed as there is a minimal time unit in VHDL.

After the informal introduction of the specification language we will give now a formal definition of the logic. Besides the VHDL variables *VVar* and signals *Sig* we use a third class of variables in the specification language:

$$y \in Aux = \bigcup_{\tau \in Types} Aux_\tau$$

is the set of *auxiliary* (or *rigid*) variables which are used to freeze some value of a VHDL variable or signal to be able to compare it with some value at another time instant. From a logical point of view the difference between variables and auxiliary variables is that the value of a variable may change along a computation, whereas the value of an auxiliary variable does not change. We use *Var* and *Var*$_\tau$ to denote the union $VVar \cup Aux \cup Sig$ resp. $VVar_\tau \cup Aux_\tau \cup Sig_\tau$.

Specification and verification of VHDL-based Hardware Designs

We extend the class of VHDL expressions by using also auxiliary variables in the construction of expressions. The set of predicates is given by the following rules:

$$p ::= \textbf{true} \mid \textit{at\_wait} \mid \texttt{ENV}\,'\textit{at\_wait} \mid \texttt{<id>}\,'\textit{at\_wait} \mid e_1^\tau = e_2^\tau \mid$$
$$e_{bool} \mid \neg p \mid p_1 \wedge p_2 \mid p_1 \vee p_2$$

The set *Form* of *first order temporal logic formulae* is given by:

$$\begin{array}{lll}
\phi ::= & p & \text{predicate} \\
\mid & \neg \phi & \text{negation} \\
\mid & \phi_1 \wedge \phi_2 & \text{conjunction} \\
\mid & \phi_1 \vee \phi_2 & \text{disjunction} \\
\mid & \Box \phi & \text{always} \\
\mid & \Diamond \phi & \text{sometimes} \\
\mid & [\phi_1 \textbf{ until } \phi_2] & \text{until} \\
\mid & [\phi_1 \textbf{ unless } \phi_2] & \text{unless (weak until)} \\
\mid & \forall y.\phi & \text{universal quantification}
\end{array}$$

Other operators may be introduced as abbreviations, e.g. $\textbf{false} := \neg\textbf{true}$, $\phi_1 \Rightarrow \phi_2 := \neg\phi_1 \vee \phi_2$, and $\textit{changed}(s) := \neg(s = s\,'\textit{last\_value})$, which expresses that the value of the signal s has changed by the last synchronization step.

We use $vvar(\phi)$, $sig(\phi)$, $aux(\phi)$, and $var(\phi)$, to denote the set of VHDL variables resp. signals, auxiliary variables, and the union of all these variables occurring in ϕ.

4.1.1 Semantics of temporal logic formulae

The semantics of a temporal logic formula is given relatively to a given computation sequence which assigns for every time instant i values to all variables and signals. In the framework of VHDL these computation sequences are given by the observations $\pi \in [\![des]\!]$. Furthermore, an assignment of auxiliary variables, which is independent of the current time instant, is needed.

Let $\alpha : \textit{Aux} \to D$ be an assignment which assigns to every auxiliary variable y of type τ an element of D_τ, and let $\pi: \mathbf{N} \to ((\textit{VVar} \cup \textit{Sig}) \to D)$ denote a computation which assigns to every time instant i a valuation of the variables and signals. The evaluation of a predicate p w.r.t. a state $\sigma: (\textit{VVar} \cup \textit{Sig}) \to D$ and an assignment α is denoted by $[\![p]\!]\sigma\alpha$.

A formula ϕ is called *valid* at time instant i w.r.t. π and α, denoted by $(\alpha, \pi, i) \models \phi$, iff

$$\begin{array}{lll}
(\alpha, \pi, i) \models p & \text{iff} & [\![p]\!]\pi(i)\,\alpha = \textbf{true} \\
(\alpha, \pi, i) \models \neg\phi & \text{iff} & \text{not } (\alpha, \pi, i) \models \phi \\
(\alpha, \pi, i) \models \phi_1 \wedge \phi_2 & \text{iff} & (\alpha, \pi, i) \models \phi_1 \text{ and } (\alpha, \pi, i) \models \phi_2
\end{array}$$

$$(\alpha, \pi, i) \models \phi_1 \vee \phi_2 \quad \text{iff} \quad (\alpha, \pi, i) \models \phi_1 \text{ or } (\alpha, \pi, i) \models \phi_2$$

$$(\alpha, \pi, i) \models \Box \phi \quad \text{iff} \quad \text{for all time instants } k \geq i: (\alpha, \pi, k) \models \phi$$

$$(\alpha, \pi, i) \models \Diamond \phi \quad \text{iff} \quad \text{there is some time instant } k \geq i \text{ with } (\alpha, \pi, k) \models \phi$$

$$(\alpha, \pi, i) \models [\phi_1 \text{ until } \phi_2] \quad \text{iff} \quad \text{there is some instant } k \geq i \text{ with } (\alpha, \pi, k) \models \phi_2 \text{ and, for all } j, i \leq j < k: (\alpha, \pi, j) \models \phi_1$$

$$(\alpha, \pi, i) \models [\phi_1 \text{ unless } \phi_2] \quad \text{iff} \quad (\alpha, \pi, i) \models [\phi_1 \text{ until } \phi_2] \text{ or } (\alpha, \pi, i) \models \Box \phi_1$$

$$(\alpha, \pi, i) \models \forall y. \phi \quad \text{iff} \quad \text{for all } d: (\alpha[y/d], \pi, i) \models \phi$$

A formula ϕ is called valid w.r.t. π iff ϕ is valid at instant 0 w.r.t. π and any assignment α (i.e. we assume that all free auxiliary variables are implicitly universally quantified):

$$\pi \models \phi \quad \text{iff} \quad \forall \alpha : (\alpha, \pi, 0) \models \phi$$

A formula ϕ is called a tautology iff it is valid for every computation π. Given a set Π of computations, ϕ is called valid for Π, denoted by $\Pi \models \phi$, iff ϕ is valid for every $\pi \in \Pi$.

The validity of an assumption/commitment specification (*assm, comm*) is defined by:

$$(\alpha, \pi, i) \models (assm, comm) \quad \text{iff} \quad (\alpha, \pi, i) \models assm \Rightarrow comm$$
$$\pi \models (assm, comm) \quad \text{iff} \quad \pi \models assm \Rightarrow comm$$

The validity of a formula ϕ depends only on the variables occurring in it. Given a set V of variables, auxiliary variables, and signals we say that a state σ is equivalent to σ' relative to V, denoted by $\sigma =_V \sigma'$, if for every $v \in V \ \sigma(v) = \sigma'(v)$. Two computations π and π' are equivalent w.r.t. V iff $\pi(i) =_V \pi'(i)$ for every instant i. $\alpha =_V \alpha'$ is defined in a similar way.

If two computations correspond on the variables of a formula ϕ, then both computations cannot be distinguished by the formula.

Lemma 4.1 *Assume that π and π' are two computations with $\pi =_{var(\phi)} \pi'$; then $(\alpha, \pi, i) \models \phi$ iff $(\alpha, \pi', i) \models \phi$.*

Another important property of the semantics of temporal formulae is the fact that it is closed under stuttering, i.e. the semantics of a formula does not change if we duplicate a state or remove a duplicated state.

Lemma 4.2 (stuttering equivalence) *Assume that π is a computation sequence and let $0 = i_0 < i_1 < i_2 < \ldots$ be a sequence of integers such that*

$\forall k \forall j : i_k < j < i_{k+1} : \pi(j) = \pi(i_k)$, and let π' be given by

$$\pi'(k) := \pi(i_k).$$

Then:

1. $(\alpha, \pi, j) \models \phi$ iff $(\alpha, \pi, i_k) \models \phi$ for $i_k < j < i_{k+1}$.
2. $(\alpha, \pi, i_k) \models \phi$ iff $(\alpha, \pi', k) \models \phi$.
3. $\pi \models \phi$ iff $\pi' \models \phi$.

Two computations π and π' are called stuttering equivalent, denoted by $\pi \sim_{st} \pi'$, iff π' is a subsequence of π as defined in Lemma 4.2 or vice versa.

Stuttering is used to introduce idle steps in the computations of a component to reflect the local steps of other components. This can be done w.l.o.g. as observables change their values only during a global synchronization step. But we should not allow stuttering of states at which a synchronization step can be performed. These states are characterized by the fact that both at_wait and ENV' at_wait are true. This information is used to identify the global synchronization points. We have to identify these global synchronization points, as e.g. inputs and $s'last\_value$ only change their values by a synchronization step. Hence, iterating these states would mean iterating the synchronization step, which is inconsistent with the VHDL semantics. Hence we say that π and π' are strong stuttering equivalent, denoted by $\pi \sim_{sst} \pi'$, iff there is a sequence $0 = i_0 < i_1 < i_2 < \ldots$ such that

- $\pi(j) = \pi(i_k)$ for all $i_k < j < i_{k+1}$
- $\pi'(k) = \pi(i_k)$
- if $\pi(i_k)(at\_wait) = \pi(i_k)(\text{ENV'}\ at\_wait) = \mathbf{true}$ then $i_{k+1} = i_k + 1$

resp. vice versa. Observe that the last condition forbids stuttering of global synchronization points.

We use $Cl[\![des]\!]$ to denote the closure of the observable semantics $[\![des]\!]$ under strong stuttering and equivalence w.r.t. $var(des)$:

$$Cl[\![des]\!] := \{\pi \mid \exists \pi' \in [\![des]\!]$$
$$\exists \pi'' \text{ with } \pi' \sim_{sst} \pi'' \text{ and } \pi =_{var(des)} \pi''\}$$

Applying Lemmata 4.1 and 4.2 to the computations of a design we obtain the following property.

Corollary 4.3 *Assume that ϕ is a temporal logic formula with $var(\phi) \setminus Aux \subseteq var(des)$; then*

$$Cl[\![des]\!] \models \phi \quad \text{iff} \quad [\![des]\!] \models \phi$$

Instead of $Cl[\![des]\!] \models \phi$ we also write in the following $des \models \phi$.

4.1.2 Specifications of structural descriptions

We will now investigate how properties of subcomponents are preserved by composition. In the following we assume that $\underline{des} = \langle \underline{ed}, \underline{ab}, \underline{conf} \rangle$ is a given design with

$$ab = sb = \langle \underline{ed}, \|_{\underline{sig},\underline{vis}}(I_1 : C_1, \ldots, I_n : C_n), \underline{gmap}, \underline{res} \rangle$$

and $\underline{conf} = \langle \underline{ed}, \underline{ab} \rangle$. Furthermore, we denote the binding of an instance $I : \overline{C}$ of the given structural description sb to an entity declaration and architecture given by the configuration $\underline{conf}$ by ed_I resp. ab_I, i.e.

$$ed_I := \underline{ed}(sb, I, C)$$
$$ab_I := \underline{ab}(sb, I, C)$$
$$\underline{des}_I := \langle ed_I, ab_I, \underline{conf} \rangle .$$

The instantiation I of the component ab_I in the architecture sb induces a substitution on the variables $var(ab_I)$. Generics are instantiated according to the corresponding generic map $\underline{gmap}$ and ports are connected to some signals according to the port map $\underline{sig}$. These substitutions should be reflected in the specification too, i.e. these renamings should be applied to a specification ϕ of ab_I to derive a specification of the instance I.

Furthermore, a specification of ab_I may contain references to its environment by the variables ENV' at_wait and ENV' $delay$. Embedding a component into a specific structure (environment) we get some information on its environment. The environment of the instance I is given by all other component instances and by the environment of sb. Hence, the environment of I is at a wait statement if all other instances $J \in \{I_1, \ldots, I_n\} \setminus \{I\}$ are at some wait statement and the environment of sb is at a wait statement. Hence the predicate ENV' at_wait in a specification of $\langle ed_I, ab_I, \underline{conf} \rangle$ should be replaced by a conjunction of all the wait predicates of the other components including the environment of sb to obtain a specification of I.

In a similar way we have to express the value of the variable ENV' $delay$ in terms of the delay variables of the components. As this variable denotes the minimal delay of all scheduled events, ENV' $delay$ has to be substituted by the minimum of the delays of the other components. Furthermore, internal variables should be renamed to avoid conflicts with variables of other components (see Section 3.4).

The renaming of variables due to the instantiation I of an architecture ab_I in the structural body sb is reflected by the substitution

$$ren_{I,sb}^{conf} : var(ab_I) \to expr$$

given by:

$$at\_wait \mapsto I'at\_wait$$

$$\text{ENV}\,'at\_wait \mapsto \text{ENV}\,'at\_wait \wedge \bigwedge_{\substack{J \in \{I_1, \ldots, I_n\} \\ J \neq I}} J\,'at\_wait$$

$$delay \mapsto I'delay$$

$$\text{ENV}\,'delay \mapsto \min(\text{ENV}\,'delay, \min_{\substack{J \in \{I_1, \ldots, I_n\} \\ J \neq I}} J'delay)$$

$$x \mapsto \begin{cases} gmap(I, x) & \text{if } x \in generics(ed_I) \\ I.x & \text{otherwise} \end{cases}$$

$$y \mapsto y$$

$$s \mapsto \begin{cases} \underline{sig(I, s)} & \text{if } s \in inports(ed_I) \\ \underline{sig(I, s)} & \text{if } s \in outports(ed_I) \text{ and} \\ & \underline{sig(I, s)} \text{ single driven} \\ I.s & \text{if } s \in outports(ed_I) \text{ and} \\ & \underline{sig(I, s)} \text{ multiple driven} \\ I.s & \text{otherwise} \end{cases}$$

The substitution $ren_{I,sb}^{conf}$ can be extended to expressions and formulae in the usual way.

The relation between a variable v of ab_I and the expression $ren_{I,sb}^{conf}(v)$ has already been used in the definition of the projection function $proj_j$ used to define the transition system $\mathcal{T}[\![sb]\!]$ (see Section 3.4). We extend the definition to computation sequences. Given a computation π we define the computation $ren_{I,sb}^{conf}(\pi)$ by

$$ren_{I,sb}^{conf}(\pi)(i) := \pi(i)[v \in var(ab_I) / [\![ren_{I,sb}^{conf}(v)]\!]\pi(i)]$$

The syntactical substitution $ren_{I,sb}^{conf}(\phi)$ coincides with the semantical substitution $ren_{I,sb}^{conf}(\pi)$ as it is expressed by the following lemma.

Lemma 4.4 (substitution lemma) *Assume that ϕ is a formula with $var(\phi) \setminus Aux \subseteq var(ab_I)$; then*

$$\pi \models ren_{I,sb}^{conf}(\phi) \quad \text{iff} \quad ren_{I,sb}^{conf}(\pi) \models \phi$$

Now we are going to characterize the computations of a structural body sb. Due to the definition of the observable semantics $[\![des]\!]$ in terms of the transition system $\mathcal{T}[\![des]\!]$ and due to the definition of $ren_{I,sb}^{conf}(\pi)$, it is obvious that with $\pi \in Cl[\![des]\!]$ the computation sequence $ren_{I,sb}^{conf}(\pi)$ is an element of $Cl[\![des_I]\!]$. To obtain a characterization of the computations we have to add some conditions concerning the signals of sb and the interconnections of its components. Some invariances between the components and the variables of sb have been expressed already in Section 3.4 by the formula Φ_{sb}. In addition we have to guarantee that input values change only by a synchronization step. As far as this concerns input signals this is guaranteed by the fact that every inport of sb is connected to some inport of some component. The only value of the environment which cannot be reconstructed from the components is its delay value. The following formula expresses that the value of ENV' $delay$ does not change whenever the environment is waiting for synchronization with the given architecture:

$$\Phi_{ENV'delay} := \Box\,(\text{ENV'}\ delay = y \land \text{ENV'}\ at\_wait \Rightarrow$$
$$[\text{ENV'}\ delay = y \text{ unless } \text{ENV'}\ delay = y \land \text{ENV'}\ at\_wait \land at\_wait])$$

Lemma 4.5

$$Cl[\![des]\!] = \bigcap_{1\le k\le n} \left\{ \pi \mid \pi \models \Box\,\Phi_{sb} \land \Phi_{ENV'delay},\ ren^{conf}_{I_k,sb}(\pi) \in Cl[\![des_{I_k}]\!] \right\}$$

Using this characterization we can show that any valid specification ϕ of a component $\underline{des}_I$ can be lifted to a valid assertion of $\underline{des}$ using the substitution $ren^{conf}_{I,sb}$. But observe that $ren^{conf}_{I,sb}(\phi)$ may contain internal variables such as $I.o$, where o is an outport of ed_I and $\underline{sig}(I,o)$ is a multiple driven signal of sb.

Lemma 4.6 *Let ϕ be a formula with $var(\phi)\setminus Aux \subseteq var(ab_I)$. If $\underline{des}_I \models \phi$ then $\underline{des} \models ren^{conf}_{I,sb}(\phi)$.*

Proof Let π be a computation of $[\![des]\!]$. Then the computation $ren^{conf}_{I,sb}(\pi)$ is an element of $Cl[\![des_I]\!]$ (by Lemma 4.5). As $\underline{des}_I \models \phi$ we have that $ren^{conf}_{I,sb}(\pi) \models \phi$. Hence, by Lemma 4.4, $\pi \models ren^{conf}_{I,sb}(\phi)$. □

4.2 Proof system

Proof rules are used to derive the properties of a composed system out of the properties of its components. These rules cover the instantiations of components and their wiring reflected by renaming component ports to the appropriate signals and bringing the resolution function into consideration for multiple driven signals. Furthermore, the rules contain weakening rules to weaken the commitment part of a specification or to strengthen its assumption part. Weakening rules are useful for hiding internal signals and deriving a formula which uses only the visible signals of a composed architecture. But to derive such a property we have to use internal signals in intermediate steps, as these are part of some components and the specification of a component may use these signals. To remove e.g. the drivers $I_{i_1}.o_{i_1},\ldots,I_{i_r}.o_{i_r}$ of a multiple driven signal $s = \underline{sig}(I_{i_1}.o_{i_1})$ we have to apply the weakening rule in conjunction with the resolution function $\underline{res}(s)$ which relates the signal value with the values of its drivers.

(R1) Instantiation Rule

The first rule deals with the instantiation of components in a structural description. According to Lemma 4.6 a valid specification of a component remains valid when embedded into a structural architecture. This leads to the rule:

$$\frac{\langle ed_{I_k}, ab_{I_k}, \underline{conf} \rangle \models (assm,\ comm)}{\langle ed, sb, \underline{conf} \rangle \models (ren^{conf}_{I_k,sb}(assm),\ ren^{conf}_{I_k,sb}(comm))},$$

where $sb = \langle ed, \|_{sig,vis}(I_1 : C_1, \ldots, I_n : C_n), gmap, \underline{res}\rangle$, $\underline{conf} = \langle \underline{ed}, \underline{ab}\rangle$, $ed_{I_k} = \underline{ed}(sb, I_k, C_k)$, $ab_{I_k} = \underline{ab}(sb, I_k, C_k)$, $var(assm, comm) \subseteq var(ab_{I_k})$, and $1 \leq k \leq n$.

(R2) Conjunction Rule
Two specifications of a design $\underline{des}$ can be combined by a conjunction.

$$\frac{\underline{des} \models (assm_1,\ comm_1) \quad \underline{des} \models (assm_2,\ comm_2)}{\underline{des} \models (assm_1 \wedge assm_2,\ comm_1 \wedge comm_2)}$$

The validity of this rule follows immediately from the definition of validity of formulae.

(R3) Weakening Rule
We can weaken a specification by weakening the commitment or strengthening the assumption. By weakening a specification we can make use of some properties of VHDL computations as it is e.g. expressed by the formulae $\Box\,\Phi_{sb}$ (see page 366) and $\Phi_{ENV'\,delay}$ (see page 380). These formulae are independent of any implementation of a VHDL architecture. They depend at most only on the structural interconnection of components.

Hence assume that $Th_{\underline{des}}(VHDL)$ denotes the set of all "implementation independent" formulae valid for all VHDL observations w.r.t. the structural information of $\underline{des}$. We do not investigate these theories in more detail; in most cases the formula Φ_{sb} is sufficient. We use

$$Th_{\underline{des}}(VHDL) \models \phi$$

to denote that ϕ is valid relative to $Th_{\underline{des}}(VHDL)$, i.e. for every computation sequence π it holds: if $\pi \models Th_{\underline{des}}(VHDL)$ then $\pi \models \phi$:

$$\frac{\underline{des} \models (assm,\ comm) \quad Th_{\underline{des}}(VHDL) \models assm' \Rightarrow assm \quad Th_{\underline{des}}(VHDL) \models comm \Rightarrow comm'}{\underline{des} \models (assm',\ comm')}$$

In most applications $Th_{\underline{des}}(VHDL) \models \phi' \Rightarrow \phi$ can be reduced to $\models (\phi' \wedge \Phi_{sb}) \Rightarrow \phi$.

(R4) Assumption Elimination Rule

An important rule is the assumption elimination rule which allows discharging of assumptions. If e.g. an assumption used in a specification derived from one component is guaranteed by a specification derived from a second component we can discharge the assumption in the first specification:

$$\frac{des \models (assm \wedge assm_1, \; comm) \qquad des \models (assm', \; assm_1)}{des \models (assm \wedge assm', \; comm)}$$

(R5) Safety Rule

Typical safety properties are invariances, mutual exclusion, deadlock freedom, and unless properties. Regarding safety properties we may derive properties from cyclic depending specifications.

A formula ϕ denotes a *safety property* iff

- $\{\pi \mid \pi \models \phi\} \neq \emptyset$
- $\pi \models \phi$ iff $\forall i \, \exists \pi'$ with $\pi_{[0..i]} \cdot \pi' \models \phi$ [9]

i.e. if every finite prefix of a computation π can be extended to a computation satisfying ϕ, then π itself satisfies ϕ.

A safety property ϕ is a safety property w.r.t. a set V of variables if the property ϕ can only be violated by a change of the values of some variable $v \in V$. We say that the i-th step of a computation π violates ϕ iff

- $\exists \pi'$ with $\pi_{[0..i]} \cdot \pi' \models \phi$ (There is no violation up to instant i.)
- $\forall \pi' \; \pi_{[0..i+1]} \cdot \pi' \not\models \phi$ (After the i-th step the computation cannot be extended to a valid computation.)

If this violation is due only to the values of V we say that it is a V-violation, i.e.

- the i-th step of π violates ϕ, and
- every π' with
  * $\pi'(j) = \pi(j) \quad 0 \leq j \leq i$
  * $\pi'(i+1) =_V \pi(i+1)$

  violates ϕ at step i as well.

A safety property ϕ is then called a *safety property w.r.t. a design entity* if it is a safety property w.r.t. the output signals of the system.

Assume that $sb = \langle ed, \|_{sig,vis}(I_1 : C_1, \ldots, I_n : C_n), gmap, \underline{res} \rangle$ is a given structural body. If we have two safety properties ψ_1 and ψ_2 relatively to

---

[9] $\pi_{[0..i]}$ denotes the initial computation up to instant i and $\beta \cdot \pi$ is the concatenation of a finite prefix β with a computation π.

Specification and verification of VHDL-based Hardware Designs

the instances I_j resp. I_k such that, for the instance I_j, ψ_1 is valid under the assumption ψ_2 and, for the instance I_k, ψ_2 is valid under the assumption ψ_1 we can prove by computational induction that ψ_1 as well as ψ_2 are valid in the structural composition. At every step in a computation I_j will not violate ψ_1 provided I_k has not violated ψ_2 up to that time instant and vice versa. Obviously, the variables of ψ_1 and ψ_2 should be visible by both instances. Therefore outports to multiple driven signals cannot be referenced in the formulae. In the following rule ϕ_i, $i = 1,2$, are the variants of ψ_1 resp. ψ_2 as they are visible by $\underline{des}_{I_k}$ and ϕ'_i, $i = 1, 2$, are the variants as they are visible by $\underline{des}_{I_j}$:

$$\frac{\begin{array}{c}\langle ed_{I_k}, ab_{I_k}, \underline{conf}\rangle \models (\phi_1,\ \phi_2) \\ \langle ed_{I_j}, ab_{I_j}, \underline{conf}\rangle \models (\phi'_2,\ \phi'_1) \\ \phi_2 \text{ safety property w.r.t. } ab_{I_k} \\ \phi'_1 \text{ safety property w.r.t. } ab_{I_j}\end{array}}{\langle ed, sb, \underline{conf}\rangle \models (\textbf{true},\ ren^{conf}_{I_k,sb}(\phi_1 \wedge \phi_2))},$$

provided that

- $var(\phi_1, \phi_2) \subseteq var(ab_{I_k})$,
- $var(\phi'_2, \phi'_1) \subseteq var(ab_{I_j})$,
- $ren^{conf}_{I_k,sb}(\phi_1) = ren^{conf}_{I_j,sb}(\phi'_1)$,
- $ren^{conf}_{I_k,sb}(\phi_2) = ren^{conf}_{I_j,sb}(\phi'_2)$,
- $sb = \langle ed, \|_{\underline{sig},\underline{vis}}(I_1 : C_1, \ldots, I_n : C_n), \underline{gmap}, \underline{res}\rangle$,
- $\underline{conf} = \langle \underline{ed}, \underline{ab}\rangle$,
- $ed_I = \underline{ed}(sb, I, C)$, $ab_I = \underline{ab}(sb, I, C)$, and
- $1 \leq k \neq j \leq n$.

(R6) Synchronization Rule

We know that a component remains at a wait statement unless all other components reach a wait statement too. Hence if two components are independently infinitely often at a wait statement they are infinitely often together at a wait statement. This fact is reflected by the following synchronization rule:

$$\frac{\langle ed, sb, \underline{conf}\rangle \models (assm,\ comm \wedge \Box\Diamond(I_k\,'at\_wait \wedge \phi_1) \wedge \Box\Diamond(I_l\,'at\_wait \wedge \phi_2))}{\langle ed, sb, \underline{conf}\rangle \models (assm,\ comm \wedge \Box\Diamond(I_k\,'at\_wait \wedge I_l\,'at\_wait \wedge \phi_1 \wedge \phi_2))}$$

where $sb = \langle ed, \|_{\underline{sig},\underline{vis}}(I_1 : C_1, \ldots, I_n : C_n), \underline{gmap}, \underline{res}\rangle$ and $1 \leq k, l \leq n$.

Observe that this rule can be derived from the weakening rule (R3) as
$\Box\Diamond(I_k\,'at\_wait\wedge\phi_1)\wedge\Box\Diamond(I_l\,'at\_wait\wedge\phi_2) \Rightarrow \Box\Diamond(I_k\,'at\_wait\wedge I_l\,'at\_wait\wedge \phi_1\wedge\phi_2)$ is valid for all VHDL computations, i.e. it can be derived from $Th_{\underline{des}}(VHDL)$ as $(\Box\Diamond I_k\,'at\_wait \wedge \Box\Diamond I_l\,'at\_wait) \Rightarrow \Box\Diamond(I_k\,'at\_wait \wedge I_l\,'at\_wait)$ is contained in $Th_{\underline{des}}(VHDL)$.

(R7) Closed System Rule

If we are at the top level of a design, i.e. we are considering a closed system without any environment, we can eliminate all variables concerning the environment. A design $\underline{des} = \langle ed, ab, conf\rangle$ is closed if the set $inports(ed)$ is empty. In that case, ENV' at_wait can be viewed to be constantly true; i.e. there is no environment which can prevent the progress of the system. Furthermore, there are no scheduled events of the environment; hence ENV' $delay$ can be substituted by ∞:

$$\frac{\underline{des} \models (assm,\ comm)\quad \underline{des}\ \text{closed}}{\underline{des} \models (assm[\text{ENV'}\ at\_wait/\textbf{true}][\text{ENV'}\ delay/\infty],\ comm[\text{ENV'}\ at\_wait/\textbf{true}][\text{ENV'}\ delay/\infty])}$$

A proof rule $\frac{\underline{des}_1\models\phi_1,\ldots,\underline{des}_k\models\phi_k}{\underline{des}\models\phi}$ is called *sound* if whenever the premise of the rule, $\underline{des}_1 \models \phi_1, \ldots, \underline{des}_k \models \phi_k$, is valid the conclusion $\underline{des} \models \phi$ is valid too.

Theorem 4.7 (soundness) *The given proof rules for VHDL designs (R1)–(R7) are sound.*

Proof The soundness of rule (R1) follows by Lemma 4.6 and the soundness of (R5) can be proved by induction on a given computation. All other rules can be proved in a straightforward manner. □

4.3 Deduction of a correctness assertion: an example

To illustrate the use of proof rules to derive properties of a composite architecture from properties of its components, we consider the example architecture described in Section 2.1. Assume that some given configuration description binds the instance M to the behaviour description of the entity description Master and the instances $S1$ and $S2$ to the behaviour description of the entity Slave.

Our goal is to verify that every request of the master module M will eventually be acknowledged by some slave component provided the progress of the system will not be blocked by its environment, i.e.

$$(\Box\Diamond\text{ENV'}\,at\_wait,\ \Box\,(Req = \,'1\,' \Rightarrow \Diamond Ack = \,'1\,'))\quad (4.5)$$

To prove this property we consider two cases — whether the requested address is '0' or '1':

$$spec := (\psi_1, \phi) \tag{4.6}$$
$$spec' := (\psi_1, \phi') \tag{4.7}$$

where

$$\psi_1 := \Box\Diamond \text{ENV'} \, at\_wait$$
$$\phi := \Box((Req = \text{'1'} \land Addr = \text{'0'}) \Rightarrow \Diamond Ack = \text{'1'}))$$
$$\phi' := \Box((Req = \text{'1'} \land Addr = \text{'1'}) \Rightarrow \Diamond Ack = \text{'1'})) \, .$$

As the two subcases are analogous we consider only the first one.

To deduce the property (4.6) we have to consider first properties of the components. To guarantee the global behaviour we require that a slave component will respond to a request by raising the Ack signal whenever the indicated address is in the range of the guarded memory. But such a reaction can only be guaranteed provided the Req signal remains high unless the acknowledge will occur. Furthermore, the reaction can only be promised under the assumption that the environment will not prevent the progress of the system, i.e. the environment has to reach a wait statement again and again. Using the abbreviations

$$\phi_1 := \Box((Req = \text{'1'} \land Addr = id) \Rightarrow$$
$$[Req = \text{'1'} \textbf{ unless } Req = \text{'1'} \land Ack = \text{'1'}])$$
$$\phi_2 := \Box((Req = \text{'1'} \land Addr = id) \Rightarrow \Diamond Ack = \text{'1'})$$

a slave component has to guarantee

$$spec_1 := (\psi_1 \land \phi_1, \phi_2) \, . \tag{4.8}$$

Furthermore, a slave component has not to react if the specified address is not in the range of its memory block. This behaviour will be guaranteed by the component provided the address line is stable as long as the request signal is high. Using the abbreviations

$$\phi_3 := \Box((Req = \text{'1'} \land Addr = a) \Rightarrow [Addr = a \textbf{ unless } Req = \text{'0'}])$$
$$\phi_4 := \Box((Req = \text{'1'} \land Addr \neq id) \Rightarrow$$
$$[Ack = \text{'0'} \textbf{ unless } Ack = \text{'0'} \land Req = \text{'0'}])$$

this property is described by:

$$spec_2 := (\phi_3, \phi_4) \, . \tag{4.9}$$

To guarantee progress of the whole system we should know that progress will not be prevented by a slave component. Hence a third specification should be valid for a slave module:

$$spec_3 := (\text{true}, \psi_2) \tag{4.10}$$

where

$$\psi_2 := \Box \Diamond \, at\_wait \, .$$

The assumptions ϕ_1 and ϕ_3 used in the specification of the slave should be guaranteed by the master module. But observe that the Ack signal of the master module is not identical with the Ack signal of some slave component. The Ack signal of the master module corresponds to the resolved signal of both acknowledge signals of the slave components. The master module will guarantee ϕ_3 without any restriction on the value of the address line. Furthermore, the master module has also to guarantee progress. Thus the required specifications of the master components are:

$$spec_4 := (\text{true}, \phi_3) \tag{4.11}$$
$$spec_5 := (\text{true}, \phi_5) \tag{4.12}$$
$$spec_6 := (\text{true}, \psi_2) \tag{4.13}$$

where

$$\phi_5 := \Box \, (Req = \text{'1'} \Rightarrow [Req = \text{'1'} \text{ unless } Req = \text{'1'} \land Ack = \text{'1'}]) \, .$$

Note that these specifications of the slave and master modules do not completely specify these components. Further formulae have to be given to specify the completion of the protocol regarding the resetting of the Req and Ack signals. But the given specifications are sufficient to derive $spec$ and $spec'$.

These specifications can be proved correct using a model checker. To do this we have to construct a labelled state/transition system out of the given VHDL descriptions as described previously. In this chapter we do not discuss the model-checking procedure and we assume that the given specifications $spec_1$–$spec_5$ are valid in the corresponding components.

In the following we discuss the deduction of $spec$ step by step. The first step towards the derivation of our goal is to apply the instantiation rule to the given specifications of the components. For the two instantiations of the slave component we obtain the following specifications:

$S1$:
$$spec'_1 := (\psi_1 \land \psi_3 \land \psi_5 \land \phi'_1, \phi'_2) \tag{4.14}$$
$$spec'_2 := (\phi_3, \phi'_4) \tag{4.15}$$
$$spec'_3 := (\text{true}, \psi_4) \tag{4.16}$$
$$\tag{4.17}$$

$S2$:

$$spec''_1 := (\psi_1 \wedge \psi_3 \wedge \psi_4 \wedge \phi''_1, \phi''_2) \quad (4.18)$$
$$spec''_2 := (\phi_3, \phi''_4) \quad (4.19)$$
$$spec''_3 := (\textbf{true}, \psi_5) \quad (4.20)$$

where

$$\psi_3 := \Box \Diamond \text{M' } at\_wait$$
$$\psi_4 := \Box \Diamond \text{S1' } at\_wait$$
$$\psi_5 := \Box \Diamond \text{S2' } at\_wait$$
$$\phi'_1 := \Box((Req = \text{'1'} \wedge Addr = \text{'1'}) \Rightarrow$$
$$[Req = \text{'1'} \textbf{ unless } Req = \text{'1'} \wedge S1.Ack = \text{'1'}])$$
$$\phi'_2 := \Box((Req = \text{'1'} \wedge Addr = \text{'1'}) \Rightarrow \Diamond S1.Ack = \text{'1'})$$
$$\phi'_4 := \Box((Req = \text{'1'} \wedge Addr \neq \text{'1'}) \Rightarrow$$
$$[S1.Ack = \text{'0'} \textbf{ unless } S1.Ack = \text{'0'} \wedge Req = \text{'0'}])$$
$$\phi''_1 := \Box((Req = \text{'1'} \wedge Addr = \text{'0'}) \Rightarrow$$
$$[Req = \text{'1'} \textbf{ unless } Req = \text{'1'} \wedge S2.Ack = \text{'1'}])$$
$$\phi''_2 := \Box((Req = \text{'1'} \wedge Addr = \text{'0'}) \Rightarrow \Diamond S2.Ack = \text{'1'})$$
$$\phi''_4 := \Box((Req = \text{'1'} \wedge Addr \neq \text{'0'}) \Rightarrow$$
$$[S2.Ack = \text{'0'} \textbf{ unless } S2.Ack = \text{'0'} \wedge Req = \text{'0'}])$$

and the instant M of Master(behaviour) satisfies the specifications:

$$spec'_4 := spec_4 \quad (4.21)$$
$$spec'_5 := spec_5 \quad (4.22)$$
$$spec'_6 := (\textbf{true}, \psi_3) \quad (4.23)$$

Observe that in the specifications of the instance M the Ack signal of the master is replaced by the Ack signal of the system as Master:Ack is an input port, whereas in the specifications of $S1$ and $S2$ the Ack signal of the slave is only substituted by the driving signals $S1.Ack$ resp. $S2.Ack$. The Ack signal of the system is related to these drivers by the resolution function of that signal. The resolution function for the Ack signal is the or function; hence the characteristic formula for this resolution function is given by

$$\xi := \Box(\ (Ack = \text{'1'} \Leftrightarrow (S1.Ack = \text{'1'} \vee S2.Ack = \text{'1'})) \wedge$$
$$(Ack = \text{'0'} \Leftrightarrow (S1.Ack = \text{'0'} \wedge S2.Ack = \text{'0'})) \ )$$

Using the knowledge of the resolution function we can deduce from the commitment ϕ'_2 of $spec'_1$ the desired commitment ϕ using the weakening rule (R3):

$$(\psi_1 \wedge \psi_3 \wedge \psi_5 \wedge \phi'_1, \phi'_2) \tag{4.24}$$

guaranteed by $S1$

$$\phi'_2 \wedge \xi \Rightarrow \phi \tag{4.25}$$

tautology

$$(\psi_1 \wedge \psi_3 \wedge \psi_5 \wedge \phi'_1, \phi) \tag{4.26}$$

applying (R3) to (4.24) and (4.25)

Hence it remains to cut off the assumptions $\psi_3 \wedge \psi_5 \wedge \phi'_1$. The assumptions ψ_3 and ψ_5 can be eliminated with $spec''_3$ and $spec'_6$ using the assumption elimination rule. Hence we get

$$(\psi_1 \wedge \phi'_1, \phi). \tag{4.27}$$

The assumption ϕ'_1 can be deduced from ϕ_5 (guaranteed by M), ϕ''_4 (guaranteed by $S2$ under the assumption ϕ_3), and the resolution function:

$$(\text{true}, \phi_5) \tag{4.28}$$

guaranteed by M

$$(\phi_3, \phi''_4) \tag{4.29}$$

guaranteed by $S2$

$$(\phi_3, \phi_5 \wedge \phi''_4) \tag{4.30}$$

applying (R2) to (4.28) and (4.29)

$$\phi_5 \wedge \phi''_4 \wedge \xi \Rightarrow \phi'_1 \tag{4.31}$$

tautology

$$(\phi_3, \phi'_1) \tag{4.32}$$

applying (R3) to (4.30) and (4.31)

Eliminating the assumption ϕ'_1 introduce the new assumption ϕ_3. But ϕ_3 is guaranteed by M without further assumption and hence we derive our goal by another application of the assumption elimination rule.

The derivation of the global specification $spec$ is summarized by the proof tree shown in Fig. 7.

5 Symbolic Timing Diagrams

In this section, a novel visual formalism called Symbolic Timing Diagrams (STD's) is introduced, which resides on top of the temporal logic (TL) introduced in the preceding section. The main advantage of this formalism is that it allows for a succinct denotation of protocol-like requirements stated about the behaviour of system components. Such requirements would be

Specification and verification of VHDL-based Hardware Designs

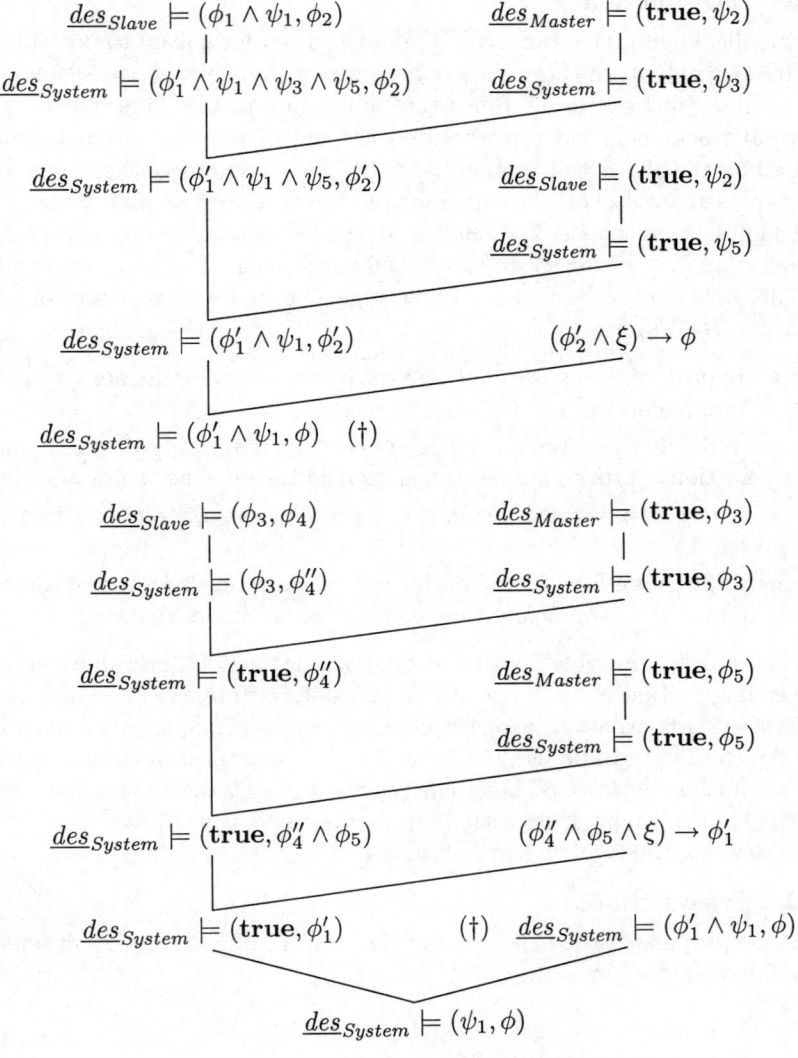

FIG. 7. Proof tree.

tedious to express using the TL-language, while their equivalent formulation using STD's is easy and natural. Since there is a translation algorithm from STD's to TL-specifications, both specification styles may be mixed, which allows us to choose the most appropriate style for each (specification or verification) task.

5.1 Introduction

Symbolic Timing Diagrams (STD's) are a visual formalism to describe requirements about the behaviour of hardware components at the system and even more abstract level. Since the publication of the pioneer work [10], several researchers have investigated the use of a specification language based on the concept of timing diagrams. They introduced languages with various semantics, and for different purposes: either as a starting point for high-level synthesis [2, 3, 39, 54, 61], or for simulation and test-pattern generation [52], or for specification and verification of system components [5, 35, 67]. To the best of our knowledge, the unique features of our formalism (STD's) are:

- support of *compositional* specifications of requirements of system components
- availability of a proof system to derive system properties from specifications of its components using *graphical* inference rules [66]
- semantics based on a *declarative* paradigm; i.e. different requirements may be stated independently[10]
- support of efficient automatic verification procedures for verification of system components using compositional model checking

STD's are "compatible" with the temporal logic (TL) introduced in the preceding section in the sense that a translation from STD's to TL exists. Due to this translation, a powerful verification technique called symbolic model checking can be used to establish the correctness of component implementations against STD-specifications. Case studies which have been carried out in cooperation with industrial partners have already proved the practical feasibility of this approach [24].

5.2 Basic notions

For the purpose of the exposition of the concept of STD's, we will refer in the following to a structure ed[11]

$$ed =_{Def} (X, typedecl)[12]$$

---

[10]Similar to a statement of *facts* in PROLOG.

[11]ed is reminiscent of the notion of a VHDL entity declaration introduced in Section 2.2; in this context, a slightly simplified notion is used.

[12]We adopt the following notational conventions. Whenever we introduce a structure declaration
$$S =_{Def} (A, B, \ldots)$$
then we refer to its components by A_S, B_S etc. A declaration of a function f of type $A \to B$ will be written
$$f : (a \in A \mapsto b_a \in B)$$
where typical variables of the domain and the range of the function are simultaneously introduced.

where X is a finite set of typed variables taken from some infinite set VAR of variable names. The set of variables declared in ed is denoted $Vars_{ed} =_{Def} X$. The type of the variables in X is given by a mapping $typedecl$,

$$typedecl : (x \in Vars_{ed} \mapsto D_x \in DOM)$$

which maps each variable $x \in Vars_{ed}$ to some (finite) value domain D_x taken from some appropriate domain DOM of value domains. Given ed, define the set Val_{ed} of all possible interpretations of the variables in $Vars_{ed}$ by

$$Val_{ed} =_{Def} \{\sigma \mid \sigma : (x \in Vars_{ed} \mapsto V_x \in typedecl_{ed}(x))\}.$$

In this context, we assume a well-ordered discrete domain $TIME$ of *time-instances* with the concrete representation

$$TIME =_{Def} \mathbf{N}.$$

The semantics of STD's will specify infinite sequences of value interpretations of the variables in $Vars_{ed}$ over $TIME$. Given ed, we define the set Obs_{ed} of all possible *observations* of the variables declared in ed by

$$Obs_{ed} =_{Def} \{obs \mid obs : (i \in TIME \mapsto \sigma_i \in Val_{ed})\}.$$

5.3 Symbolic waveforms

We will use predicates to define for a given entity declaration ed sets of (valid) valuations of the variables declared in ed at a given time instance. Similarly, symbolic waveforms will be used to define sequences of valuations of $Vars_{ed}$ over some period of time. Let $Pred_{ed}$ denote the set of predicates over Val_{ed}. A *symbolic waveform* ρ over ed is a structure

$$\rho =_{Def} (actcond, kernel)$$

where the first component $actcond$, called the activation condition of ρ, is a predicate over ed and the second, called the kernel of ρ, is a mapping

$$kernel : (\kappa \in SE \mapsto (contcond_\kappa, exitcond_\kappa) \in Pred_{ed} \times Pred_{ed})$$

where SE is some linearly ordered (possibly empty) finite set of objects called *symbolic events*, which are taken from some infinite set of symbolic events (usually represented by the set $\mathbf{N}$ of natural numbers). The ordering of the set SE_ρ is denoted by $\leq_\rho$. For technical reasons, we adjoin a unique maximal element $\top$ to SE_ρ and refer to this extended set by

$$sevents_\rho =_{Def} SE_\rho \cup \{\top\}.$$

The ordering $\leq_\rho$ naturally extends to the set $sevents_\rho$ by the definition

$\forall e \in sevents_\rho : e \leq_\rho \top$. The least element of $sevents_\rho$ w.r.t. $\leq_\rho$ is denoted by $\kappa_{0,\rho}$. Furthermore, define for any symbolic waveform ρ the relation

$$\neq_\rho =_{Def} (sevents_\rho \times sevents_\rho) \setminus \{(e,e) \mid e \in sevents_\rho\}$$

and write as usual $e_1 <_\rho e_2 \iff (e_1 \leq_\rho e_2) \wedge (e_1 \neq_\rho e_2)$. On $sevents_\rho$ we define the relation $\rightarrow_\rho$ (successor) by

$$\rightarrow_\rho =_{Def} \{(\kappa_1, \kappa_2) \in sevents_\rho \times sevents_\rho \mid \\ \kappa_1 <_\rho \kappa_2 \wedge \neg(\exists \kappa \in sevents_\rho : \kappa_1 <_\rho \kappa <_\rho \kappa_2)\}.$$

The mapping $kernel_\rho$ associates with each symbolic event $\kappa \in SE_\rho$ a symbolic event annotation ANN_κ, which is a pair $ANN_\kappa = (contcond_\kappa, exitcond_\kappa)$ of predicates called the *continuation condition* and the *exit condition* of κ, respectively. Given $\rho = (actcond, kernel)$, define

$$length_\rho =_{Def} |SE_\rho|$$

and, for $length_\rho > 0$,

$$tail_\rho =_{Def} (contcond_{kernel_\rho(\kappa_{0,\rho})}, kernel_\rho|_{SE_\rho \setminus \{\kappa_{0,\rho}\}}).$$

Observe that for $length_\rho > 0$, $length_{tail_\rho} < length_\rho$. The set of all symbolic waveforms over ed is denoted by $SymbWaves(ed)$.

5.4 Bundles of waveforms

While symbolic waveforms are used to define sequences of valuations of a set $Vars_{ed}$ of variables over some time period, we will use (finite) sets of symbolic waveforms to specify the behaviour of subsets $Y_1, Y_2, \ldots$ of variables taken from $Vars_{ed}$, whose changes over time are only loosely coupled. Such a set of symbolic waveforms is called a *bundle* of waveforms (or just bundle, for brevity). A bundle $WAVES$ over ed is a mapping

$$WAVES : (id \in SWN \mapsto \rho_{id} \in SymbWaves(ed))$$

which associates each name of some finite set SWN of symbolic waveform names, taken from some infinite set of symbolic waveform names, with a symbolic waveform over ed. The notion of a symbolic event is naturally extended to a bundle $WAVES$ by the definition

$$SEvents_{WAVES} =_{Def} \bigcup_{id \in SWN_{WAVES}} \{\langle id, \kappa \rangle \mid \kappa \in sevents_{WAVES(id)}\}.$$

A pair $e = \langle id, \kappa \rangle, e \in SEvents_{WAVES}$ is called a (symbolic) event of the bundle $WAVES$. The linear ordering $\leq_\rho$ as well as the conflict relation $\neq_\rho$ on the symbolic events in each waveform ρ induce a partial order $\preceq_{WAVES}$

respectively a conflict relation $\neq_{WAVES}$ in a bundle $WAVES$, defined by

$$\left\{ \begin{array}{c} \preceq_{WAVES} \\ \neq_{WAVES} \end{array} \right\} =_{Def} \{(e_1, e_2) \in SEvents_{WAVES} \times SEvents_{WAVES} \mid $$
$$(id_{e_1} = id_{e_2}) \wedge \kappa_{e_1} \left\{ \begin{array}{c} \leq_\rho \\ \neq_\rho \end{array} \right\} \kappa_{e_2} \text{ where } \rho = WAVES(id_{e_1})\}$$

A mapping ζ, which determines one symbolic event in each waveform of a bundle is called a *frontstate* (or front, for brevity). Given a bundle $WAVES$, define

$$Front_{WAVES} =_{Def} \{\zeta \mid \zeta : (id \in SWN_{WAVES} \mapsto $$
$$\langle id, \kappa_{id} \rangle \in SWN_{WAVES} \times sevents_{WAVES(id)}\}$$

The successor relation $\to_\rho$ defined for each symbolic waveform of a bundle $WAVES$ induces a successor relation $\to_{WAVES}$ on $Front_{WAVES}$ as follows: For $\zeta_1, \zeta_2 \in Front_{WAVES}$,

$$\zeta_1 \to_{WAVES} \zeta_2 \text{ iff } \exists E \subseteq SEvents_{WAVES} : $$

1. $E \subseteq im(\zeta_1)^{13}, E \neq \emptyset$
2. $\forall e_1 \in E : \kappa_{e_1} \to_\rho \kappa_{e_2}$ where $\rho = WAVES(id_{e_1})$ and $e_2 = \zeta_2(id_{e_1})$
3. $\forall id \in SWN_{WAVES} : \zeta_1(id) \notin E : \zeta_1(id) = \zeta_2(id)$

We call a set E of symbolic events a *step*, which causes a move from frontstate ζ_1 to ζ_2, and write $\zeta_1 \stackrel{E}{\to}_{WAVES} \zeta_2$ whenever we need to refer to the step explicitly.

$\to^*_{WAVES}$ is a partial order on $Front_{WAVES}$. Let $\zeta_{0,WAVES}$ denote the unique minimal element w.r.t. $\to^*_{WAVES}$, defined by

$$\zeta_{0,WAVES} =_{Def} (id \in SWN_{WAVES} \mapsto \langle id, \kappa_{0,\rho}\rangle \text{ where } \rho = WAVES(id))$$

Similarly, $\zeta^\top_{WAVES}$ denotes the unique maximal element w.r.t. $\to^*_{WAVES}$, defined by

$$\zeta^\top_{WAVES} =_{Def} (id \in SWN_{WAVES} \mapsto \langle id, \top\rangle)$$

A bundle $WAVES$ defines the set $Path_{WAVES}$ of sequences (paths) of frontstates starting from $\zeta_{0,WAVES}$ by

$$Path_{WAVES} =_{Def} \{(\zeta_0, \ldots, \zeta_r) \mid some\ r \geq 0, \zeta_0 = \zeta_{0,WAVES} \text{ and} $$
$$\forall i = 0 \ldots (r-1) : \zeta_i \to_{WAVES} \zeta_{i+1}\}$$

For $\pi \in Path_{WAVES}$, $\pi = (\zeta_0, \ldots, \zeta_r)$, define $length_\pi =_{Def} r$, $frontstates_\pi =_{Def} \{\zeta_0, \ldots, \zeta_r\}$, $last_\pi =_{Def} \zeta_r$ and

$$sevents_\pi =_{Def} (\bigcup_{\zeta \in frontstates_\pi} im(\zeta)) \setminus im(last_\pi)$$

---

[13] $im(f)$ denotes the image of a mapping f.

For a subset $R \in SWN_{WAVES}$, let $\pi|_R =_{Def} \{\zeta_0|_R, \ldots, \zeta_r|_R\}$ denote the elementwise restriction of π to R. Given a bundle $WAVES$, define $length_{WAVES}$, the size of $WAVES$, by

$$length_{WAVES} =_{Def} \sum_{id \in SWN_{WAVES}} length_{WAVES(id)}$$

5.5 Filter structures

Given an entity declaration ed, a filter structure γ over ed is a structure

$$\gamma =_{Def} (WAVES, CONSTRAINTS)$$

where $WAVES$ is a bundle of symbolic waveforms over ed and $CONSTRAINTS$ is a structure

$$CONSTRAINTS = (UNWIND, EXIT, PROPAGATE)$$

where $UNWIND \subseteq Path_{WAVES_\gamma}$ is a set of valid "unwinding" sequences which satisfy:

1. $\forall (\pi \in UNWIND$ where $\pi = \zeta.\pi')^{14} : \zeta = \zeta_{0, WAVES_\gamma}$ ($UNWIND$ is rooted)
2. $\forall (\pi \in UNWIND$ where $\pi = \pi_1.\zeta) : \pi_1 \in UNWIND$ ($UNWIND$ is prefix-closed)

The set $UNWIND$ defines a border $border_{UNWIND}$ by

$$border_{UNWIND} =_{Def} \{\pi \in Path_{WAVES_\gamma} \setminus UNWIND \mid \pi = \pi_1.\zeta \text{ and } \pi_1 \in UNWIND\}$$

which is partitioned into two subsets:

1. $EXIT \subseteq border_{UNWIND}$, the second component of the structure $CONSTRAINTS$, which is a set of step sequences causing exit (premature termination of activation) from an activated filter structure[15]
2. $Failure_\gamma =_{Def} border_{UNWIND} \setminus EXIT$, the set of step sequences causing failure (due to a sequence of events which are to be rejected)

Finally,

$$PROPAGATE \subseteq (\bigcup_{\pi \in UNWIND} frontstates_\pi) \setminus \{\zeta^\top_{WAVES}\},$$

the third component of the structure $CONSTRAINTS$, is a subset of frontstates, which are distinguished with the meaning that these states must eventually be left (i.e. some step must occur eventually and cause progress in the filter).

---

[14]$\zeta.\pi'$ denotes the head construct and $\pi_1.\zeta$ denotes the tail append operation on finite sequences.

[15]The concept of activation is explained in Section 5.6.

The set rel_{WAVES} of *relevant* waveforms of a bundle $WAVES$ contains those waveforms which are not empty, defined by

$$rel_{WAVES} =_{Def} \{id \in SWN_{WAVES} \mid length_{WAVES(id)} > 0\}$$

Let $front_{0,WAVES}$ define the set of symbolic events in $im(\zeta_{0,WAVES})$ restricted to the non-empty waveforms,

$$front_{0,WAVES} =_{Def} im(\zeta_{0,WAVES} \mid rel_{WAVES})$$

and $Step_{0,WAVES}$ the set of steps taken from $front_{0,WAVES}$, i.e.

$$Step_{0,WAVES} =_{Def} \{E \subseteq front_{0,WAVES} \mid E \neq \emptyset\}$$

Given a filter structure γ, define the predicates[16]

$$Activate_\gamma \equiv_{Def} \bigwedge_{id \in SWN_{WAVES_\gamma}} actcond_{WAVES_\gamma(id)}$$

$$Stable_\gamma \equiv_{Def} \bigwedge_{id \in rel_{WAVES_\gamma}} actcond_{WAVES_\gamma(id)}$$

$$PredFail_\gamma \equiv_{Def} \bigvee_{id \in rel_{WAVES_\gamma}} (\neg actcond_\rho \wedge \neg contcond_{0,\rho}$$
$$\wedge \neg exitcond_{0,\rho} \quad \text{where} \quad \rho = WAVES_\gamma(id))$$

$$PredExit_\gamma \equiv_{Def} \neg PredFail_\gamma \wedge$$
$$\bigvee_{id \in rel_{WAVES_\gamma}} (\neg actcond_\rho \wedge \neg contcond_{0,\rho}$$
$$\wedge exitcond_{0,\rho} \quad \text{where} \quad \rho = WAVES_\gamma(id))$$

For $E \in Step_{0,WAVES}$:

$$Match_\gamma(E) \equiv_{Def} \bigwedge_{e \in E} contcond_{0,WAVES_\gamma(id_e)} \wedge$$
$$\bigwedge_{e' \in (front_{0,WAVES} \setminus E)} actcond_{0,WAVES_\gamma(id_{e'})}$$

For steps $E \in Step_{0,WAVES}$, define the auxiliary function π_{WAVES} by

$$\pi_{WAVES}(E) =_{Def} (\zeta_{0,WAVES}, \zeta_1) \text{ iff } \zeta_{0,WAVES} \xrightarrow{E} WAVES \ \zeta_1$$

and the following subsets of $Step_{0,WAVES}$:

$$FailStep_\gamma =_{Def} \{E \in Step_{0,WAVES_\gamma} \mid \pi_{WAVES_\gamma}(E) \in Failure_\gamma\}$$
$$ExitStep_\gamma =_{Def} \{E \in Step_{0,WAVES_\gamma} \mid \pi_{WAVES_\gamma}(E) \in EXIT_\gamma\}$$
$$UnwindStep_\gamma =_{Def} \{E \in Step_{0,WAVES_\gamma} \mid \pi_{WAVES_\gamma}(E) \in UNWIND_\gamma\}$$

---

[16] Boolean operations ($\wedge, \vee, \neg$) are defined pointwise on predicates, e.g. $(f \wedge g) =_{Def} \lambda x. f(x) \wedge g(x)$.

5.6 Semantics of filter structures

Given an entity declaration ed, a filter structure γ over ed can be regarded as a pattern for valid sequences obs of valuations of the variables declared in ed over a period of time. In order to define the semantics $[\![\gamma]\!] \subseteq Obs_{ed}$ of a filter by induction, the notion of *unwinding* is introduced. For steps $E \in UnwindStep_\gamma$, γ^E is a new filter structure obtained by an unwinding operation from the filter structure γ, defined by

$$\gamma^E =_{Def} (WAVES^E, CONSTRAINTS^E)$$

where

$$WAVES^E =_{Def} \left(id \in rel_{WAVES_\gamma} \mapsto \left\{ \begin{array}{l} tail_{WAVES_\gamma(id)} \text{ if } \zeta_{0,WAVES}(id) \in E \\ WAVES_\gamma(id) \text{ if } \zeta_{0,WAVES}(id) \notin E \end{array} \right\} \right)$$

and

$$CONSTRAINTS^E =_{Def} (UNWIND^E, EXIT^E, PROPAGATE^E),$$

$$UNWIND^E =_{Def} \{\pi|_{rel_{WAVES}} \mid \zeta_{0,WAVES_\gamma}.\pi \in UNWIND_\gamma,$$
$$\pi = \zeta_1.\pi' \text{ and } \zeta_{0,WAVES_\gamma} \xrightarrow{E} WAVES_\gamma \zeta_1\}$$

$$EXIT^E =_{Def} \{\pi|_{rel_{WAVES}} \mid \zeta_{0,WAVES_\gamma}.\pi \in EXIT_\gamma,$$
$$\pi = \zeta_1.\pi' \text{ and } \zeta_{0,WAVES_\gamma} \xrightarrow{E} WAVES_\gamma \zeta_1\}$$

$$PROPAGATE^E =_{Def} \{\zeta|_{rel_{WAVES}} \mid \zeta \in PROPAGATE_\gamma\}$$
$$\cap \bigcup_{\pi \in UNWIND^E} frontstates_\pi$$

The size $length_\gamma$ of a filter structure γ is the size of its bundle of waveforms, i.e.

$$length_\gamma =_{Def} length_{WAVES_\gamma}$$

Observe that for steps $E \subseteq UnwindStep_\gamma$, $length_{\gamma^E} < length_\gamma$. We define the semantics $[\![\gamma]\!] \subseteq Obs_{ed}$ by induction on $length_\gamma$ as follows:

$length_\gamma = 0:$ $[\![\gamma]\!] = Obs_{ed}$
$length_\gamma > 0:$
$\quad [\![\gamma]\!] = \{obs \in Obs_{ed} \mid$
$\qquad (\forall j \geq 0 : obs(j) \models Stable_\gamma \land \zeta_{0,WAVES_\gamma} \notin PROPAGATE_\gamma)$
$\qquad \lor (\exists k \geq 0 : obs(k) \models PredExit_\gamma \land \forall j : 0 \leq j < k : obs(j) \models Stable_\gamma)$
$\qquad \lor (\exists k \geq 0 : obs(k) \models \bigvee_{E \in ExitStep_\gamma} Match_\gamma(E)$
$\qquad\quad \land \forall j : 0 \leq j < k : obs(j) \models Stable_\gamma)$
$\qquad \lor (\exists k \geq 0 : obs(k) \models \bigvee_{E \in UnwindStep_\gamma} Match_\gamma(E)$
$\qquad\quad \land \forall j : 0 \leq j < k : obs(j) \models Stable_\gamma$
$\qquad\quad \land obs^k \in [\![\gamma^E]\!])\}$[17]

---

[17] obs^k is the tail of obs starting from position k: $obs^k =_{Def} obs(k)obs(k+1)\ldots$

5.7 Symbolic Timing Diagrams

Commonly, boolean expressions are used as concrete representations of predicates; similarly, Symbolic Timing Diagrams (STD's) are used as concrete representations of filter structures over some entity declaration ed. An STD TD over ed is a structure

$$TD =_{Def} (PAR, ACTMODE, BODY)$$

where

$$PAR =_{Def} (L, localtypedecl)$$

L is a finite set of typed local variables disjoint from $Vars_{ed}$, and

$$localtypedecl : (y \in L \mapsto D_y \in DOM)$$

maps each local variable y to some (finite) value domain D_y (cf. Section 5.2). The second component of TD is a flag

$$ACTMODE \in \{initial, dynamic\}$$

called *activation mode* which is used to select the interpretation of the diagram from two alternatives: *initial* means that the diagram is activated initially, while *dynamic* means that the diagram is activated whenever the activation condition is met. Third

$$BODY =_{Def} (TDWAVES, TDCONSTRAINTS)$$

is a concrete representation of a filter structure; specifically, $TDWAVES$ represents a bundle $WAVES$ of symbolic waveforms over the extended entity declaration

$$ed_L =_{Def} (Vars_{ed} \cup L, typedecl_{ed} \cup localtypedecl)$$

where each occurrence of a predicate $cond$ is replaced by a boolean expression b_{cond} over $Vars_{ed_L}$ such that $[\![b_{cond}]\!] \equiv cond$. $TDCONSTRAINTS$ is a structure used to represent the $CONSTRAINTS$ component of a filter structure. However, instead of explicitly giving the sets of unwind and exit step sequences and the set of propagation states, STD's use seven types of constraint arcs to denote constraints on the relative ordering of symbolic events in the waveforms. We define

$$TDCONSTRAINTS = (CA^{=,!}, CA^{\preceq,!}, CA^{\neq,!}, CA^{=,?}, CA^{\preceq,?}, CA^{\neq,?}, CA^{\leadsto})$$

where the seven components are relations on $SEvents_{TD} \times SEvents_{TD}$ which fall into two categories:

1. Asymmetric relations: $CA^{\preceq,!}$, $CA^{\preceq,?}$ and $CA^{\leadsto}$ [18], the sets of

---

[18] $CA^{\leadsto}$ is a relation on $SEvents'_{TD} \times SEvents_{TD}$, where $SEvents'_{TD} =_{Def} SEvents_{TD} \cup \{e_{act}\}$ and e_{act} denotes a special symbolic event called *activation edge* of TD.

strong (!) and weak (?) precedence ($\preceq$) and the set of leads-to ($\rightsquigarrow$) constraints.

2. Symmetric relations: $CA^{=,!}$, $CA^{\neq,!}$, $CA^{=,?}$, $CA^{\neq,?}$, the sets of strong simultaneous (=) and conflict ($\neq$) and weak simultaneous and conflict constraints, respectively.

From these sets, seven relations are derived as follows:

1.
$$=^! \;=_{Def}\; (CA^{=,!})^*$$

is an equivalence on $SEvents_{TD}$. Let $EQ_S =_{Def} SEvents_{TD} \setminus =^!$.

2.
$$\prec^!_{EQ_S} \;=_{Def}\; ((CA^{\preceq,!} \cup \preceq_{TD}) \setminus =^!)^{+19}$$

where $\preceq_{TD} =_{Def} \preceq_{TDWAVES}$.
Let $\preceq^! =_{Def} (\prec^!_{EQ_S} \downarrow_{=^!} SEvents_{TD}) \cup diag(SEvents_{TD})$. We require that $\preceq^!$ is a partial order on $SEvents_{TD}$[20].

3.
$$\neq^!_{EQ_S} \;=_{Def}\; (CA^{\neq,!} \cup \neq_{TD}) \setminus =^!$$

where $\neq_{TD} =_{Def} \neq_{TDWAVES}$. Let $\neq^! =_{Def} \neq^!_{EQ_S} \downarrow_{=^!} SEvents_{TD}$.

4.
$$=^?_{EQ_S} \;=_{Def}\; (CA^{=,?} \setminus =^!)^*$$

and $=^? \;=_{Def}\; =^?_{EQ_S} \downarrow_{=^!} SEvents_{TD}$. Then $=^?$ is an equivalence on $SEvents_{TD}$. Let $EQ_W =_{Def} SEvents_{TD} \setminus =^?$.

5.
$$\prec^?_{EQ_W} \;=_{Def}\; ((CA^{\preceq,?} \cup \preceq_{TD}) \setminus =^?)^+$$

and $\preceq^? =_{Def} (\prec^?_{EQ_W} \downarrow_{=^?} SEvents_{TD}) \cup diag(SEvents_{TD})$. We require that $\preceq^?$ is a partial order on $SEvents_{TD}$.

6.
$$\neq^?_{EQ_W} \;=_{Def}\; (CA^{\neq,?} \cup \neq_{TD}) \setminus =^?$$

and $\neq^? =_{Def} \neq^?_{EQ_W} \downarrow_{=^?} SEvents_{TD}$.

---

[19] For some relation R and equivalence $\cong$ on some set M, define a relation on $M \setminus \cong$ by
$$R \setminus \cong \;=_{Def}\; \{([e]_\cong, [e']_\cong) \mid \exists e_1 \in [e]_\cong, e_2 \in [e']_\cong : (e_1, e_2) \in R\}.$$

[20] If $R_\cong$ is a relation on $M \setminus \cong$ for some set M, equivalence $\cong$ on M, define a relation on M by
$$R_\cong \downarrow_\cong M \;=_{Def}\; \{(e_1, e_2) \mid ([e_1]_\cong, [e_2]_\cong) \in R_\cong\}.$$

7.
$$\leadsto_{EQ_S} =_{Def} (CA \leadsto \setminus =^!)^+$$

and $\leadsto \ =_{Def} \ \leadsto_{EQ_S} \downarrow_{=^!SEvents_{TD}}$. We require that $\leadsto$ is antisymmetric and

$$\leadsto^{-1} \cap \preceq^! = \emptyset.$$

In the following, let $STD(ed)$ denote the set of STD's over ed.

5.8 Semantics of Symbolic Timing Diagrams

The semantics of an STD TD is defined in two steps. First the semantics of an *instantiated* STD is defined, which is obtained from TD by assigning fixed values to the local variables of TD. Let

$$TD = (PAR, ACTMODE, BODY) \in STD(ed)$$

be given; then from $val \in Val_{L_{TD}}$ we obtain an val-instance of TD, written $TD[L_{TD} \leftarrow val]$ by partial evaluation of the boolean expressions contained in TD as follows:

$$TD[L_{TD} \leftarrow val] = (PAR_\emptyset, ACTMODE_{TD}, BODY_{TD}[L_{TD} \leftarrow val])$$

where $PAR_\emptyset =_{Def} (\emptyset, \emptyset)$ and $BODY_{TD}[L_{TD} \leftarrow val]$ is obtained from $BODY_{TD}$ by replacing each occurrence of a variable $v \in L_{TD}$ in $BODY_{TD}$ by its value $val(v)$ under the instantiation mapping val. Such an instantiated STD can be regarded as an STD over ed without parameters (local variables); in this case we omit the PAR component and simply write $TD = (ACTMODE, BODY)$. An instantiated STD

$$TD = (ACTMODE, BODY)$$

where $BODY = (TDWAVES, TDCONSTRAINTS)$, defines a filter structure

$$\gamma_{TD} = (WAVES, CONSTRAINTS)$$

where $WAVES$ is obtained from $TDWAVES$ by replacing each expression b occurring in $WAVES$ by the predicate $[\![b]\!]$. The sets $UNWIND$ and $EXIT$ in the structure

$$CONSTRAINTS_\gamma = (UNWIND, EXIT, PROPAGATE)$$

are constructed from $TDCONSTRAINTS$ and the seven induced relations inductively:

$i = 0$:

$$\begin{aligned} UNWIND^0 &=_{Def} \{(\zeta_0, WAVES)\} \text{ and} \\ EXIT^0 &=_{Def} \emptyset. \end{aligned}$$

$i > 0$:

$$UNWIND^i =_{Def} \{\pi.\zeta \mid \exists E \subseteq SEvents_{WAVES} :$$
$$\pi \in UNWIND^{i-1} \wedge \pi = \pi_1.\zeta_1$$
$$\wedge \zeta_1 \to^E_{WAVES} \zeta \wedge$$
$$\neg(\exists e \in E, e' \in E^C : e =^! e') \wedge$$
$$\neg(\exists e_1, e_2 \in E : e_1 \neq^! e_2) \wedge$$
$$\neg(\exists e \in E, e' \in E^C : e' \preceq^! e) \wedge$$
$$\neg(\exists e \in E, e' \in E^C : e =^? e') \wedge$$
$$\neg(\exists e_1, e_2 \in E : e_1 \neq^? e_2) \wedge$$
$$\neg(\exists e \in E, e' \in E^C : e' \preceq^? e)$$

where $E^C =_{Def} SEvents_{WAVES} \setminus sevents_{\pi.\zeta}\}$

$$EXIT^i =_{Def} \{\pi.\zeta \mid \exists E \subseteq SEvents_{WAVES} :$$
$$\pi \in UNWIND^{i-1} \wedge \pi = \pi_1.\zeta_1$$
$$\wedge \zeta_1 \to^E_{WAVES} \zeta \wedge$$
$$\neg(\exists e \in E, e' \in E^C : e =^! e') \wedge$$
$$\neg(\exists e_1, e_2 \in E : e_1 \neq^! e_2) \wedge$$
$$\neg(\exists e \in E, e' \in E^C : e' \preceq^! e) \wedge$$
$$((\exists e \in E, e' \in E^C : e =^? e') \vee$$
$$(\exists e_1, e_2 \in E : e_1 \neq^? e_2) \vee$$
$$(\exists e \in E, e' \in E^C : e' \preceq^? e))$$

where $E^C =_{Def} SEvents_{WAVES} \setminus sevents_{\pi.\zeta}\}$.

Note that for all $\pi \in Path_{WAVES}$, $length_\pi \leq length_{WAVES}$; hence we have

Fact : $\exists i_0 \forall i \geq i_0 : UNWIND^i = EXIT^i = \emptyset$.

Now define

$UNWIND =_{Def} \bigcup_{i \geq 0} UNWIND^i$ and
$EXIT =_{Def} \bigcup_{i \geq 0} EXIT^i$ and
$PROPAGATE =_{Def} \{\zeta \in Front_{WAVES} \mid \exists e \in im(\zeta),$
$e', e'' \in SEvents_{WAVES} : \kappa_{\zeta(id_{e''})} \leq \kappa_{e''} \wedge$
$(e_{act} \rightsquigarrow e'' \vee e' \rightsquigarrow e'' \wedge \kappa_{e'} < \kappa_{\zeta(id_{e'})})\}$.

The semantics of an instantiated STD TD is based on the semantics of the associated filter structure γ_{TD} and the concept of *activation*. If the component $ACTMODE_{TD}$ of TD is "initial", then the semantics requires that an observation $obs \in Obs_{ed}$ initially satisfies $Activate_{\gamma_{TD}}$ and that the observation itself satisfies the filter γ_{TD}. If the component $ACTMODE_{TD}$ of TD is "dynamic", then the semantics requires that whenever an observation $obs \in Obs_{ed}$ satisfies $Activate_{\gamma_{TD}}$ then the rest of the observation from this time instance on must satisfy the filter γ_{TD}. Thus, for an instantiated STD TD, we define

$ACTMODE = initial$:
$\quad [\![TD]\!] =_{Def} \{obs \in Obs_{ed} \mid obs(0) \models Activate_{\gamma_{TD}} \land obs \in [\![\gamma_{TD}]\!]\}$
$ACTMODE = dynamic$:
$\quad [\![TD]\!] =_{Def} \{obs \in Obs_{ed} \mid \forall k \geq 0 : obs(k) \models Activate_{\gamma_{TD}} \rightarrow obs^k \in [\![\gamma_{TD}]\!]\}$.

The semantics of a STD TD with parameters is defined as the intersection of the semantics of all possible instantiations of TD, i.e.

$$[\![TD]\!] =_{Def} \bigcap_{val \in Val_{L_{TD}}} [\![TD[L_{TD} \leftarrow val]]\!].$$

5.9 Translation to temporal logic

It turns out that the semantics of a STD can be characterized using the temporal logic introduced in Section 4. First, recall the semantics of a filter structure γ_{TD} resulting from an instantiated STD TD over some entity declaration ed. We define $TL(\gamma_{TD})$ as a the first-order temporal logic formula over $Vars_{ed}$, which characterizes the semantics $[\![\gamma_{TD}]\!]$ of the filter γ_{TD}, by induction on $length_{\gamma_{TD}}$:

$length_{\gamma_{TD}} = 0 : \quad TL(\gamma_{TD}) \equiv \mathbf{true}$
$length_{\gamma_{TD}} > 0 :$
$TL(\gamma) \equiv \quad [TL(Stable_\gamma)$
$\qquad \begin{cases} \mathbf{unless} & \text{if } \zeta_{0,WAVES_\gamma} \notin PROPAGATE_\gamma \\ \mathbf{until} & \text{if } \zeta_{0,WAVES_\gamma} \in PROPAGATE_\gamma \end{cases}$
$\qquad (TL(PredExit_\gamma)$
$\qquad \lor \bigvee_{E \in ExitStep_\gamma} TL(Match_\gamma(E))$
$\qquad \lor \bigvee_{E \in UnwindStep_\gamma} (TL(Match_\gamma(E)) \land TL(\gamma^E))$
$\qquad)] \quad \text{where } \gamma = \gamma_{TD}.$

Note that for the predicates defined for filter structures in Section 5.5, $TL(Activate_{\gamma_{TD}})$, $TL(Stable_\gamma)$, $TL(PredExit_\gamma)$ and $TL(Match_\gamma)$ denote the corresponding boolean expressions (constructed from the expressions occurring in TD). The characteristic TL formula of an STD TD with a set L_{TD} of local variables, $L = \{y_1, \ldots, y_k\}$ for some $k \geq 0$, is defined by:

1. $ACTMODE_{TD} = initial$:

$$TL(TD) \equiv_{Def} \forall y_1 \ldots \forall y_k : TL(Activate_{\gamma_{TD}}) \land TL(\gamma_{TD}).$$

2. $ACTMODE_{TD} = dynamic$:

$$TL(TD) \equiv_{Def} \forall y_1 \ldots \forall y_k : \Box(TL(Activate_{\gamma_{TD}}) \rightarrow TL(\gamma_{TD})).$$

5.10 Graphical denotation of Symbolic Timing Diagrams

The *graphical denotation* of an STD

$$TD = (PAR, ACTMODE, BODY) \in STD(ed)$$

for some *ed*, is depicted as shown in Fig. 8, if $PAR_{TD} = (\{y_1, \ldots, y_k\}, (y \in \{y_1, \ldots, y_k\} \mapsto D_y \in DOM))$ and $ACTMODE = dynamic$. The activation bar is depicted as a double line, if $ACTMODE = initial$.

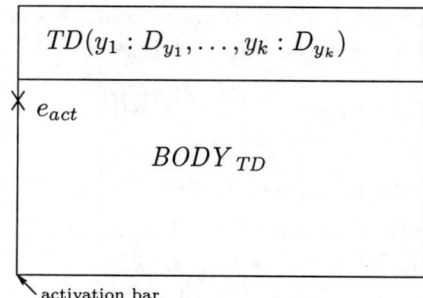

FIG. 8. Graphical denotation of an STD (*BODY* is detailed below).

Recall that the body of a STD constitutes of waveforms and constraint arcs. A waveform $\rho = TDWAVES(id)$ is depicted as shown in Fig. 9 if

$$TDWAVES(id) = (b_{actcond}, kernel_{id}) \text{ where}$$
$$kernel_{id} = (\kappa \in \{\kappa_1, \ldots, \kappa_r\} \mapsto (b^k_{contcond}, b^k_{exitcond}))$$

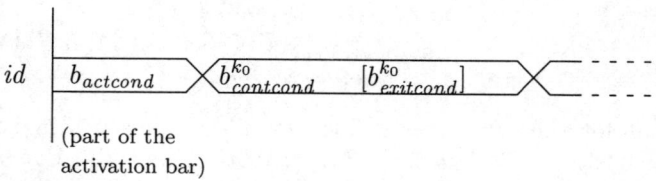

FIG. 9. Graphical denotation of a waveform.

Finally, the graphical denotations of the elements of the seven sets of constraint arcs are listed with their names in Fig. 10. Note that there are six types of *superpositions* of constraint arcs, which have special denotations.

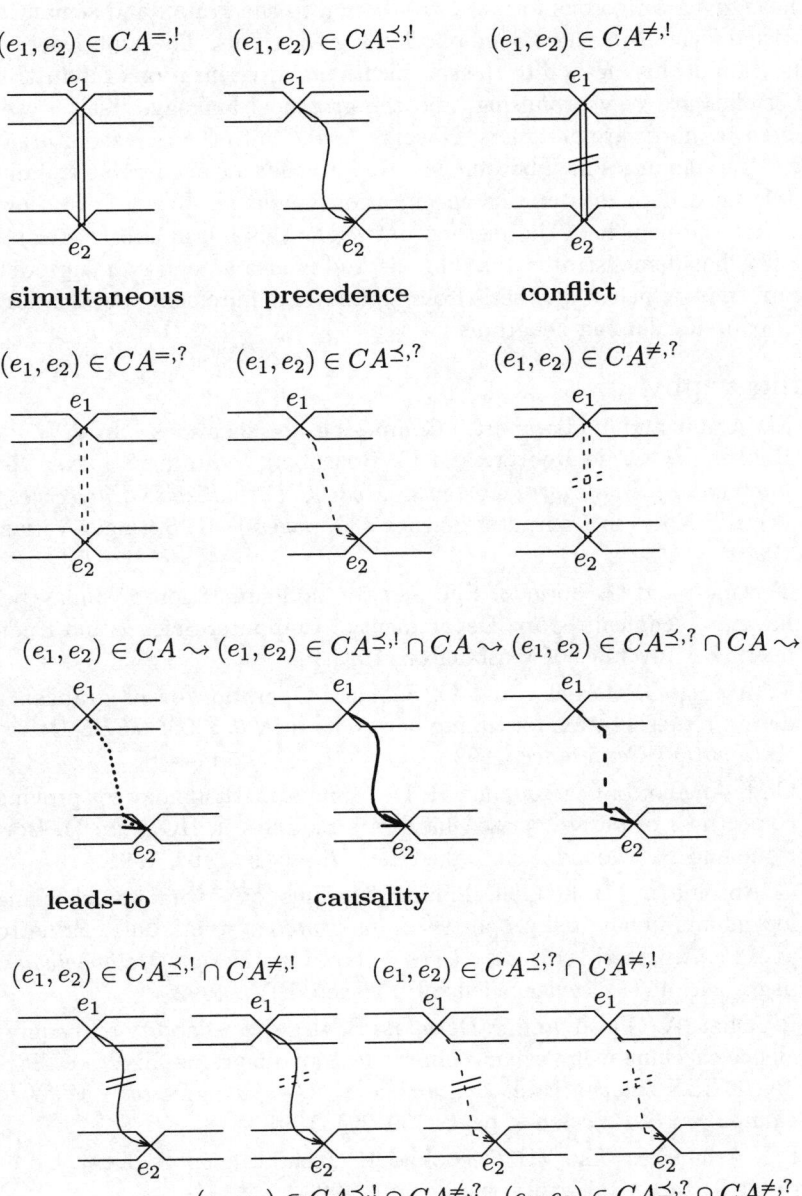

FIG. 10. Graphical denotation of constraints.

5.11 Summary

We have given a rigorous formal introduction to the syntax and semantics of a visual formalism called Symbolic Timing Diagrams. The experiences in application of this method to the specification and verification of industrial case studies are very promising, and the graphical language itself is well accepted by hardware designers. Nevertheless, due to the rich structure of STD's, the semantics may become involved, so that a considerable training effort is needed to master this specification language. We believe, however, that the benefit of the method outweighs this initial effort. Related work [54] has demonstrated that the method is also a good starting point for performing efficient synthesis from high-level requirement specifications using Symbolic Timing Diagrams.

Bibliography

1. M. Abadi and L. Lamport. Composing specifications. In J.W. de Bakker, W.-P. de Roever, and G. Rozenberg, editors, *Stepwise Refinement of Distributed Systems. Models, Formalisms, Correctness*, Lecture Notes in Computer Science 430, pages 1–41. Springer-Verlag, 1990.
2. T. Amon and G. Boriello. Specification and simulation of timing behavior. Technical report, Department of Computer Science and Engineering, University of Washington, 1993.
3. T. Amon, G. Boriello, and C. Sequin. Operation/event graphs: a design representation for timing behavior. In *29th ACM/IEEE Design Automation Conference*, 1992.
4. C.M. Angelo, L. Claesen, and H. De Man. A methodology for proving correctness of parameterized hardware modules in HOL. In D. Borrione and R. Waxman, editors, *CHDL91*, pages 43–62, 1991.
5. C. Antoine and B. Le Goff. Timing diagrams for writing and checking logical and behavioral properties of integrated systems. In P. Prinetto and P. Camurati, editors, *Correct Hardware Design Methodologies*, pages 441–453. Elsevier Science Publishers B.V., 1992.
6. P. Ashar, A. Ghosh, and S. Devadas. Boolean satisfiability and equivalence checking using general binary decision diagrams. In *Proceedings 1991 IEEE International Conference on Computer Design: VLSI in Computers & Processors*, pages 259–264, 1991.
7. P.J. Ashenden. The VHDL cookbook. Technical report, Dept. Computer Science, University of Adelaide, 1990.
8. G. Berry and L. Cosserat. The synchronous programming language Esterel and its mathematical semantics. In S.D. Brookes, editor, *CMU Seminar on Concurrency*, Lecture Notes in Computer Science 197, pages 389–449. Springer-Verlag, 1985.

9. C. Bolchini, M. Bombana, P. Cavalloro, C. Costi, F. Fummi, and G. Zaza. A design methodology for the correct specification of VLSI systems. In *EUROMICRO 93*, pages 563–570, 1993.
10. G. Boriello. *A New Interface Specification Methodology and its Application to Transducer Synthesis*. PhD thesis, U.C. Berkeley, UCB/CSD 88/430, May 1988.
11. D. Borrione, L. Pierre, and A. Salem. PREVAIL: A proof environment for VHDL descriptions. In *Proc. Advanced Research Workshop on Correct Hardware Design Methodologies*, pages 145–168, 1991.
12. R.S. Boyer and J.S. Moore. *A Computational Logic*. Academic Press, 1979.
13. R.S. Boyer and J.S. Moore. *A Computational Logic Handbook*. Academic Press, 1988.
14. R.E. Bryant. Graph-based algorithms for boolean function manipulation. *IEEE Trans. Comput.*, C-35:677–691, 1986.
15. R.E. Bryant. On the complexity of VLSI implementations and graph representations of boolean functions with application to integer multiplication. *IEEE Trans. Computers*, 40:205–213, 1991.
16. J.R. Burch, E.M. Clarke, and D.E. Long. Representing circuits more efficiently in symbolic model checking. In *28th ACM/IEEE Design Automation Conference*, 1991.
17. J.R. Burch, E.M. Clarke, K.L. McMillan, and D.L. Dill. Sequential circuit verification using symbolic model checking. In *27th ACM/IEEE Design Automation Conference*, pages 46–51, 1990.
18. E.M. Clarke, O. Grumberg, and D.E. Long. Model checking and abstraction. In *Proceedings of the 19th ACM Symposium on Principles of Programming Languages*, pages 343–354, 1992.
19. E.M. Clarke, E.A. Emerson, and A.P. Sistla. Automatic verification of finite state concurrent systems using temporal logic specifications: a practical approach. In *Proceedings of the 10th ACM Symposium on Principles of Programming Languages*, pages 117–126, 1983.
20. E.M. Clarke, E.A. Emerson, and A.P. Sistla. Automatic verification of finite-state concurrent systems using temporal logic. *ACM Trans. on Programming Languages and Systems*, 8:244–263, 1986.
21. E.M. Clarke, D.E. Long, and K.L. McMillan. A language for compositional specification and verification of finite state hardware controllers. *Proceedings of the IEEE*, 79(9):1283–1292, 1991.
22. CLSI Solutions. VFormal user's manual: formal verification for VHDL designs, 1993.
23. J.V. Cook. Verification of the C/30 microcode using the state delta verification system (SDVS). In *Proceedings of the 13th National Com-*

puter Security Conference. National Bureau of Standards/National Computer Security Center, 1990.

24. W. Damm, H. Hungar, P. Kelb, and R. Schlör. Using graphical specification languages and symbolic model checking in the verification of a production cell. In C. Lewerenz and T. Lindner, editors, *Case Study "Production Cell": A Comparative Study in Formal Specification and Verification.* FZI Publication, 1994.

25. W. Damm, B. Josko, and R. Schlör. A net-based semantics for VHDL. In *Proceedings EURO-DAC/EURO-VHDL 93*, pages 514–519, 1993.

26. W. Damm and G. Döhmen. Specifying distributed computer architectures in AADL. *Parallel Computing*, 9, 1989.

27. W. Damm, G. Döhmen, V. Gerstner, and B. Josko. Modular verification of petri nets: the temporal logic approach. In J.W. de Bakker, W.-P. de Roever, and G. Rozenberg, editors, *Stepwise Refinement of Distributed Systems. Models, Formalisms, Correctness*, Lecture Notes in Computer Science 430, pages 180–207. Springer-Verlag, 1990.

28. D. Dams, G. Döhmen, R. Gerth, P. Kelb, R. Herrmann, and H. Pargmann. Design of a VHDL/S model checker based on adaptive state and data abstraction. In *CAV 94*, 1994.

29. D. Dams, O. Grumberg, and R. Gerth. Generation of reduced models for checking fragments of CTL. In C. Courcoubetis, editor, *Computer Aided Verification*, Lecture Notes in Computer Science 697, pages 479–490. Springer-Verlag, 1993.

30. D. Déharbe and D. Borrione. Symbolic model checking of VHDL design entities. Technical Report RR 9925 -I-, Laboratoire ARTEMIS, Grenoble, December 1993.

31. G. Döhmen. Petri nets as intermediate representation between VHDL and symbolic transition systems. In *Proceedings EURO-DAC/EURO-VHDL 94*, pages 572–577, 1994.

32. E.A. Emerson. Temporal and modal logic. In J. van Leeuwen, editor, *Handbook of Theoretical Computer Science Volume B*, pages 995–1072. Elsevier, Amsterdam, 1990.

33. I.V. Filippenko. VHDL verification in the state delta verification system (SDVS). In P.A. Subrahmanyam, editor, *International Workshop on Formal Methods in VLSI Designs*, 1991.

34. S. Finn, M.P. Fourman, M. Francis, and R. Harris. Formal system design – interactive synthesis based on computer-assisted formal reasoning. In G. Musgrave and U. Lauther, editors, *Proceedings of IMEC-IFIP International Workshop on Applied Formal Methods For Correct VLSI Design*, pages Volume 1, 97–110. Elsevier, 1989.

35. M. Fujita and H. Fujisawa. Specification, verification and synthesis of control circuits with propositional temporal logic. In J.A. Darringer

and F.J. Rammig, editors, *Computer Hardware Description Languages and their Applications*, pages 265–279. Elsevier, 1990.
36. P. Glavan and D. Rosenzweig. Communicating evolving algebras. In E. Börger, editor, *Computer Science Logic*, Lecture Notes in Computer Science 702, pages 182–215. Springer-Verlag, 1993.
37. M.J.C. Gordon. HOL: a proof generating system for higher-order logic. In G. Birtwistle and P.A. Subrahmanyam, editors, *VLSI Specification, Verification and Synthesis*, pages 73–128. Kluwer, 1987.
38. M.J.C. Gordon and T.F. Melham. *Introduction to HOL: A Theorem Proving Environment for Higher-Order Logic*. Cambridge University Press, 1993.
39. W. Grass, M. Mutz, and W.-D. Tiedemann. High-level synthesis based on formal methods. In *Workshop Design Methodologies for Microelectronics and Signal Processing*, Gliwice - Cracow, Poland, 1993.
40. O. Grumberg and D.E. Long. Model checking and modular verification. In *CONCUR 91*, 1991.
41. D. Harel, A. Pnueli, J.P. Schmidt, and R. Sherman. On the formal semantics of statecharts. In *Proceeding IEEE Symposium on Logic in Computer Science*, pages 54–64, 1987.
42. D. Harel and A. Pnueli. On the development of reactive systems. In K.R. Apt, editor, *Logics and Models of Concurrent Systems*, NATO ASI Series F13, pages 477–498. Springer-Verlag, 1985.
43. J. Helbig, R. Schlör, W. Damm, G. Döhmen, and P. Kelb. VHDL/S – integrating statecharts, timing diagrams, and VHDL. *Microprocessing and Microprogramming*, 38:571–580, 1993.
44. R. Herrmann and H. Pargmann. Computing binary decision diagrams for VHDL data types. In *Proceedings EURO-DAC/EURO-VHDL 94*, pages 578–583, 1994.
45. R. Herrmann and H. Pargmann. Symbolic transition systems for VHDL specifications. Technical report, OFFIS, Oldenburg, Germany, 1994.
46. W.A. Hunt. The FM5801: a verified microprocessor. Technical Report 47, University of Texas at Austin, 1986.
47. W.A. Hunt. The mechanical verification of a microprocessor design. In D. Borrione, editor, *From HDL Descriptions to Guaranteed Correct Circuits Designs*, pages 89–129. North-Holland, 1987.
48. IEEE standard 1076–1987, VHDL language reference manual, 1988.
49. C.N. Ip and D.L. Dill. Better verification through symmetry. In D. Agnew, L. Claesen, and R. Camposano, editors, *CHDL 93*, pages 87–100, 1993.
50. B. Josko. Verifying the correctness of AADL modules using model

checking. In J.W. de Bakker, W.-P. de Roever, and G. Rozenberg, editors, *Stepwise Refinement of Distributed Systems. Models, Formalisms, Correctness*, Lecture Notes in Computer Science 430, pages 386–400. Springer-Verlag, 1990.

51. B. Josko. *Modular Specification and Verification of Reactive Systems.* Habilitationsschrift, Universität Oldenburg, 1993.

52. P.K. Khordoc, M. Dufresne, and E. Czerny. A stimulus/response system based on hierarchical timing diagrams. Technical Report 770, Université de Montreal, 1991.

53. C.D. Kloos, T. de Miguel Moro, T.R. Valladares, G.R. Filho, and A.M. López. VHDL generation from a timed extension of the formal description technique LOTOS within the FORMAT project. In *EUROMICRO 93*, pages 589–596, 1993.

54. F. Korf and R. Schlör. Interface controller synthesis from requirement specifications. In *Proceedings, The European Conference on Design Automation*, 1994.

55. F. Kröger. *Temporal Logic of Programs.* EATCS-Monographs. Springer-Verlag, 1987.

56. K.G. Larsen. Compositional theories based on an operational semantics of contexts. In J.W. de Bakker, W.-P. de Roever, and G. Rozenberg, editors, *Stepwise Refinement of Distributed Systems. Models, Formalisms, Correctness*, Lecture Notes in Computer Science 430, pages 487–518. Springer-Verlag, 1990.

57. B.H. Levy. An overview of hardware verification using the state delta verification system (SDVS). In P.A. Subrahmanyam, editor, *International Workshop on Formal Methods in VLSI Designs*, 1991.

58. R. Lipssett, C. Schaefer, and C. Ussery. *VHDL: Hardware Description and Design.* Kluwer Academic Publishers, 1991.

59. Z. Manna and A. Pnueli. *The Temporal Logic of Reactive and Concurrent Systems. Specification.* Springer-Verlag, 1992.

60. K.L. McMillian. *Symbolic Model Checking. An Approach to the State Explosion Problem.* PhD thesis, Carnegie Mellon University, Pittsburgh, 1992.

61. P. Moeschler, H.P. Amann, and F. Pellandini. High-level modelling using extended timing diagrams. In *Proceedings EURO-DAC with EURO-VHDL 93*, pages 494–499, 1993.

62. S. Olcoz and J. M. Colom. Towards a formal semantics of IEEE Std. VHDL 1076. In *EURO-DAC/EURO-VHDL'93*, pages 526–531, 1993.

63. S. Olcoz and J.M. Colom. Analysis tools applied to VHDL. In *EUROMICRO 93*, pages 597–604, 1993.

64. G.D. Plotkin. A structural approach to operational semantics. Tech-

nical Report DAIMI FN-19, Computer Science Department, Aarhus University, 1981.
65. A. Pnueli. In transition from global to modular temporal reasoning about programs. In K.R. Apt, editor, *Logics and Models of Concurrent Systems*, NATO ASI Series, Vol. F13, pages 123–144. Springer-Verlag, 1985.
66. R. Schlör. *Symbolic Timing Diagrams: A Visual Formalism for Specification and Verification of System-level Hardware Design*. PhD thesis, Universität Oldenburg, 1994 (to appear).
67. R. Schlör and W. Damm. Specification and verification of system-level hardware designs using timing diagrams. In *The European Conference on Design Automation with the European Event in ASIC Design*, pages 518–524, 1993.
68. R. Schlör and J. Helbig. Symbolic timing diagrams – visual constraint programming for system level design. Technical report, Universität Oldenburg, 1993.
69. J.P. Van Tassel. The semantics of VHDL with VAL and HOL: towards practical verification tools. Tech. rep. 196, University of Cambridge, Computer Laboratory, 1990.
70. J.P. Van Tassel. A formalisation of the VHDL simulation cycle. Tech. rep. 249, University of Cambridge, Computer Laboratory, 1992.
71. J.P. Van Tassel. *Femto-VHDL: The Semantics of a Subset of VHDL and its Embedding in the HOL Theorem-prover*. PhD thesis, University of Cambridge, 1993.
72. W.D. Tiedemann, S. Lenk, C. Grobe, and W. Grass. Introducing structure into behavioural descriptions obtained from timing diagram specifications. In *EUROMICRO 93*, pages 581–588, 1993.
73. G. Umbreit. Providing a VHDL interface for proof systems. In *European Design Automation Conference*, 1992.
74. A. Valmari. Stubborn sets for reduced state space generation. In G. Rozenberg, editor, *Advances in Petri Nets 1990*, Lecture Notes in Computer Science 483, pages 491–515. Springer-Verlag, 1989.
75. A. Valmari. On-the-fly verification with stubborn sets. In C. Courcoubetis, editor, *5th Conference on Computer-Aided Verification*, Lecture Notes in Computer Science 697. Springer-Verlag, 1993.
76. A. Valmari. A stubborn attack on state explosion. In R.P. Kurshan and E.M. Clarke, editors, *Computer-Aided Verification '90*, volume 3 of *DIMACS Series in Discrete Mathematics and Theoretical Computer Science*, pages 25–41. American Mathematical Society, 1991.
77. P. Wolper. Expressing interesting properties of programs in propositional temporal logic. In *Proceedings of the 13th ACM Symposium on Principles of Programming Languages*, pages 184–193, 1986.

Specification and Verification of Gate-level VHDL Models of Synchronous and Asynchronous Circuits

David M. Russinoff

Abstract

We present a mathematical definition of a hardware description language (HDL) that admits a semantics-preserving translation to a subset of VHDL. Our HDL includes the basic VHDL propagation delay mechanisms and gate-level circuit descriptions. We also develop formal procedures for deriving and verifying concise behavioral specifications of combinational and sequential devices. The HDL and the specification procedures have been formally encoded in the computational logic of Boyer and Moore, which provides a LISP implementation as well as a facility for mechanical proof-checking. As an application, we design, specify, and verify a circuit that achieves asynchronous communication by means of the biphase mark protocol.

1 Introduction

During the course of the design process, a typical hardware device is modeled at various levels of abstraction. The most abstract representation is generally a sequential machine, which is initially derived from a given behavioral specification. This model is then gradually refined to produce a concrete representation, such as a network of gates, which is more amenable to implementation.

A hardware design is validated by demonstrating the equivalence of these representations. This is most commonly effected through simulation. The VHSIC Hardware Description Language [2] (VHDL), which is rapidly becoming an industry standard, supports modeling and simulation of circuits at all stages of the design process. In VHDL, a circuit component is represented as an *entity*, which may be associated with various alternative *architectures*. An architecture may either specify an abstract

---

This work was sponsored in part at Computational Logic, Inc. by National Aeronautics and Space Administration Langley Research Center (NAS1-18878). The views and conclusions contained in this document are those of the author and should not be interpreted as representing the official policies, either expressed or implied, of Computational Logic, Inc., NASA Langley Research Center, or the U.S. Government.

behavioral description of a device, or provide a concrete *structural* definition in terms of simpler components. The equivalence of architectures may be confirmed through comparative simulations. Once a sufficiently low-level VHDL architecture has been derived and validated in this manner, it may be implemented directly, even automatically.

However, since exhaustive testing of complex circuits is impractical, the effectiveness of simulation as a validation method is limited. An alternative approach is provided by formal hardware verification. The object of formal verification is to prove mathematically that a given model of a hardware device satisfies a given behavioral specification. Once this is accomplished, the design problem is reduced to that of implementing the model.

Naturally, the utility of this approach requires that the specification is sufficiently abstract to provide a comprehensive description of functionality, and that the model is sufficiently concrete to allow straightforward implementation. Unfortunately, hardware verification techniques have been deficient in this regard: proofs of of high-level specifications generally depend on similarly high-level implicit assumptions. In particular, verification of sequential machine behavior has been achieved only by basing the hardware model itself on the sequential machine concept.

For the purpose of addressing this problem, we have designed a formal hardware simulation language that admits a semantics-preserving translation to a subset of VHDL. The language is based on the paradigm of *event-driven simulation* and the basic signal propagation and delay mechanisms of VHDL. In particular, it includes the VHDL "delta-delay" mechanism, which complicates its definition considerably. Since this mechanism is irrelevant to our present purpose, we shall present here a simplified version of the language, in which all delays are required to be positive. The full language definition may be found in [6].

The language that we shall describe includes behavioral modules as primitives, which we use to model gates, and structural modules, with which we represent hierarchically constructed circuits. Our goal is to derive and verify abstract specifications of these gate-level models.

First, we consider the relatively simple class of *combinational* circuits, i.e., circuits that are free of cyclic paths. Each output of such a circuit is naturally associated with a certain Boolean function of the inputs. This association is commonly stated as follows: the value of an output at any time may be computed by applying the associated function to the current input values. Obviously, this description is valid only with respect to hardware models that ignore propagation delay. We shall derive a more accurate specification of combinational circuits and verify its validity in the context of our model.

The analysis of sequential circuits is considerably more complicated. While the abstract sequential machine model is well understood, its precise relationship with the actual behavior of the hardware that it is intended to describe is not. The sequential machine characterization is traditionally based on the extravagant assumption that signal values may change only at discrete points occurring at regular time intervals. This allows the behavior of a signal to be represented abstractly as a sequence of values. The value of an output over a given interval is then expressed as a function of the sequence of past input values. Of course, the underlying model again must disregard propagation delay. This approximation seems questionable, since the functionality of the basic state-holding elements generally depends critically on the presence of delays.

We shall treat a class of sequential circuits that may be characterized as *synchronous resettable rising-edge-triggered* devices. The basic memory element employed in their construction is a resettable clocked d-flip-flop, composed of nand gates. After verifying a precise specification of the behavior of this component, we establish a procedure for deriving high-level sequential machine descriptions for this class of circuits, and prove a theorem that gives a precise statement of the relationship between the sequential machine description of a circuit and its behavior as defined by our gate-level semantics.

One advantage of our approach is that we can effectively model asynchronous communication between individually synchronous processors. In fact, we shall present the definition of a circuit in our language that consists of two independently clocked sequential modules, and prove that communication between them is achieved by means of the well known biphase mark protocol [5]. The circuit design and the proof are both based on Moore's work on asynchrony [4], which includes a formal model of asynchronous communication and a rigorous formulation of the protocol.

The syntax and semantics of our language are both based on the *S-expressions* of LISP. This decision was motivated by our desire to support its analysis with the use of the Nqthm system of Boyer and Moore [1]. Nqthm is based on a constructive formal logic for which the intended model is the domain of S-expressions. Thus, there is a correspondence between the formulas of this logic and informal propositions about S-expressions. A user of the system may extend the logic by adding axioms that correspond to definitions of computable functions over this domain.

Mechanical support for the Nqthm logic is provided by a LISP implementation that includes (1) an evaluator that computes values of functions defined in the logic, and (2) a theorem prover that may be used to derive logical consequences of the axioms. Since these theorems may be interpreted as propositions about functions of S-expressions, the prover may be used to verify mechanically the correctness of properties of these functions that have been derived by traditional (informal) mathematical methods.

All of the functions involved in the construction of our language, which we describe informally, meet the computability requirement for encoding as Nqthm definitions [1]. In fact, we have developed an Nqthm theory that formalizes these functions, including the module recognizers that form the syntax of the language, the interpreter that constitutes its semantics, and various procedures for deriving behavioral specifications of its programs. Thus, we have a complete LISP implementation of our language, provided by the Nqthm evaluator.

Moreover, all of our results, which are justified by informal (but mathematically rigorous) proofs, correspond in a natural way to Nqthm formulas. Thus, these proofs could, in principle, be checked mechanically by the Nqthm prover, thereby increasing our confidence in their validity at the the expense of some effort. In general, we have found it practical to employ the prover to check those proofs that involve extensive computation or detailed case analysis, while relying instead on the conventional social review process to detect any errors in our more intelligible proofs. In this instance, most of the results pertaining to specific circuits, including the components of the biphase mark implementation, have been mechanically verified, but at the time of this writing, most of the more general theorems have not.

Another benefit of the Nqthm formalization is that it provides a basis for a LISP implementation of the translator from our language to VHDL [3]. This potentially allows commercial VHDL synthesis tools to be used to implement our programs in silicon. As another application of more immediate interest, we have executed the translations of many of our programs using the Vantage VHDL simulator. For the simulations that we have tested, which include all of those described herein, the Vantage results were identical to those produced by our LISP-based interpreter. Aside from the practical advantage of increased efficiency, this offers evidence that we have achieved our goal of semantically capturing the VHDL subset in which we are interested. Indeed, in the absence of any comprehensive formal semantics for VHDL itself, these empirical observations provide the most convincing evidence possible.

2 Definition of the Language

2.1 S-expressions

Along with the set $\mathbf{N}$ of natural numbers, we posit a set $\mathbf{B} = \{\mathcal{T}, \mathcal{F}\}$ and an infinite set $\mathbf{L}$, the elements of which are called *Boolean* and *literal atoms*, respectively. These three sets are assumed to be pairwise disjoint, and any element of their union is called an *atom*. We further assume that no atom is an ordered pair of atoms, and we recursively define an *S-expression* to be an atom or an ordered pair of S-expressions. $\mathbf{S}$ denotes the set of all S-expressions. Three basic operations on $\mathbf{S}$ are defined: if $z = (x,y) \in \mathbf{S} \times \mathbf{S}$, then $car(z) = x$, $cdr(z) = y$, and $cons(x,y) = z$.

We also assume the existence of various distinct literal atoms, which we shall mention as we proceed. Among these is the atom NIL. A *list* is an S-expression that is either NIL or an ordered pair $z \in \mathbf{S} \times \mathbf{S}$ such that $cdr(z)$ is a list. The list NIL is denoted alternatively as (), and a non-NIL list z is denoted as $(a_1 \ldots a_n)$, where $a_1 = car(z)$ and $(a_2 \ldots a_n)$ denotes $cdr(z)$. In this case, n is the *length* of z, and $a_1, \ldots, a_n$ are its *members*. For $1 \leq i \leq n$, $nth(i, z)$ is defined to be a_i. A list is a *bit vector* if each of its members is a Boolean atom.

A function $f : \mathbf{B}^n \to \mathbf{B}$ is an n-ary Boolean function. The following Boolean functions are called *elementary*: the 0-ary functions $t0$ and $f0$, with values $\mathcal{T}$ and $\mathcal{F}$, respectively; the unary function $not1$; the binary functions $and2$, $or2$, $nand2$, $nor2$, and $xor2$; the ternary functions $and3$, $or3$, $nand3$, $nor3$, and $xor3$; the quaternary functions $and4$, $or4$, $nand4$, $nor4$, and $xor4$; and the quinary functions $and5$, $or5$, $nand5$, $nor5$, and $xor5$. The definitions of these functions are assumed to be understood.

For the purpose of encoding Boolean function calls, we also assume that each elementary Boolean function f is associated with a unique literal atom $\bar{f}$ that is denoted with the same name as f. Thus, the function $not1$ is associated with the literal atom $\overline{not1} =$ NOT1. We define a *Boolean term* over a list L of distinct literal atoms to be an S-expression that is either (a) a member of L, or (b) a list $(\bar{f} \tau_1 \ldots \tau_n)$, where f is an n-ary elementary Boolean function and each τ_i is an Boolean term over L.

Let $L = (s_1 \ldots s_k)$ be a list of distinct literal atoms and let $V = (v_1 \ldots v_k)$ be a bit vector. Then $pairlist(L, V)$ is defined to be the list $A = ((s_1, v_1) \ldots (s_k, v_k))$, which is called an *association list*. If τ is a Boolean term over L, then we define $eval(\tau, A)$ to be (a) v_i, if $\tau = s_i$, or (b) $f(eval(\tau_1, A), \ldots, eval(\tau_n, A))$, if $\tau = (\bar{f} \tau_1 \ldots \tau_n)$.

2.2 Waveforms

In the simplified version of our language on which the present work is based, our model of time is the set $\mathbf{N}$. Thus, a moment is represented by a natural number, which we take arbitrarily to be the number of picoseconds elapsed since the beginning of a simulation. For $t_1, t_2 \in \mathbf{N}$, the interval $\{t \in \mathbf{N} : t_1 \leq t < t_2\}$ will be denoted as $[t_1, t_2)$.

An *event* is an ordered pair $e = (v, t)$, where $v = value(e) \in \mathbf{B}$ and $t = time(e) \in \mathbf{N}$. Let $w = ((v_n, t_n) \ldots (v_0, t_0))$ be a list of events. If $t_i > t_{i-1}$ and $v_i \neq v_{i-1}$ for $0 < i \leq n$, and $t_0 = 0$, then w is a *waveform*. We define $\hat{w} : \mathbf{T} \to \mathbf{B}$ by $\hat{w}(t) = v_j$, where j is the greatest value of i satisfying $t_i \leq t$; $\hat{w}(t)$ is called the *value of w at t*. Note that $\hat{w}_1 = \hat{w}_2$ iff $w_1 = w_2$. If $t = t_j$, then we shall say that w *has a new value at t*. We also define the *history of w relative to t* to be the waveform $hist(w, t) = ((v_j, t_j) \ldots (v_0, t_0))$.

A *packet* is a list of waveforms, $p = (w_1 \ldots w_n)$, $n \geq 0$. For any $t \in \mathbf{N}$, the *value of p at t* is the bit vector $\hat{p}(t) = (\hat{w}_1(t) \ldots \hat{w}_n(t))$; p *has a new value at t* if any member of p does. The *history* of p relative to t is the packet $hist(p, t) = (hist(w_1, t) \ldots hist(w_n, t))$.

The behavior of each signal occurring in a circuit will be modeled as a waveform. When a waveform is considered in the context of a current time t_0, each of its members e is viewed as a past, current, or future event, according to the relationship between $time(e)$ and t_0. Past and present events are immutable, but future events are subject to deletion as they are superceded by newly scheduled events.

The fundamental operation of the simulator is the updating of a waveform w at a time t_0 by scheduling a new event $e = (v, t_v)$, where $t_0 < t_v$. This may be performed by either of two procedures, corresponding to the *transport* and *inertial* delay modes of VHDL. The simpler of these is transport mode, in which each event (v', t') with $t' \geq t_v$ is deleted from w, and e is then *consed* to the result, unless that result already has value v at t_v. The updated waveform w' is computed as the value of $transport(w, v, t_v)$, which is defined recursively as follows:

(1) Let $car(w) = (v_f, t_f)$. If $t_f \geq t_v$, then $w' = transport(cdr(w), v, t_v)$; otherwise:
(2) If $v_f = v$, then $w' = w$; otherwise:
(3) $w' = cons((v, t_v), w)$.

Alternatively, w' may be described in terms of the function $\hat{w}'$:

$$\hat{w}'(t) = \begin{cases} v & \text{if } t \geq t_v \\ \hat{w}(t) & \text{if } t < t_v. \end{cases}$$

Inertial mode is somewhat more complicated: every event (v', t') with $t' > t_0$ is deleted from w, and if $\hat{w}(t_0) \neq v$, then a single event with value v is consed to the result. If $\hat{w}(t_v) = v$, then the time of this event is the time of the last event of w that precedes t_v; otherwise, it is t_v. Note that this procedure takes the current time t_0 as an additional argument, and requires that $t_0 < t_v$. The recursive definition of $w' = inertial(w, v, t_0, t_v)$ is given as follows:

(1) Let $\bar{w} = hist(w, t_0)$. If $\hat{w}(t_0) = v$, then $w' = \bar{w}$; otherwise:
(2) Let $car(w) = (v_f, t_f)$. If $t_f \geq t_v$, then $w' = inertial(cdr(w), v, t_0, t_v)$; otherwise:
(3) If $v_f = v$, then $w' = cons((v, t_f), \bar{w})$; otherwise:
(4) $w' = cons((v, t_v), \bar{w})$.

The difference between the two propagation modes is illustrated in Fig. 1. The diagram labelled (a) represents the waveform

$$w = ((\mathcal{T}, 9)\,(\mathcal{F}, 8)\,(\mathcal{T}, 6)\,(\mathcal{F}, 5)\,(\mathcal{T}, 3)\,(\mathcal{F}, 1)\,(\mathcal{T}, 0)).$$

The results of updating w at time 1 by scheduling an event with time 7 and value $\mathcal{T}$, in both transport and inertial modes, are

$$transport(w, \mathcal{T}, 7) = ((\mathcal{T}, 6)\,(\mathcal{F}, 5)\,(\mathcal{T}, 3)\,(\mathcal{F}, 1)\,(\mathcal{T}, 0))$$

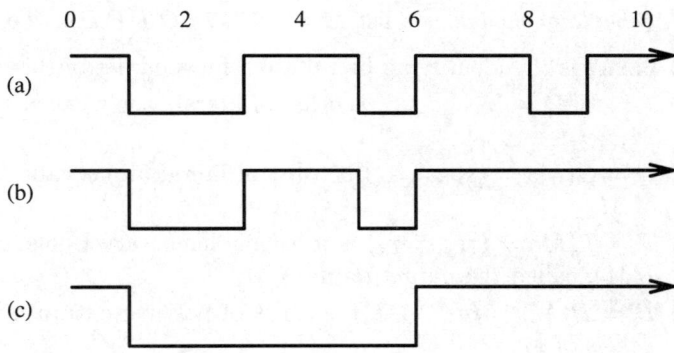

FIG. 1. Transport and inertial delay.

and
$$inertial(w, \mathcal{T}, 1,, 7) = ((\mathcal{T}, 6)\, (\mathcal{F}, 1)\, (\mathcal{T}, 0)),$$

as shown in (b) and (c), respectively.

Transport mode is often used to model wires (along which pulses of arbitrarily small duration are propagated to the delayed signal), while gate outputs are generally modeled by inertial delay. The latter, which is the VHDL default mode, will be used in all of our examples.

The following is a summary of both propagation functions. Each result may be proved by a straightforward induction. Note that (b) is consistent with our earlier informal observation that past events are immutable:

Lemma 2.1 *Let w be a waveform, let t_0, t_1, and t_v be natural numbers with $t_0 < t_v$, and let w' be either $transport(w, v, t_v)$ or $inertial(w, v, t_0, t_v)$. Then:*

(a) $\hat{w}'(t) = v$ for $t \geq t_v$;
(b) $\hat{w}'(t) = \hat{w}(t)$ for $t \leq t_0$;
(c) if $t_1 \leq t_0 \leq t_2 \leq t_v$ and $\hat{w}(t) = u$ for $t \in [t_1, t_2)$, then $\hat{w}'(t) = u$ for $t \in [t_1, t_2)$.

A similar induction shows that both procedures are "idempotent" in the following sense:

Lemma 2.2 *If w is a waveform and t_0, t_v, t'_0, t'_v are natural numbers with $t_0 < t_v$, $t'_0 < t'_v$, $t_0 < t'_0$, and $t_v < t'_v$, then:*

(a) $transport(transport(w, v, t_v), v, t'_v) = transport(w, v, t_v)$;
(b) $inertial(inertial(w, v, t_0, t_v), v, t'_0, t'_v) = inertial(w, v, t_0, t_v)$.

2.3 Behavioral Modules

The simplest programs of our language are the behavioral modules, which contain explicit information concerning propagation delay and the functional dependence of outputs on inputs.

A *behavioral module* is a list $M = (\text{BEHAV}\ I\ O\ T\ P\ D)$, where:

(1) BEHAV is the identifying literal atom for modules of this type;
(2) $I = I(M) = (r_1 \ldots r_m)$ is a list of literal atoms called the *inputs* of M;
(3) $O = O(M) = (s_1 \ldots s_n)$ is a list of literal atoms called the *outputs* of M;
(4) $T = T(M) = (\tau_1 \ldots \tau_n)$ is a list of elementary Boolean terms over $I(M)$, called the *output terms* of M;
(5) $D = D(M) = (d_1 \ldots d_n)$ is a list of positive natural numbers, the *delays* of M;
(6) $P = P(M) = (p_1 \ldots p_n)$ is a list of literal atoms called the *propagation modes* of M, each of which is either TRANSPORT or INERTIAL.

The members of the list $(r_1 \ldots r_m\ s_1 \ldots s_n)$ are required to be distinct and are called the *signals* of M.

Note that each output is associated with a term, a mode, and a delay. If every term is either an atom or a list of atoms, (i.e., contains no nested function calls), then M is *primitive*.

Gates are generally modeled as primitive modules with inertial delays. For example, we represent a simple 2-input nand gate as the primitive module **nand2**:

(BEHAV (A B) (C) ((NAND2 A B)) (2000) (INERTIAL))

We may define a similar behavioral module, with n inputs and 1 output, corresponding to each elementary n-ary Boolean function, arbitrarily taking the delay to be 2000 in each case. In the sequel, we shall refer to these primitive modules without explicitly listing their definitions.

Another example of a behavioral module is the 1-bit adder **adder1**:

(BEHAV (A B C) (L H)
 ((XOR3 A B C) (OR2 (AND2 A (OR2 B C)) (AND2 B C)))
 (12000 10000)
 (INERTIAL INERTIAL))

The two outputs of this module represent the 2-bit sum of the three input bits. Since the higher-order "carry" output bit is not expressed as an elementary function of the inputs, this is not a primitive module.

Let $s = nth(j, O(M))$ be an output of a behavioral module M and let $\tau = nth(j, T(M))$ be the corresponding term. For any bit vector V of the same length as $I(M)$, we define the *combinational value* of s w.r.t. V as $cv(s, V, M) = eval(\tau, pairlist(I(M), V))$.

We shall say that a list of waveforms is an *input* (resp., *output*) *packet* for a module M if it has the same length as $I(M)$ (resp., $O(M)$). The semantics of behavioral modules are defined by a function *exec* of four arguments: (1) a module M, (2) an input packet p_{in} for M, (3) an output packet $p_{out} = (w_1 \ldots w_n)$ for M, and (4) a number t_0. The value of $exec(M, p_{in}, p_{out}, t_0)$ is the updated output packet $p'_{out} = (w'_1 \ldots w'_n)$ that results from "executing" M at t_0. It is defined as follows: For $i = 1, \ldots, n$, let v_i be the combinational value of $nth(i, O(M))$ w.r.t. $\hat{p}_{in}(t_0)$, and let $t_i = t_0 + nth(i, D(M))$. Then w'_i is either $transport(w_i, v_i, t_i)$ or $inertial(w_i, v_i, t_0, t_i)$, according to $nth(i, P(M))$.

Our first observation concerning the behavior of $exec$ is that its value depends only on the current values of the input:

Lemma 2.3 *Let p_1 and p_2 be input packets and let p_{out} be an output packet for a behavioral module M. For any $t_0 \in \mathbf{N}$, if $\hat{p}_1(t_0) = \hat{p}_2(t_0)$, then $exec(M, p_1, p_{out}, t_0) = exec(M, p_2, p_{out}, t_0)$.*

Two other basic properties may be derived as consequences of Lemmas 2.1(b) and 2.2:

Lemma 2.4 *Let p_{in} and p_{out} be an input packet and an output packet for a behavioral module M. For any $t_0 \in \mathbf{N}$, $hist(exec(M, p_{in}, p_{out}, t_0), t_0) = hist(p_{out}, t_0)$.*

Lemma 2.5 *Let p_{in} and p_{out} be an input packet and an output packet for a behavioral module M and let t_0 and t_1 be natural numbers. If $t_0 < t_1$ and $\hat{p}_{in}(t_0) = \hat{p}_{in}(t_1)$, then*

$$exec(M, p_{in}, exec(M, p_{in}, p_{out}, t_0), t_1) = exec(M, p_{in}, p_{out}, t_0).$$

2.4 Structural Modules

Our language also includes modules that represent hierarchically constructed circuits. These structures contain information concerning interconnections among the modules of which they are composed.

A *structural module* is a list $M = (\text{STRUCT } I\ O\ S\ LI\ LO)$, where

(1) STRUCT is the identifying literal atom for modules of this type;
(2) $I = I(M) = (r_1 \ldots r_m)$ is a list of literal atoms called the *(global) inputs* of M;
(3) $O = O(M) = (s_1 \ldots s_n)$ is a list of literal atoms called the *(global) outputs* of M;
(4) $S = S(M) = (\mu_1 \ldots \mu_k)$ is a list of (structural or behavioral) modules, called the *submodules* of M;
(5) $LI = LI(M) = (A_1 \ldots A_k)$, where for $j = 1, \ldots, k$, $A_j = (a_{j1} \ldots a_{jm_j})$ is a list of literal atoms called the jth *local inputs* of M, and m_j is the length of $I(\mu_j)$;
(6) $LO = (B_1 \ldots B_k)$, where for $j = 1, \ldots, k$, $B_j = (b_{j1} \ldots b_{jn_j})$ is a list of literal atoms called the jth *local outputs* of M, and n_j is the length of $O(\mu_j)$.

The members of the list $(r_1 \ldots r_m\ b_{11} \ldots b_{1n_1} \ldots b_{k1} \ldots b_{kn_k})$, consisting of the global inputs and all local outputs, are required to be distinct and are

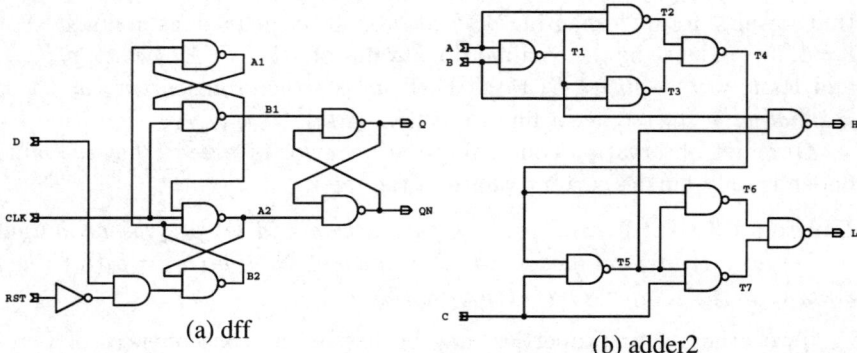

FIG. 2. Circuit Diagrams.

called the *signals* of M. There is no such constraint on the global outputs or local inputs, but each local input must be a signal of M, and each global output must be a local output.

Note that the local inputs and outputs of M correspond to its submodules. Thus, intuitively, the submodules of a structure generate signals that are distinct from each other and from the structure's inputs. Each signal may be connected to arbitrarily many submodule inputs. A signal other than a global input may serve as any number of global outputs, but global inputs and outputs are distinct.

Our first example is the structural module adder2, composed of nine nand gates and intended as a gate-level "implementation" of the behavioral module adder1:

```
(STRUCT (A B C) (L H)
  (nand2 nand2 nand2 nand2 nand2 nand2 nand2 nand2 nand2)
  ((A B) (A T1) (B T1) (T2 T3) (C T4) (T5 T4) (C T5) (T5 T1) (T7 T6))
  ((T1) (T2) (T3) (T4) (T5) (T6) (T7) (H) (L)))
```

A circuit diagram for adder2 appears in Fig. 2(b). Later, we shall compare its behavior with that of the behavioral module adder1.

An important feature of our language is that it allows cyclic signal paths, thereby providing for the modeling of state-holding devices. Figure 2(a) shows a clocked resettable d-flip-flop, which is modeled by the structural module dff:

```
(STRUCT (CLK RST D) (Q QN)
  (not1 and2 nand2 nand2 nand3 nand2 nand2 nand2)
  ((RST) (RN D) (B2 B1) (A1 CLK) (B1 CLK B2) (A2 DD) (B1 QN) (Q A2))
  ((RN) (DD) (A1) (B1) (A2) (B2) (Q) (QN)))
```

In addition to five 2-input nand gates, the submodules of dff include an inverter not1, an a 2-input and gate and2, and a 3-input nand gate nand3, the definitions of which are assumed to be understood.

We shall define the semantics of structural modules by means of a function *step*, based on the *exec* function of the preceding subsection. Note that the notions of input and output packets may be naturally applied to any module. For a structural module M, however, instead of a simple output packet, the third argument of *step* must be an object that consists of a waveform corresponding to each signal generated by each component of M. Thus, for any module M, we define a *bundle for M* to be a list B such that: (a) if M is behavioral, then B is an output packet for M; (b) if M is a structure with $S(M) = (\mu_1 \ldots \mu_k)$, then $B = (\beta_1 \ldots \beta_k)$, where β_i is a bundle for μ_i, $i = 1, \ldots, k$.

Let B be a bundle for a module M and let s be a signal of M that is not an input of M. The *waveform for s determined by B* is the waveform w that is computed as follows: (a) if M is behavioral and $s = nth(j, O(M))$, then $w = nth(j, B)$; (b) if M is structural and $s = nth(i, nth(i, LO(M)))$, then w is the waveform for $nth(j, O(nth(i, S(M))))$ determined by $nth(i, B)$.

The *output packet for M determined by B*, denoted as $outp(M, B)$, is defined as follows: (a) if M is behavioral, then $outp(M, B) = B$; (b) if M is structural with $O(M) = (s_1 \ldots s_n)$, then $outp(M, B) = (w_1 \ldots w_n)$, where for $1 \leq j \leq n$, w_j is the waveform for s_j determined by B.

Let M be a structural module with $nth(i, LI(M)) = (a_{i1} \ldots a_{in_i})$. Let p be an input packet and let B be a bundle for M. The ith *input packet determined by p and B*, denoted as $inp(i, M, p, B)$, is the input packet $(w_1 \ldots w_m)$ for $nth(i, S(M))$, where for $1 \leq j \leq m$, w_j is computed as follows: (a) if s_j is a global input $nth(k, I(M))$, then $w_j = nth(k, p)$; (b) if s_j is a local output, then w_j is the waveform for s_j determined by B.

We may now define *step*. Let p and B be an input packet and a bundle, respectively, for an arbitrary module M, and let $t \in \mathbf{T}$. Then $step(M, p, B, t)$ is the bundle B', defined as follows: (a) if M is behavioral, then $B' = exec(M, p, B, t)$ if p has a new value at t, and $B' = B$ if not; (b) if M is structural with $S(M) = (\mu_1 \ldots \mu_k)$ and $B = (\beta_1 \ldots \beta_k)$, then $B' = (\beta'_1 \ldots \beta'_k)$, where $\beta'_i = step(\mu_i, inp(i, M, p, B), \beta_i, t)$.

Thus, the execution of a structure at time t amounts to the execution of each behavioral component for which the value of some input signal changes at t.

We have the following generalization of Lemma 2.3:

Lemma 2.6 *Let p_1 and p_2 be input packets and let B be a bundle for a module M. Let $t_0 \in \mathbf{N}$. If $hist(p_1, t_0) = hist(p_2, t_0)$, then*

$$step(M, p_1, B, t_0) = step(M, p_2, B, t_0).$$

The *history* of a structural bundle $(\beta_1 \ldots \beta_k)$ relative to a time t is recursively defined as $hist(B, t) = (hist(\beta_1, t) \ldots hist(\beta_k, t))$. Lemma 2.4 may be generalized as follows:

Lemma 2.7 *Let p and B be an input packet and a bundle for a module M. For any $t_0 \in \mathbf{N}$, $hist(step(M, p, B, t_0), t_0) = hist(B, t_0)$.*

2.5 Simulation

Let p and B be an input packet and a bundle for a module M. For any $t \in \mathbf{N}$, we define $t_{next}(t, p, B, M)$ to be the minimum element of the set of all $t' \in \mathbf{N}$ that occur as times of events in the waveforms of p and B and that satisfy $t' > t$, if this set is nonempty; otherwise, $t_{next}(t, p, B, M)$ is undefined.

A simulation of M consists of repeated applications of *step*, which are performed by the function *run*. For $t_0, t_f \in \mathbf{T}$, we define $run(M, p, B, t_0, t_f)$ to be the bundle B' that is computed recursively as follows: Let $t_{next} = t_{next}(t_0, p, B, M)$. If t_{next} is defined and $t_{next} \leq t_f$, then

$$B' = run(M, p, step(M, p, B, t_{next}), t_{next}, t_f);$$

otherwise, $B' = B$.

The definition of our top-level simulation function *sim* depends on *run* as well as a function *init*, which generates an initial bundle from a module and an input packet. First, for a given module M, we define the bundle $B_0(M)$:

(1) If M is behavioral, then $B_0(M)$ is the output packet $(w_0 \ldots w_0)$ for M, where $w_0 = ((\mathcal{F}, 0))$.
(2) If M is structural and $S(M) = (\mu_1 \ldots \mu_k)$, then

$$B_0(M) = (B_0(\mu_1) \ldots B_0(\mu_k)).$$

Thus, every waveform of $B_0(M)$ is the trivial w_0, which has the constant value $\hat{w}_0(t) = \mathcal{F}$. Prior to simulation, each of these waveforms is updated by executing every behavioral component of M. The result is the bundle $init(M, p)$, defined as follows:

(1) If M is behavioral, then $init(M, p) = exec(M, p, B_0(M), 0)$.
(2) If M is structural with $S(M) = (\mu_1 \ldots \mu_k)$, then $init(M, p) = (init(\mu_1, inp(1, M, p, B_0(M))) \ldots init(\mu_k, inp(k, M, p, B_0(M))))$.

Now, given an input packet p for M and a time t, we define

$$sim(M, p, t) = run(M, p, init(M, p), 0, t).$$

As an example, simulations of the modules `adder1` and `adder2` are illustrated in Fig. 3. The waveforms corresponding to the inputs A, B, and C are

$$w_\mathtt{A} = ((\mathcal{F}, 80000)\,(\mathcal{T}, 12000)\,(\mathcal{F}, 10000)\,(\mathcal{T}, 0)),$$

$$w_\mathtt{B} = ((\mathcal{F}, 60000)\,(\mathcal{T}, 20000)\,(\mathcal{F}, 0)),$$

and

$$w_\mathtt{C} = ((\mathcal{T}, 60000)\,(\mathcal{F}, 40000)\,(\mathcal{T}, 0)),$$

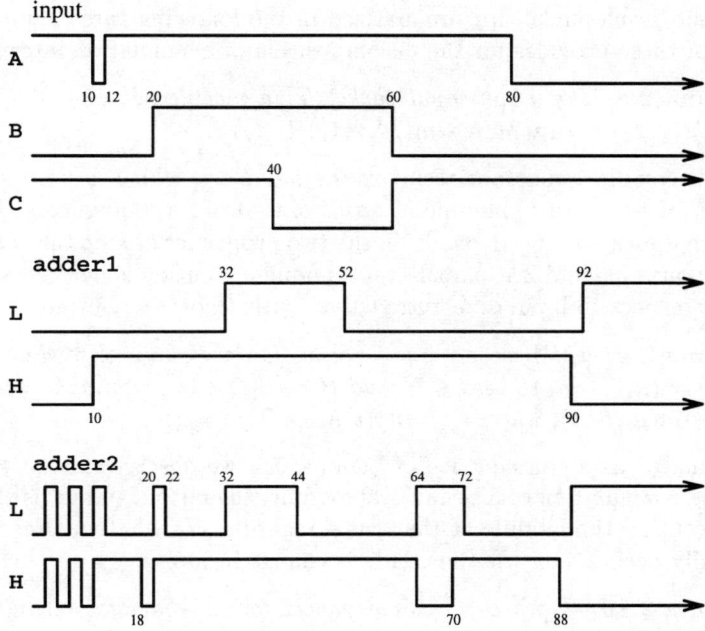

FIG. 3. Simulation of adder1 and adder2.

respectively. The resulting output of the behavioral module adder1 is

$$sim(\text{adder1}, (w_A\ w_B\ w_C), 100000) = (w_L\ w_H),$$

where

$$w_L = (((\mathcal{T}, 92000)\ (\mathcal{F}, 52000)\ (\mathcal{T}, 32000)\ (\mathcal{F}, 0)))$$

and

$$w_H = ((\mathcal{F}, 90000)\ (\mathcal{T}, 10000)\ (\mathcal{F}, 0)).$$

This example exhibits a fundamental characteristic of inertial delay, as distinguished from transport delay: an input pulse of duration less than the delay, as occurs in w_A over the interval $[10000, 12000)$, is not reflected in the output.

The corresponding simulation of the circuit adder2 produces a bundle $sim(\text{adder2}, (w_A\ w_B\ w_C), 100000)$, of the form

$$((w'_{T1})\ (w'_{T2})\ (w'_{T3})\ (w'_{T4})\ (w'_{T5})\ (w'_{T6})\ (w'_{T7})\ (w'_H)\ (w'_L)),$$

of which we illustrate the output waveforms w'_L and w'_H. Note that the behavior of adder2 is somewhat more complicated than that of adder1, although for stable inputs, the two modules eventually produce the same values.

Some basic properties of the simulator that will be critical in the subsequent development are summarized in the following three lemmas. The first of these provides for the decomposition of a simulation interval:

Lemma 2.8 *If p is an input packet for a module M, and $t_1 \leq t_2$, then $sim(M, p, t_2) = run(M, p, sim(M, p, t_1), t_1, t_2)$.*

An equally important result is the following, which describes the behavior of a structural module in terms of that of its components. Its proof (which appears in [6]) depends on the two properties of *step* that are stated in Lemmas 2.6 and 2.7, namely that module execution is neither predictive (with respect to input) nor retroactive (with respect to output):

Lemma 2.9 *Let p be an input packet for a structural module M with $S(M) = (\mu_1 \ldots \mu_k)$. Let $t \in \mathbf{N}$ and $B = (\beta_1 \ldots \beta_k) = sim(M, p, t)$. Then $\beta_i = sim(\mu_i, b_i, t)$, where $b_i = inp(i, M, p, B)$, $i = 1, \ldots, k$.*

Finally, as a consequence of Lemma 2.5, we observe that at any time during a simulation of a behavioral module, the output packet is the result of executing the module at that time, regardless of whether the execution actually occurs, i.e., whether there is change in input:

Lemma 2.10 *Let p be an input packet for a behavioral module M, let $t \in \mathbf{N}$, and let $B = sim(M, p, t)$. Then $B = exec(M, p, B, t)$.*

3 Specification of Synchronous Circuits
3.1 Combinational Modules

Before undertaking a characterization of synchronous sequential circuits, we shall consider the relatively simple class of *combinational* circuits. Let $\rho = (s_1 \ldots s_p)$ be a list of signals of a structural module M such that for each i, $1 < i \leq p$, there exists j such that s_{i-1} is a member of $nth(j, LI(M))$ and s_i is a member of $nth(j, LO(M))$. Then ρ is a *path* in M from s_1 to s_p. If $s_1 = s_p$, then ρ is a *loop* in M. An arbitrary module M is *combinational* if either (a) M is behavioral or (b) M is structural with no loops and all of its submodules are combinational.

The notion of *combinational value*, which previously applied only to outputs of behavioral modules, may be extended to combinational modules. Let s be any signal of a combinational module M and let V be a bit vector of the same length as $I(M)$:

(1) If $s = nth(j, I(M))$, then $cv(s, V, M) = nth(j, V)$.
(2) If M is structural and $s = nth(j, nth(i, LO(M)))$, where $\mu = nth(i, S(M))$ and $(a_1 \ldots a_m) = nth(i, LI(M))$, then
$cv(s, V, M) = cv(nth(j, O(\mu)), (cv(a_1, V, M) \ldots cv(a_m, V, M)), \mu)$.

We shall describe the behavior of combinational modules in terms of the function cv. Our analysis begins with the following characterization of behavioral modules:

Lemma 3.1 Let $s = nth(j, O(M))$ be the jth output of a behavioral module M, let $d = nth(j, D(M))$ be the corresponding delay, and let $w = nth(j, sim(M, p, t_f))$.

Assume that for all $t \in [t_1, t_2)$, the combinational value of s w.r.t. $\hat{p}(t)$ is v, where $t_1 + d \leq t_2$ and $t_1 \leq t_f$. Then for all $t \in [t_1 + d, t_2 + d)$, $\hat{w}(t) = v$.

Proof: Let $p_1 = sim(M, p, t_1)$. Then according to Lemma 2.10, $p_1 = exec(M, p, p_1, t_1)$. It follows from Lemma 2.1(a) that the value of $nth(j, p_1)$ is v for all $t \geq t_1 + d$.

We claim that if p' is any output packet for M such that $nth(j, p')$ has value v throughout $[t_1 + d, t_2 + d)$, then so does $nth(j, run(M, p, p', t', t_f))$, for any $t' \geq t_1$. Once this claim is proved, the lemma will follow from Lemma 2.8 upon substituting p_1 and t_1 for p' and t'.

The claim is proved by induction. It suffices to show that if p has a new value at $t'' = t_{next}(t', p, p', M)$, and $p'' = exec(M, p, p', t'')$, then $nth(j, p'')$ has value v throughout $[t_1 + d, t_2 + d)$.

If $t'' \geq t_2$, then the desired result follows from Lemma 2.1(c). Thus, we may assume $t'' < t_2$ and hence, the combinational value of s w.r.t. $\hat{p}(t'')$ is v. In this case, $nth(j, p'')$ has value v on $[t_1 + d, t'' + d)$ by Lemma 2.1(c), and on $[t'' + d, t_2 + d)$ by Lemma 2.1(a). □

Lemma 3.1 is illustrated by the simulation of adder1 shown in Fig. 3. Note, for example, that the output L of adder1, with corresponding term (XOR3 A B C), has the combinational value $\mathcal{F}$ throughout the interval from 40000 to 80000, and thus, since its delay is 12000, the actual value of the signal is $\mathcal{F}$ from 52000 to 92000. Note also that this simple behavior is not shared by the combinational module adder2.

However, we shall derive a generalization of Lemma 3.1 that provides similar (although somewhat weaker) behavioral specifications of arbitrary combinational modules. First, we associate each signal s of a combinational module M with two parameters, called the *minimum* and *maximum delays* of s, which represent the range of total delays along all paths connecting the inputs of M to s. These are defined as follows:

(1) If s is a member of $I(M)$, then $dmin(s, M) = dmax(s, M) = 0$.

(2) If M is behavioral and $s = nth(j, O(M))$, then

$$dmin(s, M) = dmax(s, M) = nth(j, D(M)).$$

(3) If M is structural and $s = nth(j, nth(i, LO(M)))$, where $\mu = nth(i, S(M))$ and $(a_1 \ldots a_m) = nth(i, LI(M))$, then

$$dmin(s, M) = dmin(nth(j, O(\mu)), \mu)$$
$$+ min(dmin(a_1, M), \ldots, dmin(a_m, M)),$$
$$dmax(s, M) = dmax(nth(j, O(\mu)), \mu)$$
$$+ max(dmax(a_1, M), \ldots, dmax(a_m, M)).$$

Lemma 3.2 *Let $s = nth(j, O(M))$ be the jth output of a combinational module M, $d = dmin(s, M)$, $d' = dmax(s, M)$, and*

$$w = nth(j, outp(M, sim(M, p, t_f))).$$

Assume that $\hat{p}$ is constant on the interval $[t_1, t_2)$, where $t_1 + d' \leq t_2$ and $t_1 \leq t_f$. Let $v = cv(s, \hat{p}(t_1), M)$. Then for all $t \in [t_1 + d', t_2 + d)$, $\hat{w}(t) = v$.

Proof: For behavioral M, the conclusion follows from Lemma 3.1. For structural M, we shall show that it holds more generally for any local output s of M and the waveform w for s determined by $B = sim(M, p, t_f)$. The proof is by induction on the length of the longest path in M terminating at s.

Suppose s is a local output, say $s = nth(j, nth(i, LO(M)))$. Let $\mu = nth(i, S(M))$, $\beta = nth(i, B)$, $(a_1 \ldots a_m) = nth(i, LI(M))$, and

$$b = inp(i, M, p, B) = (w_1 \ldots w_m).$$

Then $w = nth(j, outp(\mu, \beta))$, and by Lemma 2.9, $\beta = sim(\mu, b, t_f)$.

For $1 \leq \ell \leq m$, let $d_\ell = dmin(a_\ell, M)$, $d'_\ell = dmax(a_\ell, M)$, and $v_\ell = cv(a_\ell, \hat{p}(t_1), M)$. If a_ℓ is a local output of M, then by inductive hypothesis, $\hat{w}_\ell(t) = v_\ell$ for all $t \in [t_1 + d'_\ell, t_2 + d_\ell)$; otherwise, a_ℓ is an input, and the same is true trivially. Thus, $\hat{b}(t) = (v_1 \ldots v_m)$ for all $t \in [t_1 + \Delta, t_2 + \delta)$, where $\Delta = max(d'_1, \ldots, d'_m)$ and $\delta = min(d_1, \ldots, d_m)$.

By the definition of cv,

$$v = cv(nth(j, O(\mu)), (v_1 \ldots v_m), \mu) = cv(nth(j, O(\mu)), \hat{b}(t_1 + \Delta), \mu).$$

Since μ is combinational, $\hat{w}(t) = v$ for all

$$\begin{aligned} t &\in [t_1 + \Delta + dmax(nth(j, O(\mu)), \mu), t_2 + \delta + dmin(nth(j, O(\mu)), \mu)) \\ &= [t_1 + d', t_2 + d). \quad \square \end{aligned}$$

As an example, consider the output signal L of the combinational module adder2. By tracing all paths from the inputs to L, we may compute $cv(\text{L}, (a\ b\ c), \text{adder2})$ as a nested $nand2$ expression that may be shown to be tautologically equivalent to $xor3(a, b, c)$. By a similar calculation, we have

$$dmin(\text{L}, \text{adder2}) = 4000 \text{ and } dmax(\text{L}, \text{adder2}) = 12000.$$

Thus, according to Lemma 3.2, if $t_1 + 12000 \leq t_2$, $t_1 \leq t_f$, and the input packet p for adder2 has the constant value $\hat{p}(t) = (a\ b\ c)$ for $t \in [t_1, t_2)$, then

$$w = nth(1, outp(\text{adder2}, sim(\text{adder2}, p, t_2)))$$

has the value $\hat{w}(t) = xor3(a, b, c)$ for $t \in [t_1 + 12000, t_2 + 4000)$. This result is illustrated in Fig. 3: since the input packet has the constant value

$(T\ T\ T)$ on the interval $[20000, 40000)$, the value of the first output is $xor3(T, T, T) = T$ on the interval $[32000, 44000)$.

3.2 Sequential Modules

We shall describe a class of sequential circuits that may be characterized as *synchronous resettable rising-edge-triggered* devices. The flip-flop `dff` of Subsection 2.4 will be used as a primitive in the construction of these circuits.

Let M be a structural module with $I(M) = (r_1 \ldots r_m)$, where $m \geq 2$, $S(M) = (\mu_1 \ldots \mu_k)$, and for $i = 1, \ldots, k$, $nth(i, LI(M)) = (a_{i1} \ldots a_{im_i})$ and $nth(i, LO(M)) = (b_{i1} \ldots b_{in_i})$. Let $q \in \mathbf{N}$. Then M is a *sequential module* with multiplicity $q = mult(M)$ if either (a) $q = 0$ and $M = \mathtt{dff}$, or (b) $0 < q \leq k$ and the following conditions hold:

(1) For $1 \leq i \leq q$, μ_i is a sequential module.
(2) For $q < i \leq k$, μ_i is a combinational module.
(3) For $1 \leq i \leq k$ and $1 \leq j \leq m_i$, $a_{ij} = r_1$ iff $i \leq q$ and $j = 1$.
(4) For $1 \leq i \leq k$ and $1 \leq j \leq m_i$, $a_{ij} = r_2$ iff $i \leq q$ and $j = 2$.
(5) If $(s_1 \ldots s_p)$ is a path in M with $s_1 = s_p$, then for some i and j, where $1 \leq i \leq p$ and $1 \leq j \leq q$, s_i is a member of $nth(j, LO(M))$.
(6) If $(s_1 \ldots s_p)$ is a path in M with s_1 a global input and s_p a global output of M, then for some i and j, where $1 \leq i \leq p$ and $1 \leq j \leq q$, s_i is a member of $nth(j, LO(M))$.

Throughout the remainder of this section, we shall assume that M is a sequential module with $I(M)$, $S(M)$, $LI(M)$, and $LO(M)$ as denoted above. Note that M must have at least two inputs, r_1 and r_2, which we call the *clock* and *reset*, respectively; the other inputs are called *data*. According to (3) and (4), if $M \neq \mathtt{dff}$, then the clock and reset of M are connected to the clock and reset, respectively, of each sequential submodule of M, and to no other submodule inputs.

We define a path in M to be *combinational* if it contains no signal that is a local output of a sequential submodule. According to (5) of the definition, M contains no combinational loop; according to (6), no combinational path connects an input to an output.

We define a signal s of M to be *native* if there is no combinational path from any global input to s; the signals `Q` and `QN` of `dff` are also defined to be *native*. Thus, all outputs of M are native signals.

A native signal s of M is *registered* if either (a) $M = \mathtt{dff}$ and s is an output of M, or (b) $M \neq \mathtt{dff}$ and s is a local output b_{ij} where $i \leq q$ and $nth(j, O(\mu_i))$ is a registered signal of μ_i. This property will have special significance in connection with asynchronous communication.

Two examples of sequential modules are diagrammed in Fig. 4. The enabled d-flip-flop, `edff`, is defined to be the following structure:

```
(STRUCT
  (CLK RST EN D)
  (Q QN)
  (dff not1 nand2 nand2 nand2)
  ((CLK RST S4) (EN) (S1 Q) (D EN) (S2 S3))
  ((Q QN) (S1) (S2) (S3) (S4)))
```

Clearly, this module satisfies the definition, with $mult(\mathtt{edff}) = 1$.

The 3-bit counter count3 is a sequential module of multiplicity 3, defined as follows:

```
(STRUCT
  (CLK RST EN)
  (Q0 Q1 Q2)
  (edff edff edff and2 xor2 xor2)
  ((CLK RST EN QN0) (CLK RST EN S3) (CLK RST EN S2)
   (Q0 Q1) (S1 Q2) (Q0 Q1))
  ((Q0 QN0) (Q1 QN1) (Q2 QN2) (S1) (S2) (S3)))
```

Note that all outputs of both of these modules are registered.

3.3 Sequential Values

Our description of the behavior of sequential modules will be based on a function that computes a sequence of values for each output corresponding to a given sequence of input values. The definition of this function involves the notion of *state*. An object Σ is a *state* of M if

(1) $M = \mathtt{dff}$ and $\Sigma \in \mathbf{B}$,
(2) $mult(M) = 1$ and Σ is a state of μ_1, or
(3) $mult(M) = q > 1$ and $\Sigma = (\sigma_1 \ldots \sigma_q)$, where for $i = 1, \ldots, q$, σ_i is a state of μ_i.

Thus, a state associates a Boolean value with each flip-flop. The *reset state* $\Sigma_0(M)$ is the state for which each of these values is $\mathcal{F}$:

(1) $\Sigma_0(\mathtt{dff}) = \mathcal{F}$.
(2) If $mult(M) = 1$, then $\Sigma_0(M) = \Sigma_0(\mu_1)$.
(3) If $mult(M) = q > 1$, then $\Sigma_0(M) = (\Sigma_0(\mu_1) \ldots \Sigma_0(\mu_q))$.

A *data vector* for M is a bit vector of length $m - 2$, the components of which correspond to the data inputs of M. We shall define a function $next(V, \Sigma, M)$ that computes a state of M from a data vector V and a state Σ. This definition requires two auxiliary functions.

First, for a native signal s and a state Σ of M, we define the *native value* of s determined by Σ, denoted as $nv(s, \Sigma, M)$, as follows:

(1) $nv(\mathtt{Q}, \Sigma, \mathtt{dff}) = \Sigma$ and $nv(\mathtt{QN}, \Sigma, \mathtt{dff}) = not1(\Sigma)$.
(2) If $mult(M) = 1$ and $s = b_{1j}$, then

$$nv(s, \Sigma, M) = nv(nth(j, O(\mu_1)), \Sigma, \mu_1).$$

(3) If $mult(M) = q > 1$ and $s = b_{ij}$, where $i \leq q$, then

$$nv(s, \Sigma, M) = nv(nth(j, O(\mu_i)), nth(i, \Sigma), \mu_i).$$

(4) If $mult(M) = q \geq 1$ and $s = b_{ij}$, where $i > q$, then
$$nv(s, \Sigma, M) =$$
$$cv(nth(j, O(\mu_i)), (nv(a_{i1}, \Sigma, M) \ldots nv(a_{im_i}, \Sigma, M)), \mu_i).$$

Now, let $V = (v_3 \ldots v_m)$ and Σ be a data vector and a state of M, respectively. We define the *resultant value* of a signal s determined by V and Σ, denoted as $rv(s, V, \Sigma, M)$, as follows:

(1) If $s = r_i$ is a data input of M, then $rv(s, V, \Sigma, M) = v_i$.
(2) If s is native to M, then $rv(s, V, \Sigma, M) = nv(s, \Sigma, M)$.
(3) If $mult(M) = q > 0$ and $s = b_{ij}$, where $i > q$, then
$$rv(s, V, \Sigma, M) =$$
$$cv(nth(j, O(\mu_i)), (rv(a_{i1}, V, \Sigma, M) \ldots rv(a_{im_i}, V, \Sigma, M)), \mu_i).$$

We may now define the function *next*. Let $mult(M) = q$ and for $i = 1, \ldots, q$, let

$$L_i = (rv(a_{i1}, V, \Sigma, M) \ldots rv(a_{im_i}, V, \Sigma, M)).$$

Then $next(V, \Sigma, M) = \Sigma'$, where:

(1) If $q = 0$ (i.e., $M = \mathtt{dff}$), then $\Sigma' = v_3$.
(2) If $q = 1$, then $\Sigma' = next(L_1, \Sigma, \mu_1)$.
(3) If $q > 1$ and $\Sigma = (\sigma_1 \ldots \sigma_q)$, then

$$\Sigma' = (next(L_1, \sigma_1, \mu_1) \ldots next(L_q, \sigma_q, \mu_q)).$$

Now, let $\mathcal{V} = (V_3 \ldots V_m)$, where for $i = 3, \ldots, m$, $V_i = (v_{i1} \ldots v_{in})$ is a bit vector of length n. $\mathcal{V}$ may be viewed as a Boolean matrix, the rows of which correspond to the data inputs of M. Each column of this matrix, $\bar{V}_j = (v_{3j} \ldots v_{mj})$, where $j = 1, \ldots, n$, is a data vector for M. A sequence of $n+1$ states is determined by $\mathcal{V}$ as follows:

$$state(j, \mathcal{V}, M) = \begin{cases} \Sigma_0(M) & \text{if } j = 0 \\ next(\bar{V}_j,, state(j-1, \mathcal{V}, M), M) & \text{if } 0 < j \leq n. \end{cases}$$

For any native signal s of M, the jth *sequential value* of s determined by $\mathcal{V}$ is defined as

$$sv(j, s, \mathcal{V}, M) = nv(s, state(j, \mathcal{V}, M), M).$$

Thus, the sequential values corresponding to a given matrix of input values are determined by the functions *nv* and *next*. As an illustration, we shall analyze the behavior of these functions for the modules `edff` and

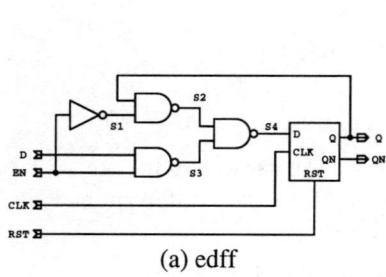
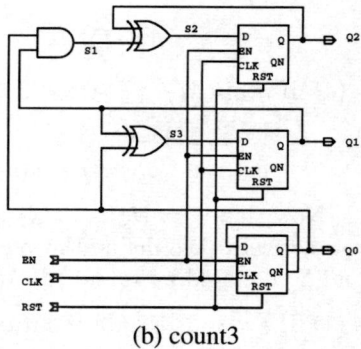

(a) edff
(b) count3

Fig. 4.

count3. Clearly, a state of edff is a state of dff, i.e., a Boolean value. If Σ is such a state and $V = (v_3\ v_4)$ is a data vector, then

$$rv(\texttt{Q}, V, \Sigma, \texttt{edff}) = nv(\texttt{Q}, V, \Sigma, \texttt{edff}) = nv(\texttt{Q}, \Sigma, \texttt{dff}) = \Sigma$$

and

$$rv(\texttt{QN}, V, \Sigma, \texttt{edff}) = nv(\texttt{QN}, V, \Sigma, \texttt{edff}) = nv(\texttt{QN}, \Sigma, \texttt{dff}) = not1(\Sigma).$$

Expanding the definition of rv, we have

$$rv(\texttt{S4}, V, \Sigma, \texttt{edff}) = nand2(nand2(not1(v_3), \Sigma), nand2(v_3, v_4)),$$

which is also the value of $next(V, \Sigma, \texttt{edff})$. A trivial calculation yields the following:

Proposition 3.3 *Let Σ and $V = (v_3\ v_4)$ be a state and a data vector for* edff. *Then*

$$nv(\texttt{Q}, V, \Sigma, \texttt{edff}) = \Sigma \text{ and } nv(\texttt{QN}, V, \Sigma, \texttt{edff}) = not1(\Sigma);$$

$$next(V, \Sigma, \texttt{edff}) = \begin{cases} v_4 & \text{if } v_3 = \mathcal{T} \\ \Sigma & \text{if } v_3 = \mathcal{F}. \end{cases}$$

A state of count3 is a vector of 3 Boolean values, corresponding to the $mult(\texttt{count3}) = 3$ occurrences of edff. If $\Sigma = (\sigma_0\ \sigma_1\ \sigma_2)$ and $V = (v_3)$ are a state and a data vector, then

$$rv(\texttt{S1}, V, \Sigma, \texttt{count3}) = and2(\sigma_0, \sigma_1),$$
$$rv(\texttt{S2}, V, \Sigma, \texttt{count3}) = xor2(and2(\sigma_0, \sigma_1), \sigma_2),$$
$$rv(\texttt{S3}, V, \Sigma, \texttt{count3}) = xor2(\sigma_0, \sigma_1),$$

and it follows from Proposition 3.3 that

Verification of Synchronous and Asynchronous Circuits   431

$next(V, \Sigma, \text{count3}) =$
$$\begin{cases} (not1(\sigma_0) \; xor2(\sigma_0, \sigma_1) \; xor2(and2(\sigma_0, \sigma_1), \sigma_2)) & \text{if } v_3 = \mathcal{T} \\ \Sigma & \text{if } v_3 = \mathcal{F}. \end{cases}$$

This result is conveniently expressed in terms of the function $inc(W)$, defined as follows for an arbitrary bit vector W:

(1) If $W = \text{NIL}$, then $inc(W) = \text{NIL}$; otherwise:
(2) If $car(W) = \mathcal{T}$, then $inc(W) = cons(\mathcal{F}, inc(cdr(W)))$; otherwise:
(3) $inc(W) = cons(\mathcal{T}, cdr(W))$.

Proposition 3.4 *Let $\Sigma = (\sigma_0 \; \sigma_1 \; \sigma_2)$ and $V = (v_3)$ be a state and a data vector for* count3. *Then*

$$nv(\text{Q0}, V, \Sigma, \text{count3}) = \sigma_0,$$
$$nv(\text{Q1}, V, \Sigma, \text{count3}) = \sigma_1,$$
$$nv(\text{Q2}, V, \Sigma, \text{count3}) = \sigma_2;$$

$$next(V, \Sigma, \text{count3}) = \begin{cases} inc(\Sigma) & \text{if } v_3 = \mathcal{T} \\ \Sigma & \text{if } v_3 = \mathcal{F}. \end{cases}$$

3.4 Behavior of dff

Naturally, the behavior of sequential modules depends on that of the primitive dff. A precise behavioral specification of dff is given by the following lemma, the proof of which is an elaboration of the informal argument found in [7]:

Lemma 3.5 *Let $t_1 + 4000 \leq t_-$, $t_- + 6000 \leq t_2$, and $t_1 \leq t_f$. Let $p = (w_{\text{CLK}} \; w_{\text{RST}} \; w_{\text{D}})$ be an input packet for* dff, *and suppose that*

$$\hat{w}_{\text{CLK}}(t) = \begin{cases} \mathcal{F} & \text{for all } t \in [t_1 - 6000, t_1) \cup [t_-, t_2) \\ \mathcal{T} & \text{for all } t \in [t_1, t_-), \end{cases}$$

$$\hat{w}_{\text{RST}}(t) = r \text{ for all } t \in [t_1 - 8000, t_1),$$

and

$$\hat{w}_{\text{D}}(t) = d \text{ for all } t \in [t_1 - 6000, t_1).$$

Let $sim(\text{dff}, p, t_f) = ((w_{\text{RN}}) \; (w_{\text{DD}}) \; (w_{\text{A1}}) \; (w_{\text{B1}}) \; (w_{\text{A2}}) \; (w_{\text{B2}}) \; (w_{\text{Q}}) \; (w_{\text{QN}}))$ and let $v = and2(not1(r), d)$. Then $\hat{w}_{\text{Q}}(t) = v$ and $\hat{w}_{\bar{Q}}(t) = not1(v)$ for all $t \in [t_1 + 6000, t_2 + 4000)$. Moreover, if these same values hold for all $t \in [t_1, t_1 + 4000)$, then they also hold for all $t \in [t_1 + 4000, t_1 + 6000)$.

Proof: By Lemmas 3.1 and 2.9, we have $\hat{w}_{\text{RN}}(t) = not1(r)$ for all $t \in [t_1 - 6000, t_1 + 2000)$. Applying the same two lemmas again, we have $\hat{w}_{\text{DD}}(t) = v$ for all $t \in [t_1 - 4000, t_1 + 2000)$. Similarly, $\hat{w}_{\text{A2}}(t) = \hat{w}_{\text{B1}}(t) = \mathcal{T}$

for $t \in [t_1 - 4000, t_1 + 2000)$, $\hat{w}_{B2}(t) = not1(v)$ for $t \in [t_1 - 2000, t_1 + 4000)$, and hence $\hat{w}_{A1}(t) = v$ for $t \in [t_1, t_1 + 4000)$.

We shall consider the case $v = \mathcal{F}$; the case $v = \mathtt{T}$ is similar. In this case, $\hat{w}_{B1}(t) = \mathcal{T}$ for $t \in [t_1 + 2000, t_1 + 6000)$, and hence $\hat{w}_{A2}(t) = \mathcal{F}$ for $t \in [t_1 + 2000, t_1 + 6000)$.

Let t' be the least time such that $t' > t_1 + 2000$ and some waveform in the set $\{w_{A1}, w_{B1}, w_{A2}, w_{B2}\}$ assumes a new value at t'. Then $\hat{w}_{A1}(t) = \hat{w}_{A2}(t) = \mathcal{F}$ and $\hat{w}_{B1}(t) = \hat{w}_{B2}(t) = \mathcal{T}$ for $t \in [t_1 + 2000, t')$. Since $t' \geq t_1 + 4000$, it follows that $\hat{w}_{B1}(t) = \hat{w}_{B2}(t) = \mathcal{T}$ and $\hat{w}_{A1}(t) = \mathcal{F}$ for $t \in [t_1 + 4000, t' + 2000)$. Similarly, $\hat{w}_{A2}(t) = \mathcal{F}$ for $t \in [t_1 + 4000, min(t' + 4000, t_- + 2000))$. Thus, only w_{A2} can possibly assume a new value at t', and this requires that $t' \geq t_- + 2000$.

Hence, $\hat{w}_{B1}(t) = \mathcal{T}$ and $\hat{w}_{A2}(t) = \mathrm{F}$ for $t \in [t_1 + 2000, t_- + 2000)$. It follows that $\hat{w}_{QN}(t) = \mathcal{T}$ for $t \in [t_1 + 4000, t_- + 4000)$, and hence $\hat{w}_Q(t) = \mathcal{F}$ for $t \in [t_1 + 6000, t_- + 4000)$.

Let t'' be the least time such that $t'' > t_1 + 6000$ and either w_Q or w_{QN} assumes a new value at t''. By an argument similar to the above, it is easily shown that $t'' \geq t_2 + 4000$. Thus, $\hat{w}_Q(t) = \mathcal{F} = u_r$ for $t \in [t_1 + 6000, t_2 + 4000)$, and $\hat{w}_{QN}(t) = \mathcal{T} = not1(u_r)$ for $t \in [t_1 + 4000, t_2 + 4000)$.

Now suppose that $\hat{w}_Q(t) = \mathcal{F}$ and $\hat{w}_{QN}(t) = \mathcal{T}$ for $t \in [t_1, t_1 + 4000)$. Then $\hat{w}_{QN}(t) = \mathcal{T}$ for $t \in [t'_1, t_2 + 4000)$. It follows that $\hat{w}_Q(t) = \mathcal{F}$ for $t \in [t_1 + 4000, t_2 + 4000)$. □

3.5 Parameters

Our objective is to impose constraints on the input to a sequential module that will allow its outputs to be described in terms of sequential values. In particular, the clock input will be required to exhibit periodic behavior. We shall call each event of its associated waveform a *rising* or *falling edge*, according to whether its value is $\mathcal{T}$ or $\mathcal{F}$. An interval between two successive rising edges is called a *cycle*. Each of the remaining inputs will be required to maintain a stable value over a prescribed interval preceding each rising edge. For the reset input r_2, this value is $\mathcal{T}$ for an initial cycle, and $\mathcal{F}$ for every cycle thereafter.

Under these constraints, we shall show that the behavior of M admits a fairly simple description. A state of M will be associated with each rising edge. This state may computed from the data values prior to the edge and the previous state by the function *next*. The values of the outputs, which may change only during a short interval following a rising edge, are the corresponding sequential values.

We shall describe the behavior of the signals of M in terms of several parameters. First, we associate with each input other than the clock a *setup time*, which represents the duration over which the signal is required to hold constant prior to a rising edge. For the case $M = \mathtt{dff}$, as suggested by Lemma 3.5, we define

$$setup(\text{RST}, \text{dff}) = 8000 \text{ and } setup(\text{D}, \text{dff}) = 6000.$$

Now suppose $mult(M) = q > 0$ and let s be any signal of M other than r_1. Assume $setup(s', M)$ has been defined for each $s' \neq s$ that lies on a combinational path starting at s. For $i = 1, \ldots, k$, let ζ_i be defined as follows:

(1) If $s \neq a_{ij}$ for all j, $1 \leq j \leq m_i$, then $\zeta_i = 0$; otherwise:
(2) If $i \leq q$, then ζ_i is the maximum $setup(nth(j, I(\mu_i)), \mu_i)$ such that $s = a_{ij}$, $j = 2, \ldots, m_i$; otherwise:
(3) $i > q$, and ζ_i is the maximum sum

$$dmax(nth(j, O(\mu_i)), \mu_i) + setup(b_{ij}, M)$$

such that $setup(b_{ij}, M) > 0$, $j = 1, \ldots, n_i$.

Then $setup(s, M) = max(\zeta_1, \ldots, \zeta_k)$.

Each native signal of M is associated with a *minimum* and a *maximum delay*, which determine an interval during which the signal's value may change following a rising edge. For the case $M = \text{dff}$, we define

$$dmin(\text{Q}, \text{dff}) = dmin(\text{QN}, \text{dff}) = 4000,$$

$$dmax(\text{Q}, \text{dff}) = dmax(\text{QN}, \text{dff}) = 6000.$$

Now suppose $mult(M) = q > 0$ and let $s = b_{ij}$ be any native signal of M:

(1) If $i \leq q$, then

$$dmin(s, M) = dmin(nth(j, O(\mu_i)), \mu_i),$$

$$dmax(s, M) = dmax(nth(j, O(\mu_i)), \mu_i).$$

(2) If $i > q$, then

$$dmin(s, M) = dmin(nth(j, O(\mu_i)), \mu_i)$$
$$+ min(dmin(a_{i1}, M), \ldots, dmin(a_{im_i}, M)),$$

$$dmax(s, M) = dmax(nth(j, O(\mu_i)), \mu_i)$$
$$+ max(dmax(a_{i1}, M), \ldots, dmax(a_{im_i}, M)).$$

We also define three parameters pertaining to the behavior of the clock input of M, called the *clock high*, the *clock low*, and the *minimum period* of M. These represent the minimum durations between a rising edge and the next falling edge, a falling edge and the next rising edge, and successive rising edges, respectively. First, we define $high(\text{dff}) = 4000$, $low(\text{dff}) = 6000$, and $per(\text{dff}) = 10000$. For $mult(M) = q > 0$, we define

$$high(M) = max(high(\mu_1), \ldots, high(\mu_q));$$

$$low(M) = max(low(\mu_1), \ldots, low(\mu_q));$$

$$per(M) = max(P_1, P_2, P_3),$$

where

$$P_1 = max\{per(\mu_i) : 1 \leq i \leq q\};$$

$$P_2 = max\{setup(r_i, M) : 2 \leq i \leq m\};$$

$$P_3 = max\{setup(b_{ij}, M) + dmax(nth(j, O(\mu_i)), \mu_i) : 1 \leq i \leq q, 1 \leq j \leq n_i\}.$$

Consider, for example, the circuits `edff` and `count3`. First, the setup times for the signals of `edff` may be computed directly from the definitions, by tracing along all combinational paths. For example,

$setup(\text{RST}, \text{edff}) = 8000,$
$setup(\text{EN}, \text{edff}) = 12000,$
$setup(\text{D}, \text{edff}) = 10000.$

The setups for `count3` follow trivially:

$setup(\text{RST}, \text{count3}) = 8000,$
$setup(\text{EN}, \text{count3}) = 12000.$

In fact, it follows from our definitions that the reset input of every sequential module is 8000.

All outputs of both of these devices are registered. It follows that the minimum and maximum delay of each output are 4000 and 6000, respectively.

Similarly, the clock high and low of each device (in fact, of any sequential device) are 4000 and 6000, respectively, as determined by `dff`. Calculation of the minimum period, on the other hand, involves a comparison of various setups and delays. In the case of `edff`, the minimum period is found to be

$$setup(\text{Q}, \text{edff}) + dmax(\text{Q}, \text{dff}) = 10000 + 6000 = 16000;$$

for `count3`, it is

$$setup(\text{Q0}, \text{count3}) + dmax(\text{Q}, \text{edff}) = 14000 + 6000 = 20000.$$

3.6 The Main Theorem

The input constraints for sequential modules will be expressed in terms of the functions *setup*, *high*, *low*, and *per*. First, we define a waveform w to be an *n-cycle pulse based at t_0 with high h, low ℓ, and period $\pi = h + \ell$* if for $k = 0, \ldots, n - 1$,

$$\hat{w}(t) = \begin{cases} \mathcal{T} & \text{for all } t \in [t_0 + k\pi, t_0 + k\pi + h) \\ \mathcal{F} & \text{for all } t \in [t_0 + k\pi + h, t_0 + (k + 1)\pi). \end{cases}$$

If $h \geq high(M)$, $\ell \geq low(M)$, and $\pi \geq per(M)$, then w is an *admissible pulse for M*.

Let $V = (v_1 \ldots v_n)$ be a bit vector and let $\pi \geq u > 0$. Let w be a waveform such that for $k = 1, \ldots, n$, $\hat{w}(t) = v_k$ for all $t \in [t_0 + k\pi - u, t_0 + k\pi)$. Then w is a *stable n-cycle waveform based at t_0 with setup u, value list V, and period π*. If $u = setup(r_2, M)$, $v_1 = \mathcal{T}$, and $v_2 = \ldots = v_r = \mathcal{F}$, then w is an admissible *reset waveform for M*.

For $i = 1, \ldots, k$, let w_i be a stable n-cycle waveform based at t_0 with value list V_i, setup u_i, and period π. Let $\mathcal{V} = (V_1 \ldots V_k)$, $U = (u_1 \ldots u_k)$, and $W = (w_1 \ldots w_k)$. Then W is a *stable n-cycle packet based at t_0 with value matrix $\mathcal{V}$, setup list U, and period π*. If $k = m - 2$ and $u_i = setup(r_{i+2}, M)$ for $i = 1, \ldots, k$, then W is an *admissible data packet for M*.

Let w_1 be an admissible $(n + 2)$-cycle pulse for M based at t_0 with period π. Let w_2 be an admissible $(n + 1)$-cycle reset waveform for M based at t_0 with period π. Let $w_3 \ldots w_m)$ be an admissible n-cycle data packet for M based at $t_0 + \pi$ with value matrix $\mathcal{V}$ and period π. Then $(w_1 \ldots w_m)$ is an *admissible n-cycle input packet for M based at t_0 with value matrix $\mathcal{V}$ and period π*.

We may now state a behavioral specification for sequential modules:

Theorem 3.6 *Let $s = nth(j, O(M))$ be the jth output of a sequential module M, $d' = dmax(s, M)$, and $w = nth(j, outp(M, sim(M, p, t_f)))$.*

Assume that p is an admissible n-cycle input packet for M based at t_0 with value matrix $\mathcal{V}$ and period π, where $t_f \geq t_0 + (n+1)\pi$. For $i = 0, \ldots, n$, let $v_i = sv(i, s, \mathcal{V}, M)$. Then w is a stable $(n + 1)$-cycle waveform based at $t_0 + \pi$ with setup $\pi - d'$, value list $(v_0 \ldots v_n)$, and period π;

Assume further that s is a registered signal of M and $v_{i-1} = v_i$, for some i, $1 \leq i \leq n$. Then $\hat{w}(t) = v_i$ for all $t \in [t_0 + (i + 1)\pi, t_0 + (i + 2)\pi)$.

Theorem 3.6 is an immediate consequence of the following:

Lemma 3.7 *Let $s = nth(j, O(M))$ be the jth output of a sequential module M, $d = dmin(s, M)$, $d' = dmax(s, M)$, and*

$$w = nth(j, outp(M, sim(M, p, t_f))).$$

Assume that p is an admissible n-cycle input packet for M based at t_0 with value matrix $\mathcal{V}$ and period π. Let $t_0 + (n+1)\pi = t_1$, $t_1 + \pi = t_2$, and assume $t_1 \leq t_f$. Let $v = sv(n, s, \mathcal{V}, M)$. Then $\hat{w}(t) = v$ for all $t \in [t_1 + d', t_2 + d)$.

Suppose further that s is a registered signal of M. If $n > 0$ and $sv(n - 1, s, \mathcal{V}, M) = v$, then $\hat{w}(t) = v$ for all $t \in [t_1 + d, t_2 + d)$.

Proof: For the case $M = \text{dff}$, the lemma is simply a restatement of Lemma 3.5. Thus, we may assume that $M \neq \text{dff}$ and proceed by induction on the structure of M. Let $\mathcal{V} = (V_3 \ldots V_m)$, where for $i = 3, \ldots, m$, $V_i = (v_{i1} \ldots v_{ir})$. For $j = 0, \ldots, n$, let $\Sigma_j = state(j, \mathcal{V}, M)$.

Let $B = sim(M, p, t_f)$, and for each signal s of M, let

$$w_s = \begin{cases} nth(i, p) & \text{if } s \text{ is a global input } r_i \\ \text{the waveform for } s \text{ determined by } B & \text{if } s \text{ is a local output } b_{ij}. \end{cases}$$

If s is not r_1 or r_2, then for $0 \leq \ell < n$, let

$$val(s, \ell) = rv(s, (v_{3(\ell+1)} \ldots v_{m(\ell+1)}), \Sigma_\ell, M).$$

If s is native, then by definition we have

$$val(s, \ell) = nv(s, \Sigma_\ell, M) = sv(\ell, s, \mathcal{V}, M).$$

Thus, for native s, we extend the definition to $\ell = n$ by

$$val(s, n) = sv(n, s, \mathcal{V}, M).$$

For any $\ell \in \mathbf{N}$, let $t^\ell = t_0 + (\ell + 1)\pi$, so that $t_1 = t^n$ and $t_2 = t^{n+1} = t^n + \pi$. We shall prove, by induction on ℓ, that the following three statements hold for each $\ell \leq n$:

(a) For each i, $1 \leq i \leq q$, $inp(i, M, p, B)$ is an admissible ℓ-cycle input packet for μ_i based at t_0 with value matrix

$$((val(a_{i3}, 0) \ldots val(a_{i3}, \ell - 1)) \ldots (val(a_{im_i}, 0) \ldots val(a_{im_i}, \ell - 1)))$$

and period π.

(b) For each native signal $s = b_{ij}$ of M,

$$\hat{w}_s(t) = val(s, \ell) \text{ for all } t \in [t^\ell + dmax(s, M), t^{\ell+1} + dmin(s, M));$$

if s is a registered signal of M, then the same is true for the interval

$$[t^\ell + dmin(s, M), t^{\ell+1} + dmin(s, M)).$$

(c) If $\ell < n$, then for each signal s of M other than r_1 and r_2,

$$\hat{w}_s(t) = val(s, \ell) \text{ for all } t \in [t^{\ell+1} - setup(s, M), t^{\ell+1}).$$

The lemma will then follow from (b), taking $\ell = n$.

Proof of (a): For $\ell = 0$, this follows from (3) and (4) in the definition of *sequential module*. For $\ell > 0$, we must also invoke the inductive hypothesis that (c) holds with ℓ replaced by $\ell - 1$.

Proof of (b): We induct on the length of the longest combinational path terminating at s. Let $s = b_{ij}$. In the base case, where $i \leq q$, the result follows from the inductive assumption that the lemma holds for the sequential submodule μ_i, Lemma 2.9, and (a). In the inductive case, where $i > q$, it follows from Lemmas 2.9 and 3.2.

Proof of (c): This is similarly proved by induction on the length of the longest combinational path terminating at s. In the base case, s is either a global input r_i, $i \geq 3$, or a local output b_{ij}, $i \leq q$. If $s = r_i$, then the claim follows directly from the admissibility of the input packet p. Suppose $s = b_{ij}$, $i \leq q$. It follows from (b) that

$$\hat{w}_s(t) = val(s, \ell) \text{ for all } t \in [t^\ell + dmax(s, M), t^{\ell+1}).$$

According to the definition of $per(M)$,

$$\pi \geq setup(b_{ij},, M) + dmax(nth(j, O(\mu_i)), \mu_i).$$

Hence,

$$t^\ell + dmax(s, M) = t^{\ell+1} - \pi + dmax(nth(j, O(\mu_i)), \mu_i) \leq t^{\ell+1} - setup(b_{ij}, M).$$

The induction is completed as in the proof of (b). □

4 Asynchronous Communication

Suppose we have a circuit in which an output of one sequential module, called the *sender*, is connected to a data input of another, called the *receiver*. Under suitable conditions on the sender's input, its output waveform is guaranteed by Theorem 3.6 to be stable with respect to the period of the sender's clock. On the other hand, in order to apply the results of Section 3 to the behavior of the receiver, we must be able to assume that its input is stable with respect to the period of its own clock. In general, this is true only for a synchronous circuit, in which the two modules are driven by the same clock. In this section, we shall examine the asynchronous case, in which the two clock inputs have different periods.

Our treatment of this problem is based on Moore's model of asynchrony [4]. In this model, the behavior of a signal is characterized abstractly by three quantities: a base time, a period, and a bit vector (representing the values assumed on successive cycles). Moore postulates that the receiver's input vector is determined by a function *asynch*, the arguments of which include the sender's output vector, the two periods, and the two base times. In this section, we shall present Moore's function *asynch* and establish the applicability of his model to certain circuits represented in our language. In Section 5, we shall employ a theorem of Moore to show that if the sender's and receiver's periods are known to be approximately equal, then communication may be achieved by means of a well known protocol.

4.1 Smooth and Quasi-smooth Waveforms

The communication protocol is motivated by the observation that if the time at which the receiver samples its input may be approximated by the sender, then the sender may successfully communicate a value by redundantly writing the value on sufficiently many successive cycles to guarantee that it is the value read by the receiver. For this purpose, the assumption that the sender's output waveform is stable is too weak; the waveform must be known to be constant on each cycle during some critical interval. With this requirement in mind, we define a stable waveform to be *smooth* if its setup time coincides with its period. Thus, w is a smooth n-cycle waveform based at t_0 with value list $V = (v_1 \ldots v_n)$ and period π if for $i = 1, \ldots, n$, $\hat{w}(t) = v_i$ for all $t \in [t_0 + (k-1)\pi, t_0 + k\pi)$.

A somewhat weaker notion of smoothness is needed to describe waveforms that are constant over some but not all cycles. First, we define a list $V = (v_1 \ldots v_n)$ to be a *generalized bit vector* if each v_i is either Boolean or the literal atom Q. In this case, we shall call w a *quasi-smooth n-cycle waveform based at t_0 with value list V and period π* if for $i = 1, \ldots, n$, either $v_i = $ Q or $\hat{w}(t) = v_i$ for all $t \in [t_0 + (k-1)\pi, t_0 + k\pi)$. (Thus, the value Q corresponds to cycles of unknown behavior.)

Our first objective is to derive a nontrivial representation of an output waveform of a sequential device as a quasi-smooth waveform. For this purpose, we make the following definition: If v is a Boolean atom and V is a bit vector, then $smooth(v, V)$ is the generalized bit vector V', where:

(1) If $V = $ NIL, then $V' = $ NIL; otherwise:
(2) If $car(V) = v$, then $V' = cons(v, smooth(v, cdr(V)))$; otherwise:
(3) $V' = cons($Q$, smooth(car(V), cdr(V)))$.

Thus, if $v = v_0$ and $V = (v_1 \ldots v_n)$, then $V' = (v'_1 \ldots v'_n)$, where for $i = 1, \ldots, n$,

$$v'_i = \begin{cases} v_i \text{ if } v_i = v_{i-1} \\ \text{Q if } v_i \neq v_{i-1}. \end{cases}$$

Lemma 4.1 *Let $s = nth(j, O(M))$ be a registered output of a sequential module M. Let $w = nth(j, outp(M, sim(M, p, t_f)))$, where p is an admissible n-cycle input packet for S based at t_0 with value matrix $\mathcal{V}$ and period π, and $t_f \geq t_0 + (n+1)\pi$.*

Let $U = (sv(0, s, \mathcal{V}, M) \ldots sv(n, s, \mathcal{V}, M))$. Then w is an n-cycle quasi-smooth waveform based at $t_0 + 2\pi$ with value list $smooth(car(U), cdr(U))$ and period π.

Proof: For $0 \leq k \leq n$, let $U_k = (sv(n-k, s, \mathcal{V}, M) \ldots sv(n, s, \mathcal{V}, M))$ and $V_k = smooth(car(U_k), cdr(U_k))$. We shall prove, by induction on k, that w is a k-cycle quasi-smooth waveform based at $t_0 + (n-k+2)\pi$ with value list V_k and period π.

The base case $k = 0$ holds vacuously. For $k > 0$, since $cdr(V_k) = V_{k-1}$, we need only consider $car(V_k)$ and the behavior of w on $[t_0 + (n-k+2)\pi, t_0 + (n-k+3)\pi)$. If $car(V_k) = $ Q, there is nothing to prove. In the remaining case, $car(V_k) = car(U_k) = car(U_{k-1})$, i.e., $sv(n - k, s, \mathcal{V}, M) = sv(n - k + 1, s, \mathcal{V}, M)$, and the result follows from Theorem 3.6. □

4.2 Describing Output as Input

Next, for a given quasi-smooth waveform with period π_s (representing that of the sender's clock), we would like to derive an alternative representation as a quasi-smooth waveform with a given period π_r (that of the receiver's clock). Let w be an n-cycle quasi-smooth waveform based at t_s (a rising edge of the sender's clock) with value list $V = (v_1 \ldots v_n)$ and period π_s. Assume $t_s \leq t_r < t_s + \pi_s$ (where t_r represents a rising edge of the receiver's clock). We shall construct a list of values $V' = warp(V, t_s, t_r, \pi_s, \pi_r)$ such that w is a quasi-smooth waveform based at t_r with value list V' and period π_r. The definition of $warp$ requires several auxiliary functions.

Let t satisfy $t_s < t \leq t_s + n\pi_s$. Choose k so that $t_s + (k - 1)\pi_s < t \leq t_s + k\pi_s$. Then $1 \leq k \leq n$. (k represents the number of cycles of the sender that intersect the interval $[t_r, t)$.) We define

$$sig(V, t_s, t, \pi_s) = \begin{cases} v_1 \text{ if } v_1 = v_2 = \ldots = v_k \\ \texttt{Q} \text{ if not.} \end{cases}$$

Under the same constraints on t, choose ℓ so that $t_s + \ell\pi_s \leq t < t_s + (\ell+1)\pi_s$. Then $0 \leq \ell \leq n$. ($t_s + \ell\pi_s$ represents the maximum sender's rising edge that is not exceeded by t.) We define

$$t_s^+(V, t_s, t, \pi_s) = t_s + \ell\pi_s$$

and

$$lst^+(V, t_s, t, \pi_s) = (v_{\ell+1} \ldots v_n).$$

Now we may define $V' = warp(V, t_s, t_r, \pi_s, \pi_r)$: If $t_r + \pi_r > t_s + n\pi_s$, then $V' = \texttt{NIL}$; otherwise,

$$V' = cons(sig, warp(lst^+, t_s^+, t_r + \pi_r, \pi_s, \pi_r)),$$

where $sig = sig(V, t_s, t_r + \pi_r, \pi_s)$, $lst^+ = lst^+(V, t_s, t_r + \pi_r, \pi_s)$, and $t_s^+ = t_s^+(V, t_s, t_r + \pi_r, \pi_s)$.

Lemma 4.2 *Let w be a quasi-smooth n-cycle waveform based at t_s with value list V and period π_s. Let $\pi_r > 0$ and $t_s \leq t_r < t_s + \pi_s$. Let $V' = warp(V, t_s, t_r, \pi_s, \pi_r)$ and let n' be the length of V'. Then w is a quasi-smooth n'-cycle waveform based at t_r with value list V' and period π_r.*

Proof: We may assume $t_r + \pi_r \leq t_s + n\pi_s$, for otherwise, $n' = 0$. Let $V = (v_1 \ldots v_n)$ and let sig, lst^+, and t_s^+ be defined as in the definition of $warp$. By induction, we may further assume that w is a quasi-smooth $(n' - 1)$-cycle waveform based at $t_r + \pi_r$ with value list $cdr(V') = $

$warp(lst^+, t_s^+, t_r + \pi_r, \pi_s, \pi_r)$ and period π_r. We need only show that either $car(V') = sig = $ Q, or $\hat{w}$ has the constant value sig on the cycle $[t_r, t_r + \pi_r)$.

Suppose $sig \neq $ Q. Choose k so that $t_s + (k-1)\pi_s < t_r + \pi_r \leq t_s + k\pi_s$. According to the definition of sig, $sig = v_1 = v_2 = \ldots = v_k$, and hence, $\hat{w}(t) = sig$ for all $t \in [t_s, t_s + k\pi_s) \supseteq [t_r, t_r + \pi_r)$. □

4.3 Eliminating Metastability

Lemmas 4.1 and 4.2 together provide a representation of a registered output waveform from the sender as a quasi-smooth waveform with respect to the receiver's clock. In order to achieve communication, we shall design a clocked state-holding device, called a *d-latch*, that converts a quasi-smooth input to a stable output. In our asynchronous circuit, this device will share the receiver's clock, and its output will be connected to the receiver's input.

The d-latch will consist of an inverter and three nand gates. Its functionality will depend on the relative delays of these components. Thus, along with our standard gates not1 and nand2, both of which have delay 2000, we shall require the following faster nand gate, fnand2:

(BEHAV (A B) ((NAND2 A B)) (1000) (INERTIAL))

We define dlatch to be the following module, which is diagrammed in Fig. 5:

```
(STRUCT (CLK D) (S2)
  (not1 nand2 nand2 fnand2)
  ((CLK) (CLK D) (S1 S3) (S0 S2))
  ((S0) (S1) (S2) (S3)))
```

Unlike all other circuits that we have encountered, the specified behavior of dlatch will also depend on the unique character of inertial delay. In particular, we shall need the following result:

Lemma 4.3 *Let $nth(j, O(M)) = s$ be an output of a behavioral module M. Let $nth(j, D(M)) = d$ and $nth(j, P(M)) = $ INERTIAL. Let p be an input packet for M, let v be the combinational value of s w.r.t. $\hat{p}(t_0)$, and let $w = nth(j, sim(M, p, t_0))$.*

(a) If $\hat{w}(t_0) = v$, then $w = hist(w, t_0)$.

(b) If $\hat{w}(t_0) \neq v$, then $w = cons((v, t_1), hist(w, t_0))$, where $t_0 < t_1 \leq t_0 + d$.

Proof: By Lemma 2.10 and the definition of *exec*,

$$w = inertial(w, v, t_0, t_0 + d).$$

The lemma follows from the definition of *inertial*. □

The behavioral specification of dlatch is an instance of the following, with $d_0 = d_1 = d_2 = 2000$ and $d_3 = 1000$.

Lemma 4.4 *Let G_0 be the inverter*

Verification of Synchronous and Asynchronous Circuits   441

$$\text{(BEHAV (A) (NOT1 A) } (d_0) \text{ (INERTIAL))}$$

and for $i = 1, 2, 3$, let G_i be the nand gate

$$\text{(BEHAV (A B) (NAND2 A B) } (d_i) \text{ (INERTIAL))},$$

where $d_1 \leq d_0$ and $d_0 + d_3 < d_1 + d_2$. Let $D = d_0 + d_1 + d_2 + d_3$. Let L be the module

$$\begin{array}{l}\text{(STRUCT (CLK) (D)}\\\quad (G_0\ G_1\ G_2\ G_3)\\\quad \text{((CLK) (CLK D) (S1 S3) (S2 S0))}\\\quad \text{((S0) (S1) (S2) (S3)))}.\end{array}$$

Let $p = (w_{\text{CLK}}\ w_{\text{D}})$ be an input packet for L, and assume that

$$\hat{w}_{\text{CLK}}(t) = \begin{cases} \mathcal{T} & \text{for all } t \in [t_+, t_-) \\ \mathcal{F} & \text{for all } t \in [t_-, t_f), \end{cases}$$

where $t_- > t_+ + D$ and $t_f > t_- + D$. Let $((w_0)\ (w_1)\ (w_2)\ (w_3)) = sim(L, p, t_f)$. Then $\hat{w}_2$ has a constant value v on $[t_- + D, t_f)$. If $\hat{w}_{\text{D}}$ has a constant value u on $[t_+, t_f)$, then $u = v$.

Proof: For each $t \in \mathbf{N}$, let $B_t = ((w_{0,t})(w_{1,t})(w_{2,t})(w_{3,t})) = sim(L, p, t)$. Then for $i = 0, \ldots, 3$, $w_i = w_{i,t_f}$. Let $t_0 = t_- + d_0$. For each $t \geq t_0$, the following results may be derived from Lemmas 3.1 and 2.9:

(a) $\hat{w}_{0,t}$ has the constant value F on $[t_+ + d_0, t_0)$;
(b) $\hat{w}_{3,t}$ has the constant value T on $[t_+ + d_0 + d_3, t_0 + d_3)$;
(c) $\hat{w}_{0,t}$ has the constant value T on $[t_0, t_f + d_0)$;
(d) $\hat{w}_{1,t}$ has the constant value T on $[t_- + d_1, t_f + d_1)$.

In particular, for each $t \geq t_0$, $\hat{w}_{0,t}$ and $\hat{w}_{1,t}$ are both constant on $[t_0, t_f)$.

By Lemma 2.9,

$$(w_{2,t}) = sim(G_2, (w_{1,t}\ w_{3,t}), t)$$

and

$$(w_{3,t}) = sim(G_3, (w_{0,t}\ w_{2,t}), t).$$

We shall apply Lemma 4.3 to both G_2 and G_3.

We shall show that for some $t_1 \in [t_0, t_- + D)$ and some $v \in \mathbf{B}$, $\hat{w}_{2,t_1}(t_1) = v$ and $\hat{w}_{3,t_1}(t_1) = not1(v)$. Let $w_{2,t_0}(t_0) = v_2$ and $w_{3,t_0}(t_0) = v_3$. We consider the following cases:

Case 1: $v_3 = not1(v_2)$. In this case, we take $t_1 = t_0$ and $v = v_2$.
Case 2: $v_3 = v_2$. By Lemma 4.3(b),

$$w_{2,t_0} = cons((not1(v_2), t_2), hist(w_{2,t_0}, t_0)),$$

where $t_0 < t_2 \leq t_0 + d_2$, and

$$w_{3,t_0} = cons((not1(v_2), t_t), hist(w_{3,t_0}, t_0)),$$

where $t_0 < t_3 \leq t_0 + d_3$.

Subcase 2a: $t_3 < t_2$. Here, $t_{next}(t_0, p, B_{t_0}, L) = t_3$. By Lemma 2.7,
$$\hat{w}_{2,t_3}(t_3) = \hat{w}_{2,t_0}(t_3) = v_2$$
and
$$\hat{w}_{3,t_3}(t_3) = \hat{w}_{3,t_0}(t_3) = not1(v_2).$$

Thus, we have $t_1 = t_3$ and $v = v_2$.

Subcase 2b: $t_2 < t_3$. In this case, $t_{next}(t_0, p, B_{t_0}, L) = t_3$, and we have
$$\hat{w}_{2,t_2}(t_2) = \hat{w}_{2,t_0}(t_2) = not1(v_2)$$
and
$$\hat{w}_{3,t_2}(t_2) = \hat{w}_{3,t_0}(t_2) = v_2.$$

In this case, $t_1 = t_2$ and $v = not1(v_2)$.

Subcase 2c: $t_2 = t_3$. We have
$$\hat{w}_{2,t_2}(t_2) = \hat{w}_{3,t_2}(t_2) = not1(v_2).$$

By Lemma 4.3(b),
$$w_{2,t_2} = cons((v_2, t_2 + d_2), w_{2,t_0}),$$
and
$$w_{3,t_2} = cons((v_2, t_2 + d_3), w_{3,t_0}).$$

It follows from our hypotheses that $d_3 < d_2$. Hence,
$$\hat{w}_{2,t_2+d_3}(t_2 + d_3) = not1(v_2)$$
and
$$\hat{w}_{3,t_2+d_3}(t_2 + d_3) = v_2.$$

Thus, $t_1 = t_2 + d_3$ and $v = not1(v_2)$.

By Lemma 4.3(a), $\hat{w}_{2,t_1} = hist(\hat{w}_{2,t_1}, t_1)$ and $\hat{w}_{3,t_1} = hist(\hat{w}_{3,t_1}, t_1)$. Hence, $t_{next}(t_1, p, B_{t_1}, L) \geq t_f$. It follows that for any $t' \in [t_1, t_f)$, $B_{t'} = B_{t_1}$, and in particular, $w_{2,t_f}(t') = w_{2,t'}(t') = w_{2,t_1}(t') = v$. Thus, w_{2,t_f} has the constant value v on $[t_1, t_f) \supseteq [t_- + D, t_f)$.

Finally, suppose that $\hat{w}_D$ has a constant value u on $[t_+, t_f)$. Then $\hat{w}_1(t) = not1(u)$ for $t \in [t_+ + d_1, t_- + d_1)$. Since $\hat{w}_3(t) = \mathcal{T}$ on $[t_+ + d_0 + d_3, t_0 + d_3)$, the combinational value corresponding to S2 is u on the intersection of these intervals, $[max(t_+ + d_1, t_+ + d_0 + d_3), min(t_- + d_1, t_0 + d_3))$. Thus, by Lemma 3.1, $\hat{w}_2(t) = u$ for $t \in [max(t_+ + d_1 + d_2, t_+ + d_0 + d_3 + d_2), min(t_- + d_1 + d_2, t_0 + d_3 + d_2))$. In particular, $\hat{w}_2(t) = u$ for $t \in [t_0, t_0 + d_3 + d_2)$. Thus, $v_2 = u$. Moreover, Subcases 2b and 2c, in which $\hat{w}$ assumes the value $not1(v_2)$ at some point in this interval, are eliminated. In the remaining cases, $v = v_2 = u$. □

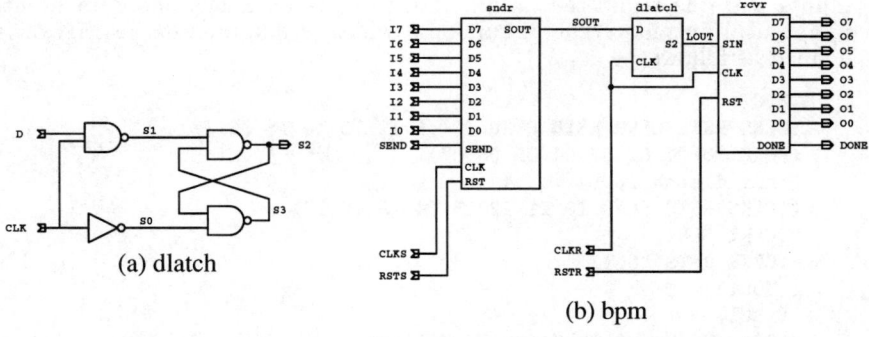

FIG. 5.

In order to avail ourselves of the results of [4], we must restate Lemma 4.4 in terms of Moore's function *det*. If V is a generalized bit vector and *oracle* is a bit vector, then $det(V, oracle)$ is the bit vector V', defined as follows:

(1) If $V = \text{NIL}$, then $V' = \text{NIL}$; otherwise:
(2) If $car(V) \in \mathbf{B}$, then $V' = cons(car(V), det(cdr(V), oracle))$; otherwise:
(3) If $oracle = \text{NIL}$, then $V' = cons(\mathcal{T}, det(cdr(V), oracle))$; otherwise:
(4) $V' = cons(car(oracle), det(cdr(V), cdr(oracle)))$.

Lemma 4.5 *Let* $p = (w_{\text{CLK}}\ w_{\text{D}})$ *be an input packet for* dlatch, *where* w_{CLK} *is an n-cycle pulse based at* t_0 *with high* $h > 7000$, *low* $\ell > 7000$, *and period* $\pi = h + \ell$, *and* w_{D} *is a quasi-smooth n-cycle waveform based at* t_0 *with value list* V *and period* π. *Let*

$$((w_0)\,(w_1)\,(w_2)\,(w_3)) = sim(\text{dlatch}, p, t_f),$$

where $t_f \geq t_0 + n\pi$. *Then for some bit vector* oracle, w_2 *is a stable n-cycle waveform based at* t_0 *with setup* $\ell - 7000$, *value list* $det(V, oracle)$, *and period* π.

Proof: We induct on n. For $n = 0$, the statement is vacuous. For $n > 0$, we may assume that w_2 is a stable $(n-1)$-cycle waveform based at $t_0 + \pi$ with setup $\ell - 7000$, value list $det(cdr(V), oracle')$, and period π. By Lemma 4.4, $\hat{w}_2$ has a constant value v on $[t_0 + h + 7000, t_0 + \pi) = [t_0 + \pi - (\ell - 7000), t_0 + \pi)$, and if $car(V) \neq \mathbf{Q}$, then $car(V) = v$. If $car(V) = \mathbf{Q}$, then let $oracle = cons(v, oracle')$; otherwise, let $oracle = oracle'$. In either case, w_2 is a stable n-cycle waveform based at t_0 with setup $\ell - 7000$, value list $det(V, oracle)$, and period π. □

4.4 The Main Theorem

In Section 5, we shall apply the results of this section to a circuit bpm, consisting of two sequential submodules, sndr and rcvr, and a dlatch:

According to the definitions that we shall present later, sndr has 9 data inputs and one registered output, SOUT, while rcvr has one data input, SIN, and 9 outputs. The circuit bpm, which is diagrammed in Fig. 5, is defined as follows:

```
(STRUCT
  (CLKS RSTS CLKR RSTR SEND I0 I1 I2 I3 I4 I5 I6 I7)
  (DONE O0 O1 O2 O3 O4 O5 O6 O7)
  (sndr dlatch rcvr)
  ((CLKS RSTS SEND I0 I1 I2 I3 I4 I5 I6 I7)
   (CLKR SOUT)
   (CLKR RSTS LOUT))
  ((SOUT)
   (LOUT)
   (DONE O0 O1 O2 O3 O4 O5 O6 O7)))
```

The following theorem summarizes our results on asynchrony, as they pertain to the module bpm. The theorem refers to Moore's function *asynch*, which is defined as follows: Let V and *oracle* be bit vectors and let $t_s, t_r, \pi_s, \pi_r \in \mathbf{N}$ such that $\pi_s > 0$, $\pi_r > 0$, and $t_s \leq t_r < t_s + \pi_s$. Then

$$asynch(V, t_s, t_r, \pi_s, \pi_r, oracle) = \\ det(warp(smooth(T, V), t_s, t_r, \pi_s, \pi_r), oracle).$$

Theorem 4.6 Let $p = (w_{\text{CLKS}}\ w_{\text{RSTS}}\ w_{\text{CLKR}}\ w_{\text{RSTR}}\ w_{\text{SEND}}\ w_0\ \ldots\ w_7)$ be an input packet for bpm, where:

(a) $(w_{\text{CLKS}} w_{\text{RSTS}} w_{\text{SEND}} w_0 \ldots w_7)$ is an admissible n_s-cycle input packet for sndr based at b_s with value matrix $\mathcal{V}$ and period π_s;

(b) w_{CLKR} is an admissible $(n_r + 2)$-cycle pulse for rcvr based at b_r with high $h > 7000$, low $\ell > 7000 + setup(\text{SIN}, \text{rcvr})$, and period $\pi_r = h + \ell$;

(c) w_{RSTR} is an admissible $(n_r + 1)$-cycle reset waveform for rcvr based at b_r with period π_r.

Let $t_r = b_r + \pi_r$. Assume that $b_s + 2\pi_s \leq t_r \leq b_s + (n_s + 2)\pi_s \leq t_r + n_r\pi_r$. Choose j so that $b_s + j\pi_s \leq t_r < b_s + (j+1)\pi_s$ and let $t_s = b_s + j\pi_s$. Assume $sv(j - 2, \text{SOUT}, \mathcal{V}, \text{sndr}) = \mathcal{T}$.

Let $U = (sv(j - 1, \text{SOUT}, \mathcal{V}, \text{sndr}) \ldots sv(n_s, \text{SOUT}, \mathcal{V}, \text{sndr}))$. Let w_{LOUT} be the waveform for LOUT determined by $sim(\text{bpm}, p, t_f)$, where $t_f \geq t_r + n_r\pi_r$. Then for some bit vector *oracle*, $(w_{\text{CLKR}}\ w_{\text{RSTR}}\ w_{\text{LOUT}})$ is an admissible input packet for rcvr based at b_r with value matrix

$$(asynch(U, t_s, t_r, \pi_s, \pi_r, oracle))$$

and period π_r.

Proof: Let w_{SOUT} be the waveform for SOUT that is determined by $sim(\text{bpm}, p, t_f)$. According to Lemma 4.1, w_{SOUT} is a quasi-smooth waveform based at t_s with value list $smooth(\mathcal{T}, U)$ and period π_s. It follows from Lemma 4.2 that w_{SOUT} is also a quasi-smooth waveform based at t_r

with value list $warp(smooth(\mathcal{T},U),t_s,t_r,\pi_s,\pi_r)$ and period π_r. Finally, by Lemma 4.5, w_{LOUT} is a stable waveform based at t_r with value list

$$det(warp(smooth(\mathcal{T},U),t_s,t_r,\pi_s,\pi_r), oracle) = \\ asynch(U,t_s,t_r,\pi_s,\pi_r,oracle)),$$

for some $oracle$, setup $\ell - 7000 > setup(\text{SIN},\text{rcvr})$, and period π_r. □

5 Biphase Mark

Moore's formulation [4] of the biphase mark protocol is based on two functions, *send* and *recv*, which represent the computations performed by the sender and the receiver, respectively. After presenting the definitions of these functions, we shall implement them in the design of the sequential modules sndr and rcvr. Then, using a theorem of Moore in combination with results of Section 4, we shall show that the circuit bpm achieves communication between these modules.

5.1 Sending

The function *send* returns a bit vector that represents an encoding of a given input bit vector msg. Each bit of msg is encoded as a bit vector called a *cell*, computed as the value of $cell(x,n,k,b)$, where b is the bit of msg to be encoded, x is the final bit of the preceding cell, and n and k are parameters of the protocol. A cell consists of two *subcells*, each of which is a uniform bit vector: a *mark* subcell of length n, followed by a *code* subcell of length k. The mark subcell is intended as a signal to the receiver that a new cell has been entered: each of its bits is $not1(x)$. The code subcell is the region in which the receiver is expected to look for information from which it will derive the value b of the encoded bit: if $b = \mathcal{T}$, then each bit of this subcell is x; if $b = \mathcal{F}$, each bit is $not1(x)$.

The definition of *cell* requires three auxiliary functions. First, the subcells are constructed by the function *listn*: for any $n \in \mathbf{N}$ and any x, $listn(n,x)$ is the uniform vector $(x \ldots x)$ of length n. Next, the two subcells are combined by the function *app*: for any two lists $L = (a_1 \ldots a_n)$ and $M = (b_1 \ldots b_m)$, $app(L,M) = (a_1 \ldots a_n\, b_1 \ldots b_m)$. Finally, the bit occurring in the code subcell is determined by the Boolean function *equal*, where $equal(x,y) = \mathcal{T}$ iff $x = y$, i.e., $equal(x,y) = not1(xor2(x,y))$.

Now, we may define

$$cell(x,n,k,b) = app(listn(n,not1(x)), listn(k, equal(x,b))),$$

and $cells(x,n,k,msg)$ is defined as:

(1) NIL, if $msg = $ NIL;
(2) $app(cell(x,n,k,car(msg)), cells(equal(x,car(msg)),n,k,cdr(msg)))$, if $msg \neq $ NIL.

The protocol includes the convention that the value $\mathcal{T}$ is transmitted until the encoded message is sent. Thus, the encoded bit vector constructed by *send* includes "pads" consisting arbitrarily many copies of $\mathcal{T}$ on both sides of the cells. The arguments of *send* include the lengths p_1 and p_2 of these pads:

$$send(msg, p_1, n, k, p_2) = \\ app(listn(p_1, \mathcal{T}), app(cells(\mathcal{T}, n, k, msg), listn(p_2, \mathcal{T}))).$$

5.2 Receiving

Next, we define $recv(i, x, j, L)$[1], which may be shown, under suitable assumptions, to be the inverse of *send*. This function recovers a bit of the encoded message from each cell by first detecting the beginning of the mark subcell, and then reading and decoding a bit at a predetermined location within the cell, which has been calculated to lie within the code subcell. Its arguments are interpreted as follows: i is the number of bits of the original message yet to be recovered, x is the last bit to have been read (from the preceding cell), j is the location within the cell of the bit to be read, and L is the remaining input stream.

The beginning of a new cell is detected by the function $scan(x, L)$, which successively removes bits from the beginning of the list L until a value different from x is found. The recursive definition follows:

(1) If $L = \text{NIL}$, then $scan(x, L) = \text{NIL}$; otherwise:

(2) If $car(L) = x$, then $scan(x, L) = scan(x, cdr(L))$; otherwise:

(3) $scan(x, L) = L$.

We shall require one other auxiliary function: If $n \in \mathbf{N}$ and L is a list, then $cdrn(n, L)$ is defined to be:

(1) L, if $n = 0$;

(2) $cdrn(n - 1, cdr(L))$, if $n > 0$.

Finally, we define $recv(i, x, j, L)$ to be the bit vector msg, where:

(1) If $i = 0$, then $msg = \text{NIL}$; otherwise:

(2) Let $S = scan(x, L)$. If $length(S) \leq k$, then $msg = \text{NIL}$; otherwise:

(3) Let $b = nth(k + 1, S)$ and $L' = cdrn(k + 1, S)$. If $b = x$, then $msg = cons(\mathcal{T}, recv(i - 1, b, j, L'))$; otherwise:

(4) $msg = cons(\mathcal{F}, recv(i - 1, b, j, L'))$.

5.3 Moore's Theorem

Moore has proved a statement of correctness of the protocol for certain values of the parameters. The lengths of the mark and code subcells generated by *send* are taken to be $n = 5$ and $k = 13$, respectively. The index

---

[1] For technical reasons, we shall slightly modify Moore's original definition of this function. Our modification does not affect the validity of any of his results.

Verification of Synchronous and Asynchronous Circuits

of the bit read by recv following the detection of an edge is $j = 10$, i.e., the eleventh bit after the edge is sampled. The theorem also depends on an assumption concerning the proximity of the two clock periods:

Theorem 5.1. (Moore) *Let $\pi_s > 0$, $\pi_r > 0$, and $17\pi_r \leq 18\pi_s \leq 19\pi_r$. Let $t_s \leq t_r < t_s + \pi_s$. Let msg be a bit vector of length k. Then for any bit vector oracle and any numbers p_1 and p_2,*

$$recv(k, \mathcal{T}, 10, asynch(send(msg, p_1, 5, 13, p_2), t_s, t_r, \pi_s, \pi_r, oracle)) = msg.$$

We shall apply Moore's theorem to the specification of the circuit bpm. The sequential submodules sndr and rcvr of bpm remain to be defined. As we present the definitions of the these modules and their components, which are diagrammed in Figs 6–10, we shall derive characterizations of their behavior that are analogous to Propositions 3.3 and 3.4. The proofs of these results are based on straightforward calculations and have all been mechanically checked. Therefore, the details of these proofs are omitted here.

5.4 Basic Components

The message that is transmitted from sndr to rcvr will consist of eight bits. It is stored (by both sndr and rcvr) in a shift register, shift8, which is constructed from eight copies of the following 3-port cell, port3:

```
(STRUCT
  (CLK RST SHIFT SIN LOAD DIN)
  (Q)
  (edff nand2 nand2 or2 nand2)
  ((CLK RST S3 S4) (DIN LOAD) (SIN SHIFT) (LOAD SHIFT) (S1 S2))
  ((Q QN) (S1) (S2) (S3) (S4)))
```

The behavior of port3 may be derived easily from that of edff (Proposition 3.3):

Proposition 5.2 *Let Σ and $V = (shift\ sin\ load\ din)$ be a state and a data vector for port3. Assume that shift and load are not both $\mathcal{T}$. Then*

$$nv(\mathtt{Q}, V, \Sigma, \mathtt{port3}) = \Sigma;$$

$$next(V, \Sigma, \mathtt{port3}) = \begin{cases} sin & \text{if } shift = \mathcal{T} \text{ and } load = \mathcal{F} \\ din & \text{if } shift = \mathcal{F} \text{ and } load = \mathcal{T} \\ \Sigma & \text{if } shift = \mathcal{F} \text{ and } load = \mathcal{F}. \end{cases}$$

The register shift8 is defined as follows:

```
(STRUCT
  (CLK RST LOAD SHIFT SIN D0 D1 D2 D3 D4 D5 D6 D7)
  (Q0 Q1 Q2 Q3 Q4 Q5 Q6 Q7)
  (port3 port3 port3 port3 port3 port3 port3 port3)
  ((CLK RST SHIFT SIN LOAD D0)
```

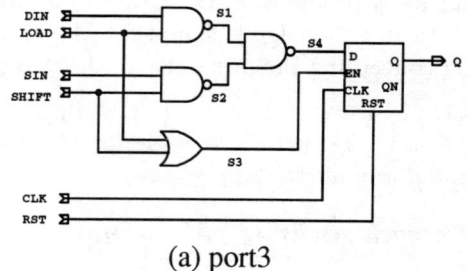

(a) port3

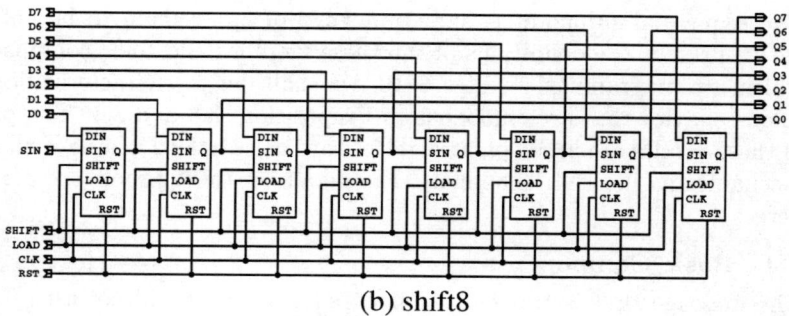

(b) shift8

FIG. 6.

```
(CLK RST SHIFT Q0 LOAD D1)
(CLK RST SHIFT Q1 LOAD D2)
(CLK RST SHIFT Q2 LOAD D3)
(CLK RST SHIFT Q3 LOAD D4)
(CLK RST SHIFT Q4 LOAD D5)
(CLK RST SHIFT Q5 LOAD D6)
(CLK RST SHIFT Q6 LOAD D7))
((Q0) (Q1) (Q2) (Q3) (Q4) (Q5) (Q6) (Q7)))
```

Proposition 5.3 *Let $\Sigma = (\sigma_0 \ldots \sigma_7)$ and $V = (load\ shift\ sin\ d_0 \ldots d_7)$ be a state and a data vector for* shift8. *Assume that shift and load are not both $\mathcal{T}$. Then*

$$nv(\mathtt{Q}i, V, \Sigma, \mathtt{shift8}) = \sigma_i,\ i = 0, \ldots, 7;$$

$$next(V, \Sigma, \mathtt{shift8}) = \begin{cases} (sin\ \sigma_0 \ldots \sigma_6) & \text{if } shift = \mathcal{T} \text{ and } load = \mathcal{F} \\ (d_0 \ldots d_7) & \text{if } shift = \mathcal{F} \text{ and } load = \mathcal{T} \\ \Sigma & \text{if } shift = \mathcal{F} \text{ and } load = \mathcal{F}. \end{cases}$$

In order to describe the shifting operation that is performed by shift8, we define, for any $b \in \mathbf{B}$ and any bit vector V,

$$shift(b, V) = \begin{cases} \mathtt{NIL} & \text{if } V = \mathtt{NIL} \\ cons(b, shift(car(V), cdr(V))) & \text{if } V \neq \mathtt{NIL}. \end{cases}$$

Verification of Synchronous and Asynchronous Circuits 449

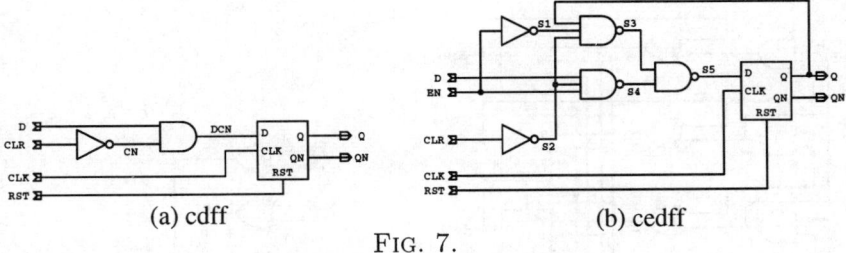

(a) cdff (b) cedff

FIG. 7.

Thus, $shift(sin, (\sigma_0 \ldots \sigma_7)) = (sin\ \sigma_0 \ldots \sigma_6)$.

In addition to dff and edff, we shall require two other versions of the flip-flop. The first of these, cdff, has an input CLR, which may be used to override the other data input D and reinitialize the state:

```
(STRUCT
  (CLK RST CLR D)
  (Q QN)
  (dff not1 nand2)
  ((CLK RST DCN) (CLR) (D CN))
  ((Q QN) (CN) (DCN)))
```

Proposition 5.4 *Let Σ and $V = (clr\ d)$ be a state and a data vector for* cdff. *Then*

$$nv(\mathtt{Q}, V, \Sigma, \mathtt{cdff}) = \Sigma \text{ and } nv(\mathtt{QN}, V, \Sigma, \mathtt{cdff}) = not1(\Sigma);$$

$$next(V, \Sigma, \mathtt{cdff}) = \begin{cases} \mathcal{F} & \text{if } clr = \mathcal{T} \\ d & \text{if } clr = \mathcal{F}. \end{cases}$$

The second, cedff, is a combination of edff and cdff:

```
(STRUCT
  (CLK RST CLR EN D)
  (Q QN)
  (dff not1 not1 nand3 nand3 nand2)
  ((CLK RST S5) (EN) (CLR) (Q S1 S2) (D S2 EN) (S3 S4))
  ((Q QN) (S1) (S2) (S3) (S4) (S5)))
```

Proposition 5.5 *Let Σ and $V = (clr\ en\ d)$ be a state and a data vector for* cedff. *Then*

$$nv(\mathtt{Q}, V, \Sigma, \mathtt{cedff}) = \Sigma \text{ and } nv(\mathtt{QN}, V, \Sigma, \mathtt{cedff}) = not1(\Sigma);$$

$$next(V, \Sigma, \mathtt{cedff}) = \begin{cases} \mathcal{F} & \text{if } clr = \mathcal{T} \\ d & \text{if } clr = \mathcal{F} \text{ and } en = \mathcal{T} \\ \Sigma & \text{if } clr = \mathcal{F} \text{ and } en = \mathcal{F}. \end{cases}$$

Using cedff, we construct the following 5-bit counter, count5:

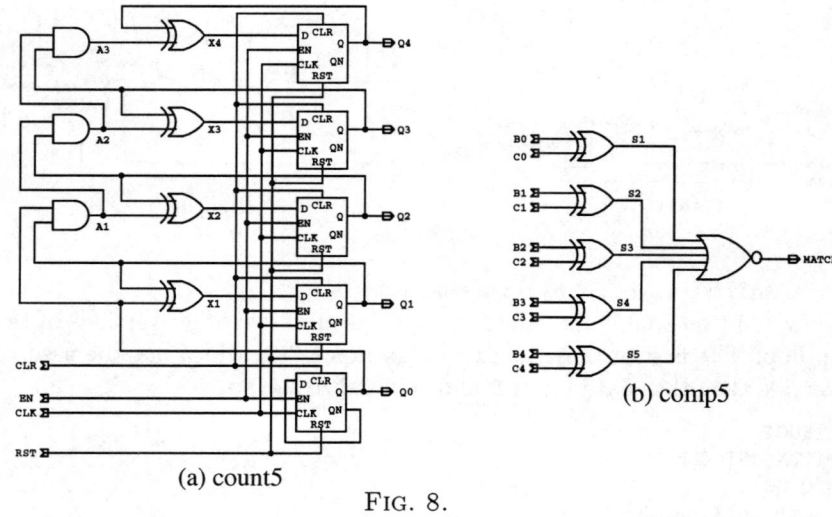

(a) count5

(b) comp5

Fig. 8.

```
(STRUCT
  (CLK RST CLR EN)
  (Q0 Q1 Q2 Q3 Q4)
  (cedff cedff cedff cedff cedff
   and2 and2 and2 xor2 xor2 xor2 xor2)
  ((CLK RST CLR EN QN0)
   (CLK RST CLR EN X1)
   (CLK RST CLR EN X2)
   (CLK RST CLR EN X3)
   (CLK RST CLR EN X4)
   (Q0 Q1) (A1 Q2) (A2 Q3) (Q0 Q1) (Q2 A1) (Q3 A2) (Q4 A3))
  ((Q0 QN0) (Q1 QN1) (Q2 QN2) (Q3 QN3) (Q4 QN4)
   (A1) (A2) (A3) (X1) (X2) (X3) (X4)))
```

Proposition 5.6 *Let $\Sigma = (\sigma_0 \ldots \sigma_4)$ and $V = (clr\ en)$ be a state and a data vector for* count5. *Then*

$$nv(\mathsf{Q}i, V, \Sigma, \mathsf{count5}) = \sigma_i,\ i = 0, \ldots, 4;$$

$$next(V, \Sigma, \mathsf{count5}) = \begin{cases} listn(5, \mathcal{F}) & \textit{if } clr = \mathcal{T} \\ inc(cnt) & \textit{if } clr = \mathcal{F} \textit{ and } en = \mathcal{T} \\ \Sigma & \textit{if } clr = \mathcal{F} \textit{ and } en = \mathcal{F}. \end{cases}$$

For convenience in representing states of both *count3* and *count5*, we define, for $k \in \mathbf{N}$ and $n \in \mathbf{N}$,

$$bv_k(n) = \begin{cases} listn(k, \mathcal{F}) & \textit{if } n = 0 \\ inc(bv_k(n-1)) & \textit{if } n > 0. \end{cases}$$

Thus, $bv_k(n)$ is the k-bit vector that represents the number n.

Verification of Synchronous and Asynchronous Circuits

We shall also require a combinational module, the following 5-bit comparator comp5:

```
(STRUCT
  (C0 B0 C1 B1 C2 B2 C3 B3 C4 B4)
  (MATCH)
  (xor2 xor2 xor2 xor2 xor2 nor5)
  ((C0 B0) (C1 B1) (C2 B2) (C3 B3) (C4 B4) (S1 S2 S3 S4 S5))
  ((S1) (S2) (S3) (S4) (S5) (MATCH)))
```

This module simply determines whether two given 5-bit vectors are equal, i.e.,

$$cv(\text{MATCH}, (c_0 b_0 c_1 b_1 \ldots c_4 b_4), \text{comp5}) = \begin{cases} \mathcal{T} & \text{if } (c_0 \ldots c_4) = (b_0 \ldots b_4) \\ \mathcal{F} & \text{if not.} \end{cases}$$

5.5 The Sender

The action of sndr is controlled by the submodule scount, which is defined as follows:

```
(STRUCT
  (CLK RST STOP BIT)
  (MARK CODE)
  (cdff count5 or2 or2 t0 f0 comp5 comp5)
  ((CLK RST STOP S1) (CLK RST S2 Q) (BIT Q) (STOP BIT) () ()
   (F Q0 F Q1 T Q2 F Q3 F Q4) (T Q0 F Q1 F Q2 F Q3 T Q4))
  ((Q QN) (Q0 Q1 Q2 Q3 Q4) (S1) (S2) (T) (F) (MARK) (CODE)))
```

A state of scount is a list $(on\ cnt)$ of two components, corresponding to the two sequential submodules, cdff and count5. As long as both data inputs are $\mathcal{F}$, the value of on remains constant. While $on = \mathcal{T}$, cnt is incremented repreatedly; while $on = \mathcal{F}$, cnt remains unchanged. If either input is $\mathcal{T}$, then on is set accordingly and cnt is reset to $bv_5(0)$. The output values are both determined by cnt:

Proposition 5.7 *Let* $\Sigma = (on\ cnt)$ *and* $V = (stop\ bit)$ *be a state and a data vector for* scount. *Then*

$$nv(\text{MARK}, V, \Sigma, \text{scount}) = \begin{cases} \mathcal{T} & \text{if } cnt = bv_5(4) \\ \mathcal{F} & \text{if } cnt \neq bv_5(4); \end{cases}$$

$$nv(\text{CODE}, V, \Sigma, \text{scount}) = \begin{cases} \mathcal{T} & \text{if } cnt = bv_5(17) \\ \mathcal{F} & \text{if } cnt \neq bv_5(17); \end{cases}$$

$$next(V, \Sigma, \text{scount}) = \begin{cases} (\mathcal{F}\ bv_5(0)) & \text{if } stop = \mathcal{T} \\ (\mathcal{T}\ bv_5(0)) & \text{if } stop = \mathcal{F} \text{ and } bit = \mathcal{T} \\ (\mathcal{T}\ inc(cnt)) & \text{if } stop = bit = \mathcal{F} \text{ and } on = \mathcal{T} \\ (\mathcal{F}\ cnt) & \text{if } stop = bit = \mathcal{F} \text{ and } on = \mathcal{F}. \end{cases}$$

The definition of sndr is as follows:

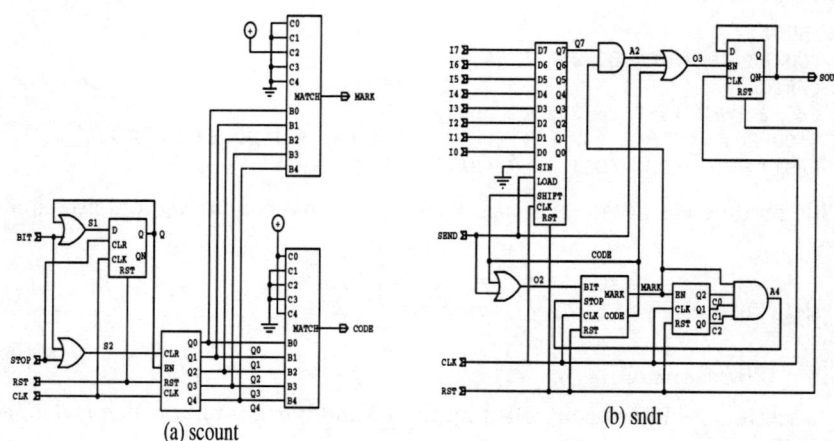

(a) scount (b) sndr

FIG. 9.

```
(STRUCT
  (CLK RST SEND I0 I1 I2 I3 I4 I5 I6 I7)
  (SOUT)
  (scount shift8 count3 edff or2 and2 and4 or3 f0)
  ((CLK RST A4 O2) (CLK RST SEND CODE F I0 I1 I2 I3 I4 I5 I6 I7)
   (CLK RST MARK) (CLK RST O3 SOUT) (CODE SEND) (Q7 MARK)
   (MARK C0 C1 C2) (A2 SEND CODE) ())
  ((MARK CODE) (Q0 Q1 Q2 Q3 Q4 Q5 Q6 Q7) (C0 C1 C2)
   (Q SOUT) (O2) (A2) (A4) (O3) (F)))
```

This module has two modes of operation. In one mode, it waits dormantly for the SEND input to become $\mathcal{T}$. When this occurs, the current values of the other eight data inputs are loaded into the shift register, the state of the flip-flop edff (which determines the output value) changes, and the controller scount begins counting. This mode is described by the following:

Proposition 5.8 *Let* $V = (s\, d_0\, \ldots\, d_7)$ *be a data vector for* sndr, *and let* $\Sigma = (\sigma_1\, \sigma_2\, \sigma_3\, \sigma_4)$ *be a state of* sndr, *where* $\sigma_1 = (on\, cnt)$. *Assume that* $on = \mathcal{F}$ *and* $cnt = bv_5(0)$. *Let* $\Sigma' = next(V, \Sigma, \text{sndr})$:

(a) *If* $s = \mathcal{T}$, *then* $\Sigma' = ((\mathcal{T}\, bv_5(0))\, (d_0\, \ldots\, d_7)\, \sigma_3\, not1(\sigma_4))$;
(b) *If* $s = \mathcal{F}$, *then* $\Sigma' = \Sigma$.

In the other mode of operation, the register contents are encoded and transmitted. Each register bit is encoded as a cell consisting of a 5-bit mark subcell and a 13-bit code subcell, as measured by scount. The number of cells that have been transmitted is recorded as the contents of count3. At the end of each mark subcell, this number is incremented. At the end of each code subcell, scount is reset and the register contents are shifted:

Proposition 5.9 Let $V = (s\, d_0\, \ldots\, d_7)$ be a data vector for sndr, and let $\Sigma = (\sigma_1\sigma_2\sigma_3\sigma_4)$ be a state of sndr, where $\sigma_1 = (oncnt)$ and $\sigma_2 = (q_0\ldots q_7)$. Assume that $s = \mathcal{F}$ and $on = \mathcal{T}$. Let $\Sigma' = next(V, \Sigma, \text{sndr})$:

(a) If $cnt = bv_5(4)$ and $\sigma_3 = bv_3(7)$, then
$$\Sigma' = ((\mathcal{F}\, bv_5(0))\, \sigma_2\, inc(\sigma_3)\, xor2(q_7, \sigma_4)).$$

(b) If $cnt = bv_5(4)$ and $\sigma_3 \neq bv_3(7)$, then
$$\Sigma' = ((\mathcal{T}\, bv_5(5))\, \sigma_2\, inc(\sigma_3)\, xor2(q_7, \sigma_4)).$$

(c) If $cnt = bv_5(17)$, then
$$\Sigma' = ((\mathcal{T}\, bv_5(0))\, shift(\mathcal{F}, \sigma_2)\, \sigma_3\, not1(\sigma_4)).$$

(d) If $cnt \neq bv_5(4)$ and $cnt \neq bv_5(17)$, then
$$\Sigma' = ((\mathcal{T}\, inc(cnt))\, \sigma_2\, \sigma_3\, \sigma_4).$$

Our main theorem on sndr is the following specification:

Proposition 5.10 Let $\mathcal{V} = (\mathcal{V}_{\text{SEND}}\, \mathcal{V}_{I0}\, \ldots\, \mathcal{V}_{I7})$ be a list of bit vectors, each of length $n \geq 144$. Let $m = n - 144$. Assume that for $j = 1, \ldots, n$,

$$nth(j, \mathcal{V}_{\text{SEND}}) = \begin{cases} \mathcal{T} & \text{if } j = m \\ \mathcal{F} & \text{if } j \neq m. \end{cases}$$

Let $d_i = nth(m, \mathcal{V}_{Ii})$, for $i = 0, \ldots, 7$. Let $sv_j = sv(j, \text{SOUT}, \mathcal{V}, \text{sndr})$, for $j = 1, \ldots, n$. Then $(sv_1\, \ldots\, sv_n) = send((d_7\, \ldots\, d_0), m, 5, 13, 0)$.

Proof: Let $\Sigma_j = state(j, \mathcal{V}, \text{sndr})$, $j = 0, \ldots, n$. By Proposition 5.8(b), for $j = 0, \ldots, m$,

$$\Sigma_j = \Sigma_0(\text{sndr}) = ((\mathcal{F}\, bv_5(0))\, listn(8, \mathcal{F})\, bv_3(0)\, \mathcal{F})$$

and hence $(sv_1\, \ldots\, sv_m) = listn(m, \mathcal{T})$. It remains to show that

$$(sv_{m+1}\, \ldots\, sv_n) = cells(\mathcal{T}, 5, 13, (d_7\, \ldots\, d_0)).$$

By Proposition 5.8(a),

$$\Sigma_{m+1} = ((\mathcal{T}\, bv_5(0))\, (d_0\, \ldots\, d_7)\, bv_3(0)\, \mathcal{T}).$$

We shall show that for all k, $0 \leq k \leq 7$, if

$$\Sigma_{m+1+18k} = ((\mathcal{T}\, bv_5(0))\, app(listn(k, \mathcal{F}), (d_0\, \ldots\, d_{7-k}))\, bv_3(k)\, x),$$

then

$$(sv_{m+1+18k}\, \ldots\, sv_n) = cells(x, 5, 13, (d_{7-k}\, \ldots\, d_0)).$$

The proposition will follow from this result upon setting $k = 0$.

The proof is by induction on $7 - k$. In the base case, $k = 7$, our assumption is that

$$\Sigma_{m+1+18k} = \Sigma_{m+127} = ((\mathcal{T}\, bv_5(0))\ app(listn(7, \mathcal{F}), (d_0))\ bv_3(7)\ x).$$

By Proposition 5.9(d), for $\ell = 0, \ldots, 4$,

$$\Sigma_{m+127+\ell} = ((\mathcal{T}\, bv_5(\ell))\ app(listn(7, \mathcal{F}), (d_0))\ bv_3(7)\ x),$$

and by Proposition 5.9(a),

$$\Sigma_{m+127+5} = \Sigma_{m+132} = ((\mathcal{F} bv_5(0)) app(listn(7,\mathcal{F}),(d_0)) bv_3(0) xor2(d_0,x)).$$

By Proposition 5.8(b), $\Sigma_{m+132+\ell} = \Sigma_{m+132}$ for $\ell = 0, \ldots, 12$. It follows that

$$\begin{aligned}(sv_{m+127}\ \ldots\ sv_n) &= app(listn(5, not1(x)), listn(13, equal(d_0, x))) \\ &= cell(x, 5, 13, d_0) \\ &= cells(x, 5, 13, (d_0)).\end{aligned}$$

In the inductive case, $k < 7$, we again have, for $\ell = 0, \ldots, 4$,

$$\Sigma_{m+1+18k+\ell} = ((\mathcal{T}\, bv_5(\ell))\ app(listn(k, \mathcal{F}), (d_0\ \ldots\ d_{7-k}))\ bv_3(k)\ x)$$

by Proposition 5.9(d). By Proposition 5.9(b) and (d), for $\ell = 5, \ldots, 17$,

$$\Sigma_{m+1+18k+\ell} = \\ ((\mathcal{T}\, bv_5(\ell))\, app(listn(k, \mathcal{F}), (d_0\ \ldots\ d_{7-k}))\, bv_3(k+1)\, xor2(d_{7-k}, x)).$$

Thus, $(sv_{m+1+18k}\ \ldots\ sv_{m+1+18k+17})$ is

$$app(listn(5, not1(x)), listn(13, equal(d_{7-k}, x))) = cell(x, 5, 13, d_{7-k}).$$

By Proposition 5.9(c), $\Sigma_{m+1+18(k+1)}$ is

$$((\mathcal{T}\, bv_5(0))\ app(listn(k+1, \mathcal{F}), (d_0\ \ldots\ d_{7-(k+1)}))\ bv_3(k+1)\ equal(d_{7-k}, x)).$$

It follows from our inductive hypothesis that

$$(sv_{m+1+18(k+1)}\ \ldots\ sv_n) = cells(equal(d_{7-k}, x), 5, 13, (d_{7-(k+1)}\ \ldots\ d_0)),$$

and hence $(sv_{m+1+18k}\ \ldots\ sv_n)$ is

$$\begin{aligned}&app(cell(x, 5, 13, d_{7-k}), cells(equal(d_{7-k}, x), 5, 13, (d_{7-(k+1)}\ \ldots\ d_0)) \\ &= cells(x, 5, 13, (d_{7-k}\ \ldots\ d_0)).\ \square\end{aligned}$$

5.6 The Receiver

The action of the receiver is controlled by a submodule, `rcount`, which is defined as follows:

Verification of Synchronous and Asynchronous Circuits

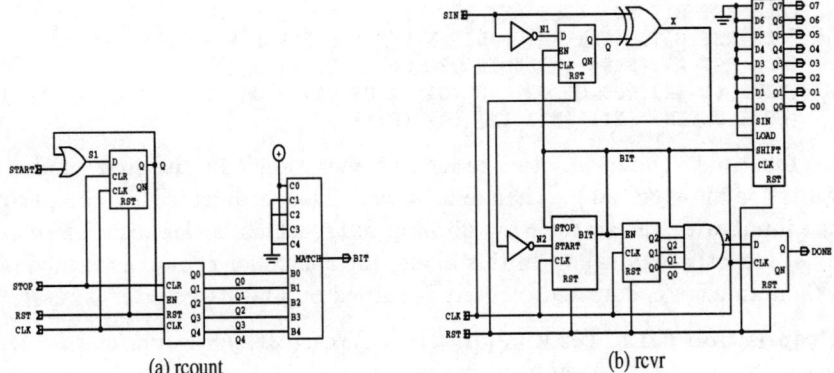

(a) rcount (b) rcvr

FIG. 10.

```
(STRUCT
  (CLK RST STOP START)
  (BIT)
  (cdff count5 or2 t0 f0 comp5)
  ((CLK RST STOP S1) (CLK RST STOP Q) (START Q)
   () () (T Q0 F Q1 F Q2 T Q3 F Q4))
  ((Q QN) (Q0 Q1 Q2 Q3 Q4) (S1) (T) (F) (BIT)))
```

The functionality of rcount is similar to that of scount. A state is again a list $(on\, cnt)$ of two components, corresponding to the two sequential submodules, cdff and count5. As long as both data inputs are $\mathcal{F}$, the value of on remains constant. While $on = \mathcal{T}$, cnt is incremented repeatedly; while $on = \mathcal{F}$, cnt remains unchanged. If STOP is $\mathcal{T}$, then on and cnt are reset to $\mathcal{F}$ and $bv_5(0)$; otherwise, if START is $\mathcal{T}$, then on is set to $\mathcal{T}$. The output value is determined by comparing cnt with $bv_5(9)$:

Proposition 5.11 *Let* $\Sigma = (on\, cnt)$ *and* $V = (stop\, start)$ *be a state and a data vector for* rcount. *Then*

$$nv(\text{BIT}, V, \Sigma, \text{rcount}) = \begin{cases} \mathcal{T} & \text{if } cnt = bv_5(9) \\ \mathcal{F} & \text{if } cnt \neq bv_5(9); \end{cases}$$

$$next(V, \Sigma, \text{rcount}) = \begin{cases} (\mathcal{F}\ bv_5(0)) & \text{if } stop = \mathcal{T} \\ (\mathcal{T}\ inc(cnt)) & \text{if } stop = \mathcal{F} \text{ and } start = on = \mathcal{T} \\ (\mathcal{T}\ cnt) & \text{if } stop = on = \mathcal{F} \text{ and } start = \mathcal{T} \\ (\mathcal{T}\ inc(cnt)) & \text{if } stop = start = \mathcal{F} \text{ and } on = \mathcal{T} \\ (\mathcal{T}\ cnt) & \text{if } stop = start = on = \mathcal{F}. \end{cases}$$

The definition of rcvr is as follows:

```
(STRUCT
  (CLK RST SIN)
  (O0 O1 O2 O3 O4 O5 O6 O7 DONE)
  (rcount edff count3 shift8 dff not1 not1 xor2 and4 f0)
  ((CLK RST BIT N2) (CLK RST BIT N1)
   (CLK RST BIT) (CLK RST F BIT X F F F F F F F)
   (CLK RST A) (SIN) (X) (SIN Q) (Q0 Q1 Q2 BIT) ())
  ((BIT) (Q QN) (Q0 Q1 Q2) (O0 O1 O2 O3 O4 O5 O6 O7)
   (DONE DONEN) (N1) (N2) (X) (A) (F)))
```

Like sndr, rcvr has two modes of operation. In the first mode, it waits for an edge, i.e., a change in input. This is detected by comparing the input with the state of the flip-flop edff, which is the negation of the most recently read value. In this mode, the controller rcount is turned off. When an edge is detected, rcount is turned on and its counter is reset:

Proposition 5.12 *Let $V = (sin)$ be a data vector for rcvr, and let $\Sigma = (\sigma_1\ \sigma_2\ \sigma_3\ \sigma_4\ \sigma_5)$ be a state of rcvr, where $\sigma_1 = (on\ cnt)$. Assume that $on = \mathcal{F}$, $cnt = bv_5(0)$, and $\sigma_5 = \mathcal{F}$. Let $\Sigma' = next(V, \Sigma, \text{rcvr})$:*

(a) *If $sin = \sigma_2$, then $\Sigma' = ((\mathcal{T}\ bv_5(0))\ \sigma_2\ \sigma_3\ \sigma_4\ \mathcal{F})$.*
(b) *If $sin \neq \sigma_2$, then $\Sigma' = \Sigma$.*

In its second mode, the receiver counts until it reaches the input bit to be sampled. At this point, the appropriate value is shifted into the register shift8, the bit counter count3 is incremented, the current input value is stored in edff, and rcount is turned off. When the eighth bit has been computed, the state of dff is altered to indicate termination:

Proposition 5.13 *Let $V = (sin)$ be a data vector for rcvr, and let $\Sigma = (\sigma_1\ \sigma_2\ \sigma_3\ \sigma_4\ \sigma_5)$ be a state of rcvr, where $\sigma_1 = (on\ cnt)$. Assume that $on = \mathcal{T}$ and $\sigma_5 = \mathcal{F}$. Let $\Sigma' = next(V, \Sigma, \text{rcvr})$:*

(a) *If $cnt = bv_5(9)$ and $\sigma_3 = bv_3(7)$, then*

$$\Sigma' = ((\mathcal{F}\ bv_5(0))\ not1(sin)\ bv_3(0))\ shift(xor2(\sigma_2, sin), \sigma_4)\ \mathcal{T}).$$

(b) *If $cnt = bv_5(9)$ and $\sigma_3 \neq bv_3(7)$, then*

$$\Sigma' = ((\mathcal{F}\ bv_5(0))\ not1(sin)\ inc(\sigma_3)\ shift(xor2(\sigma_2, sin), \sigma_4)\ \mathcal{F}).$$

(c) *If $cnt \neq bv_5(9)$, then $\Sigma' = ((\mathcal{T}\ inc(cnt))\ \sigma_2\ \sigma_3\ \sigma_4\ \mathcal{F})$.*

The specification of rcvr is given by the following lemma. For its proof, we require the following definition: If L and M are two bit vectors, then

$$push(L, M) = \begin{cases} M & \text{if } L = \text{NIL} \\ push(cdr(L), shift(car(L), M)) & \text{if } L \neq \text{NIL}. \end{cases}$$

Thus, if $L = (x_1\ \ldots\ x_\ell)$ and $M = (y_1\ \ldots\ y_m)$, where $\ell \leq m$, then

$$push(L, M) = (x_\ell\ \ldots\ x_1\ y_1\ \ldots\ y_{m-\ell}).$$

Proposition 5.14 *Let $\mathcal{V} = (V)$, where V is a bit vector of length n. Assume that $length(recv(8, \mathcal{T}, 10, V)) = 8$. Then for some m, $1 \le m \le n$,*

$$sv(j, \text{DONE}, \mathcal{V}, \text{rcvr}) = \begin{cases} \mathcal{T} & \text{if } j = m \\ \mathcal{F} & \text{if } j < m. \end{cases}$$

For $i = 1, \ldots, 7$, let $d_i = sv(m, 0i, \mathcal{V}, \text{rcvr})$. Then

$$(d_7 \ldots d_0) = recv(8, \mathcal{T}, 10, V).$$

Proof: Let $V = (v_1 \ldots v_n)$. For $j = 0, \ldots, n$, let $V_j = (v_{j+1} \ldots v_n)$ and

$$\Sigma_j = state(j, \mathcal{V}, \text{rcvr}) = ((on_j \; cnt_j) \; flg_j \; bits_j \; reg_j \; done_j).$$

We shall prove the following generalization of the desired result.

Suppose that for some j, $on_j = \mathcal{F}$, $cnt_j = bv_5(0)$, $done_i = \mathcal{F}$ for all $i \le j$, and

$$length(recv(8 - b, not1(flg_j), 10, V_j)) = 8 - b,$$

where $bits_j = bv_3(b)$. Then for some $m > j$, $done_i = \mathcal{F}$ for all $i < m$, $done_m = \mathcal{T}$, and

$$reg_m = push(recv(8 - b, not1(flg_j), 10, V_j), reg_j).$$

The proposition will then follow from the case $j = 0$.

First note that according to our assumption,

$$recv(8 - b, not1(flg_j), 10, V_j) \ne \text{NIL},$$

and hence, $scan(not1(flg_j), V_j) = V_k$ for some k, $j \le k < n - 10$. Thus, $v_i = not1(flg_j)$ for $i = j+1, \ldots, k$, and $v_{k+1} = flg_j$. From the definition of $recv$, we have

$$recv(8 - b, not1(flg_j), 10, V_j) = \\ cons(xor2(flg_j, v_{k+11}), recv(7 - k, v_{k+11}, 10, V_{k+11})),$$

and hence,

$$length(recv(7 - b, v_{k+11}, 10, V_{k+11})) = 7 - b.$$

By Proposition 5.12, $\Sigma_i = \Sigma_j$ for $i = j, \ldots, k$, and

$$\Sigma_{k+1} = ((\mathcal{T} \; bv_5(0)) \; flg_j \; bits_j \; reg_j \; \mathcal{F}).$$

By Proposition 5.13(c), for $i = 0, \ldots, 9$,

$$\Sigma_{k+1+i} = ((\mathcal{T} \; bv_5(i)) \; flg_j \; bits_j \; reg_j \; \mathcal{F}).$$

The proof is by induction on $7-b$. Consider first the base case, $b=7$. By Proposition 5.13(a),

$$\Sigma_{k+11} = ((\mathcal{F}\,bv_5(0))\,not1(v_{k+11})\,bv_3(0)\,shift(xor2(flg_j, v_{k+11}), reg_j)\,\mathcal{T}).$$

Here, the result holds for $m = k+11$, since
$$push(recv(8-b, not1(flg_j), 10, V_j), reg_j) = push((xor2(flg_j, v_{k+11})), reg_j)$$
$$= shift(xor2(flg_j, v_{k+11}), reg_j).$$

Now suppose that $b < 7$, and assume that the claim holds with b replaced with $b+1$. By Proposition 5.13(a),

$$\Sigma_{k+11} = ((\mathcal{F}bv_5(0))\,not1(v_{k+11})\,bv_3(b+1)\,shift(xor2(flg_j, v_{k+11}), reg_j)\mathcal{F}).$$

We may conclude that for some $m > k+11$, $done_i = \mathcal{F}$ for all $i < m$, $done_m = \mathcal{T}$, and

$$reg_m = push(recv(7-b, v_{k+11}, 10, V_{k+11}), shift(xor2(flg_j, v_{k+11}), reg_j))$$
$$= push(cons(xor2(flg_j, v_{k+11}), recv(7-b, v_{k+11}, 10, V_{k+11})), reg_j)$$
$$= push(recv(8-b, not1(flg_j), 10, V_j), reg_j).\ \square$$

5.7 The Main Theorem

Finally, we present our main result concerning the circuit bpm. We assume that the two clock input waveforms are admissible pulses for sndr and rcvr, respectively, with periods that conform to the constraints imposed by Moore's theorem, and that the other inputs are well-behaved with respect to the clocks, as required by Theorem 3.6. We also assume that the SEND input has the value $\mathcal{T}$ on exactly one cycle, during which an 8-bit message is read from the other data inputs. This message is then encoded and transmitted by sndr, and received, decoded, and output by rcvr. As stated in the theorem, the completion of this process is signalled by the output DONE: when its value first becomes $\mathcal{T}$, the other outputs display the decoded message.

Theorem 5.15 *Let $p_{in} = (w_{\text{CLKS}}\ w_{\text{RSTS}}\ w_{\text{CLKR}}\ w_{\text{RSTR}}\ w_{\text{SEND}}\ w_0 \ldots w_7)$ be an input packet for bpm, where:*

(a) $(\text{cLKS}w_{\text{RSTS}}w_{\text{SEND}}w_0\ldots w_7)$ is an admissible n_s-cycle input packet for sndr based at b_s with value matrix $V_s = (V_{\text{SEND}}\ V_{I0}\ \ldots\ V_{I7})$ and period π_s.

(b) w_{CLKR} is an admissible (n_r+2)-cycle pulse for rcvr based at b_r with high $h > 7000$, low $\ell > 7000 + setup(\text{SIN}, \text{rcvr})$, and period $\pi_r = h + \ell$.

(c) w_{RSTR} is an admissible (n_r+1)-cycle reset waveform for rcvr based at b_r with period π_r.

Assume $17\pi_r \le 18\pi_s \le 19\pi_r$. Suppose that for some m_s, $1 \le m_s \le n_s - 144$,

$$nth(j, V_{\text{SEND}}) = \begin{cases} \mathcal{T} & \text{if } j = m_s \\ \mathcal{F} & \text{if } j \ne m_s,\ 1 \le j \le n_s. \end{cases}$$

For $i = 0, \ldots, 7$, let $d_i = nth(m_s, V_{Ii})$. Let $t_r = b_r + \pi_r$. Assume that $b_s + 2\pi_s \leq t_r \leq b_s + (m_s + 2)\pi_s$ and $b_s + (n_s + 2)\pi_s \leq t_r + n_r\pi_r$.

Let $p_{out} = outp(\text{bpm}, sim(\text{bpm}, p_{in}, t_f))$, where $t_f \geq t_r + n_r\pi_r$. Then p_{out} is a stable n_r-cycle packet based at $t_r + \pi_r$ with value matrix V_r and period π_r, for some $V_r = (V_{\text{DONE}} V_{O0} \ldots V_{O7})$. For some m_r, $1 \leq m_r \leq n_r$,

$$nth(j, V_{\text{DONE}}) = \begin{cases} \mathcal{T} & \text{if } j = m_r \\ \mathcal{F} & \text{if } j \neq m_r, \ 1 \leq j \leq n_r, \end{cases}$$

and for $i = 0, \ldots, 7$, $nth(m_r, V_{Oi}) = d_i$.

Proof: We may assume, without loss of generality, that $n_s = m_s + 144$. For $j = 0, \ldots, n_s$, let $sv_j = sv(j, \text{SOUT}, V_s, \text{sndr})$. By Proposition 5.10,

$$(sv_1 \ldots sv_{n_s}) = send((d_7 \ldots d_0), m_s, 5, 13, 0).$$

Since $sv_0 = \mathcal{T}$, we have $sv_j = \mathcal{T}$ for all $j \leq m_s$.

Fix j so that $b_s + j\pi_s \leq t_r < b_s + (j+1)\pi_s$ and let $t_s = b_s + j\pi_s$. Then $2 \leq j \leq m_s + 2$, and hence $sv_{j-2} = \mathcal{T}$. Let

$$S = (sv_{j-1} \ldots sv_{n_s}) = send((d_7 \ldots d_0), m_s - j + 2, 5, 13, 0)$$

and let w_{LOUT} be the waveform for LOUT determined by $sim(\text{bpm}, p, t_f)$. By Theorem 4.6, $(w_{\text{CLKR}} w_{\text{RSTR}} w_{\text{LOUT}})$ is an admissible input packet for rcvr based at b_r with value matrix (A) and period π_r, where

$$A = asynch(U, t_s, t_r, \pi_s, \pi_r, oracle)$$

for some bit vector $oracle$.

Let $V_r = (V_{\text{DONE}} V_{O0} \ldots V_{O7})$, where

$$V_{\text{DONE}} = (sv(1, \text{DONE}, (A), \text{rcvr}) \ldots sv(n_r, \text{DONE}, (A), \text{rcvr}))$$

and for $i = 0, \ldots, 7$,

$$V_{Oi} = (sv(1, Oi, (A), \text{rcvr}) \ldots sv(n_r, Oi, (A), \text{rcvr})).$$

By Theorem 3.6, p_{out} is a stable n_r-cycle packet based at $b_r + \pi_r + \pi_r = t_r + \pi_r$ with value matrix V_r and period π_r.

According to Moore's Theorem, $recv(8, \mathcal{T}, 10, A) = (d_7 \ldots d_0)$. But then, by Proposition 5.14, there exists m_r such that $1 \leq m_r \leq n_r$,

$$nth(j, V_{\text{DONE}}) = \begin{cases} \mathcal{T} & \text{if } j = m_r \\ \mathcal{F} & \text{if } j \neq m_r, \ 1 \leq j \leq n_r, \end{cases}$$

and

$$(nth(m_r, V_{O7}) \ldots nth(m_r, V_{O0})) = (d_7 \ldots d_0).$$

Thus, for $i = 0, \ldots, 7$, $nth(m_r, V_{Oi}) = d_i$. □

Bibliography

1. Boyer, R. S. and Moore, J S., *A Computational Logic Handbook*, Academic Press, Boston, 1988.
2. Institute of Electrical and Electronic Engineers, *Draft Standard VHDL Language Reference Manual*, 1993.
3. Kaufmann, M., *A Translator from an HDL of David Russinoff to VHDL*, Internal Note 278, Computational Logic, Inc., July 1993.
4. Moore, J S., "A Formal model of asynchronous communication and its use in mechanically verifying a biphase mark protocol", *Formal Aspects of Computing* 6, no. 1 (1994):60-91.
5. Roden, M. S., *Digital Communication Systems Design*, Prentice-Hall, 1988.
6. Russinoff, D. M., *A Formalization of a Subset of VHDL*, Technical Report No. 98, Computational Logic, Inc., April, 1994.
7. Taub, H. and Schilling, D., *Digital Integrated Electronics*, McGraw-Hill, New York, 1977.